T5-AGL-143

ROCKHURST COLLEGE LIBRARY

0 0006 0039097 5

Date Due

International Review of Industrial
and Organizational Psychology
1987

International Review of Industrial and Organizational Psychology 1987

Edited by

Cary L. Cooper
and
Ivan T. Robertson

University of Manchester
Institute of Science & Technology UK

JOHN WILEY & SONS
Chichester · New York · Brisbane · Toronto · Singapore

Copyright© 1987 by John Wiley & Sons Ltd.

All rights reserved.

No part of this book may be reproduced by any means, or transmitted,
or translated into a machine language without
the written permission of the publisher

Library of Congress Cataloging-in-Publication Data

ISSN 0886-1528
Library of Congress Catalog Card Number 86-643874

British Library Cataloguing in Publication Data:

International review of industrial and
   organizational psychology 1987.
   1. Psychology, Industrial
   1. Cooper, Cary L.   II. Robertson, Ivan T.
      158.7   HF5548.8

ISBN 0 471 91352 9

Phototypeset by Dobbie Typesetting Service, Plymouth, Devon
Printed in Great Britain by St Edmundsbury Press, Bury St Edmunds, Suffolk

48.7
7
7

ROCKHURST COLLEGE LIBRARY

CONTRIBUTORS

Cary L. Cooper **Editor**	*Professor of Organizational Psychology, Department of Management Sciences, University of Manchester Institute of Science and Technology, UK.*
Ivan T. Robertson **Editor**	*Senior Lecturer in Organizational Psychology, Department of Management Sciences, University of Manchester Institute of Manchester Institute of Science and Technology, UK.*
Arthur G. Bedeian	*Department of Management, Louisiana State University, USA.*
Ronald J. Burke	*Faculty of Administrative Studies, York University, Canada.*
Antony J. Chapman	*Department of Psychology, University of Leeds, UK.*
Michael Frese	*Department of Psychology, University of Munich, West Germany.*
Esther R. Greenglass	*Department of Psychology, York University, Canada.*
Leonard Greenhalgh	*The Amos Tuck School of Business Administration, Dartmouth College, USA.*
Hannah Rothstein Hirsh	*Department of Management, Baruch College, City of New York University, USA.*
John E. Hunter	*Department of Psychology, Michigan State University, USA.*
Fred Luthans	*Department of Management, University of Nebraska, USA.*
Colin J. Mackay	*Medical Division, Health and Safety Executive, UK.*
Robin Martin	*MRC/ESRC Social and Applied Psychology Unit, Department of Psychology, University of Sheffield, UK.*
Mark Martinko	*Florida State University, USA.*

127041

CONTRIBUTORS

Andrew Rutherford   *Department of Production Engineering and Production Management, University of Nottingham, UK.*

Noel P. Sheehy   *Department of Psychology, University of Leeds, UK.*

Toby D. Wall   *MRC/ESRC Social and Applied Psychology Unit, Department of Psychology, University of Sheffield, UK.*

John R. Wilson   *Department of Production Engineering and Production Management, University of Nottingham, UK.*

CONTENTS

EDITORIAL FOREWORD

This second volume of the *International Review of Industrial and Organizational Psychology* contains ten chapters contributed by outstanding scholars within the industrial/organizational psychology field.

As editors we have been helped enormously by the enthusiasm and commitment of contributing authors and their ability to deliver what we requested on time.

The chapters in this volume, together with those in the 1986 volume, provide coverage of many of the major issues within the industrial and organizational psychology field. Our editorial judgement has clearly played a large role in the selection of topics for coverage, though we have canvassed the opinions of colleagues quite widely, and attempted to produce coverage that reflects the wide range of interests of contemporary industrial and organizational psychologists.

Topics scheduled for inclusion in the 1988 volume are:

Ethnic Relations at Work
Training
Leadership
Managerial Assessment
Organizational Climate
Theory Building in Industrial and Organizational Psychology
Psychological Measurement: Abilities, Skills, and Aptitudes
Cross-cultural Research in Industrial and Organizational Psychology
Career Development
Personality (Theory and Research) and Organizational Behaviour
Health Promotion at Work

CLC
ITR
August 1986

ix

International Review of Industrial and Organizational Psychology 1987
Edited by C. L. Cooper and I. T. Robertson
© 1987 John Wiley & Sons Ltd

Chapter 1

ORGANIZATION THEORY: CURRENT CONTROVERSIES, ISSUES, AND DIRECTIONS

Arthur G. Bedeian
Department of Management
Louisiana State University
USA

INTRODUCTION

The field of organization theory is alive and apparently thriving. A sense of excitement and vitality has transcended national boundaries as researchers throughout the world have turned their attention to examining organizations as distinct units in a larger system of relations. An interdisciplinary field, organization theory is defined by its focus upon the *organization as the unit of analysis* (Cummings, 1978). It has roots in sociology, political science, anthropology, and economics, and deals with questions of organization structure, processes, and outcomes within social/economic contexts.

Organization theory thus focuses on the actions of organizations viewed as total entities. This stands in contrast to the field of organizational behavior that examines the behavior of individuals and groups within the context of organizations. The distinction here is not only one of unit of analysis, but of nature of dependent variables. Within the field of organizational behavior, the relevant dependent variables are measures of individual or subunit (e.g. work clusters, departments, authority ranks) affective or behavioral reactions. By comparison, organization theory takes as its primary concerns dependent variables such as effectiveness, efficiency, and environmental relations. As a consequence, while organizations furnish a common locus of research for investigators from both fields, their questions of interest and the corresponding conceptual schemes which guide their inquiries vary (Schneider, 1985). The present review will concentrate solely on the organization theory field. Those readers interested in reviews of the organizational behavior field are referred to representative sources such as Mitchell (1979), Cummings (1982), Staw (1984), and Schneider (1985).

1

Focus and Format of the Review

The literature associated with organization theory since its emergence as a field four or so decades ago is enormous. In a review such as this it is impossible to cover all areas or to do justice to areas that have received considerable attention in the literature. In general, as the number of contributions to a research domain increases, the pressures for review and integration grow. The mass of available information becomes too large for assimilation. This pressure has produced a number of earlier reviews of the organization theory field (Cyert and MacCrimmon, 1968; Donaldson, 1985; March, 1965; Miner, 1982; Pfeffer, 1986; Scott, 1964; Scott, 1975; Nystrom and Starbuck, 1981).

My intent is not to cover the same ground again. Rather, this review will focus on current controversies and issues associated with four topics on which substantial scholarship has been conducted recently. These topics are: (1) organizational effectiveness, (2) organization-environment relations, (3) organizational learning, and (4) organizational decline. For each topic, a summary will be provided of the prevailing theoretical approaches and research trends. Theoretical issues will be discussed more fully than any particular study, and ideas are emphasized over methods. The historical works of the field will be used as a framework for interpretation. A section at the end of the review comments on the field's present state of health.

ORGANIZATIONAL EFFECTIVENESS

In a recent commentary on the state of contemporary organization theory, it was observed that research themes seem to have changed not so much because issues are resolved and phenomena understood, but rather because investigators run out of steam and interest turns to 'newer, more exciting' topics (Bedeian, 1986b). Perhaps no topic better exemplifies this observation than that of organizational effectiveness.

Although it was identified by Cummings (1982) as a reemerging area of research likely to continue to accelerate as a focus of scholarship, the last few years have seen a virtual abandonment of organizational effectiveness studies, as investigators have turned to 'hotter' topics. The latest heyday of organizational effectiveness research began building up steam in the late 1970s (Cameron, 1978; Campbell, 1976; Goodman *et al.*, 1977; Steers, 1975, 1976, 1977).

Effectiveness Models

The goal model

Initial interest in organizational effectiveness can be traced to early economic, accounting, and general management theories. Viewed historically, theorists have traditionally defined effectiveness as the meeting or surpassing of organizational goals (see, for example, Barnard, 1938). This perspective has become known as the goal model approach to the study of organizational effectiveness, since it views organizations as principally concerned with the attainment of certain end products or goals. The goal model thus rests on the implicit assumption that an organization's goals can be clearly established and that necessary human and material resources can be manipulated for goal attainment.

Various shortcomings in the goal model have been noted repeatedly. For instance, it has been observed that most contemporary organizations are multifunctional, pursuing numerous goals at the same time (Cameron, 1981a). Consequently, effectiveness in attaining one goal may be inversely related to effectiveness in attaining other goals. This suggests the likelihood that an organization will find it impossible to be effective in all areas simultaneously if it has multiple goals.

A second common criticism leveled at the goal model concerns the establishment of unambiguous criteria for measuring effectiveness. An ability to assess effectiveness on the basis of goal attainment depends upon the extent to which goals are measurable. Business firms, for example, have identifiable 'bottom line' objectives. No comparable yardstick exists for public organizations such as social welfare agencies and voluntary associations (Keating and Keating, 1981; Meyer, 1985). The determination of what constitutes goal attainment in these and similar situations can be quite unclear.

Despite these and other such criticisms, the goal model remains the dominant approach for studying organizational effectiveness (Clinebell, 1984). 'Its dominance,' as suggested by Hall (1980, p. 538), 'is linked to the fact that organizations do in fact utilize goals, as witnessed by annual reports and planning documents.' Hall further notes that 'while these can be labeled as rationalizations for past actions, goals remain a central component of most theories of organizations and of organizational effectiveness'.

The system resource model

Perhaps the most widely accepted alternative to the goal model is known as the system resource model of organizational effectiveness. Incorporating an open-systems viewpoint, this approach defines effectiveness as the degree to which an organization is successful in acquiring scarce and valued resources. The system resource model focuses on the interaction between an organization and its environment. In contrast to the goal model, inputs replace outputs as the primary consideration (Shipper and White, 1983). Organizations are viewed as involved in a continuous bargaining relationship with their environment, importing scarce resources to be returned as valued outputs. An organization's survival through time clearly depends upon its ability to establish and maintain a favorable input–output ratio. That is, to establish and maintain a greater resource intake than is required to produce its output.

Like the goal model, the system resource model has also received its share of criticism. Principal among these is that it is difficult to operationalize. While the system resource model holds that an organization is most effective when it optimizes its resource intake, it provides little guidance as to what constitutes optimum procurement. Moreover, it does not elaborate on *which* scarce and valued resources are relevant for assessing an organization's effectiveness and how, once obtained, they should be internally allocated.

More recent models for studying organizational effectiveness have been largely integrative. Two of these models, the 'multiple constituency approach' and the 'competing values approach', have generated sufficient interest to be considered separately. Each will be examined in turn.

Multiple constituency model

Individuals become involved with different organizations for various reasons. As would be anticipated, these reasons are reflected in differential preferences for performance. The multiple constituency approach (Connally, Conlon, and Deutsch, 1980) to organizational effectiveness defines effectiveness as the extent to which an organization satisfies the goals of its strategic constituents (or stakeholders). Thus, it represents an expansion of the goal model in the sense that it incorporates in the assessment process the goals of constituencies other than managers. As generally portrayed, a typical organization's constituencies (stakeholders) include society in general, customers, governments (local, state and federal), owners, employees, suppliers and competitors (Bedeian, 1986a). The multiple constituency model, thus, avoids problems of specifying and assessing organizational goals inherent in the goal model, as well as problems of identifying and assessing optimal resource acquisition as required by the system resource model.

As with its predecessors, however, critics have been quick to note several shortcomings associated with the multiple constituency model. Most notably, it incorporates several underlying value-based issues. Major among these is that selecting specific constituents to participate in assessing an organization's effectiveness involves a value judgement (Mark and Shotland, 1985). Except in instances where there is a limited constituent set or an unlikely consensus among constituents about what is important, practical constraints will prohibit an organization from satisfying *all* concerns that might interest its various constituents.

This dilemma has obvious implications for the actual measurement of organizational effectiveness. Admittedly, perceptions of an organization's effectiveness depend largely upon its constituents' frames of reference (Zammuto, 1984). As Bedeian (1986b) has observed, this presents three rather complicated measurement issues:

1. Any and all effectiveness criteria that are proposed will doubtlessly be viewed in terms of self-interest by each of the constituents involved.
2. Despite claims to the contrary, no criteria will be viewed impartially. Assessments of effectiveness do not take place in a neutral vacuum. Each criterion will likely benefit some constituents more than others.
3. Given the above considerations, in a situation in which resources are scarce, we would have every reason to expect a wide divergence and commensurate conflict in the criteria different constituents propose for assessing effectiveness.

Competing values model

The most recent approach to studying organizational effectiveness is that developed by Quinn and Rohrbaugh (1981, 1983; Rohrbaugh, 1981, 1983; Faerman and Quinn, in press). Known as the 'competing values' approach, it provides a means for integrating different models of organizational effectiveness with respect to three underlying value dimensions: (1) an internal focus versus an external focus, (2) a concern for flexibility versus a concern for control, (3) a concern for ends versus a concern for means.

Casting these underlying value dimensions on a Cartesian plane, Quinn and Rohrbaugh found a parallel with four alternative models of organizational effectiveness (see Figure 1.1). The 'human relations' model emphasizes an internal focus together with flexibility. It stresses effectiveness criteria such as cohesion and morale (as means) and human resource development (as an end). The 'open-systems' model emphasizes an external focus along with flexibility. It stresses effectiveness criteria such as innovation and readiness (as means) and organizational growth (as an end). The 'rational goal' model emphasizes an external focus, as well as control. It stresses effectiveness criteria such as planning and goal setting (as means) and productivity (as an end). Finally, the 'internal process' model emphasizes an internal focus together with control. It stresses effectiveness criteria such as the role of information management and communication (as means) and stability and predictability (as ends).

Each of the four organizational effectiveness models identified by Quinn and Rohrbaugh (1981) is embedded in a set of competing values. Indeed, while each does have a polar opposite with a directly competing emphasis, it also shares parallel

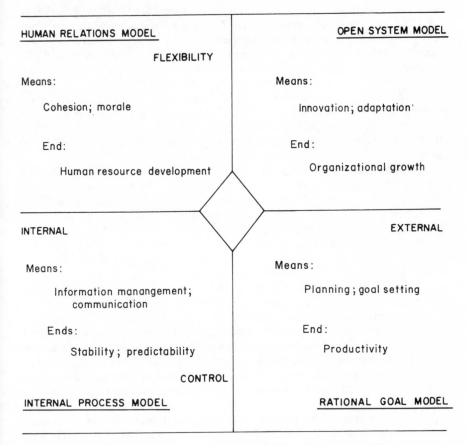

Figure 1.1 A summary of competing value dimensions and four effectiveness models
Source: based on Quinn and Rohrbaugh (1981, 1983; Rohrbaugh, 1981, 1983)

emphases with the two models it adjoins on common axes. The critical point to note, however, is that while certain pairs of effectiveness criteria reflect competing values, in practice they are not mutually exclusive. To be effective may require that an organization be both cohesive *and* productive, or stable *and* innovative.

The competing values approach clearly recognizes that multiple criteria and potentially conflicting constituent interests underlie any effort at assessing an organization's effectiveness. Moreover, given an understanding of the values different constituencies hold, it provides a basis for predicting the effectiveness criteria a constituency will likely employ in judging an organization's performance. Such knowledge should be of great value to an oganization attempting to satisfy a maximum number of stakeholders.

Measurement Concerns

As the preceding discussion suggests, irrespective of approach, assessing effectiveness is difficult and potentially controversial. Much frustration, as well as numerous methodological problems, surround the measurement of organizational effectiveness (Cameron, 1986). Several authors have even called for a moratorium on studies of organizational effectiveness and, in the extreme, have suggested that efforts to develop a theory of effectiveness be abandoned (Bluedorn, 1980; Goodman, Atkin, and Schoorman, 1982). The work of Quinn and Rohrbaugh (1981) is especially notable in integrating what has largely been a fragmentary and scattered area. The development of an accepted methodology for assessing an organization's overall effectiveness has been hampered by acknowledged measurement problems (Bedeian, 1986b).

Of particular concern in measuring effectiveness is the assessment of organizational performance across time (Cameron and Whetten, 1984). Three issues are particularly noteworthy. First, since organizations do not perform in standard units that are uniformly distributed over time, effectiveness is cyclical (Warner, 1967). Thus, the specific period or era and the actual time—short-run versus long-run—used in assessing an organization's performance may influence the resulting evaluation. Second, organizations are necessarily at different stages in their life cycles. Thus, effectiveness criteria appropriate at one stage may be unsuitable at another as organizational goals at each stage generally have a different focus (Cameron, 1981b; Cameron and Whetten, 1981; Quinn and Cameron, 1983). Third, taking a multiple constituency perspective, it is likely that an organization's constituents will change over time (Zammuto, 1982a, 1984). Moreover, the preferences of any continuing constituents are unlikely to remain stable. Measurement techniques for incorporating such changes and, in turn, determining how an organization's attempts to satisfy constituent preferences at one point in time will likely change constituent expectations for an organization's future performance simply do not exist.

A further measurement problem hampering the development of an accepted methodology for assessing effectiveness concerns the translation of criteria across levels of analysis (Mossholder and Bedeian, 1983a, 1983b). Effectiveness can be and has been conceptualized at the individual, group, and supra-system levels. It should not be assumed, however, that assessing an organization's overall effectiveness is a substitute for assessing its components or vice versa. Moreover, as Schneider (1985, p. 597) notes, it is becoming increasingly recognized that studies which include 'data derived from a focus on only one unit of analysis will likely yield relatively weak relationships because phenomena exist at multiple levels'. In the context of the present discussion, our ability to measure organizational effectiveness would be significantly enhanced by the identification of processes that operate across levels.

A final, but certainly not last, measurement problem hindering the development of an accepted methodology for assessing effectiveness concerns the appropriateness of criteria across organizations (Lewin and Minton, 1986). Research supports the view that since different types of organizations (e.g. profit versus not-for-profit) have different goals and constituencies, different criteria are appropriate for judging their performance (see, for example, Bozeman, 1982). Thus, while certain criteria (e.g. market share) may be relevant for certain types of organizations (e.g. business firms), they may have little relevance for others (e.g. public service agencies). A valid means for establishing appropriate effectiveness criteria that accurately reflect such contrasting orientations awaits development.

ORGANIZATION-ENVIRONMENT RELATIONS

Environmental relations have probably attracted more research than any other dependent variable in the organization theory field. The issue of organization-environment relations has drawn the attention of investigators for the greater part of the last two decades. Recent research, maintaining a longstanding tradition, has continued to examine environmental management strategies. Likewise, it has extended its focus in the allied areas of organization-environment 'fit' and strategic choice and environmental determinism. Of additional current interest, population ecologists have emerged in force as a vocal group attempting to explain the dynamics of organization-environment relations. The following discussion will review recent work in the areas of (1) organization-environment fit, (2) strategic choice and environmental determinism, (3) population ecology, and (4) environmental management strategies, including environmental scanning.

Organization-Environment 'Fit'

Structural contingency theory models have long dominated the study of organization design and performance (Venkatraman and Camillus, 1984). The basic proposition of these models is that performance is contingent on a fit between two or more factors, e.g. the fit between environmental demands, strategy, structure, and technology. Recently, however, structural contingency theory has drawn increasing criticism for a seeming inability to address its basic theoretical and empirical problems (e.g. Schoonhoven, 1981; Schreyogg, 1980; Takahashi, 1983).

In specific response to this mounting criticism, Van de Ven and Drazin (1985; Drazin and Van de Ven, 1985; Van de Ven, 1979) have argued that much of this criticism arises from the inadequate specification of the 'fit' concept. Van de Ven

(1979), for instance, has noted that there are at least four different conceptual meanings of fit, each with its own unique theoretical implications. Contending that little scientific progress will be made until more detailed specifications of fit are established, Van de Ven and Drazin (1985) have made a significant contribution to the organization theory literature by addressing the current confusion surrounding contingency theory models.

Focusing on three approaches to fit—selection, interaction, and systems—Van de Ven and Drazin (1985) have not only suggested alternate means for testing the fit concept, but have empirically tested their own recommendations (Drazin and Van de Ven, 1985). Their evidence provides support for the selection and systems approaches, but not the interaction approach. Commenting on the generalizability of this finding, Drazin and Van de Ven urge the design of further contingency studies to permit additional comparative evaluation of alternative approaches to fit. In doing so, they stress that the resulting complementary information can result in more comprehensive explanations of context-structure-performance relationships than any single approach to fit alone.

Strategic Choice and Environmental Determinism

Although research suggests that some form of fit between an organization's structure and its environment affects its performance, the role of managerial perceptions and strategic choice in this adaptive process is still unclear (Bourgeois, 1985). As Hrebiniak and Joyce (1985, p. 336) note, 'The prevailing assumption in recent literature is that strategic choice and environmental determinism represent mutually exclusive, competing explanations of organizational adaptation'. On the one hand, environmental determinists, focusing on objective environments as determinants of structures, have disregarded the influence of managerial perceptions on organizational adaptations. On the other hand, strategic choice advocates, emphasizing the role of managerial perceptions, have ignored the influences of objective environments. Despite the general recognition that organizations and their environments are parts of a complex interactive system both groups have assumed one-way causality. Yasai-Ardekani's (1986, p. 9) conclusion that 'objective and perceptual approaches to the study of environment-structural fit have yielded equally suspect results' should thus not be surprising.

Environmental determinists essentially view organizations as passive recipients being acted upon by their environment. By contrast, strategic choice advocates view organizations as perceptually modeling their world and taking actions accordingly. A recognition of the relevance of both the environment and top managers' choices in determining organizational performance is beginning to emerge (Astley and Van de Ven, 1983; Dess and Beard, 1984). Hrebiniak and Joyce (1985), for instance, have argued that classifying organizational adaptations as either managerially or environmentally derived is misleading. They suggest instead that strategic choice and environmental determinism are independent variables that in interaction yield four types of organizational adaptation: (1) natural selection: low strategic choice and high environmental determinism, (2) differentiation: high strategic choice and high environmental determinism, (3) strategic choice: high strategic choice and low environmental determinism, and (4) undifferentiated choice: low strategic choice and low environmental determinism. The key point emerging from Hrebiniak and Joyce's analysis is that organizational adaptation is a dynamic process in which strategic choice and environmental determinism exist simultaneously.

Hrebiniak and Joyce thus view strategic choice and environmental determinism as variables whose effects can only be understood in relation to one another. Their model of organizational adaptation suggests that strategic choice and environmental determinism never operate in isolation. In an extension of Hrebiniak and Joyce's logic, Bedeian (1986b) contends that strategic choice and environmental determinism stand in a relationship of continuous reciprocal influence in which organizations respond to their environments as well as change them. His argument is that environmental attributes and strategic choice continuously influence each other in a multidirectional interaction process that Pervin and Lewis (1978) term 'reciprocal action-transaction'. What makes the reciprocal action-transaction model even more different from traditional models is that it requires consideration of a time orientation. In traditional models, strategic choice and environmental determinism are viewed interdependently. By contrast, from a reciprocal action-transaction perspective, strategic choice and environmental determinism exist in continual interaction over time. Thus, reciprocal action-transaction derives from two factors: (1) organizations not only react to their individual environments, they also create or enact them, and (2) the resulting new environments in turn influence future organization actions, which alternately change the environments again. The continuous reciprocal influence underlying the cognitive interpretation and reinterpretation of environments by organizations hence emphasizes the need to attend to both subjective and objective phenomena as they interact across time. As two examples, recently published case studies of the historical development of the Du Pont Company (McNamee, 1983) and how the cigarette industry has protected its environmentally threatened cigarette operations (Dunbar and Wasilewski, 1985) clearly underscore the continuous reciprocal interplay of organization and environment.

Population Ecology

Following a deterministic slant, the population ecology perspective has quickly become one of the most influential approaches for explaining the dynamics of organization-environment relations. Proponents of this perspective focus on the appearance, development, and disappearance of organizations. They contend that extreme environmental demands in effect 'select out' stronger, more dominant organizational forms as 'weaker' organizations cease to exist, or survive only as markedly different forms of organization. Thus, organizational forms which are successful spread through growth and imitation, while unsuccessful forms disappear or are absorbed into other organizations. A complete development of population ecology as it applies to organizations is given by Aldrich, McKelvey, and Ulrich (1984), Aldrich and McKelvey (1983), Bidwell and Kasarda (1985), Kasarda and Bidwell (1984), McKelvey and Aldrich (1983), Ulrich (1984), and Ulrich and Barney

(1984). Astley (1985a) has recently gone beyond population ecology to develop a more encompassing community ecology perspective.

A fundamental aspect of population ecology lies in the identification of environmental niches — 'distinct combinations of resources and other constraints that are sufficient to support an organizational form' (Aldrich, 1979, p. 28). Of particular interest has been the question of niche width. That is, a population of organizations' 'tolerance for changing levels of resources, its ability to resist competitors, and its response to other factors that inhibit growth' (Carroll, 1985, p. 1266). Populations with a broad niche (generalists) have a wide tolerance, being able to reproduce in diverse circumstances. Those with a narrow niche (specialists) have more limited ranges of tolerance, being able to survive only in specific environmental conditions. To date, studies investigating the notion of niche width (Carroll, 1985; Freeman and Hannan, 1983; McPherson, 1983) have been more distinguished by their statistical manipulations than their clarity of results. Likewise, analyses of the general population ecology model have largely reported inconsistent results (Korsching, 1983; Marple, 1982, 1983; Rundall and McClain, 1982; Staber, 1985).

Criticism of the population ecology perspective has been far-reaching (Betton and Dess, 1985). Critics have claimed that the selection process incorporated in population ecology is much more complicated than presented. As Weick (1979, p 125) explains, 'their objection is that "selection" can occur in so many ways that the concept does not explain very much of what happens. It is easy to attribute everything that occurs to some kind of selection, and for this reason the explanation loses its power'. Others (McPherson, 1983; Van de Ven, Hudson and Schroeder, 1984) have noted that unless the population ecology logic is tested with longitudinal experimental evidence, it contains an inherent tautology: organizations are successful because they have survived, and they have survived because they were successful. Equally vocal are those (Astley and Fombrun, 1983; Astley and Van de Ven, 1983) who argue that environments may not really consist of open niches waiting to be filled, but rather of potential space that needs to be carved out. Additionally, there are critics (Büschges, 1985; Foo, Aliga and Puxty, 1981) who object to population ecology's virtually ignoring the role played by managerial decision makers. The population ecology perspective views organizations as adopting a passive, reactive posture in relation to environmental events. It depicts the process of selection among organizational forms continuing almost regardless of managerial decision makers. Finally, it has also been noted (Astley, 1984; Strauss, 1982) that population ecologists have focused almost exclusively on the dynamics of competition and ignored the cooperative social and political features regulating the vital intersections between organizations.

Environmental Management Strategies

Environmental scanning

Theorists rejecting the notion of a deterministic relationship between environment and structure generally argue that strategic choice plays an important role in influencing an organization's responses to its environment. In this respect, a close relationship has been repeatedly shown between performance and gathering of environmental data. On the upscale side, most research shows a positive correlation between superior performance and the extent to which organizations scan their environment (e.g. Miller and Friesen, 1980). On the downscale side, organizational decline has been repeatedly associated with a failure to adequately identify and assess environmental trends (e.g. Schendel, Patton and Riggs, 1976).

As generally conceptualized, scanning involves monitoring and evaluating events and trends in an organization's environment. Recognizing the importance of adequately identifying and assessing environmental trends, organization theorists have continued their study of formal environmental scanning activities. A two-dimensional matrix for guiding scanning activities has been developed by Camillus and Venkatraman (1984). Diffenbach (1983) and Higgins (1986) have surveyed the extent of environmental analysis in *Fortune 500* and British firms, respectively. Klein and Linneman (1984) have similarly surveyed the nature of environmental scanning in a worldwide sample of international corporations. Other more or less comprehensive studies have also been recently reported (e.g. Fahey, Narayanan, 1981; Jain, 1984; Stubbart, 1982).

Studies investigating specific hypotheses relating to environmental scanning behavior have been performed by Nishi, Schoderbek, and Schoderbek (1982; Nishi, 1979) and Culnan (1983). In a test of eight propositions, Nishi *et al.* (1982) found, among other things, that executives' scanning behaviors (surveillance and search) were related to different environmental states (dynamic versus stable), as well as to different hierarchical levels of management (upper versus lower). Culnan's (1983) findings also confirm that scanning is influenced by an organization's environment, but that the information-gathering requirements (e.g. complexity) associated with a manager's environment are related to the use of different information sources (e.g. periodicals, consultants, databases). In a methodological advance, Farh, Hoffman, and Hegarty (1984) have adapted Hambrick's (1981) environmental scanning scale for use at the subunit level. Finally, Lenz and Engledow (1986) have explored the administrative problems associated with structuring, sustaining, and using environmental scanning units in ten 'leading-edge' corporations.

Assuming a benefit from environmental scanning, the specific strategies organizations employ hopefully to manage their environment vary extensively. What have been generally classified as *direct* strategies include coopting, interlocking directorates, illegal activities, mergers, and joint ventures. More *indirect* strategies include involvement of third parties such as trade associations (e.g. National Association of Furniture Manufacturers), professional organizations (e.g. American Medical Association), and, in the US, political action committees. The extent of research on each of these strategies varies. Mergers, joint ventures, and similar coalescing activities have been extensively reviewed in the general management literature (e.g. Bedeian, 1986a) and will, thus, not be covered here. Comments, however, will be offered on a majority of the remaining identified strategies.

Coopting

A *direct* strategy for dealing with environmental uncertainty, coopting is the process of absorbing external elements into an organization's decision-making or policy-determining structure as a means of averting threats to its stability or existence.

The naming of International Union–United Auto Workers President (Emeritus) Douglas A. Fraser to the Chrysler Corporation board is a typically cited example of cooptation (Zeithaml and Zeithaml, 1984). Cooptation is selected as a strategy to manage environmental relations on the assumption that if threatening elements from the environment are absorbed or coopted into an organization, the effects of uncertainty can be partially neutralized. The classic case is the non-financial corporation that is seriously indebted to a particular bank and coopts a representative of the bank onto its board (Pennings, 1980). The notion of cooptation, however, has been more broadly defined. Hirsch (1975) has shown how the pharmaceutical industry coopted the American Medical Association. More recently, Burt (1983a, 1983b) has suggested that corporate philanthropy can be employed as a means of coopting the consumer sector of a nation's economy.

Interlocking directorates

Interlocking directorates is a second *direct* strategy for attempting to manage environmental uncertainty. The literature dealing with interlocking boards of directors is voluminous (e.g. recently, Burt, 1982, 1983a; Fennema, 1982; Mintz and Schwartz, 1985; Mizruchi, 1982; Pennings, 1980; Scott and Griff, 1984). The goal of director interlocks is to help manage external dependencies, and thus make an organization's environment more manageable. Research suggests that this is primarily accomplished in four ways: (1) establishment of horizontal coordination, whereby two or more competitors are linked, can communicate, and can jointly benefit; (2) establishment of vertical coordination, whereby an organization can reduce uncertainty concerning either its input or its outputs; (3) appointment of outside directors who can contribute information and skills from which an organization can benefit; and (4) appointment of prestigious people as directors to provide confirmation for the larger environment as to the wealth and responsibility of an organization (Bazerman and Schoorman, 1983; Mintz and Schwartz, 1981; Ornstein, 1984; Palmer, 1983; Roy, 1983; Schoorman, Bazerman, and Atkin, 1981).

Illegal activities

Interest in organizational illegality, a third *direct* strategy for managing organization-environment relations, has grown steadily (e.g. Sonnenfeld, 1981). The exact extent of such deviant behavior is, of course, unknown. Available evidence, however, suggests that it is quite extensive (Clinard, 1983a, 1983b; Ermann and Lundman, 1982; Wagel, Ermann, and Horowitz, 1981). As identified by Szwajkowski (1985), three explanatory variables appear to form the building blocks of organizational crime theory. They are: environment (press, need or distress); structure (corporate, industrial or legal); and inner-directed choice processes (pathology, intent or proactive exploitation). Szwajkowski contends that these variables may occur in isolation or combination and may be manifested in numerous ways. Moreover, he notes that their explanatory power may vary considerably across violation type and setting, with their effect differing depending upon whether relevant laws are new and uncertain or well-established and tested.

Political action committees

Of the various *indirect* strategies employed by organizations hopefully to manage their environment, political action committees (PACs) have perhaps generated the most interest. While corporations in Britain are permitted to donate money to political parties and candidates they favor, US corporations by law cannot (Useem, 1984). The US ban on direct corporate financing of political campaigns has prompted a substantial number of organizations of all types (corporate, labor, trade) to establish PACs to collect funds from employees and channel them to friendly political parties and candidates. The growth in PAC activity has spawned a good deal of concern in both the academic (e.g. Handler and Mulkern, 1982) and popular press (Grover, 1986). This concern is far too wide to chronicle here. Some researchers have concluded that PACs do have a major effect on legislative behavior (Kau and Rubin, 1981; Kau, Keenan, and Rubin, 1982). Others, however, contend that the influence of PACs is overstated (Banthin and Stelzer, 1986; Chappell, 1982; Keim, Zeithaml, and Baysinger, 1984; Malbin, 1979). Of the studies in this area, the works of Masters and his colleagues (e.g. Masters and Keim, 1985) are of particular interest. More specifically, Masters and Baysinger (1985) have developed a theoretical framework to explain variation in corporate PAC fundraising. Findings based on hypotheses derived from the model suggest that the federal government, through its actions as a purchaser and regulator, seems to have a significant impact on how corporations act in the political arena. For instance, it is not surprising to find that corporations highly affected by government attempt to influence policy making through electoral campaign financing. Similarly, Masters and Delaney (1985) have developed and tested an exploratory model to explain differences in union PAC contributions. Their findings suggest that political activity among union PACs is at least partly a function of being situated in a highly regulated economic sector. In any case, evidence is mounting to suggest that organizations, especially US corporations, are becoming increasingly involved in political activity (Baysinger, 1984; Baysinger and Woodman, 1982; Dickie, 1984; Keim, 1985; Yoffie and Bergenstein, 1985).

ORGANIZATIONAL LEARNING

Interest in oganizational learning can be traced to the early work of Cyert and March (1959, 1963; March, 1962). This interest, however, did not reach its full stride until the publication of March and Olsen's (1975, 1976) research on ambiguity and choice. A conceptually appealing notion, organizational learning has recently emerged as a key concept in the popular management press. Writing in their *Leaders: The Strategies for Taking Charge*, Bennis and Nanus (1985) see 'innovative' learning as essential for an organization's survival. Similarly, O'Toole (1985) sees 'continuous' learning as a general characteristic of organizations practicing the 'New Management', or what he terms 'Vanguard Management'.

Generally defined, organizational learning is the process by which an organization obtains knowledge about the associations between past actions, the effectiveness of those actions, and future actions (cf. Fiol and Lyles, 1985). As presented by March and Olsen (1975), organizational learning rests on two fundamental foundations: (1) rational calculation and (2) experiential learning. The notion of rational calculation incorporates the idea that organizations use expectations about future outcomes as a basis for selecting among current alternatives. Experiential learning assumes that organizations adjust their activities based on past experiences in an effort to increase their competence.

Just as in the case of 'organizational goals', the concept of organizational learning raises the issue of reification. That is, it grants to the concept of organization anthropomorphic (human) characteristics that it does not possess. Acknowledging that organizations exhibit adaptive behavior over time, it seems naïve to assume that organizations learn in the same manner as human beings. Bennis and Nanus (1985) sidestep this issue by simply declaring that organizational learning occurs at all levels in an organization—among individuals and groups as well as systemwide. Friedlander (1983) avoids this issue by coining the term 'learning organism' to include both individual and organizational learning. Perhaps most satisfactorily, Argyris (1985) states that organizational learning is produced through the actions of individuals acting as an 'agent' for an organization. Exactly how individual and organizational learning relate remains unclear. Organizational learning is, however, certainly real. In adapting over time, organizations obviously employ individual members as behavioral instruments. However, the learning process involved seems independent of individuals and to proceed uninterrupted through repeated turnover of personnel, as well as despite some variation in the actual behaviors people contribute. This would suggest that the organizational learning process is influenced not only by the specific individuals involved, but by a broad set of exogenous (i.e. social, political and structural) variables.

Organizational learning has reached its current prominence on the basis of its importance for bringing about successful change. As Friedlander (1983, p. 194) remarks, 'Learning is the process that underlies and gives birth to change. Change is the child of learning'. This reasoning, of course, reflects a basic logic that has long been a part of the literature on innovation. For instance, Shepard (1967), writing on innovation-resisting and innovation-producing organizations, considered an organization to have innovated when it had learned to do something it did not know how to do before. The conceptual overlap in the organizational learning and innovation literatures suggests that the latter might be an important knowledge base for understanding (1) how learning (innovation) is induced, (2) how to design organizations which are productive of innovations (learning), and (3) how to change an innovation (or learning) resistant organization into an innovation (or learning) producing organization. Recognizing a close relationship between strategic action and innovativeness, this conceptual overlap further suggests that the development of a strategic management capability is closely related to an organization's ability to learn and be creative. Indeed, Normann (1985) contends that a high organizational learning capability is an underlying variable explaining performance in strategic action. This contention squares completely with Shrivastava and Grant's (1985; Shrivastava, 1985) research into strategic decision-making processes and organizational learning. While their work reveals that there is no perfect organizational learning system, it underscores the necessity of developing organizational learning systems that support an organization's strategic decision-making processes.

Theories of Action

Building on their learning, organizations develop what Argyris and Schön (1978; Argyris, 1985) have termed theories of action. These theories represent beliefs that organizations hold about the environmental consequences (outcomes) of their actions. Shrivastava and Schneider (1984) contend that such theories allow employees to share organizational frames of reference and institutionalize them as consensual knowledge. Hedberg (1981), however, warns that difficulties commonly occur in relating organizational actions to specific environmental responses. He introduces the concept of myth to denote invalid theories of action which guide organizational learning. Myths are undermined as they fail to produce desired results or as exogenous events raise doubts about their validity. As this occurs, new theories of action will emerge. The theory of action generating the most convincing strategy will rule until it is no longer valid (becomes a myth). An understanding of the emergence of theories of action would be of considerable importance in comprehending the dynamics of organizational learning (Brunsson, 1985; Ford and Hegarty, 1984). To the extent that theories of action permit the sharing of oganizational frames of reference and their institutionalization as consensual knowledge, a clear implication thus emerges: what organizations learn does not depend on their environment in general, but on those elements in the environment from which they form their theories of action (Dery, 1982, 1983).

Organizational Memory

A point yet unmentioned is that experiential learning, the second fundamental foundation upon which organizational learning rests, presupposes a capacity to recall. Therefore, organizations must accumulate and maintain an adequate organizational memory (Etheredge, 1981). As described by Covington (1985), memory contributes to two organizational attributes: (1) a learning capability that informs and conditions decisions with knowledge of the past, and (2) an independent and self-sustaining identity—a continuing characteristic sense of mission. In an interesting analysis, Covington (1985) studied the organizational memory of the staff components attached to the National Security Council, the Office of Management and Budget, and the Council on Environmental Quality. Six features were identified as determinates of organizational memory: (1) staff turnover, (2) record-keeping regulations, (3) veteran-newcomer cooperation, (4) goal compatibility over time, (5) job routine, and (6) recruitment control. A study by Green, Bean, and Snavely (1983) of idea flows in an R&D lab extends our knowledge in this area further. Their results suggest that the critical key in idea management for organizational learning may be moving ideas from an organization's short-term memory into a long-term memory.

Organizational learning occurs along several simultaneous dimensions. Learning from direct experience (experiential learning) is supplemented by other forms of learning. Organizations also learn from (1) imitation, (2) novel interpretations of prosaic facts, (3) errors, and (4) superstition.

Imitative Learning

Learning through imitation results from the diffusion of experience. Imitation, or simply copying others, is a common method for increasing the amount of experience from which an organization can draw (March, 1982). Indeed, March and Sevón (1982) observe that organizations copying each other can be seen as reflecting contagion, and that such learning can be seen spreading through a population of actors like measles through a population of children. Imitation allows new organizations to start further along the learning curve and possibly out-compete older organizations (Aldrich, 1986). This copying often takes the form of 'reverse engineering' (Eells and Nehemkis, 1984), where an organization examines in detail its competitors' products as they appear in the marketplace. Imitation is thus one way for an organization to neutralize an advantage enjoyed by its competition. Citing research by Ijiri and Simon (1967), Dutton and Freedman (1985) suggest that the inability of *Fortune* 500 firms to maintain or replicate past successes may result from competitors imitating their successful techniques. This is one example of what DiMaggio and Powell (1983) have called 'mimetic processes' whereby organizations mimic each other as a means for nullifying the perceived advantages of their competitors. Commenting on such situations, Herriott, Levinthal, and March (1985), however, argue that while 'fast learners' often do better than 'slow learners', there are many plausible situations in which slow learners do better than fast learners. In a related finding, Sahal (1981) presents evidence to suggest a lack of interindustry transmission of technical know-how. Knowledge largely seems to be product and industry specific. The process of learning associated with the development of technology appears context dependent, typically isolated in the industry of its origin. Sahal (1981, p. 57) has labeled this phenomenon the 'principle of technological insularity'.

Novel Learning

A second form of organizational learning involves the novel interpretation of prosaic facts. As Smirich and Stubbart (1985) observe, successful organizations have often considered the same facts available to their competitors, but done so in a way as to invent startling insights. They cite as one example Ray Kroc and McDonald's fast-food hamburger restaurant chain. Smirich and Stubbart further note that such novel interpretations frequently occur when organizations enter an environment in which they have no experience. Not burdened by prior theories of action (myths?), they introduce novel strategies that run counter to conventional assumptions. As an example they cite Philip Morris in the beer industry. The introduction of Lite Beer through the firm's Miller Brewing unit flew in the face of traditional knowledge that a diet beer could not be sold. Such erroneous industrywide theories of action (myths) stress the fragile nature of so-called industry wisdom (Cooper and Schendel, 1983). The dynamics underlying industrywide learning have only recently been studied (Stokey, 1986). Such occurrences draw attention to the fragile nature of theories in use.

Learning from Errors

Organizations also learn through their errors. While little cumulative research is available on this form of organizational learning, its importance should not be underestimated. Dery (1982, p. 217) contends that 'the learning organization is, by definition, an erring organization'. Notably, Dery argues that error recognition is a function of interpretation rather than simply observation of events. This argument stresses the significance of converting data into information. The story is told at Proctor & Gamble (P & G) of how a crutcher (a device to mix ingredients) was left on too long and inadvertently put air bubbles into an early product, thus accidently producing a buoyant soap, Ivory. P & G was aware of the error (data), but it carried no meaning (information) until shoppers started asking for more of 'the soap that floats'. To restate Dery's position, error recognition (i.e. interpretation of events) rather than simple error detection is a basic prerequisite to organizational learning.

Superstitious Learning

Finally, organizational learning can be superstitious. This is likely to be the case in situations where organizational outcomes are affected by both random and systematic environmental effects, and where the rate of environmental change exceeds an organization's ability to adapt (Levinthal and March, 1981). In general, superstitious learning develops because cognitive limitations distort managerial perceptions of action–outcome relations in such a way that environmental responses to organizational initiatives are erroneously interpreted. Notwithstanding, organizational actions are assumed to produce intended environmental responses and subsequent actions are modified in what is judged to be an appropriate manner. Despite the fact that the real situation is substantially different from what is believed, 'learning' continues. Implications are drawn from environmental events and succeeding altered organizational actions (Rice, 1985). As an example of superstitious learning, one only need consider the marketing efforts of most major corporations. While advertising and other marketing efforts doubtlessly have an impact on consumer expenditures, the full extent and nature of their effectiveness remains unknown. Indeed, it could be easily argued that the marketplace is actually indifferent to much advertising, and that advertising expenditures are based as much on superstition as on fact.

In sum, most forms of organizational learning are adaptively rational (Comfort, 1985). As viewed by March (1982), they allow organizations to identify good alternatives for most of the choice situations they will encounter. However, March further observes that the organizational learning process can produce some surprises:

> If goals adapt rapidly to experience, learning what is likely may inhibit discovery of what is possible. If strategies are learned quickly relative to the development by competence, a decision maker will learn to use strategies that are intelligent given the existing level of competence, but may fail to invest in enough experience with a suboptimal strategy to discover that it would become a dominant choice with additional competence. (March, 1982, p. 35)

While such derivations are unlikely to occur frequently, they do provide a link between the organizational learning process and surprising results.

ORGANIZATIONAL DECLINE

Over the past decade, organizational decline has emerged as a major research topic in organization theory. Building from a small base (Whetton, 1980a), research interest in this area has grown tremendously (for a bibliography see Zammuto, 1983). Traditionally, most general theories of organization have reflected inherent biases in favor of growth. These biases have proven quite dysfunctional for managers who must deal with declining organizations. Mounting research clearly indicates that the effects of growth and decline on organizations and their members are asymmetrical (Zammuto, 1982b).

Current interest in decline can be largely traced to Hedberg, Nystrom, and Starbuck's (1976) early work on the behaviors of declining organizations in their transition from growth to non-growth. Building on this base, present research has primarily focused on both the sources and dynamics of decline (Kaufman, 1985). The following review will center on these two subjects.

Sources of Decline

In general, the types of crises that, if responded to improperly, precipitate organizational decline can be classified as either internally or externally generated. That is to say, crises may be classified as originating from either deficiencies within an organization itself or from sudden and unpredictable events or changes in an organization's environment. Whetten (1980b), building on Levine (1978), has developed a particularly useful typology for examining both internally and externally generated sources of decline. The four sources of decline which he has identified are (1) organizational atrophy, (2) vulnerability, (3) loss of legitimacy, and (4) environmental entropy. Research into these sources has been uneven.

Organizational atrophy

Unless appropriate counteractions are taken organizational atrophy is a phenomenon to be expected in any organization (Levine, 1978). It results from the breakdown of an organization's internal operating systems, leading to declining performance and weakening productive capacity. Attempts to understand why organizations are vulnerable to internal atrophy and its consequences are being made. Most impressive in this regard is the continuing work of Nystrom and Starbuck (1984a, 1984b; Starbuck 1983, 1985). Their findings suggest that many organizations fall victim to atrophy as a consequence of their accumulated past successes. Bolstered by recollections of former triumphs, they create action generators (automatic behavior programs that are similar to routinized or scripted behavior of individuals) that go unchallenged long after their usefulness has expired (Starbuck, 1983). As a consequence of clinging to inappropriate beliefs and perceptions, atrophic organizations act non-adaptively most of the time. Nystrom and Starbuck (1984a, 1984b) contend that organizations must unlearn these cognitive structures if they are to survive.

Vulnerability

Vulnerability, the second source of organizational decline identified by Whetton (1980b), is an internal property indicating a high level of fragility that limits an organization's capacity to resist environmental demands. Factors contributing to vulnerability include small size (Dalton and Kesner, 1985a), internal conflict (Gilmore and Hirschhorn, 1984; Krantz, 1985), and changes in leadership (Gilmore and Hirschhorn, 1983). Evidence suggests, however, that an organization's age may be the strongest predictor of its vulnerability. Young organizations are more likely to be vulnerable than their older counterparts because they lack initial legitimacy to claim resources, have yet to develop a wide range of adaptive skills, possess a limited capacity for learning, and wield only limited environmental influence (Storey, 1985; Wiewel and Hunter, 1985). The research in this regard is lengthy and virtually unequivocal (see, most recently, Aldrich and Auster, 1986; Altman, 1983; Carroll, 1983; Carroll and Delacroix, 1982; Delacroix and Carroll, 1983; Freeman, 1982; Freeman, Carroll, and Hannan, 1983; Hannan and Freeman, 1984). This is not to say, however, that a wide range of factors (e.g. elite sponsorship, government support in the form of subsidies or favorable tax laws, etc.) cannot mitigate selection pressures associated with youth (DiMaggio and Powell, 1983).

Loss of legitimacy

Loss of legitimacy represents a third source of decline. Organizations seek to maintain a congruence between the social values associated with their activities and the standards of acceptable behavior in the society of which they are a part (Dowling and Pfeffer, 1975). When a disparity exists between the two, there will exist a threat to organizational legitimacy. This threat may take the form of legal, economic and other social sanctions. Loss of legitimacy can thus have direct consequences for an organization's continued existence. Perhaps most significantly, failure to establish and maintain legitimacy will immeasurably inhibit an organization's ability to deflect criticism and obtain resources and other support from its surrounding environment (Berger, 1981). The exact process by which society views an organization as proper and worthy of support—that is, as legitimate—remains unexplored. It is a topic greatly in need of empirical research.

Environmental entropy

The fourth source of decline, environmental entropy, occurs when the capacity of an environment to support an organization at an existing level of activity is no longer adequate. This kind of decline typically results from market and technological shifts that render ineffective an organization's established processes of self-maintenance. The decline in demand for domestic textiles and steel provides two examples of market shifts that have prompted increased entropy in a number of economic sectors. The greatly diminished demand for mechanically based products and systems as a consequence of advancements in electronics and software would exemplify a technological shift that has given rise to similar entropy.

Based on a review of the relevant literature, Zammuto and Cameron (Zammuto, Whetten, and Cameron, 1983; Zammuto and Cameron, 1985; Cameron and Zammuto, 1983) have proposed an integrative model depicting four different types of environmental decline resulting from entropy (see Figure 1.2). The four types vary by (1) type of change in ecological niche configuration (size versus shape) and (2) the continuity of change (continuous versus discontinuous). Organizations that encounter continuous decline in the size of their ecological niche experience 'erosion'. Those that encounter a discontinuous decline in their niche's size experience 'contraction'. 'Dissolution' is experienced when a continuous change in the shape of a niche occurs. Finally, 'collapse' refers to a rapid, unanticipated shift in an organization's existing niche and the emergence of a new niche. Zammuto and Cameron's (1985) model is important because it suggests that different types of environmental entrophy result in diffenent types of organizational decline. Moreover, it underscores that to survive and prosper, organizations must select domain strategies that address the challenges presented by different environmental conditions.

Dynamics of Decline

A declining organization encounters many difficult challenges. Most notably, decline induces changes in virtually all relationships within an organization and between an organization and its environment. Research on the various organizational processes affected by decline has been uneven. It has ranged from theoretical models of organizational responses to scarcity (Nottenburg and Fedor, 1983) to analyses of stress caused by budget cuts (Jick, 1983) to suggestions for managing organizational retrenchment and death (Harris and Sutton, 1986; Robinson, 1985). The following review will survey findings on the two organizational attributes which have received the most attention in the decline literature. These are top management leadership and workforce composition.

Top management leadership

One nearly universal generalization emerges from the literature on organizational decline. Research supports the view that a declining organization's successful turnaround is dependent on the replacement of its current leadership (top management). Both recent case (Kothari and Near, 1982) and policy (O'Neill, 1986)

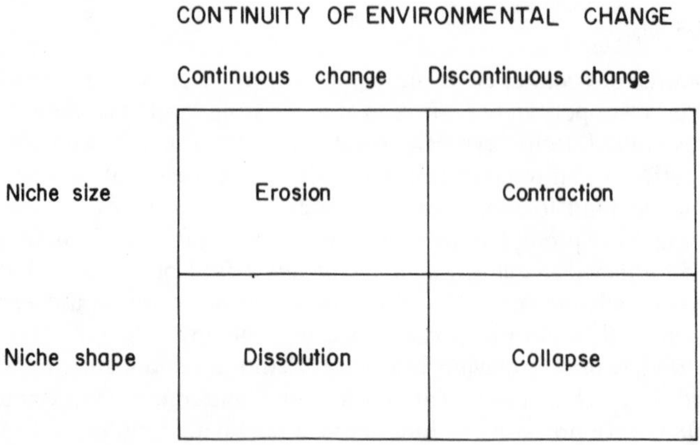

CONTINUITY OF ENVIRONMENTAL CHANGE

	Continuous change	Discontinuous change
Niche size	Erosion	Contraction
Niche shape	Dissolution	Collapse

Figure 1.2 A model of environmental decline
Source: based on Cameron and Zammuto (1983), Zammuto, Whetten, and Cameron (1985), and Zammuto and Cameron (1985)

studies offer similar results. These results are consistent with research extending back at least a decade (Hofer, 1980; Khandwalla, 1981, 1983-1984; Schendel, Patton, and Riggs, 1976; Starbuck, Greve, and Hedberg, 1978). It is generally held that outside recruitment of top management is associated with the introduction of novel viewpoints and practices (Dalton and Kesner, 1983, 1985b). New top-level managers are not shackled to existing administrative patterns and resource allocations. By voicing their opinions and questioning old knowledge, new managers can trigger organizational learning. The exact manner in which new top-level managers prompt organization recoveries deserves further research (cf. Hambrick, 1985; Tushman, Virany, and Romanelli, 1985). Especially intriguing would be a more complete understanding of what the popular press has labeled 'masters of the corporate turnaround' (Cole, 1983; Eklund, 1986).

Workforce composition

One of the most disturbing effects of decline is that while voluntary turnover of all employees typically increases, it is usually the most qualified (hence mobile) employees who leave first (Greenhalgh, 1983a, 1983b). The net consequence is a 'regression to the mean' in labor pool qualifications (Whetten, 1981). Between the human resource management and business policy literatures, this dilemma has been dealt with extensively. While general economic conditions will affect the extent to which more valuable workers exit (Levine and Wolohojian, 1983; Levine, 1984), it is generally reasoned that those most qualified do not want their record marred by failure and are drawn away by attractive job alternatives in more prosperous organizations. Thus, those employees with the greatest potential for turning around a declining organization see little incentive for making the effort. Case evidence suggests, however, that there are at least two exceptions to this pattern: (1) high-quality employees who are extremely loyal, and (2) better employees retained by promises of equal or better positions in a parent organization (Sutton, 1983). The more prescriptive business policy literature echoes the importance of enacting this second exception (Harrigan, 1984).

Perhaps the most extensive outline of a role for human resource management in a declining organization has been provided by Ferris, Schellenberg, and Zammuto (1984). Taking the Cameron and Zammuto (1983) model of environmental decline, they have developed a model identifying different roles and responsibilities within the human resource function under different conditions of environmental decline. Although the model must still be tested, it clearly suggests that organizations must take into account the capacity of their human resource managers in implementing strategic responses to decline.

Clearly, gaps yet remain in our understanding of how to manage human resources more effectively in a declining organization. Improvements in our understanding of ways to prevent the exit of key employees are especially needed. Drawing on case analyses of the declines experienced by companies such as Continental Illinois Bank and Itel Corporation, Perry (1984) suggests that in addition to increasing career opportunities in order to reduce ill-timed employee exit, organizations should strive to reduce organizational uncertainty by creating the impression that survival is guaranteed or turnaround is imminent. He indicates that this can be accomplished in numerous ways. Perhaps the most powerful means involves creating a new organizational image. In one example, he cites Lee Iacocca as spokesperson for the advertising campaign that introduced 'The New Chrysler Corporation'. Regardless of the means chosen for countering key employee loss, it is generally acknowledged that how an organization treats its employees during stressful periods is of critical importance to its long-term health (Smith, 1982).

Although the preceding review has focused on the two organizational attributes which have received the most attention in the decline literature, others should not be ignored. As identified by Greenhalgh (1983a), other major organizational attributes affected by decline include various structural properties, e.g. formalization, centralization, differentiation (Cullen, Anderson, and Baker, 1986), and administrative intensity (Goh and Evans, 1985); slack, meaning a surplus of resources over what is required to maintain equilibrium in an ecological niche; adaptive innovation (McKinley, 1984); and relationships with employees, unions, competitors, and regulatory agencies. A more complete understanding of the complex interrelated processes that occur during decline would enable a more complete response to be made to questions such as (Wilson, 1985), 'Which organizations will die?' 'Which survive?' 'What can be done to revive a wounded organization?' and 'Why did this organization decline or, in transmigrating, become a different creature?'.

CONCLUSION

A review of the literature in four topic areas in which substantial scholarship has been conducted recently suggests that the organization theory field is alive. Important work is being conducted not only in such traditional strongholds as Great Britain and the United States, but throughout Europe, Canada, Australia, Israel, and Japan. However, if the field is alive, does this (as our opening sentence suggests) mean that it is also well? In the eyes of some, the answer to this question is less certain. Organization theorists, they concede, are undoubtedly investigating important issues, but they yet wonder whether the field is progressing as a result of such investigations. As in so many other instances associated with organization theory, different opinions have emerged (Donaldson, 1985). Based on the preceding four-part literature review, the position advanced here is that progress is being made; perhaps not as quickly as some might wish, but nevertheless advances have been real. Indeed, over the past four decades, organization theory has emerged as a purposeful, coherent area of study with its own criteria and traditions.

This emergence and its accompanying progress are manifest in several ways. First, organization theorists are interested in an ever-increasing number of phenomena and are exploring these phenomena in a greater variety of ways. There are strong incentives for researchers to 'create intellectual novelty and pursue distinctive paradigms' (Astley, 1985b, p. 504). Given its multidisciplinary roots, the organization theory field has resisted advancing a given world view or a single preferred analytical perspective. This has contributed greatly to the dynamic and pluralistic growth of organization research. Moreover, it has served as a substantial safeguard against academic isolationism and conceptual stagnation.

A second manifestation of progress is the many efforts to relate organization theory to developments in other areas, especially business policy/strategic management and industrial economics. The resulting cross-fertilization of ideas has led to a wide range of issues being studied and to the development of differing methods of research. Boundaries which were once clearly labeled organizational sociology, industrial economics, business policy/strategy management, public administration, and so on, are now quite vague.

A final manifestation of progress is the growing international exchange of knowledge concerning organizations. The international editorial board of the relatively new journal *Organization Studies*, published by the European Group for Organizational Studies (EGOS), is one sign of an excitement and vitality that transcends national boundaries. In the United States, an increasing internationalization of the Academy of Management's Organization and Management Theory Division is another. Both efforts have been supported by an international emphasis long evident in traditional research outlets such as the *Administrative Science Quarterly*, and their newer counterparts such as the *Journal of Management*.

Attention to such progress is not meant to suggest that there are no reasons for concern. As suggested in the instance of organizational effectiveness studies, too often it seems that the popularity of research themes has either grown or declined in direct proportion to their marketability rather than the degree to which basic issues have been resolved and critical phenomena understood.

One consequence of this tendency to focus on 'hot' topics is what some see as an extreme iconoclasm resulting in an unhealthy fragmentation of the field (Astley, 1985b). Instead of that being a tendency to build on previous findings, a vogue seems to exist in some quarters that encourages a preoccupation with 'fad and fashion'. As Staw (1985, p. 97) has observed, this would seem to explain why a measure of organization theory research tends to be 'literature driven' rather than problem driven. One predictable consequence is that much organization research is non-cumulative and non-communicable across quarters. Needless to say, such difficulties have led to substantial and frequent disagreements. Confusion and controversy, however, are traditionally characteristic of a new and growing field of study. In this regard, organization theory has been no exception.

ACKNOWLEDGEMENTS

The critical comments of Edward R. Kemery (University of Baltimore), Robert T. Lenz (Indiana University—Indianapolis), Robert E. Quinn (State University of New York at Albany), James D. Werbel (Louisiana State University), and Raymond R. Zammuto (University of Colorado at Denver) on an earlier draft manuscript are gratefully acknowledged.

REFERENCES

Aldrich, H. (1979). *Organizations and Environments*. Engelwood Cliffs, NJ: Prentice-Hall.
Aldrich, H. (1986). *Population Perspectives on Organizations*. Uppsala: Acta Universitatis Upsaliensis.
Aldrich, H., and Auster, E. R. (1986). Even dwarfs started small: Liabilities of age and size and their strategic implications. *Research in Organizational Behavior*, **8**.
Aldrich, H., and McKelvey, B. (1983). The population perspective and the organization form concept. *Economia Aziendale*, **2** (1), 63-86.

Aldrich, H., McKelvey, B., and Ulrich, D. (1984). Design strategy from the population perspective. *Journal of Management*, **10**, 67-86.

Altman, E. I. (1983). Why businesses fail. *Journal of Business Strategy*, **3** (4), 15-21.

Argyris, C. (1982). The executive mind and double-loop learning. *Organizational Dynamics*, **11** (5), 5-22.

Argyris, C. (1985). Developing with threat and defensiveness. In *Organizational Strategy and Change*, ed. J. M. Pennings *et al.*, pp. 412-430. San Francisco: Jossey-Bass.

Argyris, C., and Schön, D. A. (1978). *Organizational Learning: A Theory of Action Perspective*, Reading, MA: Addison-Wesley.

Astley, W. G. (1984). Toward an appreciation of collective strategy. *Academy of Management Review*, **9**, 526-535.

Astley, W. G. (1985a). The two ecologies: Population and community perspectives on organizational evolution. *Administrative Science Quarterly*, **30**, 224-241.

Astley, W. G. (1985b). Administrative science as socially constructed truth. *Administrative Science Quarterly*, **30**, 497-513.

Astley, W. G., and Fombrun, C. J. (1983). Collective strategy: The social ecology of organizational environments. *Academy of Management Review*, **8**, 576-587.

Astley, W. G., and Van de Ven, A. (1983). Central perspectives and debates in organization theory. *Administrative Science Quarterly*, **28**, 245-273.

Banthin, J., and Stelzer, L. (1986). Political action committees: Facts, fancy, and morality. *Journal of Business Ethics*, **5**, 13-19.

Barnard, C. I. (1938). *The Functions of the Executive*. Cambridge: Harvard University Press.

Baysinger, B. D. (1984). Domain maintenance as an objective of business political activity: An expanded typology. *Academy of Management Review*, **9**, 248-258.

Baysinger, B. D., and Woodman, R. W. (1982). Dimensions of the public affairs/government relations function in American corporations. *Strategic Management Journal*, **3**, 27-41.

Bazerman, M. H., and Schoorman, F. D. (1983). A limited rationality model of interlocking directorates. *Academy of Management Review*, **8**, 206-217.

Bedeian, A. G. (1986a). *Management*. Hinsdale, IL: Dryden Press.

Bedeian, A. G. (1986b). Contemporary challenges in the study of organizations. *Yearly Review, Journal of Management*, **12**, 185-201.

Bennis, W., and Nanus, B. (1985). *Leaders: The Strategies for Taking Charge*. New York: Harper & Row.

Berger, P. L. (1981). New attack on the legitimacy of business. *Harvard Business Review*, **59** (11), 82-89.

Betton, J., and Dess, G. G. (1985). The applications of population ecology models to the study of organizations. *Academy of Management Review*, **10**, 750-757.

Bidwell, C. E., and Kasarda, J. D. (1985). *The Organization and its Ecosystem; A Theory of Structuring in Organizations*. Greenwich, CN: JAI Press

Bluedorn, A. C. (1980). Cutting the Gordian knot: A critique of the effectiveness traditional in organizational research. *Sociology and Social Research*, **64**, 477-497.

Bourgeois, L. J. (1985). Strategic goals, perceived uncertainty, and economic performance in volatile environments. *Academy of Management Review*, **28**, 548-573.

Bozeman, B. (1982). Organization structure and the effectiveness of public agencies: An assessment and agenda. *International Journal of Public Administration*, **4**, 235-296.

Brunsson, N. (1985). *The Irrational Organization: Irrationality as a Basis for Organizational Action and Change*. Chichester, UK: Wiley

Burt, R. S. (1982). *Toward a Structural Theory of Action*. New York: Academic Press.

Burt, R. S. (1983a). *Corporate Profits and Cooptation: Networks of Market Constraints and Directorate Ties in the American Economy*. New York: Academic Press.

Burt, R. S. (1983b). Corporate philanthropy as a cooptive relation. *Social Forces*, **62**, 419-449.

Büschges, G. (1985). [Review of *Organizational Systematics*: taxonomy, evolution, classification] *Organization Studies*, **6**, 191-193.

Cameron, K. S. (1978). Measuring organizational effectiveness in institutions of higher education. *Administrative Science Quarterly*, **23**, 604-632.

Cameron, K. S. (1981a). Domains of organizational effectiveness. *Academy of Management Journal*, **24**, 25-47.

Cameron, K. S. (1981b). The enigma of organizational effectiveness. In *New Directions for Program Evaluation: Measuring Effectiveness*, ed. D. Baugher, pp. 1-13 San Francisco: Jossey-Bass.

Cameron, K. (1986). A study of organizational effectiveness and its predictors. *Management Science*, **32**, 87-112.

Cameron, K. S., and Whetten, D. A. (1981). Perceptions of organizational effectiveness across organizational life cycles. *Administrative Science Quarterly*, **26**, 525-544.

Cameron, K. S., and Whetten, D. A. (1984). Models of the organizational life cycle: Applications to higher education. In *College and University Organization: Insights from the Behavioral Sciences*, ed. J. L. Bess, pp. 31-61 New York: New York University Press.

Cameron, K. S., and Zammuto, R. (1983). Matching managerial strategies to conditions of decline. *Human Resource Management*, **22**, 359-375.

Camillus, J. C., and Venkatraman, N. (1984). Dimensions of strategic choice. *Planning Review*, **12** (1), 26-31, 46.

Campbell, J. P. (1976). Contributions research can make in understanding organization effectiveness. *Organization and Administrative Science*, **7** (1), 29-45.

Carroll, G. R. (1983). A stochastic model of organizational mortality: Review and reanalysis. *Social Science Research*, **12**, 303-329.

Carroll, G. R. (1985). Concentration and specialization: Dynamics of niche width in populations of organizations. *American Journal of Sociology*, **90**, 1262-1283.

Carroll, G. R., and Delacroix, J. (1982). Organizational mortality in the newspaper industry of Argentina and Ireland: An ecological approach. *Administrative Science Quarterly*, **27**, 169-198.

Chappell, H. W., Jr (1982). Campaign contributions and congressional voting: A simultaneous probit-tobit model. *Review of Economics and Statistics*, **64**, 77-83.

Clinard, M. B. (1983a). *Corporate Ethics and Crime*. Beverly Hills: Sage

Clinard, M. B. (1983b). *Corporate Crime, Ethics and Middle Management*. Beverly Hills: Sage.

Clinebell, S. (1984). Organizational effectiveness: An examination of recent empirical studies and the development of the contingency view. In *Proceedings 27th Annual Conference Midwest Academy of Management*, ed. W. D. Terpening and K. R. Thompson, pp. 92-102. Notre Dame, IN: Department of Management, University of Notre Dame.

Cole, R. J. (1983). Masters of the corporate turnaround. *New York Times*, 31 July, Section 3, pp. 1, 9-10.

Comfort, L. K. (1985). Action research: A model for organizational learning. *Journal of Policy Analysis and Management*, **5**, 100-118.

Connally, T., Conlon, E. J., and Deutsch, S. J. (1980). Organizational effectiveness: A multiple-constituency approach. *Academy of Management Review*, **5**, 211-217.

Cooper, A. C., and Schendel, D. (1983). Strategic responses to technological threats. In *Business Policy and Strategy; Concepts and Readings*, ed. D. J. McCarthy, pp. 207-219. Homewood, IL: Irwin

Covington, C. R. (1985). Development of organizational memory in presidential agencies. *Administration and Society*, **17**, 171-196.

Cullen, J. B., Anderson, K. S., and Baker, D. D. (1986). Blau's theory of structural differentiation revisited: A theory of structural change or scale? *Academy of Management Journal*, **29**, 203-229.

Culnan, M. J. (1983). Environmental scanning: The effects of task complexity and source accessibility on information gathering behavior. *Decision Sciences*, **14**, 194-206.

Cummings, L. L. (1978). Toward organizational behavior. *Academy of Management Review*, **4**, 90-98.

Cummings, L. L. (1982). Organizational behavior. *Annual Review of Psychology*, **33**, 541-579.

Cyert, R. M., and MacGrimmon, K. R. (1968). Organizations. In *Handbook of Social Psychology*, 2nd edn, ed. G. Lindzey and E. Aronson, vol. 1, pp. 568-611 Reading, MA: Addison-Wesley.

Cyert, R. M., and March, J. G. (1959). A behavioral theory of organizational objectives. In *Modern Organization Theory*, ed. M. Haire, pp. 76-90. New York: Wiley.

Cyert, R. M., and March, J. G. (1963). *A Behavioral Theory of the Firm*. Englewood Cliffs, NJ: Prentice-Hall

Dalton, D. R., and Kesner, I. F. (1983). Inside/outside succession and organizational size: The pragmatics of executive replacement. *Academy of Management Journal*, **26**, 736-742.

Dalton, D. R., and Kesner, I. F. (1985a). Organizational growth: Big is beautiful. *Journal of Business Strategy*, **6**, 38-48.

Dalton, D. R., and Kesner, I. F. (1985b). Organizational performance as an antecedent of inside/outside chief executive succession: An empirical assessment. *Academy of Management Journal*, **28**, 749-762.

Delacroix, J., and Carroll, G. R. (1983). Organizational foundings: An ecological study of the newspaper industries of Argentina and Ireland. *Administrative Science Quarterly*, **28**, 274-291.

Dery, D. (1982). Erring and learning: An organizational analysis. *Accounting, Organizations and Society*, **7**, 217-223.

Dery, D. (1983). Decision-making, problem-solving and organizational learning. *Omega*, **11**, 321-328.

Dess, G. G., and Beard, D. W. (1984). Dimensions of organizational task environments. *Administrative Science Quarterly*, **29**, 52-73.

Dickie, R. B. (1984). Influence of public affairs offices on corporate planning and of corporations on government policy. *Strategic Management Journal*, **5**, 15-34.

Diffenbach, J. (1983). Corporate environmental analysis in large U. S. corporations. *Long Range Planning*, **16** (3), 107-116.

DiMaggio, P. J., and Powell, W. W. (1983). The iron cage revisited: Institutional isomorphism and collective rationality in organizational fields. *American Sociological Review*, **48**, 147-160.

Donaldson, L. (1985). *In Defence of Organization Theory: A Reply to the Critics*. Cambridge: Cambridge University Press.

Dowling, J., and Pfeffer, J. (1975). Organizational legitimacy: Social values and organizational behavior. *Pacific Sociological Review*, **18**, 122-135.

Drazin, R., and Van de Ven, A. H. (1985). Alternative forms of fit in contingency theory. *Administrative Science Quarterly*, **30**, 514-539.

Dunbar, R. L. M., and Wasilewski, N. (1985). Regulating external threats in the cigarette industry. *Administrative Science Quarterly*, **30**, 540-559.

Dutton, J. M., and Freedman, R. D. (1985). External environment and internal strategies: Calculating, experimenting, and imitating in organizations. *Advances in Strategic Management*, **3**, 39-67.

Eells, R., and Nehemkis, P. (1984). *Corporate Intelligence and Espionage*, New York, Macmillan

Eklund, C. S. (1986). Stan Hiller is old-fashioned: He fixes broken companies. *Business Week*, 31 March, pp. 74-75.

Ermann, M. D., and Lundman, R. J. (1982). *Corporate Deviance*. New York: Holt, Rinehart, & Winston.

Etheredge, L. S. (1981). Government learning: An overview. In *Handbook of Political Behavior*, ed. S. L. Long, vol. 2, pp. 73-161. New York: Plenum.

Faerman, S., and Quinn, R. E. (in press). Effectiveness: The perspective from organizational theory. *Higher Education Review*.

Fahey, L., King, W., and Narayanan, V. (1981). Environmental scanning and forecasting in strategic planning—the state-of-the-art. *Long Range Planning*, **14** (1), 32-39.

Farh, J., Hoffman, R. C., and Hegarty, W. H. (1984). Assessing environmental scanning at the subunit level: A multitrait-multimethod analysis. *Decision Sciences*, **15**, 197-220.

Fennema, M. (1982). *International networks of banks and industry*. The Hague: Martinus Hijhoff

Ferris, G. R., Schellenberg, D. A., and Zammuto, R. F. (1984). Human resource management strategies in declining industries. *Human Resource Management*, **23**, 381-394.

Fiol, C. M., and Lyles, M. A. (1985). Organizational learning. *Academy of Management Review*, **10**, 803-811.

Foo, W. F., Oliga, J. C., and Puxty, A. G. (1981). The population ecology model and management action. *Journal of Enterprise Management*, **2**, 317-325.

Ford, J. D., and Hegarty, W. H. (1984). Decision makers' beliefs about the causes and effects of structure: An exploratory study. *Academy of Management Journal*, **27**, 271-291.

Freeman, J. H. (1982). Organizational life cycles and natural selection processes. *Research in Organizational Behavior*, **4**, 1-32.

Freeman, J., Carroll, G. R., and Hannan, M. T. (1983). Age dependence in organizational death rates. *American Sociological Review*, **48**, 692-710.

Freeman, J., and Hannan, M. T. (1983). Niche width and the dynamics of organizational populations. *American Journal of Sociology*, **88**, 1116-1145.

Friedlander, F. (1983). Patterns of individual and organizational learning. In *The Executive Mind*, ed. S. Shrivastava *et al.*, pp. 192-220. San Francisco: Jossey-Bass.

Gilmore, T., and Hirschhorn, L. (1983). The downsizing dilemma: Leadership in the age of discontinuity. *Wharton Annual, 1984*, **8**, 94-104.

Gilmore, T., and Hirschhorn, L. (1984). Management challenges under conditions of retrenchment. *Human Resource Management*, **22**, 341-357.

Goh, S. C., and Evans, M. G. (1985). Organization growth and decline: The impact on direct and administrative components of a university. *Canadian Journal of Sociology*, **10**, 121-138.

Goodman, P. S., Atkin, R. S., and Schoorman, F. D. (1982). On the demise of organizational effectiveness studies. In *Organizational Effectiveness: A Comparison of Multiple Models*, ed. K. S. Cameron and D. A. Whetten, pp. 163-183. New York: Academic Press

Goodman, P. S., Pennings, J. M., et al. (eds.) (1977). *New Perspectives on Organizational Effectiveness*. San Francisco: Jossey-Bass.

Green, S. G., Bean, A.S., and Snavely, B. K. (1983). Idea management in R&D as a human information processing analog. *Human Systems Management*, **4**, 98-112.

Greenhalgh, L. (1983a). Organizational decline. *Research in the Sociology of Organizations*, **2**, 231-276.

Greenhalgh, L. (1983b). Managing the job insecurity crisis. *Human Resource Management*, **22**, 431-444.

Grover, R. (1986). Campaign reformers just can't catch up with the PACs. *Business Week*, 20 January, pp. 24-26.

Hall, R. H. (1980). Effectiveness theory and organizational effectiveness. *Journal of Applied Behavioral Science*, **16**, 536-545.

Hambrick, D. C. (1981). Environment, strategy, and power within top management teams. *Administrative Science Quarterly*, **26**, 253-276.

Hambrick, D. C. (1985). Turnaround strategies. In *Handbook of Business Strategy*, ed. W. D. Guth, pp. 10/1-10/32 Boston: Warren, Gorham & Lamont.

Handler, E., and Mulkern, J. R. (1982). *Business in Politics*. Lexington MA: Lexington Books.

Hannan, M. T., and Freeman, J. (1984). Structural inertia and organizational change. *American Sociological Review*, **49**, 149-164.

Harrigan, K. R. (1984). Managing declining businesses. *Journal of Business Strategy*, **4** (3), 74-78.

Harris, S. G., and Sutton, R. I. (1986). Functions of parting ceremonies in dying organizations. *Academy of Management Journal*, **29**, 5-30.

Hedberg, B. L. T. (1981). How organizations learn and unlearn. In *Handbook of Organizational Design*, ed. P. C. Nystrom and W. H. Starbuck, vol. 1, pp. 3-27. New York: Oxford University Press

Hedberg, B. L. T., Nystrom, P. C., and Starbuck, W. H. (1976). Camping on seesaws: Presciptions for a self-designing organization. *Administrative Science Quarterly*, **21**, 41-64.

Herriott, S. R., Levinthal, D., and March, J. G. (1985). Learning from experience in organizations. *American Economic Review* (Papers and Proceedings), **75**, 298-302.

Higgins, J. C. (1986). Progress in monitoring the sociopolitical environment of the firm. *Omega*, **14**, 49-55.

Hirsch, P. (1975). Organizational effectiveness and the institutional environment. *Administrative Science Quarterly*, **20**, 327-344.

Hofer, C. W. (1980). Designing turnaround strategies. *Journal of Business Strategy*, **1** (1), 19-31.

Hrebiniak, L. G., and Joyce, W. F. (1985). Organizational adaptation: Strategic choice and environmental determinism. *Administrative Science Quarterly*, **30**, 336-349.

Ijiri, Y., and Simon, H. A. (1967). A model of business firm growth. *Econometrica*, **35**, 348-355.

Jain, S. (1984). Environmental scanning in U.S. corporations. *Long Range Planning*, **17** (2), 117-128.

Jick, T. D. (1983), The stressful effects of budget cuts in organizations. In *Topics in Managerial Accounting*, ed. A Rosen, pp. 267-280 Toronto: McGraw-Hill

Kasarda, J. D., and Bidwell, C. E. (1984). A human ecological theory of organizational structuring. In *Sociological Human Ecology: Contemporary Issues and Applications*. In *Sociological Human Ecology: Contemporary Issues and Applications*, ed. M. Micklin and H. M. Choldin, pp. 183-236. Boulder, CO: Westview.

Kau, J. B., Keenan, D., Rubin, P. H. (1982). A general equilibrium model of congressional voting. *Quarterly Journal of Economics*, **97**, 271-293.

Kau, J. B., and Rubin, P. H. (1981). The impact of labor unions on the passage of economic legislation. *Journal of Labor Research*, **2**, 133-145.

Kaufman, H. (1985). *Time, Chance and Organizations: Natural Selection in a Perilous Environment*. Chatham, NJ: Chatham House.

Keating, B. P., and Keating, M. O. (1981). Goal setting and efficiency in social service agencies. *Long Range Planning*, **14** (1), 39-48.

Keim, G. (1985). Corporate grassroots programs in the 1980's. *California Management Review*, **28**, 110-123.

Keim, G. D., Zeithaml, C. P., and Baysinger, B. D. (1984). New directions for corporate political strategy. *Sloan Management Review*, **25** (3), 53-62.

Khandwalla, P. N. (1981). Strategy for turning around complex sick organizations. *Vikalpa*, **6** (3-4), 143-165.

Khandwalla, P. N. (1983-1984). Turnaround management of mismanaged complex organizations. *International Studies of Management and Organization*, **8** (4), 5-41.

Klein, H. E., and Linneman, R. E. (1984) Environmental assessment: An international study of corporate practice. *Journal of Business Strategy*, **5** (1), 66-75.

Korsching, P. F. (1983). The ecology of an ecological study: Comments on Marple's 'Technology Innovation and Organizational Survival'. *Sociological Quarterly*, **24**, 151-153.

Kothari, R. M., and Near, J. P. (1982). Decline and revival of a sick enterprise: A case discussion. *Indian Management*, **21** (7), 9-15.

Krantz, J. (1985). Group process under conditions of organizational decline. *Journal of Applied Behavioral Science*, **21**, 1-17.

Lenz, R. T., and Engledow, J. L. (1986). Environmental analysis units and strategic decision-making: A field study of selected 'leading-edge' corporations. *Strategic Management Journal*, **7**, 69–89.

Levine, C. H. (1978). Organizational decline and cutback management. *Public Administration Review*, **38**, 316–325.

Levine, C. H. (1984). Retrenchment, human resource erosion, and the role of the personnel manager. *Public Personnel Management Journal*, **13**, 249–263.

Levine, C. H., and Wolohojian, G. G. (1983). Retrenchment and human resources management: Combatting the discount effects of uncertainty. In *Public Personnel Management: Problems and Prospects*, ed. S. W. Hays and R. C. Kearney, pp. 175–188. Englewood Cliffs, NJ: Prentice-Hall

Levinthal, D., and March, J. G. (1981). A model of adaptive organizational search. *Journal of Economic Behavior and Organization*, **2**, 307–333.

Lewin, A. Y., and Minton, J. W. (in press). Determining organizational effectiveness: Another look, and an agenda for research. *Management Science*, **32**, 514–538.

McKelvey, B., and Aldrich, H. (1983). Populations, natural selection, and applied organizational science. *Administrative Science Quarterly*, **28**, 101–128.

McKinley, W. (1984). Organizational decline and innovation in manufacturing. In *Strategic Management of Industrial R&D*, ed. B. Bozeman, M. Crow, and A. Link), pp. 147–159 Lexington, MA: Lexington Books.

McNamee, S. J. (1983). Capital accumulation and the Du Pont Company: An historical analysis. *Organization Studies*, **4**, 201–218. Errata. *Organization Studies* (1984) **5**, 208–209.

McPherson, M. (1983). An ecology of affiliation. *American Sociological Review*, **48**, 519–532.

Malbin, M. J. (1979). Campaign financing and the 'special interests'. *Public Interest*, **56**, 21–42.

March, J. G. (1962). Some recent substantive and methodological developments in the theory of organizational decision-making. In *Essays on the Behavioral Study of Politics*, ed. A. Ranney, pp. 191–208. Urbana: University of Illinois Press.

March, J. G. (ed.) (1965). *Handbook of Organizations*. Chicago: Rand McNally.

March, J. G. (1982). Theories of choice and making decisions. *Society*, **20**, 29–39.

March, J. G., and Olsen, J. P. (1975). The uncertainty of the past: Organizational learning under ambiguity. *European Journal of Political Research*, **3**, 147–171.

March, J. G., and Olsen, J. P. (1976). *Ambiguity and Choice in Organizations* Bergen: Universitetsforlaget.

March, J. G., and Sevón, G. (1982). Gossip, information, and decision making. *Advances in Information in Organizations*, **1**, 95–105.

Mark, M. W., and Shotland, R. L. (1985). Stakeholder-based evaluations and value judgments. *Evaluation Review*, **9**, 605–626.

Marple, D. (1982). Technological innovation and organizational survival: A population ecology study of nineteenth-century American railroads. *Sociological Quarterly*, **23**, 107–116.

Marple, D. (1983). Reply to Korshing's 'The Ecology of an Ecological Study: Comments on Marple's Technological Innovation and Organizational Survival'. *Sociological Quarterly*, **24**, 155–157.

Masters, M. F., and Baysinger, B. D. (1985). The determinants of funds raised by corporate political action committees: An empirical examination. *Academy of Management Journal*, **28**, 654–664.

Masters, M. F., and Delaney, J. T. (1985). Interunion variation in congressional campaign contributions. *Industrial Relations*, **23**, 410–416.

Masters, M. F., and Keim, G. D. (1985). Determinants of PAC participation among large corporations. *Journal of Politics*, **47**, 1158–1173.

Meyer, M. W. (1985). *Limits to Bureaucratic Growth*. Berlin: Gruyter.

Miller, D., and Friesen, P. (1980). Archtypes of organizational transition. *Administrative Science Quarterly*, **25**, 268–269.

Miner, J. B. (1982). *Theories of Organizational Structure and Processes*. Hinsdale, IL: Dryden

Mintz, B., and Schwartz, M. (1981). Interlocking directorates and interest group formation. *American Sociological Review*, **46**, 851-869.

Mintz, B., and Schwartz, M. (1985). *The Power Structure of American Business* Chicago: University of Chicago Press.

Mitchell, T. R. (1979). Organizational behavior. *Annual Review of Psychology*, **30**, 243-281.

Mizruchi, M. S. (1982). *The American Corporate Network: 1904-1974*. Beverly Hills: Sage.

Mossholder, K. W., and Bedeian, A. G. (1983a). Cross-level inference and organizational research: Perspectives on interpretation and application. *Academy of Management Review*, **8**, 547-558.

Mossholder, K. W., and Bedeian, A. G. (1983b). Group interaction processes: Individual and group effects. *Group and Organization Studies*, **8**, 187-202.

Nishi, K. (1979). *Management Scanning Behavior: A Study of Information-Acquisition Behavior.* Tokyo: Saikon.

Nishi, K., Schoderbek, C., Schoderbek, P. P. (1982). Scanning the organizational environment: Some empirical results. *Human Systems Management*, **3**, 233-245.

Normann, R. (1985). Developing capabilities for organizational learning. In *Organizational Strategy and Change*, ed., J. M. Pennings *et al.*, pp. 217-248 San Francisco: Jossey-Bass.

Nottenburg, G., and Fedor, D. B. (1983). Scarcity in the environment: Organizational perceptions, interpretations and responses. *Organization Studies*, **4**, 317-337.

Nystrom, P. C., and Starbuck, W. H. (eds.) (1981). *Handbook of Organizational Design*, vols. 1-2. New York: Oxford University Press.

Nystrom, P. C., and Starbuck, W. H. (1984a). To avoid organizational crises, unlearn. *Organizational Dynamics*, **12** (4), 53-65.

Nystrom, P. C., and Starbuck, W. H. (1984b). Managing beliefs in organizations. *Journal of Applied Behavioral Science*, **20**, 277-287.

O'Neill, H. M. (1986). Turnaround strategy and recovery: What strategy do you need? *Long Range Planning*, **19** (1), 8-88.

Ornstein, M. (1984). Interlocking directorates in Canada: Intercorporate or class alliance? *Administrative Science Quarterly*, **29**, 210-231.

O'Toole, J. (1985). *Vanguard Management*. Garden City, NY: Doubleday.

Palmer, D. (1983). Broken ties: Interlocking directorates and intercorporate coordination. *Administrative Science Quarterly*, **28**, 40-55.

Pennings, J. M. (1980). *Interlocking Directorates: Origins and Consequences of Connections Among Organizations' Boards of Directors*. San Francisco: Jossey-Bass.

Perry, L. T. (1984). Key human resource strategies in an organization downturn. *Human Resource Management*, **23**, 61-75.

Pervin, L. A., and Lewis, M. (1978). Overview of the internal-external issue. In *Perspectives in Interactional Psychology*. ed. L. A. Pervin and M. Lewis, pp, 1-22 New York: Plenum.

Pfeffer, J. (1986). Organizations and organization theory. In *Handbook of Social Psychology*, 3rd edn, ed. G. Lindzey and E. Aronson, vol. 1, pp. 379-440. New York: Random House.

Quinn, R. E., and Cameron, K. (1983). Organizational life cycles and shifting criteria of effectiveness: Some preliminary evidence. *Management Science*, **29**, 33-51.

Quinn, R. E., and Rohrbaugh, J. (1981). A competing values approach to organizational effectiveness. *Public Productivity Review*, **5**, 122-140.

Quinn, R. E., and Rohrbaugh, J. (1983). A spatial model of effectiveness criteria: Towards a competing values approach to organizational analysis. *Management Science*, **29**, 363-377.

Rice, G. H., Jr (1985). Available information and superstitious decision making. *Journal of General Management*, **11** (2), 35-44.

Robinson, I. (1985). Managing retrenchment in a public service organization. *Canadian Public Administration*, **28**, 513-530.

Rohrbaugh, J. (1981). Operationalizing the competing values approach: Measuring performance in the employment service. *Public Productivity Review*, **5**, 141-159.

Rohrbaugh, J. (1983). The competing values approach: Innovation and effectiveness in the job service. In *Organizational Theory and Public Policy*, ed. R. H. Hall and R. E. Quinn, pp. 265-280. Hollywood: Sage.

Roy, W. G. (1983). The unfolding of the interlocking directorate structure of the United States. *American Sociological Review*, **48**, 248-257.

Rundall, T. G., and McClain, J. O. (1982). Environmental selection and physician supply. *American Journal of Sociology*, **87**, 1090-1112.

Sahal, D. (1981). *Patterns of Technological Innovation*. Reading, MA: Addison-Wesley.

Schendel, D., Patton, G. R., and Riggs, J. (1976). Corporate turnaround strategies: A study of profit decline and recovery. *Journal of General Management*, **3** (3), 3-11.

Schneider, B. (1985). Organizational behavior. *Annual Review of Psychology*, **36**, 573-611.

Schoonhoven, C. B. (1981). Problems with contingency theory: Testing assumptions hidden within the language of contingency 'theory'. *Administrative Science Quarterly*, **26**, 349-377.

Schoorman, F. D., Bazerman, M. H., and Atkin, R. S. (1981). Interlocking directorates: A strategy for reducing environmental uncertainty. *Academy of Management Review*, **6**, 243-251.

Schreyogg, G. (1980). Contingency and choice in organization theory. *Organization Studies*, **1**, 305-326.

Scott, J., and Griff, C. (1984). *Directors of Industry: The British Corporate Network 1904-76*. Cambridge, UK: Polity.

Scott, W. R. (1964). Theory of organizations. In *Handbook of Modern Sociology*, ed. R. E. L. Faris, pp. 485-529 Chicago: Rand McNally.

Scott, W. R. (1975). Organizational structure. *Annual Reivew of Sociology*, **1**, 1-20.

Shepard, H. A. (1967). Innovation-resisting and innovation-producing organizations. *Journal of Business*, **40**, 470-477.

Shipper, F., and White, C. S. (1983). Linking organizational effectiveness and environmental change. *Long Range Planning*, **16** (3), 99-106.

Shrivastava, P. (1985). Knowledge systems for strategic decision making. *Journal of Applied Behavioral Science*, **21**, 95-107.

Shrivastava, P., and Grant, J. H. (1985). Empirically derived models of strategic decision-making processes. *Strategic Management Journal*, **6**, 97-113.

Shrivastava, P., and Schneider, S. (1984). Organizational frames of reference. *Human Relations*, **37**, 795-809.

Smirich, L., and Stubbart, C. (1985). Strategic management in an enacted world. *Academy of Management Review*, **10**, 724-736.

Smith, M. E. (1982). Shrinking organizations: A management strategy for downsizing. *Business Quarterly*, **47** (4), 30-33.

Sonnenfeld, J. (1981). Executive apologies for price fixing: Role biased perceptions of causality. *Academy of Management Journal*, **24**, 192-198.

Staber, U. (1985). A population perspective on collective action as an organizational form: The case of trade associations. *Research in the Sociology of Organization*, **4**, 181-219.

Starbuck, W. H. (1983). Organizations as action generators. *American Sociological Review*, **48**, 91-102.

Starbuck, W. H. (1985). Acting first and thinking later: Theory versus reality in strategic change. In *Organizational Strategy and Change*, ed. J. M. Pennings *et al.* pp. 336-372. San Francisco: Jossey-Bass.

Starbuck, W. H., Greve, A., and Hedberg, B. L. T. (1978). Responding to crises: Theory and the experience of European business. In *Studies in Crisis Management*, ed. C. F. Smart and W. T. Stanbury, pp. 111-137. Toronto: Butterworth.

Staw, B. M. (1984). Organizational behavior: A review and reformation of the field's outcome variables. *Annual Review of Psychology*, **35**, 627-666.

Staw, B. M. (1985). Repairs on the road to relevance and rigor: Some unexplored issues in publishing organizational research. In *Publishing in the Organizational Sciences*, ed. L. L. Cummings and R. J. Frost, pp. 96-107. Homewood, IL: Irwin.

Steers, R. M. (1975). Problems in the measurement of organizational effectiveness. *Administrative Science Quarterly*, **20**, 546-558.

Steers, R. M. (1976). When is an organization effective? A process approach to understanding effectiveness. *Organizational Dynamics*, **5** (2), 50-63.

Steers, R. M. (1977). *Organizational Effectiveness* Santa Monica, CA: Goodyear.

Stokey, N. L. (1986). The dynamics of industry-wide learning. In *Equilibrium Analysis: Essays in Honor of Kenneth J. Arrow*, ed. W. P. Heller, R. M. Starr and D. A. Starrett, vol. 2, pp. 81-104 Cambridge: Cambridge University Press.

Storey, D. J. (1985). The problem facing new firms. *Journal of Management Studies*, **22**, 327-345.

Strauss, A. (1982). Interorganizational negotiation. *Urban Life*, **11**, 350-367.

Stubbart, C. (1982). Are environmental scanning units effective? *Long Range Planning*, **15** (3), 139-145.

Sutton, R. I. (1983). Managing organizational death. *Human Resource Management*, **22**, 391-412.

Szwajkowski, E. (1985). Organizational illegality: Theoretical integration and illustrative application. *Academy of Management Review*, **10**, 558-567.

Takahashi, N. (1983). Efficiency of management systems under uncertainty: Short-run adaptive processes. *Behaviormetrika*, **14**, 59-72.

Tushman, M. L., Virany, B., and Romanelli, E. (1985). Executive succession, strategic reorientations, and organization evolution: The minicomputer industry as a case in point. *Technology in Society*, **7**, 297-313.

Ulrich, D. (1984). Specifying external relations: Definition of and actors in an organization's environment. *Human Relations*, **37**, 245-262.

Ulrich, D., and Barney, J. B. (1984). Perspectives in organizations: Resource dependence, efficiency, and population. *Academy of Management Review*, **9**, 471-481.

Useem, M. (1984). *The Inner Circle: Large Corporations and the Rise of Business Political Activity in the U.S. and U.K.* New York: Oxford University Press.

Van de Ven, A. H. (1979). [Review of *Organizations and Environment*] *Administrative Science Quarterly*, **24**, 320-326.

Van de Ven, A. H., and Drazin, R. (1985). The concept of fit in contingency theory. *Research in Organizational Behavior*, **7**, 333-365.

Van de Ven, A. H., Hudson, R., and Schroeder, D. M. (1984). Designing new business startups: Entrepreneurial, organizational, and ecological considerations. *Journal of Management*, **10**, 87-108.

Venkatraman, N., and Camillus, J. C. (1984). Exploring the concept of 'fit' in strategic management. *Academy of Management Review*, **9**, 513-525.

Wagel, W. B., Ermann, M. D., and Horowitz, A. M. (1981). Organizational responses to imputations of deviance. *Sociological Quarterly*, **22**, 43-55.

Warner, W. K. (1967). Problems in measuring the goal attainment of voluntary organizations. *Adult Education*, **19**, 3-14.

Weick, K. E. (1979). *The Social Psychology of Organizing*, 2nd edn. Reading, MA: Addison-Wesley

Whetten, D. (1980a). Organizational decline: A neglected topic in organizational science. *Academy of Management Review*, **5**, 577-588.

Whetten, D. (1980b). Organizational decline: Causes, responses, and effects. In *The Organizational Life Cycle*, ed. J. Kimberly, R. Miles, *et al.* pp. 354-362 San Francisco: Jossey-Bass.

Whetten, D. A. (1981). Organizational responses to scarcity: Exploring the obstacles to innovative aproaches to retrenchment in education. *Educational Administration Quarterly*, **17** (3), 80-97.

Wiewel, W., and Hunter, A. (1985). The interorganizational network as a resource: A comparative case study on organizational genesis. *Administrative Science Quarterly*, **30**, 482-496.

Wilson, E. K. (1985). What counts in the death or transformation of an organization? *Social Forces*, **64**, 259-280.

Yasai-Ardekani, M. (1986). Structural adaptations to environments. *Academy of Management Review*, **11**, 9-21.

Yoffie, D. B., and Bergenstein, S. (1985). Creating political advantage: The rise of the corporate political entrepreneur. *California Management Review*, **28**, 124-139.

Zammuto, R. F. (1982a). *Assessing organizational effectiveness: Systems change, adaptation, and strategy*. Albany, NY: SUNY Press.

Zammuto, R. F. (1982b). Organizational decline and management education. *Exchange: The Organizational Behavior Teaching Journal*, **7** (3), 5-12.

Zammuto, R. F. (1983). *Bibliography on Decline and Retrenchment* Boulder, CO: National Center for Higher Education Management Systems.

Zammuto, R. F. (1984). A comparison of multiple constituency models of organizational effectiveness. *Academy of Management Review*, **9**, 606-619.

Zammuto, R. F., and Cameron, K. S. (1985). Environmental decline and organizational response. *Research in Organizational Behavior*, **7**, 223-262.

Zammuto, R. F., Whetten, D. A., and Cameron, K. S. (1983). Environmental change, enrollment decline and institutional response: Speculations on retrenchment in colleges and universities. *Peabody Journal of Education*, **60**, 93-107.

Zeithaml, C. P., and Zeithaml, V. A. (1984). Environmental management: Revising the marketing perspective. *Journal of Marketing*, **48**, 46-53.

International Review of Industrial and Organizational Psychology 1987
Edited by C. L. Cooper and I. T. Robertson
© 1987 John Wiley & Sons Ltd

Chapter 2

BEHAVIORAL APPROACHES TO ORGANIZATIONS

Fred Luthans
Department of Management
University of Nebraska
USA
and
Mark Martinko
Florida State University
USA

THEORETICAL DIMENSIONS

The old human relations approach to organizations was largely dominated by a humanistically based theoretical foundation probably best represented by the work of Douglas McGregor (1960). His now famous Theory Y served a useful purpose of drawing the attention of both academics and practising managers to the importance and complexities of the 'human side of enterprise'. However, it proved to be too simplistic.

In the 1960s, behavioral scientists such as Victor Vroom (1964) began to propose more sophisticated explanations of human behavior in organization. Taken largely from cognitively based expectancy theories rather than behavioral theories, these new foundations of orgnizational behavior tried to spell out a complex process that involved valences, instrumentalities, expectancies, effort, performance, satisfaction, role perceptions, and abilities, The widely recognized Porter and Lawler (1968) model probably best represented this approach.

Certainly these models proposed by Vroom and Porter and Lawler were a more realistic theoretical position representing the complexities of behavior in organizations than were those offered earlier by McGregor or Herzberg's two-factor theory (Herzberg, Mausner, and Snyderman, 1959). But, by the same token, these theories had strayed too far from application and a parsimonious explanation. Cognitively based expectancy theories certainly helped in the better *understanding* of organizational behavior, but they fell short on predicting and controlling employee behavior in organizations.

The Role of Operant Theory

In the past decade an operant theoretical framework has emerged to better meet the objectives of parsimony and practical application (prediction and control). Although operant theory goes way back (Skinner, 1953) as an explanation of individual behavior, its application to organizational behavior is relatively recent (Luthans and Kreitner, 1975).

Whereas the early work of Vroom and Porter and Lawler is a cognitively based theory, operant theory is an environmentally based theory. Operant theory goes way back to Skinner's important distinction between respondent and operant conditioning. That is, behavior is a function of its contingent consequences. This, of course, is the most parsimonious explanation of organizational behavior, and through the technique of organizational behavior modification or O.B. Mod. (Frederiksen, 1982; Luthans and Kreitner, 1975, 1985) has proven it can also be successfully applied in organizations.

In summary, the relatively simplistic human relations theories of McGregor and Herzberg were replaced by the relatively complex expectancy theories of Vroom and Porter and Lawler. However, to meet a more parsimonious and applications oriented theoretical foundation for behavior in organizations, operant theory emerged. More recently, some extensions of these theories have just started to become important in the study and application of behavior in organizations. In particular, attribution theory and social learning theory are the newest and potentially the most important new theoretical dimensions.

The Role of Attribution Theory

Recently, organizational behavior scholars have perceived a need and made a call for a more mid-range, compromising theoretical stance between the seemingly diametrically opposed expectancy theory on the one hand and operant theory on the other. Attribution theory and social learning theory have arrived to meet this need and answer this call.

Leaning toward the cognitive end of the continuum, attribution theory is concerned with the relationship between an individual's perception and interpersonal behavior. In other words, it is a more comprehensive theory of behavior than just a framework for motivation. Kelley (1967) stresses that attribution theory incorporates cognitive processes by which an individual interprets behavior as being caused by (or attributed to) parts of the relevant environment. Fritz Heider (1958), the generally recognized pioneer of attribution theory, believed that both internal forces (e.g. personal attributes such as ability or effort) and external forces (e.g. environmental attributes such as rules or the weather) combine additively to determine behavior. He stresses that it is the perceived, not the actual, determinants that are important to behavior. Thus, attribution theory assumes humans are rational and motivated to identify and understand the causal structure of their relevant environment.

Applied to the study of behavior in organizations, attributions so far have mainly been divided into internal (i.e. ability or effort) and external (i.e. luck or task difficulty) loci of control (Rotter, 1966). A number of studies are coming up with some very interesting and relevant findings. For example, one study found that employees under internal control are generally more satisfied with their jobs, are more likely to be in managerial positions, and are more satisfied with a participatory management style than are employees who perceive external control (Mitchell, Smyser, and Weed, 1975). Other studies have found internal managers to be better performers (Anderson, Hellriegel, and Slocum, 1977; Anderson and Schneier, 1978) and more considerate with subordinates (Pryer and Distenfano, 1971), and that they tend to follow a more strategic style of executive action (Miller, Kets de Vries, and Toulouse, 1982). In addition, attribution theory has been shown to have relevance in explaining goal-setting behavior (Dossett and Greenberg, 1981), leadership behavior (Calder, 1977; McElroy, 1982) and the poor performance of employees (Mitchell and Wood, 1980). A recent review article concludes that locus of control is related to the performance and satisfaction of organization members and may moderate the relationship between motivation and incentives (Spector, 1982).

Attribution theory seems to hold a great deal of promise for the better understanding of behavior in organizations. However, for the future, other dimensions besides the internal and external loci of control will have to be accounted for and studied. Weiner (1972), for example, suggests that a stability (fixed or variable) dimension must also be recognized. Experienced employees may have a stable internal attribution concerning effort. By the same token, employees may have a stable external attribution about task difficulty, but an unstable external attribution about luck. Besides the stability dimension, Kelley (1973) suggests that dimensions such as consensus (do others act this way in this situation?) consistency (does this person act this way in this situation at other times?) and distinctiveness (does this person act differently in other situations?) will affect the type of attributions that are made. In other words, attribution theory recognizes the complexity of human behavior and this must be part of a theory that attempts to *explain* and *understand* behavior in organizations. But unlike some of the predecessors in the cognitive approach, attribution theory does seem to have more potential for application and relevance to actual human resource management instead of being a purely academic exercise in theory building.

The Role of Social Learning Theory

Whereas attribution theory leans toward the cognitive approach, the recently emerging social learning theory leans more toward the operant end of the continuum. Mainly stemming from the work of Bandura (1976, 1977), social learning theory (SLT) accepts the principles of operant theory and the importance of environmental contingencies but then goes further. In particular, the individual (including cognitive processes), the environment (both overt and covert) and the behavior itself are viewed as interacting, reciprocal determinants in SLT.

In SLT there is more than direct learning via antecedent cues and reinforcing consequences as in operant theory. Vicarious processes or modeling are also important explanations for learning. According to Bandura, subprocesses such as attention, retention, motoric reproduction, and reinforcement are important to learning. Through these subprocesses learning can take place by observing or modeling other persons in the social environment. In other words, the person learns by observing how others act and then acquires a mental picture of the act and its consequences. Next, the person acts out the newly acquired image. Much as in operant theory, if the consequences are reinforcing, the behavior will be strengthened and tend to increase in subsequent frequency. This extended explanation of learning seems to be especially applicable and relevant to the study of behavior in organizations. For example, modeling has been successfully applied to employee training programs (Burnaska, 1976; Kraut, 1976; Latham and Saari, 1979).

Besides modeling, SLT goes beyond operant theory by emphasizing the importance of self-control. By recognizing mediating cognitions, self-regulatory processes become an important part of SLT. In particular, SLT recognizes cognitively based antecedents (e.g. goals or expectancies) and consequences (self-evaluative rewards and/or punishers). As Bandura (1976, p. 28) explains:

> The notion that behavior is controlled by its consequences is unfortunately interpreted by most people to mean that actions are at the mercy of situational influences. In fact, behavior can, and is, extensively self-regulated by self-produced consequences for one's own actions. . . . Because of their great representational and self-reactive capacities, humans are less dependent upon immediate external supports for their behavior.

In other words, self-control processes do not negate the importance of environmental contingencies, but instead allow the person to analyze and alter external regulatory contingencies rather than just mechanistically respond to them.

The self-control theoretical development has relevant linkages to practical application. One study suggested that self-management may be the 'missing link' in managerial effectiveness (Luthans and Davis, 1979). It was found that self-management procedures could be successfully used to increase the effectiveness of managers in diverse situations and there is a growing literature on its applicability to behavior in organizations (Brief and Aldag, 1981; Manz and Sims, 1980).

Figure 2.1 graphically depicts social learning theory. Its improvement over traditional theories and more limited operant theory is summarized as follows:

> Although traditional work motivation theories (like Abraham Maslow's needs hierarchy) do address the employee's need for social interaction, they fail to explain the nature of that interaction. SLT improves upon the traditional theories by assigning a prominent role to vicarious or observational learning. Similarly, SLT extends the operant model of learning—what we have called the external approach—by explaining how the individual processes environmental stimuli. This helps us understand why similar employees in similar situations often behave quite differently; the operant model is limited in its ability to explain such variations. (Kreitner and Luthans, 1984, p. 55)

In total, social learning may prove to be the most important theoretical development to date for the field of behavior in organizations. It blends the need for understanding the complexities of human behavior at work with the pragmatism of relevance and applicability to human resource management. However, by stressing the *interactive* nature of organizational behavior, some alternative research perspectives and techniques are required.

METHODOLOGICAL DIMENSIONS

If the theoretical framework recognizes employee–organization–behavior *interactions* as being the most appropriate unit of study, then alternatives to the traditional

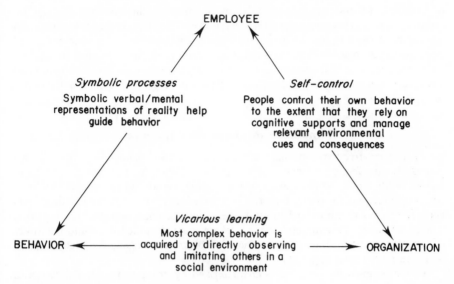

Figure 2.1 A social learning model of behavior in organizations
Source: adapted from Kreitner and Luthans (1984, p. 55)

research perspectives, designs and data-gathering techniques are needed. In particular, Figure 2.2 shows some methodological dimensions that seem more compatible with the social learning theoretic assumptions.

Etic to Emic Research Perspectives

The distinction between etic and emic research perspectives that come out of anthropology (Morey and Luthans, 1984) seem appropriate for the study of behavior in organizations. These terms were first used by Kenneth Pike who took the suffixes of the terms phon*emic* and phon*etic* from linguistic analysis. The term *emic* is used in anthropological research to denote the native or 'insider's' view of the situation. Etic is the 'outsider's', i.e. the researchers, definition of the situation.

In traditional research in organizational behavior, an etic perspective has prevailed. The researcher formulates the research questions and defines the situation (e.g. through the assignment to experimental and control groups and the identification

TRADITIONAL APPROACHES	ALTERNATIVE APPROACHES
Etic	Emic
Nomothetic	Idiographic
Quantitative	Qualitative
Questionnaires	Observations

Figure 2.2 Some alternative methodological dimensions for a social learning approach to behavior in organizations

of independent and dependent variables or through the response choices on questionnaires). However, the emic perspective has largely been ignored. An alternative methodological dimension for researching behavior in organizations would be to have the insider's, i.e. the subject's, definition of the situation. By dealing with real people in real organizations, an emic perspective for research may yield some very rich, and perhaps heretofore overlooked, research questions and data for understanding.

Nomothetic to Idiographic Research

Another alternative to traditional methods of researching behavior in organizations is to make a distinction between nomethetic and idiographic research (Luthans and Davis, 1982). About 45 years ago Gordon Allport introduced the terms to contrast the methodologies for doing research in psychology. Through the ensuing years there has been a continual debate in the behavioral sciences about which approach should be taken. This methodological debate has not spilled over into the study of behavior in organizations because there has been almost a singular preoccupation with the nomothetic approach.

In brief, nomothetic research is characterized by group-centered, standardized, and controlled environmental contexts, and quantitative methodologies. Idiographic research, on the other hand, is individual-centered, uses naturalistic environmental contexts, and depends more on qualitative methodologies. The nomothetic approach is appropriate under the theoretic assumption that people are basically the same and operate in a constant environment. However, when interactive theoretic assumptions are made, then an idiographic approach becomes more useful.

Quantitative to Qualitative Research Techniques

Still another distinction can be made between quantitative and qualitative research. This distinction is more familiar to organizational behavior researchers than are the etic–emic and nomothetic–idiographic distinctions. The argument between quantitative and qualitative research in organizational behavior has been more prevalent over the years (e.g. see Behling, 1980; Susman and Evered, 1978). However, with only a few recent exceptions (the 1979 special issue on qualitative methods in the *Administrative Science Quarterly* and the work of Van Maanen and his colleagues, 1982), quantitative research totally dominates the field.

Although the definition of qualitative research is quite vague, Van Maanen (1979, p. 520) explains that the approach 'is at best an umbrella term covering an array of interpretive techniques which seek to describe, decode, translate, and otherwise come to terms with the meaning, not the frequency, of certain more or less naturally occurring phenomena in the social world.' The quantitative approach, on the other hand, is heavily influenced by the natural science model and depends on inferential statistical analysis techniques. Quantitative research divides up the research problem into variables that use data collection techniques (e.g. questionnaires) allowing quantifiable analysis. In general, the quantitative approach concentrates on measurement and systematic evaluation, and on hypothetico-deductive testing of research questions; and gives careful attention to the criteria that may invalidate the findings (Campbell and Stanley, 1966; Cook and Campbell, 1979).

Quantitative techniques flow from the etic, nomothetic approaches that have dominated the field to date. Like the emic and idiographic approaches, qualitative techniques offer an alternative methodological dimension for researching behavior in organizations. It should be pointed out that these qualitative techniques are not a throwback to the old case approach, but instead offer the opportunity to obtain needed, rich data of interactive human behavior in real, complex organizations.

Questionnaires to Observation Techniques for Data Collection

In line with the proposals of moving from etic to emic, nomothetic to idiographic and quantitative to qualitative, is the movement from questionnaires to observation techniques. In particular, it was suggested a few years ago that there was a need for observation measures of organizational behavior in natural settings, especially under a social learning theoretical perspective (Luthans, 1979). That proposal has led to the development of a reliable and valid measurement system for managerial behavior in natural settings (Luthans and Lockwood, 1984).

Questionnaires, of course, have been used as almost the only data-gathering technique in organizational behavior research. For example, Martinko and Carter (1979) found that practically all the studies reported in the *Academy of Management Journal* in a recent 10-year period used questionnaires. Despite their prevalent use, questionnaires are recognized to have serious problems for measurement, not the least of which is the lack of demonstrated validity for the widely used standardized questionnaires (Schreisheim, Bannister, and Money, 1979; Schreisheim and Kerr, 1977). Observation techniques, on the other hand, although often talked about, have, with but a few exceptions been almost totally ignored in researching behavior in organizations. (For the exceptions, see McCall, Morrison, and Hannan, 1978, for a review of the few observation studies of managerial work, most notably Mintzberg's 1973 study and recent studies by Martinko and Gardner, 1984, 1985, and Luthans, Rosenkrantz, and Hennessey, 1985.) For the future, more of these alternative perspectives, methods, and data-gathering techniques seem desirable.

SUMMARY OF RESEARCH RESULTS

Obviously there have been a multitude of published research papers in the general area of behavior in organizations during the last several years. This review of the research literature is selective and focuses mainly on those studies which best demonstrate the behavioral management approach as suggested by Luthans and Kreitner (1975, 1985). In particular, studies which can be characterized as primarily cognitive and attitudinal in nature as well as those primarily utilizing questionnaire data have not been emphasized unless they provide particular insight into the management of reinforcement contingencies in organizations.

The review is divided into four major sections. In the first, the early work associated with the development and empirical demonstrations of the effectiveness of behavioral management principles is briefly reviewed. The second section focuses on more recent work and discusses the results of reinforcement interventions in areas such as safety, attendance, consumer behavior and performance evaluation. It also emphasizes the relative effectiveness of reinforcement contingencies such as feedback and monetary incentives. In the third section, the progress described in the first parts is carefully evaluated and the theoretical foundations, strengths, and weaknesses of the behavioral management approach in general are considered. While it is concluded that the basic behavioral management approach has been shown to be quite effective, theoretical departures such as social learning theory, goal setting, attribution theory, and broader organizational perspectives are suggested as strategies for increasing the explanatory power of behavioral management. The final section provides specific suggestions for theory building and future research.

Early Work: Model Building and Description of Applications

Although the conceptual basis for motivation and cognitively based expectancy theories of behavior in organizations was established in the 1960s (Porter and Lawler, 1968; Vroom, 1964), it is only within the last 15 years that the basic principles and paradigms of reinforcement theory have been introduced in the study and research of behavior in organizations. The first work in this area focused primarily on the description of basic reinforcement notions and accounts of their application (At Emery Air Freight, 1973; Luthans and White, 1971; Nord, 1969). As this literature evolved, several different behavioral management intervention models and processes were proposed and described (Brethower, 1972; Gilbert, 1978; Luthans and Kreitner, 1974, 1975; Miller, 1978).

Although there are some minor variations among these models, the basic process described is essentially the same. The model developed by Luthans and Kreitner (1975) called organizational behavior modification or simply O. B. Mod. is representative:

1. *identity* the problem-related performance behavior;
2. *measure* to identify baseline frequencies of the identified behavior;
3. *functionally analyze* the antecedent and consequent contingencies in the current environment;
4. *intervene* by changing the existing environmental contingencies to accelerate desired (functional) behaviors (a reinforcement intervention strategy) and decelerate undesired (dysfunctional) behaviors (an extinction or punishment intervention strategy); and
5. *evaluate* for determining behavioral change in the desired direction and bottom line improvements through systematically measuring and monitoring results.

Along with the development of the five-step O. B. Mod. paradigm came a number of demonstrations of its effectiveness in areas such as quality control, absenteeism, and supervisory training.

Quality

Some of the earliest and most sophisticated work demonstrating the effectiveness of behavioral management techniques on quality control was conducted by Adam and his associates (Adam, 1972, 1974; Adam and Scott, 1971). Using experimental/control group comparisons, this work demonstrated that behaviors associated with quality could be modified in both laboratory and industrial settings. An equally impressive report, although not methodologically rigorous, is Feeney's description of the results of feedback on quality control problems in the air freight business (At Emery Air Freight, 1973). This application indicated that feedback and praise can result in significant and immediate improvement in behaviors associated with quality. Similarly, feedback and social reinforcement was demonstrated to be an effective intervention in decreasing operator quality control problems in textile production (McCarthy, 1978).

Absenteeism

Improving attendance behavior has also been a focus of early work (e.g. Luthans and Martinko, 1976; Nord, 1970). Several studies demonstrate the effectiveness of reward systems on absenteeism (Nord, 1970; Orpen, 1978; Pedalino and Gamboa, 1974). Wallin and Johnson (1976) demonstrate that lottery systems can also have an effective impact on absenteeism. Importantly, although a variety of rewards, incentives, and intervention strategies were used in this early research, the results are almost uniformly positive.

Supervisory training

Another early application of behavioral management involved training first line supervisors (Luthans and Lyman, 1973). In these types of interventions supervisors learn the basic principles of O. B. Mod., identify key performance behaviors, measure and chart the frequencies of these behaviors, identify current contingencies and design a new set of contingencies to improve performance, apply the new set of contingencies, and evaluate the intervention to determine if behavior changes in the desired directions and bottom-line performance improves.

The supervisory training interventions have resulted in the successful modification of a wide variety of performance behaviors within a number of different organizational contexts. Ottemann and Luthans (1975) report success in a light manufacturing organization for behaviors associated with productivity, quality, and attendance. Similarly, Bourdon (1977) trained supervisors to successfully decrease quality control problems resulting from 'high bobbins' in a textile organization. Another example of improvement in both quality and productivity is provided by Luthans and Schweizer's (1979) description of an intervention in a waterbed manufacturing company.

Not-for-profit organizations have also been the target of successful interventions. Both Frederiksen (1978) and Snyder and Luthans (1982) trained supervisors and demonstrated significant increases in behaviors related to productivity and quality among staff in a mental institution and a general hospital, respectively.

Major conclusions: early work

When the above studies are considered as a whole, three major conclusions are apparent. First, behavioral management appears to be an effective approach with demonstrated success in modifying a variety of behaviors (e.g. productivity, quality, and attendance) within different organizational contexts. Second, it is clear that supervisors and practicing managers can readily learn and apply the approach. Finally, the many similarities in the literature on model development indicate that there is general consensus regarding the basic principles and procedures for applying this behavioral management approach. Thus, by the end of the 1970s, the general approach to behavioral management became established and its effectiveness as a strategy for contributing to bottom-line results was established.

More Contemporary Work on Behavioral Management

Recent work on behavioral management has focused primarily on refining various interventions and applications. This section will first examine specific interventions of feedback and incentive systems and then review the applications to attendance, safety, consumer behavior, and performance evaluation.

Feedback

An examination of early research in behavioral management indicates that feedback was the most frequently used intervention (e.g. Adam, 1974; Andrasik, Heimberg, and McNamara, 1981; Bourdon, 1977; Komaki, Waddel, and Pearce, 1977; Ottemann and Luthans, 1975; Snyder and Luthans, 1982). Feedback remains the most frequently used intervention in the more current literature as well.

Feedback has been used in a variety of mental health and social services settings as an effective consequence for modifying a wide range of staff behaviors including timely reporting, and participation in meetings, and a number of different behaviors associated with worker productivity and quality (Anderson, Crowell, Sponsel, Clarke, and Brence, 1982; Anderson, Crowell, Sucec, Gilligan, and Wikcoff, 1982; Brown, Willis, and Reid, 1981; Coles and Blunden, 1981; Frederiksen, 1978; Frederiksen, Richter, Johnson, and Solomon, 1981; Maher, 1981; Prue, Krapfl, Noah, Cannon, and Maley, 1980; Repp and Deitz, 1979a, 1979b). Feedback has also proved to be an effective intervention for workers in a variety of production settings including the manufacture of textiles (Dick, 1978), furniture (Wikcoff, Anderson, and Crowell, 1982), and rosin bags (Frost, Hopkins, and Conrad, 1981). Positive results with feedback interventions have also been realized in meat packing (Luthans, Maciag, and Rosenkrantz, 1983), the reduction of scrap (Eldridge, Lemasters, and Szypot, 1978), and theft (McNees, Gilliam, Schnelle, and Risley, 1979).

In a general review of feedback interventions, Kopelman (1982, 1986) concluded that, regardless of the setting and target behavior, the literature indicates that feedback interventions almost always work. The present review of the current literature supports Kopelman's conclusions, emphasizing the diversity of both settings and target behaviors associated with effective feedback interventions. These findings, coupled with the low or nonexistent cost of feedback interventions, suggest that they may be among the most cost-efficient and effective interventions available in behavioral management.

Monetary incentives

A second important intervention available for behavioral management is financial incentive programs. Unlike feedback, although widely used, relatively few studies have been reported on incentive pay systems. In Hills's (1979) criticism of pay as an intervention strategy for behavioral management, he notes that it tends to be ineffective because it is often tied to contingencies beyond the control of managers and their employees (e.g. longevity and economic trends). It may be that the lack of attention devoted to pay as an incentive reflects the difficulty concerned with disassociating pay from contingencies which are not productivity related rather than the lack of the effectiveness of money as a reinforcer.

In general, those studies which have investigated the use of contingent monetary incentives have found them to be extremely effective. For example, Bowles, Malott, and Dean (1981), Luthans, Paul, and Baker (1981), and Luthans, Paul, and Taylor (1985) used cash awards and paid vacations as effective incentives for recruiting new health club members and increasing key sales behaviors, respectively. Pay incentives were also found to be an effective contingency for reducing the accident rates of urban transit workers (Haynes, Pine, and Fitch, 1982) and increasing attendance (Stephens and Burroughs, 1978) and the punctuality of industrial workers (Hermann, de Montes, Dominguez, de Montes, and Hopkins, 1973). In the only studies comparing the relative effectiveness of different types of pay incentives, both Saari and Latham (1982) and Latham and Dossett (1978) found variable schedules to be superior to incentives provided on a continuous basis.

As a whole, the above studies clearly demonstrate the effectiveness of monetary incentives for increasing a variety of employee behaviors. However, additional research in this area is clearly needed for the future.

Attendance

In addition to work on interventions such as feedback and monetary incentives, recent attention has also been devoted to applications areas such as attendance. For example, Baum (1978) showed that a hierarchy of successively more severe sanctions, consistently enforced, significantly reduces the absenteeism behavior of chronic absentees. This study is particularly important since it validates the effectiveness of currently popular progressive discipline programs. Using a somewhat different strategy, Ford (1981) was able to demonstrate significant reductions in absenteeism by using post-absence interviews as a contingency. Together, these two interventions suggest that punishment may be an effective strategy for reducing absenteeism.

Experimentation regarding positive reinforcement has also yielded significant results. Stephens and Burroughs (1978) compared the relative effectiveness of two different lottery systems as contingencies for increasing attendance. Both were equally effective. Feedback accompanied by social reinforcement was found by Silva, Duncan, and Douds (1981) to be an effective strategy for increasing attendance. Finally, Durand (1983) demonstrates that a scheduled leave policy is an effective contingency in reducing unscheduled absences.

As with the earlier reports on applications of behavioral management, the literature on absenteeism and attendance control suggests that almost all programs attempted have been effective, including programs that use punishment as well as positive reinforcement. However, additional work, especially comparing the relative effectiveness of different types of interventions on attendance, is needed.

Safety

Behavioral management applications in the area of safety are probably the most recent but are developing rapidly. Charting unsafe behaviors and accident rates and providing feedback based on these data have proved to be effective in reducing safety violations in a variety of settings including a public works department (Komaki, 1977), an animal laboratory (Sulzer-Azaroff, 1978), a coal mine (Rhoton, 1980), and off-shore oil drilling (Chhokar and Wallin, 1984; Reber and Wallin, 1984; Reber, Wallin, and Chhokar, 1984). Two separate studies have investigated motor vehicle accident rates in organizations dependent on their personnel driving a lot. Larson, Schlenker, Kirchner, Carr, Domash, and Risley (1980) demonstrated reductions in police motor vehicle accident rates by providing feedback relating odometer readings and accidents. In a similar program, the accident rates of urban transit workers were reduced during a program consisting of feedback, competition, and incentives (Haynes, Pine, and Fitch, 1982).

Relatively innovative interventions have also been developed to reduce hearing loss. Zohar and Fussfield (1981) demonstrate that a token reinforcement system was related to significantly higher rates of earplug use by textile workers. Daily feedback and hearing tests were important contingencies associated with higher levels of earplug use in a metal fabrication manufacturing facility (Zohar, Cohen, and Azar, 1980).

A particularly interesting study is reported by Komaki, Collins, and Penn (1982) who report significant reductions in safety violations during poultry processing. The intervention in this study consisted of workers viewing videotaped sequences demonstrating the antecedents and consequences of unsafe behaviors. Apparently, the observation of these films resulted in what Bandura called vicarious learning (Bandura, 1977).

Sales and consumer behavior

Behavioral management applied to this area is also a recent development. The first articles applying the principles of behavior management to marketing appeared in 1980 (Nord and Peter) and 1981 (Rothschild and Gaidis). Up to this time, the earliest empirical report found was an article by Carter, Hansson, Holmberg, and Melin (1979) which demonstrated significant reductions in shoplifting through the use of prompts such as signs and warnings.

There is some literature reporting significant improvements in sales persons' behavior. Brown, Malott, Dillon, and Keeps (1980) used feedback to increase target behaviors such as approaches, greetings, courtesy, and closings. Similar behaviors were increased through paid time-off and lottery interventions reported by Luthans, Paul and Taylor (1981) and Luthans (1985). These latter studies used control group experimental designs and found a causal relationship between reinforcement contingencies and sales behaviors.

Other studies are directly aimed at consumer behavior. Mirman (1982) demonstrates that prompts appreciably modify customer orders in a restaurant.

ROCKHURST COLLEGE LIBRARY

Martinko (in press) demonstrates significant changes in brand preferences for beer as a result of both prompting and price interventions. Importantly, these latter studies demonstrate the generalization of behavior management principles to targets outside of organizations (such as consumers) which are not normally viewed as dependent on organizational contingencies. In addition, these studies suggest that the modification of behavior through antecedent conditions rather than consequence interventions is a potentially powerful, although frequently ignored, strategy for behavior change.

Performance evaluation

The generalization of behavior management to performance evaluation is a natural extension and several researchers have suggested behaviorally based performance evaluation systems (Komaki, Collins, and Thoene, 1980; Latham, Fay, and Saari, 1979; Millard, Luthans, and Ottemann, 1976; Smith and Kendall, 1963). Although there is some support for the psychometric superiority of behaviorally based performance evaluation systems (Campbell, Dunnette, Arvey, and Hellervik, 1973) the majority of the recent literature suggests that these systems are not necessarily superior to others (Jacobs, Kafry, and Zedeck, 1980; Kingstrom and Bass, 1981; Schwab, Heneman, and Decotiis, 1975). Thus, although behaviorally based performance evaluation appears to be based on solid theoretical ground, there is not enough evidence to demonstrate its superiority at this time.

Conclusions: current research

When the overall literature in the area of behavioral management is considered, it is obvious that there is a substantial amount of research. The consistency of the basic approach and the relatively great amount of positive results indicate that behavioral management is both well established and effective. As research in this area has progressed, it has become methodologically more sophisticated. Multiple baseline (e.g. Komaki, Collins, and Penn, 1982; Sulzer-Azaroff, 1978), reversals (e.g. Luthans and Maris, 1979), control group experiments (Luthans, Paul, and Baker, 1981), and replications (e.g. Luthans, Paul, and Taylor, 1985) are used in the design of the research and give confident indications of causal relationships between behavioral management interventions and performance outcomes.

Behavioral Management in Retrospect

Despite the significant achievements and advances in the theory, methods, and applications of behavioral management there have been some criticisms (Fry, 1974; Jablonsky and DeVries, 1972; Locke, 1979; Schneier, 1974). These criticisms coupled with the need for theoretical advancement stimulated a symposium a few years ago that addressed the issues associated with behavioral management (Behling, 1976; Cummings, 1976; Luthans, 1976; Mitchell, 1976; Nord, 1976). This symposium, and other recent attempts to merge rather than polarize behavioral management with the more cognitively based social learning approach (e.g. Kreitner and Luthans, 1984; Luthans and Kreitner, 1985), provide a basis for understanding recent departures from a radical behaviorist approach.

127041

Much of the criticism associated with behavioral management has been concerned with the epistemological nature of the radical behaviorist position. As Mitchell (1976) points out, the Skinnerian system is essentially atheoretical in that it is based solely on observations and closed system definitions of the principles of reinforcement. Citing Kaplan (1964), Mitchell notes that the strict behaviorist position places unnecessary limits on scientific inquiry by demanding that all theoretical concepts be directly observable and measurable. Behling (1976) supports Mitchell in suggesting that the deductive nature of the Skinnerian theoretical framework excludes theory development through induction developed from observation. He also notes that the Skinnerian system results in propositions which are not testable and verifiable.

Another perspective of the radical behaviorist position is provided by Luthans and his colleagues. As Davis and Luthans (1980) note, the basic premise of reinforcement theory (behavior is a function of its consequences) fails to provide a rich explanation of how the reinforcement process actually works. Also, Luthans and Kreitner (1985) suggest that the strict behaviorist position which implies environmental determinism and ignores cognitive processes is an untenable foundation for *explaining* organizational behavior. They do not, however, accept the position which suggests that behavior is not influenced by the environment; that it is self-determined and caused by the individual's internal needs, expectancies, and satisfactions. Rather they assume an intermediate position between environmental determinism and self-determinism represented by the social learning theory approach discussed earlier (see Figure 2.1).

The above discussions as well as several recent research reports suggest new trends and theoretical departures in behavioral management. Although there appears to be consensus that the basic principles of operant and reinforcement theory still hold, and are very valuable for predicting and controlling behavior in organizations, it now seems appropriate to extend and expand.

Departure one: social learning theory

As suggested in the introductory part of this chapter, social learning theory (SLT), originally proposed by Albert Bandura (1976, 1977), views behavior as the result of a reciprocal and interdependent interaction between the person, environment, and behavior. As explained, it is very similar to operant theory in that it focuses on antecedents, behaviors, and consequences while stressing observable variables. The key difference, however, is that SLT also recognizes that people (1) learn vicariously through the observation of others, (2) learn through covert processes in which the individual cognitively processes information about behavior and environmental contingencies, and (3) can purposely control their own behavior by managing environmental contingencies. As was pointed out, the contributions of SLT complement traditional behavioral management and broaden its applicability by helping to account for and explain cognitive processes such as goal setting, self-evaluation, and attributions.

Several key studies demonstrate that modeling, which is based on the premise that people learn vicariously, is an effective behavioral management approach. Goldstein and Sorcher (1974) describe the process of using modeling to train managers. Krumhus and Malott (1980) and Latham and Saari (1979) demonstrate improved staff and supervisory performance, respectively, as a result of training that incorporated modeling procedures. Showing videotapes displaying models experiencing environmental contingencies proved to be a particularly effective strategy for reducing unsafe behaviors (Komaki, Heinzmann, and Lawson, 1980). Several convincing demonstrations of the effectiveness of behavioral self-management also support the validity of SLT principles (Bucher and Fabricatore, 1970; Flannery, 1972; Luthans and White, 1971). More recent examples by Luthans and Davis (1979) and Ivancevich and McMahan (1982) demonstrate that self-generated feedback and contingencies effectively modify one's own behavior.

Although research in this area is still in the developing stage, the above examples from the literature provide convincing evidence that SLT is an important theoretical framework for behavioral management and can make substantial contributions toward increasing the effectiveness of its application.

Departure two: goal setting

Goal setting is a second area which has cognitively based theoretical underpinnings (Locke, 1968), but is nevertheless becoming associated with behavioral management. Although Locke (1979) would take exception to including it under behavioral management, recent reviews of the behavioral management literature have begun to incorporate goal-setting research (Rapp, Carstensen, and Prue, 1983) and there are several behavioral explanations regarding the effectiveness of goals (e.g. Lloyd, 1983; Ritschl and Hall, 1980). Essentially, from an operant perspective, goals can be considered to be antecedent conditions: cues, discriminative stimuli, and prompts.

The research on goal setting clearly demonstrates that the performance of people in specific, difficult goal setting as opposed to no goal setting or general, easy goal conditions, is superior (Dossett, Latham, and Mitchell, 1979; Ivancevich, 1976, 1977; Kim and Hamner, 1976; Latham and Saari, 1982; Latham and Yukl, 1976; and Locke, Shaw, Saari, and Latham, 1981). Not so clear is the role of participation. Of ten studies which examine the effects of assigned versus participative goals (Carroll and Tosi, 1979; Dossett, Latham, and Mitchell, 1979; French, Kay, and Meyer, 1966; Ivancevich, 1976, 1977; Latham and Mitchell, 1982; Latham, Mitchell, and Dossett, 1978; Latham and Yukl, 1975, 1976; Steers, 1975), only two indicate the superiority of participatively set goals (Latham, Mitchell, and Dossett, 1978; Latham and Yukl, 1975).

Although there are several different explanations for the differential effectiveness of various goal-setting conditions (Chacko, Stone, and Brief, 1979; Locke, Shaw, Saari, and Latham, 1981; Sauers and Martinko, 1986a, 1986b), all suggest that cognitive states regarding commitment, acceptance, and attributions may provide the most effective explanations. In particular, Sauers and Martinko (1986a, 1986b) present convincing arguments that differences in attributions regarding task performance best explain the varying levels of performance in assigned versus participative goal conditions.

Put into a behavioral management framework, the research clearly documents that goal setting is a significant antecedent condition influencing human performance in organizations. Although there are a variety of potential explanations for discrepant findings within goal-setting research, attributional explanations appear most promising and, as in the case of SLT, suggest the important role of exploring the person variable (i.e. employee cognitions) in fully understanding and explaining the dynamics of behavior in organizations.

Departure three: attribution theory

As suggested in the introductory part of the chapter, attribution theory offers a promising perspective which may facilitate better understanding of the role that cognitive processes play in behavior in organizations. As was pointed out, similar to SLT, attribution theory is complementary rather than in opposition to operant theory. Mitchell (1976) points out that the principles of reinforcement can be accepted without resorting to environmental determinism. Attribution theory suggests that it is a person's ideas, beliefs, and feeling about stimuli that shape behavior rather than the stimuli *per se*. Thus, although environmental antecedents and consequences are primary determinants of behavior, the way people perceive and feel about these consequences and their beliefs about causation also play a central role.

Although research on attribution theory applications to behavioral management was reviewed earlier, it should also be noted that several studies have demonstrated that the nature of leaders' attributions is closely related to the severity and degree of punishment which leaders elect to use (Green and Liden, 1980; Mitchell, Green, and Wood, 1981; and Mitchell and Wood, 1980). Other research indicates that motivation and performance deficits are more likely to result when people attribute failure to internal stable causes such as their ability as opposed to external unstable causes such as luck or chance (Anderson, 1983; Anderson, Horowitz, and French, 1983). In a review of both research and theory, Martinko and Gardner (1982) present a convincing argument that much of the passive and helpless behavior exhibited in organizations (often called learned helplessness) is related to subordinate attributional states.

As in the case of social learning and goal setting, the research on attributional processes may be viewed as another important link in fully understanding the relationship between behavior, environmental contingencies, and the person. Although research in this area is just beginning, the potential for further contributions is promising.

Departure four: broader organizational and contextual perspectives

Behavioral management is usually considered micro-oriented, focusing on a specific individual or group and particular environmental contingencies (rewards and punishers). In contrast, recently there have been several important contributions which employ a more macro-organizational perspective. Stonich's (1984) and Podsakoff's (1982) work are examples.

Stonich (1984) places the notion of reinforcement within a larger organizational context and examines its relationship to culture, strategy, structure, resources, and management style. His basic thesis is that reinforcement systems must be synchronized with and complement other organizational variables and processes. If all processes and systems are not fully integrated, none will function at its optimum level. At a recent symposium sponsored by the Florida Association of Behavior

Analysts (Daniels, Feeney, Komacki, and Martinko, 1986), a significant issue involved the lack of continued support for behavioral management programs, even when remarkable successes had been demonstrated. It would seem that Stonich's (1984) analysis contributes to our understanding of these types of problems, suggesting that major behavioral management interventions must be more macro-oriented, involving all major organizational systems, rather than focusing on specific individuals or groups.

In a major review of the literature, Podsakoff (1982) also takes a broad contextual perspective, attempting to identify situational factors associated with reward and punishment frequencies in organizations. Among the relationships he identifies are: (1) the use of punishment increases as the span of control becomes larger (Goodstadt and Kipnis, 1970; Kipnis and Consentino, 1969); (2) supervisors prefer to use social as opposed to monetary consequences as contingencies for poor performers (Hinton and Barrow, 1975; McFillen and New, 1979); (3) under conditions of group stress and conflict, complaint workers are rewarded at higher levels than others (Fodor, 1976; Goodstadt and Kipnis, 1970; Grey and Kipnis, 1976; Kipnis and Vanderveer 1971); (4) the levels of subordinate performance significantly influence supervisors' awards of consequences (Barrow, 1976; Farris and Lim, 1969; Fodor, 1973; Greene, 1976, Herold, 1977; Lowin and Craig, 1968; McFillen and New, 1979); and (5) leaders do not punish subordinates as severely for poor performance when they attribute it to uncontrollable dimensions (Mitchell and Wood, 1980; Wood and Mitchell, 1981).

The above studies demonstrate a broader organizational perspective in considering and researching environmental contingencies. It is expected that similar approaches in future research and theory building will broaden and strengthen the current micro-orientation of behavioral management.

Future Directions

When the literature reviewed in this article is considered, the results of behavioral management are very positive. In almost all cases where the behavioral management approach has been applied, behavioral change and improved performance have been documented. Moreover, as the research on feedback demonstrates, the interventions are more frequently simple to administer and inexpensive. Thus, the research clearly demonstrates that behavioral management is fundamentally sound and a practical approach to effective human resources management.

Despite the documented positive contributions, it is also clear that there is criticism of the radical behaviorist position. Departures from this position suggest a more moderate stance as evidenced by the reciprocal determinism implied in social learning theory. The theoretical departures represented by goal setting, attribution, and broader organizational perspectives also provide additional bases for strengthening and building upon the fundamentally sound theoretical foundation of behavioral management. The same is true of the emic, idiographic, qualitative, and observational research methodologies. They can contribute to an expanded research base for behavioral management.

For the future, there are at least four loci for research. The first, and perhaps most needed, is on comparative studies and replications. Currently the majority of the research evaluates the effectiveness of specific interventions. Thus, there are few comparative studies which, for example, evaluate the effectiveness of different levels of monetary incentives. Methodological articles (Kazdin, 1973; Komaki, 1977; Luthans and Davis, 1982; Luthans and Maris, 1979) provide guidelines for conducting behavioral management research. The article by Luthans, Paul, and Taylor (1985) is an example which demonstrates how replications can add to our knowledge of the relative efficiency of specific types of behavioral management interventions.

A second focus of future research should be on particular types of interventions in areas such as safety, productivity, quality, goal setting, consumer behavior, absenteeism, and performance evaluation. An important group of studies has already appeared in each of these areas. However, as additional focused and targeted work (particularly comparative studies) is conducted, the effectiveness of these types of interventions should increase. These developments should also result in substantially enhanced implementation techniques for performance-oriented managers.

The third major focus should be on theoretical reorientation and accommodation. As the research results in the areas of modeling and self-management suggest, incorporating the role of the person and cognition in behavioral management interventions greatly increases both explanatory potential and practical applicability. Similarly, theory building and research in the areas of goal setting, attribution, and broader organizational perspectives may also contribute to expanding both the explanatory and practical implications of behavioral management. Thus, theoretical development focusing on expanding the more limited operant-based behavioral management approach to include a consideration of the person (including cognitions), attributions, goals, and the broader organizational setting in which behavior occurs may greatly enhance the potential of behavioral management.

Finally, the alternative research methods which allow the investigation of interactions need to be more strongly advocated. There appears to be a need for qualitative (Van Maanen, 1979), idiographic (Luthans and Davis, 1982), and emic research methodologies (Morey and Luthans, 1984). Although there is considerable discussion regarding the relative merits of various research perspectives (Behling, 1980; Susman and Evered, 1978; Weick, 1979), it is clear that these alternative methodological perspectives and designs may result in additional understanding of the behavior–person–environment interaction dynamic. Moreover, it would seem that the single-subject methods, including reversal and multiple baseline designs which were developed in behavior modification research, complement and could become a very important part of the movement toward emic and idiographic methodologies. Undoubtedly, as these methods and their applications unfold, understanding of behavior in organizations will significantly increase.

REFERENCES

Adam, E. E., Jr (1972). An analysis of changes in performance quality with operant conditioning procedures. *Journal of Applied Psychology*, **56**, 480–486.

Adam, E. E., Jr (1974). Behavior modification in quality control. *Academy of Management Journal*, **18**, 662–678.

Adam, E. E., Jr, and Scott, W. E. (1971). The application of behavioral conditioning procedures to the problems of quality control, *Academy of Management Journal*, **14**, 175–193.

Anderson, C. A. (1983). Motivational and performance deficits in interpersonal settings: The effect of attributional style. *Journal of Personality and Social Psychology*, **45**, 1136-1141.

Anderson, C. A., Horowitz, L. M., and French, R. De S. (1983). Attributional style of lonely and depressed people. *Journal of Personality and Social Psychology*, **45**, 127-136.

Anderson, C. R., Hellriegel, D., and Slocum, J. W. (1977). Managerial response to environmentally induced stress. *Academy of Management Journal*, **20**, 260-272.

Anderson, C. R., and Schneier, C. E. (1978). Locus of control, leader behavior and leader performance among management students. *Academy of Management Journal*, **21**, 690-698.

Anderson, D. C., Crowell, C. R., Sponsel, S. S., Clarke, M., and Brence, J. (1982). Behavior management in the public accommodations industry: A three project demonstration. *Journal of Organizational Behavior Management*, **4**, 33-66.

Anderson, D. C., Crowell, C. R., Sucec, J., Gilligan, K. D., and Wikcoff, M. (1982). Behavior management of client contacts in a real estate brokerage: Getting agents to sell more. *Journal of Organizational Behavior Management*, **4**, 67-96.

Andrasik, F., Heimberg, J. S., and McNamara, J. R. (1981). Behavior modification of work and work-related problems. *Progress in Behavior Modification*, **11**, 118-161.

At Emery Air Freight (1973). Positive reinforcement boosts performance. *Organizational Dynamics*, **1**, 41-50.

Bandura, A. (1976). Social learning theory. In J. T. Spence, R. C. Carson, and J. W. Thibaut (eds.), *Behavioral Approaches to Therapy*. General Learning Press, Morristown, NJ, 1-46.

Bandura, A. (1977). *Social Learning Theory*. Prentice-Hall, Englewood Cliffs, NJ.

Barrow, J. C. (1976). Worker performance and task complexity as causal determinants of leader behavior, style, and flexibility. *Journal of Applied Psychology*, **61**, 433-440.

Baum, J. F. (1978). Effectiveness of an attendance control policy in reducing chronic absenteeism. *Personnel Psycholgy*, **31**, 71-81.

Behling, O. (1976). Operant conditioning approaches to employee behavior: Some issues of research methodology. *Organization and Administrative Science*, April, 43-46.

Behling, O. (1980). The case for the natural science model for research in organizational behavior and organizational theory. *Academy of Management Review*, **5**, 483-490.

Bourdon, R. D. (1977). A token economy application to management performance improvement. *Journal of Organizational Behavior Management*, **1**, 23-38.

Bowles, M. D., Malott, R. W., and Dean, M. R. (1981). The evaluation of an incentive program used to recruit health club memberships through friend referrals. *Journal of Organizational Behavior Management*, **3**, 65-72.

Brethower, D. M. (1972). *Behavioral Analyses in Business and Industry: A Total Performance System*. Behaviordelia, Kalamazoo, MI.

Brief, A. P., and Aldag, R. J. (1981). The 'self' in work organizations: A conceptual review. *Academy of Management Review*, **6**, 75-88.

Brown, K. M., Willis, B. S., and Reid, D. H. (1981). Differential effects of supervisor verbal feedback plus approval on institutional staff peformance. *Journal of Organizational Behavior Management*, **3**, 57-67.

Brown, M. G., Malott, R. W., Dillon, M. J., and Keeps, E. J. (1980). Improving customer service in a large department store through the use of training and feedback. *Journal of Organizational Behavior Management*, **2**, 251-266.

Bucher, B., and Fabricatore, J. (1970). Use of patient-administered shock to suppress hallucinations. *Behavior Therapy*, **1**, 382-385.

Burnaska, R. F. (1976). The effects of behavior modeling training upon managers' behavior and employees' perceptions. *Personnel Psychology*, **29**, 329-335.

Calder, B. J. (1977). An attribution theory of leadership. In B. Staw and G. Salancik (eds.), *New Directions in Organizational Behavior*. St Clair Press, Chicago, 179-204.

Campbell, D. T., and Stanley, J. C. (1966). *Experimental and Quasi-Experimental Designs for Research*. Rand McNally, Chicago.

Campbell, J. P., Dunnette, M. D., Arvey, R. D., and Hellervik, L. W. (1973). The development and evaluation of behaviorally based rating scales. *Journal of Applied Psychology*, **57**, 15-22.

Carroll, S. J., and Tosi, H. L. (1979). Goal characteristics and personality factors in a management by objectives program. *Administrative Science Quarterly*, **151**, 295-305.

Carter, N., Hansson, L., Holmberg, B., and Melin, L. (1979). Shoplifting reduction through the use of specific signs. *Journal of Organizational Behavior Management*, **2**, 73-84.

Chacko, T. I., Stone, T. H., and Brief, A. P. (1979). Participation in goal setting: An attributional analysis. *Academy of Management Review*, **24**, 433-438.

Chhokar, J., and Wallin, J. (1984). A field study of the effect of feedback frequency on performance. *Journal of Applied Psychology*, **69**, 524-530.

Coles, E., and Blunden, R. (1981). Maintaining new procedures using feedback to staff, a hierarchical reporting system, and a multidisciplinary management group. *Journal of Organizational Behavior Management*, **3**, 19-33.

Cook, T. D., and Campbell, D. T. (1979). *Quasi-Experimentation: Design and Analysis Issues for Field Settings*. Rand McNally, Chicago.

Cummings, L. L. (1976). Reinforcement analysis in management: An overview. *Organization and Administrative Science*, April, 41-42.

Daniels, A., Feeney, E., Komaki, J., and Martinko, M. (1986). Behavior analysis in business and industry: A specialty conference, presented by the Florida Association Behavior Analysis, Jacksonville, Florida.

Davis, T. R. V., and Luthans, F. (1980). A social learning approach to organizational behavior. *Academy of Management Review*, **5**, 281-290.

Dick, H. W. (1978). Increasing the productivity of the day relief textile machine operator. *Journal of Organizational Behavior Management*, **2**, 45-57.

Dossett, D. L., and Greenberg, C. I. (1981). Goal setting and performance evaluation: An attributional analysis. *Academy of Management Journal*, **24**, 767-779.

Dossett, D. L., Latham, G. P., and Mitchell, T. R. (1979). Effects of assigned versus participatively set goals, knowledge of results, and individual differences on employee behavior when goal difficulty is held constant. *Journal of Applied Psychology*, **64**, 291-298.

Durand, V. M. (1983). Behavioral ecology of a staff incentive program. *Behavior Modification*, **7**, 165-181.

Eldridge, L., Lemasters, S., and Szypot, B. (1978). A performance feedback intervention to reduce waste: Performance data and participant responses. *Journal of Organizational Behavior Management*, **1**, 258-266.

Farris, G. F., and Lim, F. G., Jr (1969). Effects of performance on leadership cohesiveness, influence, satisfaction, and subsequent performance. *Journal of Applied Psychology*, **53**, 490-497.

Flannery, R. B. (1972). Use of covert conditioning in the behavioral treatment of a drug-dependent college drop-out. *Journal of Counseling Psychology*, **19**, 547-550.

Fodor, E. M. (1973). Disparagement by a subordinate, ingratiation, and the use of power. *Journal of Psychology*, **84**, 181-186.

Fodor, E. M. (1976). Group stress, authoritarian style of control, and use of power. *Journal of Applied Psychology*, **61**, 313-318.

Ford, J. E. (1981). A simple punishment procedure for controlling employee absenteeism. *Journal of Organizational Behavior Management*, **3**, 71-78.

Frederiksen, L. W. (1978). Behavioral reorganization of a professional service system. *Journal of Organizational Behavior Management*, **2**, 1-10.

Frederiksen, L. W. (1982). *Handbook of Organizational Behavior Management*, Wiley, New York.

Frederiksen, L. W., Richter, W. T., Johnson, R. P., and Solomon, L. J. (1981). Specificity of performance feedback in a professional service delivery setting. *Journal of Organizational Behavior Management*, **3**, 41-53.

French, J. R. P., Kay, E., and Meyer, H. H. (1966). Participation and the appraisal system. *Human Relations*, **19**, 13-19.

Frost, J. M., Hopkins, B. L., and Conard, R. J. (1981). An analysis of the effects of feedback and reinforcement on machine paced production. *Journal of Organizational Behavior Management*, **3**, 5-14.

Fry, F. (1974). Operant conditioning and O. B. Mod.: Of mice and men. *Personnel*, **51**, 17-24.

Gilbert, T. F. (1978). *Human Competence: Engineering Worthy Performance*. McGraw-Hill, New York.

Goldstein, A. P., and Sorcher, M. (1974). Changing managerial behavior by applied learning techniques. *Training and Development Journal*, **27**, 36-39.

Goodstadt, B., and Kipnis, D. (1970). Situational influences on the use of power. *Journal of Applied Psychology*, **54**, 201-207.

Green, S. G., and Liden, R. C. (1980). Contextual and attributional influences on control decisions. *Journal of Applied Psychology*, **65**, 453-458.

Greene, C. N. (1976). A longitudinal investigation of performance reinforcing leader behavior and subordinate satisfaction and performance. *Midwest Academy of Management Proceedings*, 157-185.

Grey, R. J., and Kipnis, D. (1976). Untangling the performance appraisal dilemma: The influence of perceived oganizational context on evaluative processes. *Journal of Applied Psychology*, **61**, 329-335.

Haynes, R. S., Pine, R. C., and Fitch, H. G. (1982). Reducing accident rates with organizational behavior modification. *Academy of Management Journal*, **25**, 407-416.

Heider, F. (1958). *The Psychology of Interpersonal Relations*, Wiley, New York.

Hermann, J. A., de Montes, A. I., Dominguez, B., de Montes, F., and Hopkins, B. L. (1973). Effects of bonuses for punctuality on the tardiness of industrial workers. *Journal of Applied Behavioral Analysis*, **6**, 563-570.

Herold, D. M. (1977). Two-way influence processes in leader-follower dyads. *Academy of Management Journal*, **20**, 224-237.

Herzberg, F., Mausner, B., and Snyderman, B. B. (1959). *The Motivation to Work*, 2nd edn. Wiley, New York.

Hills, F. S. (1979). The pay-for-performance dilemma. *Personnel*, September-October, 23-31.

Hinton, B. J., and Barrow, J. C. (1975). The supervisor's reinforcing behavior as a function of reinforcements received. *Organizational Behavior and Human Performance*, **14**, 123-143.

Ivancevich, J. M. (1976). Effects of goal setting on performance and job satisfaction. *Journal of Applied Psychology*, **61**, 605-612.

Ivancevich, J. M. (1977). Different goal-setting treatments and their effects on performance and job satisfaction. *Academy of Management Journal*, **20**, 406-419.

Ivancevich, J. M., and McMahan, J. T. (1982). The effects of goal setting, external feedback and self-generated feedback on outcome variables: A field experiment. *Academy of Management Journal*, **25**, 359-372.

Jablonsky, S. F., and DeVries, D. L. (1972). Operant conditioning principles extrapolated to the theory of management. *Organizational Behavior and Human Performance*, **7**, 340-358.

Jacobs, R., Kafry, D., and Zedeck, S. (1980). Expectations of behaviorally anchored rating scales. *Personnel Psychology*, **33**, 595-640.

Kaplan, A. (1964). *The Conduct of Inquiry*. Chandler Publishing, Scranton, PA.

Kazdin, A. E. (1973). Methodological and assessment considerations in evaluating reinforcement programs in applied settings. *Journal of Applied Behavioral Analysis*, **6**, 517-553.

Kelley, H. H. (1967). Attribution theory in social psychology. In D. Levine (ed.), *Nebraska Symposium on Motivation*, vol. 15. University of Nebraska Press, Lincoln.

Kelley, H. H. (1973). The process of causal attribution. *American Psychologist*, **28**, 107-128.

Kim, J. S., and Hamner, W. C. (1976). Effect of performance feedback and goal setting on productivity and satisfaction in an organizational setting. *Journal of Applied Psychology*, 61, 48-57.

Kingstrom, P. O., and Bass, A. R. (1981). A critical analysis of studies comparing behaviorally anchored rating scales (BARS) and other rating formats. *Personnel Psychology*, 34, 263-289.

Kipnis, D., and Cosentino, J. (1969). Use of leadership powers in industry. *Journal of Applied Psychology*, 53, 460-466.

Kipnis, D., and Vanderveer, R. (1971). Ingratiation and the use of power. *Journal of Personality and Social Psychology*, 17, 280-286.

Komaki, J. (1977). Alternative evaluation strategies in work settings: Reversal and multiple baseline designs. *Journal of Organizational Behavior Management*, 1, 53-77.

Komaki, J., Collins, R. L., and Penn, P. (1982). The role of performance antecedents and consequences in work motivation. *Journal of Applied Psychology*, 67, 334-340.

Komaki, J., Collins, R. L., and Thoene, T. J. (1980). Behavioral measurement in business, industry and government. *Behavioral Assessment*, 2, 103-123.

Komaki, J., Heinzmann, A. T., and Lawson, L. (1980). Effects of training and feedback: Component analyses of behavioral safety program. *Journal of Applied Psychology*, 65, 261-270.

Komaki, J., Waddel, W. M., and Pearce, M. G. (1977). The applied behavior analysis approach and individual employees: Improving performance in two small businesses. *Organizational Behavior and Human Performance*, 19, 337-352.

Kopelman, R. E. (1982). Improving productivity through objective feedback: A review of the evidence. *National Productivity Review*, 83, 43-55.

Kopelman, R. E. (1986). *Managing Productivity in Organizations*. McGraw-Hill, New York.

Kraut, A. I. (1976). Developing managerial skills via modeling techniques: Some positive research findings—A symposium. *Personnel Psychology*, 29, 325-369.

Kreitner, R., and Luthans, F. (1984). A social learning approach to behavioral management: Radical behaviorists 'mellowing out'. *Organizational Dynamics*, Autumn, 47-65.

Krumhus, K. M., and Malott, R. W. (1980). The effects of modeling and immediate and delayed feedback in staff training. *Journal of Organizational Behavior Management*, 2, 279-294.

Larson, L. D., Schlenker, J. F., Kirchner, R., Jr, Carr, A. F., Domash, M., and Risley, T. R. (1980). Reduction of police vehicle accidents through mechanically aided supervision. *Journal of Applied Behavior Analysis*, 13, 571-581.

Latham, G. P., and Dossett, D. L. (1978). Designing incentive plans for unionized employees: A comparison of continuous and variable ration reinforcement schedules. *Personnel Psychology*, 31, 47-61.

Latham, G. P., Fay, C. H., and Saari, L. M. (1979). The development of behavioral observation scales for appraising the performance of foremen. *Personnel Psychology*, 32, 299-311.

Latham, G. P., and Mitchell, H. A. (1982). The effects of self-set, participatively set and assigned goals on performance of government employees. *Personnel Psychology*, 35, 399-404.

Latham, G. P., Mitchell, T. R., and Dossett, D. L. (1978). The importance of participative goal setting and anticipated rewards on goal difficulty and job performance. *Journal of Applied Psychology*, 63, 163-171.

Latham, G. P., and Saari, L. M. (1979). Application of social-learning theory to training supervisors through behavior modeling. *Journal of Applied Psychology*, 64, 239-346.

Latham, G. P., and Saari, L. M. (1982). The importance of union acceptance for productivity improvement through goal setting. *Personnel Psychology*, 35, 781-787.

Latham, G. P., and Yukl, G. A. (1975). Assigned versus participative goal setting with educated and uneducated wood-workers. *Journal of Applied Psychology*, 60, 299-302.

Latham, G. P., and Yukl, G. A. (1976). The effects of assigned and participative goal setting on performance and satisfaction. *Journal of Applied Psychology*, 61, 166-171.

Lloyd, M. D. (1983). Selecting systems to measure client outcome in human service agencies. *Behavioral Assessment*, 5, 55-70.

Locke, E. A. (1968). Toward a theory of task motivation and incentives. *Organizational Behavior and Human Performance*, **3**, 157-189.

Locke, E. A. (1979). The myths of behavior mod in organizations. *Academy of Management Review*, **2**, 543-553.

Locke, E. A., Shaw, K. N., Saari, L. M., and Latham, G. P. (1981). Goal setting and task performance: 1969-1980. *Psychology Bulletin*, **90**, 125-152.

Lowin, A., and Craig, J. (1968). The influence of level of performance on managerial style: An experimental object-lesson in the ambiguity of correlational data. *Organizational Behavior and Human Performance*, **3**, 440-458.

Luthans, F. (1976). An O. B. Mod approach to organizational development. *Organization and Administrative Science*. April, 47-53.

Luthans, F. (1979). Leadership: A proposal for a social learning theory base and observational and functional analysis techniques to measure leadership behavior. In J. G. Hunt and L. L. Larson (eds.), *Crosscurrents in Leadership*. Southern Illinois Press, Carbondale, 201-208.

Luthans, F., and Davis, T. R. V. (1979). Behavioral self-management: The missing link in managerial effectiveness. *Organizational Dynamics*, Summer, 42-60.

Luthans, F., and Davis, T. R. V. (1982). An idiographic approach to organizational behavior research: The use of single case experimental designs and direct measures. *Academy of Management Review*, **7**, 380-391.

Luthans, F., and Kreitner, R. (1974). The management of behavioral contingencies. *Personnel*, July-August, 7-16.

Luthans, F., and Kreitner, R. (1975). *Organizational Behavior Modification*. Scott, Foresman, & Co., Glenview, IL.

Luthans, F., and Kreitner, R. (1985). *Organizational Behavior Modification and Beyond: An Operant and Social Learning Approach*. Scott, Foresman, & Co., Glenview, IL.

Luthans, F., and Lockwood, D. L. (1984). Toward an observation system for measuring leader behavior in natural settings. In J. G. Hunt, D. Hosking, C. Schreisheim, and R. Stewart (eds.), *Leaders and Managers: International Perspectives on Managerial Behavior and Leadership*. Pergamon, New York, 117-141.

Luthans, F., and Lyman, D. (1973). Training supervisors to use organizational behavior modification. *Personnel*, September-October, 38-44.

Luthans, F., Maciag, W. S., and Rosenkrantz, S. A. (1983). O. B. Mod: Meeting the productivity challenge with human resources management. *Personnel*, March-April, 28-36.

Luthans, F., and Maris, T. L. (1979). Evaluating personnel programs through the reversal technique. *Personnel Journal*, **58**, 692-697.

Luthans, F., and Martinko, M. J. (1976). An organizational behavior modification analysis of absenteeism. *Human Resource Management*, Fall, 11-18.

Luthans, F., Paul, R., and Baker, D. (1981). An experimental analysis of the impact of contingent reinforcement on salespersons' performance behavior. *Journal of Applied Psychology*, **66**, 314-323.

Luthans, F., Paul, R., and Taylor, L. (1985). The impact of contingent reinforcement on retail salespersons' performance behaviors: A replicated field experiment. *Journal of Organizational Behavior Management*, **7**, 25-34.

Luthans, F., Rosenkrantz, S. A., and Hennessey, H. W. (1985). What do successful managers really do? An observation study of managerial activities. *Journal of Applied Behavioral Science*, **21**, 255-270.

Luthans, F., and Schweizer, J. (1979). O. B. Mod. in a small factory: How behavior modification techniques can improve total organizational performance. *Management Review*, **68**, 43-50.

Luthans, F., and White, D. D. (1971). Behavior modification: Application to manpower management. *Personnel Administration*, **34**, 41-47.

McCall, M. W., Jr, Morrison, A. M., and Hannan, R. L. (1978). Studies of managerial work: Results and methods. *Technical Report, No. 9*. Center for Creative Leadership, Greensboro, NC.

McCarthy, M. (1978). Decreasing the incidence of 'high bobbins' in a textile spinning department through a group feedback procedure. *Journal of Organizational Behavior Management*, **1**, 150-154.

McElroy, J. C. (1982). A typology of attribution leadership research. *Academy of Management Review*, **7**, 413-417.

McFillen, J. M., and New, J. R. (1979). Situational determinants of supervisor attributions and behavior. *Academy of Management Journal*, **22**, 793-809.

McGregor, D. (1960). *Human Side of Enterprise* McGraw-Hill, New York.

McNees, P., Gilliam, S. W., Schnelle, J. F., and Risley, T. (1979). Controlling employee theft through time and product identification. *Journal of Organizational Behavior Management*, **2**, 113-119.

Maher, C. A. (1981). Performance feedback to improve the planning and evaluation of instructional programs. *Journal of Organizational Behavior Management*, **3**, 33-39.

Manz, C., and Sims, H. P., Jr (1980). Self-management as a substitute for leadership: A social learning theory perspective. *Academy of Management Review*, **5**, 361-367.

Martinko, M. J. (in press). An O. B. Mod analysis of consumer behavior. *Journal of Organizational Behavior Management*.

Martinko, M. J., and Carter, N. (1979). A critical evaluation of methodology in organizational research. In E. L. Miller (ed.), *Proceedings of the 22nd Annual Conference of the Midwest Academy of Management*, 321-326.

Martinko, M. J., and Gardner, W. L. (1982). Learned helplessness: An alternative explanation for performance deficits. *Academy of Management Review*, **7**, 413-417.

Martinko, M. J., and Gardner, W. L. (1984). The observation of high performing educational managers: Methodological issues and managerial implications. In J. G. Hunt, D. Hosking, C. Schreisheim, and R. Stewart (eds.), *Leaders and Managers: International Perspectives on Managerial Behavior and Leadership*. Pergamon, New York, 142-162.

Martinko, M. J., and Gardner, W. L. (1985). Beyond structured observation: Methodological issues and new directions. *Academy of Management Review*, **10**, 676-695.

Millard, C. W., Luthans, F., and Ottemann, R. (1976). BARS: A new breakthrough for performance appraisal. *Business Horizons*, August, 70-72.

Miller, D., Kets de Vries, M. F. R., and Toulouse, J. M. (1982). Top executive locus of control and its relationship to strategy-making, structure, and environment. *Academy of Management Journal*, **25**, 237-253.

Miller, L. M. (1978). *Behavior Management: The New Science of Managing People at Work*. John Wiley, New York.

Mintzberg, H. (1973). *The Nature of Managerial Work*. Harper & Row, New York.

Mirman, R. (1982). Performance management in sales organizations. *Handbook of Organizational Behavior Management* John Wiley, New York, 427-475.

Mitchell, T. R. (1976). Cognitions and Skinner: Some questions about behavioral determinism. *Organization and Administrative Science*, April, 63-69.

Mitchell, T. R., Green, S. G., and Wood, R. E. (1981). An attributional model of leadership and the poor performing subordinate: Development and validation. *Research in Organizational Behavior*, **3**, 197-234.

Mitchell, T. R., Smyser, C. M., and Weed, S. E. (1975). Locus of control: Supervision and work satisfaction. *Academy of Management Journal*, **18**, 623-631.

Mitchell, T. R., and Wood, R. E. (1980). Supervisor's responses to subordinate poor performance: A test of an attribution model. *Organizational Behavior and Human Performance*, **25**, 123-138.

Morey, N. C., and Luthans, F. (1984). An emic perspective and ethnoscience methods for organizational research. *Academy of Management Review*, **9**, 27-36.

Nord, W. R. (1969). Beyond the teaching machine: The neglected area of operant conditioning in the theory and practice of management. *Organizational Behavior and Human Performance*, **4**, 375-401.

Nord, W. R. (1970). Improving attendance through rewards. *Personnel Administration*, 33, 37-41.

Nord, W. R. (1976). Some issues in the application of operant conditioning to the management of organizations. *Organization and Administrative Science*, April, 55-62.

Nord, W. R., and Peter, J. P. (1980). A behavior modification perspective on marketing. *Journal of Marketing*, 44, 113-119.

Orpen, C. (1978). Effects of bonuses for attendance on absenteeism of industrial workers. *Journal of Organizational Behavior Management*, 1, 118-124.

Ottemann, R., and Luthans, F. (1975). An experimental analysis of the effectiveness of an organizational behavior modification program in industry. *Proceedings of the 35th Annual Meeting of the Academy of Management*, 140-142.

Pedalino, E., and Gamboa, V. U. (1974). Behavior modification and absenteeism: Intervention in one industrial setting. *Journal of Applied Psychology*, 59, 694-698.

Podsakoff, P. M. (1982). Determinants of supervisors' use of rewards and punishments: A literature review and suggestions for further research. *Organizational Behavior and Human Performance*, 29, 58-83.

Porter, L. W., and Lawler, E. E. (1968). *Managerial Attitudes and Performance*. Irwin, Homewood, IL.

Prue, D. M., Krapfl, J. E., Noah, J. C., Cannon, S., and Maley, R. F. (1980). Managing the treatment activities of state hospital staff. *Journal of Organizational Behavior Management*, 2, 165-181.

Pryer, M. W., and Distenfano, M. K. (1971). Perceptions of leadership, job satisfaction, and internal-external control across three nursing levels. *Nursing Research*, 2, 534-537.

Rapp, S. R., Carstensen, L. L., and Prue, D. M. (1983). Organizational behavior management 1978-1982: An annotated bibliography. *Journal of Organizational Behavior Management*, 5, 5-50.

Reber, R. A., and Wallin, J. A. (1984). The effects of training, goal setting, and knowledge of results on safe behavior: A component analysis. *Academy of Management Journal*, 27, 544-560.

Reber, R. A., Wallin, J. A., and Chhokar, J. S. (1984). Reducing industrial accidents: A behavioral experiment. *Industrial Relations*, 23, 119-125.

Repp, A. C., and Deitz, D. E. (1979a). Improving administrative-related staff behaviors at a state institution. *Mental Retardation*, August, 185-192.

Repp, A. C., and Deitz, D. E. (1979b). Reinforcement based reductive procedures: Training and monitoring performance of institution staff. *Mental Retardation*, October, 221-226.

Rhoton, M. W. (1980). A procedure to improve compliance with coal mine safety regulations. *Journal of Organizational Behavior Management*, 2, 243-250.

Ritschl, E. R., and Hall, R. V. (1980). Improving MBO: An applied behavior analyst's point of view. *Journal of Organizational Behavior Management*, 2, 269-278.

Rothschild, M. L., and Gaidis, W. C. (1981). Behavioral learning theory: Its relevance to marketing and promotions. *Journal of Marketing*, 45, 70-78.

Rotter, J. B. (1966). Generalized expectancies for internal versus external control of reinforcement. *Psychological Monographs*, 80, 1-28.

Saari, L. M., and Latham, G. P. (1982). Employee reactions to continuous and variable ratio reinforcement schedules involving a monetary incentive. *Journal of Applied Psychology*, 67, 506-508.

Sauers, D. A., and Martinko, M. J. (1986a). Goal setting: An attributional perspective. Paper presented at the Annual Meeting of the Academy of Management, Chicago.

Sauers, D. A., and Martinko, M. J. (1986b). The effects of assigned versus participative goal setting and knowledge of results on satisfaction: A test of an attributional model. Paper presented at the Annual Meeting of the Academy of Management, Chicago.

Schneier, C. E. (1974). Behavior modification in management: A review and critique. *Academy of Management Journal*, 17, 528-548.

Schreisheim, C. A., Bannister, B. D., and Money, W. H. (1979). Psychometric properties of the LPC scale: An extension of Rice's review. *Academy of Management Review*, 4, 287-290.

Schreisheim, C. A., and Kerr, S. (1977). Theories and measures of leadership: A critical appraisal of current and future directions. In J. G. Hunt and L. L. Larson (eds.), *Leadership: The Cutting Edge*. Southern Illinois University Press, Carbondale, IL, 9-45.

Schwab, D. P., Heneman, H., and Decotiis, T. (1975). Behaviorally anchored rating scales: A review of the literature. *Academy of Management Proceedings*, 223.

Silva, D. B., Duncan, P. K., and Douds, D. (1981). The effects of attendance-contingent feedback and praise on attendance and work efficiency. *Journal of Organizational Behavior Management*, 3, 59-69.

Skinner, B. F. (1953). *Science and Human Behavior*. Free Press, New York.

Smith, P. C., and Kendall, L. M. (1963). The retranslation of expectations: An approach to the construction of unambiguous anchors for rating scales. *Journal of Applied Psychology*, April, 149-155.

Snyder, C., and Luthans, F. (1982). Using O. B. Mod. to increase the productivity of hospital personnel. *Personnel Administrator*, August, 67-73.

Spector, P. E. (1982). Behavior in organizations as a function of employee's locus of control. *Psychological Bulletin*, 91, 582-497.

Steers, R. M. (1975). Task-goal attributes, N-achievement, and supervisory performance. *Organizational Behavior and Human Performancce*, 13, 392-403.

Stephens, T. A., and Burroughs, W. A. (1978). An application of operant conditioning to absenteeism in a hospital setting. *Journal of Applied Psychology*, 63, 518-521.

Stonich, P. J. (1984). The performance measurement and reward system: Critical to strategic management. *Organizational Dynamics*, 12, 45-57.

Sulzer-Azaroff, B. (1978). Behavioral ecology and accident prevention. *Journal of Organizational Behavior Management*, 2, 11-44.

Susman, G. I., and Evered, R. D. (1978). An assessment of the scientific merits of action research. *Administrative Science Quarterly*, 23, 582-603.

Van Maanen, J. (1979). Reclaiming qualitative methods for organizational research: A preface. *Administrative Science Quarterly*, 24, 520-526.

Van Maanen, J., Dabbs, J. M., Jr, and Faulkner, R. R. (1982). *Varieties of Qualitative Research*, Sage Publications, Beverly Hills, CA.

Vroom, V. H. (1964). *Work and Motivation*. Wiley, New York.

Wallin, J. A., and Johnson, R. D. (1976). The positive reinforcement approach to controlling employee absenteeism. *Personnel Journal*, 55, 390-392.

Weick, K. (1979). *The Social Psychology of Organizing*, 2nd end. Addison-Wesley, Reading, MA.

Weiner, B. (1972). *Theories of Motivation*. Markham, Chicago.

Whyte, W. F. (1972). Pigeons, persons, and piece rates: Skinnerian theory in organizations. *Psychology Today*, April, 66-68, 96-100.

Wikcoff, M., Anderson, D. C., and Crowell, C. R. (1982). Behavior management in a factory setting: Increasing work efficiency. *Journal of Organizational Behavior Management*, 4, 97-127.

Wood, R. E., and Mitchell, T. R. (1981). Managerial behavior in a social context: The impact of impression management on attributions and disciplinary actions. *Organizational Behavior and Human Performance*, 28, 356-378.

Zohar, D., Cohen, A., and Azar, N. (1980). Promoting increased use of ear protectors in noise through information feedback. *Human Factors*, 22, 69-79.

Zohar, D., and Fussfeld, N. (1981). Modifying earplug wearing behavior by behavior modification techniques: An empirical evaluation. *Journal of Organizational Behavior Management*, 3, 41-52.

International Review of Industrial and Organizational Psychology 1987
Edited by C. L. Cooper and I. T. Robertson
© 1987 John Wiley & Sons Ltd

Chapter 3

JOB AND WORK DESIGN

Toby D. Wall and Robin Martin
MRC/ESRC Social and Applied Psychology Unit
Department of Psychology
University of Sheffield
UK

INTRODUCTION

Job design is an area of enduring interest within the broader field of industrial and organizational psychology. Research focuses on the charactistics of jobs and how these affect people's attitudes and behavior. Traditionally, the emphasis has been on lower-level jobs within organizations, such as clerical and shopfloor work.

Explicit psychological interest in job design can be traced back to the turn of the century, to the early days of the emergence of psychology as an academic and applied discipline in its own right. Since that time, as is typical of most areas of scientific endeavour, progress has been uneven. Periods of high research activity and rapid advance are followed by quiet times in which the momentum appears to be lost and the avenues for future inquiry are obscure. In reviewing the literature for this chapter we came to the conclusion that currently we are experiencing such a lull. There is a lower rate of publication on job design during the 1980s than there was during the 1970s.

It is clear, nevertheless, that the nature of jobs will remain an important influence over the quality of people's lives, and less research will not alter that fact. So we turned our thoughts to the kinds of influence that might serve to rekindle progress in the area. We decided to ask ourselves two questions. First, what are the major deficiencies in the literature as it stands? Second, what developments in the 'outside world' are likely to help us overcome those weaknesses and open up opportunities for innovative studies? Our tentative answers to these questions will emerge during the course of the chapter. For the present it is sufficient to signal that, with respect to the second question, we identified the application of information technology in work settings as an important stimulus. The diffusion of such microelectronic based technology into organizations is accelerating, and changing the nature of jobs in offices and on the shopfloor. It represents what some have called the 'second industrial revolution' (Halton, 1985), or the 'information technology revolution' (Forester, 1985). The diffusion of this technology raises numerous questions about how it can best be exploited, and what dangers are inherent in its use. Central among these are the implications of the technology for job design, and conversely, how psychological knowledge of job design can be deployed in the development of new technologies. It is these opportunities and challenges which should stimulate research and development studies.

This chapter is divided into four main sections. The first is a history of job design research up to the mid-1970s. This is followed by a summary of the more recent literature which is considered thematically. The third part outlines some of the weaknesses in the literature to date, by identifying important issues which are inadequately treated, and others which are neglected. Finally, the chapter concludes with a brief consideration of the implications of the 'information technology revolution' for research into job design.

A BRIEF HISTORY OF JOB DESIGN RESEARCH

It is useful to recap on some of the major early developments in job design for two reasons: first, this serves as a background against which to consider the research reviewed in the following section: second, aspects of this history have been recently revived to help analysis of the job and psychological implications of the application of information technology in work organizations. We begin this brief historical review at the usual starting point, the evolution of the 'traditional' approach to job design, that of work simplification.

Work Simplification

The major influences on traditional job design practices can be traced back to the writings of such theorists as Adam Smith (1776) and Charles Babbage (1835). A key idea in their arguments is the division of labour, which they saw as the vehicle for increasing output per man–hour. For Smith this would occur for three reasons: greater dexterity would arise when employees 'specialized' in a small part of the required work; time would be saved by not having to change from one task to another; and labour-saving inventions were more likely to appear when the focus had been narrowed in this way. Babbage added the rationale that learning times would be reduced by fragmentation of jobs and savings thus could be made both in training and by employing less skilled and therefore cheaper labour.

The writings and practical demonstrations offered by Taylor (1911) and Gilbreth (1911) contributed to the progression towards work simplification. Taylor's Scientific Management approach has many facets, but an important feature is that it built upon the principle of the division of labour and suggested that management should explicitly assume responsibility for the design of jobs, and exercise greater influence over the execution of work. This involved developing more efficient work methods and, through a combination of training, incentives, and control, ensuring these were put into practice. To the fragmentation of work into jobs comprising only a small range of the required tasks (a horizontal division of labour) was added the idea of a vertical division of labour. Here management assumed more regulation, and 'workers' less, over how and when work was to be completed. There was a separation between planning and control on the one hand, and 'doing' on the other.

The extent to which the ideas introduced by Smith, Babbage, and particularly Taylor influenced the evolution of job design is a matter of controversy among historians of the area (see, for example, Baritz, 1960; Kelly, 1982). It is certainly clear that a range of other developments, such as the moving assembly line introduced in 1914 at the Ford Motor Company at Highland Park in Michigan (Edwards, 1978) and the incorporation of the principles of the division of labour and Scientific Management into classical management theories (e.g. Gulick and Urwick, 1937), played an important part (see Davis, and Taylor, 1962; Kelly, 1982). It also seems likely that the principles of job design which emerged themselves reflected existing trends in industry. What is less in dispute is the conclusion that work simplification has been, and still is, the dominant job design paradigm. As Klein (1976, p. 14) describes:

the choices made in the design and organization of work have tended to be in the direction of rationalization, specialization and the sub-division of tasks, and the minimizing and standardization of skills . . . first in manufacturing and later in administration, the knowledge and methods of the natural sciences have been put to the task of discovering new methods of working and organizing which would give economic and predictable results.

That work simplification has spread from shopfloor jobs in manufacturing to most other areas of work is an argument offered by many commentators (e.g. Braverman, 1974; Cherns and Davis, 1975; Kraft, 1977), and its continuing influence over job design practice has been documented by Davis, Canter, and Hoffman (1955), Hedberg and Mumford (1975) and Taylor (1979).

Though clearly neither a universal nor homogeneous phenomenon, work simplification is the reference point for contemporary I/O psychology approaches to job design. These attempt to reverse the trend by creating jobs which involve a wider range of tasks over which job holders exercise greater control. The term job redesign is thus often used as it signifies a change from the dominant paradigm. The productivity argument behind this alternative approach is that more complex, responsible jobs will engender better performance through promoting work motivation, which will compensate for gains otherwise obtained by the division of labour. It is also argued that job redesign leads to greater flexibility and, by enhancing satisfaction, to an improvement in the quality of working life—itself a benefit to which employees are entitled as major contributors to their employing organizations (Mohrman et al., 1986). Research into job design can be seen as the quest to test these assumptions empirically, to examine their general validity and determine the limits within which they operate.

Early Studies of Work Simplification

Early psychological interest in job design was mainly reactive to the horizontal aspect of work simplification. It sought to document the affective and behavioral consequences of creating jobs involving the repetition of a narrow range of tasks. The vertical division of labour was an issue left relatively untouched.

In the UK some of the earliest studies of repetitive work were undertaken under the auspices of the Industrial Fatigue Research Board, which evolved into the Industrial Health Research Board funded by the Medical Research Council. These involved intensive investigations of such jobs as bicycle chain assembly, soap wrapping, tobacco weighing and packing, cartridge case assembly, and pharmaceutical product packing (e.g. Burnett, 1925; Wyatt and Ogden, 1924). The results confirmed the now accepted view that repetitive work is dissatisfying and, if taken to extremes, is not necessarily more productive. Thus Wyatt, Fraser, and Stock (1928) reported 'operatives who have experience of both uniform and varied conditions of work generally prefer the latter' (p. 25). Similarly, the Board's eleventh annual report drawing on the results of the whole programme of research concluded, 'boredom has become increasingly prominent as a factor in the industrial life of the worker, and its effects are no less important than those of fatigue' (Industrial Health Research Board, 1931, p. 30).

A later Health Board report brought a new dimension to the area. Fraser (1947) examined the association between job (and social) factors and the incidence of neurotic illness in a large sample of over 3000 employees in engineering factories. Neurosis (independently assessed by clinicians) was found to be most prevalent among those who found work boring, were engaged in asssembly, bench inspection, and tool room work, or performed jobs requiring constant attention. He summarized the results as follows: 'It may still be less important to make jobs foolproof than to design them so that they will not be disliked, found boring, or demand long periods of close attention to unvarying detail. . . . More variety, and scope for initiative and interest, could be introduced without any fundamental alteration of production programmes' (Fraser, 1947, p. 10).

In the United States similar findings were obtained. Walker and Guest's (1952) classic study, *Man on the Assembly Line*, conducted in the car industry, confirmed the relationship between simplified jobs and negative work attitudes; and Kornhauser's (1965) investigation of mental health, in the same industrial sector, supported Fraser's findings. Kornhauser concluded that 'by far the most influential attribute [of jobs] is the opportunity work offers — or fails to offer — for the use of workers' abilities and for associated feelings of interest, sense of accomplishment, personal growth and self-respect' (1965, p. 363). Simplified jobs were seen as offering few such opportunities.

Overall, this early line of research served to establish the importance of job factors to psychological wellbeing. It confirmed the intuitively accepted view that simplified, repetitive jobs were less satisfying, and introduced mental health as a relevant outcome variable (which later investigators have largely ignored). However, it generally failed to address the issue of productivity, did not move effectively into a proactive mode involving the deliberate redesign of jobs (Walker's 1950 study is an exception), and focused on the horizontal aspect of the division of labour (the range of tasks carried out) to the relative exclusion of the vertical aspect as reflected by job autonomy, control, and responsibility.

Job Enrichment

During the 1950s and 1960s research into work design was guided by two largely independent developments. Both encouraged a more proactive, change-oriented research approach by describing how jobs should be redesigned; and both challenged work simplification not only by suggesting a wider range of tasks be included in jobs, but also by advocating that more autonomy and control be afforded to employees over the execution of work. The first of these was the notion of job enrichment. The second development was that of autonomous work groups (which is considered later).

Job enrichment has its origins in the work of Herzberg and associates (1959, 1966, 1968) in the United States. In his Two-Factor Theory, Herzberg (1966) distinguished between characteristics intrinsic to jobs, such as achievement, advancement, recognition, responsibility, and the nature of the work itself; and those extrinsic to the jobs, such as company policy and administration, supervision, interpersonal relations, and work conditions. He argued that the former ('motivators') are instrumental in promoting motivation and satisfaction, whereas the latter ('hygiene factors') are only important as sources of dissatisfaction. Thus the central proposition of the theory is that sources of job satisfaction and motivation are qualitatively different from the determinants of dissatisfaction.

Research failed to confirm the Two-Factor Theory as a whole (e.g. Locke and Henne, 1986; King, 1970; Wall and Stephenson, 1970), but the focus on the importance of intrinsic job factors for satisfaction and motivation provided impetus for subsequent studies. It was from this perspective that the idea of job enrichment arose, a proposal for redesigning jobs to provide employees with greater responsibility and control over their work activities.

Herzberg's theory was effectively superseded by Hackman and Oldham's (1976) Job Characteristics Model, which built upon earlier work by Turner and Lawrence (1965) and Hackman and Lawler (1971). The Job Characteristics Model specifies five 'core job dimensions' salient to job attitudes and behaviour. These are task variety, task identity, task significance, autonomy, and task feedback. By (differentially) affecting the 'critical psychological states' of experienced meaning, responsibility, and knowledge of results, the five job characteristics are predicted to promote work motivation, work performance, and job satisfaction, and to reduce labour turnover and absenteeism. The model (through the medium of the 'motivating potential score') ascribes particular importance to autonomy and feedback. In addition, the strength of the job characteristics–outcome relationship is predicted to be affected by individual differences, in particular the level of employees' 'growth need strength'. The attitudes and behavior of those who place greater importance on challenge, using their own judgement and the opportunity for achievement at work (high growth need strength), are held to be more strongly affected by the job characteristics than are the attitudes and behavior of those with less strong growth needs.

The Job Characteristics Model did not represent a major new departure in job design. Rather, it served to summarize a previous line of research stretching back more than 15 years and to present this in a commendably explicit and digestible form. Moreover, by developing a set of measures covering each of the key variables (the Job Diagnostic Survey, Hackman and Oldham, 1975) the authors provided an attractive research package. Together these properties account for the fact that it was to become a major theoretical influence on research from its inception to the present day.

Group Work Redesign

The second major development concerns the concept of the autonomous work group. This evolved within the more general socio-technical systems approach to organizational analysis and design developed at the Tavistock Institute in Great Britain (Trist and Bamforth, 1951; see also Trist, 1981, for a more recent review). Early work at Tavistock involved intensive studies of people engaged in functionally interrelated tasks. It is thus not surprising that the focus on work design which emerged took the work group as the main unit of analysis.

A key feature of autonomous work groups is that they provide for a high degree of self-determination by employees in the management of their everyday work. Typically this involves collective control over the pace of work, distribution of tasks within the group, and the timing and organization of breaks; also participation in the training and recruitment of new members (Gulowsen, 1972). Often it also requires little or no direct supervision (Emery, 1980). In recent years autonomous work groups have been given a variety of labels including, *inter alia*, 'semi-autonomous work groups,' 'self-managing work groups,' 'self-managing work teams,' and 'self-regulating work teams'. In practice this approach has much in common with job enrichment with regard to the recommended content of work since it emphasizes the provision of autonomy, feedback, and task completeness. The focus, however, is on the group level of design and analysis.

The early history of research into autonomous work groups is punctuated by carefully documented case studies and action research projects (e.g. Davis and Valfer, 1965; Rice, 1958; Trist and Bamforth, 1951). This approach to work design has also had considerable practical success, especially in Europe, and later in the United States. In the 1970s Volvo and Saab built new car production plants which eschewed conventional production lines and were based around autonomous work groups, as did General Motors in the 1980s. Along with job enrichment, the ideas behind autonomous work groups and socio-technical systems theory more generally have played a prominent role in the quality of working life (QWL) movement which emerged in almost all Western industrial societies in the 1960s and 1970s (Mohrman *et al.*, 1986; Wall, 1982).

The influence of the autonomous work group concept on empirical research, however, developed more slowly. During the 1960s it gave rise to few studies based on designs allowing causal inference, and was not systematically evaluated in terms of its effects on attitudes and behaviour. The literature was disparate, and no focused set of studies emerged. This in part was due to its origins in a more action research oriented environment dedicated to meeting client rather than 'scientific' needs. It was also a reflection of a lack of specificity, and considerable complexity, in the underlying socio-technical systems theory (Clark, 1975; Hill, 1972; McLean and Sims, 1978). As Cherns and Davis (1975) note, the approach requires the use of a 'number of nonexistent dictionaries' in order to be put into practice. Not until the mid-1970s did interest in the socio-technical approach take root in the United States. Nevertheless, because of its clear potential, and its compatibility with contemporary values (Davis, 1976; Hertog, 1976; Klein, 1976), the approach survives to influence the direction of more recent research.

Overview

The above four perspectives continue to structure contemporary research. Work simplification remains as the predominant job design influence in practice, against which I/O approaches are contrasted. There has persisted a line of inquiry focused on the horizontal aspect of the division of labour, that which is concerned with the psychological implications of short cycle, repetitive, and paced jobs. Through the Job Characteristics Model, job enrichment persists as an approach which also emphasizes the role of individual difference variables in the explanation of its effects. Finally, the original idea of autonomous work groups which is receiving renewed attention provides a starting point for group work redesign and, through its roots in socio-technical systems theory, reminds investigators that such developments should be considered in their organizational contexts. We turn now to consider how recent research has built and elaborated upon these guiding approaches.

CONTEMPORARY RESEARCH INTO WORK DESIGN

Research since the mid-1970s clearly reflects the issues central within the history of job design, but is also characterized by an increasing diversity of perspective. In this section we attempt to represent this diversity by briefly describing some of the main themes that have guided recent investigations.

Repetitive and Machine-paced Work

Early interest in job design reactive to the horizontal aspect of work simplification has been represented by recent research into the psychological effects of repetitive and machine-paced jobs. Cox and his colleagues have examined the effects of such work both in laboratory experiments and field settings (Cox and Mackay, 1979; Cox, 1980; Cox, Mackay, and Page, 1982; Cox, Thirlaway, and Cox, 1982; Cox and Cox, 1984). They found machine-paced repetitive work to be associated with higher levels of reported stress, but that high 'attentional demands' and socializing could serve to alleviate this effect.

In a similar vein Hurrell (1985) examined the moderating effect of the Type A behaviour pattern on the relationship between paced work and psychological mood disturbance. Using a sample of nearly 3000 machine-paced letter sorters, and an equivalent sized comparison group engaged in unpaced work, he found pacing to be associated with mood state (e.g. higher tension–anxiety, anger–hostility, and depression–dejection), but there was no differential effect for subjects with high Type A scores.

A provocative paper by Broadbent (1985) suggests a more differentiated view of the relationship between job characteristics and mental health. Using data from his own research and that of NIOSH reported by Caplan et al. (1975) and LaRocco, House, and French, (1980), and also drawing on Karasek's (1979) ideas, Broadbent argued that job demands (work load and pacing) have effects primarily on anxiety, social isolation operates on depression, and repetitive, unskilled work mainly affects job dissatisfaction. He also suggested that social support, instrumental attitudes (the extent to which people work for pay as opposed to job satisfaction), and leisure satisfaction either buffer or moderate such relationships.

Other recent work on repetitiveness and pacing is described by Broadbent and Gath (1979, 1981), Dainoff, Hurrell, and Happ (1981), Murrell (1978), Murphy and Hurrell (1980), Salvendy and Smith (1981), and Smith, Hurrell, and Murphy (1981).

This area of inquiry is promising, and Broadbent's ideas in particular warrant further attention. The focus on mental health is refreshing in a field which has traditionally been rather conservative in its choice of outcome variables (as we shall discuss later). It provides a clear link between I/O and clinical psychology which is worthy of pursuit. Nevertheless, this aspect of job design has received relatively little attention in recent years, and correspondingly its empirical base is less than impressive. Studies are predominantly cross-sectional and far from definitive.

The Job Characteristics Approach and Job Enrichment

Recent research into the design of individual jobs has been strongly influenced by Hackman and Oldham's (1975, 1976) Job Characteristics Model (JCM). Published studies based on this model increased dramatically in number up to the appearance of the thorough critical review of the job characteristics approach by Roberts and Glick (1981), since which time they have diminished. We shall not attempt to repeat and update that analysis, the main conclusions of which are equally valid today. Rather, we shall look more selectively at some of the issues of continuing interest.

Despite the general influence of the JCM over research, the full model has only rarely been investigated empirically. The feature which distinguishes the JCM most clearly from its predecessors is the inclusion of the critical psychological states as intervening variables (see p. 65 for a description of the JCM). Direct examination of this part of the model has confirmed neither the predicted differential pattern of relationships between the five job characteristics and the three critical psychological states, nor that these intervening variables are required to account for the relationship between the core job dimensions on the one hand and the outcome variables on the other (e.g. Wall, Clegg, and Jackson, 1978). It appears that the critical psychological states are an unnecessary elaboration which concern for parsimony would lead one to exclude. Generally, investigators have either ignored this aspect of the JCM (e.g. Oldham, 1976; Orpen, 1979) or treated the critical psychological states as dependent variables (e.g. Baghat and Chassie, 1980; Kiggundu, 1980).

In practice, therefore, the JCM has been simplified to an approach concerned with the direct causal links between job characteristics and outcome variables, with growth need strength specified as a moderator. Its considerable influence over the literature stems from its identification of a particular set of variables and the provision of instruments to tap these. This has given a consistency of focus to the literature which other approaches have failed to achieve. We shall consider the primary causal proposition here, and address the issue of individual differences afterwards.

The central component of the JCM, along with other approaches to work design is that the specified job characteristics are posited as determinants of employees' attitudes and behaviour. The natural progression of research effort is to move from weak but expedient cross-sectional research designs, which are sufficient to suggest whether the proposition deserves further attention, to change studies with designs capable of supporting causal inference. There has been much effort of the correlational exploratory type which supports the job characteristics approach (see, for example, the meta-analysis reported by Loher et al., 1985), and it seems generally agreed that little more is needed (Roberts and Glick, 1981).

Progress with respect to building up evidence based on change studies has been disappointing. Such investigations are few and far between, and in general exhibit important design weaknesses. One interesting trend in this area has been a particular variant of the 'naturally occurring field experiment'. Here investigators have homed in on instances of organizational change which are incidental to but may have (unknown) consequences for job design (e.g. the introduction of a 4-day week, Baghat and Chassie, 1980; job moves, Keller and Holland, 1981; and technological change, Hackman, Pearce, and Wolfe, 1978). The allocation of employees to enriched, no change, and impoverished 'conditions' has then been made *post hoc* on the basis of self-report measures of job characteristics obtained both before and after the change. In the absence of either a clear rationale for predicting the effects of the organizational change for job design, or the use of independent or objective measures of job character- istics, this approach seems to offer at best only a minor advance over cross-sectional research using perceptual measures, and provides a dubious base for causal inference.

Other field change studies have involved actual, and typically deliberate, theory- related job changes (e.g. Griffeth, 1985; Griffin, 1983; Locke, Sirota, and Wolfson, 1976; Orpen, 1979). Perceived job characteristics measures have been used to confirm that the manipulation had its expected experienced counterpart. Taken as a whole the evidence from this research, in common with laboratory experiments (e.g. White and Mitchell, 1979) and longitudinal field surveys (e.g. Griffin, 1981), supports predictions concerning attitudinal and (to a lesser degree) performance effects, but is neither unproblematic nor definitive. Performance effects without corresponding motivational or attitudinal ones, and vice versa, point to theoretical deficiencies, and suggest there may be unidentified factors which promote or inhibit particular outcomes. Methodological considerations also cloud the issue: only a small proportion of the few investigations is based on strong research designs; it seems likely that failures are under-represented in the literature (but see Frank and Hackman, 1975; Lawler, Hackman, and Kaufman, 1973); and it is often difficult to ascribe changes recorded to job design itself rather than to the various associated changes which the redesign may have necessitated. A particular weakness in change studies is that the effects of job redesign have only been pursued in the short term, a few weeks to 6 months. In the absence of clear theoretical specification of an appropriate time scale for job redesign effects to appear, it is unclear whether negative findings reflect an inappropriate measurement period, or indeed if positive ones are really only short-term rather than enduring.

The above criticisms are not intended as an indictment of particular studies or investigators. Indeed, those that have undertaken change studies are to be commended. Rather it is a comment on the area as a whole. There remains a need for still more field experimentation and longitudinal research using a variety of alternative designs and techniques. Only by creating such a large body of evidence can the inevitable weaknesses in individual studies, which arise because of the many constraints inherent in working in real-life settings, be compensated for by the strengths of others. As in other areas of I/O psychology there is a paucity of change studies (cf. Griffin and Bateman, 1986), and this presumably reflects the difficulties experienced in mounting such research. We consider this more general issue later.

Another aspect of research stemming directly from the JCM concerns the measurement of job characteristics. The large majority of studies have been based on the Job Diagnostic Survey (JDS, Hackman and Oldham, 1975), used in such a way that observations of the independent and dependent variables derive from the same source, the job incumbent. Examinations of this instrument have shown that whilst the scales to measure the five core job dimensions typically exhibit high internal reliability, multivariate analysis does not always confirm the theory specified separation among them. For example, Abdel-Halim (1978), Ferratt and Reeve (1977), and Katz (1978b) obtained confirmation of the five dimensions, but Dunham (1976, 1977) Dunham, Aldag, and Brief (1977), and Green et al, (1979) did not. Schnake and Dumler (1985) similarly obtained non-confirmatory results, but went on to show that partialling out intrinsic job satisfaction changed the findings to one of support for the hypothesized structure. They concluded that the measure can be contaminated by people's affective reactions (see also Ferratt, Dunham, and Pierce, 1981).

This latter point highlights the continuing concern about the validity of attempting to measure actual job characteristics through the medium of people's perceptions of their own jobs. Hackman and Oldham (1975), in their original report on the Job Diagnostic Survey, presented limited evidence to show that perceived scores were associated with ratings of job characteristics obtained from independent sources. More recently Kiggundu (1980) showed empirical support for the JCM when using independent ratings of job characteristics (from immediate supervisors and informed coworkers) and relating these to job incumbents' attitudes. It should be noted, however, that the support was stronger where the job incumbents' own ratings were used. Algera (1983) describes comparable results. These studies (along with field experiments involving actual changes to jobs) suggest that empirical support for the job characteristics approach as a whole cannot be dismissed as simply an artifact of the use of perceptual measures of job characteristics. However, they do not rule out the possibility that such measures are subject to attributional processes which could inflate or otherwise affect the nature of the evidence obtained (see p. 72), and these processes could be sufficient to account for the results of correlational studies based solely on self-report data.

In summary, research on the relationship between job characteristics and job reactions does not contradict the main predictions embodied within the JCM. Nevertheless, it is far from satisfactory. Two particular areas of weakness are: the lack of a sufficiently substantial body of field experiments examining the effects of job redesign over appropriate periods of time; and inadequate measurement of the objective job characteristics. These weaknesses were highlighted by Roberts and Glick in 1981, and little progress is evident since then. It should also be noted that researchers have paid considerably more attention to the predicted attitudinal outcome variables (job satisfaction and intrinsic motivation) than to the behavioural ones (performance and absence). Another area of research activity promoted by the JCM, that concerned with the role of individual differences in moderating the relationships between job characteristics and outcome variables, is considered next.

Individual Differences and Other Moderator Variables

One consequence of the JCM was to promote interest in individual differences as moderators of the relationship between job characteristics and employee responses. Initially, reflecting the particular variables specified by the JCM, the focus was predominantly on growth need strength (GNS), or related constructs such as higher-order need strength.

Much research effort has gone into examining the moderating role of GNS, either as an issue in its own right, or as part of investigations into the job characteristics approach to job design more generally (e.g. Champoux, 1980; Farr, 1976; Ganster, 1980; Griffin, 1982; Hackman, Pearce, and Wolfe, 1978; Jackson, Paul, and Wall, 1981; Kemp and Cook, 1983; Lawler, Hackman, and Kaufman, 1973; Orpen, 1979; Umstot, Bell, and Mitchell, 1976; Zierden, 1980).

Recently, two meta-analyses have been published which serve to integrate empirical research in this area. Loher *et al.* (1985) limited their analysis to the five job dimensions specified by the JCM and the single outcome variable of job satisfaction. They concluded that 'we can now state with some confidence that growth need strength acts as a moderator of the relationship between job characteristics and job satisfaction' (p. 287), but also noted that the main effect was still in evidence among employees with low GNS scores. Spector (1985) examined a wider range of outcome variables, including different dimensions of work satisfaction, motivation, performance, and absenteeism, and reached an equivalent conclusion for all these variables except the last.

The underlying tendency within the research as a whole thus lends support to the moderating effect of GNS. Nevertheless, it should be noted that the meta-analyses were based on subgroup correlations, rather than the more appropriate moderated regression (Zedeck, 1971) or analysis of covariance (Jackson, Paul, and Wall, 1981). Moreover, they encompassed a substantial proportion of negative findings. It thus remains unclear if there exists a generalizable GNS effect, or whether its discovery has been obscured by the use of inadequate measurement instruments, insensitive statistical techniques (Morris, Sherman, and Mansfield., 1986; Peters and Champoux, 1979), or other factors (cf. O'Connor, Rudolf, and Peters, 1980). Once again, the bulk of investigations have been based on cross-sectional data with independent, moderator, and dependent variables all measured through self-report data. There are few investigations examining whether high GNS employees respond more positively to actual job enrichment than do their lower GNS counterparts.

The inconclusiveness of investigations into GNS no doubt encouraged the search for other individual differences and contextual variables which moderate employees' responses to job characteristics. Among those examined have been work values such as need for achievement, need for autonomy, self-esteem, and the Protestant work ethic (Ganster, 1980; Mossholder, Bedeian, and Armenakis, 1982; O'Reilly and Caldwell, 1979; Steers, 1975; Steers and Spencer, 1977; Stone, Mowday, and Porter, 1977); job longevity (Katz, 1978a, 1978b; Kemp and Cook, 1983); role stress (Abdel-Halim, 1978, 1981; Beehr, 1976; Keller, Szilagyi, and Holland, 1976); extrinsic satisfaction (Abdel-Halim, 1979; Champoux, 1980; Oldham, 1976); and organizational climate and setting (Ferris and Gilmore, 1984; Walsh, Taber, and Beehr, 1980). As for GNS, the outcome has been an inconsistent rather than a coherent pattern of findings.

It would seem inappropriate to dismiss the issue of individual differences in job design or other areas of psychological research, as some would have us do (e.g. White, 1978). Yet research to date makes it clear that no strong and consistent moderating effect is apparent. Perhaps, as Kemp and Cook (1983) observe, rather than ask the question 'Which moderators are replicable across situations?' we should be attempting to 'specify the conditions under which moderators are important' (p. 896). It is also the case that the emphasis on moderator effects has distracted attention from other contributions of individual differences to people's work attitudes and behaviours.

The Social Information Processing Approach

The central role of perceived job characteristics in the literature provided the springboard for the recent growth of interest in the social information processing (SIP) approach to work design. In its most general form the SIP approach is based on the premise that job attitudes and perceptions are socially construed, and reflect information provided by others in the workplace. In some respects this can be seen as complementing the job characteristics approach, by offering the prospect of explaining additional variance with regard to the relationship between job perceptions and reactions. In other respects, the SIP approach can be seen as an alternative and invalidating perspective, which explains the relationship between the salient variables as caused by social factors rather than by objective job differences, which job design models assume (Griffin and Bateman, 1986).

Interest in the SIP approach was fostered by two theoretical papers by Salancik and Pfeffer (1977, 1978; see also Shaw, 1980). Subsequent empirical research has been mainly in the form of laboratory experiments in which informational cues (e.g. others' views of job characteristics, and their satisfactions) were manipulated and the effects on job perceptions, attitudes, and performance observed (e.g. Adler, Skov, and Salvemini, 1985; Mitchell, Liden, and Rothman, 1985; O'Reilly and Caldwell, 1979; Shaw and Weekley, 1981; Slusher and Griffin, 1980; White and Mitchell, 1979).

Field studies, using indirect indices of social influence (e.g. professional attitudes, work-group membership and affiliation), have been reported by Oldham and Miller (1979), O'Reilly, Parlette, and Bloom (1980), Griffin (1983, a field experiment), and O'Reilly and Caldwell (1985). Within the SIP framework attention has also been paid to individual difference effects on task perceptions and other reactions (e.g. O'Connor and Barrett, 1980; O'Reilly, Parlette, and Bloom, 1980; Weiss and Shaw, 1979). A difficulty with these studies is that the nature of the social cues from the indirect sources remains undefined.

Useful reviews of the SIP literature are provided by Blau and Katerberg (1982) and Thomas and Griffin (1983). Overall, it is clear that social factors do affect people's job perceptions, attitudes, and behaviour, much as would be expected. But it also appears that these influences complement rather than invalidate the job characteristics approach. Where objective job characteristics and social cues have been examined together they have been shown to affect employee reactions independently. Much remains to be done to take the SIP approach beyond its current exploratory status, not least of which is to develop direct measures of social cues in field settings.

The Socio-technical Systems Approach and Work-group Design

Although comparisons are difficult, it seems that autonomous work groups have been more widely implemented in practice than individually oriented job design approaches. Certainly, many observers have commented on their increasing use, along with that of socio-technical analysis more generally (e.g. Cummings, 1978; Kerr, Hill, and

Broedling, 1986; Pasmore *et al.*, 1983). Paradoxically, this practical interest does not appear to be fully reflected by the recent research literature. Nevertheless, academic interest has been growing, and this is evident in three respects. First, a number of authors have attempted to make more explicit, and develop, early theoretical thinking. The work of Susman (1976) and Cummings (1978, 1982) drew wider attention to the potential of this approach to work design, and its relevance to the design of jobs for advanced manufacturing technology has been made clear by Cummings and Blumberg (1987). Second, attempts have been made to adapt the job characteristics approach to make it applicable at the level of group work design. Hackman (1977) went so far as to suggest that autonomous work groups are likely to prove more powerful than individual forms of job design since they can encompass much larger and more complete pieces of work. Hackman (1983) subsequently extended the Job Characteristics Model to apply at the group level. Similarly, Rousseau (1977) and Cummings (1982) argued for a synthesis of the two approaches. Finally, there has been a number of reviews of empirical research in the area which point to the potential benefits of autonomous work groups whilst calling for initiatives in conducting field studies with strong research designs (e.g. Cummings, Molloy, and Glen, 1977; Pasmore *et al.*, 1983).

The response to the plea for more adequate empirical examination of autonomous work groups, however, has been disappointing. Case studies and general accounts continue to describe how change agents could or have set about undertaking socio-technical systems design, and provide valuable, but nevertheless circumstantial, evidence concerning the psychological and organizational benefits (and some costs) to be expected (e.g. Walton, 1977; Lawler, 1978; Emery, 1980; Kolodny and Kiggundu, 1980; Manz and Sims, 1982; Ciborra, Migliarese, and Romano, 1984). But this literature is mainly illustrative. The move towards a more adequate empirical base has been slow. Two comparative studies have been reported by Denison (1982) and Kemp *et al.*, (1983); a longitudinal investigation by Wall (1980) and Wall and Clegg (1981); and a field experiment (examining effects over 30 months) by Wall *et al.*, (1986). All these provide evidence in support of the attitudinal and performance benefits of autonomous group work, but the latter study also suggests costs with regard to labour turnover and managerial stress.

The above research only begins to scratch the surface with respect to the effects and implications of autonomous work groups. It is sufficient to encourage greater effort in the area, but does not provide a substantial enough base from which to generalize. It is even less adequate with regard to empirical evidence on the processes which take place within autonomous work groups, and how these may account for attitudinal and behavioural effects. It should also be pointed out that whilst socio-technical theory emphasizes the joint optimization of technical and social subsystems, empirically based research has almost entirely focused only on the social dimension (Denison, 1982; Pasmore *et al.*, 1983). It is to be hoped that recent initiatives encourage more systematic, comprehensive, and extensive investigation of autonomous work groups in field settings.

Context in Theory and Practice

A general criticism of the job characteristics approach to work design was that it encouraged a narrow theoretical perspective (e.g. Roberts and Glick, 1981). Certainly, until around the 1980s work in this area paid scant attention either to other relevant theories, or to contextual factors which may affect job properties and their effects on attitudes and behaviour. In principle research on autonomous work groups is less open to such a charge, since it is axiomatic to the underlying socio-technical systems theory that interdependence among a range of variables is considered. In practice, however, even studies emanating from this background showed little systematic consideration of organizational variables.

Recent investigations have shown signs of moving towards a broader perspective. We have already noted the introduction of social information processing theory to the job design area (p. 72), and the attempt to integrate job characteristics and socio-technical systems approaches (p. 73). This diversification is apparent in a number of other respects. Several investigators have examined the link between technology and the design of jobs. Technological uncertainty and its relationship with job characteristics has been considered by Brass (1985), Clegg (1984), Jones and James (1979), Pierce (1984), and Slocum and Sims (1980). The job design implications of technological interdependence (e.g. pooled, sequential, and reciprocal) and technological type (e.g. long-linked, mediating, and intensive) have been explored by Abdel-Halim (1981), Kiggundu (1981, 1983), Rousseau (1977), and Slocum and Sims (1980). Others have considered the relationship of job design to organizational structure (Aldag and Brief, 1979; Fry and Slocum, 1984; Pierce, Dunham, and Blackburn, 1979; Porter, Lawler, and Hackman, 1975; and Vecchio and Keon, 1981); managerial and leadership practices (Cordery and Wall, 1985; Ferris and Rowland, 1981; Hulin and Roznowski, 1985; Ovalle, 1984; Zierden, 1980); functional speciality (Dunham, 1977); staffing levels (Greenberg, Wang, and Dossett, 1982; Vecchio and Susman, 1981); turbulence (Williams, 1982); goal setting (Umstot, Bell, and Mitchell, 1976; Umstot, Mitchell, and Bell, 1978); management information systems (Clegg and Fitter, 1978); and organizational climate (Ferris and Gilmore, 1984).

Another consideration to receive attention is that concerned with the implementation of new forms of work design. Although Nicholas (1982) found that job enrichment has been based largely on 'top-down' approaches, the normative position taken by many investigators, and especially socio-technical theorists, is that employees should participate in the design or redesign of their own jobs. Empirical evidence for this view is scarce. Seeborg (1978) described an experimental study which provides some support for employee involvement in the design process (see also Huse and Cummings, 1985), but a recent field experiment reported by Griffeth (1985) showed that participation did not enhance the effects of job enrichment. Neither of these studies is without interpretational difficulty, and the effectiveness of alternative approaches to implementation remains largely undocumented. More generally, as Clegg (1979) has pointed out, the process of job redesign is a 'theoretical orphanage'.

The literature relating work design to organizational context is at present fragmented. It suggests a range of factors it is plausible to take into account, but as yet there is insufficient empirical evidence to identify the most salient among these. It does, however, hold out the prospect of leading to a more realistic perspective. Here the questions posed concern the conditions under which alternative approaches to job design will be successful and, conversely, the kinds of adjustment required in organizational structures and practices in order to effectively introduce a chosen form of work design.

ISSUES FOR THEORY AND RESEARCH

The aim of this section is to highlight issues of general relevance to the development of research and theory in job and work design. Some of these are elaborations of deficiencies already touched upon in the review so far. Others concern areas for development largely neglected in the contemporary literature. We have selected five we consider to be among the most important.

A Restriction of Focus

In an earlier review of the job design literature Roberts and Glick (1981, p. 210) noted: 'Investigations have become narrower over time. A restricted set of task characteristics and moderator variables have been focused on.' This remains a feature of contemporary research, as does concentration on a severely limited range of outcome variables.

In one sense this narrowness of focus is a testimony to the appeal of existing theory and its success in bringing coherence to the research effort. In this respect the Job Characteristics Model has been a dominant influence. In another sense, however, it is an indictment of the area, and of the absence of competing theoretical perspectives. Taking the independent variables first, there is clearly more to jobs than skill variety, task identity, task significance, autonomy, and feedback. Jobs can be characterized at different levels of analysis, and in different respects. Cycle time, physical load, attentional demand, memory load, cognitive demand, time span of discretion, level and mix of responsibility, time pressure, and a range of other variables seem likely to be important in themselves as well as potential determinants of employee job attitudes and behaviour. Little attention has been paid to such factors. It is not that they have been investigated and found wanting as salient job properties, but that they have been largely ignored. The inclusion of such variables would not only open up the prospect of a more comprehensive characterization of jobs, but also offers the opportunity for job design to more adequately cover a wide range of jobs, and particularly those at higher organizational levels which have been customarily neglected (cf. Wood, 1986).

In a similar way, the job design area is characterized by concentration on a very narrow range of dependent variables. Satisfaction, motivation, attendance behaviour, and performance are undoubtedly important aspects of work experience. But so, too, are other factors, such as industrial relations attitudes, grievances, stress, accidents and safety, and health. All these, and many others, are likely to be affected by the nature of jobs. A particular dependent variable which has periodically surfaced in relation to job design, but never been systematically integrated theoretically, is that of mental health (e.g. Kornhauser, 1965; Karasek, 1979; Wall and Clegg, 1981; Broadbent, 1985). A difficulty here, however, is that most existing conceptualizations and measures of mental health focus on the absence of mental illness. Since mental illness is evident in only small proportions of typical work populations, research is hampered by the lack of adequate variance in the dependent measure. However, re-emergent interest in the notion of positive mental health and the resultant creation of more sensitive instruments (e.g. Warr, 1987) makes it possible to pursue this area of inquiry. The same point about restricted focus can be made with regard to moderator variables, although recent research has shown greater diversity in this respect (see pp. 70-72).

The general point is that theory and research are currently very narrowly conceived. This may have been functional at one stage, but the time is now ripe for a wider perspective both in substantive terms and with regard to levels and types of measurement. The particular variables suggested above are introduced only as illustrations of what might be considered. If a broader base were to be adopted, especially within single studies, then empirical evidence could contribute to the selection of relevant variables. In this way theory could be built more explicitly on factors of demonstrable significance rather than being based on content by theoretical fiat.

The Theoretical Status of Motivation

The concept of motivation is logically central to all approaches to job design. It is required in order to explain why job characteristics affect performance and other behaviour. Nevertheless, the role of motivation is poorly articulated within existing theory. In the context of autonomous work groups it is rarely explicitly considered. In the Job Characteristics Model, motivation is ascribed the status of an outcome variable and its relationship with performance (and other dependent variables) is left unspecified. This is perhaps no more than a reflection of the ubiquitous yet unsatisfactory role of motivation within I/O psychology more generally (Locke and Henne, 1986), but nonetheless requires attention.

In practice there appears to be a large number of implicit assumptions within the literature concerning how and why job design affects performance. Perhaps the most conventional yet nebulous interpretation, based on need theory, is that enriched jobs lead to feelings of wanting to exert effort and this leads to higher performance (job enrichment→motivation→performance). A second, stemming from goal-setting theory (Umstot, Mitchell, and Bell, 1978), is that the provision of autonomy requires clear performance objectives and feedback, and it is this which motivates performance (target setting/feedback→motivation→performance). A third is that people in enriched jobs feel satisfied when they perform well (Hackman and Oldham, 1980). Thus the link is performance (given complex jobs)→motivation. A fourth explanation, most closely associated with the socio-technical systems approach, focuses on 'the control of variance at source'. Here the argument is that performance benefits accrue because with control over work being in the hands of operators they can respond more rapidly and flexibly to presenting circumstances than if being directed by supervision. The explanation thus lies in the logic of the work situation (but also assumes that employees wish to deploy their effort to performance ends). Here the assumption is: autonomous work groups→rapid and flexible response to production needs→performance. Other explanations abound (e.g. labour intensification, Kelly, 1982).

It is clearly important to explore the validity of these several explanations, since they can have very different practical implications. For example, under the first explanation above there would be little benefit from enriching jobs if either the incumbents had insufficient ability to translate their enhanced motivation into performance, or the technology itself so constrained output that performance could not be raised. Similarly, performance benefits under the fourth explanation would be expected to be positively related to the amount of variance inherent in the work system. For reliable and predictable systems with little variance to control, minimal advantage would accrue from introducing autonomous work groups. More generally, the need is for research to come to grips with this issue of motivation, and to explain how job design affects performance. This implies more clearly articulated theory, closely monitored longitudinal field studies, and research designed to assess competing (or complementary) propositions.

The Dynamics of Redesigning Work

The above criticism of the status of motivation in work design theory is in fact a special case of a more general problem in the area. Too little attention has been paid to the questions of why and how the principles of work design operate with regard to each of the dependent variables. Empirical work has focused on outcome evaluations to the exclusion of documenting and explaining the processes within enriched jobs or autonomous work groups. In the latter approach to work design, for example, numerous intra-group and inter-group processes seem likely to affect both employees' attitudes and behaviour. Group cohesiveness, procedures for handling interpersonal conflict, the emergence of group norms and inter-group conflict are among the many factors which could influence the effects of this approach. Understanding of these factors may account for apparently conflicting results. Moreover, such a perspective is interesting in its own right and has important implications for the selection and training of employees for this form of work design.

Occasionally investigators have commented on such aspects of work design. Manz and Sims (1982) considered the potential for 'groupthink' in autonomous work groups; and Hackman (1983) introduced a number of group process issues in his theoretical approach to the design of work teams. One of the few empirical studies was reported by Blumberg (1980) who examined job switching within autonomous work groups in relation to job satisfaction and absenteeism. In general, however, the way in which individuals and groups respond and adapt to the challenge of redesigned work has not been on the research agenda. It ought to be, along with the related issue (introduced earlier, p. 74) concerning the process of implementing new forms of work design.

Theoretical Integration

So far our critique of job design research has applied largely within the parameters existing theory has set for itself. Here we broaden the focus by suggesting that the area might expand its boundaries and could benefit by taking on board ideas and propositions from traditionally separate areas of inquiry.

We have already drawn attention to emerging initiatives in relating work design to organizational context, and attempts to integrate the two areas both theoretically and empirically (pp. 73–74). It may be advantageous to extend this cross-fertilization into other fields. Implicit in the previous account of the dynamics of redesigned work is an integration with social psychological studies of small-group behaviour and processes. Personality theory and clinical psychology have contributions to make with regard to explanations of why job characteristics may have particular psychological effects, and clinical psychology could underpin the development of mental health as a dependent variable. Microeconomics offers the prospect of more adequate treatment of performance issues, particularly where the economic effects of work redesign appear to arise from altered labour costs rather than changed individual performance. Industrial relations perspectives are relevant, and are currently almost entirely neglected by psychologists.

A particular approach which has not been effectively adopted is open systems theory. Despite the support from within the work design area, as represented by socio-technical systems theorists, and the influential work of Katz and Kahn (1966, 1978) promoting this approach for I/O psychology more generally, it remains little more than a perspective. Its potential for guiding theory development and empirical research has not been realized. Part of the reason for this lies in the nature of the approach itself. As Klein (1976, p. 76) observed, 'It is easy to agree that the enterprise is a socio-technical system; it is a little hard to know what to do next, if one's own learning and experience is not within this tradition.' Similarly, Clark (1975, p. 184) concludes that 'socio-technical analysis is one of the best known, highly relevant, least understood and rarely applied perspectives'. Systems theory requires development both outside and inside the work design area to a level where it provides explicit and refutable predictions concerning the relationships between variables measured at different levels of analysis. Progress in this respect could be a vehicle for achieving wider theoretical integration, and provide the requisite breadth for work design theory to reflect more fully the complexities it necessarily involves.

A final issue, relevant to theory at all levels of development and integration, concerns the treatment of time. To our knowledge no established framework of work design attempts to specify even the order in which predicted effects occur, let alone the time it takes for them to be observable, or their duration. If attitudes and behaviours at work are the product of cumulative experience, how long will it take for these to be altered by changes in job characteristics? And how long will effects persist? The inclusion of such predictions would make theory much more testable and, where empirically supported, would have immense practical value. Consideration of time in this way would also underscore the need for longitudinal and experimental research designs, the general issue with which we conclude this critique.

Research Design for Causal Interpretation

In a recent review Cummings (1982) foresaw increased use of experimental and longitudinal research designs within organizational behaviour by the mid-1980s. Unfortunately, such development does not appear to have materialized, either within the field generally or in the work design area in particular. The lack of a substantial empirical base derived from field studies using designs which allow for causal inference remains a major weakness. This is not a new criticism, but one which has been raised in almost all major reviews over the last decade or more. Since the repeated call for more change studies is largely unanswered it is worthwhile considering why this is so.

A common explanation for the lack of field experiments focuses on the acceptability of work redesign within organizations. It is suggested that because such change is of unproven value (hence the research) it is not worth the risk and disruption to normal working practices. This undoubtedly is an important part of the explanation, but it cannot be the whole story. There are numerous examples of enterprises implementing new forms of work organization on their own account, within the more general QWL paradigm. As Mohrman *et al.* (1986, p. 191) concludes: 'since the mid-1970s the QWL movement has had a life of its own. There has been rapid diffusion of it and a growing body of literature, much of it in the popular and business press. Indeed, one of its most striking aspects has been the degree to which practice recently has outpaced theory and research.'

If the nature of work redesign is acceptable in practice, then maybe the lack of experimental and longitudinal research reflects that such forms of investigation place unacceptable demands on organizations. This is surely a large part of the explanation, and points to the need both to create strong research designs which minimize the intrusiveness of the research process, and to develop approaches which ensure that research is carried out in such a way that it is of evident and more immediate benefit to the organization itself. Attention should also be given to 'naturally occurring' developments within organizations which both have clear implications for the design of work and open up opportunities for access and creative research design.

Problems of access of the kind considered above clearly exist, and will remain as a greater obstacle to change studies than to correlational ones. However, they do not seem entirely sufficient to account fully for the lack of field experiments and longitudinal studies. There is a danger of externalizing in looking for explanations. Perhaps one should also look closer to home, and ask whether our own institutional structures and practices are likely to discriminate against such research. Here we can see some impediments. Long-term change studies are high risk for the individual researcher in that they can be aborted for reasons outside his or her control. Compared with correlational, survey, and laboratory research they also offer the prospect of a poor effort-to-publication ratio. With academic career prospects so strongly affected by publication rates many individuals may have reservations about committing themselves to change studies where other kinds of research offer more certain rewards. More team-based research, longer-term funding, and ascribing additional weight to field experimental studies might be ways of promoting the much needed commitment to this form of investigation. It is an issue on which to ponder!

WORK DESIGN AND THE 'INFORMATION TECHNOLOGY REVOLUTION'

By way of conclusion to this review we turn to consider the implications of information technology for future research into job and work design. As mentioned in the introduction, it appears from the literature that research in the area is in need of fresh impetus. If history is anything to go by then general critiques, such as we have just provided, are insufficient in themselves to foster major changes in emphasis. Criticism concerning the scarcity of change studies, narrowness of perspective, lack of theoretical integration, or the absence of competing conceptual frameworks will at best only exert a mild influence over future development. For more rapid change to be achieved one needs external conditions which offer new opportunities and perspectives. We believe that new technology as applied in work settings presents such an opening.

Let us look first at the implications of new technology for the nature of jobs. It currently appears that one of the effects of implementing new technology, particularly in the case of manufacturing applications, is to polarize jobs with regard to the dimensions central to work design theory. Some applications lead to much more repetitive and simplified jobs, others require operators to think, plan, and take much more responsibility for machine operation and product quality. Moreover, this polarization sometimes affects only some aspects of the job, with others remaining largely unaltered. It is worthwhile briefly considering the emerging literature in the area to illustrate the new technologies in question and how this divergence of effect arises.

One current perspective on new technology is that it will lead to deskilled or simplified shopfloor work. The argument is a general one, but has been most clearly articulated in the context of new manufacturing technology. For example, Braverman (1974), and later Shaiken (1979, 1980), considered the job content implications of the now most prevalent form of new manufacturing technology, the computer numerically controlled (CNC) machine tool. This replaces hand-controlled, general purpose machine tools which, in precision engineering companies, are traditionally operated by time-served skilled employees. Conventionally, the operator uses his or her knowledge of the properties of different metals, cutting tools, cutting and feed speeds, and so on, to translate the information on a drawing into the required end-product. With CNC technology all this information is incorporated into a program which guides the machine tool through the entire cycle, without the need for skilled human intervention. The technical advantage is that by loading different programs a whole range of different products can be made on one machine within tolerances which are less variable than those which can be achieved when direct human operation is involved.

In a similar way robots can be programmed to carry out skilled operations previously performed by human operators, such as paint spraying and spot welding. Here the technolgoy has been developed so that the robot can be programmed by copying operator movements. A skilled paint sprayer, for instance, can guide a robot arm through the physical movements necessary to achieve a given finish, and the entire sequence can be recorded on its program. The whole sequence can then be reproduced on demand.

The argument behind the deskilling prediction is basically simple. It is evident by their nature that many new manufacturing technologies can simplify existing jobs by absorbing traditional skills and knowledge into computer programs. Where previously reliance was placed on direct manual work, or the operation of general purpose machine tools in real time, the new technology allows one to distil relevant knowledge and motor skills into a program which replaces human control. Operators, if required (as is usually the case), can be left to load, unload and monitor the new technology. Where malfunctions occur they call the experts (computer programmers, tool setters, electronics engineers, etc.). The operator thus experiences reductions in task variety, task feedback, autonomy, and other salient job characteristics.

Proponents of the deskilling perspective suggest that this new technical opportunity will be grasped by organizations in order to enhance management control over production and reduce manning costs (through the hiring of less skilled labour). In this way the opportunity arises to deskill jobs which hitherto have been relatively immune from simplication, and for new technology to be used to extend the historical trend towards work simplification. The same effects have been predicted for a variety of other applications of information technology, such as computer-aided design (CAD) systems (Cooley, 1984).

Empirical support for the above work simplification argument has been forthcoming from a number of sources (see, for example, the collection of case studies reported in Butera and Thurman, 1984; also Blumberg and Gerwin, 1984; Burns et al., 1983; Scarborough and Moran, 1985). At the same time, however, investigations have shown that simplification is not a necessary outcome of the application of new technology. Many cases have been documented in which CNC and other new technology has been implemented in such a way as to enhance operator responsibility and feedback, and the loss of regular use of traditional skills has been replaced by the acquisition of new computing and engineering related skills and knowledge.

To some extent this divergence of effect reflects differences in technology, but more often arises from different strategic choices of how to manage and organize the new work (Buchanan and Boddy, 1982, 1983; Clegg and Kemp, 1986; Clegg, Kemp, and Wall, 1984; Nicholas et al., 1983; Sorge et al., 1983). Evidence is also accumulating that in uncertain production environments enriching jobs by enskilling operators and giving them control over the new technology is the better alternative with regard to productivity. By dealing with variances at source they can improve utilization and promote quality (Clegg and Wall, 1987; Cummings and Blumberg, 1987). More generally, it is evident that new technology is not being applied solely to skilled jobs, but also to ones which are inherently repetitive and short cycle and involve little discretion, as for example on assembly lines. The technologies selected, and often customized to local needs, are varied, as are the forms of implementation. One thus sees diverse effects of new technology not only between organizations but also within them, and often opposite job design effects are associated with equivalent forms of new technology.

The important general point is that new manufacturing technology is being implemented in diverse ways and this is having a polarizing effect in terms of job design. This means that more extreme differences are being created between jobs; these are towards both simplification and enrichment, and often they emphasize particular job dimensions. Add to this the fact that implementation is typically incremental and takes place alongside unaltered traditional job designs, and it becomes clear that the opportunity to mount experimentally oriented and comparative studies is improving. Also, such differences are occurring not only between organizations but also within them. This means investigations can be carried out where context is relatively constant.

Our argument, therefore, is that there is evolving, as a result of the introduction of new technology, a set of circumstances particularly conducive to experimentally oriented field studies of job design. We are now witnessing the beginnings of a move towards substantial changes in job dimensions occurring at a rate and to an extent that permits the use of strong research designs. The fact that such change arises for reasons internal to organizations, rather than being inspired by researchers or others, means they are there to be exploited. Over the next decade, and probably longer, these conditions will become more common, as more and more manufacturing organizations begin their piecemeal adoption of new technology. The rate of adoption is demonstrably accelerating (Child, 1984; Northcote and Rogers, 1984). This offers the opportunity to overcome one of the major practical impediments which has historically hampered research, the difficulty of implementing and sustaining major change in work design.

The existence of conditions which allow experimental field research into work design are not sufficient to ensure that it will occur. Also important is the question of access. Why should managements, trade unions, and others welcome the attention of researchers? This will remain somewhat of a problem. Nevertheless, there appears to be more opportunity than previously. It results from the needs of organizations. Most managements and trade unions now believe that they must follow the path of introducing new technology in order to remain competitive and survive (Mueller et al., 1986). They set out on this road driven by technical possibilities, and reach a point where they feel they can handle this side of the issue. In so doing, however, they soon realize the implications of the technology for jobs. In the light of the substantial changes that are necessary for technical reasons, their attitudes are to some extent unfrozen. They are willing to put on the agenda issues which before were not negotiable. There is, in short, a readiness to change and experiment. What is missing, however, is a conceptual framework to handle the human and organizational side of the change. Here psychologists can play a part, for the framework offered by job design theory provides a way of highlighting some of the issues and options available. Increasingly, organizations are looking beyond their own boundaries for such ideas.

The opportunity the introduction of new technology offers for revitalizing research into work design has so far been considered from the standpoint of current applications of information technology on the shopfloor. These are predominantly stand-alone systems. The next stage of development of such technology (already operating in a few hundred organizations worldwide) is flexible manufacturing systems (FMS). This application involves the integration of stand-alone systems through shared information processing. In such systems materials can be passed from one machine to another, to complete the operations required, through the use of robots, automated guided vehicles, and conveyors, with the entire sequence under the control of micro-processing technology. The further integration of FMS with production control, inventory, stock, and other organization-wide information systems offers the prospect of large-scale computer-integrated manufacturing (CIM) (see Cummings and Blumberg, 1987; Sharlt, Chang, and Salvendy, 1986).

The advent of such larger-scale applications of information technology in manufacturing is of considerable relevance to research into work design. In addition to having implications for the content of operator jobs, they will make clearer than ever the interrelationship between job design on the one hand and the larger organization on the other. Such technical systems incorporate and symbolize many features of systems theory, and provide a springboard from which a broader theoretical perspective may be easier to develop. Along with their now current stand-alone predecessors, FMS and CIM also draw attention to the narrow range of job dimensions covered by existing job design theory. It is, for example, extremely difficult to encapsulate the jobs of operators of new manufacturing technology without paying attention to the planning, problem solving, diagnostic, and system understanding aspects of their work. In other words, a job characteristic which such technology requires one to take into account is that of cognitive demand, which is overlooked by current theory in work design. In these and many other ways the introduction of new technology on the shopfloor provides a stimulus to broaden and improve the theoretical base of research into work design.

The discussion to date has been based predominantly on manufacturing applications of information technology. It may be that the opportunities foreseen turn out to be somewhat overstated, and that for other areas of application prospects for work design research and practice are less marked. Nevertheless, opportunities clearly exist. As Walton (1982) observes, there is much scope for the application of job design and social criteria more generally in understanding the effects and contributing to the design of a range of systems for clerical, managerial, and professional use.

This brings us to our concluding point. Our emphasis has been on exploiting technically induced change in work organizations in order to upgrade empirical research and theoretical development in job and work design. Such advance will be of little consequence unless it feeds back into practice. The parallel challenge is to apply current knowledge of work design to the design of new technology itself. Initiatives are already being taken in this respect, often under the banner of 'human-centred systems' (e.g. Corbett, 1985; Rosenbrock, 1983, 1985). Work on this dual front offers the prospect of providing those concerned with the psychological implications of the design of jobs with a source of ideas, and research opportunities, from which the field as a whole should benefit.

REFERENCES

Abdel-Halim, A. A. (1978). Employee affective responses to organizational stress: Moderating effects of job characteristics. *Personnel Psychology*, **31**, 561-579.

Abdel-Halim, A. A. (1979). Individual and interpersonal moderators of employee reactions to job characteristics: A re-examination. *Personnel Psychology*, **32**, 121-137.

Abdel-Halim, A. A. (1981). Effects of role stress-job design-technology interaction on employee work satisfaction. *Academy of Management Journal*, **24**, 260-273.

Adler, S., Skov, R. B., and Salvemini, N. J. (1985). Job characteristics and job satisfaction: When cause becomes consequence. *Organizational Behaviour and Human Decision Processes*, **35**, 266-278.

Aldag, R. J., and Brief, A. P. (1979). *Task Design and Employee Motivation*. Scott, Foresman: Glenview, Ill..

Algera, J. A. (1983). 'Objective' and perceived task characteristics as a determinant of reactions by task performers. *Journal of Occupational Psychology*, **56**, 95-107.

Babbage, C. (1835). *On the Economy of Machinery and Manufacturers*. Charles Knight: London.

Baghat, R. S., and Chassie, M. B. (1980). Effects of changes in job characteristics on some theory-specific attitudinal outcomes: Results from a naturally occurring quasi-experiment. *Human Relations*, **33**, 297-313.

Baritz, L. (1960). *The Servants of Power*. Wiley: New York.

Beehr, T. A. (1976). Perceived situational moderators of the relationship between subjective role ambiguity and role strain. *Journal of Applied Psychology*, **61**, 35-40.

Blau, G. J., and Katerberg, R. (1982). Toward enhancing research with the social information processing approach to job design. *Academy of Management Review*, **7**, 543-550.

Blumberg, M. (1980). Job switching in autonomous work groups: An exploratory study in a Pennsylvania coal mine. *Academy of Management Journal*, **23**, 287-306.

Blumberg, M., and Gerwin, D. (1984). Coping with advanced manufacturing technology. *Journal of Occupational Behaviour*, **5**, 113-130.

Brass, D. J. (1985). Technology and the structure of jobs: Employee satisfaction, performance, and influence. *Organizational Behavior and Human Decision Processes*, **35**, 216-240.

Braverman, H. (1974). *Labour and Monopoly Capital*. Monthly Review Press: New York.

Broadbent, D. E. (1985). The clinical impact of job design. *British Journal of Clinical Psychology*, **24**, 33-44.

Broadbent, D. E., and Gath, D. (1979). Chronic effects of repetitive and non-repetitive work. In C. J. Mackay and T. Cox (eds.), *Response to Stress: Occupational Aspects*. Independent Publishing: London.

Broadbent, D. E., and Gath, D. (1981). Symptom levels of assembly line workers. In G. Salvendy and M. Smith (eds.), *Machine Pacing and Occupational Stress*. Taylor & Francis: London.

Buchanan, D. A., and Boddy, D. (1982). Advanced technology and the quality of working life: The effects of word processing on video typists. *Journal of Occupational Psychology*, **55**, 1-11.

Buchanan, D. A., and Boddy, D. (1983). Advanced technology and the quality of working life: The effects of computerised controls on biscuit-making operators. *Journal of Occupational Psychology*, **56**, 109-119.

Burnett, I. (1925). *An Experimental Investigation into Repetitive Work*. Report no. 30, Industrial Fatigue Research Board. HMSO: London.

Burns, A., Feickert, D., Newby, M., and Winterton, J. (1983). The miners and new technology. *Industrial Relations Journal*, **14**(4), 7-20.

Butera, F., and Thurman, J. E. (1984). *Automation and Work Design*. Amsterdam: North-Holland.

Caplan, R. D., Cobb, S., Frech, J. R. P., Van Harrison, R., and Pinneau, S. R. (1975). *Job Demands and Worker Health*. NIOSH Research Report, USHEW. US Government Printing Office: Washington, DC.

Champoux, J. E. (1980). A three sample test of some extensions to the job characteristics model of work motivation. *Academy of Management Journal*, **23**, 466-478.

Cherns, A. B., and Davis, L. E. (1975). Assessment of the state of the art. In L. E. Davis and A. B. Cherns (eds.), *The Quality of Working Life* (vol. 1). Free Press: New York.

Child, J. (1984). New technology and developments in management organization. *Omega International Journal of Management Science*, **12**, 211-223.

Ciborra, C., Migliarese, P., and Romano, P. (1984). A methodological inquiry of organizational noise in sociotechnical systems. *Human Relations*, **37**, 565-588.

Clark, P. A. (1975). Intervention theory: Matching role, focus and context. In L. E. Davis and A. B. Cherns (eds.), *The Quality of Working Life* (vol. 1). Free Press: New York.

Clegg, C. W. (1979). The process of job redesign: Signposts from a theoretical orphanage? *Human Relations*, **32**, 999-1022.

Clegg, C. W. (1984). The derivation of job designs. *Journal of Occupational Behaviour*, **5**, 131-146.

Clegg, C. W., and Fitter, M. J. (1978). Information systems: The Achilles heel of job redesign? *Personnel Review*, **7**, 5-11.

Clegg, C. W., and Kemp, N. J. (1986). Information Technology: Personnel where are you? *Personnel Review*, **15**, 8-15.

Clegg, C. W., Kemp, N. J., and Wall, T. D. (1984). New Technology: Choice control and skills. In G. C. Van der Veer, M. J. Tauber, T. R. G. Green, and P. Gorny (Eds.), *Readings in Cognitive Ergonomics—Mind and Computers*. Springer-Verlag: Berlin.

Clegg, C. W., and Wall, T. D. (1987) Managing factory automation. In F. Blackler and D. Oborne (eds.), *Information Technology and People: Designing for the Future.* British Psychological Society: Leicester.

Cooley, M. (1984). Problems of automation. In T. Lupton (ed.), *Proceedings of the 1st International Conference on Human Factors in Manufacturing.* North-Holland: Amsterdam.

Corbett, J. M. (1985). Prospective work design for a human-centred CNC lathe. *Behaviour and Information Technology,* **4,** 201-214.

Cordery, J. L., and Wall, T. D. (1985). Work design and supervisory practices: A model. *Human Relations,* **38,** 425-441.

Cox, T. (1980). Repetitive work. In C. L. Cooper and R. Payne (eds.), *Current Issues in Occupational Stress.* Wiley: London.

Cox, T., and Cox, S. (1984). Job design and repetitive work. *Employment Gazette,* **92,** 97-100.

Cox, T., and Mackay, C. J. (1979). The impact of repetitive work. In R. Sell and P. Shipley (eds.), *Satisfaction in Work Design: Ergonomics and Other Approaches.* Taylor & Francis: London.

Cox, T., Mackay, C. J., and Page, H. (1982). Simulated repetitive work and self-reported mood. *Journal of Occupational Behaviour,* **3,** 247-252.

Cox, T., Thirlaway, M., and Cox, S. (1982). Repetitive work, well-being and arousal. In R. Murison (ed.), *Biological and Psychological Basis of Psychomatic Disease.* Pergamon: Oxford.

Cummings, L. L. (1982). Organizational behavior. In *Annual Review of Psychology* (vol. 33). Annual Reviews Inc.: Palo Alto, Calif.

Cummings, T. G. (1978). Self-regulating work groups: A socio-technical synthesis. *Academy of Management Review,* **3,** 625-634.

Cummings, T. G., and Blumberg, M. (1987). Advanced manufacturing technology and work design. In T. D. Wall, C. W. Clegg, and N. J. Kemp (eds.), *The Human Side of Advanced Manufacturing Technology.* Wiley: Chichester, Sussex.

Cummings, T. G., Molloy, E. S., and Glen, R. (1977). A methodological critique of fifty-eight selected work experiments. *Human Relations,* **30,** 675-708.

Dainoff, M., Hurrell, J. J., and Happ, A. (1981). A taxonomic framework for the description and evaluation of paced work. In G. Salvendy and M. J. Smith (eds.), *Stress in Machine Pacing.* Taylor & Francis: London.

Davis, L. E. (1976). Developments in job design. In P. B. Warr (ed.), *Personal Goals and Work Design.* Wiley: London.

Davis, L. E., Canter, R. R., and Hoffman, J. (1955). Current job design criteria. *Journal of Industrial Engineering,* **6,** 5-11.

Davis, L. E., and Taylor, J. C. (1962). *Design of Jobs.* Penguin: Harmondsworth, Middx.

Davis, L. E., and Valfer, E. S. (1965). Intervening responses to changes in supervisors' job designs. *Occupational Psychology,* **39,** 171-189.

Denison, D. R. (1982). Sociotechnical design and self-managing work groups: The impact of control. *Journal of Occupational Behaviour,* **3,** 297-314.

Dunham, R. B. (1976). The measurement and dimensionality of job characteristics. *Journal of Applied Psychology,* **62,** 760-763.

Dunham, R. B. (1977). Reactions to job characteristics: Moderating effects of the organisation. *Academy of Management Journal,* **20,** 42-65.

Dunham, R. B., Aldag, R., and Brief, A. (1977). Dimensionality of task design as measured by the Job Diagnostic Survey. *Academy of Manufacturing Journal,* **20,** 209-223.

Edwards, R. C. (1978). The social relations of production at the point of production. *Insurgent Sociologist,* **8,** 109-125.

Emery, F. E. (1980). Designing socio-technical systems in 'greenfield' sites. *Journal of Occupational Behaviour,* **1,** 19-27.

Farr, J. L. (1976). Task characteristics, reward contingency, and intrinsic motivation. *Organizational Behavior and Human Performance,* **16,** 294-307.

Ferratt, T. W., Dunham, R. B., and Pierce, J. L. (1981). Self-report measures of job characteristics and affective responses: An examination of discriminant validity. *Academy of Management Journal*, **24**, 780–794.

Ferratt, T. W., and Reeve, J. M. (1977). The structural integrity of the JDS and JDI when examined together. *Proceedings of the Mid-West Division of the Academy of Management*, **20**, 144–155.

Ferris, G. R., and Gilmore, D. C. (1984). The moderating role of work context in job design research: A test of competing models. *Academy of Management Journal*, **27**, 885–892.

Ferris, G. R., and Rowland, K. M. (1981). Leadership, job perceptions, and influence: A conceptual integration. *Human Relations*, **34**, 1069–1077.

Forester, T. (ed.) (1985). *The Information Technology Revolution*. Blackwell: Oxford.

Frank, L. L., and Hackman, J. R. (1975). A failure of job enrichment: The case of the change that wasn't. *Journal of Applied Behavioural Science*, **11**, 413–436.

Fraser, R. (1947). *The Incidence of Neurosis among Factory Workers*. Report no. 90, Industrial Health Research Board. HMSO: London.

Fry, L. W., and Slocum, J. W. (1984). Technology, structure, and workgroup effectiveness: A test of contingency model. *Academy of Management Journal*, **27**, 221–246.

Ganster, D. C. (1980). Individual differences and task design: A laboratory experiment. *Organizational Behavior and Human Performance*, **26**, 131–148.

Gilbreth, F. B. (1911). *Brick Laying System*. Clark: New York.

Green, S. B., Armenakis, A. A., Marber, L. D., and Bedeian, A. G. (1979). An evaluation of the response format and scale structure of the job diagnostic survey. *Human Relations*, **32**, 181–188.

Greenberg, C. I., Wang, Y., and Dossett, D. L. (1982). Effects of work group size and task size on observers' job characteristics ratings. *Basic and Applied Social Psychology*, **3**, 53–66.

Griffeth, R. W. (1985). Moderation of the effects of job enrichment by participation: A longitudinal field experiment. *Organizational Behaviour and Human Decision Processes*, **35**, 73–93.

Griffin, R. W. (1981). A longitudinal investigation of task characteristics relationships. *Academy of Management Journal*, **24**, 99–113.

Griffin, R. W. (1982). Perceived task characteristics and employee productivity and satisfaction. *Human Relations*, **35**, 927–938.

Griffin, R. W. (1983). Objective and social sources of information in task design: A field experiment. *Administrative Science Quarterly*, **28**, 184–200.

Griffin, R. W., and Bateman, T. S. (1986). Job satisfaction and organizational commitment. In C. L. Cooper and I. T. Robertson (eds.), *International Review of Industrial and Organizational Psychology*. Wiley: Chichester, Sussex.

Gulick, L., and Urwick, L. (eds.) (1937). *Papers on the Science of Administration*. Institute of Public Administration: New York.

Gulowsen, J. (1972). A measure of work group autonomy. In L. E. Davis and J. C. Taylor (eds.), *Design of Jobs*. Penguin: London.

Hackman, J. R. (1977). Work design. In J. R. Hackman and J. L. Suttle (eds.), *Improving Life at Work: Behavioral Science Approaches to Organizational Change*. Goodyear: Santa Monica, Calif..

Hackman, J. R. (1983). The design of work teams. In J. Lorsch (ed.), *Handboook of Organizational Behavior*. Prentice-Hall: Englewood Cliffs, NJ.

Hackman, J. R., and Lawler, E. E. (1971). Employee reactions to job characteristics. *Journal of Applied Psychology*, **55**, 259–286.

Hackman, J. R., and Oldham, G. (1975). Development of the Job Diagnostic Survey. *Journal of Applied Psychology*, **60**, 159–170.

Hackman, J. R., and Oldham, G. (1976). Motivation through the design of work: Test of a theory. *Organizational Behavior and Human Performance*, **16**, 250–279.

Hackman, J. R., and Oldham, G. (1980). *Work Redesign*. Addison-Wesley: Reading, Mass..

Hackman, J. R., Pearce, J. L., and Wolfe, J. C. (1978). Effects of changes in job characteristics on work attitudes and behaviors; A naturally occurring quasi-experiment. *Organizational Behavior and Human Performance*, **21**, 289-304.

Halton, J. (1985). The anatomy of computing. In T. Forester (ed.), *The Information Technology Revolution: The Complete Guide*. Blackwell: Oxford.

Hedberg, B., and Mumford, E. (1975). The design of computer systems. In E. Mumford and H. Sackman (eds.), *Human Choice and Computers*, North-Holland: New York.

Hertog, F. J. den (1976). Work structuring. In P. B. Warr (ed.), *Personal Goals and Work Design*. Wiley: London.

Herzberg, F. (1966). *Work and the Nature of Man*. World Publishing: Cleveland, Ohio.

Herzberg, F. (1968). One more time: How do you motivate employees? *Harvard Business Review*, **46**, 53-62.

Herzberg, F., Mausner, B., and Snyderman, B. (1959). *The Motivation to Work*. Wiley: New York.

Hill, C. P. (1972). *Toward a New Management Philosophy*. Gower: London.

Hulin, C. L., and Roznowski, M. (1985). Organizational technologies: Effects on the organisations' characteristics and the individuals' responses. *Research in Organizational Behavior*, **22**, 350-365.

Hurrell, J. J. (1985). Machine-paced work and the Type A behaviour pattern. *Journal of Occupational Psychology*, **58**, 15-25.

Huse, E., and Cummings, T. (1985). *Organization Development and Change*. West Publishing: St Paul, Minn..

Industrial Health Research Board (1931). *Eleventh Annual Report*. HMSO: London.

Jackson, P. R., Paul, L. J., and Wall, T. D. (1981). Individual differences as moderators of reactions to job characteristics. *Journal of Occupational Psychology*, **54**, 1-8.

Jones, A. P., and James, L. R. (1979). Psychological climate: Dimensions and relationships of individual and aggregated work environment perceptions. *Organizational Behavior and Human Performance*, **23**, 201-250.

Karasek, R. A. (1979). Job demands, job decision latitude, and mental strain: Implications for job redesign. *Administrative Science Quarterly*, **24**, 285-308.

Katz, D., and Kahn, R. L. (1966). *The Social Psychology of Organizations*. Wiley: New York.

Katz, D., and Kahn, R. L. (1978). *The Social Psychology of Organizations* (2nd edn). Wiley: New York.

Katz, R. (1978a). The influence of job longevity on employee responses to task characteristics. *Human Relations*, **31**, 703-725.

Katz, R. (1978b). Job longevity as a situational factor in job satisfaction. *Administrative Science Quarterly*, **23**, 204-223.

Keller, R. T., and Holland, W. E. (1981). Job change: A naturally occurring field experiment. *Human Relations*, **34**, 1053-1067.

Keller, R. T., Szilagyi, A., and Holland, W. E. (1976). Boundary spanning activity and employee reactions: An empirical study. *Human Relations*, **29**, 699-710.

Kelly, J. E. (1982). *Scientific Management, Job Redesign and Work Performance*. Academic Press: London.

Kemp, N. J., and Cook, J. D. (1983). Job longevity and growth need strength as joint moderators of the task design-job satisfaction relationship *Human Relations*, **36**, 883-898.

Kemp, N. J., Wall, T. D., Clegg, C. W., and Cordery, J. L. (1983). Autonomous work groups in a greenfield site. A comparative study. *Journal of Occupational Psychology*, **56**, 271-288.

Kerr, S., Hill, K. D., and Broedling, L. (1986). The first-line supervisor: Phasing out or here to stay? *Academy of Management Review*, **11**, 103-117.

Kiggundu, M. N. (1980). An empirical test of the theory of job design using multiple job ratings. *Human Relations*, **33**, 339-351.

Kiggundu, M. N. (1981). Task interdependence and the theory of job design. *Academy of Management Review*, **6**, 499-508.

Kiggundu, M. N. (1983). Task independence and job design: Test of a theory. *Organizational Behavior and Human Performance*, **31**, 145-172.

King, N. A. (1970). A clarification and evaluation of the two-factor theory of job satisfaction. *Psychological Bulletin*, 74, 18-30.

Klein, L. (1976). *New Forms of Work Organisation*. Cambridge University Press: Cambridge.

Kolodny, H. F., and Kiggundu, M. N. (1980). Towards the development of a sociotechnical systems model in woodlands mechanical harvesting. *Human Relations*, **33**, 623-645.

Kornhauser, A. (1965). *Mental Health of the Industrial Worker*. Wiley: New York.

Kraft, P. (1977). *Programmes and Managers*. Allen Lane: London.

LaRocco, J. M., House, J. S., and French, J. R. P. (1980). Social support, occupational stress, and health. *Journal of Health and Social Behaviour*, **21**, 202-218.

Lawler, E. E. (1978). The new plant revolution. *Organizational Dynamics*, **6**, 2-12.

Lawler, E. E., Hackman, J. R., and Kaufman, S. (1973). Effects of job redesign: A field experiment. *Journal of Applied Social Psychology*, **3**, 49-62.

Locke, E. A., and Henne, D. (1986). Work motivation theories. In C. L. Cooper and I. T. Robertson (eds.), *International Review of Industrial and Organizational Psychology*. Wiley: Sussex.

Locke, E. A., Sirota, D., and Wolfson, A. (1976). An experimental case study of the successes and failures of job enrichment in a government agency. *Organizational Behavior and Human Performance*, **5**, 484-500.

Loher, B. T., Noe, R. A., Moeller, N. L., and Fitzgerald, M. P. (1985). A meta-analysis of the relation of job characteristics to job satisfaction. *Journal of Applied Psychology*, **70**, 280-289.

McLean, A. J., and Sims, D. B. P. (1978). Job enrichment from theoretical poverty: The state of the art and directions for future work. *Personnel Review*, **7**, 5-10.

Manz, C. C., and Sims, H. P. (1982). The potential for 'groupthink' in autonomous work groups. *Human Relations*, **35**, 773-784.

Mitchell, T. R., Liden, R. C., and Rothman, M. (1985). Effects of normative information on task performance. *Journal of Applied Psychology*, **70**, 48-55.

Mohrman, S. A., Ledford, G. E., Lawler, E. E., and Mohrman, A. M. (1986). Quality of worklife and employee involvement. In C. L. Cooper and I. T. Robertson (eds.), *International Review of Industrial and Organizational Psychology*. Wiley: Chichester, Sussex.

Morris, J. H., Sherman, J. D., and Mansfield, E. R. (1986). Failures to detect moderating effects with ordinary least squares-moderated multiple regression: Some reasons and a remedy. *Psychological Bulletin*, **99**, 282-288.

Mossholder, K. W., Bedeian, A. G., and Armenakis, A. A. (1982). Role perceptions, satisfaction and performance: Moderating effects of self-esteem and organizational level. *Organizational Behavior and Human Performance*, **28**, 224-234.

Mueller, W. S., Clegg, C. W., Wall, T. D., Kemp, N. J., and Davies, R. (1986). Pluralist beliefs about new technology within an organization. *New Technology, Work and Employment*, **1**, 127-139.

Murphy, L. R., and Hurrell, J. J. (1980). Machine pacing and occupational stress. In R. Schwartz (ed.), *New Developments in Occupational Stress*. DHHS (NIOSH) Publication no. 81-102. US Government Printing Office: Washington, DC.

Murrell, H. (1978). Work stress and mental strain. Occasional Paper no. 6. Work Research Unit, Department of Employment: London.

Nicholas, J. (1982). The comparative impact of organization development interventions on hard criteria measures. *Academy of Management Review*, **7**, 531-542.

Nicholas, J., Warner, M., Sarge, A., and Hartman, G.(1983). Computerised machine tools, manpower training and skill polarisation: A study of British and West German manufacturing firms. In G. Winch (ed.), *Information Technology in Manufacturing Processes*. Rossendale: London.

Northcote, J., and Rodgers, P. (1984). *Micro-electronics in British Industry: The Pattern of Change*. Policy Studies Institute: London.

O'Connor, E. J., Rudolf, C. J., and Peters, L. H. (1980). Individual differences and job design reconsidered: Where do we go from here? *Academy of Management Review*, **5**, 249-254.

O'Connor, G. J., and Barrett, G. V. (1980). Informational cues and individual differences as determinants of subjective perceptions of task enrichment. *Academy of Management Journal*, **23**, 697-716.

Oldham, G. (1976). Job characteristics and internal motivation: The moderating effect of interpersonal and individual variables. *Human Relations*, **29**, 559-569.

Oldham, G., and Miller, H. E. (1979). The effect of significant other's job complexity on employee reactions to work. *Human Relations*, **32**, 247-260.

O'Reilly, C. A., and Caldwell, D. F. (1979). Informational influence as a determinant of perceived task characteristics and job satisfaction. *Journal of Applied Psychology*, **64**, 157-165.

O'Reilly, C. A., and Caldwell, D. F. (1985). The impact of normative social influence and cohesiveness on task perceptions and attitudes: A social information processing approach. *Journal of Occupational Psychology*, **58**, 193-206.

O'Reilly, C. A., Parlette, G., and Bloom, J. (1980). Perceptual measures of task characteristics: The biasing effects of differing frames of reference and job attitudes. *Academy of Management Journal*, **23**, 118-131.

Orpen, C. (1979). The effects of job enrichment on employee satisfaction, motivation and performance: A field experiment. *Human Relations*, **32**, 189-217.

Ovalle, N. K. (1984). Organizational/managerial control processes: A reconceptualization of the linkage between technology and performance. *Human Relations*, **37**, 1047-1062.

Pasmore, W., Francis, C., Haldeman, J., and Shani, A. (1983). Sociotechnical systems: A North American reflection on the empirical studies of the seventies. *Human Relations*, **35**, 1179-1204.

Peters, W. S., and Champoux, J. E. (1979). The use of moderated regression in job design decisions. *Decision Sciences*, **10**, 85-95.

Pierce, J. L. (1984). Job design and technology: A sociotechnical systems perspective. *Journal of Occupational Behaviour*, **5**, 147-154.

Pierce, J. L., Dunham, R. B., and Blackburn, R. S. (1979). Social systems structure, job design, and growth need strength: A test of congruency model. *Academy of Management Journal*, **22**, 223-240.

Porter, L. W., Lawler, E. E., and Hackman, J. R. (1975). *Behavior in Organizations*. McGraw-Hill: New York.

Rice, A. K. (1958). *Productivity and Social Organization*. Tavistock: London.

Roberts, K. H., and Glick, W. (1981). The job characteristics approach to job design: A critical review. *Journal of Applied Psychology*, **66**, 193-217.

Rosenbrock, H. H. (1983). Robots and people. *Work and People*, **66**, 193-217.

Rosenbrock, H. H. (1985). Designing automated systems: Need skill be lost? In P. Marstrand (ed.), *New Technology and the Future of Work and Skills*. Pinter: London.

Rousseau, D. M. (1977). Technological differences in job characteristics, employee satisfaction motivation: A synthesis of job design research and socio-technical systems theory. *Organizational Behavior and Human Performance*, **19**, 18-42.

Salancik, G., and Pfeffer, J. (1977). An examination of need-satisfaction models of job attitudes. *Administrative Science Quarterly*, **22**, 427-456.

Salancik, G., and Pfeffer, J. (1978). A social-information processing approach to job attitudes and task design. *Administrative Science Quarterly*, **23**, 224-253.

Salvendy, G., and Smith, M. J. (1981). *Stress in Machine Pacing*. Taylor & Francis: London.

Scarborough, H., and Moran, P. (1985). How new tech. won at Longbridge. *New Society*, **71**, 207-209.

Schnake, M. E., and Dumler, M. P. (1985). Affective response bias in the measurement of perceived task characteristics. *Journal of Occupational Psychology*, **58**, 159-166.

Seeborg, I. (1978). The influence of employee participation in job redesign. *Journal of Applied Behavioral Science*, **14**, 87–98.

Shaiken, H. (1979). Impact of new technology on employees and their organizations. Research report. International Institute for Comparative Social Research: Berlin.

Shaiken, H. (1980). Computer technology and the relations of power in the workplace. Research report. International Institute for Comparative Social Research: Berlin.

Sharlt, J., Chang, T. C., and Salvendy, G. (1986). Technical and human aspects of computer-aided manufacturing. In G. Salvendy (ed.), *Handbook of Human Factors*. Wiley: New York.

Shaw, J. B. (1980). An information processing approach to the study of job design. *Academy of Management Journal*, **1**, 41–48.

Shaw, J. B., and Weekley, J. A. (1981). The effects of socially provided task information on redesigned tasks. *Proceedings, Southern Management Association*, 64–66.

Slocum, J. W., and Sims, H. P. (1980). A typology for integrating technology, organization and job design. *Human Relations*, **33**, 193–211.

Slusher, E. A., and Griffin, R. W. (1980). Social comparison processes and task design. Working Paper. University of Missouri: Columbia, Mo.

Smith, A. (1776). *The Wealth of Nations*. Republished in 1974 by Penguin: Harmondsworth, Middx.

Smith, M. J., Hurrell, J. J., and Murphy, R. K. (1981). Stress and health effects in paced and unpaced work. In G. Salvendy and M. J. Smith (eds.), *Stress in Machine Pacing*. Taylor & Francis: London.

Sorge, A., Hartman, G., Warner, M., and Nicholas, T. (1983). *Microelectronics and Manpower in Manufacturing: Applications of Computer Numerical Control (CNC) in Great Britain and West Germany*. Gower Press: London.

Spector, P. E. (1985). Higher-order need strength as a moderator of the job scope–employee outcome relationship: A meta-analysis. *Journal of Occupational Psychology*, **58**, 119–127.

Steers, R. M. (1975). Problems in the measurement of organizational effectiveness. *Administrative Science Quarterly*, **20**, 546–558.

Steers, R. M., and Spencer, D. (1977). The role of achievement motivation in job design. *Journal of Applied Psychology*, **62**, 472–479.

Stone, E. F., Mowday, R. T., and Porter, L. W. (1977). Higher-order need strengths as moderators of the job scope–job satisfaction relationship. *Journal of Applied Psychology*, **62**, 466–471.

Susman, G. (1976). *Autonomy at Work*. Praeger: New York.

Taylor, F. W. (1911). *The Principles of Scientific Management*. Harper: New York.

Taylor, J. C. (1979). Job design criteria twenty years later. In L. E. Davis and J. C. Taylor (eds.), *Design of Jobs* (2nd edn). Goodyear: Santa Monica, Calif.

Thomas, J., and Griffin, R. W. (1983). The social information processing model of task design: A review of the literature. *Academy of Management Review*, **8**, 672–692.

Trist, E. L. (1981). The sociotechnical perspective: The evolution of sociotechnical systems as a conceptual framework and as an action research program. In A. H. Van de Ven and W. F. Joyce (eds.), *Perspectives on Organizational Design and Behavior*. Wiley: New York.

Trist, E. L., and Bamforth, K. W. (1951). Some social and psychological consequences of the long-wall method of coal-getting. *Human Relations*, **4**, 3–38.

Turner, A. N., and Lawrence, P. R. (1965). *Individual Jobs and the Worker*. Harvard University Press: Cambridge, Mass.

Umstot, D. D., Bell, C. H., and Mitchell, T. R. (1976). Effects of job enrichment and task design goals on satisfaction and productivity: Implications for job design. *Journal of Applied Psychology*, **61**, 379–394.

Umstot, D. D., Mitchell, T. R., and Bell, C. H. (1978). Goal setting and job enrichment: An integrated approach to job design. *Academy of Management Review*, **2**, 867–879.

Vecchio, R. P., and Keon, T. L. (1981). Predicting employee satisfaction from congruency among individual need, job design, and system structure. *Journal of Occupational Behaviour*, 2, 283-292.

Vecchio, R. P., and Sussman, M. (1981). Staffing sufficiency and job enrichment: Support for an optimal level theory. *Journal of Occupational Behaviour*, 2, 177-187.

Walker, C. R. (1950). The problem of the repetitive job. *Harvard Business Review*. 28, 54-58.

Walker, C. R., and Guest, R. H. (1952). *Man on the Assembly Line*. Harvard University Press: Cambridge, Mass.

Wall, T. D. (1980). Group work redesign in context: A two-phase model. In K. D. Duncan, M. Gruneberg, and D. Wallis (eds.), *Changes in Working Life*. Wiley: Chichester, Sussex.

Wall, T. D. (1982). Perspectives on job redesign. In J. E. Kelly and C. W. Clegg (eds.), *Autonomy and Control in the Workplace*. Croom Helm: London.

Wall, T. D., and Clegg, C. W. (1981). A longitudinal field study of group work redesign. *Journal of Occupational Behaviour*, 2, 31-49.

Wall, T. D., Clegg, C. W., and Jackson, P. R. (1978). An evaluation of the Job Characteristics Model. *Journal of Occupational Psychology*. 51, 183-196.

Wall, T. D., Kemp, N. J., Clegg, C. W., and Jackson, P. R. (1986). An outcome evaluation of autonomous work groups: A long-term field experiment. *Academy of Management Journal*, 29, 280-304.

Wall, T. D., and Stephenson, G. M. (1970). Herzberg's two-factor theory of job attitudes: A critical evaluation and some fresh evidence. *Industrial Relations Journal*, 1, 41-65.

Walsh, J. T., Taber, T., and Beehr, T. A. (1980). An integrated model of perceived job characteristics. *Organizational Behavior and Human Performance*, 25, 252-267.

Walton, R. E. (1977). Work innovations at Topeka: After six years. *Journal of Applied Behavioural Science*, 13, 422-433.

Walton, R. E. (1982). New perspectives on the world of work. *Human Relations*, 35, 1073-1084.

Warr, P. B. (1987). *Work Unemployment and Mental Health*. Oxford University Press: Oxford.

Weiss, H. M., and Shaw, J. B. (1979). Social influences on judgements about tasks. *Organizational Behavior and Human Performance*, 24, 126-140.

White, J. K. (1978). Individual differences and the job quality–worker response relationship: Review, integration, and comments. *Academy of Management Review*, 3, 267-280.

White, S. E., and Mitchell, T. R. (1979). Job enrichment versus social cues: A comparison and competitive test. *Journal of Applied Psychology*, 64, 1-9.

Williams, T. A. (1982). A participative design for dispersed employees in turbulent environments. *Human Relations*, 35, 1043-1058.

Wood, R. E. (1986). Task complexity: Definition of the construct. *Organizational Behavior and Human Decision Processes*, 37, 60-82.

Wyatt, S., Fraser, J. A., and Stock, F. G. L. (1928). *The Comparative Effects of Variety and Uniformity in Work*. Report no. 52, Industrial Fatigue Research Board. HMSO: London.

Wyatt, S., and Ogden, D. A. (1924). *On the Extent and Effects of Variety and Uniformity in Repetitive Work*. Report no. 26, Industrial Fatigue Research Board. HMSO: London.

Zedeck, S. (1971). Problems with the use of moderator variables. *Psychological Bulletin*, 76, 295-310.

Zierden, W. E. (1980). Congruence in the work situation: Effects of growth needs, management style, and job structure on job related satisfactions. *Journal of Occupational Behaviour*, 1, 297-310.

International Review of Industrial and Organizational Psychology 1987
Edited by C. L. Cooper and I. T. Robertson
©1987 John Wiley & Sons Ltd

Chapter 4

HUMAN INTERFACES WITH ADVANCED MANUFACTURING PROCESSES

John R. Wilson and Andrew Rutherford
*Department of Production Engineering
and Production Management
University of Nottingham
UK*

INTRODUCTION

Rapid and profound changes in technology and social systems have had implications for how, and to what extent, Western industrialized society provides work (in the sense of paid employment). Consequent marked changes are found in how the organizations through which work is carried out are structured, and in the roles of their workforces. Such developments imply a shifting scenario within which occupational ergonomists and others concerned with human factors in work systems must operate. They must adapt their models and theories, methods and criteria, in order to make a significant contribution to the design of effective, satisfying, and safe work.

There is no space in this review to do justice to all aspects of occupational ergonomics, to establish in total its relevance and potential impact on industrial systems design and operation. For instance, a number of recent reviews at the 1985 Congress of the International Ergonomics Association covered a wide area of application of ergonomics to industrial systems (e.g. Cox, 1985; Rohmert, 1985; Stewart, 1985; van Cott, 1985), and still only scratched the surface. One particular aspect of the ergonomics of the workplace must be selected for discussion. A major growth in interest in ergonomics in recent years has been in the use and effects of computers. It is not solely the direct interface between computers and their operators which has been given attention, important though this is, but also the effects on people, and their work, due to the changes in the distribution of the functions and content of work between machines and people. Despite an appearance to the contrary which may be gained from the popular and professional media, this is not just a change for office workers. The computer revolution is a revolution in the way information is manipulated, a transfer of role from people to machines. In consequence any process requiring information, which is the life blood of control, is undergoing dramatic change. The impact is therefore felt in manufacturing industry, in retail stores, in warehousing, transport, banking—indeed, in all areas of human work.

Therefore we will concentrate upon reviewing the provision of human interfaces in advanced, computer-based manufacturing. Moreover, the particular emphasis of the review will be upon information transfer through such interfaces, upon the specification in terms of form and content of systems' displays. Although we are of necessity talking about human–computer interfaces, we are not concerned with office automation or, except peripherally, with management information systems. Work in this area is being considered elsewhere in the book. In any case, it is perhaps not unfair to suggest that too much attention is often paid to the human factors of office automation to the exclusion of manufacturing computerisation, and to the use of computers solely in information handling rather than to achieve control of processes (although the two cannot be regarded as mutually exclusive, of course).

There are two underlying themes and purposes in this review. Development and implementation of computerised systems and processes necessitate the involvement of a number of professions, from engineers to ergonomists, from software designers to psychologists, from economists to sociologists. Our review is written by an ergonomist and a psychologist who work closely with engineers and computer specialists. Within our work we have become aware of certain confusions, contradictions and sometimes misuses in the ideas — and the terminology employed — involved in multidisciplinary discussions and joint research. To take just one example, the term 'model' has been found to imply very different things to different professional specialists.

Ergonomics is well known as an applied discipline, utilizing anatomical, biological, or psychological knowledge in improving the match between people and the systems they use. Here, then, we wish to explore in some depth the psychological knowledge (particularly with respect to cognition) that is available and that is required in order to specify ergonomic interfaces.

Thus we wish to provide a restatement of some of the concepts of cognitive psychology now being employed in interface design, and to discuss their particular relevance to the understanding of the information required to control systems. Also we wish to make apparent the need for a consideration of people and their information-processing capabilities in 'automated systems'. Furthermore, and from the opposite tack, we will try to make cognitive psychologists aware of how their work must be applied by ergonomics.

The remainder of the chapter will then firmly embed the vital knowledge from cognitive psychology within the context of a discussion of manufacturing process displays. First, a view will be given of occupational ergonomics applied in modern industry. Advanced manufacturing technology (AMT) will then be defined and parallels drawn with continuous process systems. The design of information displays in AMT, and the relevance of such aspects of cognition as mental models, will then be discussed. Finally, the case will be made for considering human factors in such, apparently computer-controlled, systems and machines.

OCCUPATIONAL ERGONOMICS

Sheridan (1985) has authoritatively summarized the development of the field of man–machine systems, defined as the analysis and synthesis of systems in which people and machines interact closely. He recognizes three 15-year eras. Era A,

1940-1955, saw the birth of ergonomics and human factors in a concern with (sensory) acuity, anthropometry, and activity analysis (often known as 'knobs and dials' ergonomics). Sheridan's particular perspective leads him to see 1955-1970, Era B, as one of borrowed engineering models giving a quantitative systems-theoretical base to the discipline, 'in contrast to the broader and more empirical human factors'. The third era, C, is termed computers, cognition (and, indeed, complexity). (It is also an era in which use of the word 'man' in terms such as man-machine systems is being replaced by the less misleading and contentious, if more cumbersome, 'human' or 'person'.) Although many would argue that Sheridan's human–machine systems perspective is narrower than that taken by most ergonomists, his diagnosis of present concerns, involving thinking, adaptive people interacting with complex computer-controlled processes, is one with which most would agree. The perspectives and concerns of other earlier eras are not anachronistic; there is as great a need as ever for study of equipment, workspaces, and work environments, within both traditional and newer industries. However, the concept of the person in the system as a decision maker handling information, rather than as a physical actuator handling objects, is one which underlies much current occupational human factors thinking. Whilst we should never forget that worker health problems existed before the advent of the VDU, and that many people in the UK at least will be working in traditional factories and offices for some considerable time to come, nevertheless the major impact of occupational ergonomics in the next 10 years will be through the provision of effective interfaces and jobs for people working with computerized systems.

What then is the ergonomist's approach to design and evaluation of human-machine (computer) systems? As part of their somewhat controversial comparison of European ergonomics and US human factors, de Montmollin and Bainbridge (1985) saw the former as now being primarily concerned with explanation (rather than classification); specific contexts (rather than generalizations); actual consequences of particular interfaces for operators (rather than merely specifying an optimum); field study or variable-rich simulations (rather than reliance upon laboratory experimentation); and a concentration upon cognitive rather than physical aspects of work, and particularly upon *how* people think rather than upon the workload 'cost' of such processes. Leaving aside the correctness or, indeed, usefulness of their cultural comparison, the European position as they explain it provides the basic framework of the approach ergonomists must take in order to develop better human interfaces in advanced manufacturing.

In general human factors terms, the Committee on Human Factors of the US National Research Council has identified six areas of research need: human decision making, eliciting expert judgements, supervisory control systems, user–computer interaction, population group differences, and applied methods (NRC, 1983). All of these can be seen as relevant to manufacturing systems, but perhaps particularly the first, third, and fourth. However, we would add to these six another key area for human factors and especially ergonomists — the design and organization of the work available for people in the system. Especially we are concerned with technology and job introduction and implementation, and with job design. That there is an intimate connection between job design and support, and the specification of the interface, will be discussed later. For now we would stress our disagreement with the type of profession/area of interest classification proposed by Buchanan and Bessant (1985). They see ergonomists as analysing the relationships between operators and computer controls; psychologists as considering employee attitudes and work life quality; and sociologists as being concerned with the effects of technology on social structure, conflict, and the relationship between operators and managers. Such pre-occupations are said to have led practitioners to a fragmented view: 'Ergonomists ignore the motivational and political implications of technical change. Sociologists and work psychologists overlook the physical nature and capabilities of computing technology and the skills required to operate it effectively (Buchanan and Bessant, 1985, p. 293). Our approach as ergonomists, and that of close colleagues in occupational psychology, provides the antithesis to such a perspective. The physical, cognitive, and organizational aspects of work must be viewed as interacting. Any attempt to consider, say, a human–machine interface (physical or cognitive) without reference to the job design, training, and organization communication consequences will be doomed to failure.

ADVANCED MANUFACTURING TECHNOLOGY

Some Basic Terminology

This review considers aspects of the human factors implicit in advanced manufacturing technology (AMT), and particularly the development of human interface graphic displays for computerized manufacturing processes. At the risk of appearing tedious it is useful here to define what could be included in the term AMT. Just as information technology (IT) could be taken to include smoke signals, parchment, pen and paper, etc., but in fact is reserved for systems involving the confluence of computers and telecommunications, so AMT means more than a new generation of manufacturing processes. Again as with IT it should, in its true widest sense, be seen as embracing not just hardware and software but the people using it and the organizations and environments in which they do so.

Advanced manufacturing technology is usually taken as comprising the whole family of modern manufacturing practices generally taking advantage of computerization to achieve benefits of efficiency, flexibility, and eventually, costs and competitiveness. Its adoption as a rule requires changes in management systems as well as in manufacturing practice.

There would appear to be two distinct ends to the spectrum of AMT, defined by the extent and the degree of integration with which the technology is applied. At one end we have the concept of the factory of the future, using computer-integrated manufacturing (CIM); at the other we have isolated items of automated, or computer-controlled, plant — 'islands of automation'.

Unfortunately, a whole language of abbreviations and acronyms has grown up around AMT. (Perhaps in order to preserve a mystique!) Using these as sparingly as possible, the 'family' of AMT has been summarized in Department of Trade and Industry literature as including computer-aided design (CAD), computer-aided manufacturing (CAM) and computer-aided production management (CAPM). Robots and flexible manufacturing (or machining) systems (FMS) — a number of individual machining units and integrated handling systems under joint computer control — may be seen either as separate strands of AMT or as a part of CAM. Within CAPM. are included data systems for processing and control of ordering, inventory, sales, etc.

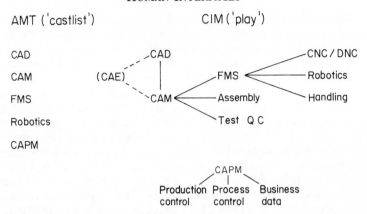

Figure 4.1 Elements of advanced manufacturing technology and computer-integrated manufacturing

It is important to distinguish more clearly the concept and scope of AMT, CIM, and FMS (see Figure 4.1). If AMT were to be conceptualized as a play's castlist, an inventory of available technologies, then CIM would be the play itself with its script, dynamic interaction between actors, ad libs and 'fluffs'. CIM thus comprises the integration and organization of all the processes of production, from the conceptual design stage to product delivery, within a computer integrated system. Thus CIM includes CAD/CAM (or computer-aided engineering — CAE), computer or direct numerical control (CNC and DNC), robots and FMS, incorporates machining, assembly, testing and other processes, and is integrated with the necessary business planning and control systems such as forecasting, production and inventory control, costing and sales processing.

In comparison with FMS, CIM is mainly concerned with the information processing tasks at all levels of the factory and its management, whereas FMS provides the essential computer controlled manufacturing tools and systems for CIM to execute the computer generated plans and schedules that take account of a total system rather than just one cell or shop. One could also say that CIM integrates 'FMS islands' with the overall computer network, the business system, with different design and manufacturing databases of the company and allows the optimization of the data flow and eventually all activities at a much broader level than FMS. (Ranky, 1986, p. 4)

Other authorities would widen the definition of CIM, in a way acceptable to ergonomists, to include the organization of people within all company functions and levels, since integration, interrelationships, and communication are the organizational keys within CIM. (For basic references see Advanced Manufacturing Technology, 1985; Department of Trade and Industry, 1984; Mortimer, 1982: NEDO, 1985; Smith, 1983; Ranky, 1986; SME, 1985.)

Levels of process and interface

Human interfaces with advanced manufacturing processes can perhaps be divided, somewhat arbitrarily, into two broad categories. There are those where the operator has overview and potential control of an FMS or wider systems of shop floor automation. He or she will be optimizing and troubleshooting a system of operations and flows, of banks of machines, conveyors, robots, and stores. Sharit (1985) and Sinclair (1986) present an ergonomics perspective in such interfaces, from the laboratory simulation and the field study respectively.

However, there is an argument that, due primarily to cost considerations (Postlethwaite, 1984), the next step, the total-CIM factory, will not necessarily have a great impact in the UK for the foreseeable future. Indeed, CIM has been said to be some way from being achieved technically (King, 1984) and 'larger-scale FMS' are in reality few and far between (Wall, 1985). Even more pessimistic is the Ingersoll Engineers report 'Integrated Manufacture' (quoted by Davies and Yates, 1986) which says that CIM exists hardly anywhere in the world and that few of the computer systems controlling machinery in factories live up to CIM's requirements of simplicity and lower product cost. The trade and technical press have articles with diametrically opposing viewpoints, often in the same issues. There are those extolling the achievable benefits of CIM and implying that companies not following this route will perish (e.g. Greenhalgh, 1986). Contradicting this are articles which conclude that CIM, or elements of it, has been oversold technically and financially (e.g. Palframan, 1984). Good journalism, agreed, but what is implied are two equally plausible visions of computer technology in manufacturing industry. Thus what we frequently see now, and may well do so for the foreseeable future, are at best 'islands of automation' of an organization's key process(es). As a consequence we would require interfaces to be developed which allow human control over these islands of automation, individual automated manufacturing processes of cutting, forming, joining, etc.

For human control of both types of process, the CIM/FMS concept or the individual machine or centre, parallels can be drawn with the longer established area of continuous process control in, for instance, the power generation, chemical, and food-processing industries. King (1984, p. 357) sees such a parallel also: future manufacturing systems being operated on a 24-hour basis; small numbers of personnel quickly performing installation, service, maintenance, or supply and collection tasks before withdrawing; and collaboration, coordination, monitoring, and control being conducted from a control centre utilizing continuous displays of systems state. Perhaps the key will be in the conceptualization of the manufacturing operative of the future having supervisory control, or at least the potential for it, of his/her machine. The four modes of supervisory control have been defined as 'monitor', 'intervene', 'teach', and 'plan' (Sheridan, 1976), and to these we can perhaps add a fifth, 'learn' (NRC, 1984). Such, then, could be said to be the human functions within advanced manufacturing systems of the future. They might also be more simply classified into two modes: of optimization (tuning) of the process, and fault detection and fault management (Schneider et al., 1982).

An exposition of what the changes in industrial systems have meant to the people who work in them has been made by Sheridan (1985). Four interrelated trends have made subtle but profound differences to the study of human–machine systems. The first trend consists of the new roles for operators; we have prefixes 'super' and 'tele' as in supervisory control and teleoperators, and the removal of the person up and away in physical relation to the process. A second trend is towards multiperson, multidata, and multiple criteria systems. Third is increasing emphasis upon cognitive models and approach. Fourth and finally, and in reaction to the increased system complexity, the greater evaluative role for human operators, and the lack of observability of cognitive events, is the greater emphasis upon decision aids and normative models to assist the operators.

The US National Research Council (NRC, 1983, pp. 50–51) has identified five categories of human factors problems in supervisory control. These are the investigation and specification of displays, command function, operators' mental models, workload imposed by the tasks, and proficiency and susceptibility to error of the operators. Thinking about the extension of the supervisory control mode to manufacturing processes, and taking into account our view of the remit of ergonomics as discussed earlier and important contemporary issues in work design generally, we would prefer to add two other concerns to these five. These are good job design (in terms of intrinsic characteristics, extrinsic context factors, and environmental characteristics) and the related problem area of training, learning, and support.

It can be argued, indeed, that the two greatest issues facing occupational ergonomics in manufacturing systems are those of job design and system implementation, and of the display of information to the operator. From them will flow the nature of the command, workload, error susceptibility, and so on that are implied. Furthermore, job design and information display are intimately related, in that in complex 'black box' technology to all intents and purposes the display *is* the system for the operators. Their tasks and roles will be defined by the information displayed, in terms of its form and content.

DISPLAYS FOR ADVANCED MANUFACTURING SYSTEMS

Displays as the Process Window

Ergonomists have long had interests in displays specification. Any number of basic texts have included large sections on display classification and utilization and on design criteria. Traditionally displays may be grouped as being quantitative (analogue or digital), qualitative, signals and warnings, status indicators, representational, or alpha-numeric (e.g. Kantowitz and Sorkin, 1983; McCormick and Sanders, 1982), with criteria of visibility, legibility, and comprehension being given for scales, markings, colours, states, etc. One recent branch of display ergonomics has been the transfer and adaptation of traditional media criteria for use with VDUs (e.g. NRC, 1983; Shurtleff, 1980).

Within process control we can see from the 1940s to 1980 a gradual evolution of the process control human–machine interface. According to Brouwers (1984) developments were from large analogue displays in local panels, to control room centralization, to smaller digitized interfaces, and then back to decentralization and miniaturization of the interface, with the pervasive introduction of online computers to enhance operator information and high-level control. From about 1980, however, there has been more drastic change, following the introduction of 'so-called distributed information systems' (Johannsen *et al.*, 1985). The hundreds of conventional displays and controls, even alarm and anunciator panels, are rapidly being replaced by VDUs, usually CRTs.

One of the key areas for debate at present is the extent to which distributed information systems or CRTs can replace more traditional displays, and the consequent advantages and disadvantages. VDU-based instrumentation requires active selection of 'information screens', a thorough knowledge of variable identifications, and well-developed mental models for the operators (Johannsen et al., 1985). The

> information is limited spatially and delivered sequentially. If one recalls that one of the problems met by the operator in the development of his operating images is to make a coherent whole. . . , to assemble the . . . pieces [and] to find relationships between apparently isolated phenomena, one understands that this method of presentation a priori hardly favours this establishment of relationships. One needs to be already initiated to make sense of it. (DeKeyser, 1985, p. 9).

On the other hand, CRTs allow presentation of information in different ways, as well as processing of it;

> 'dynamic mimics are of interest . . . because they make the largest number of types of information explicit . . . [and] VDU graphics may have the potential for making all types of information explicit' (Bainbridge, 1981, p. 55).

Bainbridge identified four basic 'one variable–one display' types of display as (1) geographical/spatial; (2) static mimic (topological diagram of physical links between process parts, often with actual variable values shown separately); (3) dynamic mimic (topological diagram including variable values, often VDU based); and (4) conventional scale instruments. Of these four, she perceived by far the greatest interest amongst her colleagues to be in the dynamic mimic displays, and also in others which show abstractions and combinations of data at a higher level than individual process state variables. DeKeyser (1985) perhaps puts information displays in process control in context with her analysis of information sources used during preparation, start-up, normal operation, and finish phases of continuous casting. Even during start-up, the critical phase when information need is greatest, the use of wall-mimic boards and CRTs was minimal compared to that of a giant display of main process parameters and, especially, of direct views of the plant and intercom communications.

Schneider et al. (1982) consider that the key questions in designing a human-machine interface are: what type of information and how much should be presented, how should it be presented, how should it be manipulated by the operator, and how should the work station be physically arranged? In fact, probably the most important issue is the effectiveness of conveying information about underlying functional structures of the process, about causal relationships between variables and the functions relating them. Increasing technological complexity, the move from observable to 'black box' industrial processes, has led to the increasing importance of displays in providing systems' transparency (Maass, 1983). Such technological complexity and the corresponding complexity in work are said by Kautto et al. (1984) to break the link or integration between knowledge and skills, the former normally being formed through practice of the latter. The knowledge now required for control activity exceeds the limits of individual experiences, and the opportunity to practise practical skills is reduced. Greater degrees of abstraction in the information handled emphasize the separation of knowledge and skill. The authors support the production and enhancement of operator knowledge and skill in complex processes by what they define as 'theoretical thinking'. Such theoretical understanding, defined along three dimensions of the systemic organization of knowledge, generic depth of explanation, and verbal/conceptual form of information appearance, must be assisted by the system. This, then, defines goals for the decomposition and presentation to the operator of process information.

In a similar vein, Goodstein (1985) and Rasmussen (1984), within the framework of the latter's well-known model of human behaviour in terms of skill-based, rule-based, and knowledge-based behaviours, relate information needs, types, and levels. Examples of the information content required are given for combinations of systems focus (our term) — e.g. plant, subsystem, equipment, or component levels — and levels of abstraction in the way the system is being thought about — e.g. physical form, physical function, generalized function, abstract function, or functional purpose. Based upon such frameworks, Goodstein (1985, p. 7-3) states that information from the system should support operator knowledge (what process is under consideration, how it is implemented and what its intended purpose is. It should support operators' deliberations on goals, priorities, values, etc., as memory aid and feedback mechanism, and should support operator actions by informing about what to do and how to do it. From this he develops a 'display window' format.

Prediction and the development of strategies in new situations — the use of knowledge-based as well as rule-based and skill-based behaviours — must be made possible. We must provide information such that operators can orientate themselves with the process whilst monitoring it, in order that intervention, optimization, start-up, etc., can be effective and timely, and such that operator learning can be enhanced and accelerated.

The Use of Display Format Guidelines

The early consideration of the psychological aspects of interfacing advocated the application of quasi-cognitive criteria, such as consistency, naturalness, and simplicity in software interface design (Foley and Wallace, 1974). Since then, a lot of effort has gone into the production of more specific guidelines, which essentially try to encapsulate knowledge acquired from one or more sources, into a task, and to some extent context-independent form that can direct design (e.g. Engel and Granada, 1975; Kriloff, 1976; MIL-STD-1472C, 1983; Ramsey and Atwood, 1979; Smith and Aucella, 1983; Smith and Mosier, 1984). However, the basic notion and the practical utility of providing such guidelines have not gone without question (e.g. Miller, 1976; Mosier and Smith, 1986; Reisner and Langdon, 1984; Boxtel and Slappendel, 1981).

Mosier and Smith (1986) surveyed a large group of people (130) who had received a copy of the Smith and Aucella (1983) report. Several problems in the practical application of guidelines were identified. The problem most frequently encountered was that the guidelines were found to be too general to be interpreted confidently in any particular context. Another problem was determining the priority ordering of guidelines which conflicted, or were incompatible. Unfortunately, there is no simple solution to this problem as the priority of ordering of guidelines is often dependent upon the particular job context.

Boxtel and Slappendel (1981) comment that the presentation of independent guidelines as reported in the literature does not promote the appreciation that to produce a satisfactory interface display format requires the integrated application of coding methods. They suggest that the basis for such integrated designs should be the manner in which the coded information will be employed by the human operator. Consequently, determining the nature of the human operator's task is an essential part of the interface design.

A severe critic of general design guidelines and a long-term advocate of the approach which emphasizes the importance of the human operators' tasks is Robert Miller. Essentially, he argues that the nature of the task should be the principal consideration in designing a user–computer software interface (e.g. Miller, 1976). The human user has a goal when operating the computer and therefore an important consideration in the design of the interface should be the goal and subgoal structure of the task. However, as it is the context in which the goal structure is manifested that defines the task, any interface display format must represent both of these components. As it is the nature of the task that determines the necessary information and its optimum manner of presentation, only by considering the task nature will it be possible to determine the interface requirements.

A good illustration of the problems associated with the application of interface software design guidelines is provided by Reisner and Langdon (1984). They report the redesign of a small interactive graphics system. In attempting to design an easy-to-use interface by applying design guidelines, they noted that 'the path from guidelines to design is far from clear'.

In accord with the responses to the Mosier and Smith survey, they found great difficulty in determining which guidelines were appropriate in particular contexts, and what the order of priority should be in situations where there were conflicting guidelines. In fact, Reisner and Langdon resolved these guideline problems by considering the demands that the operators would make on the interface as they employed the graphics system. In other words, the nature of the operator's task was used as a means of determining the interface requirements.

On the basis of such evidence and argument it would seem resonable to conclude that, while design guidelines are useful for setting what may be considered as design constraints, to provide a design orientation and for the detail of interface design, the approach advocated by Miller must be adopted.

OPERATOR MENTAL MODELS
The Need to Know the User's Model

Whether we talk of continuous process plant, CIM, or islands of automation, the displays of process physical form, function, and state must be compatible with the internal representations which operators have of the system, and which themselves allow mental models to be built up. Users are said to navigate their way around a system by using the information given to them and their conceptual model of the system (Rubinstein and Hersh, 1984, p. 43). (Indeed, Stassen (1976) has claimed that all forms of human behaviour involve, or are explainable in terms of, some internal representation or model of the system being controlled or observed. However, the validity of such a statement depends upon the definition of human behaviour.

Presumably, Stassen's definition of human behaviour is much more restricted than that employed by many psychologists, who happily discuss the behaviour of cognitive processing modules, or even single neuronal cell responses.)

The influence of the system on the user's internal representation can be two-way, with the display format influencing internal representation also (Pikaar and Twente, 1981). One simple illustration of this is provided by the map of the London Underground. By its station positioning and straight line format, removal of extraneous detail, and having a schematic form, this map provides a representation of the real world that enables passengers to more easily interpret and use the transport system. It can be suggested that this simplified view of the system is so strong that the map will be the image (or model) of the majority of people if they are suddenly asked to think about the London Underground (rather than images of tunnels, trains, etc.). Furthermore, from anecdotes it would seem that the mental model so formed by users interferes with their overground navigation (orientation and destination finding) in London, and their ability to utilize less abstract representations of similar systems (e.g. the original Paris Metro map).

> Operating in the knowledge-based mode implies the use of a set of mental representations or models of the system with which one is dealing. These serve as references of expected behaviour/functioning/structure against which actual conditions can be compared in order to identify state and to predict the effects of changes. . . . Various 'mental tools' are often employed to perform transformations on the system . . . [which] enable one either to aggregate/decompose (parts of) the system so as to change the resolution or level in the detail of attention with which one views the system, or they permit a change in the level of abstraction with which the system is considered (Goodstein, 1983, pp. 63–64).

Contemporary ergonomics and human factors texts are increasingly including statements on the necessity of knowing and designing for the user's model of the system, such as 'information being presented about the system behaviour must fit with the existing internal model of the system because that is the reference for change' (Kantowitz and Sorkin, 1983, p. 380) or 'the designer is obliged to ensure the users have or construct an appropriate user model' (Thimbley, 1984, p. 171). There are even design guidelines for model consideration and use (e.g. Rubinstein and Hersh, 1984). It seems appropriate here to restate some of the basic psychological literature referring to mental models, remembering that this should be read in the context of (largely graphical) information displays for manufacturing processes.

The Notion of Mental Models

In an ideal world, the objective and unambiguous description of the nature of the human operator's task would conform to the human operator's concept of the task. To apply Norman's (1986) terminology, the *designer's mental model* of the *target system* should be identical to the *user's mental model*. However, the user's mental model of a target system often does not match the mental model of the target system held by an expert user such as the designer. Non-expert models may be incomplete, limited in their ability to determine consequences, unstable, have fuzzy spheres of application, include redundancy, and maintain redundancy to allow the general application of a single mental model, rather than engage in the mental effort of increasing efficiency by developing separate, more specific mental models (Norman, 1983).

One of the most considered accounts of the nature and use of mental models is provided by Johnson-Laird (1981, 1983). Johnson-Laird describes mental models simply as particular (but not necessarily veridical) representational forms of external reality. Mental models enable the simulation of the 'real' world and on this basis allow inferences to be drawn and meaning to be determined.

Johnson-Laird also places mental models in terms of other representational constructs. He regards mental models as being the basis and referents of (parsed) propositional representations via procedural semantics (e.g. Woods, 1981; see also Miller and Johnson-Laird, 1976). In this account Johnson-Laird adheres to the verbally based notion of a proposition such as proposed by Kintsch (e.g. 1974), rather than the lower level, brain (cf. machine) code propositions, such as discussed by Pylyshyn (e.g. 1973, 1978). Schemata (e.g. Norman and Bobrow, 1976; Rumelhart, 1980), scripts (e.g. Schanck and Abelson, 1977), frames (e.g. Minsky, 1975), etc., provide the particular sets of procedures for constructing mental models (see Figure 4.2). In other words, when a mental model is constructed, a schema or a

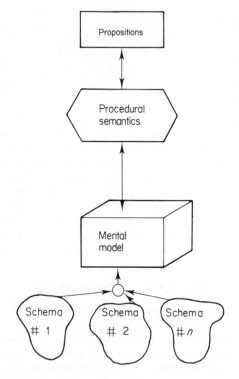

Figure 4.2 The relationship between various descriptions of psychological representational forms

set of schemata are instantiated (Rumelhart, 1984). Although the notion of schemata is not restricted to sets of procedures for representing external reality (e.g. Norman and Bobrow, 1979; Norman, 1981; Schmidt, 1975), the distinction between schemata and mental models would seem to be primarily between levels of description or, perhaps more accurately, forms of abstraction (Rutherford, 1986).

The notion of mental models has much currency in pure and applied psychology (e.g. Falzon, 1982; Gentner and Stevens, 1983; Jagacinski and Miller, 1978; Johnson-Laird, 1983; Kieras and Bovair, 1984; Rumelhart and Norman, 1981; Venemans, 1981). One consequence of this notion is that the main task of human computer software interface design is seen as the attempt to achieve compatibility between the representational form of the users' mental model and that manifested by the display and response format of the computer software interface (Falzon, 1982). Designers must construct an effective 'external myth' to curry the idea of what is required of the user, in other words to create the intended user conceptual model (Rubinstein and Hersh, 1984).

Stated in such a manner, it would seem a simple job to design a user-compatible software interface. All that has to be done is to determine the form of the user's mental model of the target system and replicate this in the design of the software interface. Unfortunately, however, it is not this easy. To begin with, it is not a simple task to determine the user's mental model of a target system, especially as it is likely to change as the user modifies the model in the light of experience. And, of course, even if a stable user mental model is perfectly described, it may still be incorrect in that the predictions it makes do not match with the operation of the target system. (See Norman (1983) for further discussion of these points.) Obviously, there would be little point in designing a software interface that inaccurately represented the target system and gave rise to erroneous actions.

Although much research was and is being carried out with respect to the development of mental models (e.g. Anderson, 1983; Bott, 1978; Gentner and Stevens, 1983), fortunately, in most applied situations the people subjected to mental model investigation will be experienced in their particular task(s) and therefore can be expected to have developed a stable and appropriate (i.e. functionally correct) mental model of the target system.

The work reported by Falzon (1982) provides a good example of the relationship between the analysis of the nature of the operator's task and the application of the notion of mental models to interface software design. Falzon conducted a study with the goal of reducing some of the difficulties experienced by air traffic controllers in directing aircraft. He explains that the air traffic control system display presents one particular representational form of reality. This, as with all representational forms, makes some information explicit and other information implicit (Marr, 1982; see also Palmer, 1978). (Roughly, the degree of implicitness of information is proportional to the complexity of the algorithm(s) that must operate on the representation to compute the required information.)

On the basis of the task requirements, the operator also creates a representation of reality. The explicit information in this representation is determined by the purpose of the representation. The goal of person–machine communication is to achieve compatibility between these two representations.

Examination of the air traffic controller's task reveals that the goal is to maintain safe separations between aircraft. Consequently, the information that the air traffic controller requires to be made explicit is the *future* separations between *pairs* of aircraft (Lafon-Milon, 1981). However, the display format presently employed by air traffic controllers provides information regarding the *present* state of *individual* aircraft.

Consequently, in order to achieve a representation compatible with their mental model, air traffic controllers are required to transform the information presented by the air traffic display. This is time consuming and potentially a source of error. In addition, both of these negative performance aspects are highlighted during stressful, busy periods.

Armed with such an insight into the air traffic controller's mental model, Falzon (1982) suggests two display formats which explicitly represent the required information. In such situations, where it is possible to explicitly represent the required information in more than one form, the issue of selecting the most appropriate display format arises.

Determining the Optimum Display Format

The problem of developing the best form of graphic representation for conveying information has been addressed by Simcox (1983). Although Simcox's work is illustrated and tested on mathematical type graphs (e.g. histograms), he claims that his design methodology is applicable to all graphic forms. The design methodology advocated by Simcox breaks into various stages and parts, but essentially, it follows the procedure outlined here, where the purpose of the display is considered and on this basis the information required to be made explicit is identified. Subsequent to this, Simcox proposes a design process that applies psychological design principles to prototype construction, with a behaviourally based test and evaluation stage. Iterative prototype construction, test, and evaluation are regarded as the best means of achieving an optimum display format.

Simcox identifies four major design parameters: objects, encoding features, groupings, and relations and reference points. The perception and effect of these parameters is determined by the manner of, and constraints on, our psychological processing. Simcox identifies sensitivity, linearity, and capacity as the psychological constraints, although it is worth pointing out that the view of limited capacity in terms of processing resource as presented by Simcox is not unchallenged (e.g. Allport, 1980).

The criterion for determining the best display format is presented as a simple account of display reading. Although Simcox does not present it exactly in such terms, the essential aspect of the account is that if the initially encoded representation of the display does not conform to that of the user's mental model, a reparsing process is initiated to achieve a match. The greater the reparsing required, the greater the processing resources required. As more reparsing is carried out, so the chances of errors increase and the time to acquire information upon which to base a response increases.

Although Simcox can provide many firm statements as to the most appropriate form of representation to achieve a certain purpose within a particular context, his advocacy of an iterative design and evaluation procedure indicates the complexity of potential interactions between graphic display features. This distinction, between the ability to determine what information should be made explicit and the uncertainty as to the best means of presenting this on a display, has a parallel with the computational theory and implementation characterizations of process described by Marr (1982).

Peruch *et al.* (1984) suggest that the most appropriate form of graphic display is that which provides the same (non-redundant) information for psychological processing as is normally encountered in real life. However, a simple adherence to this view may lead to conflict with the previous principle of making explicit that information employed in the user's mental model of the system. For example, Falzon (1982) rejects the notion that a three-dimensional (facsimile) representation would be more appropriate for air traffic controllers, even though it would have greater similarity to the form of the information available in the real world. Falzon argues that as operators do not base their decisions on a 3-D model, there is no point in providing such a display format. A 3-D representation would need to be processed to obtain the information to be mapped into the air traffic controller's mental model. Instead, using available technology, this information can be predetermined and presented explicitly.

However, air traffic control perhaps is an exceptional example of a human task. The control of aircraft flight paths is something very few people have attempted, or have ever needed to attempt. By definition, more common human tasks will be performed more often. As all impinging information has to be parsed in some manner to enter into the representational system, it should not be surprising to find such well-rehearsed tasks, employing real world information, being performed very efficiently. As the person's processing system has evolved and developed to cope with particular real world situations, it is to be expected that many or most naturally occurring tasks already will be carried out by a system employing the optimum mental model and parser.

This account reconciles the orientation towards display format design suggested by the notion of mental models and the viewpoint of Peruch *et al.* (1984). In situations where 'natural' operations, or operations that have some analogy with 'natural' operations, are being displayed, the strategy of 'present [ing] the human operator with isomorphic situations for his processing methods' (Peruch *et al.*, 1984) is unlikely to be improved upon. However, in circumstances where novel or 'artificial' operations have to be displayed, performance is likely to be facilitated by adopting the strategy of display format design that attempts to achieve compatibility with the user's mental model.

HUMAN-CENTRED ADVANCED MANUFACTURING TECHNOLOGY
The Case for Human Interfaces in AMT

At first sight it would appear that there is a paradox in our consideration of human (control) interfaces in advanced manufacturing systems. The move to computer-controlled manufacturing, whether in islands, or CNC machinery, or FMS or CIM, should offer considerable advantages in speed, accuracy, consistency and, over time, cost. Why, then, introduce a human interface for essentially automated processes? The case for this has several elements which overlap to a considerable extent.

It is argued that advances in automation will not necessarily displace human capabilities: the 'desire to eliminate human intervention seems to be wishful management thinking' (Buchanan and Bessant, 1985). Increasingly it is recognized that developments in automation have not, in fact, lessened the need for consideration of human factors in systems design; operator roles may change but their importance to systems efficiency is not diminished. We do not yet have the 'unmanned factory' (Brouwers, 1984), a prime reason being the inability of computers to deal with disturbances or unforeseen events, as well as some tasks being unsuitable for automation (Hwang et al., 1984, p. 844; Margulies and Zemanek, 1983). Even in robotics, where a simple view might be that the person is irrelevant almost by definition, Parsons (1985) has defined nine types of human task. Several examples are being reported where early design decisions to eliminate human skills have proved technically and organizationally infeasible during systems development (e.g. Henning et al., 1984).

Thus the great paradox of modern industrial systems is that what is intended as a move towards greater automation often does not imply, indeed may be incompatible with, people-less organizations. Bainbridge (1983) has clearly pointed out a number of ironies of moves to automation. The more advanced a system the more crucial may be the role of the human operator. Attempts to eliminate human operators often leave them to perform an arbitrary collection of tasks the designer cannot, in the final event, automate. Furthermore, moves to automate may be prompted by a designer's view of unreliable and inefficient human operators, but in fact designers' errors themselves can be a major source of operating problems.

If we cannot, and do not wish to, fully automate our manufacturing systems then we run the risk of providing only fragmentary, low-level jobs, of misusing and under-utilizing human abilities. The consequences of this can be demotivation bringing in its train physical and mental health problems. Labour relations difficulties will increase if the workforce see themselves as undervalued by management, with even the low level of attention required of them being given unwillingly so that work quality may suffer. A further consequence is waste of an important company resource of tacit craft knowledge (Jones, 1984; Karasek, et al. 1982; Martin, 1983; Rosenbrock, 1983). As Margulies and Zemanek (1983, p. 123) put it, to 'escape the vicious circle of designing stupid jobs to fit stupid people, thus making people stupid enough to cope with the stupidity of their jobs, we obviously have to start with the jobs'. The need for good job design, for a symbiotic relationship between people and the systems they use, is particularly acute in situations of technological change and computerization (Butera and Thurman, 1984). Rosenbrock illustrates graphically the nonsense of human resource waste in two analogies (Rosenbrock, 1981, 1983). He describes two jobs: light bulb assembly and press operation. For each he makes the point that a general purpose robot could easily be found to do the jobs, but that an engineer would object due to the great versatility and potential of the artifact being wasted; a simple and cheap pick and place device could be used. Why then, he argues, would we not use a machine for tasks which are much beneath its ability when we habitually give people work which involves incomparably greater waste of ability?

Above, it was stated that humans must be on hand in automated systems, to make interventions where necessary. These must occur in emergencies or cases of system faults, but can also enhance systems flexibility (Benchimol, 1984); ' the nature and limitations of the computer control system and the high cost of error made management more dependant on effective human intervention than with simpler batch production methods' (Buchanan and Bessant, 1985, p. 306). Within the context of islands of automation it is predicted that set-up, maintenance, and innovation will all be enhanced by incorporation of a human interface which allows a skilled, integrated role for the operator.

The Realization of Human–Computer Interfaces

With many computer manufacturers recognizing the commercial value of 'user-friendly' systems, a good deal of human factors research has been instigated and conducted under the auspices of these organizations. One unfortunate consequence is the commercial confidentiality required of such research, resulting in some extremely vague and opaque publications, or none at all on some aspects. The reduced circulation of, and greater difficulty in obtaining, such research reports not only can be frustrating but, when viewed from a more global scientific rather than commercial perspective, also is very wasteful.

Such circumstances, together with the recent proliferation of journal titles and conference proceedings publications, seem to have overwhelmed the traditional citation index and even computer-based methods of literature search! Obtaining a representative collection of published work now can be a time-consuming occupation, requiring some degree of good fortune, if not many appropriate contacts.

Whatever the reasons, set alongside the relatively great volume of published work on human–computer interfaces in the office or in the nuclear, chemical, and other continuous process control industries there is a paucity of recent published work on practical applications of human interfaces in computer-controlled manufaturing. Examples are appearing, however. At the CIM/FMS end, Sinclair (1986) examines the ergonomics implications of the automated factory, especially the information flows and their effects on tasks. Despite the conceptual nature of this paper, it has emanated in part from development work in the field. Sharit (1985) reports on laboratory simulations of supervisory control of an FMS (commenting incidentally on the lack of similar work in, presumably, the USA). Some projects within a German manufacturing technologies programme have concerned 'humane' work design in FMS (e.g. Brödner, 1983) although the exact extent of interface development along ergonomics lines is difficult to establish.

At a medium level of technology integration, a number of authors have reported developments of human interfaces for CNC machine tools; for instance, for examples in Germany see Fähnrich and Raether (1985) or Martin (1983). In the UK possibly the most well-known example is the human-centred technology development work under Rosenbrock at Manchester, including work design for a human-centred CNC lathe (Corbett, 1985). Considering automation of individual processes, or single units of manufacturing capacity, any work in this area can perhaps be considered as related to that for machining cells and FMS but also as an extension to the history of design of interfaces for traditional industrial machines. An example, interestingly triggered by technological imperatives, is work involving the authors at Nottingham University in which human (supervisory) control is to be designed into an automated materials forging process.

CONCLUSIONS

We do not have to take a 'technocentric' approach to AMT design; we can take an 'anthropocentric' approach (Brödner, 1983, 1985), perhaps better termed a 'human-centred' approach. Technology is *not* deterministic *per se*; systems designers and engineers do have a choice. Whether we are talking of FMS or stand-alone islands of automation, there are considerable advantages for the acceptance, effective and full utilization, and flexibility of AMT in the provision of human interfaces and of skilled, responsible jobs for operators. People and the new machines must act together, tolerate and compensate for each other in synergy (Nemes, 1983). 'The optimal relationship between the human and computer in an FMS is one of shared responsibility and decision-making' (Hwang *et al.*, 1984, p. 842). To go back to the seminal paper of Jordan (1963), in his criticism of rigid adherence to a Fitts List approach to allocation of function, people and machines must be seen as complementary not comparable. We should not just give people an 'odd job' selection of tasks at which they are better than machines. Their jobs should consist of fully integrated sets of tasks, and of graded difficulty to allow learning (Whitfield, 1967).

'New technology . . . can be used to correct or even reverse the historical process of subordinating men and women to machines and eliminating initiative and control in their work, and to develop a manufacturing technology which is subordinate to human skill and co-operate with it' (Council for Science and Society, quoted in Martin, 1983). Even those human scientists who may not go as far as Noble (1983), in his three-part thought-provoking attack upon the dangers to society implicit in new technology, should actively seek to promote the role of people in the control of advanced manufacturing technology. Automation and its benefits for the enterprises using it can and must be achieved whilst maximizing the degree of skilled control allowed to its operators. Once there is management and system designer realization of this, then one route for enhancing operator control is through manufacturing process displays matched to, and allowing increase in, the operators' understanding of that process.

ACKNOWLEDGEMENT

Part of the work for this chapter was funded by The Application of Computers to Manufacturing. Engineering Directorate of SERC, GRD 30242.

REFERENCES

Advanced Manufacturing Technology (1985). State of the art. Special reports collection by editors. *Advanced Manufacturing Technology*, July, 66–91.

Allport, D. A. (1980). Attention and performance. In *Cognitive Psychology: New Directions* (ed. G. Claxton). Routledge & Kegan Paul, London.

Anderson, A. (1983). Semantic and social aspects of meaning in task oriented dialogue. Doctoral thesis. Department of Psychology, University of Glasgow.

Bainbridge, L. (1981). Displaying process structure. *Proceedings of the 1st European Annual Conference on Human Decision Making and Manual Control*. Delft University, 25–27 May 1981, pp. 54–61.

Bainbridge, L. (1983). Ironies of automation. In *Analysis, Design and Evaluation of Man-Machine Systems* (ed. G. Johannsen and J. E. Rijnsdorp). Pergamon, Oxford. pp. 129–135.

Benchimol, G. (1984). An interactive EDP for enlarging humane potential. In *Proceedings of 1st International Conference on Human Factors in Manufacturing* (ed. T. Lupton), pp. 87-97. North-Holland, Amsterdam.

Bott, R. A. (1978). A study of complex learning, theory and methodologies. Unpublished doctoral dissertation. University of California, San Diego.

Boxtel, A. J. B. van, and Slappendel, C. (1981). The structuring of information on visual display units. In *Proceedings of the 1st European Annual Conference on Human Decision Making and Manual Control*, Delft University, 25-27 May 1981.

Brödner, P. (1983). Humane work design for man-machine systems—a challenge to engineers and labour scientists. In *Analysis, Design and Evaluation of Man-Machine Systems* (ed. G. Johannsen and J. E. Rijnsdorp). Pergamon, Oxford. pp. 157-163.

Brödner, P. (1985). Qualification based production—the superior choice to the 'unmanned factory'. In *Analysis, Design and Evaluation of Man-Machine Systems: Invited Papers* (ed. G. Johannsen, G. Mancini, and L. Martensen). Pre-prints of 2nd IFAC/IFIP/IFORS/IEA Conference, Varese, September, pp. 18-22.

Brouwers, A. A. F. (1984). Automation and the human operator; effects in process operations. Institution of Chemical Engineers Symposium Series, no. 90, pp. 179-190.

Buchanan, D. A., and Bessant, J. (1985). Failure, uncertainty and control: The role of operators in a computer integrated production system. *Journal of Management Studies*, **22**, 292-308.

Butera, F., and Thurman, J. E. (1984). *Automation and Work Design*, Elsevier/North-Holland, Amsterdam.

Corbett, J. M. (1985). Prospective work design of a human-centred CNC lathe. *Behaviour and Information Technology*, **4**, 201-214.

Cott, H. P. van (1985). High technology and human needs. *Ergonomics*, **28**, 1135-1142.

Cox, T. (1985). The nature and measurement of stress. *Ergonomics*, **28**, 1155-1163.

Davies, J., and Yates, T. (1986). Too early for the factory of the future. *New Scientist*, 2 January, 40-42.

DeKeyser (1985). Technical assistance to the operator in case of incident. Paper presented at the NATO ASI, Intelligent Decision Aids for the Process Environment, San Miniato, September.

De Montmollin, M., and Bainbridge, L. (1985). Ergonomics or human factors? *Human Factors Society Bulletin*, **28**, 6, 1-3.

Department of Trade and Industry (1984). Advanced Manufacturing Technology. Leaflets on the 'AMT Awareness/IT in Industry' campaigns, DTI, London.

Engel, S. E., and Granada, R. E. (1975). Guidelines for man/display interfaces. Technical Report TR 00.2720. IBM Corporation, Poughkeepsie, New York.

Fähnrich, K.-P., and Raether, C. (1985). Human computer interaction in the production—a systematic approach to the design of CNC tools. In *Towards the Factory of the Future* (ed. H.-J. Bullinger and H. J. Warnecke), pp. 876-881. Springer-Verlag, Berlin.

Falzon, P. (1982). Display structures: compatibility with the operator's mental representation and reasoning processes. In *Proceedings of the 2nd European Annual Conference on Human Decision Making and Manual Control*. University of Bonn, 2-4 June 1982.

Foley, J. D., and Wallace, V. L. (1974). The art of natural graphic man-machine conversation. *Proc. IEEE*, **62**, 462-471.

Gentner, D., and Stevens, A. L. (1983). (eds.) *Mental Models*. LEA, NJ.

Goodstein, L. P. (1983). An integrated display set for process operators. In *Analysis, Design and Evaluation of Man-Machine Systems* (ed. G. Johannsen and J. E. Rijnsdorp), pp. 63-70. Pergamon, Oxford.

Goodstein, L. P. (1985). Computer aided operation of complex systems. Experimental testing and evaluation. Final Report of the NKA Projects LIT-3.2 and -3.3. Riso National Laboratory, Denmark (LIT(85)5, Riso-M-2532).

Greenhalgh, K. (1986). Averting the computer-aided disaster. *Automation*, March, 33.

Henning, K., Ijewski, P., and Schurmann, B. (1984). Design of man–machine interfaces and work content in a container transfer process. In *Design of Work in Automated Manufacturing Systems* (ed. T. Martin), pp. 23–28. Pergamon, Oxford.

Hwang, S., Barfield, W., Chang, T., and Salvendy, G. A. (1984). Integration of humans and computers in the operation and control of flexible manufacturing systems. *International Journal of Production Research*, **22**, 841–856.

Jagacinski, R. J., and Miller, R. A. (1978). Describing the human operator's internal model of a dynamic system. *Human Factors*, **20**, 425–433.

Johannsen, G., Rijnsdorp, J. E., and Tamura, H. (1985). Matching user needs and technologies of displays and graphics. In *Analysis, Design and Evaluation of Man–Machine Systems: Invited Papers* (ed. G. Johanssen, G. Mancini, and L. Martensen). Pre-prints of 2nd IFAC/IFIP/IFORS/IEA Conference, Varese, September, pp. 46–56.

Johnson-Laird, P. N. (1981). Mental models in cognitive science. In *Perspectives on Cognitive Science* (ed. D. A. Norman). Ablex/LEA, NJ.

Johnson-Laird, P. N. (1983). *Mental Models*. Cambridge University Press, Cambridge.

Jones, B. (1984). Division of labour and distribution of tacit knowledge in the automation of metal machinery. In *Design of Work in Automated Manufacturing Systems* (ed. T. Martin), pp. 19–22. Pergamon, Oxford.

Jordan, N. (1963). Allocations of functions between man and machines in automated systems. *Journal of Applied Psychology*, **47**, 161–165.

Kantowitz, B. H., and Sorkin, R. D. (1983). *Human Factors*. Wiley, Chichester.

Karasek, R. A., Schwartz, J., Theorell, T., Pieper, C., and Schnall, P. (1982). *Job Characteristics, Occupation and Coronary Heart Disease*. US Department of Health, Washington, DC.

Kautto, A., Norros, L., Ranta, J., and Heimbürger, H. (1984). The role of visual information in improving the acquisition of adequate work orientation. Institution of Chemical Engineers Symposium Series, no. 90, 97–113.

Kieras, P. E., and Bovair, S. (1984). The role of a mental model in learning to operate a device. *Cognitive Science*, **8**, 255–273.

King, J. R. (1984). Is there any future for man in man–machine manufacturing systems? In *Proceedings of 1st International Conference on Human Factors in Manufacturing* (ed. T. Lupton), pp. 353–358. North-Holland, Amsterdam.

Kintsch, W. (1974). *The Representation of Meaning in Memory*. LEA, NJ.

Kriloff, H. Z. (1976). Human factor considerations for interactive display systems. In *Proceedings of ACM/SIGGRAPH Workshop: User-oriented Design of Inter-active Graphics Systems* (ed. S. Treu), 14–15 October, Pittsburgh, PA.

Lafon-Milon, M. T. (1981). Représentation mentale de la séparation verticale au cours du diagnostic dans le contrôle aerieu: 3-représentation des états futurs. *Rapport INRIA*, no. CO R66. INRIA, Le Chesnay, France.

Maass, S. (1983). Why systems transparency? In *The Psychology of Computer Use* (ed. T. R. G. Green, S. J. Payne, and G. C. van der Veer), pp. 19–28. Academic Press, London.

McCormick, E. J., and Sanders, M. S. (1982). *Human Factors in Engineering and Design*, 5th edn. McGraw-Hill, New York.

Margulies, F., and Zemanek, H. (1983). Man's role in man–machine systems. In *Analysis, Design and Evaluation of Man–Machine Systems* (ed. G. Johanssen and J. E. Rijnsdorp). Pergamon, Oxford, pp. 121–128.

Marr, D. (1982). *Vision: A Computational Investigation into the Human Representation and Processing of Visual Information*. W. H. Freeman, San Francisco.

Martin, T. (1983). Human software requirements engineering for computer-controlled manufacturing systems. In *Analysis, Design and Evaluation of Man–Machine Systems* (ed. G. Johannsen and J. E. Rijnsdorp). Pergamon, Oxford. pp. 151–156.

Miller, G. A., and Johnson-Laird, P. N. (1976). *Language and Perception*. Cambridge University Press, Cambridge.

Miller, R. B. (1976). The human task as reference for system interface design. In *Proceedings of ACM/SIGGRAPH Workshop: User oriented Design of Inter-active Graphics Systems* (ed. S. Treu), 14-15 October, Pittsburgh, PA.

MIL-STD-1472C (1983). *Military Standard: Human Engineering Design Criteria for Military Systems, Equipment and Facilities*, revised. US Department of Defense, Washington, DC.

Minsky, M. (1975). A framework for representing knowledge. In *The Psychology of Computer Vision* (ed. P. H. Winson). McGraw-Hill, New York.

Mortimer, J. (1982). *The FMS Report: Ingersoll Engineers*. IFS (Publications) Ltd, Bedford.

Mosier, J. N., and Smith, S. L. (1986). Application of guidelines for designing user interface software. *Behaviour and Information Technology*, **5**, 39-46.

NEDO (1985). *Advanced Manufacturing Technology*. National Economic Development Office, London.

Nemes, L. (1983). Man-machine synergy in highly automated manufacturing systems. In *Analysis, Design and Evaluation of Man-Machine Systems* (ed. G. Johannsen and J. E. Rijnsdorp), pp. 145-150. Pergamon, Oxford.

Noble, D. F. (1983). Present tense technology — Parts 1, 2, and 3. *Democracy*, **3**, 2, 8-24; **3**, 3, 70-82; **3**, 4, 71-93.

Norman, D. A. (1981). Categorisation of action slips. *Psychological Review*, **88**, 1-15.

Norman, D. A. (1983). Some observations on mental models. In *Mental Models* (ed. D. Gentner and A. L. Stevens). LEA, NJ.

Norman, D. A. (1986). Cognitive engineering. In *User Centred System Design* (ed. D. A. Norman and S. W. Draper). LEA, NJ.

Norman, D. A., and Bobrow, D. G. (1976). On the role of active memory, processes in perception and cognition. In *The Structure of Human Memory* (ed. C. N. Cofer). Freeman, San Francisco.

Norman, D. A., and Bobrow, D. G. (1979). Descriptions: An intermediate stage in memory retrieval. *Cognitive Psychology*, **11**, 107-123.

NRC (National Research Council) (1983). *Research Needs for Human Factors*. National Academy Press, Washington, DC.

NRC (National Research Council) (1984). *Research and Modelling of Supervisory Control Behaviour* (ed. T. B. Sheridan and R. T. Hennessey). National Academy Press, Washington.

Palframan, D. (1984). Was CAD too much of a con? *Technology*, 26 March.

Palmer, S. E. (1978). Fundamental aspects of cognitive representation. In *Cognition and Categorisation* (ed. E. Rosch and B. B. Lloyd). LEA, NJ.

Parsons, H. M. (1985). Automation and the individual: Comprehensive and comparative views. *Human Factors*, **27**, 99-112.

Peruch, P., Cavallo, V., Deutsch, C., and Pailhous, J. (1984). Real time graphic simulation of visual effects of egomotion. In *Readings on Cognitive Ergonomics — Mind and Computers* (ed. G. C. van der Meer, M. J. Tauber, T. R. G. Green and P. Gorny). Springer-Verlag, Berlin.

Pikaar, R. N., and Twente, T. H. (1981). How people discover input/output relationships. *Proceedings of the 1st European Annual Conference on Human Decision Making and Manual Control*. Delft University, 25-27 May 1981.

Postlethwaite, A. (1984). Industry can't afford high tech. *New Technology*, 5 November.

Pylyshyn, Z. W. (1973). What the mind's eye tells the mind's brain: a critique of mental imagery. *Psychological Bulletin*, **80**, 1-24.

Pylyshyn, Z. W. (1978). Computational models and empirical constraints. *Behavioural and Brain Sciences*, **1**, 93-128.

Ramsey, H. R., and Atwood, M. E. (1979). Human factors in computer systems: a review of the literature. Science Applications Inc., Report no. SA1-79-111-DEN, Englewood, CO.

Ranky, P. G. (1986). *Computer Integrated Manufacturing*, Prentice-Hall, London.

Rasmussen, J. (1984). Strategies for state identification and diagnosis in supervisory control tasks, and design of computer-based support systems. In *Advances in Man–Machine Systems Research*, vol. 1. (ed. W. B. Rouse). JAI Press, London.

Reisner, P., and Langdon, G. G. (1984). Human factors redesign and test of a graphics system. In *Proc. Computer Graphics*, Tokyo, 24–27 April. Japan Management Association, Tokyo, pp. T3-5/1-17.

Rohmert, W. (1985). Ergonomics and manufacturing industry. *Ergonomics*, **28**, 1115–1134.

Rosenbrock, H. H. (1981). Engineers and the work that people do. WRU Occasional Paper no. 21. Work Research Unit, London.

Rosenbrock, H. H. (1983). Developing a technology which provides satisfactory work. Address to the International Research Symposium on New Techniques and Ergonomics, Valenciennes, May.

Rubinstein, R., and Hersh, H. (1984). *The Human Factor: Designing Computer Systems for People*. Digital Press, Burlington, MA.

Rumelhart, D. E. (1980). Schemata: the building blocks of cognition. In *Theoretical Issues in Reading Comprehension* (ed. R. Spiro, B. Bruce, and W. Brewer). LEA, NJ.

Rumelhart, D. E. (1984). Understanding understanding. In *Understanding Reading Comprehension* (ed. J. Flood). International Reading Association, DE.

Rumelhart, D. E., and Norman, D. A. (1981). Analogical processes in learning. In *Cognitive Skills and their Acquisition* (ed. J. R. Anderson). Erebaum, Hillsdale, NJ.

Rutherford, A. (1986). The use of physical context information in psychological processing: an investigation into the environmental context reinstatement effect. Doctoral thesis. Department of Psychology, University of Glasgow.

Schanck, R. C., and Abelson, R. P. (1977). *Scripts, Plan, Goals and Understanding*. LEA, NJ.

Schmidt, R. A. (1975). A schema theory of discrete motor skill learning. *Psychological Review*. **82**, 225–260.

Schneider, H. W., van der Veldt, R. J., and Stassen, H. G. A. (1982). The role of overview displays in human supervisory control. In *Proceedings of the 2nd Annual European Conference on Human Decision Making and Manual Control*, University of Bonn, 2–4 June 1982.

Sharit, J. (1985), Supervisory control of a flexible manufacturing system. *Human Factors*, **27**, 47–59.

Sheridan, T. B. (1976). Toward a general model of supervisory control. In *Monitoring Behaviour and Supervisory Control* (ed. T. Sheridan and G. Johannsen), pp. 271–280. Plenum, New York.

Sheridan, T. B. (1985). Forty-five years of man–machine systems: history and trends. In *Analysis, Design and Evaluation of Man–Machine Systems: Invited Papers* (ed. G. Johannsen, G. Mancini, and L. Martensen). Pre-prints of 2nd IFAC/IFIP/IFORS/IEA Conference, Varese, September, pp. 5–13.

Shurtleff, D. A. (1980). *How to Make Displays Legible*, Human Interface Design, La Miranda, CA.

Simcox, W. A. (1983). Cognitive considerations in the design of graphic representations. Unpublished doctoral dissertation, Tufts University, MA.

Sinclair, M. A. (1986). Ergonomics aspects of the automated factory. *Ergonomics*, **29**, 1507–1523.

SME (1985). *Computer-integrated Manufacturing*. Society of Manufacturing Engineers, Dearborn, MI.

Smith, S. L., and Aucella, A. F. (1983). Design guidelines for the user interface to computer-based information systems. Technical Report ESD-TR-83-122. USAF Electronics Systems Division, Hauscom Air Force Base, MA. (NTIS no. AD A127 345).

Smith, S. L., and Mosier, J. N. (1984). Design guidelines for user–system interface software. Technical Report ESD-TR-84-190. USAF Electronics Systems Division, Hauscom Air Force Base, MA (NTIS no. AD A154 907).

Smith, W. A. (1983). *A Guide to CADCAM*. Institution of Production Engineers in association with the Numerical Engineering Society, London.

Stassen, H. (1976). Man as a controller. In *Introduction to Human Engineering* (ed. K. F. Kvaiss and J. Moraal). Verlag TUV, Rheinland GmbH.

Stewart, T. (1985). Ergonomics of the office. *Ergonomics*, **28**, 1165-1177.

Thimbley, H. (1984). User interface design: generative user engineering principles. In *Fundamentals of Human-Computer Interaction* (ed. A. Monk). Academic Press, London.

Venemans, P. (1981). Prediction and state in simple dynamic systems: what is learned? *Proceedings of the 1st European Annual Conference on Human Decision Making and Manual Control*. Delft University, 25-27 May 1981.

Wall, T. D. (1985). Information technology and shop floor jobs: Opportunities and challenges for psychologists. *Occupational Psychology Newsletter*, **19**, 3-10.

Whitfield, D. (1967). Human skill as a determinate of allocation of function. In *The Human Operator in Complex Systems* (ed. T. Singleton, R. Easterby, and D. Whitfield), pp. 54-60. Taylor & Francis, London.

Woods, W. A. (1981). Procedural semantics. In *Elements of Discourse Understanding* (ed. A. K. Joshi, I. Sag, and B. L. Webber). Cambridge University Press, Cambridge.

International Review of Industrial and Organizational Psychology 1987
Edited by C. L. Cooper and I. T. Robertson
©John Wiley & Sons Ltd

Chapter 5

HUMAN-COMPUTER INTERACTION IN THE OFFICE

Michael Frese
Department of Psychology
University of Munich
West Germany

INTRODUCTION

There is no doubt that computers have already changed work and will continue to do so in the future. According to some estimates, 40-50 per cent of all American workers will deal daily with a computer by the end of this century (Giuliano, 1982). The following technological trends are likely to appear in the future (see, for example, Otway and Peltu, 1983):

— stronger interconnectedness of computers;
— a proliferation of software so that many different programs are at our disposal and many will have to be learned;
— an increasing integration of software so that a writer can interchange between, for example, graphics, (business-)calculations, using a database, putting a thought on a notepad, and writing a text;
— an integration of traditional uses of the computer and the telephone (teleconferencing, electronic mail and mailbox, voice-mail, telecopying, etc.);
— an increasing use of decision support systems (e.g. in the work of the insurance sales person);
— the use of huge databases that are integrated into daily work; additionally, filing will be done electronically.

In spite of the obvious importance of this new technology, there is curiously little interest among industrial and organizational psychologists in dealing with the topic of human-computer interaction at the workplace; there are very few contributions on this topic in the major journals (e.g. *Journal of Applied Psychology*). On the other hand, there is actually ample literature on psychological issues in human-computer interaction as documented in two literature guides (Rödiger, 1985; Williams and Burch, 1985) but this research was mainly done within the frameworks of human factors and cognitive science (as in the three journals *International Journal of Man-Machine Studies, Behavior and Information Technology,* and *Human-Computer Interaction*). In addition, there has been a score of edited volumes on this topic, e.g. Balzert, 1983; Bennett, Case, Saudelin, and Smith, 1984; Borman and Curtis, 1985;

Bullinger, 1985; Cakir, 1983; Green, Payne, and Veer, 1983; Janda, 1983; Mantei and Orbeton, 1986; Norman and Draper, 1986; Schauer and Tauber, 1984; Shackel, 1985a; Thomas and Schneider, 1984; Veer, Tauber, Green, and Gorny, 1984; also, several textbooks have appeared, e.g. Monk, 1984; Nickerson, 1986; Shneiderman, 1980).

The emphasis here will be on computer-related work in the office (of course, human–computer issues cannot be divided neatly into those that relate to the office and those that do not). I have concentrated on European and American research that was published after 1980. Industrial and organizational psychology is usually interested in the study of organizational problems, long- and short-term difficulties for the workers (stress), how one can improve productivity, individual differences, and in recommendations for job design. Therefore, these are the topics of this review: What are the organizational conditions of human–computer interaction? What are potential stress problems? How can the human–computer interaction be optimized (in terms of improving the system and training the worker)? The question of individual differences: how can industrial psychologists influence the design process and what kind of guidelines are useful? Additionally, some general ('big') controversies that pervade different issues of human–computer interaction will be elaborated.

Actually, the emphasis on office automation would also call for reviewing the literature on combining microprocessors with the telephone (telecommunication), but this could not have been done within the space constraints of this chapter. This is a pity because telecommunication will probably change society and the way we live and work more than the computer alone. The following topics were also *not* pursued although they may be touched upon at times: hardware ergonomics (cf. Cakir, Hart, and Stewart, 1979; Monk, 1984; Nickerson, 1986; Spinas, Troy, and Ulich, 1983), robotics, CAD/CAM systems (computer-aided design, computer-aided manufacturing) or computer-integrated manufacturing, management information systems, and psychological issues in programming (Schauer and Tauber, 1983; Weinberg, 1971). Expert systems (Hayes-Roth, Waterman, and Lenat, 1983) were also not considered except as a tool in supporting human–computer interaction.

THE 'BIG' CONTROVERSIES IN
HUMAN–COMPUTER INTERACTION

There are essentially three 'big', partly overlapping controversies: (1) low-level vs. high-level approaches; (2) human control vs. machine control at work; and (3) computer as a normal (albeit complicated) tool vs. as something new. I call these controversies 'big' because they pervade several different specific areas of research and application and because they stem from deep philosophical and value differences.

Level-of-Analysis Controversy

The level-of-analysis-controversy is curiously reminiscent of the debate on a molecular vs. molar learning theory between Hull and Tolman about 50 years ago. The molecular school of thought argues for an analysis of the lowest level, combining this with precise operational measurement, and mathematical laws. For example, Card, Moran, and Newell (1983) and Newell and Card (1985) argue for this kind of low-level analysis that 'there is a small number of information-processing operators, that the user's behavior is describable as a sequence of these, and that the time the user requires to act is the sum of the times of the individual operators' (Card *et al.*, 1983, p. 139). They describe the human as consisting of long-term memory, working memory (i.e. visual image store and auditory image store), the perceptual processor, the cognitive processor, and the motor processor. Each processor needs a certain amount of time (specified in milliseconds); e.g. the cognitive processor needs about 70 msec. So, for example, the time a person needs for pressing 'yes' when two symbols are identical and 'no' when they are not is calculated to be 310 msec after the presentation of the second symbol: 1 perceptual processor for perceiving the second symbol (100 msec) + 1 cognitive processor for matching first and second symbol (70 msec) + 1 cognitive processor for deciding what to answer (70 msec) + 1 motor processor (70 msec). Their keystroke model is similarly elementaristic; it proposes, for example, that in order to evaluate a move on a word processor, the number of keystrokes should be counted (and when designing it, minimized). Card *et al.*'s argument for their approach seems to be threefold: (1) an approximate quantification is better than none; (2) only a hard science approach (providing quantified laws) will be accepted by designers; and (3) this approach allows for an analysis of design alternatives *before* they are actually designed.

An alternative school of thought emphasizes molar, high-level approaches (Norman, 1986b; Carroll, 1986; Greif, 1986a). This is well exemplified in the volume edited by Norman and Draper (1986). Although the editors pursue a pluralistic approach, the contributions are usually high-level ideas, metaphors (e.g. design in architecture and design of interfaces), and paradigms rather than detailed, ready-to-use, quantifiable, low-level concepts. An example is Norman's (1986a) chapter on cognitive engineering. He specifies an action theory framework consisting of goals, intentions, action specifications, execution, perception, interpretation, and evaluation. These are high-level concepts that cannot be measured in milliseconds. He then goes on to contrast the designer's model with the user's model, emphasizing the differences and the fact that the user cannot directly recognize the designer's model, but can only work via the system's image. Clearly, this approach lacks the detail of Card *et al.*'s but may be more applicable to workplace issues.

Human Control vs. Machine Control

The second 'big' controversy—human control vs. machine control—is not yet out in the open but looms behind many issues (Boddy and Buchanan, 1982; Brown, 1986). It is related to the question of which kind of division of functions between human and machine should be aimed for (Price, 1985). Personal control can be defined as having an impact on the conditions and on one's activities in correspondence with some higher-order goal. (Frese, 1984b, in press, a). This implies that people are able to decide on their goal, their plans to reach the goal, the use of feedback, and the conditions under which they work. These decisions may refer to the sequence of how one does things, the timeframe (how quickly and when) and the content of the goals, plans, use of feedback, and conditions (Frese, in press, a). There are several factors which can be conceptualized to be prerequisites of a sense of control although they are not identical to control: (1) transparency of the system

(Maass, 1983; Brown, 1986) (however, a system may be transparent but not controllable), (2) predictability of the system (however, it may be predictable without being controllable), (3) functionality of the system, i.e. it is possible to achieve one's goals with the tools at hand (however, functionality does not assure controllability), and (4) skills concerned with how to develop plans and put them into action (however, one may be skillful but the system still does not allow decision points).

A very clear statement on the controversy between human control and machine control for the blue-collar sector has been made by Kern and Schumann (1984). In their sociological study of managing new technology in the machine-producing sector, they distinguished two production 'philosophies': a non-ideological–empirical approach to rationalization and a narrow-minded, technological approach. The latter implies that the technology is driven to its limits so as to automatize as completely as possible. The rest that cannot (yet) be done by technical means or is uneconomical to do with machines is left to humans (e.g. putting the raw material into the computer-driven lathe). The former approach takes into consideration the knowledge of the skilled workers and tries to teach the necessary skills to master the computer-driven lathe, e.g. teaching programming or working together with the programmers on the problems at hand. There is evidence that the non-ideological position is more functional, at least for reaching production goals in Western societies (cf. also Corbett, 1985).

One area in which there is a particularly lively debate on the issue of control is piloting airplanes. There is a call for actually reducing the achieved level of automation because this level might have led to a 'sterile cockpit' with ensuing accidents (Sundermeyer and Haack-Vörsmann, 1983; Wiener, 1985; Wohl, 1982). This is reminiscent of the old concept in industrial psychology where the human being should be an 'active operator' *vis-à-vis* automated systems (Hacker, 1978).

A similar reasoning applies even to expert systems (e.g. Coombs and Alty, 1984). Traditional conceptualizations of expert systems (e.g. Feigenbaum and McCorduck, 1984) have emphasized that expert systems are better than experts and should replace them or at least tell them what to do next. In contrast to this is the position that expert systems should give advice to the expert (e.g. via large databases), but that the expert should always be in control. One reason for the latter position lies in the fact that experts at the workplace typically have legal and moral responsibilities; only human beings can take responsibility (Fitter and Sime, 1980) and only they will care in a moral sense about what happens as a result of their expertise (Sabini and Silver, 1985). While the standard argument is that the responsibility for an expert system may lie with the programmer, complicated systems are usually not transparent even for the programmer. Fitter and Sime quote cases in which automation engineers who had designed the system had to experiment with it to find out how the system worked. When expert systems become truly able to learn, the issue of responsibility will become hopelessly muddled.

The issue of control comes up in the use of computers in the office as well (Kaye and Sutton, 1985). Gregory and Nussbaum (1982) maintain in their pessimistic review that the increasing introduction of computers will lead to more machine control, tighter (machine-) supervision, social isolation and little freedom of movement, as well as the deskilling of machine operators. To support their position they quote published IBM projections and Glenn and Feldberg's (1977) paper. A good example of attempting to use the computer to streamline social contact in the office, and thus reduce control is the suggestion by Cashman (1985) that the 'coordinator tool' should allow social contact only when this is in line with the official tasks that a person is supposed to do. Bjorn-Andersen (1983) found that there was a higher degree of structure, preprogramming, and formalization in computerized banks leading to a reduction in choices for the individual worker. Buchanan and Boddy (1982) found in their case study of word processing that management control became tighter after the introduction of computers. However, all of them agree that this is a management decision and not a necessary consequence of using computers (also Ellis, 1984; Schardt and Knepel, 1981; Spinas, in press). Similarly, Cornelius (1985) maintains that it is an organizational choice whether there is more machine or human control and he paints several scenarios for a bank office in 1990 which differ from one another in control and skill utilization. Pava (1983) concurs with this line of argument and describes how office work design is usually organized according to two rationality criteria: (1) streamlining office work in some linear fashion and (2) optimizing discrete components of office work (e.g. typing and telephoning) by introducing new machines and/or new organizational approaches. He points out several problems with these approaches and advocates a sociotechnical design concept for the office in which control is enhanced.

Thus, the issue of control comes up again and again in organizational design of computer work, as well as in the use of computers as tools and in usability guidelines (cf. Benbasat and Wand, 1984; DIN 66234, 1984; Frese, in press, a). Controllability is important because it has an impact on the functionality, the usability, and the user friendliness of the system. The question of control may, however, also be dependent on the user. Novices (or infrequent users) of a specific system may at first need some guidance from the system, while experts want control over the system and can make use of it (Benbasat and Wand, 1984; Shneiderman, 1980).

Computers as Tools?

The last 'big' controversy—the computer as a normal tool or as something new that has a larger impact on our being, thinking, and feeling than earlier technologies—has been debated philosophically, starting with Turing's (1950) test of artificial intelligence and leading to Turkle's (1984) discussion of the computer being like a 'second self'. Human factor workers side more with conceptualizing computers as just another (albeit quite complicated and powerful) tool, while scientists in the areas of artificial intelligence and some social critics are in the other camp. Weizenbaum (1976) warned that increased computer use will lead to a reduction in qualititive reasoning because it will be replaced by thinking mainly about problems that can be easily quantified. Taking this critique one step further, Volpert (1985) argues that the employment of computers and particularly expert systems at the workplace will lead to intellectual and creative deficits, to a Taylorization of expert work, and to a reduction of social relationships; and that computers offer an easy dream world to those individuals who have problems finding social and responsible contacts with others.

This view is to be contrasted with the concept that computers are tools that can have positive or negative consequences depending upon the organizational conditions under which they are used and the sophistication of hardware and software design (e.g. Dzida, Hoffmann, and Valder, 1984; Ulich and Troy, 1986). This position is implied in the work of most human factor researchers and industrial and organizational psychologists since recommendations, guidelines, better design, improved functionality and usability, and finally, higher user friendliness should decrease negative effects and make computers more usable in working on one's tasks.

ORGANIZATIONAL FRAMEWORK AND CONSEQUENCES OF COMPUTER USE

Acceptance of Computer Use in the Organization

In many European countries, particularly in West Germany, computers were looked upon with some suspicion by the general public and by the blue- and white-collar workers (Lange, 1984; v. Rosenstiel, 1984). Therefore, attitudes to and acceptance of computer technology received some attention (cf. Helmreich, 1985; Reichwald, undated). The following factors seem to increase acceptance:

— prior knowledge of computers (Frese, 1984a; Hiltz, 1983);
— participation when introducing new technology at the workplace (see also next chapter);
— good training (this is so important that we deal with it in a separate section);
— good hardware ergonomics (Radl, undated);
— concrete working conditions after introduction of computers, particularly control at work (Eller, 1984), job complexity (Müller-Böling, 1984), and low stress levels (e.g. small response time, machine does not break down often; Müller-Böling, 1984);
— no loss of qualifications with introduction of computers (Weltz, undated);
— anticipation of positive personal and social consequences of computer use, e.g. better working conditions, personal advancement (Frese, 1984a).

Introducing Computers at the Workplace

There is no doubt that the process by which management introduces the computer at the workplace is crucial to whether the computer system will be accepted or whether there will be resistance to change. Resistance to change seldom manifests itself in open revolt (e.g. strikes, sabotage). More often there are indirect measures of resistance, e.g. reduction of output, keeping information to oneself, working strictly according to work rules, and not using the new system (Baroudi, Olson, and Ives, 1986; Hirschheim, Land, and Smithson, 1985; Weltz, undated). The psychological theory of reactance (Wicklund, 1974) may best explain these phenomena. Reactance appears when freedom is taken away and control is reduced. A further consequence of non-control is learned helplessness (Seligman, 1975). Wortman and Brehm (1975) have argued that the first response to non-control is reactance, and that after a period of time in non-control situations helplessness ensues. Since helplessness has cognitive, motivational, and behavioral consequences, a helpless worker may not be able to learn to use a new system, or may not be motivated to get to know it, and may stay passive — not in the sense of not working, but in the sense of trying to avoid the use of new technology.

Ever since the publication of the classic paper by Coch and French (1948), the standard answer of organizational psychologists to reduce the problem of reactance and helplessness is participation in the process of introducing new technology. Even though there is near unanimity among social scientists on the importance of participation, this recommendation is often not heeded in practice (Gottschall, Mickler, and Neubert, 1985; Spinas, in press; Sydow, 1984). Unfortunately, when participation is tried, it is often employed too late and there is too little of it (Weltz and Lullies, 1983). It is too late because the reactance frequently starts when the very first steps are made by management: e.g. analysis of current situation or needs assessment. At this point rumors and anxieties arise, as well as feelings that things cannot be influenced any more because everything has already been decided (Weltz and Lullies, 1983). Anxiety is usually high when workplace change is anticipated since old routines and old skills may become obsolete, the social situation may change and consequently a loss of social status is feared, and finally, there is always the threat of unemployment if this is not clearly and convincingly denied by management (Frese and Wendel, in preparation). Older people, particularly, may be fearful about whether they are still able to learn a completely new system. Thus, participation has to start right after management begins to deliberate on technological changes, even if it is not known at this point what the changes will look like. User participation takes time and training and often the system is ordered before the users can effectively participate (Eason, 1982).

There is too little participation because the professional organizers of technological change try to make a perfect plan that allows little end-user influence (Weltz, undated). They do this because they are under pressure to produce 'cost-effective results'. These savings are often compared to unrealistic estimates by the companies selling hardware and software. The fact that there is too little and too late preparation leads to passive resistance. This in turn can force management to use more authoritative measures: a vicious circle results.

Another problem is that end-users do not know enough about the technology to be able to effectively participate. Weltz (undated) argues that there are two types of experts, the system's expert and the 'usage' expert. The 'usage' expert's interest in the system concerns only its tool aspect. The end-users are usually the ones who have higher expertise in the usage aspect of the system because they know the tasks and how to do them. Unfortunately, however, the system's experts tend to dominate the introductory process which may lead to non-optimal solutions from a usage point of view. Thus, participation of end-users can also enhance the system's functionality.

Therefore, the following steps in participation should be followed (see Briefs, Ciborra, and Schneider, 1983, and Mumford, 1980, for case studies and Spinas, Troy, and Ulich, 1983, for guidelines):

—People should be trained for participation.
—Participation should start at the point of needs assessment and feasibility study (Johansen and Baker, 1984), e.g. with a subjective activity analysis (Ulich, 1981).
—A system should be installed on a trial basis so that it can be elaborated and amended (Eason, 1982).

—Early information should be given; it should be understandable, i.e. it should be concrete, related to the concrete tasks and work procedures—and not technically oriented (Weltz, undated).

—There should be no perfect plan (Weltz, undated).

There are, of course, several problems related to participation:

—Who should be included in the participatory scheme (representatives, all end-users)?
—How can participation work when one system is introduced for several thousands of employees?
—There may be overly high expectations associated with participation.
—The users do not know enough about the system to be really able to participate.
—The users are conservative and aim primarily to minimize all changes.
—Management allows only pseudo-participation without any real input from the end-users.

Consequences of Computer Use

There are good reviews on the consequences of computer use (e.g. Bjorn-Andersen and Rasmussen, 1980; Kling, 1980; Iacono and Kling, in press). In our context, three outcome variables are of particular interest: the impact of new technology (1) on social relations, (2) on control and skill utilization, and (3) on the organization.

Impact on social relations

There are very few empirical studies on this issue. However, there is some evidence for the existence of lower staff and supervisor support in computerized office work than in non-computerized work (Sauter et al., 1983). Volpert (1985) and Rosenstiel (1984) argue that the introduction of computers results in increased isolation. One reason for this may be that computer systems integrate filing, getting information, deciding, and communicating. This results in less moving around, less going to the next room, etc.—all of which used to enhance informal social contacts (Salvendy, 1984; Weltz, 1982). This contrasts with informal reports that there are even stronger social ties because the computer is a constant topic of discussion. White-collar workers often do not work the whole day with computers but only some part of it (Ruch, 1986); thus, they share computers—a welcome chance for social interaction. Depending upon how the allocation of space, the division of work, and the social situation are organized, positive or negative effects on social relations are possible. However, a negative impact of computer work on the intensity of social relations is likely to happen in many organizations.

Impact on control at work and skills utilization

There is some evidence that the introduction of computers may lead to an increase in control at work and in skill utilization in the blue-collar section (Kern and Schumann, 1984; in contrast to this, see Frese and Zapf, 1987) but that there is a danger that employees' control at the white-collar level will be decreased (Buchanan and Boddy, 1982; Ellis, 1984; Hoos, 1960, 1983; Iacono and Kling, in press; Mowshowitz, 1976; Rödiger, 1985; Sauter *et al.*, 1983; Schardt and Knepel, 1981; Sydow *et al.*, 1981; however, see in contrast Reichwald, 1983, and the differentiated picture drawn by Gottschall *et al.*, 1985). Note that the prevailing tendency occurring in a particular organization is dependent upon how the work is organized (Iacono and Kling, in press).

Impact on the organization

Although it is not possible to generalize across different organizations or across different countries, some trends can be ascertained.

(1) Computers are usually introduced in an evolutionary fashion—step by step with only a few changes taking place at each point in time (Pomfrett, Olphert, and Eason, 1985, p. 847). All in all, there are fewer changes than one might assume (De Brabander *et al.*, 1981; Frese and Zapf, 1987).

(2) Any introduction of computers into the organization has some implications for the power structure of the organization (Kling, 1980) since information is redistributed and new avenues of information flow are produced. Those controlling computer resources become more powerful (Bjorn-Andersen and Rasmussen, 1980). Suggestions for or against certain systems are, therefore, often based on this power issue rather than on purely functional grounds.

(3) The advent of large mainframes in the 1960s led to an increase in centralization (Spinas, 1984); but this tendency was reduced again with the use of personal computers (Reichwald, 1983). Today, with the use of large databases and support systems for specialists (e.g. in the banking and insurance industry), there may be a tendency to recentralize. However, the meaning of centralization may become more difficult to ascertain, because there are systems that increase both the decision latitude for decentralized units and the centralization of information that gives the headquarters a great deal of knowledge on the day-to-day operations of the units (Ellis, 1984).

(4) With the fluctuation of centralization, the power of computer departments in organizations may undergo change as well.

(5) Earlier studies showed trends towards specialization when computers were introduced (partly motivated by the costs of hardware) (Bjorn-Andersen *et al.*, 1979). However, since hardware is becoming cheaper, this trend may be stopped and even reversed (Bjorn-Andersen, 1985). There are cases in the banking and insurance industry, for example, where the worker is responsible for all areas of insurance (e.g. car, life, and house insurance). This was introduced to enhance rapport with the customers (Gottschall *et al.*, 1985; Spinas, 1984).

(6) Recently, concern over invasion of privacy has become dominant—especially in some European countries and particularly in the labor unions. Bjorn-Andersen and Rasmussen (1980) report a case of a French insurance company where all the doors including the toilet door could only be opened by a plastic card being put into some terminal. Thus, management could develop a profile of movement for each person. After a strike, this project was cancelled. Computerized personnel information systems can also be used to quickly develop personal profiles of individuals since, for example, the following data are available: trends in sickness days, number of children at home, smoking and drinking (people often pay with a

computerized card in the company cafeteria), trends in average keystrokes per day and which telephone numbers have been called how often. These data can then be used for lay-offs and firing, putting people on half-day jobs or realigning departments. The point is not so much that this information was not available before the advent of personnel information systems, but that the scattered data can now be more easily combined and cheaply collected and made accessible to management.

Conclusion

There is overall agreement, with just a few dissenting voices, that the so-called technological determinism (of the Blauner, 1964, variety) is wrong. There is overwhelming evidence that there is a *danger* of Taylorization of office work with the advent of computers. This could occur by bringing to the office the kind of division of labor that is boring and tedious with planning of work being placed outside of the working person's control. This is typical of much of blue-collar work today (Dieckhoff, Dieckhoff, and Roth, 1982). There is also evidence, however, that it is possible to use alternative (often sociotechnical) job design methods and, additionally, that it pays to proceed with a more holistic and humane approach (Kaye and Sutton, 1985; Margulies and Zemanek, 1983; Pava, 1983; Ranney and Carder, 1984; Ruch, 1986; Spinas, 1984, 1986; Ulich, 1981; Walton and Vittori, 1983; however, contradictory to this is Hedberg, 1980). Thus, it is not the technology that determines the human consequences of computer use, but how computer use is organized (Driscoll, 1982; Haider and Rohmert, 1983; Iacono and Kling, in press; Ulich and Troy, 1986).

Empirically, depending upon the hierarchical position of a worker and whether a worker has a data entry job, a data recall job, or a job involving an intensive dialogue with the computer (Sydow, 1984), computer use has different impacts. At the lowest level, the advent of computers created the keypunch operators who typically hold a Tayloristic job *par excellence*. Further technological development will probably reduce the number of workers in this area. At one level higher up, the introduction of word processing may downgrade the working conditions for the secretaries if a typing pool is introduced at the same time, but upgrade the typists' jobs in an already existing typing pool. At the level of specialists, decision-support systems can sometimes lead to a polarization of skills (some are downgraded, doing routine work that is essentially prescribed by the system, and some are upgraded, doing the complicated cases) or to upgrading of the job because of higher use of skills (Gottschall *et al.*, 1985). Job enrichment can be easily achieved at this level. Even at the low managerial level, as long as there is high interdependency of the systems, task constraints may develop (Bjorn-Andersen, Eason, and Robey, 1986) and there may also be tighter supervision (Wynne and Otway, 1983).

Thus, the general conclusion is that the impact of the use of computer technology is variable and depends on the type of jobs and, in the last analysis, on organizational decisions. This has optimistic implications—in so far as improvements of the working conditions are possible and can be achieved in the process of change, but it also implies a high degree of responsibility for the organization to optimize the adaptation of the technology to human needs.

STRESS

The question of whether stress at work has increased after introducing computers or decreased must be answered very similarly to the issue of organizational effects of modern technology: it depends. Thus, there are studies on people working with computers which show higher stress-effects (Frese, Saupe, and Semmer, 1981; Johansson and Aronsson, 1984; Schardt and Knepel, 1981), lower stress-effects (Kalimo and Leppänen, 1985), and equivocal outcomes (Frese & Zapf, 1987; Sauter et al., 1983; Turner and Karasek, 1984). If the job produces high stressors and little control, negative effects are to be expected.

There is now ample evidence in industrial psychology which indicates that two aspects of the workplace should be investigated under the heading of stress and strain: the stressors and the resources (Frese, in press, a). Lack of resources may have direct negative effects and/or may interact with stressors to produce negative effects, since stressors have a higher impact if resources are low. Stress-effects may manifest themselves in occupational ill-health and in disease (more on this in Cooper and Marshall, 1976). Examples of resources at the workplace are control or descretion level at work (Frese, 1984b; Frese, in press, a; Karasek, 1979; Karasek et al., 1981; Semmer, 1984), amount of skill utilization (Karasek, 1979), and social support (House, 1981; Frese, in preparation b). Therefore, two questions are to be dealt with: (1) Are there new (computer-related) stressors at work? (2) Are there new (computer-related) resources or threats to resources?

New Stressors in Computer-aided Work?

Physical stressors

A major part of research on potential negative effects of the use of a video display terminal (VDT) has been directed to the study of posture effects, radiation effects, and medical effects on the visual system. This literature is not reviewed here. However, it is plausible that purely physical stressors can feed into psychosomatic problems. There is evidence that VDT work is physiologically demanding on the eye (Haider, Kundi, and Weissenböck, 1980; Stark and Johnston, 1984; Smith, 1984; Wilkins, 1985). However, this does not necessarily produce *eye-strain*: sometimes it does (Gunnarson, 1984), sometimes it does not (Hartmann and Zwahlen, 1985; Howarth and Istance, 1985). Obviously, this depends on how badly or how well the VDT is designed from a hardware ergonomics point of view (Stammerjohn, Smith, and Cohen, 1981; cf. Cako et al.'s 1979 discussion of this). But there is an additional and not quite so obvious point: eye-strain is not only a function of the specific demand on the eye but also of general stress at work. There are three psychosomatic processes by which general stress at work may lead to eye-strain (cf. Frese, in press, b, for a similar reasoning for musculoskeletal complaints): (1) Every stressor demands some coping attempt. Since humans have only a limited processing capacity, stressors reduce the available processing capacity that is left for the original task. Thus, the task becomes objectively more difficult (this also explains a lower performance rate under stress; Dainoff, 1984). (2) When there are high background psychological stressors, higher muscular tension ensues as a general psychological response; this also affects eye fatigue. (3) High background stress leads to a stronger pain sensation.

The psychosomatic reactions most easily appear in that organ that is most strongly in demand and strained in a physiological sense. Since general stress at work has an impact on eye-strain in jobs that put an emphasis on work with the eye, this reasoning allows us to interpret the finding that there is an association of eye-strain with time spent on a VDT in 'bad' jobs (like data entry by typists who have high stressors and little control) but not in 'good' jobs (like programmers or secretaries with a wide range of tasks) (e.g. Coe *et al.*, 1980; Dainoff, *et al.*, 1981; Läubli *et al.*, 1980; Smith, 1984; Smith *et al.*, 1981; Cakir, 1981). Apparently, additional psychological stressors in 'bad' jobs contribute to eye-strain.

Thus, there is evidence that VDT work is psychologically demanding on the eyes and that this *plus* a workplace with little control and high stressors can lead to eye-strain. Other (psycho)somatic reactions to the VDT workplace have been described as headaches and backaches (Cakir, 1981). A similar reasoning might apply here, although the latter may be a function of bad ergonomic design that forces the worker to lean forward, thus not having a support of a chairback.

Psychological stressors

It is necessary to ask whether there are new psychological stressors related to working with a computer and/or whether some well-known stressors become more pronounced in computer work. There are five stress problems that fit into that category: response time and computer breakdowns, feeling rushed, constantly feeling supervised, invasion of privacy, and the abstractness of computer work. A sixth stressor is the threat of unemployment which is not new but has become increasingly important with the advent of a powerful new technology.

System response times and breakdowns have been shown to be a major stressor in computer-related work (Johansson and Aronsson, 1984). (They are, of course, not entirely new to computer systems. Machine breakdowns or organizational problems have been disturbing in non-computerized industry, as well; Semmer, 1982). In a way, it is paradoxical that slow system response times of the computer and breakdowns should count as a stressor. One might think that they would be welcomed as beneficial rest periods (or thinking periods). The stress-effect has been explained as being due to unpredictability of events (Boucsein, Greif, and Wittekamp, 1984) or it may be due to the interruption of a plan. Miller (1968) and Cakir (1986) gave recommendations on response times. In general, low response times have been suggested. However, Shneiderman (1986) warned that very short response times may also add to feelings of being rushed — as a further stressor. In fact, research has not been entirely consistent in showing the lowest stress-effects with low response times (Kuhmann *et al.*, in press; Martin and Corl, 1986; Schaefer *et al.*, 1986). However, the question arises whether laboratory studies, like the ones by Kuhmann *et al.* and Schaefer *et al.*, where response times of 8 sec were actually overall less stressful than those of 2 sec, can simulate the time pressures that exist in normal work which may be the most important contributor to the annoyance with long system response times.

In a thorough review, Shneiderman (1984b) argues that it is necessary to differentiate between system response time and thinking time. When the system response time becomes much longer than thinking time, it becomes a stressor. The stress characteristic of system response time is also dependent on what the user expects to be a normal response time. This may be one factor explaining why high variability of the response times is most often reported as being stressful. Stable expectations cannot be developed in this case.

The effects of breakdowns and response times will most probably also depend on organizational issues, namely how the workers are paid (e.g. some piece rate system), whether they are under public pressure to render results (e.g. in an airline ticket office), or whether or not their workload is adjusted to breakdowns or slow system response times.

Thus, the aversiveness of response times may be a function of being rushed. Johansson and Aronsson (1984) and Weltz (1982) have argued that the *feeling of being rushed and the feeling of high concentration* are produced by working with a VDT. The cursor constantly blinks, signalling readiness for further input. The typewriter used to provide for a mixture of high-concentration tasks like writing and low-concentration tasks like getting up, fetching folders, and putting paper in the machine. This mixture of tasks also made it possible to rest for very short (nearly not noticeable) periods of time. These tasks are now streamlined into the system. One user described the work with the VDT as 'simpler, yes, but somehow more strenuous' (Spinas, 1986, p. 12). Again, these feelings may gain added importance because rushing people used to be done by supervisors in the office (if at all) and not by machines. Now it is more difficult to consciously ward off the time pressure.

There is new potential to *supervise* white-collar workers. Many computer programs provide a convenient log of how many keystrokes a worker has made per day. This kind of information creates a dehumanizing atmosphere (Smith, 1984) and is probably one of the reasons why anxiety is often quite high when computers are introduced in the office.

A similar issue is *invasion of privacy* which is surprisingly little researched. Computers allow for the easy combination of data that are, singly and taken individually, relatively innocuous. With the use of computers for registering citizens, keeping track of their financial situation and prosecuting criminals, the danger of invasion of privacy in society is widely feared (Rosenstiel, 1984). Similar fears come up in industry, as well, when many work-related and private data are stored and combined.

Abstractness of work may be another potential stressor (Volpert, 1985; Weltz, 1982) although it has not been researched much. This may be a more important problem in the blue-collar sector (e.g. in the printing industry where concrete handling of lead letters was replaced by computerized type-setting). But even in white-collar work, people used to handle paper, folders, and numbers in a relatively concrete way. There was a one-to-one relationship between a piece of paper and the information on it. This relationship is gone in computer-aided work. Abstractness may be of added importance in telecommunication (which we do not discuss here). There may be a 'natural' need in humans to handle things in a concrete manner (a 'full action' means that both thinking and handling something are combined; see Hacker, 1985). This may also be a reason why 'direct manipulation' is a successful interaction mode. Lack of concreteness may lead to two problems: (1) a feeling of unreality towards the objects — this might have more negative consequences in war games than in office work; (2) a fear of making errors because the errors are made with a medium that is not discernible. An example that was reported to me in a company might illustrate this. When a data system was introduced one secretary kept a column of names constant and by mistake changed their addresses around in the second column. Such an error is, of course, impossible to make on paper.

The last stress factor to be mentioned here is *fear of unemployment*. While simulation studies of national economies have given equivocal results on the problem of unemployment, there is no doubt that many companies introduce computers to reduce the number of workers. This leads to fear of unemployment, which in turn leads to high stress-effects (Pelzmann, Winkler, and Zewell, 1985).

Does this list of stressors imply that computers have led to a higher degree of overall stress at work? I do not think that this conclusion is warranted. Some stressors have been minimized, e.g. anxieties about making a 'typo', or having to retype texts over and over again after small changes. Additionally, computers can be used to reduce the demands on working memory, another potential stressor (Hacker, 1983). It depends on the organization of work as to whether the net stress-effect has increased and the net resources have reduced.

New Threats to Resources in Computer-aided Work

There are four major resources at work: control at work, development of skills, information support, and social support. It has already been stated that there is a tendency to reduce *control* in the computerized office. Control *vis-à-vis* the system may mean to have options, to be able to adjust computer programs to one's own job requirements and to one's liking, to develop one's own masks (screen layouts) or patterns of interaction, to be able to choose the tasks and the task order, and to time them at one's own pace—in short, to be master of the system. As already stated, control depends on the system and on the organizational context. Therefore, it is not surprising to find different results on control perception in computer-aided work (Buchanan and Boddy, 1982; Rafaeli and Sutton, 1986; Sauter *et al.*, 1983; Turner and Karasek, 1984). However, there is no doubt that control decreases strain and increases job satisfaction. Indirect or direct evidence for this can be found in Bikson and Gutek (1983), Smith *et al.* (1981), Troy (1986), Turner and Karasek (1984), and Ulich (1986).

Without *skills*, there is little chance to master the machine. Skills can be used to change the program, to adapt it to one's needs, and to develop clever solutions for complicated problems. Thus, skills can help to reduce the effects of stress (Greif, 1986b). One prerequisite for skill utilization is that work is complex enough (the relationship between control and complexity is itself quite complicated and cannot be pursued here; see Frese, in press, a). Hacker (1983, 1985) has shown that complexity of work leads to positive consequences. However, this is only true given a certain skill level. Another prerequisite is that skills are to a certain extent private. This means that it is up to the workers to decide to employ them. If they are not private, a skillful problem solution might be programmed into the system. In this case, the skillful accomplishment is not at the worker's disposal any more, but is a resource of the machine. Thus, it cannnot count as a resource for the individual's stress management because it does not increase a sense of self-confidence and it cannot be used to reduce unexpected stressors. On the contrary, in such a case the job has been reduced to a potentially more monotonous work situation. Thus, skill utilization by the workers should be kept (and enhanced) in computer-aided work. This may not be a problem at the present time because the systems are nowadays still complex enough to actually necessitate an increase in skills. But with increasing employment of 'intelligent' systems in the future there is a danger that skill utilization will be decreased.

One frequent phenomenon in computerized office systems is that units of *information* are hierarchically organized according to their access so that one needs to know certain codes in order to get information that is reserved for those higher up in the hierarchy. Since official task descriptions are seldom complete or even adequate, and since they determine the information policy of the system, this leads to a person not having the needed information. Since one reason for regulating access to information may be the privacy issue, there might be a trade-off here between the problem of invasion of privacy and the question of information support.

Social support is a resource that buffers the effects of stressors on psychological and psychosomatic problems (House, 1981). Since social support is dependent on social contacts, the frequently mentioned problem of social isolation as a result of computer-aided work is important. Computer-aided work, e.g. for the specialist, can lead to less social contact (Smith, 1984; Turner and Karasek, 1984). In the past, the specialist used to move around and ask other people for information. This may not be necessary after a system has been introduced. However, to my knowledge there is little systematic research relating this problem to the stress field.

In summary, there are dangers of increasing stressors as well as reducing resources in computer-aided work. However, this is dependent on the particular organizational context in which the work is done. As a matter of fact, resources can be increased and stressors decreased with the introduction of computers in the workplace as well. Resources are usually enhanced when some kind of mixed work is instituted, e.g. when a secretary not only types but also does scheduling and financing, writes letters on her own, etc. (Ruch, 1986; Troy, 1986; Ulich and Troy, 1986).

Our emphasis on organizational conditions leads to the general warning that even the best designed computer screens and keyboards (from a hardware ergonomics point of view), as well as the best software ergonomics, do not help if the organizational environment produces stressors and decreases resources (see Hacker, 1983, Rödiger, 1985).

COGNITIVE OPTIMIZATION OF HUMAN-COMPUTER INTERACTION

Cognitive optimization of human-computer interaction can be done by increasing the individual's skills to deal with the system and/or by optimizing the system. Both increasing skills and optimizing systems are related to the question of how a human makes sense of the system—the mental model. Training is a direct way of teaching the 'sense' of the system; but designing the system should similarly be oriented to implicit or explicit mental models. Therefore, I shall first discuss the concept of mental model, then the optimization of skills (training), and finally, optimization of the system.

Mental Models

It is nowadays nearly a truism that a person using a computer has to develop some kind of mental model of the functioning of the system and that even a novice will approach a computer with some kind of mental model in mind (overviews: Carroll, 1984; Jagodzinski, 1983; Rohr and Tauber, 1984). In other words, the user has some kind of conceptualization of the functions of the system and of how one has to deal with the system. These mental models may be of the metaphor kind, e.g. using the analogy of a typewriter when first using a word-processing system, or may be a knowledge of the rules to be used in a system. It is useful to make the mental model explicit for the user (Kieras and Bovair, 1984) because wrong mental models may lead to wrong or inefficient approaches to the machine (Bayman and Mayer, 1984). However, this is not always so; in certain circumstances a wrong mental model may be more functional than a correct one that is just a little incomplete: a wrong home heat regulation theory (valve theory) saves more energy than the correct feedback theory which does not take into consideration other thermal laws (Kempton, 1986). Norman (1983a) observes the following characteristics of mental models: They are incomplete, they are not 'run' easily, they are unstable (and parts of them forgotten), they have no firm boundaries, they are unscientific (and even superstitious), and they are parsimonious. In short, they are not in any way a neat and non-contradictable set of ideas as in a scientific model.

Essentially, the following conceptualizations of mental models in research on human–computer interaction can be differentiated: (1) the mental model may refer to action or to knowledge of the world; (2) the mental model may or may not be thought of as consisting of hierarchies; (3) the mental model may be of the production theory type or be more holistic, like the schema theories; and (4) the mental model may be analog or analytic.

(1) Various theories have distinguished action-oriented models from models that explain and describe the world. Miller, Galanter, and Pribram (1960) distinguished image (the description) from plans (the action-oriented model), Hacker (1978) an operative image system from other non-operative cognitions, Young (1983) a surrogate model from a task/action model, Anderson (1983) declarative from procedural knowledge, Carroll (1984) conceptual from mapping analysis, and diSassa (1986) structural from functional models. Not all of these distinctions are exactly alike but most agree that there are mental structures for description and/or analysis as well as mental structures for action. The relationship between these two different kinds of mental models still needs to be elaborated: it is likely that in the last analysis the action-oriented models are the important ones and the conceptual and analytic ones are subservient (Hacker, 1978). This may be one of the reasons why functional models are more useful in learning about computer systems (diSassa, 1986).

(2) The mental model can be conceptualized as being hierarchically organized (e.g. Anderson, 1983; Gallistel, 1980; Miller, Galanter, and Pribram, 1960) or not (Neisser, 1976). Most cognitive theorists assume now that there is some kind of hierarchy, but that processing may also run counter to a strict hierarchial model (heterarchical conceptualization; Gallistel, 1980).

(3) Many theorists in the area of human–computer interaction think of the mental model as consisting of production rules (Anderson, 1983; Card *et al.*, 1983; Polson

and Kieras, 1985). The alternative would assume a less elementaristic notion, as in the concept of schema (Bartlett, 1932; Neisser,1985). The production system consists of low-level molecular production rules (e.g. given a certain goal and certain conditions, act X should be performed). In contrast, schemata are more high-level molar concepts—often thought to have some *Gestalt* character—that cannot be broken down into smaller units. Schemata are flexible, anticipatory devices that can have internal conceptualizations of movements and trajectories (Neisser, 1985) often related to images. An integration of both views has been suggested (Waern, 1985): high-level schemata are used in novel situations or in non-redundant environments, while low-level automatisms of the production system kind are used in overlearned skills. In fact, lower-level skills are more easily disturbed, either by thoughts (in the fable the centipede cannot walk any more after being asked how he moves his hundred legs) or by novel inputs from the environment, while the higher regulation level can easily deal with novel input (at the expense of being less efficient). This integrative view has to answer the difficult question, of course, of by which process a high-level schema can be transformed into a low-level production system in the process of learning an action.

Elementaristic production systems can explain the process of automation easier (through the chunking process) than schema theories (Anderson, 1983). On the other hand, schema theories are better equipped to deal with metaphors, images, the incompleteness and flexibility of mental models, the active, changing, and constructive nature of mental models, and their *Gestalt*-like nature.

(4) The mental models may be either analog or analytic. This is somewhat related to the above point. While images and schemata are typically analog mental models, production rules are more analytic. Metaphors (Carroll and Thomas, 1982) play a role when learning a computer system. The typewriter metaphor is typically used by novices when approaching a word-processing system. Metaphors are analog mental models. It has been suggested that novices start with models of an analog type and become more analytic with time.

Hammond and Barnard (1984, p. 131) specify in some more detail what the user needs to know in order to work with a computer system: 'Knowledge of the domain', 'Knowledge of the computer version of the domain', 'Knowledge of the workbase version of the domain', 'Knowledge of the problem', 'Knowledge of system operations', 'Knowledge of physical interface', 'Knowledge of interface dialogue', 'Knowledge of natural language', and 'Knowledge of other machines and procedures'. This list is quite impressive, and other authors, like Greif (1986b), add that one should also know the potential errors. Riley (1986) contends that a user should have an understanding that is internally coherent, valid, and integrated.

Seen from this perspective, it is not surprising that people make serious errors with computers and that learning takes a long time. Additionally, this complex set of issues makes the design of software quite complicated. In any case a system designer has to take into consideration the users' mental model—otherwise the system may not be functional and usable.

Optimizing Skills: Training

In order to develop a mental model, training is necessary (although not all training is geared towards developing mental models). But training does not only optimize the interaction with the system but can also decrease potential stress-effects. Workers who are not well-trained use descriptors for the computer that signify that they see themselves as servants of the system ('he wants to') in contrast to the well-trained workers (Ulich and Troy, 1986). Although, in general, organizations perceive the need for the training of skills in the area of human–computer interaction, they usually do not provide enough time and resources (Bjorn-Andersen, 1985; Gottschall *et al.*, 1985). Training research has concentrated on programming (which will not be dealt with here; see Boulay and O'Shea, 1981; Mayer, 1975, 1976; Owen, 1986) and word processing on which substantial work has been done at the IBM Watson Research Center (e.g. Carroll *et al.*, 1985; Carroll and Mack, 1984; Mack, Lewis, and Carroll, 1983).

The less complicated the commands, the rules, and the interface of a system, and the more the person knows right from the start, the less there is a need for training. However, even for 'fool-proof' systems, such as Apple's LISA with its desktop metaphor, some type of training will be needed. They are difficult to learn, even for persons who know other word-processing systems (Carroll and Mazur, 1985). Training is necessary even if so-called on-line tutorials or manuals are provided. Manuals are not used much (Carroll and Mack, 1983; Scharer, 1983) and tutorials are often not helpful (Carroll and Mazur, 1985; Greif, 1986a).

Most training programs can be conveniently grouped as in Table 5.1 (although there are really never 'pure' types of training program). Sequential training programs do not explain the background of the system and the laws and rules regulating it, but essentially present a correct sequence of steps and have the student practice them. Thus, they work within a behavioristic tradition. Most computer-driven tutorials follow this kind of reasoning, presenting a step and then asking the person to perform the respective action (Carroll and Mazur, 1985; Greif, 1986a). Unfortunately, many commercially available training programs do the same (Greif, 1986b). In contrast, an integrated–systematic training program explains the background for the computer program, the reasons behind the commands, how they are related, which metaphors are used, how the commands pertain to general rules and heuristics — in short, to some mental model. These explanations are action-oriented. In other words, an integrated–systematic program tries to build up complete and full action. This implies that all levels of regulation are implicated in the action: the intellectual level, on which rules, metaphors, and heuristics are regulated, as well as the lower levels, e.g. the sensorimotor level of regulation (cf. Hacker, 1985). In a sequential program, only the lower levels of regulation are trained (however, the trainee may well develop some kind of action-oriented and even systematic mental model in spite of the training program). Thus, integrated–systematic training stems

TABLE 5.1 — Types of Training Programs

| | | TRAINING PROCESS | |
		SEQUENTIAL	INTEGRATED-SYSTEMATIC
Development of the Mental Model		Passive	
		Active	

from an implicit or explicit theory of action (Norman, 1986a; Frese and Sabini, 1985; Volpert, 1981). In general, integrated-systematic forms of training seem to work better than sequential programs (Frese *et al.*, in preparation; Greif, 1986a; Hacker, Rühle, and Schneider, 1978; Kieras and Bovair, 1984; Volpert, Frommann, and Munzert, 1984; a good description of such a training is given in Greif, 1986b). Moreover, integrated-systematic training is better adapted to how people go about learning; humans give spontaneous interpretations, generalize from experience (even when they refer to very shaky data), and perform their first steps on the computer in accordance with some preestablished metaphors (Carroll and Mack, 1984; Douglas and Moran, 1983). Usually, computer-naïve people take a typewriting metaphor when they work with a word-processing system and make the 'appropriate' mistakes (Mack, 1984; Waern, 1985).

The second dimension of Table 5.1, 'active-passive', is related to an action theory approach as well. Carroll and Mack (1984) vividly describe how trainees proceed *actively* and exploringly with a word-processing task rather than passively following instructions (as some manuals would presuppose) (cf. also Waern and Rabenius, 1985). Training that emphasizes exploratory behavior fares better than more traditional procedures (Carroll *et al.*, 1985; Greif, 1986a; Frese *et al.*, 1986; cf. Carroll and Rosson, in press, for a theoretical discussion on this issue). Unfortunately, it is nearly impossible to neatly differentiate between the four cells of Table 5.1; it is particularly difficult to develop an active training program that is not integrated-systematic since people spontaneously develop models with some degree of integration. Frese *et al.* (1986) have tried to test three of the four cells against each other with the active and integrated-systematic training being the most effective cell.

There are five more issues in training: (1) Training of what? (2) Treatment of errors. (3) Transfer. (4) Local experts. (5) Individual differences.

(1) Training should not just deal with those few tasks that appear in a particular job description but should be broader so that the user really understands the system. Riley (1986) has suggested that user understanding of a system implies a conceptualization with some internal coherence, a correct representation of the system, and an integration of this knowledge into other areas of knowledge. This principle of broad training objectives is particularly important for computer-based work because even well-established software programs often have serious flaws. To deal with these flaws, one has to know a great deal more than is necessary to do just the task in hand. Furthermore, the official job description seldom represents all the tasks that a worker really does. Bjorn-Andersen (1985) suggests that training should also include democratic participatory and exploratory behavior at the workplace.

(2) Making errors produces anxiety, particularly in the novice. There are essentially three suggestions for dealing with them. First, the training program does not allow errors or minimizes the chances to make errors, as in the no-surprise editor (Mack, 1985) or in the training wheels approach (Carroll and Carrithers, 1984). Second, the system facilitates retrieval from error, e.g. with an 'undo' button (Carroll *et al.*, 1985). Third, trainees are encouraged to make errors (a sort of error training) and errors are used in a specific procedure to develop a mental model of the system (Greif, 1986a, 1986b).

(3) Since it is nearly certain that workers will have to use different systems in the course of their working life, the question of transfer between systems is important. Carroll and Mazur (1985) report how people have many problems with the supposedly easy direct manipulation interface of LISA. Since all of the subjects in this study had known other systems before, some of the problems might actually have been instances of negative transfer. Examples of the difficulties of transfer are also given in Karat *et al.* (1986). This is an area with relatively little research. Research is particularly needed for answering the question of which *basic* skills a person should acquire to deal with *different* kinds of programs. An additional issue is to transfer the skills learned in some course to one's daily work. This is a particular problem with courses that are not task-oriented and that take place outside work. Therefore, training should be oriented to the concrete work that has to be done, transfer tasks should be given so that the workers can solve their daily work problems, and check-ups and additional 'refreshing-the-memory' training should be given.

(4) In most companies some people will become the explicit or implicit local experts for given departments (Scharer, 1983). A system of local experts should be developed by the company because people like to ask other people about the procedures to be taken and because the local expert can stimulate further learning of the system and support the long-range learning effects.

(5) There may be individual differences in the ways people learn. For example, people with low spatial memory are poor in learning line as well as full-screen editors (Gomez and Egan, 1983). People may even differ in their preference for either of the two dimensions of training, stated above. There may be learning strategies that are sequential or integrated–systematic (Veer and Beishuizen, undated). Similarly, some people like just to be active (without reading a lot beforehand) and others want to read a good deal before they start to learn a word-processing system (Frese *et al.*, 1986; Schulte-Göcking, 1987).

In conclusion, there is evidence that training should be action-oriented and should teach an explicit mental model, the training goals should be broader than just teaching the officially described tasks, errors should be minimized in the training process or explicitly taught, overcoming problems of transfer should be an integral part of training, local experts should be encouraged, and individual differences should be taken into consideration.

Optimizing the System

The optimization of system parameters has been the research area to which scientists and human factor workers have contributed most actively. It cannot and shall not be completely summarized here. Obviously, a system has to be compatible with prior mental models, it has to present an obvious system's image and has to be self-explanatory, it has to give clear feedback and decrease mental overload to be useful for the development of an adequate mental model. Furthermore, it has to have a clear layout or mask (Morland, 1983). I shall pick out some issues for discussion here that seem to be of major (and increasing) importance: help facilities, different types of interaction modes, and errors.

Help facilities

Manuals and on-line help systems are usually constructed for the novice. Nevertheless, novices do not use them under 'normal' working conditions (expert users refer to them more often) (Mack, Lewis, and Carroll, 1983; Scharer, 1983). This is not surprising because 'to ask a question, one must know enough to know what is not known' (Miyake and Norman, 1979). It is often the expert's task to help users develop the right questions (Pollak, 1985; McKendree and Carroll, 1986).

Novices frequently do not understand computer jargon, do not know how to get to the appropriate help message, or do not want to plow through a lot of information. Users like to ask their peers for advice (Lang, Auld, and Lang, 1982; O'Malley, 1986); therefore many offices have 'local experts' who have the (sometimes informal) function of providing human help (Bannon, 1986; Scharer, 1983).

Manuals Manuals are not read, warnings are not heeded, even clear recommendations by the computer are sometimes not understood. Sullivan and Chapanis (1983) suggest the following rules for writing manuals: simple language, short and active sentences, order of description parallel to action steps, complete and specific description of action, one thing at a time, headings and subheadings, lists instead of prose. Carroll *et al.* (1986) have suggested a more radical approach. They constructed a 'minimal manual' with a minimum of words, which is directed towards error recognition and error recovery and which is task-oriented. It presupposes that the user will only consult the manual as a starting point. Compared with a commercially available longer manual, this minimal manual leads to better performance, although it does not give advance organizers (Foss, Rosson, and Smith, 1982), it is not complete, and it does not have a clear hierarchical outline.

On-line help systems O'Malley *et al.* (1983) distinguish the following user needs with regard to help functions: quick reference (e.g. verification of a command name), task-specific help (the user knows the problem but not the command for solving it), and full explanation of the capabilities of the system. By and large, on-line help systems usually deal only with the first two needs.

Help facilities may be either passive (the user has to call upon it) or active (the help is initiated and/or selected by the system). Cohill and Williges (1985) studied the effects of help being initiated and selected either by the user or by the system, and whether the help was presented on-line or as hard copy. The best condition was the user initiated and selected help that was printed on hard copy.

Depending upon design, on-line help systems may either be the same for everybody or differ according to the expert level of the user. Help systems that adjust to the user level of expertise can be designed as knowledge-based help systems (Fischer *et al.*, 1985; Dzida, Hoffmann, and Valder, 1984). These help systems may sometimes have the form of excursions that do not change the state of task operations (Darlington, Dzida, and Herda, 1983). One prerequisite for knowledge-based help systems is to develop some kind of user model for the system. Chin (1986) describes an example of how to do this: the system records errors and the difficulty levels of commands used correctly and incorrectly. The records are then compared with some preestablished pattern of errors and command knowledge stored in the system. Thus, the system has an *a priori* categorization for typical errors and levels of competence of novices, beginners, intermediates, and experts. On the basis of this comparison, the system assigns the user to one of these categories and then gives appropriate help (e.g. more explanations to the novice and just a shorthand description to the intermediate (cf. also Williges *et al.*, 1985).

Interaction mode

Usually, users develop their mental models from interacting with a system. Thus, the surface structure of the system is important. There are different modes by which a person can interact with a computer. These interaction modes may be based on menu, command language, natural language, and direct manipulation.

Menu vs. command vs. natural language Conventionally, menu, command language, and natural language systems are differentiated. Menus display the different commands that can be used. They can either pop up when ticked (as in the Macintosh system) or may be displayed more permanently. They can also be embedded in a text which is particularly useful in data systems (Koved and Shneiderman, 1986). They can display icons or commands with a short explanation. Finally, the menus may just display commands and thus help the user to remember the commands. The menu contents may be touched with the help of a mouse, the finger, or a light-pen, or activated by moving the cursor with the keyboard. From a memory point of view, menus allow for recognition rather than for recall which is why menus are easier to learn.

Command language systems, on the other hand, rely on recall. In a pure command language system, the user has to know the different commands (thus, it is similar to a programming language even if just used for word processing). However, these systems are often complemented by named function keys which actually act as menus (this time presented on the keyboard instead of on the screen).

A natural language system is based on our own natural language (e.g. English). We tell the computer in our language what we want it to do. Unfortunately, there are no systems that really understand natural language in a 'natural' way. Thus, the systems that exist are relatively restricted (e.g. they are not able to understand when there is a small typing error in the natural language command). Therefore, it is quite difficult to test the usefulness of different natural language systems. Small and Weldon (1983) used a trick to enable to compare a real natural language system with a command-based system in a query task. In the natural language condition, the user's requests were displayed to another (hidden) human experimenter who interpreted the questions, reacted to the requests, and gave the appropriate answers. Surprisingly, the natural language system did not fare very well. Although it was not less accurate than the command system, it produced slower results.

This may reinforce the skepticism towards natural language approaches. Shneiderman (1980) argues accordingly that constrained natural language systems make for negative transfer from real natural language, that the differences between computers and people get confused, that natural language systems are unreliable and will always be so. The negative transfer effect of natural language commands was observed by Scapin (1981), as well.

Other empirical studies comparing performance with command, menu, and natural language systems do not render entirely consistent results. Hauptmann and Green

(1983) conclude that there are few differences between these systems in the time it takes to operate and in satisfaction because the structure and constraints of the programs wipe out all other effects. The natural language group was most annoyed by the constraints of the commands that they could use. (Examples of how to overcome the problems of constraints in natural language programs are given by Hayes and Reddy, 1983.) Natural language also showed most verbosity (that did not translate into slower work in this study, however).

Comparing command and menu systems that are on the market, Whiteside et al. (1985) found few differences between them. Although their best system turned out to be a command system, other command systems were doing rather badly. Users' attitudes (satisfaction) are in general not a good indicator of performance (Barnard et al., 1981; Frese et al., 1986)—this was also true in the Whiteside et al. study.

It has been argued that menu systems are better for beginners and command language systems better for experts (Nickerson, 1986). However, contrary to this popular wisdom, there is evidence that those systems that are easier to learn are also easier to use for both experts and novices alike (Roberts and Moran, 1983; Whiteside et al., 1985; cf. Stelovsky and Sugaya, 1985, and Norman, 1983b, for the pros and cons of menus and command language systems).

A special topic in command language: naming Two questions are particularly important in designing command languages: how the commands should be named and how they should be abbreviated. (They are, of course, not only relevant in connection with command languages but are especially important here.)

As Carroll (1982) argues and shows empirically, names are never completely arbitrary entities but are paradigmatic—only a certain range of names is possible and a specific name can only stand for a restricted number of objects (or processes). When observing naming behavior for files, 85 per cent were organized into paradigms (like Text1, Text2, etc.). In experiments, congruent names for commands (e.g. up/down, raise/lower, but not up/lower) are better remembered and used more efficiently in problem-solving tasks. The data for 'hierarchicalness' of names are less clear but this issue seems to be less important. Similarly, the 'suggestiveness' of command names plays a crucial role in learning an internal model and for performance accuracy (Rosenberg, 1982).

There are two controversies regarding command names that have not yet been fully resolved: are general terms better than specific ones, and are self-generated terms and abbreviations better than other-generated ones? First, Barnard et al. (1982) showed that specific command names were more efficiently used and produced better memory effects (albeit not all of these differences were significant) than more general names (see also Rosenberg and Moran, 1985, on this topic). Scapin (1982), on the other hand, found the opposite effect.

One of the factors responsible for this contradiction may be the question of self-generation of names. Scapin (1982) used self-generated names, in contrast to the imposed command names used by Barnard et al. (1982). It might be assumed that self-generated names are more easily remembered. However, there are some experiments that show the opposite effect (e.g. Grudin and Barnard, 1985, for abbreviating words). Jones and Landauer (1985) may have resolved this issue: they argue and show experimentally that the advantage of self-generation of names is lost when the subjects do not know anything about the context. Thus, the best naming is done by the person who knows the context and uses a strategy of congruence and consistency. General commands may be better learned under these conditions as well.

A special topic in menu systems: breadth vs. depth   A crucial question is how to arrange a menu. The literature converges on the suggestion that the depth of a menu should not be large (i.e. there should only be a few levels in the menu tree). This speaks for broad menus (Kiger, 1984; Landauer and Nachbar, 1985; Tullis, 1985). But could it be that there is an optimal breadth of menu? Landauer and Nachbar's and Tullis's studies propose that the broader the menu, the better. Kiger's research, on the other hand, calls for an optimality criterion; the breadth should be around eight entries; this is in accord with G. A. Miller's (1956) estimate of the short-term memory capacity.

Direct manipulation   Shneiderman (1982b, 1983a) coined this term to mean a system that continuously represents the object of interest, in which a complex syntax is replaced by physical action, and which makes the impact of incremental operations immediately visible. In other words, 'what you see is what you get'. In contrast to, for example, a command language which gives an abstract representation of the tasks, direct manipulation models the world that a person works on (Hutchins *et al.*, 1986). An example (albeit not necessarily a perfect one) of direct manipulation is the desktop metaphor of the Xerox Star System and Macintosh. A better example is the direct manipulation of data (Hutchins *et al.*, 1986): when a graphic shows that there are two distinct subgroups in a datapool, one subgroup is circled and it, as well as the respective statistics (e.g. the correlation for this subgroup), becomes visible in a second window.

The advantages of direct manipulation are that novices can learn the functions quickly, that work is rapid, error messages are rarely needed, users see immediately whether an action leads to a goal, actions are reversible at any time, and the system is comprehensible (Shneiderman, 1982b). Therefore, the operator feels in control at all times.

A direct manipulation interface has some drawbacks as well. For example, a repetitive operation can be done more easily with a formula (symbolic description), accuracy may be more difficult to achieve with direct manipulation devices, and finally, direct manipulation interfaces give control over objects of goals but not over the program of the computer (Hutchins *et al.*, 1986).

As the Macintosh programs are usually considered to come close to the concept of direct manipulation (e.g. by Fähnrich and Ziegler, 1985), the question arises whether they lead to better performance than, for example, menu systems. This is generally assumed but not frequently shown. The evidence for the superiority of the desktop metaphor is not unequivocal (Dumais and Jones, 1985; Whiteside *et al.*, 1985).

Direct manipulation often implies graphic representations (but note that a full-screen editor is also more direct than a line editor and that graphic *representation* does not necessarily imply direct manipulation. An overview of graphic representation is given by Gorny (1984). In general, graphic representations are of value, as long as a real-world model of the task is useful and functional, and the user is accustomed to this kind of representation (Boecker, Fischer, and Nieper, 1986; Cole, 1986; Powers *et al.*, 1984; Rohr, 1984; Widdel and Kaster, 1985; see also Preece's, 1983, critical discussion).

Errors and treatment of errors

Within his action-theoretic approach, Norman (1984b) distinguishes slips from mistakes. Slips are inappropriate actions, where the intention was correct (example: a person inadvertently deletes a whole file without wanting to). Slips can occur because of faulty activation of schemata (an example is the capture error: a person who wants to change his coat in the bedroom, undresses and goes to bed) and from faulty triggering of active schemata (Norman, 1981).

Mistakes are caused by inappropriate intentions (example: a person wanted to delete a file and finds out afterwards that she still needs it). The concept of mistakes is related to inefficiency of action (see Schönpflug, 1985; Semmer and Frese, 1985), since we often label something as a mistake when the goal is not achieved as fast and with as little effort as would have been possible. Another aspect of mistake is misdiagnosis that is enhanced by a tendency to search only for confirming evidence and to use partial explanations (Norman, 1984b).

In human–computer interaction, most 'errors' are not really human errors at all but are due to the inability of the computer program to decipher unclear commands (Lewis and Norman, 1986). To make matters worse, many programs give error messages that the user is not able to understand (examples in Lewis and Norman, 1986). There are two ways to deal with human 'errors':

1. Avoid errors. Direct manipulation is one way to avoid errors. It is also possible to program for errors, e.g. small misspellings of commands are 'understood' by the system. Additionally, a system may facilitate the retrieval of a document name by allowing the user to recall those parts of the name that he still remembers — e.g. when he had stored it, when he last worked on it — or the approximate name (Branscomb and Thomas, 1984). If the system gives clear feedback (e.g. in which mode a user is working and is consistent, fewer errors develop (Lewis and Norman, 1986).
2. Give adequate feedback when errors have happened. Dean (1982) and Shneiderman (1982a) give recommendations (see also Isa *et al.*, 1983). At the very least, error messages should be polite and constructive, specific and oriented towards the user.

INDIVIDUAL DIFFERENCES

Although we can be quite confident that individual differences play a role in human–computer interaction, there is yet little systematic research. Therefore, we cannot tell with certainty which person variables are particularly important (Muylwijk, Veer, and Waern, 1983; Veer *et al.*, 198). Likely candidates are cognitive styles (Robertson, 1985), action styles (Frese, Stewart, and Hannover, in press), and learning styles. For example, one would hypothesize that the kinds of errors made by impulsive workers (errors of commision) would be different from those made by reflective workers (errors of omission). An impulsive worker may need an 'undo' command more often than a reflective worker. Similarly, the action styles of planfulness and goal-orientation (Frese *et al.*, in press) might influence which strategy is preferred. A highly planful person wants to lay out the plan of work beforehand, a person with low planfulness will start right away, completing the plan as he goes; differences in preferences for planning tools will depend upon planfulness. Finally, learning strategies can be more holistic or more serialistic (Pask and Scott, 1972), or can be oriented towards learning by doing (without looking at a manual) vs. learning by studying manuals first (Frese *et al.*, 1986; Schulte-Göcking, 1987). It has been argued that, in a way, these different strategies and styles call for differences in 'metacommunication' between human and computer (Veer *et al.*, 1985).

It is important to note that these styles and strategies should not only be considered as independent or intervening variables, but also as potentially dependent variables. Work can have a socializing effect (Frese, 1982), e.g. increasing planfulness, goal-orientation, reflectiveness, and algorithmic thinking.

Additionally, it has been suggested that work be organized differentially to fit the particular needs, styles, and concepts of the worker. This should not be thought of as a static concept in which some expert prescribes each person's adequate design, but as a dynamic process in which the individual develops and adapts the work situation (Ulich, 1983). Thus, this concept is related to the issue of control. With the advent of computer systems, an individualized path to work design seems to be more feasible than with traditional technology (Ulich, 1986). This implies that the system gives options. Aside from the default option (which may be particularly useful for the novice), the program should permit choices for how to do a task and which tools to use when. It should also be possible to 'reprogram' the system. Reprogramming does not mean that the source program is changed but that adaptations of the programs to one's individual needs are easily made. This implies, of course, that the user has learned the skills for 'reprogramming'. Moreover, individualization can imply that one can develop certain individualized paths of skill development at the workplace. While the latter suggestion may sound a bit utopian, there are indications in the literature that individualizing work increases work efficiency (Ackermann, 1986; Geiselman and Samet, 1982; Sasso, 1985; Zülch and Starringer, 1984).

GUIDELINES FOR HUMAN–COMPUTER INTERACTION AND THE DESIGN PROCESS

The Design Process

It has been repeatedly suggested that the interface design be radically separated from the design of the system *per se* (Branscomb and Thomas, 1984; Norman, 1983a). This makes it possible to change the interface design without having to change the whole system; thus, it can be improved after more knowledge on interface design has been accumulated. Furthermore, the design of the interface demands different skills from those required for the design of the system *per se* and might, therefore, be produced by different programmers.

However, this recommendation is not heeded very often. Moreover, most designers know very little about ergonomic considerations (Gould and Lewis, 1983) and use them even less. This is not just a 'bad' attitude towards the importance of psychology and human factors; there are also systematic reasons. Besides the obvious problems that there are technical constraints of limited memory and processing capacity, that designers work under very high time pressure, and that they usually are not really quite finished with the products in their own terms when the products are installed or arrive on the market (e.g. a product that still has bugs is thrown on the market), there are psychological constraints. The designers have difficulties in putting themselves into the shoes of the user, because the designers' tasks are different from those of the user (also the designer usually does not know much about the user's tasks; Smith and Mosier, 1984). Because of this, the qualifications and mental models of the designer are different as well.

The designer has a certain model in her mind of the system to be built. She then produces a system with a certain 'image'. It is this image that the user builds his model from (Norman, 1986a). The difficulty is that the user cannot directly perceive what the designer really meant, and problems could creep in while transforming the designer's model into a system and transforming the system's image into a user's model. (Hooper, 1986, actually uses the analogy of 'false façade' to characterize the image.) This issue becomes even more complicated when the psychologist enters the field and produces his own model of the system, of the user's model of the designer's model, etc. (Streitz, 1985). The designer and the user often do not both come up with that model of the system which is necessary to guarantee the functioning of the system. One important reason for this is that models are developed for certain tasks but the designer works on a different task from that of the user. This leads (again) to the demand that the user should be given high control over the system's functioning. In that case, the individual is able to adapt the system to his own model (and his own tasks), reducing the potential differences between the designer's model and his own (Greenberg and Witten, 1985; Huddleston, 1984; Raum, 1984; Rich, 1983; Ulich and Troy, 1986).

A variant of the differences between mental models is the fact that designers usually think about system-immanent problems (their tasks). The user on the other hand does not care about the system *per se* but only about its usefulness for doing his job. For example, the designer may emphasize a clean and logical structure of the program and the menus; but this 'cleanness' that the designer is proud of may actually impede the user's work because he has to plow through a lot of unnecessary menus (Hammond *et al.*, 1983). In addition to the designer being an expert in something different, the designer's expertise itself can have negative repercussions for the design process. Experts are usually bad teachers of novices because they have automized many procedures and are not able to verbalize them adequately, much less understand potential problems that a novice might have with them.

For all these reasons, psychology has to provide aids for the designers. There are essentially five approaches to help in the design of a program for human users; they are, of course, not mutually exclusive: (1) providing a set of quantitative psychological laws; (2) prototyping; (3) including the user in the design team; (4) providing theories, metaphors and analogies for the design; (5) giving guidelines and standards with a discussion of trade-offs. The last is probably the most important one and will therefore be considered separately and in a little more detail.

The first approach — providing a set of *quantitative laws* — has been suggested and followed by Card *et al.* (1983). This approach has several drawbacks from an industrial psychological point of view:

a. It is a question of whether their model can be adequately applied to the workplace. Just a single emotion (e.g. anger that the sequence of operations is prescribed in detail) would add an immeasurable amount of time to the postulated times for the cognitive processes. Similarly, a high-level goal, e.g. not wanting to work with a computer, has an impact on each low-level keystroke.

b. The low-level nature of their analysis and their little concern for ecological validity may lead to the wrong conclusions. Since they actually suppose that they have covered a large part of human–computer interaction, the lack of completeness of their approach is problematic. In their keystroke model, there is no systematic consideration of errors, 'nor are preferences for alternative command names, errors induced by complex command syntax, unusual sequencing of subtasks, comprehensibility of screen displays or menu structures, effectiveness of errors messages, help facilities, or documentation' considered (Shneiderman, 1984b, p. 236).

c. Since so many pieces for an applied science are missing, there is an aura of pseudo-exactness in their quantitative approach. Since quantitative approaches are preferred by computer scientists, this may lead to using those recommendations that are based on quantitative laws at the expense of other issues.

d. The emphasis is one-sided. The shortest possible command string (that follows from their model) may ignore issues of comprehensibility and memorability (Shneiderman, 1984b). Important (and high-level) design questions, such as why direct manipulation may be better than a simple command language approach, cannot be treated within their approach. It is also difficult to discuss trade-offs within their concepts (e.g. the trade-off between speed of work and creativity).

e. Productivity is seen primarily as a question of how many keystrokes or how many processors are involved. This implies a very short-term efficiency model which is typical of Taylor (1911) and Gilbreth (1919) and which does not take into account long-term needs. Thus, problems that are potentially associated with lower-level solutions may ensue; e.g. reducing the complexity of work may increase monotony (Greif and Holling, 1986).

f. Card *et al.* (1983) may have a wrong conception of the design process itself. Carroll and Rosson (1984) describe the design process as being neither in Card *et al.*'s sense top-down (using a general conception, e.g. a task description or a general law of psychology first and then delineating the steps from it) nor bottom-up (solving parts of the problem and then combining them into a whole), but as a mixture of all possible procedures. This often leads to a rejection of all solutions that had been entertained at the beginning of the design process.

Note that these points of critique do not call into question Card *et al.*'s substantive contributions in their specific areas. Obviously the level of analysis must depend on the question that is asked. If the research question is to design a keyboard then their model may be quite adequate. If the question is to integrate the computer in the workplace, their model is not so useful.

The (rapid) *prototyping* approach (e.g. Budde *et al.*, 1984; Gould and Lewis, 1983; Floyd, 1984; Richards, Boies, and Gould, 1986; Wixon *et al.*, 1983) is advantageous as it explicates potential user problems with the design at a very early stage of the game, thus enabling the designer to change the design and then test it again. Jörgensen (1984) argues for prototyping because designing a system is so complicated that one is never able to predict whether the system is satisfactory without empirically checking it. This presupposes, of course, that the relevant features are included in the prototype and that the relevant group of users is tested. Furthermore, a set of 'benchmark' tests or acceptance tests has to be developed (Carroll and Rosson, 1984; Roberts and Moran, 1983; Shneiderman, 1983b). Prototyping is an iterative process — a successive approximation to some goal (or benchmark). However, note that the iterative design process often includes changing one's goals (Carroll and Rosson, 1984). Although prototyping can be done without much theory behind it, it is useful to provide a background theory to analyze the results and draw the right conclusion from the evaluation of the prototype.

Potential pitfalls of this approach are that the prototypes are usually tested in an artificial context and that the prototype typically lacks certain necessary functions. Moreover, there is some debate whether users are really competent in providing ideas about good designs (Jörgensen, 1984).

Including the user in the design team is certainly one of the best ways to increase control for the user, to enhance mutual understanding between users and designers, and to ensure that the system is functional. Rapid prototyping is one form of inclusion, but including the user in the design team is another one. Potential drawbacks of this approach are that many users do not know the potentials of the computer, that the software is often designed for many different groups of users, and that the user may be too much concerned about her (novice) status now to suggest design ideas that will help her (as an expert) later.

Theories, metaphors, and analogies can aid the designer to use the right approaches — even if the 'nitty-gritty' of design is not explicated. Several analogies are discussed in Norman and Draper's (1986) book, e.g. architecture or theater. Two types of theories have been particularly useful for design consideration: keystroke theories (Card *et al.*, 1983; Hammer and Rouse, 1982; Schiele and Pelz, 1985) and action theories (Frese & Sabini, 1985; Hacker, 1985; Norman, 1986a; Rasmussen, 1983).

Guidelines

Guidelines and checklists are the most important aids for designers because they can orient the designer to the major problems and solutions of a user-centered design. These guidelines must be firmly rooted in psychological theory and research. There are now many published guidelines for improving different aspects of human-computer interaction (e.g. Branscomb and Thomas, 1984; Davis and Swezey, 1983; Döbele-Berger, Martin, and Martin, 1984; Dzida, 1985; Engel and Granada, 1975; Hannemyr and Innocent, 1985; Maguire, 1982; Spinas, Troy, and Ulich, 1983; Williges and Williges, 1983; Ulich, 1985). It is impossible to discuss them all or even a good number of them. Instead, I want, first, to suggest a hierarchy of guidelines and then to focus on one set of guidelines that have stirred up some controversies recently — the German suggestions for DIN Standards on the design of the human-computer dialogue.

A hierarchy of guidelines

The various guidelines discuss recommendations on quite different levels. It is, therefore, useful to provide some hierarchy among these guidelines as suggested in Table 5.2 (space constraints do not allow me to spell out the mesolevel and microlevel guidelines).

The assumption of Table 5.2 is that system design should be seen within the overall organizational framework. There should be participation in the introductory process. the organization should be decentralized so that more decisions can be made at each individual workplace; similarly, this applies to control over organizational decision making. Training needs to be adequate. Finally, it is a basic organizational decision which approach is taken *vis-à-vis* division of labor. From the standpoint of industrial psychology, the demand is put forward that the division of labor between the machine and human and between workers should be jointly optimized. This is, of course, an old demand of the sociotechnical approach (Emery and Thorsrud, 1976; Pava, 1983).

TABLE 5.2 — The Hierarchy of Guidelines

Tier 1:   Organizational Level
— Participation in the introductory process
— Decentralization
— Control over organizational decision
— Adequate training
— Overall optimization of the human–human division and the human–computer division of labor
Tier 2:   Workplace Level
— Practicability
— No damage to health or reduction of wellbeing
— Providing for social interactions
— Enhancement of personality
Tier 3:   Task Level
— Variety
— Task significance
— Task identity
— Controllability over task decisions
— Learning potential
Tier 4:   Macrocriteria for Computer Systems (short-term/long-term)
— Functionality
— Usability
— User friendliness
Tier 5:   Mesocriteria for Computer Systems
Example I: Specific criterion for usability: error reduction, error tolerance
Example II: Controllability
Tier 6:   Microcriteria for Computer Systems
Example I: System understands synonyms for commands, provides an 'undo' command
Example II: Default option plus easy change of layout, function keys, order of menus, menu content, reminders, command names, etc.

This means that division of labor should be reduced to allow higher variety, task significance and identity, controllability, and increase of learning potential. At each point, the question should be asked whether a technical decision has repercussions for the division of labor. This stands in contrast to just optimizing the technical subsystem—without regard to the workers involved.

Design should take into consideration the workplace as a whole. Therefore, the four criteria (suggested by different authors, e.g. Hacker, 1978; Ulich, 1986) of a good workplace are of importance. (By the way, we do not assume that the criteria suggested are orthogonal; they most probably correlate considerably and have a large overlap.) Practicability implies that the workplace is organized in such a way that the tasks can be accomplished (Hacker, 1978)—in a way, this is the workplace equivalent of the functionality of a computer system. The second criterion is that the workplace should not damage the workers' health (including psychosocial health) nor reduce their wellbeing. This issue is, of course, related to stress at work. A long-term stress at work (and low resources) may lead to ill-health and reduction of wellbeing. This is similarly true of lack of social interactions at the workplace. Finally, the workplace should allow one to advance one's personality (Hacker, 1978). Since the workplace has an influence on workers' intelligence and creativity, emotional growth and growth of self-confidence, and active (or passive) approaches to life (Frese, 1982), workplace design can be seen as enhancing (or thwarting) personality growth.

Four of the five criteria of the design of tasks are related to Hackman and Oldham's (1975) criteria for job motivation. Task variety signifies that different tasks (requiring different skills) are performed; task identity means that the worker completes a 'whole piece' of work rather than a meaningless part; task significance implies that the task is important for other people (or other people's work); controllability (Hackman and Oldham call it autonomy) refers to being able to decide on the content of the subtasks, on the order of the tasks, on the methods for solving the tasks, and on the timeframe in which to do the tasks. Finally, learning potential means that the tasks should be reasonably complex and should thus allow one to develop one's abilities and skills.

Roughly, the macrocriteria for the design of computer systems (Tier 4) can be grouped into three categories: Functionality, usability, and user friendliness. Each of them can have a short-term and a long-term meaning. (Of course, there is again an overlap between these different categories—often a functional system is easier to use and might have positive consequences to the user—but there are also differences.)

Functionality refers to whether a computer program allows and enhances the completion of the task. Thus, this term is oriented to the task outside the computer system. A short-term issue of functionality is, for example, whether the computer system models real-world tasks. A long-term issue is whether the user can redesign the system to fit the specifics of the tasks better (controllability) or whether the system can be adjusted to different approaches to the tasks. Some programs are high in functionality because they help to do the job, and low in usability, perhaps because of a bad command language (e.g. early spreadsheet programs; cf. Norman, 1986a).

Usability refers to whether the system is hard or easy to use. Examples of design issues of usability are tolerance of user errors, what kind of feedback the system gives, and whether it is consistent, self-explanatory, and corresponds to users' expectations (see also Shackel, 1985b). In the short term, the issue of learnability is important. In the long run, adaptability to one's own style of working may be more important. It should be emphasized that the test of whether a system is usable has to be performed at the workplace, and not in the laboratory. For rather subtle reasons, the use of an apparently good system may be rejected (Eason, 1984).

Although this is not usually done, usability should be conceptually differentiated from *user friendliness* which means literally that the system is 'friendly' towards the user, i.e. that the system has no long- or short-term negative effects but positive effects on the user (it might also be liked best). A user-friendly system should not produce stress. The long-term effect is related to wellbeing and personality enhancement. For a short-term measure, human factor workers have frequently employed user satisfaction scales. However, user satisfaction is usually measured in a rather superficial manner. It would be productive to follow Bruggemann, Groskurth, and Ulich's (1975) suggestions on differentiating levels of satisfaction: (1) progressive satisfaction in which the level of aspiration of what the system should look like is increased; (2) stabilized satisfaction (level of aspiration is kept constant); (3) resigned satisfaction (level of aspiration is lowered to fit the system); (4) pseudo-satisfaction in which defense mechanisms prevail; (5) fixated dissatisfaction (dissatisfaction but no attempt to change the situation); and (6) constructive dissatisfaction in which the level of aspiration is kept up but one tries to change the system to match the aspirations.

We are not able to fully discuss Tiers 5 and 6 of the hierarchy because hundreds of recommendations apply at these levels. The examples may suffice. Error reduction is a more specific criterion of usability (and is related to functionality). Error reduction is achieved when synonyms for commands are recognized by the computer system and when there is an 'undo' command. Controllability may be related to functionality, usability, and user friendliness. Examples for controllability on the microlevel are given in Table 5.2.

The importance of presenting the guidelines as a hierarchical model is that each of these lower-level criteria can and should be related to the upper-level criteria. This underscores again the importance of organizational decisions.

The German guidelines on the human–computer dialogue

If the German suggestions for guidelines (DIN 66 234, part 8, 1984; see also Dzida, 1985, and Paetau, 1985) are approved officially, it will be one of the first attempts to nationally streamline the human factors consideration of software and encourage industry to respond. The standards are partly based on a study by Dzida, Herda, and Itzfeldt (1978). They have stirred up some controversies, since it is argued that it is too early to propose standards that might lead to inflexible use (e.g. Smith, 1986). The following five standards have been proposed—each one described by way of many examples: (1) task adequateness, which supports doing a task without adding load through system characteristics; (2) self-explanatory, i.e. the system is either immediately understandable or (full or partial) explanations are given on request; (3) user controllability, which implies that the user can modify the speed, and has a say in the number and the order of tools and the way the tasks are handled; (4) reliability, which means consistency with user expectations and internal consistency; and (5) error tolerance and transparency, i.e. the system accepts small errors and it explains when errors have occurred.

These standards clearly refer to different levels in the above hierarchy but they can be related to the criteria for a good workplace. Unlike some other German standards, these standards are relatively loose guidelines that are supposed to be optimized depending upon tasks and user groups. This stands in contrast to Smith's (1986) worries that they would lead to inflexibility. Obviously, there are trade-offs when applying these recommendations, as is true of all guidelines (Norman, 1983b). For example, a self-explanatory system may lack controllability since a system with maximal controllability can be changed into a new system that could not be predicted by the programmer (and thus no self-explanatory tools could be developed). Although these guidelines are supplemented by examples, designers may have difficulties using them, as is true of other guidelines (Mosier and Smith, 1986). It would be useful to develop data bases that could counsel the designers on each of their design tasks.

CONCLUSION

In this review the five major areas of interest to industrial and organizational psychology — organizational conditions, stress, cognitive optimization of human — computer interaction, individual differences, and design suggestions — have been summarized. The major conclusion has been that issues of human–computer interaction cannot and should not be separated from organizational issues. In the last analysis, organizational decisions on how the computer is used will contribute towards either positive or negative consequences in the employment of new technology. However, there is a sequel to this general statement: if the organization should, for example, decide on increasing control *vis-à-vis* a system, the question arises as to whether such a system exists and what should be the parameters of its design. Therefore, it is necessary that issues like control are taken seriously on each level — on the organizational level, the workplace level, the task level, and the levels of software ergonomics (macrocriteria, mesocriteria, and microcriteria for computer systems), and that concrete design suggestions are developed.

Unfortunately, as it turns out, organizational decisions are constrained less often by technology than by the marketing strategies of the hardware-producing companies (Cakir, 1981) and by restrictive conceptualizations of balancing costs and benefits. For example, when hardware was expensive, separate and centralized word-processing units were pushed by the producers and were estimated to be profitable. However, as pointed out by the economist Reichwald (1982), this 'profitability' turned out to be high only when the number of keystrokes was used as sole criterion of productivity. When other aspects were included — such as an increase in the total organizational time it takes to finish a letter, an increase in mistakes and in complicated and bureaucratic procedures, a reduction in the efficiency of specialists, etc. — centralized word-processing units are no longer seen to increase productivity. Developing national guidelines for software design, as in the Federal Republic of Germany, may enlarge our concept of cost–benefit analysis and encourage the production of adequate software that allows for different options and is functional, usable, and user friendly.

What can we say about the so-called 'big' controversies with which we started our review? From the perspective of industrial and organizational psychology, high-level (molar) approaches seem to be more adequate. However, low-level approaches can also be useful as long as they are subsumed under an overall organizational approach to the workplace.

The issue of control at work and controllability of the sytem is of high importance since control plays a role at the organizational level, the workplace and tasks levels, and each level of human–computer design. Furthermore, controllability has an impact not only on stress-effects, but also on performance and on the creativity with which an organization can accommodate to new environmental demands or to technological changes. Since it is likely that technological changes will be more frequent in the future, controllability for the individual workers has an ever more important function in the survival of industrial organizations.

The question of whether computers are seen as tools or as something beyond them may be dependent on the factor of controllability. If the computer is controllable and if the division of labor between human and machine is organized so that the human is firmly in control of the important procedures, decisions, and timeframes, it is more likely that the computer will be perceived as a tool. However, should controllability be reduced, then the computer is not a tool for those people who work with it, but only for the masters in the background. In such a case, stronger resistance introducing and using computers at the workplace is a more likely result.

This review has shown that we have already accumulated a fair amount of knowledge on some low-level issues of software design, but that these issues have to be integrated into a larger framework. Thus, it is necessary to develop an industrial and organizational psychology of computer use, system design, and integration of system design into an overall organizational design, so that we can minimize negative consequences of computer use and optimize productive and creative use of this powerful tool.

ACKNOWLEDGEMENTS

Thanks are due to L. Beerman, F. Glover, H. Gstalter, W. Kannheiser, J. Lang, and B. Zang for reading an earlier draft of the chapter and giving very useful suggestions.

REFERENCES

Ackermann, D. (1986). A pilot study on the effects of individualization in man–computer interaction. *Proceedings of the 2nd IFAC/IFIP/IFORS/IEA conference on analysis, design and evaluation. Varese.* London: Pergamon.

Anderson, J. R. (1983). *The Architecture of Cognition.* Cambridge, Massachusetts: Harvard University Press.

Baecker, R., Marcus, A. (1986). Design principles for the enhanced presentation of computer program source text. *Proceedings of the CHI '86 Conference on Human Factors in Computing Systems* (pp. 51–58). Boston.

Baitsch, C. (1986). Designing attempt 2: Personnel administration in private industry. In E. Ulich (ed.), *Computer-aided Office Work* (pp. 29–35). Zürich: ETH, Lehrstuhl für Arbeits- und Organisationspsychologie.

Balzert, H. (ed.) (1983). Software Ergonomie. *Berichte des German chapter of the ACM*. Stuttgart: Teubner.

Bannon, L. J. (1986). Helping users help another. In D. A. Norman and S. W. Draper (eds.), *User Centered Systems Design*. San Diego: Erlbaum.

Barnard, P. J., Hammond, N. V., MacLean, A., and Morton, J. (1982). Learning and remembering interactive commands in a text-editing task. *Behaviour and Information Technology*, **1**, 347-358.

Barnard, P. J., Hammond, N. V., Morton, J., and Long, J. B. (1981). Consistency and compatibility in human-computer dialogue. *International Journal of Man-Machine Studies*, **15**, 87-134.

Baroudi, J. J., Olson, M. H., and Ives, B. (1986). An empirical study of the impact of user involvement on system usage and information satisfaction. *Communications of the ACM*, **29**, 232-242.

Bartlett, F. C. (1932). *Remembering: A Study in Experimental and Social Psychology*. Melbourne: Cambridge University Press.

Bayman, P., and Mayer, R. E. (1984). Instructional manipulation of users' mental models for electronic calculators. *International Journal of Man-Machine Studies*, **20**, 189-199.

Benbasat, I., and Wand, Y. (1984). A structured approach to designing human-computer dialogues. *International Journal of Man-Machine Studies*, **21**, 105-126.

Bennett, J., Case, D., Sandelin, J., and Smith, M. (1984). *Visual Display Terminals: Usability Issues and Health Concerns*. Englewood Cliffs: Prentice Hall.

Bikson, T. K., and Gutek, B. A. (1983). Advanced office systems: An empirical look at use and satisfaction. *AFIPS Conference proceedings, National Computer Conference* (pp. 319-327).

Bjorn-Andersen, N. (1983). The changing roles of secretaries and clerks. In H. J. Otway and M. Peltu (eds.), *New Office Technology: Human and Organizational Aspects* (pp. 120-137). London: Frances Pinter.

Bjorn-Andersen, N., Eason, K., and Robey, D. (1986). *Managing Computer Impact: An International Study of Management and Organization*. Norwood, New Jersey: Ablex.

Bjorn-Andersen, N., Hedberg, B., Mercer, D., Mumford, E., and Sole, A. (1979). *The Impact of Systems Change in Organizations*. Alphen: Sijthoff and Noordhoff.

Bjorn-Andersen, N., and Rasmussen, L. B. (1980). Social implications of computer systems. In H. T. Smith and T. R. G. Green (eds.), *Human Interaction with Computers* (pp. 98-123). London: Academic Press.

Bjorn-Andersen, N. (1985). Training for subjection or participation. In B. Shackel (ed.), *Human-Computer Interaction* (pp. 839-846). Amsterdam: Elsevier.

Blauner, R. (1964). *Alienation and Freedom: The Factory Worker and His Industry*. Chicago: University of Chicago Press.

Boecker, H. D., Fischer, G., and Nieper, H. (1986). The enhancement of understanding through visual representations. *Proceedings of the CHI '86 Conference on Human Factors in Computing Systems* (pp. 44-50). Boston.

Boddy, D., and Buchanan, D. A. (1982). Information technology and the experience of work. In L. Bannon, U. Barry and O. Holst (eds.), *Information Technology* (pp. 144-157). Dublin: Tycooly International.

Boies, S., Wood, W., and Zimmer, W. (1986). Managing the design of user-computer interfaces. *Proceedings of the CHI '86 Conference on Human Factors in Computing Systems* (pp. 340-342). Boston.

Borman, L., and Curtis, B. (eds.) (1985). *Proceedings of the CHI '85 Conference on Human Factors in Computing Systems*. San Francisco.

Boucsein, W., Greif, S., and Wittekamp, J. (1984). Systemresponsezeiten als Belastungsfaktor bei Bildschirm-Dialogtätigkeiten. *Zeitschrift für Arbeitswissenschaft*, **38**, 113-122.

Boulay, du, B., and O'Shea, T. (1981). Teaching novices programming. In M. J. Coombs and J. L. Alty (eds.) *Computing Skills and User Interface* (pp. 147-201). NY: Academic Press.

Branscomb, L. M., and Thomas, J. C. (1984). Ease of use. A system challenge. *IBM Systems Journal*, **23**, 224-235.

Briefs, U., Ciborra, C., and Schneider, L. (eds.) (1983). *Systems Design for, with, and by the Users*. Amsterdam: North-Holland.

Brown, J. S. (1986). From cognitive to social ergonomics and beyond. In D. A. Norman and S. W. Draper (eds.), *User Centered Systems Design*. Hillsdale, Erlbaum.

Bruggemann, A., Groskurth. P., and Ulich, E. (1975). *Arbeitszufriedenheit*. Wien: Huber.

Buchanan, D. A., and Boddy, D. (1982). Advanced technology and the quality of working life: The effects of word processing on video typists. *Journal of Occupational Psychology*, **55**, 1-11.

Budde, R., Kuhlenkamp, K., Mathiassen, L., and Züllighoven, H. (1984). *Approaches to Prototyping*. Berlin: Springer.

Bullinger, H.-J. (ed.) (1985). *Software-Ergonomie '85*. Stuttgart: Teubner.

Cakir, A. (1981). Belastung und Beanspruchung bei Bildschirmtätigkeiten. In Frese, M. (ed.) *Stress im Büro* (pp. 46-71). Bern: Huber.

Cakir, A. (1986). Short paper towards an ergonomic design of software. *Behaviour and Information Technology*, **5**, 63-70.

Cakir, A. (ed.) (1983). *Bildschirmarbeit*. Berlin: Springer.

Cakir, A., Hart, D. J., and Stewart, T. F. M. (1979). *The VDT manual: Ergonomics, Workplace Design, Health and Safety, Task Organization*. Darmstadt: IFRA.

Card, S. K., Moran, T. P., and Newell, A. (1983). *The Psychology of Human–Computer Interaction*. Hilladale, NJ: Erlbaum.

Carroll, J. M. (1982). Learning, using and designing filenames and command paradigms. *Behaviour and Information Technology*, **1**, 327-346.

Carroll, J. M. (1984). *Mental Models and Software Human Factors: An Overview*. Yorktown NY: IBM Watson Research Center RC 10616.

Carroll, J. M. (1986). Science is soft at the frontier. *Talk at the ACM conference CHI '86*. Boston.

Carroll, J. M. and Carrithers, C. (1984). Training wheels in a user interface. *Communications of the ACM*, **27**, 800-806.

Carroll, J. M., and Mack, R. L. (1983). Actively learning to use a word processor. In W. E. Cooper (ed.), *Cognitive Aspects of Skilled Typewriting*. New York: Springer.

Carroll, J. M., and Mack, R. L. (1984). Learning to use a word processor: By doing, by thinking, and by knowing. In J. C. Thomas and M. L. Schneider (eds.), *Human Factors in Computer Systems* (pp. 13-51). Norwood, New Jersey: Ablex.

Carroll, J. M., Mack, R. L., Grischkowsky, N. L., and Robertson, S. R. (1985). Exploring exploring a word processor. *Human–Computer Interaction*, **1**, 283-307.

Carroll, J. M., and Mazur, S. A. (1985). *LisaLearning*. Yorktown: IBM Watson Research Center RC 11427.

Carroll, J. M., and Rosson, M. B. (1984). Usability specifications as a tool in development. In H. R. Hartson (ed.), *Advances in Human-Computer Interaction*. Norwood: Ablex Publishing.

Carroll, J. M., and Rosson, M. B. (in press). Paradox of the active user. In J. M. Carroll (ed.), *Interfacing Thought: Cognitive Aspects of Human–Computer Interaction*. Bradford Books/MIT Press.

Carroll, J. M., Smith-Kerker, P. L., Ford, J. R. and Mazur, S. A. (1986). *The Minimal Manual*. Yorktown: IBM Watson Research Center RC 11637.

Carroll, J. M., and Thomas, J. C. (1982). Metaphor and the cognitive representation of computing systems. *IEEE Transactions on Systems, Man, and Cybernetics*, **12**, 107-116.

Cashman, P. M. (1985). *Interfaces in organizations. Supporting Group Work*. San Francisco: Talk at the ACM conference CHI '85.

Chin, D. N. (1986). User modeling in UC, the UNIX consultant. *Proceedings of the CHI '86 Conference on Human Factors in Computing Systems*. Boston.

Coch, L., and French, J. R. P. (1948). Overcoming resistance to change. *Human Relations*, **19**, 39-56.

Coe, J. B., Cuttle, K., McClellon, W. C., Warden, N. J., and Turner, P. J. (1980). *Visual Display Units: A Review of Potential Problems Associated with their Use.* Wellington: New Zealand Department of Health.

Cohill, A. M., and Williges, R. C. (1985). Retrieval of HELP information for novice users of interactive computer systems. *Human Factors*, **27**, 335-343.

Cole, W. G. (1986). Medical cognitive graphics. *Proceedings of the CHI '86 Conference on Human Factors in Computing Systems* (pp. 91-95). Boston.

Coombs, M., and Alty, J. (1984). Expert systems: An alternative paradigm. *International Journal of Man-Machine Studies*, **20**, 21-43.

Cooper, C. L., and Marshall, J. (1976). Occupational sources of stress: A review of the literature relating to coronary heart disease and mental ill health. *Journal of Occupational Psychology*, **49**, 11-28.

Corbett, J. M. (1985). Prospective work design of human-centred CNC lathe. *Behaviour and Information Technology*, **4**, 201-214.

Cornelius, D. (1985). Scenario: Büro 1990. *Arbeitswissenschaft für Arbeitnehmer.* Düsseldorf: Deutscher Gewerkschaftsbund.

Dainhoff, M. J. (1982). Occupational stress factors in visual display terminal (VDT) operation: A review of empirical research. *Behaviour and Information Technology*, **1**, 141-176.

Dainoff, M. (1984). A model for human efficiency: Relating health, comfort and performance in the automated office workstation. In G. Salvendy (ed.), *Human Computer Interaction* (pp. 355-360). Amsterdam, Holland: Elsevier.

Dainoff, M. J., Happ, A., and Crane, P. (1981). Visual fatigue and occupational stress in VDT operators. *Human Factors*, **23**, 421-438.

Darlington, J., Dzida, W., and Herda, S. (1983). The role of excursions in interactive systems. *International Journal of Man-Machine Studies*. **18**, 101-112.

Davis, E. G., and Swezey, R. W. (1983). Human factors guidelines in computer graphics: A case study. *International Journal of Man-Machine Studies*, **18**, 113-133.

De Brabander, B., Vanlommel, E., Deschoolmeester, D., and Leyder, R. (1981). The impact of computer-use on organisation structure. In B. Shackel (ed.), *Man-Computer Interaction* (pp. 309-346). Dordrecht: Sigthoff and Noordhoff.

Dean, M. (1982). How a computer should talk to people. *IBM Systems Journal*, **21**, 424-453.

Dieckhoff, K., Dieckhoff, J., and Roth, V. (1982). Soziale Aspekte des technisch-organisatorischen Wandels in der Textverarbeitung. In Institut für angewandte Arbeitswissenschaft (ed.) *Folgewirkungen neuer Technologien in der Textverarbeitung.* Köln: Institut für angewandte Arbeitswissenschaft.

DIN 66 234 Teil 8 Entwurf (1984). *Bildschirmarbeitsplätze*: Grundsätze der Dialoggestaltung. (Deutsches Institut für Normung).

diSessa, A. A. (1986). Models of computation. In D. A. Norman and S. W. Draper (eds.), *User Centered Systems Design.* Hillsdale: Erlbaum.

Döbele-Berger, C., Martin, H., and Martin, P. (1984) *Gestaltung von Bildschirmmasken — Ableitung einer Checkliste.* Fachgebiet Arbeitswissenschaft, Gesamthochschule Kassel.

Douglas, S. A., and Moran, T. P. (1983). Learning text editor semantics by analogy. *Proceedings of the CHI '85 Conference on Human Factors in Computing Systems* (pp. 207-211). Boston.

Driscoll, J. W. (1982). How to humanize office automation. *Office: Technology and People*, **1**, 167-176.

Dumais, S. T., and Jones, W. P. (1985). A comparison of symbolic and spatial filing. *Proceedings of the CHI '85 Conference on Human Factors in Computing Systems* (pp. 127-130). San Francisco.

Dzida, W. (1985). Ergonomische Normen für die Dialoggestaltung. Wem nützen die Gestaltungsgrundsätze im Entwurf DIN 66234, Teil 8? In H.-J. Bullinger (ed.), *Software Ergonomie '85* (pp. 430-444). Stuttgart: Teubner.

Dzida, W., Herda, S., and Itzfeldt, W. D. (1978). User-perceived quality of interactive systems. *IEEE Transactions on Software Engineering SE-4*, 270-276.

Dzida, W., Hoffmann, C., and Valder, W. (1984). Wissensbasierte Dialogunterstützung. In H. Schauer and M. J. Tauber (eds.), *Psychologie der Computerbenutzung* (pp. 164-210). Wien: Oldenbourg.

Eason, K. D. (1982). The process of introducing information technology. *Behaviour and Information Technology*, **1**, 197-213.

Eason, K. D. (1984). Towards the experimental study of usability. *Behaviour and Information Technology*, **3**, 133-143.

Eller, E. C. (1984). Eine längsschnittanalytische Betrachtung von Einstellungen zur EDV und Arbeitszufriedenheit von Angestellten. In Berufsverband Deutscher Psychologen (ed.), *Arbeit in moderner Technik* (pp. 295-314). Duisburg: Eigendruck.

Ellis, P. (1984). Office planning and design: The impact of organizational change due to advanced information technology. *Behaviour and Information Technology*, **3**, 221-233.

Emery, F., and Thorsrud, E. (1976). *Democracy at Work: The Report of the Norwegian Industrial Democracy Program*. Leiden: Nijhoff.

Engel, S., and Granada, R. (1975). *Guidelines for Man/Display Interfaces*. New York: IBM Technical Report TR 00.2720.

Fähnrich, K.-P., and Ziegler, J. (1985). Direkte Manipulation als Interaktionsform an Arbeitsplatzrechnern. In H.-J. Bullinger (ed.), *Software-Ergonomie '85* (pp. 75-85). Stuttgart: Teubner.

Feigenbaum, E. A., and McCorduck (1984). *The Fifth Generation: Artificial Intelligence and Japan's Computer Challenge to the World*. New York: Signet.

Fischer, G., Lemke, A., and Schwab, T. (1985). Knowledge-based help systems. *Proceedings of the CHI '85 Conference on Human Factors in Computing Systems* (pp. 161-167). San Francisco.

Fitter, M., and Sime, M. (1980). Creating responsive computers: Responsibility and shared decision making. In H. T. Smith, and T. R. G. Green (eds.) *Human Interaction with Computers* (pp. 39-66). London: Academic Press.

Floyd, C. (1984). A systematic look at prototyping. In R. Budde, K. Kuhlenkamp, L. Mathiasen, and H. Züllighoven (eds.), *Approaches to Prototyping* (pp. 1-18). Berlin: Springer.

Foss, D. A., Rosson, M. B., and Smith, P. L. (1982). Reducing manual labor: Experimental analysis of learning aids for a text-editor. *Proceedings of the Conference on Human Factors of Computer Systems*. Gaithersberg, MD: National Bureau of Standarts.

Frese, M. (1982). Occupational socialization and psychological development: An underemphasized research perspective in industrial psychology. *Journal of Occupational Psychology*. **55**, 209-224.

Frese, M. (1984). Einstellungen zur Technologie und Computern: Entwicklung von Messinstrumenten. In Berufsverband Deutscher Psychologen (ed.), *Arbeit in moderner Technik* (pp. 97-108). Duisburg: Selbstverlag.

Frese, M. (1984). Transition in jobs, occupational socialization and stain. In V. L. Allen and E. v. d. Vliert (eds.), *Role Transitions* (pp. 239-252). New York: Plenum.

Frese, M. (in press) (a). A theory of control and complexity: Implications for software design and integration of computer systems into the work place. In M. Frese, E. Ulich and W. Dzida (eds.), *Psychological Issues of Human-Computer Interaction in the Work Place*. Amsterdam: North-Holland.

Frese, M. (in press) (b). *Stress at Work, Coping Strategies, and Musculoskeletal Complaints*.

Frese, M. (in prep.). *Social support as a moderator of the relationship between stress at work and psychological dysfuntioning*.

Frese, M., Albrecht, K., Altmann, A., Lang, J., v. Papstein, P., Peyerl, R., Prümper, J., Schulte-Göcking, H., Wankmüller, I., and Wendel, R. (1986). *The effects of an active development of the mental model in the training process: Experimental results on a word processing system*. München: Dept. of Psychology, University.

Frese, M., Saupe, R., and Semmer, N. (1981). Stress am Arbeitsplatz von Schreibkräften: Ein Vergleich zweier Stichproben. In M. Frese (ed.), *Stress im Büro* (pp. 225-251). Bern: Huber.

Frese, M., and Sabini, J. (eds.) (1985). *Goal Oriented Behavior: The Concept of Action in Psychology*. Hillsdale, NJ: Erlbaum.

Frese, M., Stewart, J., and Hannover, B. (1987). Goal-orientation and planfulness: Action styles as personality concepts. *Journal of Personality and Social Psychology*, **52**(6).

Frese, M., and Wendel, R. (in prep.). *Die Einführung von neuen Technologien am Arbeitsplatz: Gefahren und Chancen*.

Frese, M., and Zapf, D. (1987). Die Einführung von neuen Techniken am Arbeitsplatz verändert Qualifikationsanforderungen, Handlungsspielraum und Stressoren kaum. Ergebnisse einer Längsschnittuntersuchung. *Zeitschrift für Arbeitswissenschaften*, **41**, 7-14.

Gallistel, C. R. (1980). *The Organization of Action: A New Synthesis*. London: Lawrence Erlbaum.

Gallistel, C. R. (1985). Motivation, intention, and emotion: Goal directed behavior from a cognitive-neuroethological perspective. In M. Frese and J. Sabini (eds.), *Goal Directed Behavior* (pp. 48-66). Hillsdale: Erlbaum.

Geiselman, R. E., and Samet, M. G. (1982). Personalized versus fixed formats for computer-displayed intelligence messages. *IEEE Transactions on Systems, Man, and Cybernetics*, *SMC-12*, 490-495.

Gilbreth, F. B. (1919). *Applied motion study*. New York: Macmillan.

Giuliano, V. E. (1982). The mechanization of office work. *Scientific American*, **247**, 148-165.

Glenn, E. N., and Feldberg, R. L. (1977). Degraded and deskilled: The proletarization of clerical work. *Social Problems*, **25**, 52-64.

Gomez, L. M., and Egan, D. E. (1983). How interface design determines who has difficulty learning to use a text editor. (pp. 176-181) *Proceedings of the CHI '83 Conference on Human Factors in Computing Systems*. Boston.

Gorny, P. (1984). Zur Manipulation visueller Information. In H. Schauer and M. J. Tauber (eds.), *Psychologie der Computerbenutzung* (pp. 55-88). Wien: Oldenbourg.

Gottschall, K., Mickler, O., and Neubert, J. (1985). *Computerunterstützte Verwaltung*. Frankfurt: Campus.

Gould, J. D., and Lewis, C. (1983). Designing for usability-key principles and what designers think. *Proceedings of the CHI '85 Conference on Human Factors in Computing Systems* (pp. 50-53). Boston.

Gould, J. D., Lewis, C., and Barnes, V. (1985). Effects of cursor speed on text-editing. *Proceedings of the CHI '85 Conference on Human Factors in Computing Systems*. (pp. 7-10). San Francisco.

Green, T. R. G., Payne, S. J., and v.d. Veer, G. C. (eds.) (1983). *The Psychology of Computer Use*. London: Academic Press.

Greenberg, S., and Witten, I. H. (1985). Adaptive personalized interface—A question of viability. *Behaviour and Information Technology*, **4**, 31-45.

Gregory, J., and Nussbaum, K. (1982). Race against time: Automation of the office. *Office: Technology and People*, **1**, 197-236.

Greif, S. (1986a). Job design and computer training. *Bulletin of the British Psychological Society,* **39**, 166-169.

Greif, S. (1986b). Neue Kommunikationstechnologien—Entlastung oder mehr Stress? In K. Pullig, U. Schaetzel, and J. Scholz (eds.), *Stress, Reihe Betriebswirtschaftliche Weiterbildung* (Vol. 8). Hamburg: Windmuehle Verlag.

Greif, S., and Holling, H. (1986). Neue Technologien. In D. Frey and S. Greif (eds.), *Sozialpsychologie* (2nd ed.) München: Urban and Schwarzenberg.

Grudin, J., and Banard, P. (1985). When does an abbreviation become a word? And related questions. *Proceedings of the CHI '85 Conference on Human Factors in Computing Systems* (pp. 121-125). San Francisco.

Gunnarson, E. (1984). The impact of organisational factors on visual strain in clerical VDT work. In B. G. F. Cohen (ed.), *Human Aspects in Office Automation* (pp. 43-61). Amsterdam: Elsevier.

Hacker, W. (1978). *Allgemeine Arbeits- und Ingeneurpsychologie* (2nd ed.). Bern: Verlag Hans Huber.

Hacker, W. (1983). Psychische Beanspruchungen bei Text- und Datenverarbeitungstätigkeiten an Bildschirmgeräten: Ermittlung und Gestaltung. *Zeitschrift für Psychologie Supplement,* **5**, 24-41.

Hacker, W. (1985). Activity: A fruitful concept in industrial psychology. In M. Frese and J. Sabini (eds.), *Goal Directed Behavior* (pp. 262-284). Hillsdale: Erlbaum.

Hacker, W., Rühle, R., and Schneider, N. (1978). Effektivitätssteigerung durch neue Verfahren zum Erlernen leistungsbestimmender geistiger Teiltätigkeiten. *Sozialistische Arbeitswissenschaft,* **22**, 363-368.

Hackman, J. R., and Oldham, G. R. (1975). Development of job diagnostic survey. *Journal of Applied Psychology.* **60**, 159-170.

Haider, E., and Rohmert, W. (1983). Beziehungen zwischen Technologien und Organisations-merkmalen in der Textverarbeitung. *Zeitschrift für Arbeitswissenschaft,* **37**, 211-214.

Haider, M., Kundi, M., and Weissenböck, X. (1980). Work related strain to VDU with different colored characters. In E. Grandjean and E. Vigliani (eds.), *Ergonomic Aspects of Visual Display Terminals.* London: Taylor and Francis.

Hammer, J. M., and Rouse, W. B. (1982). The human as a constrained optimal editor. *IEEE Transactions on Systems, Man, and Cybernetics, SMC-12,* 777-784.

Hammond, N., and Barnard, P. (1984). Dialogue design: Characteristics of user knowledge. In A. Monk (ed.), *Fundamentals of Human–Computer Interaction* (pp. 127-164). London: Academic Press.

Hammond, N., Jorgenson, A., MacLean, A., Barnard, P., and Long, J. (1983). Design practice and interface usability: Evidence from interviews with designers. *Proceedings of the CHI '83 Conference on Human Factors in Computing Systems* (pp. 40-44). Boston.

Hannemyr, G. and Innocent, P. R. (1985). A network user interface: Incorporating human factors guidelines into the ISO standard for open systems interconnection. *Behaviour and Information Technology,* **4**, 309-326.

Hartmann, A. L., and Zwahlen, H. T. (1985). Mehr Augenbeschwerden durch Bildschirmarbeit? *Sozial- und Präventivmedizin,* **30**, 280-281.

Hauptmann, A. G., and Green, B. F. (1983). A comparison of command, menu-selection and natural-language computer programs. *Behaviour and Information Technology,* **2**, 163-178.

Hayes, P. J., and Reddy, R. D. (1983). Steps toward graceful interaction in spoken and written man–machine communication. *International Journal of Man–Machine Studies,* **19**, 231-284.

Hayes-Roth, R., Waterman, D. A., and Lenat, D. B. (eds.) (1983). *Building Expert Systems.* London: Addison-Wesley.

Hedberg, B. (1980). Using computerized information systems to design better organizations and jobs. In Bjorn-Andersen, N. (ed.), *The Human Side of Information Processing* (pp. 19-37). Amsterdam: North-Holland.

Helmreich, R. (1985). Human aspects of office systems: User acceptance research results. In B. Shackel (ed.), *Human-Computer Interaction* (pp. 715-718). Amsterdam: Elsevier.

Hiltz, S. R. (1983). A study of the determinants of acceptance of computer-medited communication systems. *SIGCHI Bulletin*, **14**, 16-17.

Hirschheim, R. A., Land, F. F., and Smithson, S. (1985). Implementing computer-based information systems in organizations: Issues and strategies: In B. Shackel (ed.), *Human-Computer Interaction* (pp. 855-863) North-Holland.

Hooper, K. (1986). Architectural design: An analogy. In D. A. Norman and S. W. Draper (ed.), *User-Centered System Design*. Hillsdale: L. Erlbaum.

Hoos, I. R. (1960). When the computer takes over the office. *Harvard Business Review*, **38**, 102-112.

Hoos, I. R. (1983). When the computer takes over the office — Update. *Office: Technology and People*, **2**, 69-77.

Howath, P. A., and Istance, H. O. (1985). The association between visual discomfort and the use of visual display units. *Behaviour and Information Technology*, **4**, 131-149.

House, J. S. (1981). *Work Stress and Social Support*. London: Addison-Wesley.

Huddleston, J. H. F. (1984). What individuality means for systems design. *Behaviour and Information Technology*, **3**, 85-91.

Hutchins, E., Hollan, J. D., and Norman, D. A. (1986). Direct manipulation interfaces. In D. A. Norman and S. W. Draper (eds.), *User-Centered System Design*. Hillsdale: Erlbaum.

Iacono, S., and Kling, R. (in press). Changing office technologies and transformation of clerical jobs: A historical perspective. In R. Kraut (ed.), *Technology and the Transformation of White-Collar Work*. Hillsdale: Erlbaum.

Isa, B. S., Boyle, J. M., Neal, A. S., and Simons, R. M. A methodology for objectively evaluating error messages. *Proceedings of the CHI '83 Conference on Human Factors in Computing Systems* (pp. 68-71). Boston.

Jagodzinski, A. P. (1983). A theoretical basis for the representation of on-line computer systems to naive users. *International Journal of Man-Machine Studies*, **18**, 215-252.

Janda, A. (1983). *Proceedings of the CHI '83 Conference on Human Factors in Computing Systems*. Boston.

Jörgensen, A. H. (1984). On the psychology of prototyping. In Budde, R., Kuhlenkamp, K., Mathiassen, L., and Züllighoven, H. (eds.), *Approaches to Prototyping* (pp. 278-289). Berlin: Springer.

Johansen, R., and Baker, E. (1984). User needs workshops: A new approach to anticipating user needs for advanced office systems. *Office: Technology and People*, **2**, 103-119.

Johansson, G., and Aronsson, G. (1984). Stress reactions in computerized administrative work. *Journal of Occupational Behaviour*. **5**, 159-181.

Jones, W. P., and Landauer, T. K. (1985). Context and self-selection effects in name learning. *Behaviour and Information Technology*, **4**, 3-17.

Kalimo, R., and Leppänen, A. (1985). Feedback from VDTs, performance control and stress in text preparation in the printing industry. *Journal of Occupational Psychology*, **58**, 27-38.

Karasek, R. A. (1979). Job demands, job decision latitude and mental strain: Implications for job redesign. *Administrative Science Quarterly*. **24**, 285-308.

Karasek, R. A., Bader, D., Marxner, R., Ahlbom, A., and Theorell, T. (1981). Job design latitude, job demands, and cardiovascular disease: A prospective study of Swedish men. *American Journal of Public Health*, **71**, 634-705.

Karat, J., Boyes, L., Weisgerber, S., and Schafer, C. (1986). Transfer between word processing systems. *Proceedings of the CHI '86 Conference on Human Factors in Computing Systems* (p. 67-71). Boston.

Katz, C. (1986). Office of the future: Trends and premises. In E. Ulich (ed.), *Computer-aided Office Work* (pp. 36-39). Zürich. ETH, Lehrstuhl für Arbeits- und Organisatiospsychologie.

Kaye, A. R., and Sutton, M. J. D. (1985). Productivity and quality of working life for office principals and the implications for office automation. *Office: Technology and People*, **2**, 267-286.
Kempton, W. (1986). Two theories of home heat control. *Cognitive Science*, **10**, 75-90.
Kern, H., and Schumann, M. (1984). *Das Ende der Arbeitsteilung? Rationalisierung in der industriellen Produktion: Bestandsaufnahme, Trendbestimmung*. München: Beck.
Kieras, D. E., and Bovair, S. (1984). The role of a mental model in learning to operate a device. *Cognitive Science*, **8**, 255-273.
Kiger, J. I. (1984). The depth/breadth trade-off in the design of menu-driven user interfaces. *International Journal of Man-Machine Studies*, **20**, 201-213.
Kling, R. (1980). Social analyses of computing: Theoretical perspectives in recent empirical research. *Computing Surveys*, **12**, 61-110.
Klockare, B., and Norrby, K. (1983). A swedish model for systems development in public administration. In U. Briefs, C. Ciboorra and L. Schneider (eds.), *Systems Design for, with, and by the Users* (pp. 119-127). Amsterdam: North-Holland Publishing Company.
Koved, L., and Shneiderman, B. (1986). Embedded menus: Selecting items in context. *Communications of the ACM*, **29**, 312-318.
Kuhmann, W., Boucsein, W., Schäfer, F., and Alexander, J. (in press). Experimental investigation of psychophysiological stress reactions induced by different system-response times in man–computer-interaction. *Ergonomics*.
Läubli, T., Hünting, W., and Grandjean, E. (1980). Visual impairments in VDU operators related to environmental conditions. *Ergonomics*, **24**, 933.
Landauer, T. K., and Nachbar, D. W. (1985). Selection from alphabetic and numeric menu trees using a touch screen: Breath, depth and width. *Proceedings of the CHI '85 Conference on Human Factors in Computing Systems* (pp. 73-78). San Francisco.
Landy, F. L. (1985). *Psychology of Work Behavior*. Homewood, Illinois: The Drosey Press.
Lang, K., Auld, R., and Lang, T. (1982). The goals and methods of computer users. *International Journal of Man-Machine Studies*, **17**, 375-399.
Lange, K. (1984). Zwischen Hoffen und Bangen. *Bild der Wissenschaft*. (1), 63-71.
Lewis, C., and Norman, D. A. (1986). Designing for error. In D. A. Norman and S. W. Draper (eds.), *User-Centered System Design*. Hillsdale: Erlbaum.
Long, J., Hammond, N., Barnard, P., Morton J., and Clark, I. (1983). Introducing the interactive computer at work. *Behaviour and Information Technology*, **2**, 39-106.
Maass, S. (1983). Why systems transparency? In T. R. G. Green, S. J. Payne and G. C. van der Veer (eds.), *The Psychology of Computer Use* (pp. 19-28). London: Academic Press.
Mack, R. (1984). *Understanding Text-Editing: Evidence from Predictions and Description Given by Computer-Naive People*. Yorktown: IBM Watson Research Center RC 10333.
Mack, R. (1985). Identifying and designing toward new user expectations in a prototype text-editor. *Proceedings of the CHI '85 Conference on Human Factors in Computing Systems* (pp. 139-141). San Francisco.
Mack, R. L. Lewis, C. H., and Carroll, J. M. (1983). Learning to use word processors: Problems and prospects. *ACM Transactions on Office Information Systems*, **1**, 254-271.
Maguire, M. (1982). An evaluation of published recommendations on the design of man–Computer dialogues. *International Journal of Man-Machine Studies*, **16**, 237-261.
Mantei, M., and Orbeton, Peter (eds.) (1986) *Proceedings of the CHI '86 Conference on Human Factors in Computing Systems*. Boston.
Margulies, F., and Zemanek, H. (1983). Man's role in man-machine systems. In G. Johannsen and J. E. Rijnsdorp (eds.) *IFAC Analysis, Design, and Evaluations of Man-Machine Systems* (pp. 121-128). Oxford, Pergamon.
Martin, G. L., and Corl, K. G. (1986). System response time effects on user productivity. *Behaviour and Information Technology*, **5**, 3-13.

Mayer, R. E. (1975). Different problem-solving competencies established in learning computer programming with and without meaningful models. *Journal of Educational Psychology*, **67**, 725-734.

Mayer, R. E. (1976). Some conditions of meaningful learning for computer programming: Advanced organizers and subject control of frame order. *Journal of Educational Psychology*, **68**, 143-150.

McKendree, J., and Carroll, J. M. (1986). Advising roles of computer consultant. *Proceedings of the CHI '86 Conference on Human Factors in Computing Systems* (pp. 35-40). Boston.

Miller, G. A. (1956). The magical number seven, plus or minus two: Some limits on our capacity for processing information. *Psychological Review*, **63**, 81-97.

Miller, G. A., Galanter, E., and Pribram, K. H. (1960). *Plans and the Structure of Behavior*. London: Holt.

Miller, R. B. (1968). Response time in man-computer conversational interactions. *Proceedings Spring Joint Computer Conference*, **33**, (pp. 267-277). Montvale: AFIPS Press.

Miyake, N., and Norman, D. A. (1979). To ask a question, one must know enough to know what is not known. *Journal of Verbal Learning and Verbal Behavior*, **18**, 357-364.'

Monk, A. (ed.) (1984). *Fundamentals of Human-Computer Interaction*. London: Academic Press.

Moran, T. P. (1981). An applied psychology of the user. *Computing Surveys*, **13**, 1-11.

Morland, V. D. (1983). Human factors guidelines for terminal interface design. *Communications of the ACM*, **26**, 484-494.

Mosier, J. N., and Smith, S. L. (1986). Application of guidelines for designing user interface software. *Behaviour and Information Technology*, **5**, 39-46.

Mowshowitz, A. (1976). *The Conquest of Will, Information Processing in Human Affairs*. Reading: Addison-Wesley.

Müller-Böling, D. (1984). Durch bessere Technik zu mehr Akzeptanz. *Office Management*, **11**, 1064-1066.

Mumford, E. (1980). The participative design of clerical information systems. In N. Bjorn-Andersen (ed.), *The Human Side of Information Processing* (pp. 91-107). Amsterdam: North-Holland.

Neisser, U. (1976). *Cognition and Reality: Principles and Implications of Cognitive Psychology*. San Francisco: W. H. Freeman.

Neisser, U. (1985). The role of invariant structures in the control of movement. In M. Frese and J. Sabini (eds.), *Goal directed behavior* (pp. 97-109). Hillsdale: Erlbaum.

Newell, A., and Card, S. K. (1985). The prospects for psychological science in human-computer interaction. *Human-Computer Interaction*, **1**, 209-242.

Nickerson, R. S. (1986). *Using Computers: The Human Factors of Information Systems*. London: The MIT Press.

Norman, D. A. (1981). Categorization of action slips. *Psychological Review*, **88**, 1-15.

Norman, D. A. (1983a). Some observations on mental models. In D. Gentner and A. L. Stevens (eds.), *Mental Models* (pp. 7-14). Hillsdale: Erlbaum.

Norman, D. A. (1983b). Design principles for human-computer interfaces. *Proceedings of the CHI '83 Conference on Human Factors in Computing Systems* (pp. 1-10). Boston.

Norman, D. A. (1984a). Stages and levels in human-machine interaction. *International Journal of Man-Machine Studies*, **21**, 365-375.

Norman, D. A. (1984b). *Working Papers on Errors and Error Detection*. San Diego: Univ. of California.

Norman, D. A. (1986a). Cognitive engineering. In D. A. Norman and S. W. Draper (eds.), *User Centered Systems Designs*. Hillsdale: Erlbaum.

Norman, D. A. (1986b). Interface design doesn't matter. *Talk at the ACM conference CHI '86*. Boston.

Norman, D. A., and Draper, S. W. (eds.) (1986). *User Centered System Design*. Hillsdale: Erlbaum.

Nullmeier, E., and Rödiger, K.-H. (1985). *Bibliographie zur Gestaltung von Dialogschnittstellen.* Berlin: Technische Universität Berlin.

O'Malley, C., Smolensky, P., Bannon, L., Conway, E., Graham, J., Sokolov, J., and Monty, M. L. (1983). A proposal for user centered system documentation. *Proceedings of the CHI '83 Conference on Human Factors in Computing Systems.* Boston.

O'Malley, C. (1986). Helping users help themselves. In D. A. Norman and S. W. Draper (eds.), *User Centered Systems Design.* Hillsdale: Erlbaum.

Otway, H. J., and Peltu, M. (1983). *New Office Technology: Human and Organizational Aspects.* London: Pinter.

Owen, D. (1986). Naive theories of computation. In D. A. Norman and S. W. Draper (eds.), *User Centered System Design.* Hillsdale: Erlbaum.

Paetau, M. (1985). The cognitive regulation of human action as a guideline for evaluating the man-compute dialogue. In B. Shackel (ed.), *Human-Computer Interaction* (pp. 731–736). Amsterdam: North-Holland.

Pask, G., and Scott, B. C. E. (1972). Learning strategies and individual competence. *International Journal of Man-Machine Studies,* **4,** 217–253.

Pava, C. H. P. (1983). *Managing New Office Technology.* New York: Free Press.

Pelzmann, L., Winkler, N., and Zewell, E. (1985). Antizipation von Arbeitslosigkeit. In T. Kieselbach and A. Wacker (eds.), *Individuelle und gesellschaftliche Kosten der Massenarbeitslosigkeit* (pp. 256–268). Weinheim: Beltz.

Picot, A., Klingenberg, H., and Kränzle, H. (1982). Office technology: A report on attitudes and channel selection from field studies in Germany. In M. Burgoon (ed.), *Communication Yearbook* Vol. 6 (pp. 674–692). London: Sage Publications.

Pollak, M. E. (1985). Information sought and information provided: An empirical study of user/expert dialogues. *Proceedings of the CHI '85 Conference on Human Factors in Computing Systems* (pp. 155–159). San Francisco.

Polson, P. G., and Kieras, D. E. (1985). A quantitive model of the learning and performance of text editing knowledge. *Proceedings of the CHI '85 Conference on Human Factors in Computing Systems* (pp. 207–212). San Francisco.

Pomfrett, S. M., Olphert, C. W., and Eason, K. D. (1985). Work organisation implications of word processing. In B. Shackel (ed.), *Human-Computer Interaction* (pp. 847–854). Amsterdam: Elsevier.

Powers, M., Lashley, C., Sanchez, P., and Schneiderman, B. (1984). An experimental comparison of tabular and graphic data presentation. *International Journal of Man-Machine Studies,* **20,** 545–566.

Preece, J. (1983). Graphs are not straightforward. In T. R. G. Green, S. J. Payne and G. C. v.d. Veer (eds.), *The Psychology of Computer Use* (pp. 41–56). London: Academic Press.

Price, H. E. (1985). The allocation of functions in systems. *Human Factors,* **27,** 33–45.

Radl G. W. (undated). *Zur Notwendigkeit der Akzeptanzforschung bei der Entwicklung neuer Systeme der Bürotechnik.* Düsseldorf: Akzente.

Rafaeli, A., and Sutton, R. I. (1986). Word processing technology and perceptions of control among clerical workers. *Behaviour and Information Technology,* **5,** 31–37.

Ranney, J. M., and Carder, C. E. (1984). Socio-technical design methods in office settings: Two cases. *Office: Technology and People,* **2,** 169–186.

Rasmussen, J. (1983). Skills, rules and knowledge; signals, signs, and symbols, and other distinctions in human performance models. *IEEE Transactions on Systems, Man, and Cybernetics, SMC-13,* 257–266.

Raum, H. (1984). Aufgabenabhängige Gestaltung des Informationsangebots bei Bildschirmarbeit. *Schweizerische Zeitschrift für Psychologie und ihre Anwendungen,* **43,** 25–33.

Reichwald, R. (undated). *Zur Notwendigkeit der Akzeptanzforschung bei der Entwicklung neuer Systeme der Bürotechnik.* Düsseldorf: Akzente.

Reichwald, R. (1982). Neue Systeme der Bürotechnik und Büroarbeitsgestaltung: Problem-zusammenhänge. In R. Reichwald (ed.), *Neue Systeme der Bürotechnik*. Berlin: Schmidt.

Reichwald, R. (1983). Bürotechnik, Bürokratisierung und das Zentralisierungsproblem: Grundüberlegungen zur Gestaltung der Büroarbeit. In A. Cakir (ed.), *Bildschirmarbeit* (pp. 23-46). Berlin: Springer.

Rich, E. (1983). Users are individuals: Individualizing user models. *International Journal of Man-Machine Studies*, **18**, 199-214.

Richards, J. T., Boies, S. J., and Gould, J. D. (1986). Rapid prototyping and systems development: Examination of an interface toolkit for voice and telephone applications. *Proceedings of the CHI '86 Conference on Human Factors in Computing Systems* (pp. 216-220). Boston.

Riley, M. (1986). User understanding. In D. A. Norman and S. W. Draper (eds.), *User Centered Systems Design*. Hillsdale: Erlbaum.

Roberts, T. L., and Moran, T. P. (1983). The evaluation of text editors: Methodology and empirical results. *Communications of the ACM*, **26**, 265-283.

Robertson, I. T. (1985). Human information-processing strategies and style. *Behaviour and Information Technology*. **4**, 19-29.

Rödiger, K. H. (1985). Beiträge der Softwareergonomie zu den frühen Phasen der Software-Entwicklung. In H.-J. Bullinger (ed.), *Software-Ergonomie '85* (pp. 455-464). Stuttgart: Teubner.

Rohr, G. (1984). Understanding visual symbols. *Proceedings of IEEE workshop on visual languages* (pp. 184-191). Hiroshima.

Rohr, G., and Tauber, M. J. (1984). Representational frameworks and models for human-computer interfaces. In G. C. van der Veer, M. J. Tauber, T. R. G. Green, and P. Gorny (eds.), *Readings on Cognitive Ergonomics: Mind and Computers* (pp. 8-26). Berlin: Springer.

Rosenberg, J. K. (1982). Evaluating the suggestiveness of command names. *Behaviour and Information Technology*, **1**, 371-400.

Rosenberg, J. K., and Moran, T. P. (1985). Generic commands. In B. Shackel (ed.), *Human--Computer Interaction* (pp. 254-250). Amsterdam: Elsevier.

Rosenstiel, v. L. (1984). Aufgaben der Arbeits- und Betriebspsychologie bei sich wandelnden Technologien, Organisationstrukturen und Werthaltungen. In Berufsverband Deutscher Psychologen (ed.), *Arbeit in moderner Technik* (pp. 15-50). Duisburg: Eigendruck.

Ruch, L. (1986). The use of word processors: A survey in Switzerland's Federal Government Administration. In E. Ulich (ed.), *Computer-aided Office Work* (pp. 17-23). Zürich: ETH, Lehrstuhl für Arbeits- und Organisationspsychologie.

Sabini, J., and Silver, M. (1985). On the captivity of the will: Sympathy, caring, a moral sense of the human. *Journal for the Theory of Social Behaviour*, **15**, 24-37.

Salvendy, G. (1984). Research issues in the ergonomics, behavioral, organizational and management aspects of office automation. In B. G. F. Cohen (ed.), *Human Aspects in Office Automation* (pp. 115-127). Amsterdam: Elsevier.

Sasso, R. (1985). Personalising the software interface. In B. Shackel (ed.), *Human--Computer Interaction* (pp. 355-362). Amsterdam: Elsevier.

Sauter, S., Gottlieb, M. S., Jones, K. C., Dodsen, V., and Rohrer, K. M. (1983). Job and health implications of VDT use: Initial results of the Wisconsin-NIOSH Study. *Communications of the ACM*, **26**, 284-294.

Scapin, D. L. (1981). Computer commands in restricted natural language: Some aspects of memory and experience. *Human Factors*, **23**, 365-375.

Scapin, D. L. (1982). Generation effect, structuring, and computer commands. *Behaviour and Information Technology*, **1**, 401-410.

Schaefer, F., Kuhmann, W., Boucsein, W., and Alexander, J. (1986). Beanspruchung durch Bildschirmtätigkeit bei experimentell variierten Systemresponsezeiten. *Zeitschrift für Arbeitswissenschaft*, **40**, 31-38.

Schardt, L. P., and Knepel, W. (1981). Psychische Beanspruchungen kaufmännischer Angestellter bei computergestützter Sachbearbeitung. In M. Frese (ed.), *Stress im Büro* (pp. 125-158). Bern: Huber.

Scharer, L. L. (1983). User training: Less is more. *Datamation*, **29**, 175-182.

Schauer, H., and Tauber, M. (eds.) (1983). *Psychologie des Programmierens*. Wien: Oldenbourg.

Schauer, H., and Tauber, M. (eds.) (1984). *Psychologie der Computerbenutzung*. Wien: Oldenbourg.

Schiele, F., and Pelz, W. H. (1985). Eine Studie zue empirischen Überprüfung der Benutzerfreundlichkeit von Textverarbeitungs- und Tabellenkalkulationsprogrammen. In H.-J. Bullinger (ed.), *Software Ergonomie '85* (pp. 239-250). Stuttgart: Teubner.

Schönpflug, W. (1985). Goal directed behavior as a source of stress: Psychological origins and consequences of inefficiency. In M. Frese and J. Sabini (eds.), *Goal Directed Behavior* (pp. 172-188). Hillsdale: Erlbaum.

Schulte-Göcking (1987). *Lernprozesse an Textsystemen: Der Einfluss von Lernstil, Handlungsstil, Problemlösekompetenz und Persönlichkeitsmerkmalen auf den Lernerfolg*. München: Institut für Psychologie, Univ. München.

Seligman, M. B. P. (1975). *Learning helplessness*. San Francisco: Freeman.

Semmer, N. (1982). Stress at work, stress in private life and psychological well-being. In W. Bachmann and I. Udris (eds.), *Mental Load and Stress in Activity: European Approaches* (pp. 42-55). Amsterdam: Elsevier.

Semmer, N. (1984). Stressbezogene Tätigkeitsanalyse: Psychologische Untersuchungen zur Analyse von Stress am Arbeitsplatz. Weinheim: Beltz.

Semmer, N., and Frese, M. (1985). Action theory in clinical psychology. In M. Frese and J. Sabini (eds.), *Goal Directed Behavior* (pp. 296-310). Hillsdale: Erlbaum.

Shackel, B. (1985a). *Human-Computer Interaction*. Amsterdam: Elsevier, North-Holland.

Shackel, B. (1985b). Human factors and usability: Whence and whither. In H.-J. Bullinger (ed.), *Software-Ergonomie '85* (pp. 1-13). Stuttgart: Teubner.

Shneiderman, B. (1980). *Software Psychology*, Cambridge, Massachusetts: Winthrop Publishers.

Shneiderman, B. (1982a). System message design: Guidelines and experimental results. In H. Badre and B. Shneiderman (eds.), *Directions in Human-Computer Interaction* (pp. 55-78). Norwood New Jersey. Ablex Publishing Co.

Shneiderman, B. (1982b). The future of interactive systems and the emergence of direct manipulation. *Behaviour and Information Technology*, **1**, 237-256.

Shneiderman, B. (1983a). Direct manipulation: A step beyond programming languages. *Computer*, **16**, 57-69.

Shneiderman, B. (1983b). Human factors of interactive software. In G. Goos and J. Hartmanis (eds.), *Lecture Notes in Computer Science* (pp. 9-29). Berlin: Springer.

Shneiderman, B. (1984a). Response time and display rate in human performance with computers. *Computing Survey*, **16**, 265-285.

Shneiderman, B. (1984b). *Review of Card, S. K., Moran, T. P., Newell, A.: The Psychology of Human-Computer Interaction*. Datamation, **30**, 236-240.

Shneiderman, B. (1986). Seven plus or minus two central issues in human-computer interaction. *Proceedings of the CHI '86 Conference on Human Factors in Computing Systems*. Boston.

Small, D. W., and Weldon, L. J. (1983). An experimental comparison of natural and structured query languages. *Human factors*, **25**, 253-263.

Smith, M. J. (1984). Health issues in VDT work. In J. Bennett, D. Case, Sandelin, J. and Smith, M. (eds.), *Visual Display Terminals: Usability Issues and Health Concerns* (p. 193-228). Englewood Cliffs: Prentice Hall.

Smith, M. J., Cohen, B. G. F., Stammerjohn, L. W., Jr. and Happ, A. (1981). An investigation of health complaints and job stress in video display operations. *Human Factors*, **23**, 387-400.

Smith, S. L. (1986). Standards versus guidelines for designing user interface software. *Behaviour and Information Technology*, **5**, 47-61.

Smith, S. L., and Mosier, J. N. (1984). The user interface to computer-based information systems: A survey of current software design practice. *Behaviour and Information Technology*, **3**, 195-203.

Spinas, P. (1984). Bildschirmeinsatz und psycho-soziale Folgen für die Beschäftigten. In Berufsverband Deutscher Psychologen (ed.), *Arbeit in moderner Technik* (pp. 503-516). Duisburg: Eigendruck.

Spinas, P. (1986). Analysis of dialogue systems: Field study. In E. Ulich (ed.), *Computer-aided Office Work* (pp. 9-16). Zürich: ETH, Lehrstuhl für Arbeits- und Organisationpsychologie.

Spinas, P. (in press). *VDU-work and user-friendly human–computer-interaction: Analysis of dialogue structures*. In M. Frese, E. Ulich and W. Dzida (eds.) *Psychological Issues of Human–Computer Interaction in the Work Place*. Amsterdam: North-Holland.

Spinas, P., Troy, N., and Ulich, E. (1983). *Leitfaden zur Einführung und Gestaltung von Arbeit mit Bildschirmsystemen*. München: CW-Publikationen.

Stammerjohn, L. W., Smith, M. J., and Cohen, B. G. F. (1981). Evaluation of work station design factors in VDT operations. *Human Factors*, **23**, 401-412.

Stark, L. W., and Johnston, P. G. (1984). Visual fatigue and VDT workplace. In J. Bennet, D. Case, J. Sandeli and M. Smith (eds.), *Visual Display Terminals: Usability Issues and Health Concerns* (pp. 229-270). Englewood Cliffs: Prentice Hall.

Stelovsky, J., and Sugaya, H. (1985). Command languages vs. menus or both? In H.-J. Bullinger (ed.), *Software-Ergonomie '85* (pp. 129-141). Stuttgart: Teubner.

Stevens, G. C. (1983). User-friendly computer systems? A critical examination of the concept. *Behaviour and Information Technology*, **2**, 3-16.

Streitz, N. (1985). Die Rolle von mentalen und konzeptuellen Modellen in der Mensch-Computer-Interaction: Konsequenzen für die Software-Ergonomie? In H.-J. Bullinger (ed.), *Software-Ergonomie '85* (pp. 280-292). Stuttgart: Teubner.

Sullivan, M. A., and Chapanis, A. (1983). Human factoring a text editor manual. *Behaviour and Information Technology*, **2**, 113-125.

Sundermeyer, P., and Haack-Vörsmann, L. (1983). On-board flight path planning as a new job concept for pilots. In G. Johannsen and J. E. Rijusdorp (eds.), *IFAC Analysis, Design, and Evaluations of Man–Machine Systems*. (pp. 197-203). Oxford: Pergamon.

Sydow, J. (1984). Sociotechnical change and perceived work situations. Some conceptual propositions and an empirical investigation in different office settings. *Office: Technology and People*, **2**, 121-132.

Sydow, J., Hattke, W., and Staehle, W. H. (1981). Situative Analyse der Bildschirmarbeit. *Zeitschrift für Organisation*, **50**, 215-223.

Szyperski, N. (1984). Das elektronische Büro. *Bild der Wissenschaft*, **1**, 73-98.

Taylor, F. W. (1911). *The Principles of Scientific Work*. New York: Harper and Row.

Thomas, J. C. and Schneider, M. L. (eds.) (1984). *Human Factors in Computing Systems*. Norwood: Ablex.

Troy, N. (1986). Designing attempt 1: Secretariats in a federal agency. In E. Ulich (ed.), *Computer-aided Office Work* (pp. 24-29). Zürich: ETH, Lehrstuhl für Arbeits- und Organisationspsychologie.

Tullis, T. S. (1985). Designing a menu-based interface to an operating system. *Proceedings of the CHI '85 Conference on Human Factors in Computing Systems* (pp. 79-84). San Francisco.

Turing, A. (1950). Computing machinery and intelligence. In E. A. Feigenbaum and J. Feldman (eds.), *Computers and Thought*. New York: McGraw Hill.

Turkle, S. (1984). *The Second Self: Computers and the Human Spirit*. NY: Simon and Schuster.

Turner, J. A., and Karasek, R. A. (1984). Software ergonomics: Effects of computer application design parameters on operator task performance and health. *Ergonomics*, **27**, 663-690.

Ulich, E. (1981). Möglichkeiten autonomieorientierter Arbeitsgestaltung. In M. Frese (ed.), *Stress im Büro* (pp. 159-177). Bern: Huber.

Ulich, E. (1983). Differentielle Arbeitsgestaltung—ein Diskussionsbeitrag. *Zeitschrift für Arbeitswissenschaft*, **37**, 12-15.

Ulich, E. (1985). Einige Anmerkungen zur Software-Psychologie. *Sysdata*, **10**, 53-58.

Ulich, E. (1986). Towards the design of user-oriented dialogue systems: Experiments. In E. Ulich (ed.), *Computer-aided Office Work* (pp. 6-9). Zürich: ETH, Lehrstuhl fuer Arbeits- und Organisationspsychologie.

Ulich, E., and Troy, N. (1986). Job organisation and allocation of functions between man and computer. In Klix, F. and Wandke, H. (eds.) *Man–Computer Interaction Research. MACINTER I* (pp. 421-427). Amsterdam: Elsevier, North Holland.

v. d. Veer, G., and Beishuizen, J. J. (undated). *Learning Styles in Conversation—A Practical Application of Pask's Learning Theory to Human–Computer Interaction.* Amsterdam: Manuscript.

v. d. Veer, G. C., Tauber, M. J., Green, T. R. G., and Gorny, P. (eds.) (1984). *Readings on Cognitive Ergonomics: Mind and Computers.* Berlin: Springer.

v. d. Veer, G., Tauber, M. J., Waern, Y., and v. Muylwijk, B. v. (1985). On the interaction between system and user characteristics. *Behaviour and Information Technology*, **4**, 289-308.

v. Muylwijk, B., v. d. Veer, G., and Waern, Y. (1983). On the implications of user variability in open systems. *Behaviour and Information Technology*, **2**, 313-326.

Volpert, W. (1981). *Sensumotorisches Lernen: Zur Theorie des Trainings in Industrie und Sport.* Frankfurt am Main: Fachbuchhandlung für Psychologie (3rd. ed.).

Volpert, W. (1985). *Zauberlehrlinge: Die gefährliche Liebe zum Computer.* Weinheim: Beltz.

Volpert, W. (1986). Gestaltbildung im Handeln: Zur psychologischen Kritik des mechanischen Weltbildes. *Gestalt Theory*, **8**, 43-60.

Volpert, W., Frommann, R., and Munzert, J. (1984). Die Wirkung allgemeiner heuristischer Regeln im Lernprozess—eine experimentelle Studie. Zeitschrift für Arbeitswissenschaft, **38**, 235-239.

Waern, Y. (1985). Learning computerized tasks as related to prior task knowledge. *International Journal of Man-Machine Studies*, **22**, 441-455.

Waern, Y., and Rabenius, L. (1985). *On the Role of Models in Instructing Novice Users of a Word Processing System.* Reprint: Department of Psychology Univ. of Stockholm.

Walton, R. E., and Vittori, W. (1983). New information technology: Organizational problem or opportunity? *Office: Technology and People*, **1**, 249-273.

Weinberg, G. M. (1971). *The Psychology of Computer Programming.* New York: Van Nostrand Reinhold.

Weizenbaum, J. (1976). *Computer Power and Human Reason: From Judgement to Calculation.* San Francisco: W. H. Freeman and Company.

Weltz, F. (undated). *Mitarbeiter-Befürchtungen und Managemetn-Fehler: Soziologische Aspekte bei der Einführung neuer Bürotechnologien.* Düsseldorf: Akzente.

Weltz, F. (1982). Arbeitsplatzgestaltung an Bildschirmarbeitsplätzen aus soziologischer Sicht. *AFA-Informationen*, **35**, 15-20.

Weltz, F., and Bollinger, H. (in press). *Mitarbeiterbeteiligung bei technisch-organisatorischen Veründergungen im Verwaltungsbereich.* Sozialwissenschaftliche Projektgruppe München.

Weltz, F. and Lullies, V. (1983). *Innovation im Büro: Das Beispiel Textverarbeitung.* Frankfurt: Campus.

Whiteside, J., Jones, S., Levy, P. S., and Wixon, D. (1985). User performance with command, menu, and iconic interfaces. *Proceedings of the CHI '85 Conference on Human Factors in Computing Systems* (pp. 185-191). San Francisco.

Wicklund, R. A. (1974). *Freedom and Reactance.* Hillsdale: Lawrence Erlbaum.

Widdel, H., and Kaster, J. (1985). Untersuchung zur formalen Transparenz eines Menüsystems. In H.-J. Bullinger (ed.), *Software-Ergonomie '85* (pp. 228-238). Stuttgart: Teubner.

Wiener, E. L. (1985). Beyond the sterile cockpit. *Human Factors*, **27**, 75-90.

Wilkins, A. J. (1985). Visual discomfort and cathode ray tube displays. In B. Shackel (ed.), *Human-Computer Interaction* (pp. 75-80). Amsterdam: Elsevier.

Williams, B. O., and Burch, J. L. (1985). *Human Foundations of Advanced Computing Technology: The Guide to the Select Literature*. Lawrence, Kansas: The Report Store.

Williges, R. C., Elkerton, J., Pittman, J. A., and Cohill, A. M. (1985). Providing online assistance to inexperienced computer users. In B. Shackel (ed.), *Human-Computer Interaction* (pp. 765-770). Amsterdam: Elsevier.

Williges, R. C., and Williges, B. H. (1983). Human-computer dialogue design considerations. In G. Johannsen and J. E. Rijusdorp (eds.), *IFAC Analysis, design, and evlauations of man-machine systems* (pp. 239-246.) Oxford: Pergamon.

Wixon, D., Whiteside, J., Good, M., and Jones, S. Building a user-defined interface. *Proceedings of the CHI '83 Conference on Human Factors in Computing Systems* (pp. 24-27). Boston.

Wohl, J. G. (1982). Information automation and the Apollo program: A retrospective. *IEEE Transactions on Systems, Man, and Cybernetics, SMC-12,* 469-478.

Wortman, C. B., and Brehm, J. W. (1975). Responses to uncontrollable outcomes: An integration of reactance theory and the learned helplessness model. In L. Berkowitz (ed.), *Advances in Experimental Social Psychology.* New York: Academic Press.

Wynne, B., and Otway, H. J. (1983). Information technology, power and managers. *Office: Technology and People,* **2,** 43-56.

Young, R. M. (1983). Surrogates and mappings: Two kinds of conceptual models for interactive devices. In D. Gentner and A. L. Stevens (eds.), *Mental Models* (pp. 35-52). Hillsdale: Erlbaum.

Zülch, G., and Starringer, M. (1984). Differentielle Arbeitsgestaltung in Fertigungen für elektronische Flachbaugruppen. *Zeitschrift für Arbeitswissenschaft,* **38,** 211-217.

International Review of Industrial and Organizational Psychology 1987
Edited by C. L. Cooper and I. T. Robertson
© 1987 John Wiley & Sons Ltd

Chapter 6

OCCUPATIONAL STRESS AND HEALTH: SOME CURRENT ISSUES

Colin J. Mackay
Medical Division
Health and Safety Executive
Bootle
UK
and
Cary L. Cooper
Department of Management Sciences
University of Manchester
Institute of Science and Technology
UK

INTRODUCTION

Of all the areas of industrial and organizational psychology, the literature relating to occupational stress continues to be one of the fastest growing. The debate has been fuelled by a number of quite disparate but nevertheless overlapping concerns, some of which are to do with the fundamental nature of the stress concept and others which are most practically oriented and are to do with the demands inherent in contemporary working life. For example, there are some issues which bear upon the utility of the stress concept and some of the continuing methodological problems with which the topic is still beset (Lazarus *et al.*, 1985; Dohrenwend and Shrout, 1985; Kasl, 1986). On a more practical level, it has been estimated that at any one time (in the USA) approximately 8 to 10 per cent of the workforce are experiencing disabling emotional or somatic ill-health; that 30 per cent suffer from a fluctuating array of minor psychological discomforts and physical ailments, and that stress-related symptoms contribute to absenteeism, lost productivity, and company health care costs to the tune of $50–75 billion annually (Brodsky, 1984). There are a number of responses to this problem. On an individual level workers' compensation claims for stress-related disorders have proliferated during the last 15 years in courts throughout the United States (Davis, 1985; Appelson, 1983), and many large organizations are or have implemented stress management initiatives to tackle the various manifestations of what is seen to be a growing occupational health problem

*The views expressed are those of the authors.

(Taylor *et al.*, 1986). Traditional occupational stress research has focused primarily upon psychosocial variables (conflict ambiguity and other role-related demands, for example) as well as sociotechnical ones (machine pacing, constrained posture, shift work), but newer and equally legitimate areas are arising which have biomedical as well as psychological components. For example, it is becoming increasingly recognized that acute workplace incidents (accidents, accidental poisoning) may trigger post-traumatic stress disorders (Schottenfeld and Cullen, 1986) and these should be seen as a new class of occupational stress problem (Mackay and Lucas, 1986). Research into stress has also been given an added impetus by the very rapid change to new technology which is still spreading rapidly throughout Western industrialized nations. The sheer complexity of the topic has also made it a rich and fertile hunting ground for researchers. Research, however, cannot be the endpoint. The translation of research findings into sensible guidance to organizations will prove troublesome, and only comparatively recently has the critical need for research that vigorously evaluates the many potential strategies for handling stress been acknowledged.

There has been in the last 10 years a gamut of overviews, reviews, and compilations as well as numerous conference proceedings devoted to this topic, either in book or periodical form—all of which are comparatively easy to access (Beehr and Newman, 1978; Cooper and Marshall, 1980; Cooper and Payne, 1978, 1980; Gardell, 1982; Holt, 1982; House, 1981; Hurrell and Colligan, 1982; Kahn, 1981; Kahn *et al.*, 1982; Kasl, 1974, 1978; Kasl and Cobb, 1983; Levi, 1972; Mackay and Cox, 1979; McGrath, 1976; McLean, 1979; Moss, 1981; Sharit and Salvendy, 1982; Shostak, 1980). For subsequent reviewers the problem becomes not so much the sheer volume of information and research findings but the variability in approach, in hypotheses, and in the subsequent lack of comparability between studies. Predominantly, studies in the occupational stress area have been concerned primarily with eliciting cause and effect relationships between working conditions and undesirable health outcomes; the latter have indicated reversible and irreversible structural and functional changes, symptoms of disease and illness and mortality. Even with comparatively straightforward epidemiological problems, decisions upon the likelihood of cause and effect relationships being present are not easy to make. Bradford-Hill (1965) has provided a comprehensive list of criteria by which to judge the likelihood of causal effects being present. Included in his list are strengths of association, consistency, specificity, existence of relationships in time, presence of dose-response effects, coherence, and biological plausibility. Imposing epidemiological criteria upon occupational stress research may not be entirely fair but if causal relationships are sought, such rigour is demanded. Nevertheless, in order to reliably demonstrate causal links such criteria are necessary, but only in a small number of studies is consideration given to these points even when they are purported to show cause and effect relationships between occupational psychosocial factors and disease outcomes (broadly conceived).

Although the long-term outcome may be disease, stress effects may be manifested in other ways. The scope of such manifestations obviously defines the legitimate field of interest and, in particular, has implications for the choice of measurement and assessment techniques. One epidemiologist has provided a working definition of disease as 'disability or failure in performance of a task' (Kagan, 1975). Structural impairments at the cellular level obviously have implications for organ dysfunction. Individual effectiveness or performance may also be degraded. Human reliability, human error, and safety are therefore legitimate concerns. Indeed, there are empirical links between the experience of stressful life events and accidents (Sheehan *et al.*, 1981; Levenson *et al.*, 1980). Certainly, the quantification of human reliability presents measurement problems at least as difficult, if not more so, as those processes and outcomes concerned with 'disease' (Swain and Guttman, 1980; Rassmussen, 1979). Empirical links are, at the present, tenuous but nevertheless promising (Broadbent *et al.*, 1982; Stuart and Brown, 1981). However, these methodological issues are not specifically addressed in the present chapter.

Psychosocial Factors and Disease in the Workplace

The extent to which psychosocial factors can elicit disease and illness cannot be seen in isolation. Their presumed causes and effects must be evaluated against other, and more reliably established, risk factors. In their recent review, commissioned as a report to the Office of Technology, US Congress, concerned with determining cancer risks from the environment, Doll and Peto (1981) discussed 'unidentified' causes of the disease. They state:

> Two categories of environmental factors that we have ignored and may therefore be classed with 'unknown factors' are that of psychological mechanisms and some form of breakdown of immunological control, both of which have been suggested at intervals throughout this century to play some part in the production of cancer. It is possible, of course, that psychological factors could have some effect, e.g., by modulating hormonal secretions, but we know of no good evidence that they do nor that they affect the incidence of cancer in any other way, except insofar as they lead people to smoke, drink, overeat, or enjoy some other harmful habit.

A similarly sceptical approach was taken recently by the Industrial Injuries Advisory Council (1981) in the UK in discussing occupational causations of illness and disease. The fact that ischaemic heart disease (ICD Code 410–414) is excluded from the revised schedule of industrial diseases is not of particular relevance to our present concern except in so far as, in reviewing the evidence, the council appear to be similarly unconvinced of the relevance of existing studies on psychosocial effects:

> Coronary disease is our leading cause of death (156,000 deaths in 1979), and was responsible for 185,000 spells of certified incapacity for work in the year 1978/79. It is quite commonly believed by the general public that stress at work can be responsible for the disease, but the epidemiological evidence in support of this belief is slender and still controversial. Far more important components of its complex aetiology are cigarette smoking, diet, lack of exercise, raised blood pressure and obesity.

The significance of these statements lies not so much in their unwillingness to consider 'psychological' factors (relating to cognition, perception, and personality, for example) but the implication that these other (so-called) well-established risk factors are not in any way linked to factors in the workplace, which may elicit or predispose to these undesirable behaviours or effects (diet, smoking). In contrast, a distinguished group of biomedical and behavioural scientists was convened in 1978 by the National Heart, Lung and Blood Institute of the United States to evaluate the available data related to the Type A coronary-prone behaviour pattern. They concluded (Cooper et al., 1981): 'Type A behaviour . . . is associated with an increased risk of clinically apparent coronary heart disease in employed, middle-aged US citizens. This risk is greater than that imposed by age, elevated values of systolic blood pressure and serum cholesterol, or smoking and appears to be of the same order of magnitude as the relative risk associated with the latter three of these factors.'

Reviewers the evaluators of material have, of course, a particular remit, their own preexisting beliefs, values, and convictions, and although policy-making and policy-influencing bodies have clearly recognized the need to consider psychosocial aspects of health and disease (e.g. the WHO Working Group on Health Aspects of Wellbeing in Working Places (World Health Organization 1980)), the overall impact of research findings in this area has been generally of a low order. Successful intervention strategies (identification of those at an elevated risk, job redesign, policies directed at social change) will depend upon reliable research findings and interpretation of these. This in turn will depend upon sound conceptual frameworks and methodology and it is in this area that problems have arisen in the past.

CONCEPTS AND METHODS

Our chief aim in this chapter is to discuss some of the conceptual and methodological problems which have fuelled controversy in the area of occupational stress which are in a sense persistent and remain unresolved. Second, we would like to review some of the recent research findings in a number of *selected* areas where progress over the last few years has been made but where differences of opinion and approach remain. Finally, we would like to address the more practical problems of prevention and management of stress in the workplace but within the context provided by the first two sections. Much of the early work concerned with stress in the workplace grew out of laboratory-based models largely concerned with effects of environmental demands and task manipulations upon performance. Such approaches do have a part to play in solving contemporary problems but the thrust of most current work, both in Europe and North America has been concerned with impacts of stressful working conditions upon health and wellbeing. Nevertheless, performance degradation in so far as it affects organizational effectiveness and as a putative index of stress problems in the individual, remains an important consideration.

Reviews of the occupational stress literature are always confronted by the dilemma of either defining precisely the usage of the term or dispensing with it entirely. Since the approach to definition adopted has profound implications regarding interpretation, methodology, and approaches to stress reduction such differences must be considered. We do not intend to examine each of these in detail (see, for example, Cooper and Marshall, 1976; Davidson and Cooper, 1980; McGrath, 1976; Cox and Mackay, 1981), rather to remind the reader of them. Essentially the term has been used in four different ways (Cox and Mackay, 1981).

1. *As a stimulus* Here stress is viewed as an independent variable; as a characteristic of the environment. Its roots may be found within the engineering psychology

literature as well as that of occupational epidemiology. A sudden accident or encounter with a traumatic event, or exposure to adverse environments, conform to this paradigm (Fisher, 1985). An important consideration is that such external stress may be more or less objectively quantified.

2. *As a response* Many conceptualizations depict stress as a bodily response to some externally imposed demand. Stress has thus been conceived of as a pattern of psychological changes (acute) or as stress-related disease (chronic). These may be behavioural, affective, or somatic disturbances (withdrawal, migraine, palmar sweating, raised catecholamine levels). Although these are often described as 'stress' or 'stress-related', the mechanisms and pathways by which such states become manifest are not elucidated since many of these bodily effects may be caused by a variety of extrinsic risk factors and intrinsic physiological changes neither of which may be relevant. Moreover, more recent laboratory and, indeed, field studies have indicated considerable individual response specificity of psychological systems suggesting that the notion of a well-defined non-specific pattern of response cannot be empirically corroborated. A practical example of the use of this form of definition is when workforce members are recruited into a stress management programme on the basis of blood pressure scores over a certain cut-off level or similarly elevated symptom checklist scores.

3. *As a perception* A prevalent view in much of contemporary writing in the stress field is that of stress arising from perceptual and cognitive processes, which led to physiological or psychological sequelae. The rationale behind this approach is discussed more fully below. The point here is that in many studies an objective evaluation/quantification of the working environment derived from, say, a job description or task analysis has been replaced by a worker's subjective description or appraisal of the working environment or some psychometrically extracted dimension of it (e.g. perceived autonomy). Kasl (1986) has argued that whilst a subjectivist interpretation may be more appropriate, without an objective assessment of environmental conditions and without other methdological safeguards such approaches, on their own, may be biased and thus misleading. (See below.)

4. *As a transaction* The above three definitions are unhelpful because they cannot incorporate the very large differences in perception, reaction, and response. The fourth and most elaborate (and elaborated) approach views stress not as a fixed component of either the environment or of individual response but as a process operating in time. The bases of such a model are the components of which they are constructed, the strengths of the relationships between the individual components and the nature of the feedback and feedforward paths. Here the time constants may be fast (milliseconds) or slow ($\geqslant$ 20–30 years) depending upon relationships between different components of the model. Essentially this approach to stress emphasizes the *control* aspects of the process and this may be seen as essentially a cybernetic model. The components, however, remain important and we would see the following as important (see Figure 6.1).

(a) The discrepancy between the demands placed upon the individual and their capacity (skills, resources) to deal with those demands (McGrath, 1976). We regard the *perception* of such variables as being at least as important as objective quantification, but the latter is important.

(b) The discrepancy or imbalance between 'internally derived' stresses (Fisher, 1985), internal demands (Cox and Mackay, 1981), and resources provided for the individual by the working environment. Elsewhere this has been described as the needs–supplies fit (Caplan, 1983; Harrison, 1976). Here, internally generated demands are those which depend upon the values and needs held or required by the individual. These values dictate aims and ambitions and may be translated into the willingness and motivation to perform ongoing tasks.

(c) The appraisal process, which combines the two pairs of external–internal components in a way which decides whether or not a discrepancy exists and presents a problem now or in the future for the individual. Coping which involves cognitive, behavioural, and physiological components is the result. In the context of the work situation failure to cope is clearly important (Sells, 1970). The speed at which the various components are changing (very quickly (seconds) or very slowly (over years)) clearly influences how the individual reacts. It is important to note that powerful *feedback* mechanisms are operating and these have implications for methodological issues.

Establishing Causal Relationships

Despite recent sophisticated attempts at modelling the stress process using techniques such as LISREL (Brenner *et al.*, 1985), methodological problems in this area still exist. To establish the causal nature of relationships, in addition to showing a correlation between presumed cause and effect, it is necessary to rule out competing or alternative hypotheses. In many studies, even if researchers wished to rule out such threats to validity, they would be unable to because of two main drawbacks: (1) the over-reliance upon subjective measures: (2) the use of cross-sectional designs. There are, however, some notable exceptions (Parkes, 1982). The important alternative hypotheses may be grouped into three classes (Frese, 1986): (1) when stress at work is measured subjectively a correlation between subjective stress and symptoms (psychosomatic complaints) may be spurious—the correlation is explained by a third set of variables; (2) when stress is measured objectively and a correlation with complaints is found, 'third variable confounding' may still exist; (3) reverse, or at least bi-directional, causation may be operating.

Class 1 Third variable confounding (subjective measures)
(see also Kasl, 1986)

These may be separated into five subsets.

(a) Conceptual overlap between measures of exposure and measures of outcome.
(b) Response bias: the measures of both exposure and outcome are subject to stable response tendencies. These may be due to the design of the instruments themselves or because of social desirability effects.
(c) Response bias: influence of personality/trait effects on the measures of both exposure and outcome.
(d) Demand characteristics of the research setting (Orne, 1961) and experimenter effects.

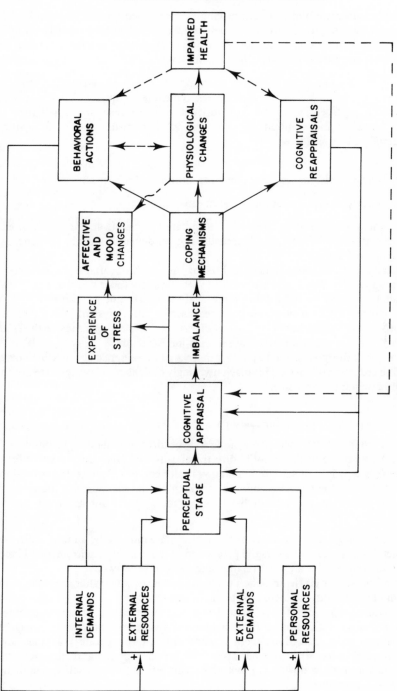

Figure 6.1 A Transactional Model of Occupational Stress

(e) Possible misattribution of symptoms to presumed causes especially in retrospective designs. This effect is well known in epidemiology as 'effort after' or 'search for meaning'. The suggested job stresses may become a legitimate 'cause' of the individual's symptoms or disease.

One way to eliminate these threats to internal validity is to use an objective index of work stress. Objective here represents measurement techniques which do not rely upon subjective perception/appraisal of work demands. Even so, one cannot always rule out 'third variable confounding' even in such circumstances. The following must therefore be considered.

Class 2   Third variable confounding (objective measures of job stress)

The following possible confounding factors may apply.

(a) Low-status jobs are often the ones with greatest demands and are more often associated with job insecurity. Insecurity, not job demands, may be influencing symptoms (Fein, 1976).

(b) Similarly, low pay and financial troubles may act as 'third variable confounders'.

(c) The low socioeconomic status associated with the above (poor housing, nutrition, alcohol use) may be the driving force in disease risk, not job factors.

(d) Age effects. There may be selective recruitment into stressful jobs for older populations. The higher prevalence of disease in the latter may thus be the true factor, not the ostensible association with job demands.

(c) Those with the most stressful jobs are motivated to influence events which may lead to reduction of stress. This may unwittingly or deliberately exaggerate health complaints and symptoms.

Class 3   Reverse or bi-directional causality

The third group of factors which may indirectly or directly generate spurious causal interpretations concerns reverse of bi-directional causality. Here the presence of the outcome (e.g. a painful or serious debilitating health condition) alters the perception and/or reporting of exposure to stressful working conditions. Some of the reasons for this phenomenon have already been alluded to. The relevant subgroups are as follows:

(a) The physiological/biochemical/psychological state induced by an illness/disease directly influences or distorts the perception of the working environment. There may or may not be a causal relationship between the two.

(b) An indirect effect via the initiation of coping processes which alter the attribution of disease causality in favour of putative work factors.

(c) Survival or selection effects. First, less assertive or demonstrative workers — these characteristics arising from concurrent symptoms and disease — may be given the more hazardous work / more difficult to operate machines and experience more stress-related problems. Second, ongoing difficulties and illness may lead to downward mobility (drift) either through self or company selection procedures.

SETTINGS FOR STUDIES OF OCCUPATIONAL STRESS

Apart from problems of measurement the investigator wishing to unravel some of these confounding factors is faced with the choice between a number of contexts in which the study or investigation can be set. Four general types of setting generally appropriate for occupational stress studies can be distinguished: laboratory studies, simulations, field studies, and clinical investigations. Each has both unique and shared advantages and disadvantages. Often the choice of setting is determined by availability of resources, expertise, and personal preference. In many programmes of research only a single setting is used and, typically in the area of stress, field studies have tended to dominate. The relative advantages and disadvantages of each approach have been extensively discussed with the respect to the literature on stress (Cullen and Siegrist, 1984). In general, field studies tend to maximize realism but with a cost in precision and a threat to aspects of internal validity. Laboratory studies tend to maximize precision at a cost to realism and pose a threat to external validity.

Laboratory Studies

Two particular drawbacks are associated with laboratory studies. The first is the considerable limitation on both the severity and duration of imposed demands. Ethical considerations predominate although there are other difficulties. The second drawback concerns the problems of realism. Since current theories of stress emphasize the perception and cognitive appraisal of demands, the ability of laboratory situations to successfully mimic perceived threat to any substantial degree must always be questioned.

The necessarily short duration of experimental situations also severely limits the extent to which the temporal factors in the mechanism which underlie the stress response can be established. All of these drawbacks are well known. Nevertheless, clever experimental designs and manipulations can largely overcome some of these drawbacks. Moreover, they have a number of advantages over other approaches. Random allocation of experimental units to conditions and systematic data collection mean that all possible interaction between variables of interest can be established and reliable dose-response relationships achieved. Within the present context, thoughtfully conducted and designed laboratory studies have an important role. Analogues of job characteristics such as task complexity or theoretical concepts such as 'underload' and 'overload' are particularly appropriate for laboratory investigation. The psychophysiological studies of Marrianne Frankenhaeuser and her colleagues are an example of a laboratory approach that can provide extremely valuable information (Frankenhaeuser, 1980). Studies involving the manipulation of physical environmental characteristics in exposure chamber studies (such as noise) are obviously relevant here. So are the laboratory analogues of concepts such as 'learned helplessness' in which experimental studies have played a major part (Seligman, 1975). Perceptions of imposed demands can also be manipulated. Laboratory studies of aversive simulation (Averill, 1973; Glass and Singer, 1972), where perception of control is manipulated, have proved particularly powerful techniques in examining theoretical constructs such as cognitive appraisal of threat.

Task demands have also been investigated with respect to subjective evaluations of workload. A laboratory study which differentiates between objective and perceived levels of demand has been described by Sales (1969). Using an anagram-solving task, Sales manipulated two conditions of objective workload: an underload condition in which subjects were kept waiting for anagrams for approximately 30 per cent of the time, and an overload condition where 3.5 per cent more anagrams were provided than could be decoded in the time allowed. Subjects were divided into those who reported high levels of subjective workload and those who reported low subjective workload. Data for two dependent variables are of relevance here: (1) reported interest in and enjoyment of the task, and (2) changes in serum cholesterol. On both these variables an interaction between subjective and objective workload occurred. Subjects in the overload condition who reported low subjective workload and those in the underload condition who reported feeling overloaded both reported high levels of interest and enjoyment in the task. Those given the overload conditions and who felt overloaded and those given the underload conditons and who felt underloaded, had low levels of interest in the task. These latter groups also showed increases in serum cholesterol. The former groups, who showed greater interest and enjoyment in the task, exhibited decreases in serum cholesterol. Sales further analysed these data and found that levels of subjective overload were negatively correlated with scores on the verbal section of the Scholastic Aptitude Test (SAT). Individuals with high levels of verbal ability reported low subjective workload, whilst high subjective workload was reported by those with relatively low verbal ability. A negative correlation between interest in the task and changes in serum cholesterol was also found. These data seem to be in general agreement with the contention that the effects of environmental demands (in this case from a task) are mediated foremost by perceptual factors. One of the primary determinants of the occurrence of psychological (interest in task) and physiological (serum cholesterol) correlates of stress is that of the individual's capability to deal with demand. These examples indicate that carefully conceived laboratory studies are of relevance in studies of adjustment. The investigation of task-inherent demands appears particularly appropriate for laboratory settings.

Experimental Simulation

Experimental simulations appear to combine the precision demanded by laboratory studies with the realism provided by field studies, but at the same time minimizing some of the threats to the latter such as non-random allocation of experimental units and unsystematic data collection. However, McGrath (1970) has highlighted three potential weaknesses of simulation strategies. First is the problem of fidelity or realism. Although simulators minimize the contrived nature of laboratory situations, the extent to which they can mimic real-life situations, influence cognitive appraisals, and hence appropriate levels of perceived threat, is not clear. Similarly, the extent to which motivation and observed behaviour are representative of actual conditions is difficult to assess. The second problem is one of resources, particularly cost. This in turn will depend very largely upon what is being simulated. Experience suggests that experimental simulation of a moderately complex system, yielding multiple outcome measures, with a number of variables and subject replications, may be the most expensive strategy option. The third problem is the danger of overconcern with attempts to increase the realism of the simulation at the expense of data collection.

Nevertheless, laboratory simulations of stressful situations can be worthwhile. One of the authors has been involved in a series of studies at Nottingham concerned with the pyschophysiological response to repetitive work (Mackay *et al.*, 1979; Cox and Mackay, 1979; Cox *et al.*, 1982). These studies were based upon simulation of a variety of repetitive tasks together with industrial field surveys of repetitive working practices and the responses to them. Two types of simulation were employed. The first was concerned with the simulation of paced repetitive work tasks. To create a realistic 'shopfloor' environment, a small workshop (approximately 90 m^2) was established, housing a conveyor belt. Using this belt, a machine-paced button-sorting process was developed, which involved three separate tasks operating in sequence. The tasks, loading, sorting, and minding were chosen to reflect and combine various aspects of unskilled and semiskilled industrial work. Loading and sorting were treated as 'repetitive' tasks and minding as a non-repetitive 'at work' control. Buttons are chosen as convenient material for this experiment: the project was not specifically concerned with work in the button-manufacturing industry.

The first task in the sorting process was loading. This consisted of placing buttons, face upwards, onto the moving belt at predetermined rates. Black discs were marked at regular intervals (372 mm) towards the front of the belt as targets onto which the button had to be accurately placed. As the buttons passed down the belt, a second person was required to inspect them for faults: sorting. Faulty buttons were rejected by being pushed to the back of the belt. The operational definition of sorting was the detection and rejection of faulty buttons: 10 per cent of all the buttons used had faults. The third task was machine minding. The minder was required to sit at the end of the belt and watch over the collection of the buttons, tidying up any spillage, and reporting any breakdowns.

The repetitive tasks varied in two ways: in the level of activity of the motor response, and in the degree of attention or in the attentional strategy demanded. Loading required a more regular and active response than sorting where an active response was related to the detection of a faulty button. Although the minder's task appeared the least simulating, unlike the other two it had no repetitive components, and it was less constrained by response requirements. All three tasks shared the same physical environment.

A period of training (15 minutes) was given on both repetitive tasks, to enable the loader to adapt to the speed of the belt and to the required pace of working, and to familiarize the sorter with the different faults present in the button used. Training appeared to overcome initial practice effects (Cox *et al.*, 1982). Following the short training period, participants worked for two more 45-minute periods during the afternoon. Participants were employed for 1 week, and worked for 1 day at each task (Tuesday and Thursday). Subjects were recruited through advertisements placed in the local press, which offered temporary unskilled work. Those selected were women, who by self-report were in a good state of general health. Background information about each subject was obtained before work started.

The simulated working arrangement proved to be very useful for studying the effects of different types of repetitive task and for manipulating factors of interest, notably degree of pacing and type of payment method, and for studying the psychophysiological responses of interest (urine catecholamines, continuously monitored cardiac activity, self-reported stress and arousal).

The second type of simulation carried out in this experiment took a slightly different approach. This involved three women recruited from advertisements in the local newspaper working on a part-time basis for 3 months. An industrial task supplied by a local electronics factory formed the basis for the work. It involved the assembly of simple components using a small hand-operated press. The task was self-paced but each worker was required to assemble several hundred finished articles each day which would be checked for quality and dispatched to the factory. This type of approach, whilst being based on only a few subjects, allows moderately long-term adjustment to work to be investigated. Also, by taking multiple measures from the same individual over many weeks, investigation of individual differences in pattern of responding can be assessed. Thus, both self-reported stress and self-reported arousal showed long-term changes indicative of a gradual adjustment to the work routine (Mackay et al., 1978; Mackay, 1980).

Field Studies

Because stress is essentially a complex multifactorial process concerned largely with chronic effects, field settings are often the only ones in which such phenomena can be studied. One is typically examining systems that are fundamentally dynamic. Individuals are growing and changing in interaction with one another and with the environment even in the absence of an imposed intervention. The complex interplay and links between environmental demands (life events), individual perceptions of threat, conflict, and harm, and their impact on pathophysiological processes cannot be satisfactorily handled by either experimental laboratory or simulation approaches. Nevertheless, good field studies are difficult to undertake.

Disadvantages with field studies are those concerned with procedural aspects and measurement problems. Often access to desired populations is difficult if not impossible, and the time and effort needed for this necessary part of field investigation should not be underestimated. Time to interview individuals or administer questionnaires is often linked to, for example, production constraints. In community or domestic settings this may be less of a problem. Because many of the available tests have been designed for those with above average comprehension and reading ability they are often not appropriate for the lower socioeconomic groups. Careful modification and piloting are made even more difficult if only limited access is possible. Moreover, there is often a great desire to collect more data from the respondent than is possible within a given data collection session. Often the data are collected haphazardly and unsystematically. Analysis and interpretation are made even more difficult, particularly when there are large numbers of missing data (physiological data are particularly at risk). The valid inferences which the investigator wishes to make about cause and effect relationships may be difficult to make.

Study Designs

The discussion of appropriate study settings leads directly to issues concerned with study design. In many cases the choice of setting dictates the type of study design employed. Further, there are often other constraints on resources which hinder the investigator. When considering design decisions with respect to studies of occupational stress there are a number of key issues. The general principles of experimental design are well known to psychologists and epidemiologists and will not be discussed here except to emphasize that control is achieved by randomized assignment to treatments. Other generic design methods are available. Cook and Campbell (1979) have placed special emphasis on quasi-experimental approaches. These are experiments that have treatments, outcome measures, and experimental units but do not use random assignment to create the comparisons from which treatment-caused change is inferred. Instead, the comparisons depend on non-equivalent groups that differ from each other in many ways other than the presence of a treatment whose effects are being tested. Cook and Campbell state:

> The task confronting persons who try to interpret the results from quasi-experiments is basically one of separating the effects of a treatment from those due to the initial noncomparability between the average units in each treatment group: only the effects of the treatment are of research interest. To achieve this separation of effects, the researcher has to explicate the specific threats to valid causal inference that random assignment rules out and then in some way deal with these threats. In a sense, quasi-experiments require making explicit the irrelevant causal forces hidden within the *ceteris paribus* of random assignment.

There are a number of threats to the validity of such studies including differential learning, ageing, and maturation effects. A further type of study which relies upon passive observation is also widely employed. Here, *passive* refers to the non-intrusive, non-interventionist nature of the study.

Typically the design is a cross-sectional one with all the measures taken at the same time (although some may refer to past events in a retrospective sense). Cook and Campbell (1979) suggest:

> For all these techniques, it was assumed that statistical controls were adequate substitutes for experimental controls and that the functions served by random assignment, isolation, and the rest could be served just as effectively by passive measurement and statistical manipulation. The belief became widespread that random assignment was not necessary because one could validly conceptualize and measure all of the ways in which the people experiencing different treatments differed before the treatment was ever implemented. Also one could rule out any effects of such initial group differences by statistical adjustment alone. Similarly, some researchers believed that all extraneous sources of variation in the dependent variable (that isolation and reliable measurement largely deal with) could be conceptualized, validly measured, and then partialled out of the dependent variable.

Descriptive occupational epidemiology, which falls into this type of passive observational design, can seldom offer definitive causal interpretations, and health differences in occupational groups cannot be simply interpreted by *a posteriori* intuitive judgements about the stressfulness of various occupations since later evidence may not quite support intuition (Kasl, 1978). Many occupational studies attempt to determine morbidity and mortality differences between groups of workers and then search for environmental factors in the workplace which may explain the differences. An alternative approach is to examine a population exposed to a hazardous agent (an organic solvent, a suspected carcinogen) and then to seek health differences between an exposed group and a non-exposed reference group. With some agents and observed diseases the causal link is comparatively easy to make (asbestos and mesothelioma, nickel carbonyl and nasal carcinoma). With others, inferring a causal link with any degree of reliability proves difficult. The main reasons are well known. The most powerful include selection effects both into and out of jobs, particularly because of health effects; illness behaviour; difficulty of determining duration and degree of exposure; and ascribing observed occupational effects to occuptional causes where in fact non-occupational factors are at play. Such confounding factors are legion. Even when occupational factors are known to play a causal role in differential occupational mortality and morbidity rates there may often be competing explanations.

An illustrative example of this type of study design is the study of occupational morbidity rates of mental health disorders carried out by Colligan, Smith, and Hurrell (1977). It must be emphasized, however, that the investigators themselves were aware of the limitations of this approach. The aim of the study was to try to provide a basis for identifying and selecting specific occupations which may be at an elevated risk of mental health problems because of job stress. Using admission records of community health centres throughout the state of Tennessee (1972–1974), these authors were able to assess the incidence rate of diagnosed mental health disorders for 130 occupations. Occupations chosen were those employing 1000 or more individuals. Colligan and co-workers based their evidence upon the sample frequency of admission for each occupation relative to the working population frequency of that occupation. It was shown that health technicians exhibited the highest incidence of mental disorders, closely followed by waiters and waitresses, practical nurses, and inspectors. A second analysis was carried out on the basis of a comparison of the observed frequency of admissions per occupation in the sample with the expected frequency based upon population (census) data. Those with scores significantly exceeding what would be expected by chance were waiters and waitresses, labourers and operatives, practical nurses, secretaries, nurses' aides, and inspectors. The authors rightly point out that inferences regarding the causal direction of the relationship between occupation and incidence of mental health disorders are not justified by this type of study design. For example, of the top 22 occupations 6 were related to hospital/health care operations. Whilst it is clear that there may be particularly severe stressful demands in the work of nurses (Parkes, 1982) other explanations of the observed differences in incidence rates are equally likely. Thus, sex sampling bias, willingness to report mental illness by health care professionals, earlier detection and treatment seeking, and predisposition to or preexisting mental health problems are equally plausible explanations. Thus the obtained occupational incidence rates may be more reflective of occupational differences in reporting tendencies and accessibility to treatment than actual incidence of mental health disorders.

To overcome these problems of interpretation which detract from retrospective designs, prospective approaches are helpful although they themselves may not always succeed. Kasl (1986) has provided a list of criteria which would provide the strongest design in the occupational stress area. These are as follows:

1. The cohort is picked up prior to exposure.
2. The environmental condition (exposure) is objectively defined and quantified.
3. Self-selection into and out of exposure conditions is minimized by exploiting opportunities for 'natural experiments' (see Parkes, 1982) and (generally) changes in the work setting that lead to highly comparable groups of exposed and unexposed individuals.
4. Potential confounding variables, primarily biological risk factors and initial health status, and their influence monitored in analysis.
5. There is an adequate period of follow-up so that there is a sufficient length of exposure to enable the cohort to pass through crucial periods of adaptation and disease causation and manifestation.
6. Mediating processes are studied, and vulnerability factors that interact with exposure are included.

SOME CURRENT ISSUES

Social Support

Since the mid-1970s the role of social factors in influencing health and wellbeing has been extensively studied. This follows the publication of three general reviews of the field implicating the impact of positive social factors upon health status (Cassel, 1976; Cobb, 1976; Kaplan et al., 1977) together with specific studies on occupational groups (Caplan et al, 1975). Since then, published research on social support has increased at a geometric rate (House and Kahn, 1985). For recent reviews of the prospect for further developments in this area, epidemiological and more general reviews see Berkman (1986), Broadhead et al. (1983), and Cohen and Syme (1985) respectively. The primary component of the social environment hypothesized to mediate the undesirable effects of stress on the individual is the degree or nature of social support received by the individual. However, there is not complete agreement as to what constitutes social support or the mechanisms by which its purported effects occur (see Gore, 1981; House and Kahn, 1985; Thoits, 1982; Leavy, 1983; Kessler et al., 1985, for methodological and conceptual reviews). House (1981) has suggested that supportive social relationships operate in three possible ways to alleviate work stress. First, support can directly enhance health by supplying human needs for affection, approval, social contact, and security. Second, by reducing interpersonal tensions and anxieties support may directly reduce levels of stress and thus improve health. These two pathways may be considered to be main effects. The third effect of support is a buffering or interactive one. This has been the predominant view of social support; it buffers the impact of stress upon manifestations of strain. That is, it operates as an *effect modifier*. The term 'buffer' has, however, led to some confusion and misinterpretation.

The original conceptualization (LaRocco et al., 1980; House, 1981) viewed the buffering impact of social support as moderating the effect of work demands upon measured outcomes. Stated at its simplest, the relationship between stress and strain is strongest in those with low levels of social support. The effect of support only becomes apparent in high-stress environments. Perceived social support may, of course, operate to influence the *subjective* reporting of stress or in some other way operate as a confounding factor (see earlier). Overall, therefore it is not surprising that studies have reported inconsistent findings. Several studies have reported the presence of moderating effects but the effects have often been specific rather than general. LaRocco *et al.* (1980) reported that social support moderated the effects of stressors on health outcomes such as depression and somatic complaints, but they found no evidence of buffering on job-related strains such as job dissatisfaction and boredom. Sandler and Lakey (1982) found social support buffered the impact of critical life events on depression and anxiety for persons with internal but not external locus of control. Kobasa and Puccetti (1983) reported that support from the boss buffered the effect of critical life events on illness symptoms but that family support did not.

One of the more comprehensive studies to have supported the buffering hypothesis comes from Winnubst *et al.* (1982) in a study of Dutch employees in several large organizations. Although they found evidence of main effects such that social support was negatively correlated with job stressors, psychological strains, and heart and somatic complaints, some evidence for a conditioning effect was found for psychological and behavioural strains and blood pressure. Other studies showing some support for the buffering effects are by Karasek (1982), Abdel-Halim (1982), and Seers *et al.* (1983). Elsewhere, studies have failed to demonstrate the presence of buffering effects (Aneshensel and Stone, 1982; Blau, 1981; Ganellen and Blaney, 1984; LaRocco and Jones, 1978). A recent study of Jayaratne and Chess (1984) examined the relationship between work stress (role conflict and ambiguity), work-related strains (job dissatisfaction, emotional exhaustion, and depersonalization), health-related strains (anxiety, depression, irritability, and somatic complaints), and emotional support. Main effects of support were in evidence but buffering effects of co-worker and supervisor support could not be demonstrated. A recent large-scale study attempted to address some of these outstanding issues by examining main effects of social support on strain outcomes, interactive or moderating effects of social support in combination with work stressors, and higher-order interactions involving social support, stressors and personal and job variables (sex, educational level, job type). No evidence for higher-order interactive effects was found nor did the data indicate the presence of buffering effects of social support. Overall, the results of this study support the reduction of harmful job demands and role characteristics together with augmentation of personal skills and social support which appeared to have a direct effect upon affective and somatic outcomes. Although the pattern of results, especially regarding buffering effects, is not uniformly consistent, the evidence cannot be completely dismissed as some have suggested (Wallston *et al.*, 1983; Kasl and Wells, 1985). The assembled data point towards considerable specificity as regards settings, measures of stress and strain, locus of support, and type of support (Henderson and Argyle, 1985).

Vulnerability to Stress at Work

One of the most fertile areas in the occupational stress literature has been the identification of personal characteristics which may increase the resistance (Antonovsky, 1979) to the effects of stress, or, conversely, may lead to vulnerability and increased health problems. Whilst a number of such individual resources have been described, much of the work in this area has concerned mediating effects of locus of control (including 'hardiness') and the Type A/B coronary-prone behaviour pattern. The belief that one's sense of control influences reactions to stress has been expressed frequently with research focusing on the locus of control concept or approximate constructs including environmental mastery (Pearlin and Schooler, 1978), fatalism (Wheaton, 1980), coherence (Antonovsky, 1979), and sense of control (Kohn, 1972).

In a study of work stress, Keenan and McBain (1979) reported that among 'externals' role ambiguity was related to tension at work, but this was not true of internals. Data from the 1979 and 1971 panels of the National Longitudinal Survey of Middle-aged Men (a shortened version of the Rotter scale being used) showed that the relationship between job and economic stressors upon psychophysiological distress was mediated by locus of control beliefs (Krause and Stryker, 1984). Detailed examination of the data revealed that men with moderately internal locus of control orientations coped more effectively with stress than those whose locus of control beliefs may be classified as extreme internal, extreme external, or moderately external. It was suggested by these authors that the underlying factor which separates moderate internals from the remaining locus of control types may be the ability to initiate actions that are intended to counteract the effects of stressful occurrences. Evidence that the mechanisms by which the locus of control exerts its effect is related to coping comes from a longitudinal study conducted by Parkes (1984). This study examined the role of coping style and appraisal (possibilities for intervention) described by a group of student nurses. The results indicated that internals were much more adaptive in their use of coping behaviours in relation to different types of appraisal than were externals. Part of this adaptive response may be the ability of internals to use sources of social support much more effectively than externals (Sandler and Lakey, 1982). Lefcourt et al. (1984) showed that the moderating effects of social supports largely occur among those who are less generally affiliative and more highly autonomous, suggesting that social supports may be most beneficial to those who are more instrumental and sparing in their approach to social interactions.

A model of vulnerability and resistance to stress has been presented by Kobasa and co-workers (e.g. Kobasa, 1979a, 1979b; Kobasa et al., 1982). They suggest that persons who remain healthy after experiencing high degrees of life stress have a constellation of personality characteristics that differentiate them from those who become ill. This constellation has been labelled 'the hardy personality' and comprises three dimensions: control, commitment, and challenge. Control concerns the feeling and belief that life events may be influenced rather than that one is helpless when confronted with adversity. Commitment reflects a generalized sense of purpose and meaningfulness that is expressed as a tendency to become actively involved in events rather than remaining passively uninvolved. Challenge suggests that life events are perceived not as an onerous burden one is weighed down by, but instead as a normal part of life that provides an opportunity for development. This similarity between hardiness and previously implicated moderators of the effects of life stress, such as locus of control and sensation seeking, should be noted (cf. Kobasa and Puccetti, 1983).

Kobasa (1979a) studied a group of executives whose retrospective reports indicated that they had experienced equivalent high levels of stressful events. Half the subjects reported becoming ill after experiencing the stress, whereas the other half did not. Although demographic variables did not distinguish between the groups, measures of hardiness did. Because level of stress was not varied, these results did not address whether hardiness should be viewed as a stress-buffer or an independent reducer of vulnerability. However, there have been two reports of the longitudinal study of these subjects in which life stress level was a variable (Kobasa *et al.*, 1982; Kobasa *et al.*, 1981). A main effect for hardiness was found in both studies.

Type A Behaviour Pattern

Friedman and Rosenman (1974) who pioneered the A/B typology define the Type A behaviour pattern as an action–emotion complex that can be any person who is aggressively involved in a chronic, incessant struggle to achieve more and more in less and less time. It is characterized by intense competitiveness, a sense of being under time pressure, and easily provoked hostility, and has been shown to be an independent risk factor for coronary heart disease (CHD) in case control and prospective studies (Haynes *et al.*, 1983; Jenkins, 1978; Rosenman *et al.*, 1975), to relate to coronary artery disease (CAD), as revealed by coronary angiography (Williams *et al.*, 1980), and to predict reinfarction in patients following an earlier infarct (Jenkins *et al.*, 1976). Studies failing to link Type A/B with pathology have been reported. Dimsdale *et al.* (1978) showed that Type A failed to predict the presence of coronary artery disease in a cohort of patients undergoing angiography. In a large but methodologically weak study of post myocardial infarction patients, presence of Type A did not predict reinfarction rates, and in a prospective study of coronary heart disease Shekelle *et al.* (1985) were unable to show a relationship between Type A and subsequent CHD. For a recent review and critical evaluation of the epidemiological evidence linking Type A behaviour to coronary disease risk see Matthews and Haynes (1986).

While earlier studies essentially classified respondents into global Type A or B (or subdivisions within these), more recent analyses have shown that at least five components can be identified, two of which appear to be crucial: fast, explosive, emphatic speech (which relates primarily to overall assessment of Type A) and hostility (Dembroski and MacDougall, in press). In a reanalysis of the Dimsdale *et al.* (1978) data the original finding of no relationship between global Type A and CAD was confirmed but hostility was significantly higher in patients with CAD (MacDougall *et al.*, 1985).

Recently, one of the authors (Davidson and Cooper, 1981) presented a model and an extensive review of the relationship between Type A behaviour patterns and the work environment, based upon interpretation of the relevant research findings to date. From that detailed review, the following six major, general conclusions pertaining to Type A behaviour and the work environment can be presented:

1. Susceptible Type A individuals tend to be professional/technical and managerial persons, aged between 36 and 55 years of age and living in urban environments.
2. Work stressors which enhance Type A behaviour patterns tend to be those which may lead to decreased levels of perceived control. The work environment factors which have been isolated as fitting into this category include: job involvement,

responsibility for people and things, role ambiguity, role conflict, over-promotion, lack of participation in decision making, poor relationships at work, and work overload.

3. Control conflict can result from the above mentioned high-risk work environment factors, which can cause susceptible individuals to form degrees of uncertainty in relation to goal setting, task performance, information processing, and organizational control. In the Type A person, unlike the Type B person, these conditions can then result in control conflict, i.e. conflict between preferred and actual available control.

4. Type A maladaptive coping behaviours include enhanced feelings of time urgency and a tendency to suppress symptoms and fatigue. Thus, Type As impose deadlines on themselves, increase goals and deny physical and psychological symptoms under pressure.

5. Symptoms of the Type A behaviour pattern include CHD, hypertension, increased cholesterol and norepinephrine levels, lack of exercise, smoking, and poor family relations.

6. Changing Type A behaviour. Type A behaviour modification programs with both CHD patients and healthy subjects have reported significant declines in serum cholesterol levels and blood pressure levels, lowered frequencies of subsequent coronary events, increased work productivity, and improved family relationships. These modification programs involve such exercises as relaxation, behavioural speed changes, and work environment behavioural drills; e.g. allotting free time periods, having fewer meetings, scheduling telephone calls, and so on.

Therefore, it becomes clear that there is a need for further prospective research in this area of stress and individual differences, especially in the area aimed at isolating and determining the specific work environment variables which enhance Type A behaviour. As yet, no prospective research project is known which has followed a sample of employees from their job application and interview situation through their careers, in order to investigate changes in, and influences on, Type A behaviour patterns. Finally, there is an obvious need for the introduction of more Type A behaviour modification programs for workers, and perhaps more emphasis should also be directed toward changing the Type A behaviour pattern socialization process, which appears to be so prevalent in urban, middle-class home environments (Davidson and Cooper, 1981).

Job socialization and job strain

In a number of publications, Karasek (e.g. 1979, 1981) has drawn attention to the fact that failure to distinguish between job stressors and job decision latitude probably accounts for many of the findings in the earlier stress and job satisfaction literature which indicated that, for example, executives and assembly line workers could both have stressful jobs but have widely different job satisfaction scores. The model proposed by Karasek suggests that the different combinations of demand and discretion characteristic of jobs may account for the discrepant findings in the literature. Low demand and low discretion are associated with passive jobs where low discretion leads to loss of ability to make decisions, solve problems, and tackle challenges, with atrophication of unused skills. High-demand, high-discretion jobs are termed 'active jobs' where challenges are matched with possibilities for alternative methods of coping. Problems typically arise with high-demand, low-discretion jobs where the individual is faced with a difficult situation and yet no satisfactory actions can be taken. A number of studies both in the US and Sweden have indicated that combinations of high demand and low discretion are associated with coronary heart disease risk from both retrospective and prospective studies (Karasek, 1982; Shaw and Riskind, 1983; Alfredsson and Theorell, 1983). Karasek's model finds support in both laboratory studies of stress and from simulations of industrial work. The effort and distress model (Frankenhauezer and Johansson, 1982) suggests that tasks with high demand but control over work pace are associated with subjectively reported effort but not 'distress' and with a physiological response characterized by adrenaline but not cortisol excretion. Lack of control, however, is associated with distress and cortisol excretion. Studies in industrial settings tend to confirm these findings (Johansson and Sanden, 1982).

Repetitive Work

Over the last decade there has been a considerable shift away from concern wholly about white-collar/managerial stresses to concerns about machine-paced and repetitive work. There have been various attempts to classify such work depending upon type and level of demands (Cox and Mackay, 1979; Dainoff et al., 1981; Murrell, 1964). Salvendy (1981) and Smith (1985) has classified paced work by the demand imposed on human-paced and machine-paced work.

Human paced

1. Unpaced
2. Socially or group paced
3. Self-paced within the context of management objectives over long time periods (e.g. over a day)
4. Incentive paced depending upon motivation/desire to earn extra pay.

Machine paced

1. Work-paced activities defined by cycle time. The shorter the cycle time the less opportunity to allocate effort and vary the rate of performance.
2. Paced work with buffer stocks. Not connected to other workers or machines.
3. Continuous paced operations based upon conveyor assembly lines. Here the worker is part of a much larger production system and his individual performance may be a rate-limiting step.
4. Discrete paced operations with breaks every so often can involve either a single operator or linked operators and may be self-activated by the operator or the machine. This gives the operator time for rest pauses or stock piling of components.

In so far as loss of control or low control is a major determinant of stress-related problems the differences in the above as far as influence over control are concerned are crucial. Thus, short cycle time, machine-paced work seems to afford the least amount of worker control, especially if the process is machine activated (Smith, 1985). Added demands arise when the process is part of a much larger one involving other machines and other operators. Cox (1985) has associated such repetitive working practices with underutilization of skill or skill potential, contributing to habituation, loss of ability to attend properly, and drowsiness. Restricted levels of stimulation and perceptual repetition are also important considerations. It is likely that the distress experienced (with consequent physiological manifestations) is in part determined by the operators' effort to combat falling levels of arousal in the presence of external pacing.

A number of recent studies both in the US and Europe have examined the impact of such work upon health and wellbeing. Although some studies have failed to find effects of cycle time (Broadbent and Gath, 1981) others have been able to show that there are critical cut-off levels below which problems arise (Frankenhaeuser and Gardell, 1976; Smith, Hurrell, and Murphy, 1981). Lack of control (Karasek, 1981), work pressure (Wilkes et al., 1981), and payment system (Cox et al., 1983) are all important in determining adverse subjective, physiological, or health outcomes. Moreover, such production methods are increasingly becoming incorporated into the design of new technology operations. These are discussed below.

New Technology and VDU Usage

One of the supposed advantages of new technology based upon VDU use is the ability of the user to interact intelligently with a computer system in ways compatible with human limitations in information-processing capacity. Essentially this approach envisages the VDU as an intelligent tool working at the bequest of the user. However, a cursory task analysis of many existing VDU-based jobs indicates that such jobs contain undesirable features characteristic of some forms of repetitive work, e.g. they fail to provide tasks which fit existing patterns of skill (or training is inadequate) and so fail to meet the individual's need for challenging and interesting work (Mackay and Cox, 1984).

The handful of studies undertaken so far on occupation stress factors inherent in some forms of VDU-based work support these general assertions. Some studies have shown high levels of reported psychological distress amongst VDU operators (Elias et al., 1982; Ghinghirelli, 1982). Others report no significant differences between users and controls (Binaschi et al., 1982). It is most likely that in most of these studies VDU work is confounded with undesirable job characteristics. The problem seems not to be the technology but the nature of work being undertaken (Sauter et al., 1983). Thus, in Gunnarsson and Ostberg's (1977) study, monotony experienced during VDU operation was clearly related to perceived feelings of lack of controllability and low levels of variety. Smith et al. (1980) report that rigid work procedures, high production standards, and constant pressure for performance were reflected in measures of self-reported stress and work demands which were substantially in excess of established norms (Caplan et al., 1975). Their respondents also complained of negative effects on their emotional health as well as musculoskeletal and visual problems. However, their data from other VDU sites suggest that perceived flexibility, autonomy, and control over how work is to be carried out act as attenuating factors in the experience of stress. In these operators the greatest problems were those concerned with ambiguity over career development and future job activities.

One of the crucial variables in determining stress-related symptoms in VDU operators is linked with the perception of control by the system (or conversely, lack of control by the operator). Such control is evident in a number of ways. First, in some systems the processing power of the machine is exploited to monitor such an operator. In many instances this information is used to determine levels of remuneration via piece-rate payment systems. Not unnaturally this level of control is often resented, is regarded with suspicion by many operators, and, understandably, is associated with feelings of fatigue and stress. Second, long response times from the computer, or those which are variable in length, cause uncertainty and frustration. Third, technical disturbances and breakdowns, when they occur frequently, serve only to exacerbate these problems (Wallin et al., 1983; Dainoff et al., 1981). All these factors substantially increase the mental load upon the operator and inevitably lead to fatigue. Thus Johannson (1979) and Johansson and Aronson (1981) have shown that these aspects of machine control lead to marked psychoneuroendocrine mobilization in VDU operators as evidenced by increased urinary catecholamine levels. These effects do not subside when the person has stopped working but have chronic effects.

VDU task design must therefore seek to minimize repetitive elements in the operator's task by introducing variability in workload throughout the day, instead of long periods of concentrated work, whilst ensuring that the load is predictable. This should be coupled with job design features which allow the individual to have some discretion in how work is allocated over work periods and, by so doing, introduce feelings of personal control and cater for individual differences in the need for brief pauses in work. Apart from these quantitative aspects of the VDU task, the qualitative features should also be examined. All too often data entry tasks require only the use of simple psychomotor skills, where only minimal exercise of intellectual abilities is possible. Thus work should be designed to be mentally challenging but within the scope of individual operator's capabilities. Ideally, the shift should be towards the use of the VDU as a tool for carrying out a much larger, enriched job, rather than regarding the VDU user as solely a machine operator. Where more or less continuous work is unavoidable some form of work–rest break schedule must be considered.

Rest pauses

In most tasks, natural breaks or pauses occur as a consequence of the inherent organization of the work. These informal breaks help to maintain performance by preventing the onset of fatigue. In some VDU work, e.g. those data entry tasks requiring continuous and sustained attention and concentration, together with high data entry rates, such naturally occurring breaks are less frequent. In situations where this type of task cannot be organized in any other way, and where natural breaks in work do not occur, the introduction of rest pauses should help attention and concentration to be maintained. It is difficult to be specific about guidance on rest pauses, since it is likely that if strictly laid down rest pauses are adhered to they will often be found to be unnecessarily prolonged and frustrating for some, and, in other circumstances, too short to prevent the onset of fatigue. The most satisfactory length of pause can only be determined by consideration of the individual operator's job, but some general statements can be made.

1. Some of the symptoms reported by operators are often the result of the effort expended in order to maintain performance in the face of accumulating fatigue. Rest pauses should therefore be arranged so that they are taken prior to the onset of fatigue, not as a recuperative period from it. Rest should be introduced when performance is at a maximum, just before a reduction in productivity. The timing of rest is more important than the length of the rest period, although optimal rest period lengths can also be determined for individual jobs (Ghiselli and Brown, 1948).

2. Short, frequently occurring pauses appear to be more satisfactory than longer ones taken occasionally.

3. Ideally the break should be taken away from the VDU.

4. Rest periods may be more useful for relatively ineffective workers; better workers seem to develop more efficient procedures and therefore have less need for rest.

5. Rest periods are more effective with work requiring concentration than with jobs that are more or less automatic and leave the employee free to daydream, converse with others, or follow similar monotony-reducing strategies.

6. A report issued by the Department of Health of New Zealand finds (Coe *et al.*, 1980) that although fatigue-like complaints about the eyes are not alleviated by mandated formal breaks, they are alleviated by informal breaks, that is, time spent not viewing the screen, which may include time spent performing other work tasks. These findings are consistent with recent work in occupational stress which emphasizes the need to allow individual operators discretion in the way tasks are carried out. Individual control over the nature and pace of work enables effort to be distributed optimally throughout the working day.

The job should be designed, therefore, to permit natural breaks, or changes in patterns of activity, as an integral part of the tasks to be performed. This may involve, for example, a mix of VDU-based and non-VDU-based work.

When the operator's job consists of a variety of tasks, some of which may involve occasional use of a VDU, minor faults in the ergonomics of the equipment may not be crucial. Conversely, when intense and continuous operation is required, the need for optimum workplace and screen characteristics become critical. However, solutions based entirely upon attention to ergonomic factors are not a panacea for low motivation and poor morale; work design and organizational factors are likely to be more important in determining the operator's overall acceptability of the computer. Thus in determining the acceptability of the system and minimizing possible indirect ill-health effects we would link work design and organizational factors with primary prevention.

The switch from orthodox office paper handling routines to VDU-based systems provides an opportunity for job enrichment and enlargement. Job flexibility and some control over work allocation should enable the promotion and utilization of individual skills. Whilst these are ideal outcomes stemming from the introduction of a computer system, they are only achieved by careful and thoughtful planning and implemention. The approach which appears to offer the most advantages and which is the most likely to achieve these objectives is that in which designers and users of the system, particularly VDU operators themselves, are jointly involved throughout the various phases of design and implementation.

We are beginning to understand something of the psychological demands inherent in VDU operation. We are not yet at a stage where very detailed recommendations can be given in order to optimize VDU task design, partly because of incomplete knowledge of possible health effects, either in the short or long term, and partly because what existing knowledge is available has been slow to be implemented.

Prevention and Management

Our eventual aim in studying occupational stress must be to provide some form of intervention aimed at reducing the problem. Here we meet an immediate dilemma. Where can limited resources and effort best be aimed? Interventions in the past have been targeted at the individual and particularly at the notion of the manager-at-risk. To some extent these views have been encouraged by the idea of the coronary-prone behaviour pattern and also by the recent developments in the health promotion literature (O'Donnell and Ainsworth, 1984). Such programmes do not typically address the environmental sources of stress, only workers' perceptions of 'distress', for example, in terms of symptomatology (Kasl, 1986). Others, however, have suggested that since much of the job-related distress can only be seen within the context of individual background and experiences, individualistic–psycho-therapeutic methods should be explored (Firth, 1985; Firth and Shapiro, 1986).

Understanding the processes involved in long-term work stress requires an appreciation of its impact on an individual basis since the experience of stress is largely determined by perceptual and cognitive evaluations of a particular work situation. Indeed, in many instances, the problem may be caused by environmental (i.e. work-based) demands which are inappropriate and not congruent with the person's skills and capabilities. Work demands may eventually overwhelm a person's capacity to deal with them (in the case of overload). On the other hand, the job may be unstimulating and unchallenging, and skills, perhaps developed over many years, may be suddenly underutilized, as in the case of underload. Similarly, there may be a discrepancy between the person's need for self-esteem, development, and satisfaction and the capacity of the working environment to meet these needs and values. Work demands which require constant striving to meet inappropriate targets and deadlines, or to produce very high-quality work under time constraints, inevitably lead to defeat and frustration in the short term, lowered evaluation of self-worth and poor mental health in the long term. Any event or situation within a working environment is a potential cause of stress experienced within the individual. The potency of the stimulus or stimuli leading to such experiences will depend on the meaning attributable to it/them, on the appraisal of ability to meet demands, and on the effectiveness of coping mechanisms. These are the essential elements of the transactional approach to stress (Cox and Mackay, 1981). The timing, frequency, intensity, and duration of the unpleasant effects evoked by conditions at work influence the potential harmfulness of work-related stress (Brodsky, 1984). Depending upon a range of factors, prolonged or severe symptomatology may impel the person to visit an occupational physician or family doctor. At this stage it is often difficult to disentangle the effects of work problems from those of non-work ones. And even if the physician is aware of the contribution a particular work difficulty is making to the patient's condition there is little he can usually do to influence the employing organization.

Choice of Strategy: Prevention or Management

Unfortunately, only a few studies have attempted critically to evaluate job stress reduction techniques. In their comprehensive and critical review of both personal and organizational strategies for handling job stress, Newman and Beehr (1979) conclude:

> Perhaps the most glaring impression we received from the review was the lack of evaluative research in this domain. Most of the strategies reviewed were based upon professional opinions and related research. Very few have been evaluated directly with any sort of scientific rigor. In spite of this weak empirical base, many personal and organisational strategies for handling stress have been espoused. Although some of these strategies seem to glow with an aura of face validity, there remains the extremely difficult task of empirically validating their effectiveness. Until this is done practitioners have little more than their common sense and visceral instincts to rely on as they attempt to develop badly needed preventive and curative stress management programmes.

Since 1979, there have been a number of published and unpublished studies providing a more rigorous evaluation of the various stress management options; on the individual level, clinically based strategies include biofeedback, muscle relaxation, and cognitive restructuring. In a critical review of such techniques, Murphy (1984) concludes that they may have significant benefits for individual wellbeing apart from other advantages, including the following. First, they can be quickly evaluated and established without major disruption to work routines. Second, they can encompass the need to take into account individual perceptions and reactions, and are thus tailored to individual needs. Third, they can combat non-work as well as work-based stress problems (which may interact synergistically). Fourth, they can be incorporated into existing employer assistance / health education packages.

The fundamental problem with such 'stress inoculation appoaches' is that for the most part they are designed solely to help the person cope with poorly designed working environments. Ganster et al. (1982) have suggested that stress management training should only be used to supplement organizational change / job redesign programmes in order to deal with stressors which cannot be designed out of the job very easily (e.g. seasonal workloads). Thus management at the secondary level (helping the person to cope) should be used to supplement attempts to identify and restructure sources of stress in the work environment—organizational, ergonomic, or psychosocial (Murphy, 1984; Broadbent, 1985).

Individuals with stress-related problems can also be helped by counselling services. On both an individual and an organizational level stress can be envisaged as a 'problem' and thus attempts at 'problem solving' are appropriate.

For many individuals part of the difficulty is in actually defining what the problem is. Most persons experiencing stress are unable to unravel the complex personal, work, and non-work factors which contribute to their feelings of uneasiness or distress. It is the meaning of each of these for the individual which is important, as is the coming to terms with those which are immutable and the changing of those which can be changed (Brodsky, 1984). Counsellors can help the worker to manage neurotic anxiety, take preventive and therapeutic measures to improve health and reduce health concerns, identify and reduce sources of family dissatisfaction, and discover personality traits that might contribute to the maintenance of a stressful situation (Field and Olsen, 1980; Rosenman and Friedman, 1977). During this process, the worker may discover that part of the problem stems from either personality difficulties or inappropriateness of training of personal skills. Whereas the former may be difficult to alter, the latter may be more conducive to manipulation by retraining or job change. Suggesting, however, that the worker leave the place of work, either temporarily or permanently, is not always in the individual's best interest and this should be considered only as a last resort. The nature of the problem identified during the counselling process has a number of implications.

If a difficulty has clearly arisen from within the individual then the process needs to help to resolve the problem within the individual, whilst always recognizing that this may have organizational consequences. On the other hand, if the problem is one largely imposed on him/her by circumstances, whether organizational or otherwise, then the consultation probably needs to be more concerned with strategies for resolving the situation. There must be, therefore, some mechanism by which decisions affecting the organization can be fed back, issues of confidentiality notwithstanding.

REFERENCES

Abdel-Halim, A. A. (1982). Social support and managerial affective responses to job stress. *Journal of Occupational Behaviour*, **3**, 281–295.

Alfredsson, L., and Theorell, T. (1983). Job characteristics of occupations and myocardial infarction risk—effect of possible confounding factors. *Social Science and Medicine*, **17**, 852–872.

Aneshensel, C. S., and Stone, J. D. (1982). Stress and depression: A test of the buffering model of social support. *Archives of General Psychiatry*, **39**, 1392–1396.

Antonovsky, A. (1974). Conceptual and methodological problems in the study of resistance resources and stressful life events. In Dohrenwend B. S. and Dohrenwend, B. P. (eds.), *Stressful Life Events: Their Nature and Effects* (pp. 245–258). New York: Wiley.

Antonovsky, A. (1979). *Health, Stress and Coping*. San Francisco: Jossey Bass.

Appelson, G. (1983). Stress on stress: Compensation cases growing. *American Bar Association Journal*, **69**, 142–143.

Averill, J. R. (1973). Personal control over aversive stimuli and its relation to stress. *Psychological Bulletin*, **80**, 286–303.

Beehr, T. A., and Newman, J. E. (1978). Job stress, employee health and organisational effectiveness. A facet analysis, model and literature review. *Personnel Psychology*, **31**, 665–699.

Berkman, L. F. (1986). Social networks, support and health: taking the next Step forward. *American Journal of Epidemiology*, **123**, 559–562.

Binashi, S., Albonico, G., Gelli, E., and Morelli di Popolo, M. R., (1982). Study on subjective symptomatology of fatigue in VDU operators. In Granjean, E., and Vigliani, E. (eds.), *Ergonomic Aspects of Visual Display Terminals* (pp. 219–225). London: Taylor & Francis.

Blau, G. (1981). An empirical investigation of job stress, social support, service length, and job strain. *Organizational Behaviour and Human Performance*, **27**, 279-302.

Bradford-Hill, A. (1965). *A Short Textbook of Medical Statistics*. Oxford: The University Press.

Brand, R. J., and Jenkins, C. D. (1975). Coronary heart disease in the Western Collaborative Group Study: Final follow up experience of 8½ years. *Journal of the American Medical Association*, **233**, 872.

Brenner, S.-O., Sorbom, D., and Wallius, E. (1985). The stress chain: A longitudinal confirmatory study of teacher stress, coping and social support. *Journal of Occupational Psychology*, **58**, 1-13.

Broadbent, D. E. (1985). The clinical impact of job design. *British Journal of Clinical Psychology*, **24**, 75-84.

Broadbent, D. E., Cooper, P. F., Fitzgerald, P., and Parkes, K. R. (1982). The Cognitive Failures Questionnaire and its correlates. *British Journal of Clinical Psychology*, **21**, 1-16.

Broadbent, D. E., and Gath, D. (1981). Ill-health on the line: Sorting myth from fact. *Department of Employment Gazette*, September, 89-93.

Broadhead, W. E., Kaplan, B. H., Shermon, A. J., Wagner, E. H., Schoenback, V. J., Grimson, R., Heyden, S., Tibbling G., and Gehlbach, S. H. (1983). The epidemiological evidence for a relationship between social support and health. *American Journal of Epidemiology*, **117**, 521-537.

Brodsky, C. (1984). Long-term work stress. *Psychosomatics*, **25**, 361-368.

Caplan, R. D., Cobb, S., French, J. R. P. J., Harrison, R. van and Pinneau, S. R. J. (1975). *Job demands and worker health*. NIOSH Research Report, HEW Publication 75-160, US Dept of Health Education and Welfare, Washington, DC.

Cassel, J. (1976). The contribution of the social environment to host resistance. *American Journal of Epidemiology*, **104**, (2), 107-122.

Cobb, S. (1976). Social support as a moderator of life stress. *Psychosomatic Medicine*. **38**, 300-314.

Coe, J. B., Cuttle, K., McClellan, W. C., and Warden, N. J. (1980). *Visual display units. A review of the potential health problems associated with their use*. Wellington NZ Regional Occupational Health Unit, New Zealand Department of Health.

Colligan, M. J., Smith, M. J., and Hurrell, J. J. (1977). Occupational incidence rates of mental health disorders. *Journal of Human Stress*, **3**, 34-42.

Cook, T. D., and Campbell, D. T. (1979). *Quasi-Experimentation: Design and Analysis Issues for Field Settings*. Chicago: Rand McNally.

Cooper, C. L., and Marshall, J. (1976). Occupational sources of stress. A review of the literature relating to coronary heart disease and mental ill health. *Journal of Occupational Psychology*, **49**, 11-28.

Cooper, C. L., and Marshall, J. (eds.) (1980). *White Collar and Professional Stress*.

Cooper, C. L., and Payne, R. (eds.) (1978). *Stress at Work*. Chichester: Wiley.

Cooper, C. L., and Payne, R. (eds.) (1980). *Current Concerns in Occupational Stress*. Chichester: Wiley.

Cooper, T., Detre, T., and Weiss, S. M. (1981). Coronary prone behaviour and coronary heart disease: a critical review. *Circulation*. **63**, 1199-1215.

Cox, T. (1985). Repetitive work: Occupational stress and health. In Cooper, C. L., and Smith M. J. (eds.), *Job Stress and Blue Collar Work*. London: Wiley.

Cox, T., and Mackay, C. J. (1979). Impact of repetitive work. In Sell, R., and Shipley, P. (eds.), *Satisfactions in Job Design*. London: Taylor and Francis.

Cox, T., and Mackay, C. J. (1981). A transactional approach to occupational stress. In Corlett, J., and Richardson, J. (eds.), *Stress, Productivity and Work Design*. Chichester: Wiley.

Cox, S., Cox, T., Thirlaway, M., and Mackay, C. J. (1983). Effects of simulated repetitive work on urinary catecholamine excretion. *Ergonomics*, **25**, 1129-1141.

Cox, T., Mackay, C. J., and Page, H. (1982). Simulated repetitive work and self-reported mood. *Journal of Occupational Behaviour*, **3**, 247-252.

Cullen, J., and Siegrist, J. (eds.), (1984). *Breakdown in Human Adaptation to Stress*. Commission of the European Communities. Dordrecht: Martinus Nijhoff.

Dainoff, M. J., Happ, A., and Crane, P. (1981). Visual fatigue and occupational stress in VDT operators. *Human Factors*, **23**, 421–438.

Dainoff, M. J., Hurrell, J., and Happ, A. (1981). A taxonomic framework for the description and evaluation of paced work. In Salvendy, G., and Smith, M. J. (eds.), *Machine Pacing and Occupational Stress*. London: Taylor & Francis.

Davidson, M. J., and Cooper, C. L. (1980). Type A coronary-prone behaviour in the work environment. *Journal of Occupational Medicine*, **22**, 375–383.

Davidson, M. J., and Cooper, C. L. (1981). A model of occupational stress. *Journal of Occupational Medicine*, **23**, 564–574.

Davis, J. (1985). Workers' compensation claims for stress-related disorders. *Journal of Occupational Medicine*, **27**, 821–825.

Dembroski, T. M., and MacDougall, J. M. (in press). Beyond global Type A: Relationships of paralinguistic attributes, hostility and anger into coronary heart disease. In Field, T., McCabe, P., and Schneiderman, N. (eds.), *Stress and Coping*. Erlbaum.

Dimsdale, J. E., Hackett, T. P., Hutter, A. M. *et al.* (1978). Type A personality and the extent of coronary atherosclerosis. *American Journal of Cardiology*, **42**, 583–586.

Dimsdale, J. E., *et al.* (1979). Type A behaviour and angiographic findings. *Journal of Psychosomatic Research*, **23**, 273.

Dohrenwend, B. P., and Shrout, P. E. (1985). 'Hassles' in the conceptualization and measurement of life stress variables. *American Psychologist*, **40**, 780–785.

Doll, R., and Peto, R. (1981). *The Causes of Cancer*. Oxford: The University Press.

Elias, R., Cail, F., Tisserand, M., Christmann, H. (1982). Investigations in operators workings with CRT display terminals: Relationships between task content and psychophysiological alterations. In Grandjean, E., and Vigliani, E. (eds.), *Ergonomic Aspects of Visual Display Terminals* (pp. 211–217). London: Taylor & Francis.

Fein, M. (1976). Motivation for work. In Dybin, R. (ed.), *Handbook of Work, Organization and Society*. Chicago: Rand McNally.

Field, J. R., and Olsen, J. (1980). Stress management. A multimodal approach. *Psychotherapy and Psychosomatics*. **34**, 233–240.

Firth, J. (1985). Personal meanings of occupational stress: Cases from the clinic. *Journal of Occupational Psychology*, **58**, 139–148.

Firth, J., and Shapiro, D. A. (1986). An evaluation of psychotherapy for job-related distress. *Journal of Occupational Psychology*, **59**, 111–119.

Fisher, S. (1985). Control and blue collar work. In Cooper, C. L., and Smith, M. L. (eds.), *Job Stress and Blue Collar Work*. London: Wiley.

Frankenhaeuser, M. 1980). Psychobiological aspects of life stress. In Levine, S., and Ursin, H. (eds.), *Coping and Health*. New York: Plenum.

Frankenhaeuser, M., and Gardell, B. (1976). Underload and overload in working life: Outline of a multidisciplinary approach. *Journal of Human Stress*, **2**, 35–46.

Frankenhaeuser, M. and Johansson, J. (1982). Stress at work: psychobiological and psychosocial aspects. Paper presented at 20th International Congress of Applied Psychology, Edinburgh, 25–31 July.

Frese, M. (1985). Stress at work and psychosomatic complaints: A causal interpretation. *Journal of Applied Psychology*, **70**, 314–328.

Friedman, M., and Rosenman, R. (1974). *Type A Behavior and Your Heart*. New York: Knopf.

Ganellen, R. J., and Blaney, P. H. (1984). Hardiness and social support as moderators of the effects of life stress. *Journal of Personality and Social Psychology*, **47**, 156–163.

Ganster, D. C., Mayes, B. T., Sime, W. E., and Tharp, G. D. (1982). Managing occupational stress. A field experiment. *Journal of Applied Psychology*. **67**, 533–542.

Gardell, B. (1982). Scandinavian research on stress in working life. *International Journal of Health Services*, **12**, 31-41.

Ghinghirelli, L. (1982). Collection of subjective opinions on use of VDUs. In Grandjean, E. and Vigliani, G. (eds.), *Ergonomic Aspects of Visual Display Terminals* (pp. 227-231). London: Taylor & Francis.

Ghiselli, E. E., and Brown, C. W. (1948). *Personnel and Industrial Psychology*. New York: McGraw-Hill.

Glass, D. C., and Singer, J. E. (1972). *Urban Stress. Experiments on Noise and Social Stressors*. New York: Academic Press.

Gore, S. (1981). Stress-buffering functions of social supports: An appraisal and clarification of research models. In Dohrenwend, B. S., and Dohrenwend, B. P. (eds.) *Stress Life Events and Their Contexts* (pp. 202-222). New York: Prodist.

Gunnarsson, E., and Ostberg, O. (1977). *The Physical and Psychological Working Environment in a Terminal-based Computer Storage and Retrieval System*. Report No. 35. National Board of Occupational Safety and Health, Stockholm.

Harrison, R. van (1976). Job stress as person environment misfit. A Symposium presented at the 84th Annual Convention of the American Psychological Association, Michigan.

Haynes, S. G., Feinleib, M., and Kannel, W. B. (1980). The relationship of psychosocial factors to coronary heart disease in the Framingham Study: III Eight year incidence of coronary heart disease. *American Journal of Epidemiology*, **III**, 37.

Henderson, M., and Argyle, A. (1985). Social support by four categories of work colleagues: Relationships between activities, stress and satisfaction. *Journal of Occupational Behaviour*, **6**, 229-239.

Holt, R. R. (1982). Occupational stress. In Goldberger L., and Brenitz, S. (eds.), *Handbook of Stress*. New York: Free Press.

House, J. S. (1981). *Work Stress and Social Support*. Reading, Mass. Addison-Wesley.

House, J. S., and Kahn, R. L. (1985). Measures and concepts of social support. In Cohen, S., and Syme, L. (eds.), *Social Support and Health*. New York: Academic Press.

Hurrell, J. J., and Colligan, M. J. (1982). Psychological job stress. In Rom, W. I. N. (ed.), *Environmental and Occupational Medicine*. Boston, Mass.: Little Brown.

Industrial Injuries Advisory Council (1981). *Industrial Diseases: A Review of the Schedule and the Question of Individual Proof*. London: HMSO.

Jayaratne, S., and Chess, W. A. (1984). The effects of emotional support on perceived job stress and strain. *Journal of Applied Behavioural Science*, **20**, 141-153.

Jenkins, C. D. (1978). Behavioural risk factors in coronary heart disease. *Annual Review of Medicine*, **29**, 543.

Jenkins, C. D., Zyzanski, S. J., and Rosenman, R. H. (1976). Risk of myocardial infarction in middle-aged men with manifest coronary heart disease. *Circulation*, **53**, 342.

Johansson, G. (1979). Psychoneuroendocrine reactions to mechanised and computerised work routines: In Mackay, C. J., and Cox, T. (eds.), *Response to Stress: Occupational Aspects*. Guildford: IPC Science and Technology Press.

Johansson, G., and Aronsson, G. (1981). Stress reactions in computerised administrative work. Supplement 50. Reports from the Department of Psychology, The University of Stockholm.

Johansson, G., and Sanden, P. (1982). Mental load and job satisfaction of control room operators. Report No 40. Department of Psychology, University of Stockholm.

Kagan, A. (1975). Epidemiology, disease and emotion. In Levi, L. (ed.), *Emotion — Their Parameters and Measurement*. New York: Raven Press.

Kahn, R. L., Hein, K., House, J., Jasl, S. V., and McLean, A. A. (1982). Report on stress in organizational settings. In Elliot, G. R., and Gisdorfer, C. (eds.), *Stress and Human Health*. New York: Springer.

Kaplan, B. H., Cassel, J. L., and Gore, S. (1977). Social support and health. *Medical Care*, **15** (5) (Suppl.) 47-58.

Karasek, R. A. (1979). Job demands, job decision latitude and mental strain, implications for job redesign. *Administrative Science Quarterly*, **24**, 285–308.

Karasek, R. A. (1981). Job socialization and job strain: The implications of two related psychosocial mechanisms for job design. In Gardell, B., and Johansson, G. (eds.), *Working Life*. Chichester: Wiley.

Karasek, R. A. (1982). Stress at work cardiovascular disease. Mimeograph. New York. Columbia University, Department of Industrial Engineering and Operations Research.

Kasl, S. V. (1974). Work and mental health. In O'Toole, J. (ed.), *Work and the Quality of Life*. Cambridge Mass.: MIT Press.

Kasl, S. V. (1978). Epidemiological contributions to the study of work stress. In Cooper, C. and Payne, R. (eds.), *Stress at Work*. Chichester: Wiley.

Kasl, S. V. (1986). Stress and disease in the workplace. A methodological commentary on the accumulated evidence. In Cataldo, M. F., and Coates, T. J. (eds.), *Health and Industry. A Behavioural Medicine Perspective*. New York: Wiley.

Kasl, S. V., and Cobb, S. (1983). Psychological and social stresses in the workplace. In Levy, B. S., and Wegman, D. H. (eds.), *Occupational Health*. Boston, Mass.: Little Brown.

Kasl, S. V., and Wells, J. A. (1985). Work and the family: Social support and health in the middle years. In Cohen, S., and Syme, L. (eds.), *Social Support and Health*. New York: Academic Press.

Keenan, A., and McBain, G. C. M. (1979). Effects of Type A behaviour, intolerance of ambiguity, and locus of control on the relationship between role stress and work-related outcomes. *Journal of Occupational Psychology*, **52**, 277–285.

Kessler, R. C., Price, R. H., and Wortman, C. B. (1985). Social factors in psychopathology: Stress, social support, and coping processes. *Annual Review of Psychology*, **36**, 531–572.

Kobasa, S. C. (1979a). Stressful life events, personality and health: An inquiry into hardiness. *Journal of Personality and Social Psychology*, **37**, 1–11.

Kobasa, S. C. (1979b). Personality and resistance to illness. *American Journal of Community Psychology*, **7**, 413–423.

Kobasa, S. C. (1982). Commitment and coping in stress resistance among lawyers. *Journal of Personality and Social Psychology*, **42**, 707–717.

Kobasa, S. C., Maddi, S. R., and Courington, S. (1981). Personality and constitution as mediators in the stress–illness relationship. *Journal of Health and Social Behaviour*, **22**, 368–378.

Kobasa, S. C., Maddi, S. R., and Kahn, S. (1982). Hardiness and health; a prospective study. *Journal of Personality and Social Psychology*, **42**, 168–177.

Kobasa, S. C., and Puccetti, M. C. (1983). Personality and social resources in stress-resistance. *Journal of Personality and Social Psychology*, **45**, 839–850.

Kohn, M. (1972). Class, family and schizophrenia. *Social Forces*, **50**, 295.

Krause, N., and Stryker, S. (1984). Stress and well-being: The buffering role of locus of control beliefs. *Social Science and Medicine*, **18**, 783–790.

LaRocco, J. M., House, J. S., and French, J. R. P. (1980). Social support, occupational stress, and health. *Journal of Health and Social Behaviour*, **21**, 202–218.

LaRocco, J. M., and Jones, A. P. (1978). Coworker and leader support as moderators of stress-strain relationships in work situations. *Journal of Applied Psychology*, **63**, 629–634.

Lazarus, R. S., DenLongis, A., Folkman, S., and Gruen, R. (1985). Stress and adaptational outcomes. *American Psychologist*. **40**, 770–779.

Leavy, R. L. (1983). Social support and psychological disorder: A review. *Journal of Community Psychology*, **11**, 3–21.

Lefcourt, H. M., Martin, R. A., and Saleh, W. E. (1984). Locus of control and social support: Interactive moderators of stress. *Journal of Personality and Social Psychology*. **47**, 378–389.

Levenson, H., Hirschfield, M. A., and Hirschfield, A. H. (1980). Industrial accidents and recent life events. *Journal of Occupational Medicine*, **22**, 53–57.

Levi, L. (1972). Stress and distress in response to psychosocial stimuli *Acta Medica Scandinavica* (Suppl.) p. 528.

MacDougall, J. M., Dembroski, T. M., and Dimsdale, J. E. (1985). Components of Type A, hostility and anger. In further relationships to angiographic findings. *Health Psychology*, **4**, 137.

McGrath, J. E. (1970). Major methodological issues. In McGrath, J. E. (ed.), *Social and Psychological Factors in Stress*. New York: Holt, Rinehart, & Winston.

McGrath, J. E. (1976). Stress and behaviour in organisations. In Dunnette, M. D. (ed.), *Handbook of Industrial and Organizational Psychology*. Chicago: Rand McNally.

Mackay, C. J. (1980). The measurement of mood and psychophysiological activity using self-report techniques. In Martin, I., and Venables, P. H. (eds.), *Techniques in Psychophysiology*. Chichester: Wiley.

Mackay, C. J., and Cox, T. (1979). *Response to Stress: Occupational Aspects*. Guildford: IPC Science and Technology Press.

Mackay, C. J., and Cox, T. (1984). Occupational stress associated with visual display unit operation. In Pearce, B. G. (ed.), *Health Hazards of VDUs?* Chichester: Wiley.

Mackay, C. J., Cox, T., Burrows, G. C., and Lazzerini, A. J. (1978). An inventory for the measurement of self-reported stress and arousal. *British Journal of Social and Clinical Psychology*, **17**, 283-284.

Mackay, C. J., Cox, T., Watts, C., Thirlaway, M., and Lazzerini, A. J. (1979). Physiological correlates of repetitive work. In Mackay, C. J., and Cox, T. (eds.), *Response to Stress. Occupational Aspects*. Guildford: IPC.

Mackay, C. J., and Lucas, E. G. (1986). Occupational aspects of whole person health care. In Christie, M. J., and Mellett, P. G. (eds.), *The Psychosomatic Approach: Contemporary Practice of Whole Person Health Care*. London: Wiley.

McLean, A. A. (1979). *Work Stress*. Reading, Mass.: Addison-Wesley.

Matthews, K. A., and Haynes, S. G. (1986). Type A behaviour pattern and coronary disease risk. *American Journal of Epidemiology*, **123**, 923-960.

Moss, L. (1981). *Management Stress*. Reading, Mass.: Addison-Wesley.

Murphy, L. R. (1984). Occupational stress management: A review and appraisal. *Journal of Occupational Psychology*, **57**, 1-15.

Murrell, K. (1964). Laboratory studies in paced work, 1 and 2. *International Journal of Production Research*, **2**, 169-185.

Newman, J. D., and Beehr, T. (1979). Personal and organisational strategies for handling job stress: A review of research and opinion. *Personnel Psychology*, **32**, 1-43.

O'Donnell, M. P., and Ainsworth, T. (1984). *Health Promotion in the Workplace*. New York: Wiley.

Orne, M. T. (1961). On the social psychology of the psychological experiment with particular reference to demand characteristics and their implications. *American Psychologist*, **17**, 776-783.

Parkes, K. R. (1982). Occupational stress in student nurses: A natural experiment. *Journal of Applied Psychology*, **67**, 784-796.

Parkes, K. R. (1984). Locus of control, cognitive appraisal and coping in stressful episodes. *Journal of Personality and Social Psychology*, **46**, 655-668.

Pearlin, L., and Schooler, C. (1978). The structure of coping. *Journal of Health and Social Behaviour*, **19**, 2.

Rassmussen, J. (1979). On the structure of knowledge—a morphology of mental models in a man-machine system context. *Report No. Risø-M-2192*, Risiønal Laboratory, DK-4000, Roskilde, Denmark.

Rosenman, R. H., and Friedman, M. (1977). Modifying Type A behaviour patterns. *Journal of Psychosomatic Research*. **21**, 323-331.

Sales, S. M. (1969). Differences among individuals in attentive, behavioural, biochemical and physiological responses to variations in workload. Unpublished Ph.D. thesis. University of Michigan.

Salvendy, G. (1981). Classification and characteristics of paced work. In Salvendy, G., and Smith, M. J. (eds.), *Machine Pacing and Occupational Stress*. London: Taylor & Francis.

Sandler, I. N., and Lakey, B. (1982). Locus of control as a stress moderator. The role of control perceptions and social support. *American Journal of Community Psychology*. **10**, 65-80.

Sauter, S. L., Gottlieb, M. S., Jones, K. C., Dodson, V. N., and Rohrer, K. M. (1983). Job and health implications of VDT use: Initial results of the Wisconsin-NIOSH Study. *Communications of the ACM*, **26**, 285-294.

Schottenfeld, R. S., and Cullen, M. R. (1986). Recognition of occupation-induced posttraumatic stress disorders. *Journal of Occupational Medicine*, **28**, (5), 365-369.

Seers, A., McGee, G. W., Serey, T. T., and Graen, G. B. (1983). The interaction of job stress and social support: A strong inference investigation. *Academy of Management Journal*, **26**, 273-284.

Seligman, M. H. P. (1975). *Helplessness: On Depression, Development and Death*. San Francisco: Freeman.

Sells, S. B. (1970). On the nature of stress. In McGrath, J. E. (ed.), *Social and Psychological Factors in Stress*. New York: Holt, Rinehart and Winston.

Sharit, J., and Salvendy, G. (1982). Occupational stress: Review and appraisal. *Human Factors*, **24**, 129-162.

Shaw, J. B., and Riskind, J. H. (1983). Predicting job stress using data from the position analysis questionnaire. *Journal of Applied Psychology*, **68**, 253-261.

Sheehan, D. V., O'Donnell, J. O., Fitzgerald, A., Hervig, L., and Ward, H. (1981-1982). Psychosocial predictors of accident/error rates in nursing students: A prospective study. *International Journal of Psychiatry in Medicine*, **11**, 125-136.

Shekelle, R. B., Hulley, S. B., and Neaton, J. D. (1985). The MRFIT behaviour pattern study: II. Type A behaviour and the incidence of coronary heart disease. *American Journal of Epidemiology*, **122**, 559-570.

Shostak, A. B. (1980). *Blue-collar Stress*. Reading, Mass.: Addison-Wesley.

Smith, M. J. (1985). Machine paced work and stress. In Cooper, C. L. and Smith, M. J. (eds.), *Job Stress and Blue Collar Work*. London: Wiley.

Smith, M. J., Cohen, B. G. F., and Stammerjohn, L. W. (1981). An investigation of health complaints and job stress in video display operations. *Human Factors*, **23**, 387-400.

Smith, M. J. Hurrell, J., and Murphy, R. K. (1981). Stress and health effects in paced and unpaced work. In Salvendy, G., and Smith, M. J. (eds.), *Machine Pacing and Occupational Stress*. London: Taylor & Francis.

Smith, M. J., Stammerjohn, L. W., Cohen, B. G. F., and Lalich, N. R. (1980). *Job Stress in Video Display Operations*. National Institute of Occupational Safety and Health, Cincinnati, Ohio.

Stuart, J. C., and Brown, O. M. (1981). The relationship of stress and coping ability to incidence of disease and accidents. *Journal of Psychosomatic Research*, **25**, 255-260.

Swain, A., and Guttman, R. S. (1980). *Handbook of Human Reliability Analysis with Emphasis on Nuclear Power Plant Applications*. Sandia Laboratories Nuclear Regulatory Commission NUREG/CR 1278.

Taylor, C. B., Agras, S. W. Sevelius, G. (1986). Managing hypertension in the workplace. In Cataldo, M. F., and Coates, T. J. (eds.), *Health and Industry. A Behavioural Medicine Perspective*. New York: Wiley.

Thoits, P. A. (1982). Conceptual, methodological, and theoretical problems in studying social support as a buffer against life stress. *Journal of Health and Social Behaviour*, **23**, 145-159.

Wallin, L., Winkvist, E., and Svensson, G. (1983). *Terminalanvandares arbetsmiljo—en enkatstudie vid Volvo i Goteborg* (The work environment of terminal users—a questionnaire study of Volvo in Gothenburg, in Swedish). Gothenburg, Sweden: A. B. Volvo.

Wallston, B. S., Alagna, S. W., DeVellis, B. M., and Devellis, R. F. (1983). Social support and physical health. *Health Psychology*, **2**, 367–391.

Wheaton, B. (1980). The sociogenesis of psychological disorder: An attributional theory. *Journal of Health and Social Behaviour*, **21**, 100–110.

Wilkes, B., Stammerjohn, L., and Lalich, N. (1981). Job demands and worker health in machine paced poultry inspection. *Scandinavian Journal of Work Environment and Health*, Supplement, **4**, 12–19.

Williams, R. B., *et al.* (1980). Type A behaviour, hostility and coronary atherosclerosis. *Psychosomatic Medicine*. **42**, 539.

Winnubst, J. A. M., Marcelissen, F. H. G., and Kleber, R. J. (1982). Effects of social support in the stressor-strain relationship: A Dutch sample. *Social Science and Medicine*, **16**, 475–482.

World Health Organization (1980). *Health Aspects of Well-being in Working places*. EURO Reports and Studies, 31. Regional Office for Europe. Copenhagen.

International Review of Industrial and Organizational Psychology 1987
Edited by C. L. Cooper and I. T. Robertson
©1987 John Wiley & Sons Ltd

Chapter 7

INDUSTRIAL ACCIDENTS

Noel P. Sheehy and Antony J. Chapman
Department of Psychology
University of Leeds
UK

It might seem obvious to say that industrial accidents are usually a consequence of human error, but the implications of such a statement need to be emphasized. Human behaviour is multicausal: there are many facets to it; and errors can be complex. Hence any attempts to identify 'the' cause of an accident, or even to identify clusters of primary causes, are destined to fail. In accident investigations 'cause' is often a difficult notion. Society at large has expected to be given causal explanations, but such explanations—involving several dozen variables, and interactions between those variables—have not met the pragmatic need for action to reduce the likelihood of similar occurrences.

In this review of industrial accidents the view taken is that good theory cannot develop without frequent, direct input from practice, the practice needs theory to order and evelute its activity (David, Foot, Chapman, and Sheehy, 1986). The chapter begins with a consideration of issues in accident reporting; it proceeds to a treatment, in turn, of individual, environmental, and organizational factors; and then to prevention, with passing reference to ergonomic factors.

ACCIDENT REPORTING

In a review of accident reporting systems Adams and Hartwell (1977) noted that such systems have not usually been designed for information surveillance. Most of them have grown, in unplanned ways, to meet specific organizational, medical, and legal needs. Also, most of them fail to elicit ergonomic information (Anderson, 1983), and consequently accumulated accident data can have only limited impact when new equipment and machinery is being designed.

Andreassend (1983) has clarified a useful distinction between primary accident *classes* and accident *types*. Accident classes are crude subdivisions of accidents (e.g. burns, falls, 'lost time') which provide descriptions and thereby classifications of accidents in terms of consequential similarities. Differentiation within accident classes is normally based upon the uses to which data may be put. Generally, the primary accident classes (e.g. 'transport', 'machinery') are easily defined, but accident types (e.g. 'driving', 'operating') are more difficult because of their functional significance.

Accident-reporting systems have concentrated on providing information in primary accident classes, and this has placed severe limitations on their usefulness. Taking back pain as an example, Nordby (1982) has pointed out that in the USA low back pain is the most common element in workers' compensation claims. In many cases the cause of such pain is accidental exposure to excessive lifting stress. Usually the effects of such stress do not appear immediately but, when workers report lumbar injury, it is often apparent that its severity could have been reduced or avoided through prior monitoring of minor lifting hazards and minor injuries. Although back pain is prevalent, Manning (1985) has noted that it is difficult to obtain information on it from conventional accident-reporting systems.

Some accident reporting systems are subsystems of larger health surveillance systems. These subsystems are advantageous to the extent that they place the accident in a broad and informative health context; but inquiries of a specialized nature are then difficult to accommodate (John, Marsh, and Enterline, 1983). However, safety officers and managers are increasingly concerned to sensitize accident surveillance systems to covert, latent injury (e.g. Shindell and Goldberg, 1981) and thereby accommodate more specialized investigations. If this trend continues it is probable that accident surveillance systems will increase in size and complexity, chiefly through integration and expansion within broad-based occupational health surveillance systems.

The inauguration of the Swedish Information System on Occupational Accidents and Disease (ISA) is a move in this direction at a national level. It is based on claims for work injury insurance and responds to a need for information in four areas: (1) preventable risks, (2) preventive methods, (3) cost–benefit analysis (i.e. cost of accidental injury against the cost of its prevention), and (4) willingness to seek a solution at political and organizational levels. It is too early for national information systems, such as the ISA, to provide detailed information on industrial and agent specific tasks. However, from a political perspective, they are already crucial because they quantify risks and costs in relative terms; consequently, they can be used to identify priority areas for intervention (Andersson and Lagerlof, 1983).

Adams, Barlow, and Hiddlestone (1981), pursuing suggestions of Adams and Hartwell for improving accident reporting, designed and tested a highly structured accident reporting schedule. It contained, for example, sections designed to elicit information on the injury agent, the behavioural antecedents of the accident, situational variables, and task variables. While highly structured 'categorical' systems do give rise to large amounts of welcome information, some of the data may be deceptive. Definitional precision is difficult to achieve, and categorical information may give a false impression of reliability. Moreover, once categorical labels (e.g. 'misjudgement') are made available they tend to be used and the data elicited through the system tend to support, in self-perpetuating fashion, the implicit theories of accident causation underlying the system's development. For example, Edwards (1981), in examining the detailed structure of two accident surveillance systems, found that the model of accident causation implicit in each was one which emphasized victim culpability: however, that model was supported by the bias towards collecting information on *victim characteristics* in isolation from other pertinent features of accidents. With such incestuous derivations accident statistics are unlikely to provide appropriate tests of accident causation hypotheses.

One further point noted by Adams et al. (1981) is that, to make meaningful statements about the relative contributions of different variables, and to facilitate interactive analyses between sets of categories, there needs to be a planned overlap between data categories. Though innovations of this kind are important, they do not tackle the criticism that accident reports paint a grossly misleading picture — in so far as they cannot begin to cater for the complexity of emotional responses associated with the occurrence, prevention, and investigation of accidents.

The same researchers (Adams *et al.*, 1981) conducted an analysis of almost 10 000 injuries over a 4-year period. They reported that the well-known 'Black Monday' effect, first observed by Powell, Hale, Martin, and Simon (1971), was absent from their data. Instead, the most salient feature in their data was the injury distribution according to 'time since last break': there was a relatively large incidence of accidents during the first 40 minutes following a break, with a peak at 40 minutes which was sustained for half an hour. The kinds of descriptions obtained with the Adams *et al.* system were essentially consequential (e.g. 'failure to allow for physical properties of the material') and, therefore, do not provide the detail required to develop safety innovations. We believe, from a prevention point of view, that accident statistics of this kind have little to offer other than to indicate the presence or otherwise of a particular problem. Fundamentally, the limitation of most accident data is that they do not provide a measure of *exposure* and, in the absence of independent measures of exposure, the data are next to impossible to interpret (see Hodge and Richardson, 1985).

Accidents are relatively rare events and usually it is necessary to wait a considerable period of time, perhaps several months or years, in order to build up a reasonable sample for study. Komaki, Barwick, and Scott (1978) have shown that while large samples can be obtained by incorporating cases of minor injuries the ensuing data are not necessarily more reliable simply because the sample is large. This is because the definition has been widened in order to accommodate different injuries. There is likely to be wide variation in the reporting of 'normal' and 'commonplace' injuries plus constantly shifting perceptions of injury severity (see Bull, 1985). Whether an injury is perceived and reported as 'severe' will tend to depend on availability and proximity of medical care.

There is a growing consensus that, from the perspectives of understanding accident causation (Sheehy, 1981) and prevention (Glendon and Hale, 1985), further in-depth analysis of accident statistics is an exercise of limited value. Glendon and Hale (1985) have provided a good demonstration of the limitations of accident data: they conducted a detailed analysis of accidents among a population of young adults on an employment training programme in the UK, and they found that a mere 20 per cent of the variance in accident severity could be explained by as many as 21 predictor variables in a discriminant function analysis.

Criticisms of accident analyses based upon statistics stem partly from dissatisfaction with the treatment of accidents as *events* rather than as *processes*. Routine tasks are experienced in everyday life as continuous, meaningful processes, and the psychological investigation of tasks conventionally gives appropriate emphasis to the continuity (Kay, 1971). The occurrence in the workplace of an unforeseen outcome with serious consequences typically prompts a redefinition, and this entails a narrow perception of the whole sequence as an event. Taylor (1981) has gone so far as to suggest that accidents should be viewed as inherently meaningless events which are separated from the meaningful antecedents and consequences. Improving accident reporting systems involves recognition of a fundamental problem: the collection of categorical data allows for completeness but at the expense of creating arbitrary discontinuities in the accident sequence. The collection of process reports—e.g. through verbal protocols (see Bainbridge, 1979)—preserves the integrity of the process but, on the other hand, such reports rarely conform to a single structure and they vary in their degree of explicitness.

Potentially the use of intelligent knowledge-based computer systems to collect and analyse data provides a technology to help extract advantages from both approaches to the investigation of accidents. First, implied moral responsibility is reduced in person–computer dialogue. Second, computers are systematic and so increase the likelihood that complete reports are obtained on all accidents. Third, the computer can generate hypotheses and query users about their assessments of those hypotheses. Fourth, in principle users can query the computer and those queries can be used as an integral part of the accident report. Fifth, with rapid advances in computational linguistics, computers are increasingly capable of receiving large quantities of continuous text (e.g. transcripts of verbal protocols) and analysing those texts. Intelligent computer–user dialogue provides prospects for a more efficient and effective way of eliciting information on accidents than conventional person–person investigation. There is already a small number of computer-based data registration systems commercially available for popular mainframe and minicomputers and potentially their intelligence can be upgraded (Whyte, 1982). Finally, computerized record keeping will facilitate the application of simulation methodology, an approach to theory testing advocated by Smillie and Ayoub (1976/1977) which has yet to be fully exploited.

INDIVIDUAL DIFFERENCES

Accident Proneness

Undoubtedly 'accident proneness', originally described by Greenwood and Woods (1919), has been the most important concept in the study of individual differences in accident causation. In reviewing the history and status of this controversial concept McKenna (1983) referred to two problematic issues. First, inappropriate statistical techniques have persistently been used to investigate proneness. The unequal liability to accidents within the population is described reasonably well by a negative binomial distribution and better than by a poisson distribution (Boyle, 1980a); but acceptance of the negative binomial model rests on the assumption, usually untenable, that exposure and biases in accident reporting are equally distributed across the population in question. Second, the concept is used loosely and inconsistently. McKenna (1983) has proposed replacing the term 'proneness' with the more neutral 'differential accident involvement'. The adoption of his proposal could circumvent the long-standing incongruency between the meaning of the concept and the way it should be investigated. Also it would probably weaken the practice of attempting to show that small groups of individuals are allegedly responsible for the majority of accidents. We would agree with McKenna that differential accident involvement amounts to a hypothesis to be tested rather than an explanation for events.

Personality Characteristics

While there is no evidence to suggest that accident proneness is a genetic trait (see McKenna, 1983), the question remains open as to whether personality characteristics and accident liability are related. Probably personality characteristics influence stress-coping styles which in turn affect accident involvement. For example, Studenski (1981) reported that, among coalminers in low, medium, and high accident rate mines, the experience of an accident produced a temporary sharp increase in anxiety among the miners. However, in mines with extremely high accident rates the opposite occurred, and possibly this is because through unsound statistical reasoning an accident is sometimes taken to portend a period of relative safety.

Various studies have reported associations between indices of accidents, illness, and personality. So, for example, Stuart and Brown (1981) found that levels of self-reported stress correlate with accident and disease liability; Schenk and Rausche (1979) found that neuroticism discriminates between high and low accident drivers; Allodi and Montgomery (1979) found that a positive history of medical, surgical, and psychosomatic episodes differentiated a group of 255 workers who had accidents from 215 no-accident controls; Jimenez (1977) found that workers with three or more accidents during a 6-month period had higher levels of aggressiveness than a comparison no-accident group; and Mayer (1981) found a weak non-significant relationship between qualitative performance on the Porteus Maze Test and incidence of reported accidents among 80 workers.

A basic difficulty with these and similar studies is that they are *retrospective* and so causal connections between personal dispositions and differences in accident liability are difficult to infer. Suppose, for example, that the focus is on stress as a causal factor. There are substantial reports to the effect that workload increases the level of perceived stress and the probability of accidental injuries (e.g. Cellier, 1980). Usually, however, the occurrence of an accident itself causes additional stress (Hart and Bartolussi, 1984), as does the supervening criticism from supervisors and managers (Franasczuk and Kopaczewska, 1978). Plainly, retrospective studies cannot discriminate between the stress that 'caused' the accident and the stress produced by its occurrence.

Many retrospective studies, like many non-retrospective studies, can be criticized on other methodological grounds too. For example, it is not uncommon for dependent and independent variables to be confounded: Allodi and Montgomery (1979) used medically-related dependent variables to discriminate between their accident and non-accident groups, and thereby almost certainly confounded their variables. In many cases a difference observed *post hoc* between accident and non-accident groups forms the basis for an explanation of differential accident liability, and this can promote confusion. Of course, some retrospective studies have not been analysed simplistically. For instance, Metts (1982) studied 302 work injuries and found that smokers had a relatively greater risk of accident involvement. One way of interpreting this finding would be to treat the difference as providing an explanation for the differential accident liability. A better interpretation, pursued by Metts, is to see the difference as requiring explanation. Metts reported that the relationship between smoking and accident liability was due to specific conflict on certain kinds of tasks, rather than smoking as such.

Life Events

Differential accident involvement is not necessarily a stable, trait-like phenomenon. Individuals may have a bout of accidents because of general stress induced by a 'life event'. Levenson, Hirschfeld, and Hirschfeld (1980) have reported above average pre-accident life-event frequency among groups of accident victims, and in general strong links have been drawn between coping styles, mental health, and work performance (Defares, Brandjes, Nass, and Ploeg, 1984).

Like studies of personality characteristics, a fundamental difficulty with the investigation of life events is that studies are almost always retrospective: it is impossible from such studies to identify strong, unambiguous associations between life events and accidents. There is also a general difficulty with this type of research, and it is that people tend to forget large numbers of events, especially negative events (see Jenkins, Hurst, and Rose, 1979). Moreover, a critical incident, such as an accident, may strengthen memories of otherwise 'ambient' stressors and these subsequently may be imbued with special significance (Jenkins et al., 1979).

A salient possibility demanding investigation is that accidents may be precipitated by the drug and alcohol use associated with attempts to manage a crisis. In other words, in part at least, the link between accidents and critical life events may be mediated by the effects of drugs which may be taken in unusually large quantities around the period of a crisis. If there is a strong link between critical life events and accident liability then, from a management point of view, the most efficient method of reducing excessive risk of accidents is probably through education about substance abuse. Most people are not aware of their general vulnerability during periods of intense stress (see Levenson, 1980). For example, it may be commonly recognized that stress is associated with sleep loss, but it is not so well recognized that sleep loss is associated with industrial accidents (Lavie, Kremerman, and Wiel, 1982). The link between accidents and sleep loss may be causal on some occasions but on others it may be mediated by different stress-provoking factors. Making individuals more aware of their vulnerability may in itself be sufficient to facilitate extra caution.

Differential accident liability correlates with problem drinking and social isolation (Wellman, 1982), and this points to the importance of viewing transient liability as an indicator of stress. Many people, at one time or another, resort to drugs, including alcohol, as a way of coping (Midanik, 1983). The hypothesis that alcohol consumption and industrial accidents may be related causally has strong face validity, and laboratory work shows clear decremental effects on sensory-motor functioning (Wolkenberg, Gold, and Tichauer, 1975).

Most of the research on accidents and alcohol consumption has examined groups of unknown or suspected alcoholics (e.g. Levens, 1976; White, 1978). Research on employees who manifest chronic episodes of drinking or sustained heavy drinking is rare. This is due in part to the fact that the effects of heavy alcoholism are likely to be determined by the nature of the jobs. Little is known of the specific effects of alcohol on performance of particular tasks. Performance decrements with high concentrations of blood alcohol are certain to occur (Price and Hicks, 1979) but the extent of decrements at low levels (e.g. through casual midday drinking) has not been studied.

The limited evidence available suggests that the effects of alcohol are not simple but are determined by the nature of the task, the ability of the worker, the safety margins adopted, and the alcohol experience of the worker (Shain, 1982). Manello (1979) reported details of a study of railroad employees which showed that 20 per cent of men on 'standby' arrived at work 'hung over' and a further 20 per cent arrived drunk. Pelz (1976) quotes West German statistics which suggest that alcohol is a contributing or major cause of 7-10 per cent of cases of industrial injury, and in the USA Parker and Brody (1981) found that 10 per cent of women and 19 per cent of men were occupational alcoholics (i.e. repetitive excessive drinkers).

Alcohol is the diluent in a large proportion of over-the-counter proprietary medications, and in a North American survey 85 per cent of 10 000 interviewees indicated that they either did not follow the advice on the packaging of drugs they were taking or they did not understand its significance (Tabor, 1982). Silverman (1981a, 1981b, 1981c) has provided a comprehensive review of the psycho-pharmacological properties of commonly available pharmaceutical preparations, but virtually nothing is known about the extent of use and abuse of over-the-counter drugs. There is urgent need for large-scale epidemiological studies of alcohol and drug usage patterns in industry. Preventive measures currently in use are crude, and they are used haphazardly. Essentially there are three management options: terminate the contracts of employees who are intoxicated when involved in an accident; or design and implement employee assistance programmes; or tackle addiction and abuse problems through general education. It is impossible to judge the efficiency and effectiveness of these solutions. Evaluative studies are required as a priority.

Perception of Risk

Often it has been assumed that discrepancies between objective risk distributions, as measured by accident statistics (i.e. reported accidents), and their subjective representatives may be a contributory factor in accidents (see Amsalem, Defranoux, and Bach, 1977; Edwards and Hahn, 1980). Vasilescu (1978), for example, obtained questionnaire responses from 328 workers and found that whereas the probability of occupational illness was usually estimated accurately, danger of accidents was underestimated. In an earlier study he identified 'spatial balancing of probability' as possibly a factor contributing to the discrepancies in estimates (Vasilescu, 1977). An increase in the objective probability of an accident may generate proportionate denial of its likelihood (i.e. perceived probability).

The link hypothesized here between risk and accident is perceptual: discrepancies between subjective estimates of risk and their objective counterparts leave people poorly prepared to detect and cope with potential hazards. The larger the under-estimation of objective risk the greater the probability that potentially dangerous situations will become accident situations. Conversely, one might predict that when subjective risk distributions approximate objective distributions the incidence of accidents should be minimized. However, in practice the incidence does not then approach zero (see Ostberg, 1980). This is partly because objective assessments of risk are not inherently more reliable than subjective assessments (Sheehy and Chapman, 1985). A distinction has to be drawn between two kinds of objective risk: 'true' objective risk and 'actual' objective risk. True objective risk is notional: it refers to the true risk associated with a particular activity. Actual objective risk is judged from exposure data: it is calculated on the basis of what is known about the incidence of injury accidents. Injury-producing accidents are not always reported and exposure data are not always available; hence, 'objective' risk, pragmatically, is an opinion and thereby is akin to subjective risk.

From the standpoint of prevention the distinction between subjective and objective risk remains important. Objective risk is normative, in the sense that it is based on events that are known to have happened, and it cannot be disproved because it is a post-accident assessment. The shape of the objective risk distribution is altered by additional accidents and by unusual accidents, but whatever its shape it cannot be declared untenable. Subjective risk is context-sensitive and reflects anticipations which can easily be shown to be wrong. Thus, subjective and objective risk serve different functions and it would be wrong to presume the superiority of objective risk.

Brown (1980) has argued that conventional hypotheses about the relationship between subjective and objective risk (see Näätänen and Summala, 1975) are oversimplified. In particular he maintains that subjective risk is weighted by the perceived likelihood of correcting errors. Subjective risk is a function of decision error probabilities and error correction probabilities. Thus, increasing people's awareness of the discrepancy between assessed objective risk and their perceptions of that risk will not necessarily bring about a reduction in accidents. Often safety requires taking sufficient precautions to permit opportunities to rectify errors.

Reason (1979), working from a different perspective, has reached the same conclusion. He has argued that increased automation tends to eliminate possibilities for error repair and therefore indirectly increases the probability of certain kinds of accident. It would seem that accident reduction is more likely to come from training in error correction skills than it is from informing individuals of their perceptual errors (Bailey, 1983). Through simulation techniques, training in error correction has been particularly effective in reducing control room accidents in high-risk technology plants (e.g. Marshall and Baker, 1985). Blignaut (1979a), using a simulator to teach novice miners about signals of possible rockfalls, has shown that the ability to switch between the production and safety aspects of the task can be an essential element of successful training. Production and safety were often seen as separate mining tasks, and successful perception of hazards appeared to be associated with the facility to switch between production and safety response modes.

The disparity between subjective and objective risk causes problems from a management point of view. Kasper (1980) has provided a detailed analysis of the nature of these problems, and he has identified four specific issues. First, the disparity encourages the use of propaganda in order to communicate and promote the 'objective' position. Second, there is an erosion of trust between those responsible for estimating the objective risks (the 'experts') and those who arrive at different conclusions daily (the workforce or public). Third, decisions about safety priorities are complicated: subjective estimates cannot be disregarded for they may imply a different set of priorities from those implied by the expert assessments. Fourth, experts and managers are likely to be called repeatedly to explain uncertainties about the effects of their assessments and decisions. Kasper's analysis suggests that attempts to discriminate against subjective estimates of risk, from the expert or 'objective' perspective, are unlikely to bring about the desired changes in subjective evaluations. Usually what is required is a cooperative effort between experts and those who are most directly affected by their assessments. In this way a rational risk appraisal is more likely to be possible and the tangible safety benefits are more likely to endure.

ENVIRONMENTAL FACTORS

This section is confined to evidence bearing on the alleged unavoidability of accidents. Theoreticians and practitioners differ in their attitudes towards safety, but the idea that accidents are unavoidable events, whose causes are located in uncontrollable, capricious forces, appeals to those who adopt a fatalistic stance with regard to accidents. Evidence from the last decade, about the influence of environmental and biological factors, suggests that some proportion of accidents may indeed be unavoidable. If so, there are important consequences for future attempts to reduce the number of accidents below any 'natural' level.

Although it does not have any foundation is psychobiology, biorhythm theory has attracted the interest of some safety practitioners (Pittner and Owens, 1975; Schwarz, 1976). The theory suggests that the percentage of accidents occurring on 'critical days' (days on which 'cycles' of intellectual, emotional, and physical capacity change) will be much higher than the percentage occurring on other days. A large number of non-significant findings has been reported (e.g. Carvey and Nibler, 1977; Khalil and Kurucz, 1977; Persinger, Cooke, and Jones, 1978; Soutar and Weaver, 1983), and critics have suggested that positive findings may be due to unreliable coding methods (Chaffin and Skadburg, 1979).

Industrial accidents have been found in some studies to correlate with a range of geophysical variables, such as lunar phase (Templer, Veleber, and Brooner, 1982), geomagnetic variation (Persinger and Nolan, 1984), and weather changes (Charry and Hawkshire, 1981; Persinger and Levesque, 1983). A problem with these studies is that the mechanism of the effect has not been specified, although it has been hypothesized that the pineal gland may be playing a role (Templer *et al.*, 1982). It is difficult to imagine how this hypothesis could be tested adequately and how a causal, rather than a correlational, association could be established unambiguously.

From a safety management point of view it is important to consider the potentially damaging impact of this kind of evidence. Most individuals experience occasional 'off days' and an explanation couched in terms of biorhythm changes may have compelling face validity to the layperson. But acceptance of a biorhythm view may induce a complacent or impotent attitude towards safety. Educational counter-measures may be needed to counter that attitude and to promote a balanced picture of the effects of environmental factors; a positive attitude towards accident avoidance should be encouraged. For example, biorhythm can easily be confused with circadian rhythm. Disturbances to circadian rhythm associated with shift work have been linked to increased accident rates but even these effects may be eliminated by well-established safety programmes (Levin, Oler, and Whiteside, 1985).

ORGANIZATIONAL FACTORS

The traditional emphasis in industry on the role of individual differences, task analysis, and the design of the worker–machine interface reflects an implicit belief that the important determinants of accidents are to be found in the events immediately preceding, or present during, the time of an accident. This is an overly restrictive view which has tended to divert attention from the importance of organizational factors. The importance of organizational factors was demonstrated early in the 1970s by Powell *et al.* (1971), and by now their importance in high-risk industrial technologies is well recognized (Perrow, 1984). Often in these technologies the individual is regarded as too inconsequential to justify a change in safety practices, and the potentially catastrophic consequences of an accident are sufficient to discourage individuals from wishing to claim prime responsibility.

Although recognized as important, organizational variables have not been studied as intensively as individual differences. However, job satisfaction has received considerable attention, and is associated with accident rates (Pestonjee, Singh, and Ahmad, 1977), probably because satisfaction is a general indicator of all aspects of organizational climate, including safety climate. Smith, Cohen, Cohen, and Cleveland (1978) conducted a questionnaire study in 42 pairs of plants in six industries matched by workforce, industrial category, and location. Low-accident companies were significantly better than high-accident companies in terms of management commitment to safety, use of experienced shopfloor staff (rather than supervisors) in employee training, the standard of selection procedures, and lower staff turnover and absenteeism. These findings support Cohen's (1977) earlier suggestion that successful safety programmes are not just characterized by their high internal validity and external face validity but by their integration into other work programmes and practices.

Chisholm and Eskenazl (1983) found that, judged against workers at a matched comparison plant, workers at the Three Mile Island nuclear reactor reported higher levels of tension during the 1979 crisis. This was probably a reaction to the crisis, rather than a direct precipitating factor. Unusually high levels of stress were also observed among residents of Three Mile Island during the 1979 crisis (Baum, Fleming, and Singer, 1983; Bromet, 1982; Cleary and Houts, 1984; Davidson, Baum, and Collins, 1982). These studies demonstrate the importance of organizational and social factors but, in the absence of a theoretical framework, their practical significance for accident prevention and crisis management remains indeterminate.

In practice responsibility for safety programmes is often assigned to individual staff, rather than diffused into the line organization (see Steventon, 1983), and safety has often been used to reinforce hierarchical managerial structures. Frequently recommendations arising from acute accident problems have not been accepted because they would disturb those structures (see Firenze, 1978; Hammer, 1976; Pasmore and Friedlander, 1982), and sometimes a paternalistic senior management seems to guide and censor the work practices at shopfloor level. However, Syroit (1985) has shown that, although the effectiveness of an educational intervention (viz. a video safety programme) can produce observable changes in attitudes to safety at the shop floor, serious accident rates tend to remain unaltered until senior management is positive in its responsibility for managing safety. For example, amongst naval personnel increased levels of responsibility are associated with lower accident rates (Hoiberg, 1980).

In the USA the existence of health and safety committees within organizational units does not uniformly affect accident rates (Boden, Hall, Levenstein, and Punnett, 1984), and this suggests some ineffective communications between decision makers, at the committee level, and decision takers on the shop floor. However, there is considerable individual variation in the success of health and safety committees, and their differential success rates may be due partly to the broader industrial relations context in which the committees function.

Beaumont (1983) has suggested that, compared with management, unions tend to have a more viable approach to safety because they tend to see problem-solving and negotiation strategies as complementary activities, whereas management tends to see them as substitutes. Thus, a managerial approach to safety is usually a problem-solving one and this usually leads to a top-down imposition of a safety solution. A negotiation approach, because it is more pragmatic, tends to facilitate piecemeal improvements which have an enduring cumulative effect. Future studies should examine the form and effectiveness of union representation on health and safety committees.

In accounting for the effectiveness of a number of safety innovations in the industrial gases industry, Griffiths (1985) has summarized the significance of the management contribution as follows: 'safety in industry is above all a responsibility of management, and unless this is understood other measures will not be successful in abolishing accidents and injuries' (p. 61). In a detailed study, of safety management, Stevenson (1980) suggested that one of the strongest barriers to effective managerial involvement in safety is a reluctance to accept safety as an important performance criterion. Probably this reluctance is due in part to the fact that safety is measured in negative quantities (i.e. the absence of accidents), and the outcome of safety innovations will only be realized in the long term. This package of disadvantages means that safety is a comparatively 'remote', non-essential managerial task.

Through generating competition, organizational boundaries can discourage the kinds of cooperative work required to secure acceptable levels of individual and group safety (see Tuttle, Dachler, and Schneider, 1975). Production methods which require shift working can also pose safety problems (see Bell and Telman, 1980; Tilley, Wilkinson, Warren, Watson, and Drud, 1982). Research, then, has focused on these and other specific organizational aspects of safety problems, but there have been few attempts to take a broader theoretical perspective on the significance of organizational factors for safety.

Within a sociotechnical systems perspective organizations can be conceptualized as comprising four subsystems: production, adaptation, training, and integration (Cherns and Wacker, 1978). The technical infrastructures of organizations interact with each of these subsystems, and effective safety management can be conceptualized as requiring the optimization of the social–technical interface. However, relative to individuals, organizations are slow to accommodate new safety measures, and safety programmes are often forced to assimilate undesirable aspects of the organization in order to gain widespread acceptance of management level (Firenze, 1978; Pasmore and Friedlander, 1982).

Cherns (1977) identified ten principles which serve as a blueprint for designing optimum sociotechnical systems, and these have since been reviewed and elaborated by Robinson (1982). Robinson argued that the sociotechnical systems approach provides a repertoire of strategic tools capable of dealing meaningfully with the problems of health and safety at an organizational level. Within the sociotechnical systems approach individuals can be imagined as risk controllers for the technologies they are expected to operate. This view is shared by researchers working within a traditional cognitive approach (Norman, 1981; Reason, 1979). Reason argues that increasing automation increases the probability of action slips. We would add that the inflexibility of some automated work stations means that when errors are detected as they are about to occur opportunities for human intervention may often be severely curtailed. For instance, on modern mainframe computers minor typographical slips by software engineers can lead to large property damage accidents. For robotics and flexible manufacturing systems Percival (1984) has identified as of paramount importance the need to re-examine the appropriateness of conventional safety axioms. The particularly important contribution of the sociotechnical systems approach is the emphasis it places on the integration of safety into the structure of the organization. Each innovation will only be permitted to have an effect in so far as the organization assimilates it.

PREVENTION

The idea that society tolerates certain 'acceptable' risks (see Sheehy and Chapman, 1984) has important implications for accident prevention. Only rarely have those implications been explicitly recognized in the theory of accident prevention. Cliff (1984) has proposed a tripartite classification of preventive measures — primary, secondary, and tertiary measures — to acknowledge the significance of acceptable accident rates. *Primary prevention* involves human factors, including engineering and legal innovations, designed to avoid accidents. *Secondary prevention* presumes that the primary measures will often fail to eliminate accidents and so includes measures designed to pattern the kind and severity of injuries likely to be sustained in an accident: the provision of protective clothing and safety goggles and the design and placement of bumpers on cars are examples of secondary preventions. *Tertiary prevention* presumes that both primary and secondary measures will often fail; it has been defined as the prevention of serious pathological consequences (Waters and Cliff, 1983), and it demands exceptionally sophisticated and expensive resources to ensure that victims recover and lead a normal life. At any one time, groups of accidents can be described in terms of the proportion of accidents prevented by primary, secondary, and tertiary measures, and this distribution is one measure of society's acceptance of the costs of accident prevention. Sheehy and Chapman (1985) have argued that some kinds of prevention are judged unacceptable because of the enormous social costs involved. They argue, for example, that better vehicle design might reduce the numbers of fatal injuries to pedestrians, but the medical and social service costs of treating critically ill and permanently handicapped individuals normally exceed the costs of fatal injury.

Psychological intervention can be associated with any of the three categories of prevention. Traditionally, training has been viewed as a primary preventive measure, although aspects of first aid training and crisis management constitute secondary preventions; rehabilitation programmes are an example of tertiary prevention. However, although psychological interventions can have a partial role to play in each of the three preventive categories, strategic countermeasures cannot materialize in any of the categories unless there is a coordinated, multidisciplinary effort. In order for this to occur it will be necessary to specify how the three classes of prevention are related. These relationships are not likely to prove simple: for instance, Saari and Lahtela (1981) found that workers' job experience was an important predictor of accident occurrence, but experiential factors have been found to be unrelated to injury severity (Bennett and Passmore, 1985).

In an early 1970s review Hale and Hale (1972) concluded that there were then almost as many studies showing positive safety training effects as there were studies showing negligible effects. A mid-1980s review by Hale (1984) indicates that the pattern has changed little during the intervening period. He suggests that training is still seen as a unitary variable. Arguing against the simplicity of that view, he has proposed a safety training classification based on the stages of perception and response to danger which precede an accident: hazard seeking, hazard recognition, assessment of the importance of the hazard, allocation of responsibility, decision to act, and the action sequence.

Hale's classification is referred to below as the chapter turns to the approaches and methods adopted in safety training: applied behaviour analysis; responsibility allocation, feedback, committee management, and crisis management. By way of general background to the remaining commentary on accident prevention we would point out that at least until the mid-1970s the consensus view about the potential of safety research was predominantly pessimistic (e.g. Chelius, 1974). For example, Ellis (1975) concluded that 'unless much better evaluative research begins to be undertaken, all of the innovative safety programmes in the future may well result in a waste of time and effort' (p. 187). More specifically, research had been predominantly correlational, inadequate operationally, excessively theoretical, and practices of using small samples and 'interpreting' non-significant correlations were not uncommon. Since that time there has been a general movement towards tackling some of these shortcomings by using larger samples, more refined operational definitions (e.g. through applied behaviour analysis) and hypothesis testing through quasi-experimental designs applied to field studies. Methodologically, there is now a preference for using multiple, rather than single, baseline measures, using 'withdrawal' designs, and using entire organizations rather than organizational sub-units.

Applied Behaviour Analysis

The use of applied behaviour analysis (Fitch, Hermann, and Hopkins, 1976) has been at the forefront of attempts to go beyond the study of accident behaviour, and it has been particularly effective in demonstrating that accident reduction and safety are not synonymous terms: accident reduction is but one objective of safety interventions, albeit the most important. The rationale for drawing upon applied behaviour analysis is that many accidents arise from unsafe work practices and, theoretically guided, fine-grain behavioural analysis permits the identification and elimination of unsafe behaviours. It has also been argued that repeated measurement of safe and unsafe work practices, implicit in this approach, provides an accurate index of the safety climate within organizations and so permits the identification of trends and sudden changes in safety (Fitch et al., 1976; Komaki et al., 1978; Smith, 1976).

Applied behaviour analysis has been used to develop programmes to reduce violations of mining regulations (Rhoton, 1980), to increase the use of protective eye apparatus (Smith, Anger, and Uslan, 1978), to increase earplug use (Zohar, 1980; Zohar, Cohen, and Azar, 1980), and to reduce traffic-related injuries among police officers (Larson, Schnelle, Kirchner, Carr, Domach, and Risley, 1980). It has also been used to bring about non-specific reductions in safety hazards (Komaki, Collins, and Penn, 1982; Komaki, Heinzman, and Lawson, 1980; Petersen, 1982; Sulzer-Azaroff and Santamaria, 1980).

A limitation to many of these studies is that the samples used were relatively small, being less than one hundred. Also it is often impossible to rule out the effects of concurrent changes in other organizational practices. For example, Pasmore and Friedlander (1982) reported an attempt to reduce an 'epidemic' of tenosynovitis (damage to the muscles in the wrist, forearm, and shoulder): nearly one-third of the personnel in a plant employing 355 people had sought treatment for soreness. Although a radical sociotechnical systems redesign was proposed, a scaled-down plan was adopted for financial reasons. By the fourth year of the programme a reduction of 95 per cent of tenosynovitis had been achieved. However, during the same period major management and production changes had been introduced which made it impossible to determine how much of the reduction was due to the safety programme.

Organizations sometimes change in ways which are unexpected, and when designing a long-term study it is obviously not practicable to allow for every possible eventuality. Nonetheless, some general precautionary steps often permit comment on the probable significance of unplanned and unforeseen changes. All successfully established organizations maintain a large archive of performance data, and often it is possible to take concurrent measures on non-safety variables which offer insights into the effects of safety programmes and their interactions with other company programmes. Just as it is important for management to diffuse safety considerations into the line organization, so it is important for practitioner–researchers to take account of the fact that safety programmes do not exist in isolation from other areas of organizational life. It is reasonable to expect safety professionals to take a broad view of safety innovations even to the extent of taking measures on non-safety programmes in order to understand the overall effect of the safety programme.

Regrettably, while positive correlations between safety innovations and accident reduction are almost always taken as evidence for the success of the innovations, negative results are often dismissed as attributable to extrinsic, non-safety factors (Pasmore and Friedlander's, 1982, study is an exception). A more balanced appraisal is to be encouraged—in particular, by taking performance measures on concurrent non-safety programmes plus precautionary or anticipatory measures on general organizational variables—and it is important to recognize that the nature of some tasks may place limits on the extent to which accidents and unsafe behaviour can be reduced. This is illustrated by Ostberg's (1980) study of the risks run by 731 forestry workers in ten forestry situations. The fellers were found to have an accurate knowledge of the kinds and levels of risks in typical felling situations, and it was impossible to achieve further substantial improvements in safety practices without attempting a total sociotechnical systems redesign of the forestry industry. Every industry has a characteristic profile of 'normal' accidents which reflects a basic demonstration of acceptable risk for that industry (Lowrance, 1976; Perrow, 1984).

The idea of an accepted level of risk is distinct from the idea of risk homeostasis. The former reflects a social evaluation of acceptable cost in pursuit of a valued industrial life-style. Risk homeostasis refers to a hypothesis that individuals have a preferred level of risk which is more or less constant (O'Neill, 1977; Wilde and Murdoch, 1982). There is some controversy over the evidence for (e.g. Hamer, 1981; Orr, 1982) and against (Lund and Zandor, 1984; McKenna, 1985; Robertson, 1981) the homeostasis hypothesis. Much of the controversy centres on the appropriateness of the exposure denominator used in calculating accident rates (Wilde, 1984). McKenna (1985) has levelled a number of other criticisms against the concept. These include: failure to discriminate between individual and societal risk homeostasis, failure to specify the mechanisms involved in achieving homeostasis, and failure to specify *a priori* whether gains in safety in one domain will be matched by increased risks in the same or different domains.

The risk homeostasis hypothesis is important for the evaluation of safety innovations because it predicts that improvements in safety may encourage riskier behaviour and so the overall level of risk and the overall accident rate will remain much the same. Tanner (1979, 1981) has provided striking evidence that in industries where there is rapid feedback about accidents individuals may use the data to regulate the risks they run in a highly controlled and therefore predictable way. An unusually clear-cut effect of control was reported by Hermann (1979) who in several studies used a composite index of medical disability (rather than simple event counting) to quantify accident rates. In the first study the baseline mean medical disability index was 177 prior to the introduction of a safety programme. This dropped to 79 during the intervention phase and rose to 366 afterwards. Similar effects were observed in two further studies. In these cases the safety innovation appeared to act as a suppressor. Once removed there was a large compensatory increase which in fact was followed by a reduction to the normal level.

Responsibility Allocation

Responsibility allocation refers to the allocation and acceptance of responsibility for action and, for example, has been used by Hale (1984) in his classification of training interventions. Several authors (e.g. Schlegel, 1979; Trist, Susman, and Brown, 1977) have argued that accident prevention is most effective when responsibility for safety procedures can be apportioned by the workers involved in their acceptance. The crucial factor is to ensure that assignation of responsibility does not routinely carry culpability in the event of an accident.

The importance of accepting responsibility is illustrated in Abeytunga and Hale's (1982) examination of the training needs of construction site supervisors. They found that 64 per cent of hazards identified during a site inspection were regarded as being the responsibility of someone other than the supervisors. Training programmes designed to improve the supervisors' seeking and recognition of hazards would probably have had a negligible impact on site safety, regardless of the internal and external validity of those programmes. What was needed was a training programme which would facilitate the acceptance of implicative associations between hazard seeking, hazard recognition, and responsibility acceptance.

McKenna (1978), McKenna and Hale (1982), and Perusse (1980) have all reported that the main effect of first aid training is to facilitate a more rational attitude towards responsibility allocation. In turn this probably affects individuals' motivations to eliminate perceived hazard. Kjellen and Baneryd (1983) reported that worker discussion groups also facilitated greater individual acceptance of responsibility for safety, and this suggests that safety programmes might be directed more towards encouraging individuals to see safety as a matter of personal responsibility. What is implied here is more than simply changing people's attitudes towards safety. Sometimes there may be a negligible relationship between safety attitudes and accident involvement (e.g. Murphy, 1981) because a positive affective response does not necessarily imply a tendency to accept responsibility for potentially dangerous actions. Thus, Reber and Wallin (1983) wrote behaviourally specific safety rules for twelve departments of a farm machinery plant. They found significant negative correlations between rule compliance and injury rates, suggesting that it is essential to tackle safety at both a behavioural and an attitudinal level.

Feedback

Preventive measures of a feedback kind, which are based on periodic observation, praise, and criticism, can be highly effective (see Lagerlof, 1982; Rhoton, 1980). There is reliable evidence to suggest that fear-arousing communications consistently produce increases in intentional and behavioural measures of message acceptance (see Sutton, 1982), and there is also evidence that negative incentives (see Pirani and Reynolds, 1976) tend to be less effective than positive incentives (see Zohar and Fussfeld, 1981).

Fellner and Sulzer-Azaroff (1984) provided written feedback for mill workers on safe and unsafe practices and conditions. There was found after 6 months to have been an improvement in safety performance in eight of the seventeen divisions in the mill. Apparently the absence of improvements in the remaining divisions may have been due to differences in division size and supervisory practices. This again emphasizes the need for large-scale studies which potentially can help identify the role and importance of organizational and training factors extraneous to the experimental programme.

Adams et al. (1981) have reported that computerized accident statistics facilitate the distribution of informational feedback. They noted a sharp reduction in accidents following such an innovation in an Australian steel-processing plant, and their observations support the view that feedback may affect behaviour independently of safety goal setting (Locke, Shaw, Saari, and Latham, 1981). Also, Chhokar and Wallin (1984) have shown that feedback is essential in order to sustain improvements initiated by alternative non-feedback means, and in a review of evaluation studies on training for industrial inspection tasks Embrey (1979) emphasized that feeding back knowledge of results is important in training for hazard recognition and diagnosis.

Safety Committees

Particularly in North America, interest has been accelerating in the effectiveness of health and safety committees within organizations. These committees aim to exploit elements of established grievance procedures through collective bargaining.

Cooke and Gautschi (1981) examined data from 113 manufacturing firms collected between 1970 and 1976. They found a small non-significant reduction in 'lost time' accidents associated with the introduction of such committees. They did not attempt specific predictions of injury rates from committee characteristics, but the need for more detailed investigation has been called for by Boden et al. (1984) who have distinguished two possible committee benefits: improvements in objective safety conditions and practices, and reductions in perceived hazardousness.

In studying 127 manufacturing firms, Boden *et al.* failed to find a relationship between the existence of health and safety committees and either the number or proportion of safety inspections arising from complaints. However, detailed study of thirteen of the firms revealed that perceived effectiveness of the committees correlated positively with management commitment to health and safety, the overall level of factory safety, the vitality of committee meetings, and the number of positive inspection reports. Thus, health and safety committees may not only increase perceived effectiveness of safety interventions, but also increase safety on some objective criteria. Further studies are required to determine the specific effects of such committees.

In considering the role of organizational factors, above, it was pointed out that safety must be set into the broader context of organizational life. Thus it is important to determine whether safety committees are more likely to emerge in firms with good safety records than in firms with poorer records. Also, the relationship between the prevailing industrial relations climate and the activity and effectiveness of such committees needs to be explored. One possibility is that health and safety committees are only likely to flourish in organizations experienced in negotiations.

Crisis Management

Comparatively little attention has been paid to the role of crisis management in accident prevention. McKenna and Glendon (1980) have suggested that in first aid training, which can be viewed as incorporating a simulation of accidental injury, there exists a benign alternative to horror which produces motivational changes in the face of perceived danger.

Glicken (1982) has said that, following serious industrial accidents, victims can be expected to manifest reactions for 4 to 6 weeks. He identified five stages of reaction: shock and numbness; guilt depression and anxiety; anger and defensive reactions to criticisms of the victim and the organization; denial of any causal role in the accident, accompanied by hostility towards the employer; and uneasy acceptance of the accident. None of these stages is well understood but, in particular, the consequences of catastrophic work accidents for the recovery of the workforce from shock, and for the future conduct of organizational life, are poorly understood.

Glicken's accompanying suggestion that management should be involved in managing recovery services for the victim is an important one. He provides a stage framework with which to conceptualize the management of personnel recovery. The stages he describes were used initially by Kubler-Ross (1970) to describe the ways in which terminally ill patients cope with their own dying and death and similar stages have been observed among patients recovering from surgery (Ray, 1982). It is fairly certain that the 'stages' are not fixed sequentially and behaviours characteristic of more then one stage can be simultaneously manifested during recovery from trauma. Thus, the stage theory framework should be treated as a general model of crisis recovery for individuals.

Early referral to vocational rehabilitation reduces experiences of depression and fear as well as facilitating an appropriate locus of control (Lindley, 1981). The client–counsellor relationship is crucial and its intensity may be the most important predictor of victim rehabilitation (Garcia, 1982). Social and cultural factors also play an important mediating role in victim rehabilitation (Katz and Shurka, 1977; Kotlarz, 1983), and there is only a partial, and therefore optimal, role for managed organizational intervention at the recovery stages.

A large proportion of multinational and national firms provide programmes to help employees cope with a range of personal, work-related difficulties (e.g. alcoholism), and there are good grounds for believing that these programmes have important contributions to make in promoting safety (see Shain and Groenveld, 1980). First, they facilitate rehabilitation; and thereby they directly benefit the organization. Second, they play a role in accident prevention by encouraging more rational attitudes to accident causation and, in the long term, to prevention too.

CONCLUSION

This selective review of the literature has identified trends relevant to future research and practice. Of much significance is an increasing reluctance to treat accident statistics as appropriate data for theory testing. This trend is likely to continue until accident reporting systems are improved so that the accruing data are of higher quality. Computer-based information gathering could provide a means to this end, but design guidelines have yet to be worked out. It would be folly to import into computer-based systems all of the characteristics of existing systems. The development of blueprints for intelligent computer-based occupational health information systems is needed as a priority. Some advance in this direction has been made, including a re-evaluation of research models for the investigation of industrial accidents (Andersson, Johnasson, Linden, Svanstrom, and Svanstrom, 1978).

Reviews of taxonomies of human error (Reason, 1985) and their relevance to industrial accidents (Rasmussen, 1982) reflect attempts to achieve a closer integration of human error theories and accident and safety theories. In a recent review of the concept of 'deviation' in accident control Kjellen (1984) has outlined some preliminary considerations for the design of comprehensive information systems for accident prevention. Further work in this direction is to be encouraged.

It is difficult to regulate stress in industry. Personnel selection according to personality profile would almost certainly meet staunch resistance from all quarters. Unfortunately, there are as yet few industry-specific data on the kinds of stress employees are likely to encounter and the ways potential stressors can be managed. The data required are of the sort provided by Gertman and Haney (1985). Among control room operators, they found that attenuation of crisis-induced stress can be achieved by reducing individual workload while maintaining individual involvement and responsibility.

There is a need to aim for closer integration of the accident/safety literature and the organizational literature. In descriptive terminology there has been some shift towards synthesis. For example, during the last decade the concept of 'safety climate' has entered the accident and safety literature, but its relationship with 'organizational climate' has not been described. Heinrich's (1936) ideas about accident causation and prevention have provided the theoretical core of safety programmes for half a century, but current trends are towards augmenting these by, for example, placing management practices in a more central role than hitherto has been common (e.g. Weaver, 1980).

From a safety perspective the most important lesson from organizational research is that often the individual is not the most appropriate unit for analysis. Industrial accidents can be conceptualized as a loss of system control (Hensley, 1985; Weaver, 1980), and hence solutions at the systems level are required. A next step must be to consider how organizations structure and manage the hazards within their domain. In this regard the extensive literature on the management of high-risk technologies might provide a useful interface between organizational theories and accident/error theories (Jakosimovich, 1984). One consequence of progress in this direction will be the encouragement of debate about the nature of industrial risk, particularly large-scale risk, and public perceptions of its management (Harding and Eiser, 1984; Hohenemser, Kates, and Slovic, 1983). Industry is likely to find in future that its management of production technology will have increasing import for wider social health issues. This is explicitly recognized in the report of the National Research Council (1985) on injury in America where recommendations are made for an injury research and training agenda.

With regard to safety training, the potential gains associated with the enforcement of even a vigorous campaign may be marginal. For instance, Mendeloff (1984) found that a panel of safety engineers, concerned with fatal injuries, considered that only 50 per cent of safety violations were detectable on the day of the accident. This points to a need for safety campaigns to incorporate training in hazard detection as well as recognition and response. Once detected, hazards will remain part of the *status quo* until individuals decide to accept responsibility for eliminating them. Positive attitudes towards safety do not guarantee positive actions towards hazard attenuation. Programmes designed to increase rule compliance suggest that, pragmatically considered, it may be most effective to proceed by changing behaviour systematically and permit attitudinal re-education to proceed as an indirect consequence.

Safety practices need to be updated to take account of new hazards (some of which are yet to be detected) posed by automated production processes. This need has been recognized by theoreticians (Reason, 1979) and practitioners (Percival, 1984). With the possible exception of training of control room operators (see Duncan and Gray, 1975; Marshall and Baker, 1985) there have been few advances in the systematic detection of new industrial hazards and safety programmes to manage them (see Ayoub, 1982a, 1982b, 1982c). It seems certain that increased computer automation means that human operators will spend less time on manual tasks and more on problem-solving tasks (Rouse, 1985), and this raises new work and adaptation problems (Sheridan, Vamos, and Aida, 1985).

Our concluding message is that there is a need to encourage synthesis at the theoretical level in order to develop frameworks capable of responding to the complexity of problems encountered in practice. Just as a tricycle needs its three wheels for balance and direction, so psychology needs practice as well as theory and research. The practice, or applied, dimension is vital to psychologists if we are to maintain proper contact with reality and if we are to be sure that we are working on substantive issues. Given predictions like '5.5 million alive in the USA in 1980 will die from accidental injuries' (Whitfield, Zador, and Fife, 1985), the need to pursue the applied dimension is urgent.

REFERENCES

Abeytunga, P. K., and Hale, A. R. (1982). Supervisors' perceptions of hazards on construction sites. Paper presented at the Twentieth Congress of the International Association of Applied Psychology, Edinburgh, September.

Adams, N. L., Barlow, A., and Hiddlestone, J. (1981). Obtaining ergonomics information about industrial accidents: A five-year analysis. *Applied Ergonomics*, **12**, 71-81.

Adams, N. L., and Hartwell, N. M. (1977). Accident reporting systems: A basic problem area in industrial psychology. *Journal of Occupational Psychology*, **50**, 285-298.

Allodi, F., and Montgomery, R. (1979). Psychosocial aspects of occupational injury. *Social Psychiatry*, **14**, 25-29.

Amsalem, A., Defranoux, G., and Bach, A. (1977). Contribution of work analysis to the improvement of the 'scaling-machine' driver post. *Travail Humain*, **40**, 63-72.

Anderson, D. M. (1983). From accident report to design problems: A study of accidents on board ship. *Ergonomics*, **26**, 43-50.

Andersson, R., Johansson, B., Linden, K., Svanstrom, K., and Svanstrom, L. (1978). Development of a model for research on occupational accidents. *Journal of Occupational Accidents*, **1**, 341-352.

Andersson, R., and Lagerlof, E. (1983). Accident data in the new Swedish information system on occupational injuries. *Ergonomics*, **26**, 33-42.

Andreassend, D. C. (1983). Standard accident definitions: Primary accident classes and accident types. *Australian Road Research*, **13**, 10-24.

Ayoub, M. A. (1982a). Control of manual lifting hazards: I. Training in safe handling. *Journal of Occupational Medicine*, **24**, 573-577.

Ayoub, M. A. (1982b). Control of manual lifting hazards: II. Job design. *Journal of Occupational Medicine*, **24**, 668-676.

Ayoub, M. A. (1982c). Control of manual lifting hazards: III. Pre-employment screening. *Journal of Occupational Medicine*, **24**, 751-761.

Bailey, R. W. (1983). *Human Error in Computer Systems*. Englewood Cliffs, New Jersey: Prentice-Hall.

Bainbridge, L. (1979). Verbal reports as evidence of the process operator's knowledge. *International Journal of Man-Machine Studies*, **11**, 411-436.

Barjonet, P. E. (1980). Representation of road accident causes in relation to social influence. *Travail Humain*, **43**, 243-253.

Baum, A., Fleming, R., and Singer, J. E. (1983). Coping with victimization by technological disaster. *Journal of Social Issues*, **39**, 117-138.

Beaumont, P. B. (1983). *Safety at Work and the Unions*. London: Croom Helm.

Bell, C. R., and Telman, N. (1980). Errors, accidents and injuries in rotating shift-work. A field study. *International Review of Applied Psychology*, **29**, 271-291.

Bennett, J. D., and Passmore, D. L. (1985). Multinomial logit analysis of injury severity in US underground bituminous coal mines, 1975-1982. *Accident Analysis and Prevention*, **17**, 399-408.

Blignaut, C. J. H. (1979a). The perception of hazard. I. Hazard analysis and the contribution of visual search to hazard perception. *Ergonomics*, **22**, 991-999.

Blignaut, C. J. H. (1979b). The perception of hazard. II. The contribution of signal detection to hazard perception. *Egonomics*, **22**, 1177-1183.

Boden, L. I., Hall, J. A., Levenstein, C., and Punnett, L. (1984). The impact of health and safety committees. *Journal of Occupational Medicine*, **26**, 829-834.

Boyle, A. J. (1980a). A model of accident liability based on the normal distribution. Paper presented at The British Psychological Society's London Conference, December.

Boyle, A. J. (1980b). 'Found experiments' in accident research: Report of a study of accident rates and implications for future research. *Journal of Occupational Psychology*, **53**, 53-64.

Bromet, E. J. (1982). Mental health of residents near the Three Mile Island Reactor. *Journal of Preventive Psychiatry*, **1**, 225-276.

Brown, I. D. (1980). Error correction probability as a determinant of drivers' subjective risk. In D. J. Oborne and J. A. Levis (eds.), *Human Factors in Transport Research*, vol. 2, User Factors: Comfort, the Environment and Behaviour. London: Academic Press.

Bull, J. P. (1985). Disabilities caused by road traffic accidents and their relation to severity scores. *Accident Analysis and Prevention*, **17**, 389-397.

Carvey, D. W., and Nibler, R. G. (1977). Biorhythmic cycles and the incidence of industrial accidents. *Personnel Psychology*, **30**, 447-454.

Cellier, J. M. (1980). Workload and safety in a task of handling. *Travail Humain*, **43**, 3-16.

Chaffin, R., and Skadburg, J. (1979). Effect of scoring set on biorhythm data. *Journal of Applied Psychology*, **64**, 213-217.

Charry, J. M., and Hawkshire, F. B. (1981). Effects of atmospheric electricity on some substrates of disordered social behavior. *Journal of Personality and Social Psychology*, **41**, 185-197.

Chelius, J. R. (1974). The control of industrial accidents: Economic theory and empirical evidence. *Law and Contemporary Problems*, **80**, 700-729.

Cherns, A. B. (1977). Can behavioural science help design organizations? *Organizational Dynamics*, **1**, 44-64.

Cherns, A. B., and Wacker, G. J. (1978). Analyzing social systems: An application of Parson's microsystem model to the organizational level and the sociotechnical perspective. *Human Relations*, **31**, 823-841.

Chhokar, J. S., and Wallin, J. A. (1984). Improving safety through applied behavior analysis. *Journal of Safety Research*, **15**, 141-151.

Chisholm, R. F., and Eskenazl, B. (1983). The nature and predictors of job related tension in a crisis situation: To the Three Mile Island accident. *Academy of Management Journal*, **26**, 385-405.

Cleary, P. D., and Houts, P. S. (1984). The psychological impact of the Three Mile Island incident. *Journal of Human Stress*, **10**, 28-34.

Cliff, K. S. (1984). *Accidents: Causes, Prevention and Services*. London: Croom Helm.

Cohen, A. (1977). Factors in successful safety programs. *Journal of Safety Research*, **9**, 168-178.

Cooke, W. N., and Gautschi, F. H. (1981). OHSA, plant safety programs, and injury reduction. *Industrial Relations*, **20**, 245-257.

David, S. S. J., Foot, H. C., Chapman, A. J., and Sheehy, N. P. (1986). Peripheral vision and the aetiology of child pedestrian accidents. *British Journal of Psychology*, **77**, 117-135.

Davidson, L. M., Baum, A., and Collins, D. L. (1982). Stress and control-related problems at Three Mile Island. *Journal of Applied Psychology*, **12**, 349-359.

Defares, P. B., Brandjes, M., Nass, C. H. T., and Ploeg, J. D. (1984). Coping styles and vulnerability of women at work in residential settings. *Ergonomics*, **27**, 527-545.

Duncan, K. D., and Gray, M. J. (1975). An evaluation of a fault finding training course for refinery process operators. *Journal of Occupational Psychology*, **48**, 199-218.

Edwards, D. S., and Hahn, C. P. (1980). A chance to happen. *Journal of Safety Research*, **12**, 59-67.

Edwards, M. (1981). The design of an accident investigation procedure. *Applied Ergonomics*, **12**, 111-115.

Ellis, L. (1975). A review of research on efforts to promote occupational safety. *Journal of Safety Research*, **7**, 180-189.

Embrey, D. E. (1979). Approaches to training for industrial inspection. *Applied Ergonomics*, **10**, 139-144.

Fellner, D. J., and Sulzer-Azaroff, B. (1984). Increasing industrial safety practices and conditions through posted feedback. *Journal of Safety Research*, **15**, 7-21.

Ferguson, J. C., McNally, M. S., and Booth, R. F. (1985). Accidental injuries among naval personnel by occupation, duty status and pay grade. *Accident Analysis and Prevention*, **17**, 79–86.

Firenze, R. J. (1978). *The Process of Hazard Control*. Dubuqus, Iowa: Kendell Hunt.

Fitch, H. G., Hermann, J., and Hopkins, B. L. (1976). Safe and unsafe behaviour and modification. *Journal of Occupational Medicine*, **18**, 618–622.

Franasczuk, I., and Kopaczewska, Z. (1978). Investigative methods of psychological selection of workers as the element of accident prophylaxis in in-plant transport. *Przeglad Psychologiczny*, **21**, 143–165.

Garcia, K. M. (1982). A psychological and demographic investigation of the rehabilitation counseling process. *Dissertation Abstracts International*, **43**, 3-B, 851–852.

Gertman, D. I., and Hanney, L. N. (1985). Personality and stress—what impact on decision making? In D. J. Oborne, (ed.), *Contemporary Ergonomics 1985*. London: Taylor & Francis.

Glendon, I., and Hale, A. R. (1985). *A Study of 1700 Accidents on the Youth Opportunities Programme*. Sheffield: Manpower Services Commission.

Glicken, M. D. (1982). Managing a crisis intervention program. *Personnel Journal*, **61**, 292–296.

Greenwood, M., and Woods, M. (1919). The incidence of industrial accidents upon individuals with special reference to multiple accidents. Industrial Fatigue Research Board, Report Number 4. London: HMSO.

Griffiths, D. K. (1985). Safety attitudes of management. *Ergonomics*, **28**, 61–67.

Hale, A. R. (1984). Is safety training worthwhile? *Journal of Occupational Accidents*, **6**, 17–33.

Hale, A. R., and Hale, M. (1972). Review of the industrial accident research literature. Research paper. Committee on Health and Safety at Work. London: HMSO.

Hamer, M. (1981). Do compulsory seat belts save lives? *New Scientist*, **89**, 461.

Hammer, W. (1976). *Occupational Safety Management and Engineering*. Englewood Cliffs, New Jersey: Prentice-Hall.

Harding, C. M., and Eiser, J. R. (1984). Characterizing the perceived risks and benefits of some health issues. *Risk Analysis*, **4**, 131–141.

Hart, S. A., and Bartolussi, M. R. (1984). Pilot errors as a source of workload. *Human Factors*, **26**, 545–556.

Heinrich, H. (1936). *Industrial Accident Prevention*. New York: McGraw-Hill.

Hermann, J. A. (1979). Effects of a safety program on the accident frequency and severity rate of automobile workers. *Dissertation Abstracts International*, **39**, 11-B, 5625–5626.

Hodge, G. A., and Richardson, A. J. (1985). The role of accident exposure in transport system safety evaluation. *Journal of Advanced Transportation*, **19**, 179–213.

Hohenemser, C., Kates, R. W., and Slovic, P. (1983). The nature of technological hazard. *Science*, **220**, 328–384.

Hoiberg, A. (1980). Sex and occupation differences in hospitalization rates among navy enlisted personnel. *Journal of Occupational Medicine*, **22**, 685–690.

Jakosimovich, V. (1984). A review of plant specific PRAs. *Risk Analysis*, **4**, 255–266.

Jenkins, C. D., Hurst, M. W., and Rose, R. M. (1979). Life changes. Do people really remember? *Archives of General Psychiatry*, **36**, 379–384.

Jimenez, P. P. (1977). Aggressiveness as a cause of accidents. *Revista-de-Psicologia-General-y-Applicada*, **32**, 573–579.

John, L. R., Marsh, G. M., and Enterline, P. E. (1983). Evaluating occupational hazards using information known only to employers: A comparative study. *British Journal of Industrial Medicine*, **40**, 346–352.

Kasper, R. G. (1980). Perceptions of risk and their effects on decision making. In R. C. Schwing and W. A. Albers (eds.), *Societal Risk Assessment*. London: Plenum.

Katz, S., and Shurka, E. (1977). The influence of contextual variables on the evaluation of the physically disabled by the nondisabled. *Rehabilitation Literature*, **38**, 369–373.

Kay, H. (1971). Accidents: Some facts and theories. In P. B. Warr (ed.), *Psychology at Work*. Harmondsworth: Penguin.

Khalil, T. M., and Kurucz, C. N. (1977). The influence of 'biorhythm' on accident occurrence and performance. *Ergonomics*, **20**, 389-398.

Kjellen, U. (1982). An evaluation of safety information systems in six medium-sized and large firms. *Journal of Occupational Accidents*, **3**, 273-288.

Kjellen, U. (1984). The deviation concept in occupational accident control—1. *Accident Analysis and Prevention*, **16**, 289-306.

Kjellen, U., and Baneryd, K. (1982). Changing the local safety and health practices at work within the explosives industry. *Ergonomics*, **26**, 863-877.

Kjellen, U., and Larsson, T. J. (1981). Investigating accidents and reducing risks—a dynamic approach. *Journal of Occupational Accidents*, **3**, 129-140.

Komaki, J., Barwick, K. D., and Scott, L. R. (1978). A behavioral approach to occupational safety: Pinpointing and reinforcing safe performance in a food manufacturing plant. *Journal of Applied Psychology*, **63**, 434-445.

Komaki, J., Collins, R. L., and Penn, P. (1982). The role of performance antecedents in work motivation. *Journal of Applied Psychology*, **67**, 334-340.

Komaki, J., Heinzman, A. T., and Lawson, L. (1980). Effect of training and feedback: Component analysis of a behavioral safety program. *Journal of Applied Psychology*, **65**, 261-272.

Kotlarz, G. M. (1983). Depressive reactions and antidepressive activity in Anglo and Mexican American males with physical injuries and disability filing for workers' compensation. *Dissertation Abstracts International*, **44**, 4-B, 1242.

Kubler-Ross, E. (1970). *On Death and Dying*. London: Tavistock.

Lagerlof, E. (1982). Accident reduction in forestry through risk identification, risk consciousness and work organization change. Paper presented at the Twentieth Congress International Association of Applied Psychology, Edinburgh, September.

Larson, L. D., Schnelle, J. F., Kirchner, R., Jr, Carr, A. F., Domach, M., and Risley, T. R. (1980). Reduction of police vehicle accidents through mechanically aided supervision. *Journal of Applied Behavior Analysis*, **13**, 571-581.

Lavie, P., Kremerman, S., and Wiel, M. (1982). Sleep disorders and safety at work in industry workers. *Accident Analysis and Prevention*, **14**, 311-314.

Levens, E. (1976). The cost benefit and cost effectiveness of occupational alcoholism programs. *Professional Safety*, November, 36-41.

Levenson, H. (1980). Industrial accidents and recent life events. *Journal of Occupational Medicine*, **22**, 53-57.

Levenson, H., Hirschfeld, M. L., and Hirschfeld, A. H. (1980). Industrial accidents and recent life events. *Journal of Occupational Medicine*, **22**, 53-57.

Levin, L., Oler, J., and Whiteside, J. P. (1985). Injury incidence in a paint company. *Accident Analysis and Prevention*, **17**, 67-73.

Lindley, E. M. (1981). Early referral and depression, fear and locus of control in industrially injured individuals. *Dissertation Abstracts International*, **42**, 2-B, 749.

Locke, E. A. Shaw, K. N., Saari, L. M., and Latham, G. P. (1981). Goal setting and task performance: 1969-1980. *Psychological Bulletin*, **90**, 125-152.

Lowrance, W. W. (1976). *On Acceptable Risk*. Los Alton, California: Kaufman.

Lund, A. K., and Zandor, P. (1984). Mandatory belt use and driver risk taking. *Risk Analysis*, **4**, 41-53.

McKenna, F. P. (1983). Accident proneness: A conceptual analysis. *Accident Analysis and Prevention*, **15**, 65-71.

McKenna, F. (1985). Do safety measures really work? An examination of the risk homeostasis theory. *Ergonomics*, **28**, 489-498.

McKenna, F. (1985). Does risk homeostasis theory represent a serious threat to ergonomics? In D. J. Oborne (ed.), *Contemporary Ergonomics 1985*. London: Taylor & Francis.

McKenna, S. P. (1978). The effects of first aid training on safety: A field study of approaches and methods. Ph.D. thesis, University of Aston, Birmingham.

McKenna, S. P., and Glendon, A. I. (1980). First aid training. Can it help prevent accidents? *Safety Surveyor*, **8**, 22-28.

McKenna, S. P., and Hale, A. R. (1981). The effect of emergency first aid training on the incidence of accidents in factories. *Journal of Occupational Accidents*, **3**, 101-114.

McKenna, S. P., and Hale, A. R. (1982). Changing behavior towards danger: The effect of first aid training. *Journal of Occupational Accidents*, **4**, 47-60.

Manello, T. A. (1979). Problem drinking among railroad workers: Extent, impact and solutions. University Research Corporation Monograph Series no. 5530, Wisconsin N. W., Washington DC 20015.

Manning, D. P. (1985). Use of an accident model to investigate and record causes of back injury. *Ergonomics*, **28**, 237-243.

Marshall, E., and Baker, S. M. (1985). Strategies for the prevention of control room based accidents in nuclear plants. In D. J. Oborne (ed.), *Contemporary Ergonomics 1985*. London: Taylor & Francis.

Mayer, H. E. (1981). On the relationship between an industrial worker's qualitative performance on Porteus Maze Tests and reported incidence of industrial accidents. *Dissertation Abstracts International*, **41**, 12-B, 4445.

Mendeloff, J. (1984). The role of OHSA violations in serious workplace accidents. *Journal of Occupational Medicine*, **26**, 353-360.

Metts, A. (1982). The relationship between work injuries and smoking habits among a group of cotton textile workers. *Dissertation Abstracts International*, **42**, 11-B, 4373.

Midanik, L. (1983). Alcohol problems and depressive symptoms in a national survey. In B. Stimmel (ed.), *Psychological Constructs of Alcoholism and Substance Abuse*. New York: Hawarth Press.

Murphy, D. J. (1981). Farm safety attitudes and accident involvement. *Accident Analysis and Prevention*, **13**, 331-337.

Näätänen, R., and Summala, H. (1975). A simple method for simulating danger-related aspects of behavior in hazardous activities. *Accident Analysis and Prevention*, **7**, 63-70.

National Research Council (1985). *Injury in America: A Continuing Public Health Problem*. Washington, DC: National Research Council.

Nordby, E. J. (1982). Epidemiology and diagnosis in low back injury. *Occupational Health and Safety*, **3**, 38-41.

Norman, D. A. (1981). Categorization of action slips. *Psychological Review*, **88**, 1-15.

O'Neill, B. (1977). A decision-theory model of danger compensation. *Accident Analysis and Prevention*, **9**, 157-166.

Orr, L. D. (1982). Incentives and efficiency in automobile safety regulations. *Quarterly Review of Economics and Business*, **22**, 43-65.

Ostberg, O. (1980). Risk perception and work behavior in forestry: Implications for accident prevention policy. *Accident Analysis and Prevention*, **12**, 189-200.

Parker, D. A., and Brody, J. A. (1981). *Risk Factors for Occupational Alcoholism and Alcohol Problems*. Alcoholism in the Workplace Monograph Series. Rockville, Maryland: NIAAA.

Pasmore, W. A., and Friedlander, F. (1982). An action-research program for increasing employee involvement in problem solving. *Administrative Science Quarterly*, **27**, 343-362.

Pelz, J. (1976). Alkohol als ursache von arbeitsunfallen, arbeitssicherheit, arzneimittel, losemittel. *Berufsgenussenschaft*, **28**, 45-46.

Percival, N. (1984). Safety aspects of robots and flexible manufacturing systems. In T. Lupton (ed.), *Human Factors in Manufacturing*. London: IFS and North-Holland.

Perrow, C. (1984). *Normal Accidents: Living with High-Risk Technologies*. New York: Basic Books.

Persinger, M. A., Cooke, W. J., and Jones, J. T. (1978). No evidence for relationship between biorhythms and industrial accidents. *Perceptual and Motor Skills*, **46**, 423-426.

Persinger, M. A., and Levesque, B. F. (1983). Geophysical variables and behavior: XII. The weather matrix accommodates large portions of variance of measured daily mood. *Perceptual and Motor Skills*, **58**, 868-870.

Persinger, M. A., and Nolan, M. (1984). Geophysical variables and behavior: XX. Weekly numbers of mining accidents and the weather matrix: The importance of geomagnetic variation and barometric pressure. *Perceptual and Motor Skills*, **59**, 719-722.

Perusse, M. (1980). Dimensions of perception and recognition of danger. Ph.D. thesis, University of Aston, Birmingham.

Pestonjee, D. M., Singh, A. P., and Ahmad, N. (1977). Job satisfaction and accidents. *Indian Journal of Industrial Relations*, **13**, 65-71.

Petersen, D. (1982). *Human Error Reduction and Safety Management*. New York: Garland STPM.

Pirani, M., and Reynolds, J. (1976). Gearing up for safety. *Personnel Management*, **5**, 25-29.

Pittner, E. D., and Owens, P. (1975). Chance or destiny? A review and test of the biorhythm theory. *Professional Safety*, **20**, 42-46.

Powell, P. I., Hale, M., Martin, J., and Simon, M. (1971). *2000 Accidents: A Shop Floor Study of Their Causes*. London: National Institute for Industrial Psychology.

Price, D. L., and Hicks, T. G. (1979). The effects of alcohol on performance of a production assembly task. *Ergonomics*, **22**, 37-41.

Rasmussen, J. (1982). Human errors. A taxonomy for describing human malfunction in industrial installations. *Journal of Occupational Accidents*, **4**, 311-333.

Ray, C. (1982). The surgical patient: Psychological stress and coping resources. In J. R. Eiser (ed.), *Social Psychology and Behavioral Medicine*. Chichester: Wiley.

Reason, J. T. (1979). Actions not as planned: The price of automation. In G. Underwood and R. Stevens (eds.), *Aspects of Consciousness*, vol. 1, Psychological Issues. London: Academic Press.

Reason, J. T. (1985). Slips and mistakes: Two distinct classes of human error? In D. J. Oborne, (ed.), *Contemporary Ergonomics 1985*. London: Taylor & Francis.

Reber, R. A., and Wallin, J. A. (1983). Validation of a behavioral measure of occupational safety. *Journal of Organizational Behavior Management*, **5**, 69-77.

Rhoton, W. W. (1980). A procedure to improve compliance with coal mine safety regulations. *Journal of Organizational Behavior Management*, **2**, 243-249.

Robertson, L. S. (1981). Automobile safety regulations and death reductions in the United States. *American Journal of Public Health*, **71**, 818-822.

Robinson, G. H. (1982). Accidents and socio-technical systems: Principles for design. *Accident Analysis and Prevention*, **14**, 121-130.

Rouse, N. B. (1985). Models of human problem solving: Detection, changes and compensation for system failures. *Automatica*, **19**, 613-625.

Saari, J., and Lahtela, J. (1981). Work conditions and accidents in three industries. *Scandinavian Journal of Environmental Health*, **7**, 97-105.

Schenk, J., and Rausche, A. (1979). The personality of accident prone drivers. *Psychologie und Praxis*, **23**, 179-186.

Schlegel, J. (1979). New contributions of psychology to accident prevention. *Bulletin de Psychologie*, **33**, 241-247.

Schwarz, G. R. (1976). A look at the matter of susceptibility to work errors as related to biorhythm. *Professional Safety*, **21**, 34-39.

Shain, M. (1982). Alcohol, drugs and safety: An updated perspective on problems and their management in the workplace. *Accident Analysis and Prevention*, **14**, 239-246.

Shain, M., and Groenveld, J. (1980). *Employee Assistance Programs: Philosophy, Theory and Practice*. Lexington.

Sheehy, N. P. (1981). The interview in accident investigation: Methodological pitfalls. *Ergonomics*, **24**, 437-446.

Sheehy, N. P., and Chapman, A. J. (1984). Accidents and safety. In A. Gale and A. J. Chapman (eds.), *Psychology and Social Problems: An Introduction to Applied Psychology*. Chichester: Wiley.

Sheehy, N. P., and Chapman, A. J. (1985). Post hoc assessment of children's accident vulnerability: The psychological basis of legal judgments. In T. Garling and J. Valsiner (eds.), *Children within Environments: Towards a Psychology of Accident Prevention*. New York: Plenum.

Sheehy, N. P., and Chapman, A. J. (1985). Applications of safety related IT to traffic accidents. In D. J. Oborne (ed.), *Contemporary Ergonomics 1985*. London: Taylor & Francis.

Sheridan, T. B., Vamos, T., and Aida, S. (1985). Adapting automation to man, culture and society. *Automatica*, **19**, 605-612.

Shindell, S., and Goldberg, M. (1981). Surveillance systems: What to include and why. *Occupational Health and Safety*, **50**, 34-39 and 56.

Silverman, H. M. (1981a). Potential effects of medications at work, I. *Occupational Health and Safety*, **50**, 48-50.

Silverman, H. M. (1981b). Potential effects of medications at work, II. *Occupational Health and Safety*, **50**, 33-35.

Silverman, M. H. (1981c). Potential effects of medications at work, III. *Occupational Health and Safety*, **50**, 26-31.

Smillie, R., and Ayoub, M. (1976/1977). Accident causation theories: A simulation approach. *Journal of Occupational Accidents*, **1**, 47-68.

Smith, M., Cohen, H., Cohen, A., and Cleveland, R. (1978). Characteristics of successful safety programs. *Journal of Safety Research*, **10**, 5-15.

Smith, M. J., Anger, W. K., and Uslan, S. S. (1978). Behavioral modification applied to occupational safety. *Journal of Safety Research*, **10**, 87-88.

Smith, P. C. (1976). Behaviors, results and organizational effectiveness: The problem of criteria. In M. Dunnette (ed.), *Handbook of Industrial and Organizational Psychology*. Chicago: Rand McNally.

Soutar, G. N., and Weaver, J. R. (1983). Biorhythms and the incidence of industrial accidents. *Journal of Safety Research*, **14**, 167-172.

Stevenson, A. (1980). *Planned Safety Management*. London: Alan Osborne.

Steventon, J. (1983). Fire safety in hospitals. *Ergonomics*, **26**, 747-754.

Stuart, J. C., and Brown, B. M. (1981). The relationship of stress and coping ability to the incidence of diseases and accidents. *Journal of Psychosomatic Research*, **25**, 255-260.

Studenski, R. (1981). Level of danger anxiety and work accidents. *Przeglad Psychologiczny*, **24**, 137-145.

Sulzer-Azaroff, B., and Santamaria, D. M. C. (1980). Industrial safety hazard reduction through performance feedback. *Journal of Applied Behavior Analysis*, **13**, 287-295.

Sutton, S. R. (1982). Fear-arousing communications: A critical examination of theory and research. In J. R. Eiser (ed.), *Social Psychology and Behavioral Medicine*. Chichester: Wiley.

Syriot, J. (1985). Effect of a video-taped safety program on attitudes towards safety: A field experiment. Paper presented at the West European Conference on the Psychology of Work and Organization, Aachen, Federal Republic of Germany, April.

Tabor, M. (1982). Minimizing the menace of OTC drugs. *Occupational Health and Safety*, **May**, 14-19.

Tanner, P. H. (1979). Risk: Taken or controlled? *Journal of Navigation*, **32**, 395-413.

Tanner, P. H. (1981). A model of a population composed of individuals regulating their own level of risk. Paper presented at the Third UKSC Conference on Computer Simulation, Harrogate, UK, May.

Tarrants, W. (1980). *The Measurement of Safety Performance*. New York: Garland STPM Press.

Taylor, D. H. (1981). The hermeneutics of accidents and safety. *Ergonomics*, **24**, 487-495.

Templer, D. I., Veleber, D. M., and Brooner, R. K. (1982). Geophysical variables and behavior: VI. Lunar phase and accident injuries: A difference between night and day. *Perceptual and Motor Skills*, **55**, 280-282.

Tilley, A. J., Wilkinson, R. T., Warren, P. S. G., Watson, B., and Drud, M. (1982). The sleep and performance of shift workers. *Human Factors*, **24**, 629-641.

Trist, E. L., Susman, G. I., and Brown, G. R. (1977). An experiment in autonomous working in an American underground coal mine. *Human Relations*, **30**, 201-236.

Tuttle, T. C., Dachler, H. P., and Schneider, B. (1975). Organizational Psychology. In B. L. Margolis and W. H. Kroes (eds.), *The Human Side of Accident Prevention*. Springfield, Illinois: Charles C. Thomas.

Vasilescu, I. P. (1977). A factor in risk-taking behavior: The evaluation of danger in industrial work: I. Estimating accident probability. *Revista-de-Psychologie*, **23**, 447-461.

Vasilescu, I. P. (1978). Risk-taking behavior: Evaluation of danger in industrial work: II. *Revista-de-Psychologie*, **24**, 95-102.

Waters, S. W. E., and Cliff, K. S. (1983). *Community Medicine: A Textbook for Nurses and Health Visitors*. London: Croom Helm.

Weaver, D. A. (1980). TOR analysis—an entry to safety management systems assessment. *Professional Safety*, **September**, 34-40.

Wellman, R. J. (1982). Accident proneness in police officers: Personality factors and problem drinking as predictors of injury claims of state troopers. *Dissertation Abstracts International*, **43**, 2-B, 538.

White, A. C. (1978). Drinking and accidents. *British Journal of Addiction*, **73**, 321-322.

Whitfield, R. A., Zador, P., and Fife, D. (1985). Projected mortality from injuries. *Accident Analysis and Prevention*, **17**, 67-73.

Whyte, A. A. (1982). Occupational health information systems. *Occupational Health and Safety*. **3**, 14-19.

Wilde, G. J. S. (1984). Evidence refuting the theory of risk homeostasis? A rejoinder to Frank P. McKenna. *Ergonomics*, **27**, 297-304.

Wilde, G. J. S., and Murdoch, P. (1982). Incentive systems for accident-free and violation-free driving in the general population. *Ergonomics*, **25**, 879-880.

Wolkenberg, R. C., Gold, C., and Tichauer, E. R. (1975). Delayed effects of acute alcoholic intoxication on performance with reference to work safety. *Journal of Safety Research*, **7**, 104-118.

Zohar, D. (1980). Promoting the use of personal protective equipment by behavior modification techniques. *Journal of Safety Research*, **12**, 78-85.

Zohar, D., Cohen, A., and Azar, N. (1980). Promoting increased use of ear protectors in noise through information feedback. *Human Factors*, **22**, 69-79.

Zohar, D., and Fussfeld, N. (1981). A systems approach to organizational behavior modification: Theoretical considerations and empirical evidence. *International Review of Applied Psychology*, **30**, 491-505.

International Review of Industrial and Organizational Psychology 1987
Edited by C. L. Cooper and I. T. Robertson
©1987 John Wiley & Sons Ltd

Chapter 8

INTERPERSONAL CONFLICTS IN ORGANIZATIONS

Leonard Greenhalgh
*The Amos Tuck School of Business Administration
Dartmouth College
USA*

Conflict is a ubiquitous phenomenon, pervading virtually all organizational processes (Dahrendorf, 1959; Lewin, 1948; Thomas, 1976). It is experienced whenever organizational actors do not agree on rights, issues, allocations, details, or procedures (Boulding, 1966; March and Simon, 1958; Kilmann and Thomas, 1978; Pondy, 1966; Robbins, 1974; Schmidt and Kochan, 1972). Although it has some positive functions (Brett, 1980; Coser, 1956; Deutsch, 1973; Pfeffer, 1981; Pondy, 1967; Simmel, 1955; Thomas, 1976; Walton, 1969), conflict more often is seen as a threat to organizational efficiency and effectiveness (March and Simon, 1958), given that our views of organizations tend to be shaped by order models (Burrell and Morgan, 1979; Horton, 1964).

The discussion that follows addresses the generic case of interpersonal conflict, and for clarity, most references are to the simple dyad. Intergroup and interorganizational conflicts have emerging properties that cannot be reduced to the dyad level of analysis but nevertheless share many of the properties and dynamics of interpersonal conflicts, especially in so far as the conflict becomes focused between agents of the larger constituencies. The discussion is not intended to apply to intrapersonal (intrapsychic) conflicts (see, for example, Deutsch, 1973).

Three basic alternatives exist for dealing with interpersonal conflicts: resolution, domination, and negotiation. Conflict resolution involves cognitive readjustment whereby the apparent disagreement is no longer experienced as highly salient (Greenhalgh, 1985, 1986; cf. March and Simon, 1958). Resolution therefore obviates the need for agreement, whereas the second alternative, domination, ignores the wishes of the other party and thereby treats agreement as inconsequential. With regard to domination, most definitions of power involve the notion of getting someone to do something he or she would not do in the absence of influence. If one party has supreme power, his or her will can prevail despite disagreement, and the conflict is suppressed. Negotiation, the third alternative, involves reaching agreement concerning the matter in dispute. The agreement represents a commitment to abide by the jointly approved settlement to the dispute. Negotiation may be adversarial in tone or it may be collaborative, but the focus is always on joint solutions that more or less meet mutual needs.

These three basic alternatives—resolution, domination, and negotiation—are conceptually distinct and each is, by itself, potentially capable of terminating a conflict. In practice, however, negotiated settlements are likely to be somewhat influenced by both the power of the parties and the parties' efforts to achieve cognitive readjustments.

For example, dominance is only rarely effective as the sole means of dealing with conflict. First, power tends to be reciprocal (see, for example, Mechanic, 1962), therefore it is uncommon for one party to have such a massive power advantage that the power holder does not care if the other party strongly disagrees. Second, dominance only suppresses conflict, therefore it only deals with the symptoms. The intensity of feelings that attend the conflict remains or even increases (Dahrendorf, 1959) and the conflict becomes manifest in less manageable forms such as passive aggression or subtle acts of sabotage.

Similarly, conflicts rarely are fully resolved through cognitive readjustment. Communication improvement was a normative approach to such cognitive readjustments within the human relations school (Nord, 1974). The idea was, if the parties could understand each other's point of view better, they would discover the misunderstandings that led to their perceiving a conflictful relationship, which in fact did not exist. When this approach was attempted in organizational situations lacking perfect harmony of goals and interests, the well-meaning actors often found that a clearer understanding of the dispute brought the conflict into sharper focus and thereby made it more acute.

Because dominance is an unstable approach and resolution impractical in most long-term relationships—and therefore in most organizational situations—actors must negotiate, and this is by far the most prominent means of dealing with conflict in organizations. Negotiation consequently pervades virtually all organizational interactions in which one party must agree with another. Examples span a wide range, including peer rivalry, superior—subordinate disagreements, differences with customers or suppliers, achievement of consensus within various types of task forces, and the behavior of coalitions within the organization's power-elite.

Negotiation therefore is viewed best as a multifaceted process that includes elements of power and cognitive adjustment, although not in such large amounts that the conflict disappears. Agreements are shaped by influence and by shifts in actors' perceptions of the situation. Thus, to understand the determinants of negotiated outcomes, one needs to consider the interaction of power, cognitive adjustment, and negotiation. These dynamics are usefully summarized in an integrative model.

The purpose of this chapter is to present such a model and to review major thrusts in the research literature that have elaborated various aspects of the model. The model serves an important function in drawing together a diffuse line of inquiry that has seen cumulative development only in narrow areas. This chapter is not intended to be a comprehensive review, but rather points to some important gaps in the body of knowledge concerning the determinants of negotiated outcomes of conflict situations. It thereby suggests a research agenda for scholars interested in this topic.

THE MODEL

Figure 8.1 summarizes a model of the determinants of negotiated outcomes of interpersonal conflicts in organizations. It shows the interrelationships between individual predispositions, power, perceptions, tactics, roles, utility structures, expectations, the intervention of third parties, and situational factors. The relationships between pairs of these variables have thus far tended to be studied separately, with little attention given to the complexities of how the relationships interact to affect the achievement of agreement. The discussion that follows explains the interrelationships one would expect on the basis of existing theory and research, and identifies key studies supporting those relationships.

Negotiated Outcomes

Walton and McKersie (1965) defined negotiation as 'the deliberate interaction of two or more . . . social units which are attempting to define or redefine the terms of their interdependence' (p. 3). The outcome of this process is a joint commitment to abide by a course of action (Gamson, 1968). The joint commitment is analytically reducible to the parties' two individual commitments, which presume antecedent individual decisions to settle the conflict rather than perpetuate it. Most of the research on this topic has concerned the individuals' antecedent decisions (see, for example, Bazerman, 1986). Particular attention has been given to the interaction of two interdependent decision makers by game theorists (e.g. Axelrod, 1984; Luce and Raiffa, 1957) and by psychologists studying game-theoretical decision making. Less research attention has been given, *per se*, to commitment to a jointly agreed upon course of action (Kiesler, 1971), and less still to the notion of joint commitment. As a result, scholars studying negotiated agreements rarely examine in detail the central phenomenon of their inquiry (see Zartman, 1977).

In addition to the further study that needs to be done on the process of agreement, research attention needs to be given to the content of the outcome. One crucial outcome of most negotiations is the subsequent interpersonal relationship between the parties. Only in the rare cases when the parties will never interact again — and when the reputations they develop as a result of their performance are inconsequential — will the ongoing relationship be insignificant. Even if the conflict is genuinely episodic, a positive feedback loop exists such that the use of relationship-impairing tactics erodes the relationship in a way that makes the use of such tactics more appropriate (see Deutsch, 1973, p. 365). Despite its importance, little attention has been given to this aspect of a negotiation. The neglect may be attributable to three major factors.

The first is the strong influence of economics-oriented game theorists on the paradigms used to study negotiations (Rubin and Brown, 1975). Their theories of negotiation 'begin with the simple and obvious notion that bargainers compare the costs and benefits of no agreement with the costs and benefits of no settlement' (Bacharach and Lawler, 1981). In this conceptualization, damage to the relationship is, at best, dismissed as being somehow factored into the cost of no settlement and, therefore, unworthy of special attention (cf. Folger and Poole, 1984, p. 37). The narrow view of the bargaining dyad that results from that conceptualization encourages scholars uncritically to use sterile simulations (see Shubik, 1968) to research rich phenomena (see, for example, Allport, 1968; Gergen, 1969; Harré and Secord, 1972; Schlenker and Bonoma, 1978; Wachtel, 1980; Zartman, 1977; for a contrary view, see Berkowitz and Donnerstein, 1982). For example, vast numbers of studies of negotiation are reported in Rubin and Brown (1975) that use the Prisoner's Dilemma simulation despite its poor external validity (Greenhalgh, Neslin,

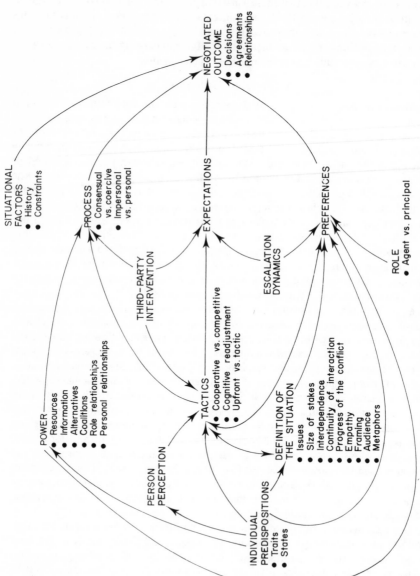

Figure 8.1 Determinants of negotiated outcomes of organizational conflicts: an integrative model

and Gilkey, 1985; Streufert and Suefeld, 1977). That simulation, and most of the research based on it, considers only the utilities of the participants for a narrow set of outcomes (Wilmot and Wilmot, 1978). However, unless the participants are and will remain anonymous strangers, post-simulation debriefing sessions reveal a strong, and sometimes paramount, concern with the effect of tactical choices on ongoing interpersonal relationships, an important outcome for many subjects that is not accommodated in the payoff matrix.

The second reason for neglect of relationships is the dominance of the classical experimental paradigms in social psychology under which the bulk of the research on negotiations has been conducted. To eliminate the confounding effects of a previous relationship, the paired subjects tend to be strangers. Thus, in the laboratory there is a very real choice as to whether to engage in or withdraw from negotiations that may not be experienced in real-world negotiations in an organizational context. US defense contractors do not have free choice in whether to deal with governments; subordinates seldom have choice in whether to deal with their bosses; and a sales division usually has to deal with the company's corresponding supply division. This artifact of experimental social–psychological methods seems to have colored the theories it investigates, with consequent limitations in adequacy and generalizability.

The third reason for scholars' neglect of interpersonal relationships as an aspect of negotiated outcomes is that scholars—especially those in the United States— have been somewhat culture-bound in their conceptualization of the scope of negotiations. Americans display a tendency to assume that a negotiation is over once an 'agreement' has been reached, and that the terms of the agreement are immutable. In other cultures, agreements are viewed as more tentative, envisioning that the terms must be revised if subsequently they no longer meet the needs of either party. In the latter case, the agreement is a mutual commitment to a relationship in which needs are mutually met, rather than to specific terms (see Tung, 1984).

Culture-boundedness can be seen in Fisher and Ury's (1981) prescriptive book, *Getting to Yes*, in which negotiators are urged to be highly aware of their best alternatives to a negotiated agreement. If sufficient weight were given to the importance of relationships, these authors might urge negotiators to take a different view and avoid sacrificing a relationship for a marginally better (in narrowly defined economic terms) outcome outside the exchange relationship. As an illustration, if one partner in a strong marriage cannot obtain something from the other marital partner, he or she might be ill advised to seek out the 'best alternative' means of gratification from an outside party, because doing so might damage the marital relationship. Analogous considerations will likely be salient in any long-term interdependent relationship.

The failure to adequately research relationships between negotiators is the more puzzling because Walton and McKersie (1965) devoted considerable attention to the topic in their seminal work, *A Behavioral Theory of Labor Negotiations*. Their concept of 'attitudinal structuring' in essence refers to managing the relationship between the parties, while concurrently determining the economic content of negotiated outcomes. In contrast to the considerable volume of follow-up studies of Walton and McKersie's concepts of distributive and integrative bargaining, almost no further work has been done on attitudinal structuring.

The next four sections of this chapter explain the four primary determinants of outcomes identified in Figure 8.1: situational factors, the negotiation process, the negotiators' preferences, and their expectations.

Situational Factors

Situational factors are the first determinant of negotiated outcomes. The history of the relationship (defined broadly to include anticipated future interactions) is an important situational factor that can affect the outcome of a negotiation (Deutsch, 1973; Filley, 1975; Rahim, 1986; Rubin and Brown, 1975; Walton and McKersie, 1965; Wehr, 1979). If previous encounters have generated enmity, an aggrieved party is likely to seek outcomes that will leave the other party at a disadvantage. Or, if the history of social exchange has left one party indebted to the other, or one party wants to become indebted to the other in order to create an exchange balance that will favor future transactions, then the dynamics of protracted 'logrolling' transactions will affect the current negotiated outcome (Pruitt, 1981, 1983).

Other situational factors may take the form of constraints (Bacharach and Lawler, 1981; Wehr, 1979). The Robinson–Patman Act is a legal constraint that prohibits certain outcomes of the buying or selling of industrial goods. Industry goals in pattern bargaining can be a constituency-imposed constraint on the outcomes of labor-management contract negotiations (Walton and McKersie, 1965). Social mores may constrain the exploitation of the disadvantaged by the advantaged in various societal transactions (Laue and Cormick, 1973). Or, the parties may experience rules by which their actions in the conflict situation are constrained (Dunlop, 1958; Thibaut and Kelley, 1959; Thomas, 1976).

The setting of the negotiation is another situational factor that can affect outcomes. For example, whether the person has a claim to the physical environment in which the negotiation takes place may make a difference in how the negotiation culminates (Martindale, 1971; Rubin and Brown, 1975). The colloquial reference to this factor is 'on whose turf' the negotiation will be conducted. The effect may not be direct, but rather may be articulated through other variables. A neutral setting may foster a less coercive process (Walton, 1969); the presence of one party's symbols of office may make power a more prominent factor (Pfeffer, 1981); even the shape of the negotiation table may have symbolic importance (Rubin and Brown, 1975); an uncomfortable physical environment may give rise to the use of tougher tactics, and so on.

The seating arrangements affect outcomes, especially in multiparty negotiations. A large volume of research has investigated the effects of seating arrangements on intragroup communication (Shaw, 1976); articulation of one's position depends on the ability to communicate, therefore it seems reasonable that seating arrangements would affect outcomes. Certainly visual accessibility can affect whether negotiators are fair, seek mutual gain, and avoid harming each other (see, for example, Carnevale, Pruitt, and Seilheimer, 1981; Lewis and Fry, 1977; Morley and Stephenson, 1977), therefore physical arrangements that permit face-to-face communication may be a significant factor in determining the outcomes of negotiations (Tedeschi, Schlenker, and Bonoma, 1973).

The social environment may be even more important than the physical environment. Some corporate cultures, for instance, encourage competition between employees, with few constraints on tactics. In other corporate cultures, the cooperation and harmony of 'teamwork' is emphasized, and conflict discouraged. In addition, certain social institutions exist for the regulation of conflict (Deutsch, 1973; Wehr, 1979) that directly affect the outcomes of conflict, especially in the case of collective bargaining (Dunlop, 1958).

Finally, time pressure may be an important situational factor (Tedeschi et al., 1973). Its psychological impact is a negotiator's desire to end the negotiation quickly (Pruitt, 1981), and thus it may not be a property of the negotiation context, but rather may be manipulated tactically by the other negotiator (Rubin and Brown, 1975; Walton and McKersie, 1965) or by a third party (Carnevale and Lawler, 1986).

The desire to end the negotiation quickly could be hypothesized to reduce intransigence, since toughness tends to draw out the negotiation process (see, for example, Stevens, 1963). One could also hypothesize that the negotiator's urgency would discourage integrative solutions because there would be less time to explore such possibilities (Walton and McKersie, 1965). If both these hypotheses held true, the effect of time pressure would be the predominance of simple, expedient compromises. Most of the reported research suggests that negotiators become more cooperative under time pressure (Pruitt, 1981; Rubin and Brown, 1975), although the research conducted by Carnevale and Lawler (1986) indicates that negotiators' individualistic/cooperative orientation affects their bargaining behavior under time pressure: for individualistically oriented negotiators, time pressure produced greater competitiveness, whereas it produced greater cooperativeness for cooperatively oriented negotiators. Furthermore, time pressure is usually found to lead to poorer joint outcomes (see, for example, Yukl, Malone, Hayslip, and Pamin, 1976). Thus, the effects of time pressure are complex and warrant further research attention — particularly involving multiattribute negotiations — given the prevalence of time pressure in important negotiations such as collective bargaining (Dunlop and Healy, 1955).

Negotiation Process

The second primary determinant of negotiated outcomes is the nature of the negotiation process. Whereas tactics involve the behaviors of individual negotiators, process describes interaction within the dyad (or larger grouping of parties). This aspect of negotiation has received surprisingly little research attention (Folger and Poole, 1984). Perhaps the most basic process typology involves the distinction between consensual and coercive processes. In the case of a consensual process, all parties involved must consent to the settlement, therefore the outcomes are likely to be compromises worked out in such a way as to jointly optimize the achieved utilities of the negotiators. A coercive process tends to result in outcomes that are less of a compromise: for example, in many cases a majority-voted outcome will serve the interests of the majority coalition at the expense of other parties (Deutsch, 1973); alternatively, a judgement can be rendered by an individual of higher authority which is binding on the parties (Zartman, 1977).

Another process distinction involves the extent to which the negotiation is personal vs. impersonal (Folger and Poole, 1984, p. 61). As negotiators shift attention from objective issues to personal characteristics of the other party, the process becomes more personal (Whyte, 1951). No matter how impersonal the grounds for negotiation, the negotiators will seldom be able to ignore the other party as an individual. A process that is highly reactive to the negotiators' personalities, however, can be detrimental to reaching settlement. Donohue (1978) found that when compatibilities between individuals become emphasized, negotiators focus more on each other's personality characteristics and less on the issues, resulting in an exchange of personal attacks. Minor issues irrelevant to the substantive objectives of negotiation may become prominent as negotiators become increasingly concerned with face saving; in fact, the original objectives may become entirely lost. What then results is a high-cost, zero-sum game, where the stakes are personal dignity and self-esteem (Williams, 1975).

Several authors have developed models of the process by which a conflict unfolds over time (see, for example, Coleman, 1957; Folger and Poole, 1984; Goldman, 1966; Kriesberg; 1973; Pondy, 1967; Thomas, 1976; Walton, 1969). Thus far, the empirical research attention given to these models has been inadequate in light of the potential for improving our understanding of conflict. The inattention is understandable given the reward structures experienced by most academic researchers. Intensive longitudinal study of complex, highly variable events is risky, time consuming, and not encouraged by some of the major journals in the field. Therefore, it is understandable that most scholars choose to conduct what is often less insightful research by means of classic bivariate social psychological experiments. Nevertheless, the result of this inattention is that we understand *that* some variables affect negotiation without understanding *how* the effect occurs. A keener understanding of the effects of established explanatory variables on negotiation subprocesses would greatly enhance the body of knowledge and clarify many of the 'mixed results' that have been reported across studies of the same phenomena.

Factors affecting process

The process of a negotiation is related to the power of the actors and the tactics they use, moderated by third-party intervention. In regard to power, as categorized by means of the French and Raven (1959) typology, it seems likely that personal, persuasive forms of power such as referent and expert will be associated with a consensual process while the more dominating forms of positional power such as legitimate, reward, and punishment will be associated with a coercive process. Note that in this model, power is not depicted as a direct determinant of outcomes. In the introduction, power solutions (dominance) were differentiated from negotiated solutions: an essential condition of a negotiated solution is agreement, which by definition is precluded if power determines outcomes directly.

Negotiators' tactics affect the process of negotiation in that they set the tone. The most basic distinction is between tactics that are cooperative and those that are competitive (Axelrod, 1984; Deutsch, 1965; Rubin and Brown, 1975). Table 8.1, below, summarizes the specific tactics that are likely to be associated with each polar orientation. Cooperative tactics are likely to engender a consensual process, and competitive tactics a coercive process.

Third-party Intervention Third parties in a conflict differ from principals in their roles and interests in the outcome. However, being a third party is in practice a matter of degree rather than a dichotomous classification. At the extreme is someone whose designated role is to constructively intervene in the process and who has no interest whatsoever in the outcomes of either party. These roles have been professionalized as arbitrators and mediators. Arbitrators issue judgements (Anderson, 1981; Notz, Starke, and Atwell, 1983) while mediators facilitate communication between the parties (Kochan and Jick, 1978; Wall, 1981; see Kolb, 1983, for a study of differences in approach).

Brett and Goldberg (1983) have suggested an additional third-party role combining the functions of mediation and arbitration, namely, that of the 'mediator-adviser'. The mediator-adviser's responsibility is to facilitate communication (like a mediator) and offer a professional judgement as to a fair outcome (like an arbitrator); however, that judgement is (unlike an arbitrator's) non-binding. Each role—arbitrator, mediator, mediator-adviser—has certain advantages in specific situations. Sometimes, change agents and other consultants need to assume such roles (see, for example, Walton, 1969).

The more familiar situation in organizations is when an organizational actor intervenes who is somewhat tangential to the conflict situation, and whose interests are only indirectly affected. Often, a superior serves in this role in disputes between lower-level employees (Sheppard, 1983). Third-party effectiveness in such situations depends on creating the perception of even-handedness and, often, allowing the parties to vent pent-up emotions that are interfering with the relationship (Greenhalgh, 1986).

The presence of a third party enhances the process by raising the visibility of the interaction between the negotiators (Deutsch, 1973). Cooperation is usually valued over competition in intraorganizational interactions, due to the prevalence of norms favoring teamwork as a means of accomplishing the organization's goals. The third party is an audience (see Rubin and Brown, 1975) whose presence fosters normative behavior, hence the link to tactics (Thomas, 1976), which in turn affect the process. More specifically, the no-holds-barred tactics that a competitive negotiator may be able to rationalize are seen as more risky when a third party is observing. For these reasons, the more powerful, prestigious, trusted, and neutral is the third party, the greater is the constraining effect (Greenhalgh, 1985).

Preferences

Bargaining exchanges typically involve one or more issues concerning how resources, broadly defined, are to be allocated among the parties (Rubin and Brown, 1975). Conflict exists because the parties value what is at stake, therefore it is important to understand in detail the utilities which the parties attach to the possible outcomes. Researchers have too often assumed that subjects have simple, stable, unified preferences and that these are perfectly shaped by role-playing instructions in laboratory studies. The result of these assumptions is that a large gap remains in our understanding of negotiated outcomes of conflict situations.

Negotiation researchers have recognized the importance of both tangible (e.g. money) and intangible (i.e. face-saving) negotiator utilities (Fisher, 1964; Ikle, 1964; Rubin and Brown, 1975; Schelling, 1960; Stevens, 1963; Walton and McKersie, 1965). Most of the social-psychological research on this topic has concerned tangible issues. The typical study involves examining the effect of increasing incentive magnitude, which is usually accomplished by varying the stakes of a Prisoner's Dilemma simulation (Rubin and Brown, 1975). Such research has limited external validity because rarely is there a single issue at stake that has a simple relationship between marginal utility and marginal change in the negotiated outcome (Tedeschi et al., 1973). A few studies have considered multiattribute negotiations (e.g. Druckman, 1977; Eliashberg, LaTour, Rangaswamy, and Stern, 1986; Froman and Cohen, 1970; Greenhalgh and Neslin, 1981; Kelley, 1966; Neale and Bazerman, 1983), but the research thrust in this area has yet to gain momentum. Because of its large potential contribution to our understanding of complex, real-world negotiation, it is worth pausing to consider the opportunities and challenges of using complex measures to capture negotiators' preferences for multiattribute outcomes.

Neslin and Greenhalgh undertook a series of laboratory studies that simulated multiattribute negotiations in collective bargaining (Greenhalgh and Neslin, 1981) and corporate sales/purchasing (Neslin and Greenhalgh, 1983, 1986). Multiattribute preferences were measured by means of conjoint analysis, a monotone analysis of variance technique originally developed by mathematical psychologists and adapted and refined by marketing researchers (Green and Rao, 1971).

Conjoint analysis is particularly suited to negotiation research because it can be used to operationalize the two key elements of each negotiator's preference structure: the utility of the various issues at stake and the utility of impasse. This measurement technique reflects the real-world negotiator's need to decide among various outcome packages: individual issue utilities are typically derived from subjects' rank ordering of a sample of outcome packages. The utility of an impasse is also measured directly by having subjects identify the point in the hierarchy of outcome packages at which they would prefer no settlement to the next worst outcome package, equivalent to what Thibaut and Kelley (1959) term the 'comparison level for alternatives.' This permits operational definition of the negotiator's resistance point (or reservation value), an important datum for most game-theoretical bargaining solutions (e.g. Nash, 1950). Data generated using conjoint analysis show that negotiator preferences can be a key predictor of negotiated outcomes, with the effects of other variables (power and personality) on outcomes being articulated through preferences (Greenhalgh et al., 1985).

The high external validity of this approach comes at some expense. The burden on subjects is large, and becomes overwhelming if more than seven attributes are used (see Green and Srinivasan, 1978). The research itself is labor-intensive, and experimental control in a rich-context simulation is inevitably constrained. The approach also poses serious theoretical problems, the most prominent of which is the questionable validity of combining utility data from different negotiators (see Luce and Raiffa, 1957). Nevertheless, the methodology offers significant advantages over classical laboratory studies that assume uniform, stable preferences across subjects: that assumption is proven to be erroneous whenever utility structures are measured, in that subjects form idiosyncratic preferences despite uniform role-playing instructions (Chertkoff, 1971), and utilities for outcome packages may shift as the negotiation proceeds (Walton and McKersie, 1965).

Another topic worthy of further research attention is the extent to which utilities have linear effects on negotiators' behavior. A set of outcomes can be ordered in terms of increasing utility (Von Neumann and Morgenstern, 1947) but there may be discontinuities in negotiators' responses to increasingly valued outcomes

(Tedeschi *et al.*, 1973). In particular, level of aspiration may change how the negotiator responds to settlements at, above, and below that level (Siegel, 1957). Siegel and Fouraker (1960) define the negotiator's level of aspiration as 'the particular achievement goal for which he strives,' and expect a behavior shift because 'a bargainer with a high level of aspiration will have considerable bargaining strength because of his reluctance to make concessions in the region of his aspiration level' (p. 60). The sophisticated multiattribute measurement techniques available today would permit empirical assessment of such discontinuities and any associated behavioral shifts.

In effect, aspiration levels are outcome goals (Siegel and Fouraker, 1960) that induce negotiators to strive harder for certain outcomes than for others that have perhaps even higher utility. Theorists need to turn to motivational theories which are more sophisticated than simple utility maximization to explain this phenomenon. Promising candidates are the goal-setting theories of motivation (Locke, Shaw, Saari, and Latham, 1981) and expectancy theory (Lawler, 1973; Vroom, 1964). Although a great deal of research has been conducted on these topics in a classic job performance context, little empirical work has been done to explicitly apply these theories to the motivation of negotiators (see Huber and Neale, 1984).

Still another topic requiring further research attention is how negotiators make the necessary cognitive readjustments when they have to accept settlements below their pre-negotiation resistance points. This may occur when the other party's power proves more formidable than expected, or when they become reluctant to sacrifice the quality of the relationship. The cognitive readjustment necessary to make the decision to accept the settlement may take the form of a preference shift ('that previously unacceptable outcome is more attractive if I can keep this relationship intact'), an attributional cognition, or both (see Zajonc and Markus, 1982). Empirical research is needed to address this issue.

Factors influencing preferences

Preferences are the subjective utilities assigned to outcomes. Because they are subjective, they are influenced by the individual predispositions of the negotiators (Greenhalgh *et al.*, 1985). As examples, compared to a risk-seeking negotiator, a risk-averse negotiator is more likely to prefer a low-risk, low potential payoff outcome to a high-risk, high potential payoff outcome (see, for example, Harnett, Cummings and Hughes, 1968); similarly, a negotiator who has little tolerance for delayed gratification will tend to prefer outcomes with immediate payoffs.

A particularly interesting—and as yet underresearched—effect of individual predispositions on preferences involves negotiators' utility for tangible outcomes relative to their utility for preserving and even enhancing the relationship. Gilkey and his colleagues studied this phenomenon from the perspective of gender differences. On the basis of differences in childhood socialization, they predicted that feminine negotiators would have higher utility for fostering the relationship with the other party than would their masculine counterparts. Data from in-depth interviews conducted by a clinical psychologist and two laboratory studies using the interviewed subjects confirmed the basic hypothesis. Feminine negotiators were more concerned with the longer-term relationships and consequently were motivated to avoid relationship-impairing tactics, even when this meant sacrificing economic payoffs (Gilkey and Greenhalgh, 1984; Greenhalgh, Gilkey and Pufahl, 1984).

These findings raise some interesting points for further theory building and empirical investigation. The negotiation point of view can shed new light on long-standing research questions. Students of interpersonal and group behavior in organizations for decades have been interested in actors' differential interest in relationships vs. tasks. In the leadership literature, this took the form of the leader's orientation toward 'consideration' vs. 'initiating structure' (see, for example, Fiedler, 1967; Fleishman, 1957; House and Baetz, 1979). In the group dynamics literature, the analogous group roles were 'task specialists' vs. 'socioemotional specialists' (see, for example, Bales and Slater, 1955).

Leaders in either a group or a leader–follower dyad can usefully be considered negotiators (Hollander, 1978; Mintzberg, 1973), in that they need to reconcile more or less incompatible interests in order to achieve their goals to some degree. From this point of view, those stalled lines of research can be seen as an attempt to discover the individuals' relative utilities for relationships vs. other outcomes of organizational conflicts. The measurement techniques now exist for operationalizing those tradeoffs, and the individual differences that give rise to tradeoff choices will likely be strongly linked to subjects' childhood socialization experiences (Gilligan, 1982).

The role taken by negotiators — e.g. negotiating on their own behalf vs. negotiating as an agent for some constituency — also affects preferences (Druckman, 1977; Hermann and Kogan, 1968; Klimoski, 1978; Walton and McKersie, 1965). Greenhalgh, Neslin, and Gilkey (1985) confirmed this phenomenon in a laboratory study in which uniform preference instructions gave rise to idiosyncratic adopted preferences. They discovered that preference structure is determined by two factors: first, the constituency's preferences that are communicated to the negotiator in his or her agent role; and second, the underlying preferences based on the negotiator's personal values.

Negotiators' experience of their roles can be deliberate and calculative, as in the case of accountability beliefs, or unconscious, as in the case of acquired loyalty (see Rubin and Brown, 1975). Accountability implies evaluation of the role performance by the constituency and the application of sanctions in response to the adequacy of the negotiators' representation. Little empirical research has been conducted on this topic (see Gruder, 1971; McKersie, Perry, and Walton, 1965). Several authors have noted the function of third parties in easing accountability pressures (see, for example, Walton and McKersie, 1965): negotiators are more comfortable making unpopular concessions when their actions can be attributed to pressure from a third party (Pruitt and Johnson, 1970). In the absence of experienced accountability, negotiators' loyalty to their constituencies is expected to emerge with group cohesion (Druckman, 1967). The effects of loyalty to the constituency on negotiators' intransigence were demonstrated in a study by Blake and Mouton (1961), although intransigence was, perhaps inadvertently, encouraged in the study by inducing participants to define the situation as a contest to be won, thereby evoking negotiators' sports metaphors (the impact of sports metaphors on negotiators' definition of the situation is discussed in detail below).

Preferences are not static. In the course of negotiations, they may change, just as expectations may change. A fascinating phenomenon resulting in a preference change is the escalation dynamics of bidding behavior (Staw, 1976). Briefly, instead of withdrawing from an unfavorable situation, people actually increase their commitment to the obviously detrimental course of action they are pursuing. Bazerman (1986 p. 68) defines such non-rational escalation as 'the degree to which an individual escalates commitment to a previously selected course of action to a point beyond that which a rational model of decision making would prescribe.' Such escalation of commitment has an effect on preferences because the attractiveness of the outcome package in which the negotiator has already invested time, energy, and perhaps even financial resources increases above the objective costs of attaining it (see, for example, Bazerman, Beekun, and Schoorman, 1982; Bazerman, Giuliano, and Appelman, 1984; Brockner and Rubin, 1985; Caldwell and O'Reilly, 1982; Deutsch, 1973; Neale and Bazerman, 1985; Northcraft and Wolf, 1984; Shubik, 1971; Staw and Ross, 1978; Teger, 1980; Walsh, Henderson and Deighton, 1986).

The final determinant of preferences is the tactics used by the other party. For example, if a negotiator takes the cooperative, problem-solving approach of integrative bargaining (Walton and McKersie, 1965), he or she is likely to focus on underlying interests rather than current positions (Fisher and Ury, 1981; Pruitt, 1981; Thomas, 1976). Doing so may alter the other party's preferences as outcomes not previously considered become recognized to be alternative ways of meeting needs. For example, a manager opposing pressure to reduce his or her workforce may shift the discussion to the more basic need to save money. This would make salient higher management's preferences for alternative cost-cutting strategies (see Greenhalgh, McKersie, and Gilkey, 1986).

Expectations

The fourth primary determinant is the expectations of the parties, which are generated by the negotiator in assessing the other party on a number of dimensions, many of them individual difference variables (Harsanyi, 1962). A particularly interesting trait is what Tedeschi, Schlenker, and Bonoma (1973, p. 97) call 'chronic self-confidence . . . a generalized expectancy of success . . . derived from an individual's past history of achievements.' Expectations affect outcomes in that unless fairness norms (Harnett and Cummings, 1980; Nash, 1950; Schelling, 1960) dominate, parties with lower expectations will achieve lower outcomes (Donohue, 1978; Blau, 1964; Schelling, 1960). This happens because a negotiator will tend to continue pressing the other party for concessions until the proposed solution is at or above the negotiator's expected minimum (Hessel, 1984). Unless perfect symmetry exists between negotiators, the lower the expectations, the lower will be the agreed-upon outcome, to the point that the decisions of each negotiator may be relatively independent of the other party's actions (Harnett and Cummings, 1980; Harsanyi, 1962; Kelley, Beckman, and Fisher, 1967; Pruitt and Drews, 1969).

The studies that have investigated this construct evidence a need for greater conceptual clarity and more precision in the use of terms. Expectations have been viewed by different researchers as predicted outcomes, desired feasible outcomes (i.e. the most desirable of the set of outcomes the negotiator views as actually attainable), and minimum outcomes (representing the very least value the negotiator expects to achieve in the negotiation). The term *expectations* denotes the negotiator's predicted outcome in the model; aspirations and minimum acceptable payoffs are accommodated in the model within preference structure.

Factors affecting negotiators' expectations

An important role of third parties is to make negotiators' expectations more realistic (see, for example, Carnevale and Pegnetter, 1985; Douglas, 1962). Particularly when the process is shaped by competitive tactics, negotiators become influenced by their own rhetoric about what are reasonable demands, and their expectations rise accordingly (Bazerman and Neale, 1983). Status group membership also has been shown to affect negotiators' initial expectations (Walsh, Greenhalgh, and Fairfield, 1986). A skillful third party will dampen such expectations without alienating the parties (Farber, 1981; Neale and Bazerman, 1983).

Negotiation tactics themselves can also have a dampening effect on the *other party's* expectations. The parties will not agree to an outcome until the proposed solution is at or above a negotiator's expectations. To achieve agreement in positional bargaining (Fisher and Ury, 1981) negotiators can either raise their offer or lower the other's expectations. The latter can be influenced by the negotiators' intransigence (Pruitt, 1981), by convincing the other that the other's alternatives are less feasible or less attractive than the other believes, or by threats that raise the cost of failure to agree (which indirectly lowers expectations by lowering the net perceived value of existing expected outcomes).

The effect of tactics on expectations is probably influenced by the personalities of the negotiators. Harnett and Cummings (1972) found a relationship between risk-taking propensity and the difference between expected gain and actual gain. Relative status has also been found to have an effect on both expectations and the way the negotiator treats the other party (Harsanyi, 1962).

Tactics

Tactics are the set of behaviors undertaken by negotiators to gain their desired ends (Bacharach and Lawler, 1981). This usage of the construct is less specific than that of Brett (1984), who differentiates tactics, as individual acts, from strategy as the goal-directed pattern that describes the set.

A large volume of research has been generated about negotiation tactics. A basic distinction is between cooperative and competitive tactics. Competitive tactics are oriented toward pursuing self-interest, whereas cooperative tactics are oriented towards serving mutual interests. Table 8.1, though not exhaustive, summarizes the literature on tactics that can be grouped by means of this typology.

Tactical objectives

Working from a perspective strongly influenced by economic game theory, Walton and McKersie (1965) differentiated distributive from integrative bargaining. Distributive tactics are competitive in the sense that their objective is to pursue gain with little regard for the needs of the other party. Intregrative tactics are those which 'integrate . . . the parties' interests and hence yield high joint benefit'

TABLE 8.1 — Specific Tactics Likely to be Associated with Cooperative and Competitive Orientations

CATEGORY OF TACTICS BASIC ORIENTATION	APPROACH COOPERATIVE	COMPETITIVE	SOURCE AXELROD, 1984; DEUTSCH, 1973
Tactical objective	Integrative	Distributive	Walton and McKersie, 1965
Bidding tactics	Principled	Postional	Fisher and Ury, 1981
Concessions	Soft concessionary behavior	Tough concessionary behavior	Siegel and Fouraker, 1960; Komorita and Brenner, 1968
Information seeking	Empathic inquiries	Socratic dialog	Greenhalgh, Gilkey, and Pufahl, 1984
Information sending	Soft posturing	Tough posturing	Wall, 1985; Martin and Sims, 1964
Forthrightness	Honest	Deceptive	Deutsch, 1973; Lewicki, 1983
Discolosure	Full disclosure	Information withholding	Martin and Sims, 1964
Basis of persuasion	Empathic appeals	Focus on own needs	Folger and Poole, 1984
Definition of issues	Jointly developing the agenda	Imposing the agenda	Bacharach and Lawler, 1981
Argumentation	Active listening	Debate	Thomas, 1976
Justification	Explaining situation	Demanding compliance	Kipnis and Schmidt, 1983; Pruitt and Rubin, 1986
Sanctions	Non-contingent concessions	Threats and promises	Bacharach and Lawler, 1981; Pruitt, 1981; Pruitt and Rubin, 1986
Manipulating comfort/discomfort	Putting at ease	Disturbing composure	Potter, 1948

(Pruitt, 1983, p. 35; see also Follett, 1940). In game-theoretical terms, integrative bargaining represents a search for positive-sum rather than zero-sum solutions. Thus, when the payoffs are not inherently zero-sum (see Raiffa, 1982) and the set of feasible outcomes and their utilities to each party are known to all the parties, an integrative solution is the only rational outcome.

The rationality of seeking an integrative solution is based on the notion of Pareto optimality. Negotiators would only seek a solution known to be suboptimal if their motives were economically irrational — such as when they wanted to harm the other party (Tedeschi et al., 1973). Economic irrationality may not simply be the result of malevolence (see, for example, Berkowitz, 1962); it may indicate a definition of the situation that involves 'beating the opponent' rather than maximizing one's own gain (Thomas, 1976). Such rivalistic motivation (Siegel and Fouraker, 1960) is likely to arise when sports metaphors dominate a negotiator's definition of the situation.

In many cases, the set of feasible solutions and their utilities to the parties are not known. When this happens, integrative bargaining involves mutual problem solving in which the parties discover or create novel solutions (see Blake, Shepard, and Mouton, 1964; Carnevale and Isen, 1986; Deutsch, 1973; Walton and McKersie, 1965).

Most of the collective bargaining literature has focused on distributive bargaining, probably reflecting the extent to which that approach dominates labor–management relations in the United States. A flurry of recent research has explored integrative bargaining, although some of this work has begun to blur the distinction between distributive and integrative bargaining. For instance, 'logrolling' (see, for example, Froman and Cohen, 1970)—trading concessions on each other's high-priority issues in multiattribute negotiations—is posited as an example of integrative bargaining. In the absence of preference measurement, it is not clear, *a priori*, that a logrolling outcome package yields higher joint utility than an outcome package involving a simple compromise on each issue. The gain in joint utility seems to be a necessary condition for an integrative solution (Thomas, 1976); therefore, instead of investigating integrative bargaining, researchers may be investigating serial contingent distributive bargaining.

In terms of process, researchers have often failed to distinguish the integrative activity of mutual problem solving from evidence of creativity in seeking individual gain with little consideration for the needs of the other party—a distributive activity.

A substantial proportion of the social–psychological literature focuses on mixed-motive bargaining, in which subjects benefit from cooperating *and* competing, and need to make a choice of tactics (Deutsch, 1973). The Prisoner's Dilemma simulation (Axelrod, 1984; Rapoport and Chammah, 1965) is the quintessential mixed-motive situation: each subject is required to decide on the competitive tactic of confessing or the cooperative tactic of remaining silent without knowing what the other party has decided; the payoff is contingent on the other party's decision. This simulation highlights the central role of trust in mutual cooperation (Pruitt, 1981; for a discussion of the importance of trust in collective bargaining, see Walton and McKersie, 1965).

Bidding tactics

Fisher and Ury (1981) contrast 'positional' and 'principled' bargaining tactics. In positional bargaining, negotiators articulate their self-interest by communicating an offer, and the other party responds with a counter-offer. These tactics are positional in the sense that both parties apparently commit themselves to competing positions. In principled bargaining, the parties jointly agree on an objective criterion by which to judge settlements. In practice, this distinction sometimes breaks down: when the parties foresee that different objective criteria are more or less advantageous, the discussion can shift from taking positions on desired outcomes to taking positions on which criteria to apply (compare the discussion of achieving 'unobtrusive control' by manipulating the premises of decision making in Perrow, 1972). Research needs to be undertaken to investigate the conditions under which negotiators will engage in good-faith principled bargaining rather than give the appearance of doing so as a subterfuge for positional bargaining.

Concessions

Concessions are steps toward reconciliation in positional negotiation. Although a large concession may appear to be a benevolent gesture, or may reflect an actual shift in the negotiator's preferences, it may well be a planned manoeuvre on the negotiator's part. For instance, soft concessionary behavior (i.e. making large concessions and/or conceding frequently) is a commonly employed tactic used to elicit greater concessions from the other party (Brett, 1984). Despite a possible manipulative intent, this tactic is considered to be cooperative in that the concession is a positive move toward mutual agreement, as opposed to tough concessionary behavior, which is to the advantage of one party and not the other (Bartos, 1970).

Consistent with Osgood's (1962) strategy of reciprocity, negotiators engage in soft concessionary behavior expecting the other party to reciprocate their moves. Reciprocation, however, may or may not occur. Soft concessionary behavior may instead have the opposite effect by increasing or supporting the other party's high aspiration levels, thereby encouraging that party to assume tough concessionary tactics or to engage in no concessionary behavior at all (Bartos, 1970; Komorita and Brenner, 1968; Siegel and Fouraker, 1960). The result would likely be an impasse, unless the negotiator conceded to such an extent as to meet the other party's aspiration level, or the other party began to concede as well. Tough concessionary behavior, with a high initial offer and small concessions, has been found in some instances to be a more effective tactic (see, for example, Bacharach and Lawler, 1981; Chertkoff and Esser, 1976; Rubin and Brown, 1975), although the relative effectiveness of soft vs. tough concessionary behavior varies across situations and deserves further research.

There also exist some hybrid tactics that fall between the cooperative and competitive poles. One such hybrid tactic is matching (Komorita and Esser, 1975; McGillicuddy, Pruitt, and Syna, 1984; Pruitt, 1981), in which one party simply mirrors the concessionary behavior of the other. Research is particularly needed on the individual predispositions that are associated with choosing this tactic, the situational factors that give rise to it, and the effects of using that tactic on the relationship between the parties. Another hybrid is the 'reformed sinner' tactic (Folger and Poole, 1984), which involves tough concessionary behavior at the outset and subsequent cooperative behavior (Pruitt and Kimmel, 1977). Research is needed on the origin and nature of the *negotiators'* implicit theories of human behavior that give rise to the choice of this tactic.

Information seeking

A negotiator cannot work effectively toward mutual benefit if he or she does not know the preference structure of the other party (Pruitt, 1981; Walton and McKersie, 1965). Inquiries regarding this information can therefore be instrumental in determining ways to accommodate the other party's needs, as well as the negotiator's own needs. Because such empathic inquiries (Greenhalgh *et al.*, 1984) facilitate joint problem solving, it is considered to be a cooperative tactic. Furthermore, empathic inquiries can help clarify and prioritize underlying interests of the other party that are not immediately obvious to the other party.

The competitive counterpart of empathic inquiries is to ask questions in such a way as to lead the other party to think in ways that will benefit the questioner. This approach is self-serving rather than empathic. An extreme case of this is seen in the courtroom when a lawyer is 'leading a witness' to give testimony that does not fairly represent the witness's own sense making. Folger and Poole (1984) suggest that this tactic may in practice inhibit dealing with the conflict because it works against both parties' fully articulating their differences.

Information sending

Tough and soft posturing are tacit tactics used to relay information regarding the negotiator's position as strong, weak, or neutral and are intended to influence the other party's perceptions (Tedeschi et al., 1973; Wall, 1985; cf. Goffman, 1959). Soft posturing is a cooperative tactic that demonstrates the negotiator's interest in the other party's wellbeing, and the negotiator's willingness to find accommodative solutions. Tough posturing, on the other hand, is competitive in that it puts the other party on the defensive and is disruptive to the formulation of mutually adaptive solutions. Wall (1985) offers some examples of soft posturing: expressing deference or general inability through one's gestures, facial expressions, and dress; being purposefully consistent and predictable in one's negotiating style; and acting in a friendly and unintimidating manner. He also cites examples of tough posturing; expressing non-deference through openly hostile behavior; ignoring the other party; and taking the other party by surprise. Posturing techniques also can be a useful means of communicating or emphasizing one's preference structure or bargaining position.

Forthrightness and disclosure

Negotiators can take advantage of the other party's ignorance through the closely related tactics of deception (Lewicki, 1983) and withholding information (Martin and Sims, 1964). Deception entails negotiators' intentional alteration of the representation of their situation, preferences, or other relevant information to the other party, for the purpose of enhancing the negotiators' potential for a successful outcome (see Ekman, 1985). Withholding information is not alteration of truth *per se*, but may none the less be considered a form of deception: by providing only incomplete information, the negotiator intentionally misleads the other party or allows the other party to draw incorrect conclusions (Bachrach and Baratz, 1963; Deutsch, 1973; Walton and McKersie, 1965).

Both deception and partial disclosure of information are competitive negotiating techniques that are used to the sole advantage of the negotiator, and to the clear disadvantage of the other party (Thomas, 1976). These tactics impede communication, and thereby resist the process of joint problem solving. Honesty and full disclosure, on the other hand, characterize a cooperative negotiation in which information is openly shared; these tactics promote open communication and, therefore, the development of mutually beneficial settlements.

Basis of persuasion

An empathic appeal is an influence tactic in which negotiators attempt to gain agreement by stating benefits from the other party's perspective (Raven and Kruglanski, 1970; Walton and McKersie, 1965). It is cooperative in the sense that the focus is on mutual interests even when the motivation of the negotiator using this tactic is self-serving. By contrast, negotiators might attempt to persuade the other party by drawing attention only to their own needs. This tactic is competitive in that negotiators take only their own interests into consideration (see Thomas, 1976).

Folger and Poole (1984) point out that this egocentric tactic is likely to be observed in the early stages of most conflicts, due to the negotiators' focus of attention.

Definition of issues

Negotiators can impose the agenda of negotiable issues according to their own priorities of interests, without accepting input from the other party. This is a competitive tactic, in that the negotiators force the other party to accommodate their priorities, undermining the importance of the other party's priorities (Bacharach and Lawler, 1981). A more cooperative approach is to suggest that the parties jointly develop the agenda, thereby equally recognizing the needs and concerns of the other party as well as the negotiators' own, and maximizing the potential for joint problem solving (Walton and McKersie, 1965).

Argumentation

The conversation that goes on between the parties may be oriented toward stating positions in a debating mode or, at the other extreme, non-directive probing to learn the other party's position. Debating is inherently competitive (Thomas, 1976), in that the objective is to overwhelm the other party with superior logic (Wall, 1985). By contrast, active listening, unless it is intended to elicit information that will be used exploitively, is cooperative in the sense that its purpose is to ensure that both parties' interests are fully articulated (see, for example, Johnson, 1967; Rogers and Roethlisberger, 1952).

Justification

Negotiators can request compliance, or they can demand it. If negotiators request compliance, they are obliged to give the other party some reason to comply. Toward that end, negotiators can explain the situation in an attempt to justify the rationale for why the other party should agree to the terms (Raven and Kruglanski, 1970). If negotiators demand compliance, on the other hand, they need not explain the situation because it is not viewed as important that the other party understand. When negotiators set forth a demand, power is a strong factor in compliance (Bacharach and Lawler, 1981; Bachrach and Baratz, 1963; Kipnis and Schmidt, 1983). Explaining the situation is a cooperative tactic in that it represents an effort to enlist support, thereby encouraging participative decision making. Demanding compliance is a competitive tactic that fails to recognize the other party as a valuable collaborator in decision making (Thomas, 1976).

Implied sanctions

Threats and promises are two tactics by which negotiators make a commitment of action dependent upon the other party's behavior (Pruitt, 1981). Threats are 'negative' commitments that say, 'If you do not comply with my request, I will punish you with x' (Bachrach and Baratz, 1963). Promises are 'positive' commitments that say, 'If you comply with my request, I will reward you with y' (Pruitt and Rubin, 1986).

Note that threats and promises are not actions *per se*, but potential actions contingent upon the other party's compliant behavior. As such, they depend on negotiators' ability to *monitor* compliance and their commitment (as perceived by the other party) to carry out the threats (Pruitt, 1981). Threats are clearly competitive tactics in the sense that they are sanctions intended to shape the other party's behavior, to the sole advantage of the negotiator issuing the threats. Threats tend to put the receiver on the defensive and, in so doing, may reduce the level of positive communication and mutual problem-solving efforts (Wehr, 1979).

Although promises do not tend to raise the other party's defenses, they probably should: promises are in effect threats that say, 'If you do not comply with my request, I will not reward you with *y*.' Therefore, promises are also competitive tactics intended to benefit the negotiator at some expense to the other party. Non-congingent concessions, on the other hand, are a cooperative means of reducing the difference between negotiators' positions and of demonstrating willingness to move toward a mutually agreeable settlement. Non-contingent concessions are actual (not potential) actions and, as implied in the adjective, are not contingent upon the other party's behavior; they therefore differ significantly from sanctions used against the other party.

Manipulating comfort/discomfort

Disturbing composure is a tactic by which an opponent is 'set up to attack' (compare the characterization of 'gamesmanship' in Potter, 1948). The negotiator puts the other party—who is construed as an opponent—off his or her guard (e.g. by causing delays, to create impatience or agitation, or by otherwise inducing the other party to experience diminished competence) and then takes advantage of the opponent's lowered resistance to yielding (Pruitt and Rubin, 1986). Disturbing composure is competitive in that individual benefit, not joint benefit, is the main objective. The negotiator can create an environment more conducive to joint problem solving by putting the other party at ease—that is, by maintaining comfortable verbal and non-verbal communication so as not to cause the other party unrest or agitation.

Explicit vs. Tactic Negotiation

The cooperative–competitive classification is only one dimension along which negotiation tactics can be categorized. A second distinction that has been made is between tactics that are explicit and those that are tacit. The most common distinction between explicit and tacit negotiation behavior has been made in reference to communication between the parties (Karrass, 1970; Pruitt, 1981; Schelling, 1964; Wall, 1985; Walton and McKersie, 1965). Specifically, negotiators can exchange information about their motivational structures either by explicit or by tacit means: explicit communication entails openly discussing their aspirations, preferences, and constraints, and openly inquiring about those of the other party; tacit communication entails indirectly expressing their motives through verbal intimations and non-verbal gestures and body language for the other party to decipher. Some authors have characterized the difference in terms of formal vs. informal influence attempts (Bacharach, 1983; McGrath, 1966, Notz *et al*, 1983); others have characterized the difference in terms of persuasive arguments vs. manipulation (Gilman, 1962; Mowday, 1978; Tedeschi, Schlenker, and Lindskold, 1972). Explicit communication is by nature intentional and directed toward the other party, but tacit communication is sometimes unconscious, not necessarily intended to influence the party and may take the form of an informative 'slip'. The explicit and tacit dimension has also been referred to as the extent to which parties characterize their interaction as a 'negotiation' (Bacharach, 1983; Bacharach and Lawler, 1981; Strauss, 1978). For instance, there are many circumstances, such as in friendship and family relationships, where agreements are made without the parties ever stating them explicitly, or ever being conscious of bargaining as such. These are colloquially referred to as 'understandings'. Bacharach (1983) makes the observation that labor-management conflict tends to be handled explicitly while other intraorganizational conflict tends to be handled tacitly. Negotiations can be dominated either by explicit or by tacit patterns of communication; however, in most instances tacit bargaining complements explicit bargaining (Pruitt, 1971; Wall, 1985).

Although explicit communication styles are more often associated with cooperative, integrative bargaining situations, and tacit styles with competitive, distributive negotiations, this is not always the case. In interactions where social norms discourage explicit bargaining, implicit information exchange is the preferred channel of communication. Tacit signals may be used to coordinate expectations and aspirations, or may be used as a means of saving face in a situation where explicit communication could cause social embarassment (Wall, 1985). In such instances, tacit behavior is not the result of competitive objectives but, on the contrary, a means toward cooperative relations. Likewise, explicit communication styles do not always foster cooperative, integrative bargaining. Explicit communication may actually damage relations when the information exchange serves to clarify—and thus intensify—substantive, irreconcilable differences. In addition, Pruitt (1981, p. 171) noted three limitations of explicit communication that could hamper the joint formulation of integrative solutions:

1. Negotiators are often confused as to their own true motives, and may thus be unable to transmit a clear and undistorted picture regarding those motives.

2. Recipients often do not believe explicit information when they hear it, suspecting ulterior motives. A negotiator may, for example, overemphasize his or her reasons for not conceding in order to elicit greater concessions from the other party.

3. Recipients may misconstrue the explicit information of the other party.

In addition to distinguishing communication patterns, explicit and tacit negotiating behavior have been considered tactics per se; negotiators can assume a general explicit or tacit negotiating style as a means to some end (Tedeschi et al., 1973). For example, negotiators may purposefully maintain a generalized tacit approach to a bargaining situation in order to remain non-committal, such as when the negotiators do not explicitly commit themselves to some action yet merely hint at it, and as a result preserve the option of not following through with that 'proposal'. The following scenario illustrates this point: a salesman, negotiating the sale of a new sterero component, lowers the price to $450. The buyer comments, '$450 is somewhat more reasonable, but I still can't see how you can expect anyone to pay that price without even a warranty!' The implicit message is that the buyer will settle for that price if the salesman includes a warranty. Yet the buyer has not committed herself to that action, and leaves open the possibility for further negotiation (such as a 10-year vs. 5-year warranty). A second example illustrates another way explicit or tacit behavior can be used as a tactic: a negotiator is intentionally open and upfront about his motives in order to appear honest and cooperative; his purpose is to elicit reciprocative honesty and cooperation from the other party.

Finally, just as tactics can be classified on a cooperative/competitive dimension, so can they be classified on an explicit/tacit dimension. Some tactics, distinct from whatever ends they may serve, are explicit or 'upfront' in nature and others more tacit. Full discolosure, jointly developing the agenda, concessionary behavior, and debating are examples of explicit tactics. Posturing, deception, withholding information, and disturbing composure are examples of tactics that are likely to be more tacit in nature.

Thus, the explicit/tacit dimension has been approached in the literature in at least three different ways: explicit and tacit modes of communicating negotiators' motivational structures to one another; explicit and tacit behavior employed deliberately as tactics to achieve some end; and tactics that are by nature either explicit or tacit, regardless of whether the negotiator realizes the conequences of being explicit or tacit.

These approaches can be easily confused, but they are conceptually distinct. Although one might assume that an implicit information exchange is necessarily associated with tacit tactics, this is not always the case. For example, a small concession is an explicit tactic that tacitly informs the other party that the negotiator's aspirations are relatively high, or that the issue at hand is of high priority; note that the negotiator need not state these motives explicitly. In addition, although one might assume that using explicit behavior as a tactic to get the other party to behave in some particular way includes only the use of explicit tactics, this is not always the case. For example, a negotiator may make a point of being explicit in order to appear honest and trustworthy, and yet may liberally use tacit tactics, such as a smile or demonstrative deference, to complement and add credibility to the more explicit tactics. Finally, there is no necessary connection between explicit/tacit communication and using explicit/tacit behavior as a tactic: negotiators can assume an explicit or tacit communication style either intentionally or unintentionally. For example, negotiators may communicate their motivational structure mainly through gestures, indirect comments, and other tacit means, although they may not be intentionally utilizing such tacit behaviors as a tactic toward achieving some end. In fact, the negotiators may be quite unaware of their communication style. While the first approach has been extensively dealt with in the literature, the last two approaches to the explicit/tacit dimension have received little attention. More theoretical as well as empirical attention is warranted on this multifaceted dimension of negotiation.

Ingratiation

A special type of tacit tactic is ingratiation. A widely accepted definition of ingratiation is 'a class of strategic behaviors illicitly designed to influence a particular other person concerning the attractiveness of one's personal qualities' (Jones, 1975; p. 11). Negotiators ingratiate in order to win the other party's favor. What the ingratiators hope to gain by this may be increased concessions from, or simply improved relations with, the other party. Four types of ingratiation tactics have been identified: conformity, other enhancement, self-enhancement, and non-verbal behavior (see Jones, 1975, for a detailed discussion).

Conformity, one of the most commonly used ingratiation tactics (Lefebvre, 1973), includes the negotiators' stating of their views and values in line with those of the other party, and likewise conforming their behavior to meet the preferences of the other party. Other enhancement and self-enhancement have been observed most extensively in superior–subordinate relations, where the ingratiating subordinate is dependent upon the superior. Other enhancement usually takes the form of compliments and praise, whereas self-enhancement includes name dropping, associating with 'the right' people, self-degradation in areas the other may perceive as threatening, and demonstrating deference in order to inspire or increase feelings of social responsibility in the other party. Finally, non-verbal behavior, including smiling, eye contact, and other body language, acts on the emotional state of the recipient, usually unbeknown to that party. Ingratiators must be careful not to 'overingratiate' when employing any of these four ingratiation tactics, as the detection of the ingratiators' ulterior motive may create the impression of insincerity and may lessen their overall credibility. Thus ingratiation is by its very nature a tacit tactic.

Kauffmann and Steiner (1968) found the probability of negotiators to employ ingratiation tactics to be influenced by: the amount of difference between the ingratiator's and the target's values, the power balance, and their personalities. Most ingratiation was found to occur in conditions where the perceived probability of an overture leading to reward was high and the risk of detection low. Less ingratiation was found when the option to ingratiate was obvious and most likely to be detected by the target.

Individual differences in ingratiation have been largely ignored (Pandey, 1978); yet, two personality variables in particular have been noted to influence the initiation and outcome of ingratiation overtures — Machiavellianism and authoritarianism. The findings concerning these two variables, however, have not been consistent. (For research relevant to Machiavellianism, see Christie and Geis, 1970; Jones, Gergen, and Davis, 1962; Pandey, 1978, 1981a; Pandey and Rostogi, 1979. For research relevant to authoritarianism, see Adorno, Frankel-Brunswik, Levinson, and Sanford, 1950.)

In addition, degree of self-esteem has been shown to influence both the use of overtures and the target's responses to ingratiation. Jones (1975) found that low self-esteem people are highly sensitive to personal evaluations about themselves, and thus have great incentive to attain social approval or be considered attractive by others. Hence, low self-esteem people will more readily ingratiate. Baron (1974) noted a tendency for low self-esteem individuals to evaluate unknown others less favorably than did those with high self-esteem. His findings imply that ingratiators would be wise to compliment relatively unfamiliar targets with low self-esteem, in order to elevate the targets' self-esteem and therefore their opinion of the ingratiator.

Yet another personality trait found to be related to ingratiation is gender. Most notably, more ingratiation overtures were found to appear in heterogeneous than homogeneous interactions, indicating that ingratiators may perceive less risk of their ulterior motives being discovered by a person of the opposite sex than of the same sex (Lefebvre, 1973). Also, gender differences were found to affect a negotiator's choice of ingratiation tactics. For example, females were found to rely more on modesty in their self-presentations than males, perhaps as a means of maintaining congeniality and smoothness in their relationships (Allen and Levine, 1969).

The ingratiators' response to the power of the target has been extensively studied (Fodor, 1973a, 1973b; Kauffmann and Steiner, 1968; Pandey, 1978, 1981b, 1984; Tjosvold, 1978). By making themselves more attractive, ingratiators can influence the decisions of power holders in the ingratiators' favor. If the strategy is successfully implemented, ingratiation can thus increase the ingratiators' own power (Steiner, 1970).

Factors Affecting Negotiators' Tactics

Power

Bacharach and Lawler (1981) view the tactics negotiators use to be strongly linked to their power. They define power in terms of the other party's dependence, reflecting their book's strong orientation toward collective bargaining. Other forms of power are available to negotiators, as explained below, thus it is reasonable to expect that negotiators' felt power, from whatever source, will affect their choice of tactics. Kipnis and Schmidt (1983), for instance, note that the greater the power differential between two negotiators, the more likely the use of directive tactics, or demands. Laue and Cormick (1973) provide an interesting argument that where the power distribution is grossly asymmetrical, an important role of third parties is to empower the weaker party so as to facilitate meaningful negotiation (see also Wehr, 1979).

Person perception

Tactics tend to be somewhat tailored to the nature of the other party, therefore person perception is an important factor in choice of tactics. Although this seems to be an obvious point, surprisingly little research has been done to investigate it. In one study, Walsh, Greenhalgh, and Fairfield (1986) found that the degree of generosity of the opening bid was influenced by the age of the other party, in conjunction with the age of the negotiators doing the bidding. Person perception is largely colored, in turn, by the individual characteristics of the perceiver (Shrauger and Altrocchi, 1964; Zalkind and Costello, 1964). Jones (1954), for instance, found 'authoritarian' individuals to perceive others in terms of power relationships, and less in terms of personality characteristics. Bernstein and Davis (1982) found individuals with high perspective-taking ability to be more accurate in person perception than those less empathic, and furthermore, to exhibit increasing accuracy with longer exposure time as opposed to less empathic individuals, who showed no such improvement.

Individual predispositions

A host of individual differences have been shown to be directly related to tactics (e.g. Bell and Blakeney, 1977; Jones and Melcher, 1982; Jones and White, 1985;

Pruitt, 1981; Thomas, 1976). These are comprehensively summarized by Rubin and Brown (1975) and need not be detailed here. Individual predispositions can be thought of as states and traits. Traits are enduring predispositions that tend to be manifest in behavior across situations but which in real life are manifest somewhat inconsistently (Endler and Magnusson, 1976; Mischel, 1968). The concept of personality is usually taken to summarize an individual's set of traits. A subset of personality, thus defined, is the individual's hierarchy of predispositions to respond in conflict situations (Berkowitz, 1962; Blake and Mouton, 1964).

States are predispositions to behave in a particular way that are momentary and perhaps even situation-specific. A negotiator may enjoy dealing with another party in a particular interaction (a state) but may not be generally sociable (a trait). The research on the effect of negotiators' individual predispositions has been heavily biased toward traits; obviously, researchers need to correct this imbalance, since states can have an important impact on the way the conflict proceeds (Folger and Poole, 1984).

Definition of the situation

Deutsch (1973) notes that 'each participant in a social interaction responds to the other in terms of his perceptions and cognitions of the other; these may or may not correspond to the other's actualities' (p. 7). Despite its recognized importance, a negotiator's conceptualization of the conflict has received surprisingly little research attention (Thomas, 1976).

People involved in a conflict can define the situation in ways that encourage the use of divisive tactics. Greenhalgh (1985, 1986) identifies six bipolar dimensions that are likely to affect choice of tactics:

1. Issues: Matters of principle are much more difficult to resolve than are issues that are obviously and easily divisible (Deutsch, 1973; Fisher, 1964; Williams, 1975). Parties who believe they are upholding principles are likely to be intransigent and therefore choose tactics that will preclude any compromise.
2. Interdependence: If the interdependence between the two parties is conceptualized as zero-sum — whereby one party can gain only at the other's expense — the parties will use tactics that are more competitive than will be the case if the interdependence is seen as non-constant sum — whereby both parties can gain by means of a creative solution, or both parties will suffer if a joint solution is not generated (Walton and McKersie, 1965).
3. Size of stakes: People who perceive high stakes tend to choose inflexible tactics: they are reluctant to make concessions to achieve a negotiated settlement because doing so involves high perceived sacrifice (Deutsch, 1973; Fisher, 1964; Williams, 1975).
4. A special case of high stakes occurs in continuous situations when the outcome is perceived to set a precedent on the basis of which future outcomes will be settled (Deutsch, 1973; Fisher, 1964): conceding in the current conflict is seen as committing the person to make similar sacrifices in future disputes involving the same issues (Williams, 1975). The anticipation of an unfavorable precedent thus reverses the usual conflict-ameliorating effect of a continuous time horizon (see next dimension).

5. Continuity of interaction: An episodic view of the conflict situation envisions the current conflict as an isolated event, as if the relationship had no history and no future (Caplow, 1968; Gruder, 1971; Roering, Slusher, and Schooler, 1975; Rubin and Brown, 1975). Such a view creates the same intractable consequences as a zero-sum view. By contrast, a continuous view—one in which the current dispute is seen as a single event within a long-term relationship— downplays the importance of maximizing one's gain in the present transaction (see Walton, 1969), since current concessions obligate the other party to reciprocate in future transactions. The parties will choose competitive or cooperative tactics accordingly.

6. Progress of the conflict: Disputes can be escalating or stable (see Thomas, 1976). An escalating dispute is difficult to settle because one party feels more harmed than the other and wishes to 'even the score' before resorting to cooperative tactics that will result in a settlement (Wehr, 1979). Each party has an idiosyncratic assessment of the severity of inflicted harm and experienced harm, and these assessments are likely to be biased (Deutsch, 1973): the same objective harmful act is likely to be judged as more severe when it is received rather than inflicted on someone else. Escalation also involves a positive feedback loop because it causes the relationship between the parties to deteriorate (Raven and Kruglanski, 1970). As a result, conflicts are inherently prone to escalation (see Coleman, 1957).

Figure 8.1 shows that definition of the situation can not only influence tactics, but reciprocally can be influenced by tactics. Cognitive readjustment can be used as a tactic whereby one party uses persuasion to alter the other party's definition of the situation. The party using this tactic can, for instance, build in a 'cooling off' period during which emotionally inflated stakes can return to a more realistic level, emphasize mutual gain and point out mutual problems, and convince the other party that equal harm has been experienced by both parties. Furthermore, Williams (1975) suggested that a negotiator can focus attention on divisible issues (i.e. deemphasize principles) and, if individual issues are not divisible, increase the number of negotiable points in order to make concessions on the *set* of negotiable issues divisible. A negotiator can also remind the other party that the relationship is long term and, to reduce the perceived size of the stakes, assure the other party that the proposed settlement will not threaten the long-run security of the parties.

Jervis (1970) suggested another cognitive restructuring tactic: a negotiator can 'decouple' his or her concession making from any signs of 'softness' by making it clear that such an action does not set a precedent for future concessions on his or her party. In the same way, a negotiator can influence the other party's definition of the situation by explicitly agreeing that a particular settlement *per se* will not set any precedents. Such tactical interventions as described above may also be self-directed, wherein the party actively attempts to adjust his or her own cognitions. For example, negotiators may recognize that they are conceiving the situation as zero-sum, and actively seek to discover positive-sum solutions.

Another important factor in definition of the situation is the extent to which the person takes the perspective of the other party. Egocentric definitions of the situation tend to focus attention on self-interest rather than mutual interest, which in turn results in the choice of competitive over cooperative tactics. An empathic definition of the situation occurs when the negotiator takes the perspective of the other party. Perspective taking has been induced in laboratory studies (see, for example, Deutsch and Krauss, 1962), but in real-world negotiations its occurrence depends on the negotiators' predispositions toward perspective taking (Bazerman and Neale, 1983; Davis, 1981; Gilkey and Greenhalgh, 1984; Greenhalgh et al., 1984). Deutsch (1973, p. 354) observes that 'the ability to place oneself in the other's shoes is notoriously underplayed and underdeveloped in most people, and . . . this ability is impaired by stress and inadequate information'.

Yet another potentially important aspect of the negotiator's definition of the situation is framing. Building on prospect theory (Kahneman and Tversky, 1979), Bazerman (1983, 1986) shows that in risk situations negotiators' decision making deviates systematically from rationality in response to a shift in perspective from the potential gain to the potential loss implied in the same risk situation. Decision making is shaped by assessment of negative utility when the focus in on loss potential and positive utility when on the complementary gain potential (Bazerman, 1984). The former orientation should lead to the choice of aggressive, risky tactics, while the latter should lead to more conservative tactics (see also Thaler, 1985; Tversky and Kahneman, 1981). Note that the effect of framing on utility structure explains the arrow in Figure 8.1 from definition of the situation to preferences. It is largely through this linkage that the effect of framing on tactics is articulated.

Negotiators sometimes have to take into account the reaction of their constituency. When the interaction is highly visible and the constituency's reaction is important to the negotiators (Rubin and Brown, 1975), they may redefine the situation as a three-way negotiation: the negotiator, his or her consistency, and the other negotiator are all significant parties in such a situation (Frey and Adams, 1972; Harnett and Cummings, 1980). Management of the negotiator–constituency relationship has been described in depth by Walton and McKersie (1965). The relationship can be managed outside the interaction between the negotiators, but when the situation is defined to include the constituency, it is likely that the tactics used will be shaped by the audience's anticipated reaction (Blake et al., 1964; Thomas, 1976).

For example, Carnevale, Pruitt, and Britton (1979) found that surveillance by a constituency encouraged the use of such competitive tactics as positioned commitments, threats, and arguments. These tactics resulted in poorer outcomes, evidencing the strength of the negotiators' motivation to appear responsive to their constituencies. Studies by Organ (1971) and by Shure, Meeker, and Hansford (1965) demonstrated that negotiators tended to comply with their constituents' advice concerning how to deal with the other party. A later study by Benton and Druckman (1974) found that, in the absence of specific advice, negotiators monitored by their constituencies used tougher, more aggressive tactics that tended to give rise to distributive bargaining and discouraged integrative bargaining (see also Hornstein and Johnson, 1966; Lamm and Kogan, 1970; Stern and Pearse, 1968).

The audience need not be the negotiator's constituency in order to affect negotiation behavior. Brown (1968), for instance, demonstrated that the feedback of an audience of peers can have a powerful effect on retaliatory response to a loss of face. It seems likely that the effect will be stronger when the audience is the negotiator's constituency, because their reactions will be more salient and therefore experienced more strongly. Furthermore, it is worth noting that the audience effect may occur even when the audience is not physically present: it is an evaluative audience's psychological presence that affects the negotiator (Rubin and Brown, 1975). Finally, when the audience is a third party intervening in the conflict, the use of divisive tactics that might further escalate the conflict is severely constrained (Thomas, 1976).

People's guiding metaphors (Greer, 1969) have a strong effect on their definition of the situation. Novel situations are defined in terms of familiar situations through the use of metaphorical comparison, and individuals' choice of guiding metaphors is shared and habitual. The most prevalent guiding metaphor used to defined conflict siuations in US organizations is the sports metaphor, reflecting a cultural preoccupation with 'winning' any contested situation. The other party is defined as an 'opponent' who must be 'beaten'. This is an unfortunate choice of metaphors from the standpoint of making the conflict amenable to a negotiated solution. Sports events are domination-oriented, thus favoring exploitive power solutions over more equitable negotiated solutions. They are also episodic and zero-sum, and encourage use of any tactics—no matter how harmful to the relationship—that are not explicitly proscribed by the perceived 'game rules'. The negotiators tend to adopt a rivalistic strategy (Siegel and Fouraker, 1960) in which the objective is to maximize the difference between their own gain and that of their 'rivals' (see Shubik, 1971), even when doing so involves some sacrifice in their own absolute payoffs (see Tropper, 1972).

Definition of the situation is, in turn, determined by individual differences. For example, a recent study by Greenhalgh, Gilkey, and Pufahl (1984) showed that masculine negotiators were likely to define the situation as episodic and zero-sum, whereas feminine negotiators were likely to do the opposite. This difference was traced to differences in childhood socialization, whereby boys play competitive games and girls play relationship-enhancing games (Gilligan, 1982). In addition to the fundamental difference in orientation that this differential socialization engenders, definition of the situation is shaped directly and strongly by the prevalence of sports metaphors among masculine negotiators (Greenhalgh, 1985).

Preferences

Negotiators' preferences constitute the final factor affecting tactics. As explained earlier, the negotiator's preference structure consists of utilities for each issue at stake and the utility of impasse. The latter is the point at which the negotiator is indifferent between accepting an outcome package and withdrawing from the negotiation, presumably to achieve an outcome of equal utility from another party. Preference structure affects tactics because a negotiator who has a high impasse utility perceives attractive alternatives and can therefore risk the consequences of such competitive tactics as tough posturing (Wall, 1985), tough concessionary behavior (Siegel and Fouraker, 1960), and demanding compliance (Kipnis and Schmidt, 1983).

Power

As noted earlier, most definitions of power involve the notion of inducing the other person to do something he or she would not otherwise do (see, for example, Blau, 1964; Dahl, 1957; Emerson, 1962; Salancik and Pfeffer, 1977; Thibaut and

Kelley, 1959; Wrong, 1979). Power can therefore be conceptualized as a *propensity* to control the other's behavior (e.g. Cartwright, 1965; March, 1955) or the *act* of achieving a behavior change (see Deutsch, 1973; cf. Pfeffer's (1981) usage of the terms 'power' and 'politics'). The propensity and the act are, in practice, closely related (Wrong, 1968, 1979). The result of a series of laboratory studies is that the more powerful party tends to use that power in negotiations (see Pruitt, 1981; Rubin and Brown, 1975). The power propensity affects tactics, whereas the power act determines whether the process will be consensual or coercive. Power tends to be bilateral rather than unilateral (Cobb, 1980; Herold, 1977; Mechanic, 1962; Salancik and Pfeffer, 1977), therefore the effect on process and tactics results from the *interaction* of the power of the two parties (Pfeffer, 1981).

Sources of negotiators' power

The control of resources is one determinant of a negotiator's power to achieve favorable outcomes (Deutsch, 1973; Kipnis and Schmidt, 1983). Resources take many forms, including money, expertise, opportunities, property rights, access, and votes. Such power is countered by the other party's control of resources, and is a function of the negotiator's dependence on that particular party (Bacharach, 1983; Bacharach and Lawler, 1981; Emerson, 1962; Pfeffer, 1981; Thompson, 1967). Thus, the alternative options for achieving objectives also determine the negotiator's power. Power is therefore closely and reciprocally related to preferences (see Figure 8.1). The utility of an impasse operationalizes the negotiator's dependence on the other party, because preferences determine dependency on a particular party, and power arising from dependency determines the resistance point within the hierarchy of preferences for alternative outcomes (Eliashberg *et al.*, 1986).

An important variant of resource control is the ability to control the other party's access to his or her resources (see the discussion of 'ecological power' in Deutsch, 1973). This is accomplished in the laboratory by such devices as letting a subject control the gate in the Acme-Bolt trucking game (Deutsch and Krauss, 1960). In organizational situations, such control may take the form of veto power, removal of constraints, or providing necessary cooperation.

Moving from resource control as a source of power to its use in generating compliance, the parties are likely to *experience* it as reward power (French and Raven, 1959). The control of resources implies the right to allocate them, and when such allocation is made contingent on the other party's compliance, the controller is exercising reward power. To the extent that resources of value can be withheld from the other party, the controller of resources is exercising punishment power.

When individuals act together to combine the resources they control or other forms of power in a conflict situation, they have formed a coalition (Caplow, 1968). Coalition membership increases the power of the negotiator to obtain favourable outcomes. The research literature on coalitions is large and diverse (see, for example, Folger and Poole, 1984; Gamson, 1964; Komorita and Chertkoff, 1973; Murnighan, 1978; Rubin and Brown, 1975; Stevenson, Pearce, and Porter, 1985; Tedeschi *et al.*, 1973) and will not be summarized here, given that the main focus of this chapter is the psychological dynamics of negotiation within the simple dyad. Suffice it to say that coalition membership is an important source of power experienced by negotiators in an organizational context.

Reward and punishment power can be mobilized even when the negotiator holds no office and controls no explicit resources. The power forms arise whenever one actor can manage the other's affect. These power bases have been explored in the literature on groups, where non-hierarchical actors make approval, affection, favors, and attention (vs. ostracism) contingent on the recipients of such valued outcomes exhibiting desired behaviors (Cartwright and Zander, 1962; Shaw, 1976).

Power arises from organizational conditions other than the control of resources. It can also arise from role relationships. Legitimate power (French and Raven, 1959) is one such example. Equivalent to most concepts of 'authority' (Merton, 1961; Simon, 1976; Weber, 1947), it is a superior's right to demand compliance from a subordinate, and exists independently of forms of position power based on resource control such as reward and punishment (Katz and Kahn, 1966). In laboratory studies, it is often simulated by manipulating status differentials (see, for example, Faley and Tedeschi, 1971; Rekosh and Feigenbaum, 1966; Rubin and Brown, 1975), which are closely correlated with legitimate power in real organizational settings (Barnard, 1946; Deutsch, 1973; Shaw, 1976).

In theory, legitimate power relationships are specified in the organization chart, which is equivalent to an obedience chart — a symbolic representation of who should obey whom in an organization. In practice, however, the theory of strategic contingencies (Crozier, 1964; Cyert and March, 1963; Hickson, Hinings, Lee, Schneck, and Pennings, 1971) suggests that some directives will carry greater legitimacy depending on how crucial is the organizational subunit from which they emanate (Clegg, 1975). Legitimate power is only effective in so far as subordinates accede to it (March and Simon, 1958; Mechanic, 1962); the socialization process is usually strong enough that people in organizations accept the vast majority of directives from authority figures (see Berger and Luckmann, 1966; Edwards, 1976). This is probably more true in the United States than in countries where there is more industrial democracy (Pfeffer, 1981). Finally, legitimate power is more effective to the extent that its users articulate organizational norms (see Deutsch, 1973).

Power also arises from personal relationships. Referent power (French and Raven, 1959) is a good example of this phenomenon. Most persuasive appeals depend heavily on aspects of the interpersonal rather than interrole dynamics. Personal relationships are a function of the personalities of the negotiators. For example, a basic bond of interpersonal attraction depends on the similarity of the personalities of the negotiators (Byrne and Griffitt, 1973; Cronbach and Gleser, 1953; Heider, 1958; Newcomb, 1956). At the organizational level of analysis, an analogous phenomenon occurs. Groups with the greatest persuasive effect in a conflict situation are those with organizational values that are similar to those of the leader (Enz, 1986).

Finally, power can arise from the control of information (Tedeschi et al., 1973). It can be experienced two ways by those who are being influenced. The first way is consistent with the French and Raven (1959) notion of expert power, in which a person is willing to be influenced by an expert in the relevant area because the expert is recognized as having superior knowledge that can guide wise choices. In practice, the attribution of expertise and therefore the willingness to comply with influence attempts is often generalized beyond the ascertainable domain of expertise.

Summarizing empirical research on this phenomenon, Folger and Poole (1984) point to a distinction between positive and negative forms of expert power that is useful in that the form shapes the character of the tactics used. The second way of experiencing information-based power is through the control of information as a resource *per se* (Bariff and Galbraith, 1978), such as when it can be provided or withheld (see Raven and Kruglanski, 1970), or filtered in a way that shapes decisions favorably (Pettigrew, 1972).

DISCUSSION

This chapter has presented a model that summarizes the factors that are hypothesized to jointly act in specified ways to determine the outcomes of conflicts. The model is intended to be applicable to a wide variety of human conflicts, inasmuch as conflict is considered a generic phenomenon: indeed, the inaugural issue of the *Journal of Conflict Resolution* emphasized that very point. The title of the chapter restricts the scope to conflicts in organizations, and most of the examples and reported research are directly or indirectly applicable to organizations, but the model should be a useful heuristic device to guide research on conflicts in other contexts.

The model is deliberately limited in scope in that it addresses only interpersonal conflicts. The advantage of this approach is that diverse phenomena can be integrated at a common level of analysis, namely, how each phenomenon is experienced by a key actor in a conflict. This approach is conceptually feasible because even large collectivities—as large as nations—take conflictful actions through key actors who experience the conflict and make decisions on the basis of that experience (Gamson, 1968). Thus, concepts that emerge at higher levels of analysis—such as coalition formation—are accommodated in the model through their effects on the individual actor in the conflict. A more complex model would have to be developed to handle higher-level phenomena; the mission of this chapter was more modest in scope.

If the model were to be made more complex, a high priority would be to include processes that unfold over time. At present, the model can only identify the major variables that have been established or hypothesized to affect negotiated outcomes. It is non-specific about how those effects occur because a conflict involves subprocesses that unfold over time, and these are not specified in the model.

The model also is of limited scope in that it concerns only negotiated outcomes. Many conflicts are terminated by means of one party dominating the other. A necessary condition for this occurrence, by definition, is for the dominator to have an overwhelming power advantage, but this is not always a sufficient condition. A more comprehensive model would identify the factors that determine the choice of domination by the more powerful party. For example, dominance is more likely to be attempted when the power holder has a high need for power (McClelland, 1958; Winter, 1973) and a low relationship orientation (Fleishman, 1973); when the situation is perceived to be a crisis that does not permit the more time-consuming process of negotiation; when the costs of implementation and control in terms of resistance to coercion are low; when the other party is untrustworthy; and when the situation is terminal (Caplow, 1968)—that is, when the conflict-settling exercise of power eliminates the other party from the relationship.

Other conflicts are terminated through the cognitive restructuring process identified as 'conflict resolution'. An enhanced model would include the factors that lead to the choice of resolution in conflict situations. Such factors might include the key actors' being conflict avoiders (Kilmann and Thomas, 1977) who are quite willing to deny the conflict; the subsidence of fleeting emotional states that have temporarily magnified the subjective importance of the conflict; and issues in conflict that involve an equity issue that can be addressed through cognitive readjustment (Adams, 1965).

Given that the model focuses on key actors' experience of interpersonal conflict, it is not surprising that the model and the research cited to substantiate it are primarily psychological in nature. Therefore it is appropriate at this point to issue the additional caveat that other disciplines—such as sociology, political science, economics, anthropology—provide equally valid and, indeed, essential perspectives from which to view conflicts.

In addition to the more general considerations outlined above, the model as it stands suggests a number of areas in which further research seems particularly needed. As well as the points mentioned earlier in the text, several conflict phenomena still need to be addressed.

The most voluminously researched relationship is the influence of personality on tactics. That research stream has been so intensive because social psychologists have investigated a fairly narrow set of paradigms. Two shortcomings of this body of research, however, make this a fertile ground for further research. First, as noted earlier, the simulations predominantly used by social psychologists have limited generalizability to organizational settings. Replication of those studies should be undertaken using more realistic simulations of conflicts that actually occur in organizations (Shubik, 1968), and these would involve the more realistic continuous relationships. At the same time, personality should be assessed in a more comprehensive manner. Self-reports on a paper-and-pencil test measuring a single trait lose most of the multifaceted impact of individual differences. On the other hand, comprehensive personality assessment (see, for example, Greenhalgh et al., 1985) is very labor-intensive and yields complex data sets. Nevertheless, so long as researchers use simplistic measures of personality, the real significance of negotiators' individual predispositions is likely to go undetected.

The position of individuals acting in an informal third-party role is also underresearched. Much attention has been given to this topic as it relates to collective bargaining, very little to interventions outside the institutional structure of labor-management contract administration such as by co-workers, ombudspersons, and consultants.

Social psychologists have favored a narrow set of mixed-motive simulations, and this has led to extensive study of research questions by means of those simulations. An important case in point is the disproportionate emphasis on cooperative vs. competitive tactics as an outcome variable. In fact, relatively little is known about the causes and consequences of cooperating and competing outside those simulations.

Not enough research has been done on what happens when the role of the negotiator is that of agent rather than a principal. Most people play agent roles in almost all their organizational interactions, yet most research tries to generalize from simulations involving principals.

A wealth of understanding of organizational negotiations is to be gained from an understanding of the effects of varying definitions of the situation. For example, whether the parties consider the negotiation to be a single episode or just one transaction within a continuous relationship can make an enormous difference in choice of tactics. Most studies simulate episodic negotiations despite the fact that few real-world situations are purely episodic. Researchers need to rise to the challenge of manipulating episodic-continuous time horizons, even though such manipulations are made difficult because of strong predispositions due to individual differences. As a second example, creative research is needed on how negotiators' guiding metaphors (Greer, 1969) affect their negotiation behavior. This research would ideally extend beyond personal metaphors to address negotiators' basic schemata.

Power arising from coalitions is also underresearched. A very basic question in this context, for instance, is the extent to which individuals coalesce primarily for economic advantage—that is, because their preferences are compatible—rather than due to predispositions for social bonding—that is, because they are sociometrically compatible (Stevenson *et al.*, 1985). Furthermore, the role of trust in determining the formation and behavior of a coalition, which seems vital in organizational settings, has yet to be researched in enough depth.

Much of the work to be done needs to advance beyond interpersonal conflict and address collectivities more complex than the dyad. The difficulty of conducting research in groups more complex than the dyad is the geometrically increasing complexity and the loss of control and analytical rigor. This encourages researchers to reduce the analysis to the level of the dyad, with some justification. Most negotiations within and between larger collectivities involve key events in which one coalition's spokesperson interacts with another's (this happens if for no other reason than because it is hard to attend to more than one dyadic exchange at a time). Given appropriate caution concerning the dangers of reductionism, the dyad is a useful if imperfect unit of analysis even in multiparty negotiations, but such research must be conducted concurrently with more holistic techniques so that scholars understand the emerging properties of multiparty negotiations that do not exist at the dyad level of analysis.

Finally, further work needs to be done to elaborate and improve the model itself. The interrelations depicted in the model are based on what is presently known about the variables specified. As new knowledge emerges concerning these variables and new variables come to be recognized as important, the model will become richer and better defined. As such, this chapter is a starting point in the quest for integrative, cumulative research in this important subject area.

ACKNOWLEDGEMENTS

The author wishes to thank Susan M. Pufahl for her invaluable help in exploring and organizing the relevant literatures and writing first drafts of some sections. Thanks are also due to James P. Walsh for his helpful comments on an earlier draft, and Nancy L. Gunn Harsha for her painstaking work in typing and retyping successive drafts of this manuscript.

REFERENCES

Adams, J. S. (1965). Inequity in social exchange. In *Advances in Experimental Social Psychology*, vol. 2, L. Berkowitz (ed.). New York: Academic Press, 267–300.

Adorno, T. W., Frankel-Brunswik, E., Levinson, D. J., and Sanford, R. N. (1950). *The Authoritarian Personality.* New York: Harper.

Allen, V. L., and Levine, J. M. (1969). Consensus and conformity. *Journal of Experimental and Social Psychology,* **5**, 389–399.

Allport, G. W. (1968). The historical background of modern psychology. In *The Handbook of Social Psychology,* vol. 1, G. Linzey and E. Aronson (eds.). Reading, MA: Addison-Wesley.

Anderson, J. C. (1981). The impact of arbitration: A methodological assessment. *Industrial Relations,* **20**, 129–148.

Axelrod, R. (1984) *The Evolution of Cooperation.* New York: Basic Books.

Bacharach, S. B. (1983). Bargaining within organizations. In *Negotiating in Organizations,* M. H. Bazerman and R. J. Lewicki (eds.). Beverly Hills: Sage Publications.

Bacharach, S. B., and Lawler, E. J. (1981). Power and tactics in bargaining. *Industrial and Labor Relations Review,* **34**, 219–233.

Bachrach, P., and Baratz, M. S. (1963). *Decisions and nondecisions: An analytical framework. American Political Science Review,* **57**, 632–642.

Bales, R. F., and Slater, P. E. (1955). Role differentiation in small decision-making groups. In *The Family, Socialization, and Interaction Process,* T. Parsons and R. F. Bales (eds.). Glencoe, IL: Free Press.

Bariff, M. L., and Galbraith, J. R. (1978). Intraorganizational power considerations for designing information systems. *Accounting, Organizations and Society,* **3**, 15–27.

Barnard, C. I. (1946). Functions and pathology of status systems in formal organizations. In *Industry and Society,* W. F. Whyte (ed.). New York: McGraw-Hill.

Baron, P. (1974). Self-esteem, ingratiation, and evaluation of unknown others. *Journal of Personality and Social Psychology,* **30**, 104–109.

Bartos, O. J. (1970). Determinants and consequences of toughness. In *The Structure of Conflict,* P. Swingle (ed.). New York: Academic Press.

Bazerman, M. H. (1983). Negotiator judgment: A critical look at the rationality assumption. *American Behavioral Scientist,* **27**, 211–228.

Bazerman, M. H. (1984). The relevance of Kahneman and Tversky's concept of framing to organizational behavior. *Journal of Management,* **10**, 333–343.

Bazerman, M. H. (1986). *Judgment in Managerial Decision Making.* New York: Wiley.

Bazerman, M. H., Beekun, R. I., and Schoorman, F. D. (1982). Performance evaluation in a dynamic context: The impact of a prior commitment to the ratee. *Journal of Applied Psychology,* **67**, 873–876.

Bazerman, M. H., Giuliano, T., and Appelman, A. (1984). Escalation in individual and group decision making. *Organizational Behavior and Human Performance,* **33**, 141–152.

Bazerman, M. H., and Neale, M. A. (1983). Heuristics in negotiation: Limitations to effective dispute resolution. In *Negotiating in Organizations,* M. H. Bazerman and R. J. Lewicki (eds.), Beverly Hills: Sage Publications.

Bell, E. C., and Blakeney, R. N. (1977). Personality correlates of conflict resolution modes. *Human Relations,* **30**, 849–857.

Benton, A. A., and Druckman, D. (1974). Constituents' bargaining orientation and intergroup negotiations. *Journal of Applied Social Psychology,* **4**, 141–150.

Berger, P. L., and Luckmann, T. (1966). *The Social Construction of Reality.* Garden City, NY: Anchor.

Berkowitz, L. (1962). *Aggression: A Social Psychological Analysis.* New York: McGraw-Hill.

Berkowitz, L., and Donnerstein, E. (1982). External validity is more than skin deep: Some answers to criticisms of laboratory experiments. *American Psychologist,* **37**, 245–257.

Bernstein, W., and Davis, M. (1982). Perspective taking, self-consciousness, and accuracy in person perception. *Basic and Applied Social Psychology,* **3**, 1–19.

Blake, R. R., and Mouton, J. S. (1961). Loyalty of representatives to ingroup positions during intergroup competition. *Sociometry,* **24**, 177–183.

Blake, R. R., and Mouton, J. S. (1964). *The Managerial Grid*. Houston, TX: Gulf.

Blake, R. R., Shepard, H. A., and Mouton, J. S. (1964). *Managing Intergroup Conflict in Industry*. Houston, TX: Gulf.

Blau, P. M. (1964). *Exchange and Power in Social Life*. New York: Wiley.

Boulding, K. B. (1966). *Conflict and Defense*. New York: Harper & Row.

Brett, J. M. (1980). Behavioral research on unions and union–management systems. In *Research in Organizational Behavior*, vol. 2, B. M. Staw and L. L. Cummings (eds.). Greenwich, CT: JAI Press.

Brett, J. M. (1984). Managing organizational conflict. *Professional Psychology: Research and Practice*, **15**, 664–678.

Brett, J. M., and Goldberg, S. B. (1983). Mediator-advisers: A new third-party role. In *Negotiating in Organizations*, M. H. Bazerman and R. J. Lewicki (eds.). Beverly Hills, Sage Publications.

Brockner, J., and Rubin J. Z. (1985). *Entrapment in Escalating Conflicts*. New York: Springer-Verlag.

Brown, B. R. (1968). The effects of need to maintain face on interpersonal bargaining. *Journal of Experimental Social Psychology*, **4**, 107–122.

Burns, J. M. (1978). *Leadership*. New York: Harper Colophon.

Burrell, G., and Morgan, G. (1979). *Sociological Paradigms and Organisational Analysis*. London: Heinemann.

Byrne, D., and Griffitt, W. (1973). Interpersonal attraction. *Annual Review of Psychology*, **24**, 317–336.

Caldwell, D. F., and O'Reilly, C. A. (1982). Responses to failures: The effects of choices and responsibility on impression management. *Academy of Management Journal*, **25**, 121–136.

Caplow, T. (1968). *Two Against One: Coalitions in Triads*. Englewood Cliffs, NJ: Prentice-Hall.

Carnevale, P. J. D., and Isen, A. M. (1986). The influence of positive affect and visual access on the discovery of integrative solutions to bilateral negotiation. *Organizational Behavior and Human Decision Processes*, **37**, 1–13.

Carnevale, P. J. D., and Lawler, E. J. (1986). Time pressure and the development of integrative agreements in bilateral negotiations. *Journal of Conflict Resolution*, **30**, 636–659.

Carnevale, P. J. D., and Pegnetter, R. (1985). The selection of mediation tactics in public sector disputes: A contingency analysis. *Journal of Social Issues*, **41**, 65–82.

Carnevale, P. J. D., Pruitt, D. G., and Britton, S. D. (1979). Looking tough: The negotiator under constituent surveillance. *Personality and Social Psychology Bulletin*, **5**, 118–121.

Carnevale, P. J. D., Pruitt, D. G., and Seilheimer, S. D. (1981). Looking and competing: Accountability and visual access in integrative bargaining. *Journal of Personality and Social Psychology*, **40**, 111–120.

Cartwright, D. (1965). Influence, leadership, control. In *Handbook of Organizations*, J. G. March (ed.). Chicago: Rand McNally.

Cartwright, D., and Zander, A. (1962). *Group Dynamics* (2nd edn.). Evanston, IL: Row, Peterson.

Chertkoff, J. M. (1971). Coalition formation as a function of differences in resources. *Journal of Conflict Resolution*. **15**, 371–384.

Chertkoff, J. M., and Esser, J. K. (1976). A review of experiments in explicit bargaining. *Journal of Experimental Social Psychology*, **12**, 464–486.

Christie, R., and Geis, F. L. (1970). *Studies in Machiavellianism*. New York: Academic Press.

Clegg, S. (1975). *Power, Rule, and Domination: A Critical and Empirical Understanding of Power in Sociological Theory and Organizational Life*. Boston, MA: Routledge & Kegan Paul.

Cobb, A. T. (1980). Informal influence in the formal organization: Perceived sources of power among work unit peers. *Academy of Management Journal*, **23**, 155–161.

Coleman, J. S. (1957). *Community Conflict*. New York: Free Press.

Coser, L. (1956). *The Function of Social Conflict*. Glencoe, IL: Free Press.

Cronbach. L. J., and Gleser, G. G. (1953). Assessing similarity between profiles. *Psychological Bulletin*, **50**, 456–473.

Crozier, M. (1964). *The Bureaucratic Phenomenon*. Chicago: University of Chicago Press.

Cyert, R. M., and March, J. G. (1963). *A Behavioral Theory of the Firm*. Englewood Cliffs, NJ: Prentice-Hall.

Dahl, R. A. (1957). The concept of power. *Behavioral Science*, **2**, 201–218.

Dahrendorf, R. (1959). *Class and Class Conflict in Industrial Society*. Stanford: Stanford University Press.

Davis, M. (1981). A multidimensional approach to individual differences in empathy. *JSAS Catalogue of Selected Documents in Psychology*, **10**, 85.

Deutsch, M. (1965). Conflict and its resolution. Paper presented at the American Psychological Association.

Deutsch, M. (1973). *The Resolution of Conflict*. New Haven, CT: Yale University Press.

Deutsch, M., and Krauss, R. M. (1960). The effect of threat upon interpersonal bargaining. *Journal of Abnormal and Social Psychology*, **61**, 181–189.

Deutsch, M., and Krauss, R. M. (1962). Studies of interpersonal bargaining. *Journal of Conflict Resolution*, **6**, 52–76.

Donohue, W. A. (1978). An empirical framework for examining negotiation processes and outcomes. *Communication Monographs*, **45**, 247–257.

Douglas, A. (1962). *Industrial Peacemaking*. New York: Columbia University Press.

Druckman, D. (1967). Dogmatism, prenegotiation experience, and simulated group representation as determinants of dyadic behavior in a bargaining situation. *Journal of Personality and Social Psychology*, **6**, 279–290.

Druckman, D. (1977). Boundary role conflict: Negotiation as dual responsiveness. *Journal of Conflict Resolution*, **21**, 639–662.

Dunlop, J. T. (1958). *Industrial Relations Systems*. New York: Holt-Dryden.

Dunlop, J. T., and Healy, J. J. (1955). *Collective Bargaining: Principles and Cases*. Homewood, IL: Irwin.

Edwards, R. C. (1976). Individual traits and organizational incentives: What makes a 'good' worker? *Journal of Human Resources*, **11**, 51–68.

Ekman, P. (1985). *Telling Lies*. New York: Norton.

Eliashberg, J., LaTour, S. A., Rangaswamy, A., and Stern, L. W. (1986). Assessing the predictive accuracy of two utility-based theories in a marketing channel negotiation context. *Journal of Marketing Research*, **23**, 101–110.

Emerson, M. (1962). Power-dependence relations. *American Sociological Review*, **27**, 31–41.

Endler, N. S., and Magnusson, D. (1976). Toward an interactional psychology of personality. *Psychological Bulletin*, **83**, 956–974.

Enz, C. A. (1986). *Power and Shared Values in the Corporate Culture*. Ann Arbor, MI: UMI Research Press.

Faley, T., and Tedeschi, J. T. (1971). Status and reactions to threats. *Journal of Personality and Social Psychology*, **17**, 192–199.

Farber, H. S. (1981). An analysis of 'splitting-the-difference' in interest arbitration. *Industrial and Labor Relations Review*, **34**, 66–74.

Fiedler, F. A. (1967). *A Theory of Leadership Effectiveness*. New York: McGraw-Hill.

Filley, A. C. (1975). *Interpersonal Conflict Resolution*. Glenview, IL: Scott, Foresman.

Fisher, R. (1964). Fractionating conflict. In *International Conflict and Behavioral Science: The Craigville Papers*, R. Fisher (ed.). New York: Basic Books.

Fisher, R., and Ury, W. (1981). *Getting to Yes: Negotiating Agreement without Giving In*. Boston, MA: Houghton Mifflin.

Fleishman, E. A. (1957). The Leadership Opinion Questionnaire. In *Leader Behavior: Its Description and Measurement*, R. M. Stogdill and A. E. Coons (eds.). Columbus: Ohio State University, Bureau of Business Research.

Fleishman, E. A. (1973). Twenty years of consideration and structure. In *Current Developments in the Study of Leadership*, E. A. Fleishman and J. G. Hunt (eds.). Carbondale, IL: Southern Illinois University Press.

Fodor, E. M. (1973a). Disparagement by a subordinate, ingratiation, and the use of power. *Journal of Social Psychology*, **84**, 181-186.

Fodor, E. M. (1973b). Group stress, ingratiation, and the use of power. *Journal of Social Psychology*, **91**, 345-346.

Folger, J. P., and Poole, M. S. (1984). *Working Through Conflict: A Communication Perspective.* Glenview, IL: Scott, Foresman.

Follett, M. P. (1940). Constructive conflict. In *Dynamic Administration: The Collected Papers of Mary Parker Follett*, H. C. Metcalf and L. Urwick (eds.). New York: Harper.

French, J. R. P., Jr, and Raven, B. (1959). The bases of social power. In *Studies in Social Power*, D. Cartwright (ed.). Ann Arbor, MI: Institute for Social Research.

Frey, R. L., and Adams J. S. (1972). The negotiator's dilemma: Simultaneous in-group and out-group conflict. *Journal of Experimental Social Psychology*. **8**, 331-346.

Froman, L. A., Jr, and Cohen, M. D. (1970). Compromise and logroll: Comparing the efficiency of two bargaining processes. *Behavioral Science*, **15**, 180-183.

Gamson, W. A. (1964). Experimental studies of coalition formation. In *Advances in Experimental Social Psychology*, vol. 1, L. Berkowitz (ed.). New York: Academic Press.

Gamson, W. A. (1968). *Power and Discontent.* Homewood, IL: Dorsey.

Gergen, K. J. (1969). *The Psychology of Behavior Exchange.* Reading, MA: Addison-Wesley.

Gilkey, R. W., and Greenhalgh, L. (1984). Developing effective negotiation approaches among professional women in organizations. Paper presented at the Third Annual Conference on Women and Organizations, Boston.

Gilligan, C. (1982). *In a Different Voice.* Cambridge, MA: Harvard University Press.

Gilman, G. (1962). An inquiry into the nature and use of authority. In *Organization Theory and Industrial Practice*, M. Haire (ed.). New York: Wiley.

Goffman, E. (1959). *The Presentation of Self in Everyday Life.* New York: Doubleday Anchor.

Goldman, R. M. (1966). A theory of conflict processes and organizational offices. *Journal of Conflict Resolution*, **10**, 328-343.

Green, P. E., and Rao, V. R. (1971). Conjoint measurement for quantifying judgmental data. *Journal of Marketing Research*, **8**, 355-363.

Green, P. E., and Srinivasan, V. (1978). Conjoint analysis in consumer research: Issues and outlook. *Journal of Consumer Research*, **5**, 103-123.

Greenhalgh, L. (1985). A diagnostic model for conflict management. Paper presented at the Academy of Management Annual Meeting, San Diego.

Greenhalgh, L. (1986) Managing conflict. *Sloan Management Review*, **27**, 45-51.

Greenhalgh, L., Gilkey, R. W., and Pufahl, S. M. (1984). Effects of sex-role differences on approach to business negotiations. Paper presented at the Academy of Management Annual Meeting, Boston.

Greenhalgh, L., McKersie, R. B., and Gilkey, R. W. (1986). Rebalancing the work force at IBM: A case study of redeployment and revitalization. *Organizational Dynamics*, **14**, 30-47.

Greenhalgh, L., and Neslin, S. A. (1981). Conjoint analysis of negotiator preferences. *Journal of Conflict Resolution*, **25**, 301-327.

Greenhalgh, L., Neslin, S. A., and Gilkey, R. W. (1985). The effects of negotiator preferences, situational power, and negotiator personality on outcomes of business negotiations. *Academy of Management Journal*, **28**, 9-33.

Greer, S. (1969). *The Logic of Social Inquiry.* Chicago: Aldine.

Gruder, C. L. (1971). Relationships with opponent and partner in mixed-motive bargaining. *Journal of Conflict Resolution*, **15**, 403-416.

Harnett, D. L., and Cummings, L. L. (1972). Bargaining behavior in an asymmetrical triad. In *Social Choice*, B. Lieberman (ed.). New York: Gordon & Breach.

Harnett, D. L., and Cummings, L. L. (1980). *Bargaining Behavior: An International Study*. Houston, TX: Dame.

Harnett, D. L., Cummings, L. L., and Hughes, G. D. (1968). The influence of risk-taking propensity on bargaining behavior. *Behavioral Science*, **13**, 1-11.

Harre, R., and Secord, P. F. (1972). *The Explanation of Social Behavior*. Oxford. Blackwell.

Harsanyi, J. C. (1962) Bargaining in ignorance of the opponent's utility function. *Journal of Conflict Resolution*, **1**, 29-38.

Heider, F. (1958). *The Psychology of Interpersonal Relations*. New York: Wiley.

Hermann, M. G., and Kogan, N. (1968). Negotiation in leader and delegate groups. *Journal of Conflict Resolution*, **12**, 332-344.

Herold, D. M. (1977). Two way influence processes in leader–follower dyads. *Academy of Management Journal*, **20**, 224-237.

Hessel, M. (1984). Mutual perceptions in bargaining: A quantitative approach. *Behavioral Science*, **29**, 221-232.

Hickson, D. J., Hinings, C. R., Lee, C. A., Schneck, R. E., and Pennings, J. N. (1971). A strategic contingencies theory of intraorganizational power. *Administrative Science Quarterly*, **16**, 216-229.

Hollander, E. P. (1978). *Leadership Dynamics*. New York: Free Press.

Hornstein, H. A., and Johnson, D. W. (1966). The effects of process analysis and ties to his group upon the negotiator's attitudes toward the outcomes of negotiations. *Journal of Applied Behavioral Science*, **2**, 449-463.

Horton, J. (1964). Alienation and anomie. *British Journal of Sociology*, **15**, 283-300.

House, R. J., and Baetz, M. L. (1979). Leadership: Some generalizations and new research directions. In *Research in Organizational Behavior*, B. M. Staw (ed.). Greenwich, CT: JAI Press.

Huber, V. L., and Neale, M. A. (1984). Effects of cognitive heuristics and goals on negotiator performance and subsequent goal setting. Unpublished manuscript, University of Utah.

Ikle, F. C. (1964). *How Nations Negotiate*. New York: Harper & Row.

Jervis, R. (1970). *The Logic of Images in International Relations*. Princeton, NJ: Princeton University Press.

Johnson, D. F., and Tullar, W. L. (1972). Study of third party intervention, face-saving and bargaining behavior. *Journal of Experimental Social Psychology*. **8**, 319-330.

Johnson, D. W. (1967). Use of role reversal in intergroup competition. *Journal of Personality and Social Psychology*, **7**, 135-141.

Jones, E. E. (1954). Authoritarianism as a determinant of first-impressions formation. *Journal of Personality*, **23**, 107-127.

Jones, E. E. (1975). *Ingratiation*. New York: Irvington.

Jones, E. E., Gergen, K. J., and Davis, E. E. (1962). Some determinants of reactions to being approved or disapproved as a person. *Psychological Monograph*, **76**, whole no. 521.

Jones, R. E., and Melcher, B. H. (1982). Personality and the preference for modes of conflict resolution. *Human Relations*, **35**, 649-658.

Jones, R. E., and White, C. S. (1985). Relationships among personality, conflict resolution styles, and task effectiveness. *Group and Organization Studies*, **10**, 152-167.

Kahneman, D., and Tversky, A. (1979). Prospect theory: An analysis of decision under risk. *Econometrica*, **47**, 263-291.

Karrass, C. L. (1970). *The Negotiating Game*. New York: Thomas Y. Crowell.

Katz, D. and Kahn, R. L. (1966). *The Social Psychology of Organizations*. New York: Wiley.

Kauffmann, D., and Steiner, I. (1968). Some variables affecting the use of conformity as an ingratiation technique. *Journal of Experimental Social Psychology*, **4**, 400-414.

Kelley, H. H. (1966). A classroom study of the dilemmas in interpersonal negotiations. In *Strategic Interaction and Conflict: Original Papers and Discussion*, K. Archibald (ed.). Berkeley, CA: Institute of International Studies.

Kelley, H. H., Beckman, L. L., and Fischer, C. S. (1967). Negotiating the division of a reward under incomplete information. *Journal of Experimental Social Psychology*, **3**, 361-398.

Kerr, C. (1954). Industrial conflict and its resolution. *American Journal of Sociology*, **60**, 230-245.

Kiesler, C. A. (1971). *The Psychology of Commitment*. New York: Academic Press.

Kilmann, R. H., and Thomas, K. W. (1977). Developing a forced-choice measure of conflict-handling behavior: The 'MODE' instrument. *Educational and Psychological Measurement*, **37**, 309-325.

Kilmann, R. H., and Thomas, K. W. (1978). Four perspectives on conflict management: An attributional framework for organizing descriptive and normative theory. *Academy of Management Review*, **3**, 59-68.

Kipnis, D., and Schmidt, S. M. (1983). An influence perspective on bargaining within organizations. In *Negotiating in Organizations*, M. H. Bazerman and R. J. Lewicki (eds.). Beverly Hills: Sage Publications.

Kipnis, D., and Vanderveer, R. (1971). Ingratiation and the use of power. *Journal of Personality and Social Psychology*, **17**, 280-286.

Klimoski, R. J. (1978). Simulation methodologies in experimental research on negotiations by respresentatives. *Journal of Conflict Resolution*, **22**, 61-77.

Kochan, T. A., and Jick, T. D. (1978). A theory of public sector mediation process. *Journal of Conflict Resolution*. **22**, 209-240.

Kolb, D. M. (1983). *The Mediators*. Cambridge: MIT Press.

Komorita, S. S., and Brenner, A. R. (1968). Bargaining and group decision making. *Journal of Personality and Social Psychology*, **9**, 15-20.

Komorita, S. S., and Chertkoff, J. M. (1973). A bargaining theory of coalition formation. *Psychological Review*, **80**, 149-162.

Komorita, S. S., and Esser, J. K. (1975). Frequency of reciprocated concessions in bargaining. *Journal of Personality and Social Psychology*, **32**, 699-705.

Kriesberg, L. (1973). *The Sociology of Social Conflict*. Englewood Cliffs, NJ: Prentice-Hall.

Lamm, H., and Kogan, N. (1970). Risk-taking in the context of intergroup negotiation. *Journal of Experimental Social Psychology*, **6**, 351-363.

Laue, J., and Cormick, G. (1973). The ethics of social intervention: Community crisis intervention programs. St Louis, MO: Community Crisis Intervention Center, Washington University.

Lawler, E. E. (1973). *Motivation in Work Organizations*. Monterey, CA: Brooks-Cole.

Lefebvre, L. M. (1973). An experimental approach to the use of ingratiation tactics under homogeneous and heterogeneous dyads. *European Journal of Social Psychology*, **3**, 427-445.

Lewicki, R. J. (1983). Lying and deception: A behavioral model. In *Negotiating in Organizations*, M. H. Bazerman and R. J. Lewicki (eds.). Beverly Hills: Sage Publications.

Lewin, K. (1948). *Resolving Social Conflicts: Selected Papers on Group Dynamics*. New York: Harper & Brothers.

Lewis, S. A., and Fry, W. R. (1977). Effects of visual access and orientation on the discovery of integrative bargaining alternatives. *Organizational Behavior and Human Performance*, **20**, 75-92.

Locke, E. A., Shaw, K. N., Saari, L. M., and Latham, G. P. (1981). Goal setting and task performance: 1969-1980. *Psychological Bulletin*, **90**, 125-152.

Luce, R. D., and Raiffa, H. (1957). *Games and Decisions*. New York: Wiley.

McClelland, D. C. (1958). Methods of measuring human motivation. In *Motives in Fantasy, Action and Society*, J. W. Atkinson (ed.). Princeton, NJ: Van Nostrand.

McGillicuddy, N. B., Pruitt, D. G., and Syna, H. (1984). Perceptions of firmness and strength in negotiation. *Personality and Social Psychology Bulletin*, **10**, 402-409.

McGrath, J. E. (1966) A social psychological approach to the study of negotiation. In *Studies on Behavior in Organizations: A Symposium*, R. V. Bowers (ed.). Athens: University of Georgia Press.

McKersie, R. B., Perry, C. R., and Walton, R. E. (1965). Intraorganizational bargaining in labor negotations. *Journal of Conflict Resolution*, **9**, 463–481.

March, J. G. (1955). An introduction to the theory and measurement of influence. *American Political Science Review*, **49**, 431–451.

March, J. G., and Simon, H. A. (1958). *Organizations*. New York: Wiley.

Martin, N. H., and Sims, J. H. (1964). Power, politics, and influence. In *Readings in Managerial Psychology*, H. J. Leavitt and L. R. Pondy (eds.). Chicago: University of Chicago Press.

Martindale, D. A. (1971). Territorial dominance behavior in dyadic verbal interactions. *Proceedings of the 79th Annual Convention of the American Psychological Association.* **6**, 305–306.

Mechanic, D. (1962). Sources of power of lower participants in complex organizations. *Administrative Science Quarterly*, **7**, 349–364.

Merton, R. K. (1961). Bureaucratic structure and personality. In *Complex Organizations: A Sociological Reader*, A. Etzioni (ed.). New York: Holt, Rinehart, & Winston.

Michener, H. A., Plazewski, J. G., and Vaske, J. J. (1979). Ingratiation tactics channeled by target values and threat capability. *Journal of Personality*, **47**, 35–56.

Mintzberg, H. (1973). *The Nature of Managerial Work*, New York: Harper & Row.

Mischel, W. (1968). *Personality and Assessment*. New York: Wiley.

Morley, I., and Stephenson, G. (1977). *The Social Psychology of Bargaining*. London: George Allen & Unwin.

Mowday, R. T. (1978). The exercise of upward influence in organizations. *Administrative Science Quarterly*, **23**, 137–156.

Murnighan, J. K. (1978). Models of coalition behavior: Game theoretic, social psychological, and political perspectives. *Psychological Bulletin*, **85**, 1130–1135.

Nash, J. F. (1950). The bargaining problem. *Econometrica*, **18**, 155–162.

Neale, M. A., and Bazerman, M. H. (1983). The impact of perspective taking ability on the negotiation process under alternative forms of arbitration. *Industrial and Labor Relations Review*, **36**, 378–388.

Neale, M. A., and Bazerman, M. H. (1985). Perspectives for understanding negotiation: Viewing negotiation as a judgmental process. *Journal of Conflict Resolution*, **29**, 33–55.

Neslin, S. A., and Greenhalgh, L. (1983). An experimental investigation of Nash's theory of cooperative games as a predictor of the outcomes of buyer–seller negotiations. *Journal of Marketing Research*, **20**, 368–379.

Neslin, S. A., and Greenhalgh, L. (1986). The ability of Nash's theory of cooperative games to predict the outcomes of buyer–seller negotiations: A dyad-level test. *Management Science*, **32**, 480–498.

Newcomb, T. M. (1956). The prediction of interpersonal attraction. *American Psychologist*, **11**, 575–586.

Nord, W. R. (1974). The failure of current applied behavioral science — a Marxian perspective. *Journal of Applied Behavioral Science*, **10**, 557–578.

Northcraft, G. B., and Wolf, G. (1984). Dollars, sense, and sunk costs: A life-cycle model of resource allocation decisions. *Academy of Management Review*, **9**, 225–234.

Notz, W. W., Starke, F. A., and Atwell, J. (1983). The manager as arbitrator: Conflicts over scarce resources. In *Negotiating in Organizations*, M. H. Bazerman, and R. J. Lewicki (eds.). Beverly Hills: Sage Publications.

Organ, D. W. (1971). Some variables affecting boundary role behavior. *Sociometry*, **34**, 524–537.

Osgood, X. (1962). *An Alternative to War and Surrender*. Urbana, IL: University of Illinois Press.

Pandey, J. (1978). Ingratiation: A review of literature and relevance of its study in organizational setting. *Indian Journal of Industrial Relations*, **13**, 381–393.

Pandey, J. (1981a). Effects of machiavellianism and degree of organizational formalization on ingratiation. *Psychologia*, **24**, 41–46.

Pandey, J. (1981b). A note about social power through ingratiation among workers. *Journal of Occupational Psychology*, **54**, 65–67.

Pandey, J. (1984). Ingratiation as a function of organizational characteristics and supervisory styles. *International Review of Applied Psychology*, **3**, 381–394.

Pandey, J., and Rostogi, R. (1979). Machiavellianism and ingratiation. *Journal of Social Psychology*, **108**, 221–225.

Perrow, C. (1972). *Complex Organizations: A Critical Essay*. Glenview, IL: Scott, Foresman.

Pettigrew, A. (1972). Information control as a power resource. *Sociology*, **6**, 187–204.

Pfeffer, J. (1981). *Power in Organizations*. Marshfield, MA: Pitman.

Pondy, L. R. (1966). A systems theory of organizational conflict. *Academy of Management Journal*, **9**, 246–256.

Pondy, L. R. (1967). Organizational conflict: Concepts and models. *Administrative Science Quarterly*, **12**, 296–320.

Potter, S. (1948). *The Theory and Practice of Gamesmanship: The Art of Winning Games Without Actually Cheating*. New York: Holt.

Pruitt, D. G. (1971). Indirect communication and the search for agreement in negotiation. *Journal of Applied Social Psychology*, **1**, 205–239.

Pruitt, D. G. (1981). *Negotiation Behavior*. New York: Academic Press.

Pruitt, D. G. (1983). Achieving integrative agreements. In *Negotiating In Organizations*, M. H. Bazerman and R. J. Lewicki (eds.). Beverly Hills: Sage Publications.

Pruitt, D. G., and Drews, J. L. (1969). The effect of time pressure, time elapsed, and the opponent's concession rate on behavior in negotiation. *Journal of Experimental Social Psychology*, **5**, 43–60.

Pruitt, D. G., and Johnson, D. F. (1970). Mediation as an aid to face saving in negotiation. *Journal of Personality and Social Psychology*, **14**, 239–246.

Pruitt, D. G., and Kimmel, M. J. (1977). Twenty years of experimental gaming: Critique, synthesis, and suggestions for the future. *Annual Review of Psychology*, **28**, 363–392.

Pruitt, D. G., and Rubin, J. Z. (1986). *Social Conflict: Escalation, Stalemate, and Settlement*. New York: Random House.

Rahim, M. A. (1965). *Managing Conflict in Organizations*. New York: Praeger.

Raiffa, H. (1982). *The Art and Science of Negotiation*. Cambridge, MA: Harvard University Press.

Rapoport, A., and Chammah, A. M. (1965). *Prisoner's Dilemma*. Ann Arbor, MI: University of Michigan Press.

Raven, B. H., and Kruglanski, A. W. (1970). Conflict and power. In *The Structure of Conflict*, P. Swingle (ed.). New York: Academic Press.

Rekosh, J. H., and Feigenbaum, K. D. (1966). The necessity of mutual trust for cooperative behavior in a two-person game. *Journal of Social Psychology*, **69**, 149–154.

Robbins, S. P. (1974). *Managing Organizational Conflict: A Nontraditional Approach*. Englewood Cliffs, NJ: Prentice-Hall.

Roering, K. J., Slusher, A., and Schooler, R. D. (1975). Commitment of further interaction in marketing transactions. *Journal of Applied Psychology*, **60**, 386–388.

Rogers, C. R., and Roethlisberger, F. J. (1952). Barriers and gateways to communication. *Harvard Business Review*, **30**, 46–52.

Rubin, J. Z., and Brown, B. R. (1975). *The Social Psychology of Bargaining and Negotiation*. New York: Academic Press.

Salancik, G., and Pfeffer, J. (1977). Who gets power — and how they hold on to it: A strategic-contingency model of power. *Organizational Dynamics*, **5**, 3–21.

Schelling, T. C. (1960). *The Strategy of Conflict*. New York: Oxford University Press.

Schelling, T. C. (1964). Bargaining communication and limited war. In *Readings in Managerial Psychology*, H. J. Leavitt and L. R. Pondy (eds.). Chicago: University of Chicago Press.

Schlenker, B. R., and Bonoma, T. V. (1978). Fun and games: The validity of games for the study of conflict. *Journal of Conflict Resolution*, **22**, 7-33.

Schmidt, S. M., and Kochan, T. A. (1972). Conflict: Toward conceptual clarity. *Administrative Science Quarterly*, **17**, 359-370.

Shaw, M. E. (1976). *Group Dynamics: The Psychology of Small Group Behavior* (2nd edn.). New York: McGraw-Hill.

Sheppard, B. H. (1983). Managers as inquisitors: Some lessons from the law. In *Negotiating in Organizations*, M. H. Bazerman and R. J. Lewicki (eds.). Beverly Hills: Sage Publications.

Shrauger, S., and Altrocchi, J. (1964). The personality of the perceiver as a factor in person perception. *Psychological Bulletin*, **62**, 299-308.

Shubik, M. (1968). On the study of disarmament and escalation. *Journal of Conflict Resolution*, **12**, 83-101.

Shubik, M. (1971). The dollar auction game: A paradox in noncooperative behavior and escalation. *Journal of Conflict Resolution*, **15**, 109-111.

Shure, G. H., Meeker, R. J., and Hansford, E. A. (1965). The effectiveness of pacifist strategies in bargaining games. *Journal of Conflict Resolution*, **9**, 106-117.

Siegel, S. (1957). Level of aspiration and decision making. *Psychological Review*, **64**, 253-262.

Siegel, S., and Fouraker, L. E. (1960). *Bargaining and Group Decision-making: Experiments in Bilateral Monopoly*. New York: McGraw-Hill.

Simmel, G. (1955). *Conflict*. New York: Free Press.

Simons, H. A. (1976). *Administrative Behavior* (3rd edn). New York: Free Press.

Staw, B. M. (1976). Knee-deep in the big muddy: A study of escalating commitment to a chosen course of action. *Organizational Behavior and Human Performance*, **16**, 27-44.

Staw, B. M., and Ross, J. (1978). Commitment to a policy decision: A multitheoretical perspective. *Administrative Science Quarterly*, **23**, 40-64.

Steiner, I. V. (1970). Perceived freedom. In *Advances in Experimental Social Psychology*, vol. 5, L. Berkowitz (ed.) New York: Academic Press.

Stern, I., and Pearse, R. F. (1968). Collective bargaining: A union's program for reducing conflict. *Personnel*, **45**, 61-72.

Stevens, C. M. (1963). *Strategy and Collective Bargaining Negotiation*. New York: McGraw-Hill.

Stevenson, W. B., Pearce, J. L., and Porter, L. W. (1985). The concept of 'coalition' in organization theory and research. *Academy of Management Review*, **10**, 256-268.

Strauss, A. (1978). *Negotiations: Varieties, Contexts, Processes, and Social Order*. San Francisco: Jossey-Bass.

Streufert, S., and Suefeld, P. (1977). Simulation as a research method: A problem in communication. *Journal of Applied Social Psychology*, **7**, 281-285.

Tedeschi, J. T., Schlenker, B. R., and Bonoma, T. V. (1973). *Conflict, Power, and Games*. Chicago: Aldine.

Tedeschi, J. T., Schlenker, B. R., and Lindskold, S. (1972). The exercise of power and influence. In *The Social Influence Processes*, J. T. Tedeschi (ed.). Chicago: Aldine.

Teger, A. I. (1980). *Too Much Invested to Quit*. New York: Pergamon.

Thaler, R. (1985). Using mental accounting in a theory of purchasing behavior. *Marketing Science*, **4**, 12-13.

Thibaut, J. W., and Kelley, H. H. (1959). *The Social Psychology of Groups*. New York: Wiley.

Thomas, K. W. (1976). Conflict and conflict management. In *Handbook of Industrial and Organizational Behavior*, M. D. Dunnette (ed.). Chicago: Rand McNally.

Thompson, J. D. (1967). *Organizations in Action*. New York: McGraw-Hill.

Tjosvold, D. (1978). Affirmation of the high-power person and his position: Ingratiation in conflict. *Journal of Applied Psychology*, **8**, 230-243.

Tropper, R. (1972). The consequences of investment in the process of conflict. *Journal of Conflict Resolution*, **16**, 97-98.

Tung, R. L. (1984). *Business Negotiations with the Japanese*. Lexington, MA: Lexington Books.

Tversky, A., and Kahneman, D. (1981). The framing of decisions and the psychology of choice. *Science*, **211**, 453–463.

Von Neumann, J., and Morgenstern, O. (1947). *Theory of Games and Economic Behavior*, (2nd edn). Princeton, NJ: Princeton University Press.

Vroom, V. (1964). *Work and Motivation*. New York: Wiley.

Wachtel, P. L. (1980). Investigation and its discontents: Some constraints on progress in psychological research. *American Psychologist*, **35**, 399–408.

Wall, J. A. (1981). Mediation: An analysis, review, and proposed research. *Journal of Conflict Resolution*, **25**, 157–180.

Wall, J. A. (1985). *Negotiation: Theory and Practice*. Glenview, IL: Scott, Foresman.

Walsh, J. P., Greenhalgh, L., and Fairfield, M. (1986). Effects of age-based status group membership on bargaining behavior. Paper presented at the American Psychological Association Annual Convention, Washington, DC.

Walton, R. E. (1969). *Interpersonal Peacemaking: Confrontations and Third Party Consultation*. Reading, MA: Addison-Wesley.

Walton, R. E., and McKersie, R. B. (1965). *A Behaviorial Theory of Labor Negotiations*. New York: McGraw-Hill.

Weber, M. (1947). *The Theory of Social and Economic Organization*. New York: Oxford University Press.

Wehr, P. (1979). *Conflict Regulation*. Boulder, CO: Westview.

Whyte, W. F. (1951). *Patterns for Industrial Peace*. New York: Harper Brothers.

Williams, R. M. (1975). Successful intergroup relations: Methods of resolving or efficiently using conflicts. Keynote address delivered at the Fifth Annual Alpha Kappa Delta Sociological Research Symposium, Richmond, VA.

Wilmot, J. H., and Wilmot, W. W. (1978). *Interpersonal Conflict*. Dubuque, IA: Wm C. Brown.

Winter, D. G. (1973). *The Power Motive*. New York: Free Press.

Wrong, D. H. (1968). Some problems in defining social power. *American Journal of Sociology*, **73**, 673–681.

Wrong, D. H. (1979). *Power: Its Forms, Bases, and Uses*. New York: Harper & Row.

Yukl, G. A., Malone, M. P., Hayslip, B., and Pamin, T. A. (1976). The effects of time pressure and issue settlement order on integrative bargaining. *Sociometry*, **39**, 277–281.

Zajonc, R. B. and Markus, H. (1982). Affective and cognitive factors in preferences. *Journal of Consumer Research*, **9**, 123–131.

Zalkind, S. S., and Costello, T. W. (1964). Perception: Implications for administration. In *Readings in Managerial Psychology*, H. J. Leavitt and L. R. Pondy (eds.). Chicago: University of Chicago Press.

Zartman, I. W. (1977). Negotiation as a joint decision-making process. *Journal of Conflict Resolution*, **21**, 619–638.

International Review of Industrial and Organizational Psychology 1987
Edited by C. L. Cooper and I. T. Robertson
©1987 John Wiley & Sons Ltd

Chapter 9

WORK AND FAMILY

Ronald J. Burke
Faculty of Administrative Studies, York University, Canada
and Esther R. Greenglass
Department of Psychology, York University, Canada

INTRODUCTION

In contemporary society, work and family roles are among the most important ones for the majority of people. Moreover, it is in the work and family domains that people generally spend most of their time. Given the salience of work and family roles it is not surprising that considerable research has been directed to the study of behavioral, sociological, and organizational aspects of these domains as well as implications for the individual. Researchers have devoted considerable attention to an understanding of family dynamics and organizational behavior. While there is a plethora of information on each of these domains, little research attention has been directed to understanding the reciprocal relationship between them. Research and theory that have begun disentangling the relationship between work and family tend to be scattered across a wide range of sources and disciplines.

The purpose of this chapter is to review and evaluate research and theory that have been directed to understanding the relationship between work and family. The erosion of the 'myth of separate worlds' (Kanter, 1977) will be discussed, followed by a consideration of the ways in which the domains of work and family have been integrated in research and theory. Considerable attention will be directed to a discussion of the ways in which work impacts on the family, including how occupational stressors affect the spouse; the experiences of children; and the implications of wives' employment for the family, and particularly the husband.

Of equal importance is consideration of the effects of the family on work. This review examines topics such as the relationship between family and job satisfaction, the decision of wives to work, family stress and work experience, and the family as a social support system, with particular reference to sex differences and their structural implications for social support. No review of the interrelationship of work and family would be complete without consideration of the topic of role conflict and its implications. The chapter will discuss theoretical models of role conflict, sources of role conflict, and coping with role conflict. The review will also consider the research relating to the division of time among dual-career couples — an increasing phenomenon given the trends toward increasing education and employment particularly among married women. Finally, new and innovative research methodologies are discussed. The methodologies reviewed here are significant for their fresh approach to the work–family interface and represent both structural and empirical alternatives to current methodologies which, in attempting to adhere to the scientific model, may be masking important social and psychological phenomena which may be uncovered only by employing multivariate, multilevel approaches to the problem.

In summary, the 'open systems' approach to the study of work and family and the assumption of interdependence between the two domains allows for the integration of people's life experiences, giving a more comprehensive picture of the individual. As social scientists we may forget that it is one and the same person who is a parent, for example, and a worker. Understanding the implications of that reality is what this review is about.

WORK AND FAMILY—THE MYTH OF SEPARATE WORLDS

It has only been in the past decade that researchers have become interested in the relationship between work and family. First, the designers of organizations themselves have attempted to separate the two spheres for fear that the socio-emotional character of family relationships would undermine the strictly rational, task-centered relationships which were presumed to exist in the workplace. Thus, organizations were located some distance from where families lived. Second, academics themselves have contributed to the myth of separate worlds. Specialists in the area of work come primarily from the fields of organizational psychology, industrial sociology, and industrial relations. Specialists in the area of the family come primarily from the fields of family sociology, human development, and marital counseling. Few individual scholars have the breadth of expertise which spans *both* work and the family. Thus, there has not been a good deal of research which has integrated both fields and studied the work–family interface.

Job incumbents themselves have also contributed to the separation of work and family. Bartolomé and Evans (1979) found that most male managers they investigated upheld as an ideal life style one in which professional and private lives were both separate and independent. Similar findings have been reported by Piotrkowski (1978), Dyer (1964), and Renshaw (1974). Thus job incumbents have been found either to deny connections between work and family, to be unaware of any connections, or to act when in one domain as if the other did not exist. Kanter (1977) has persuasively argued that the myth of separate worlds fits the interests of the modern corporation.

This situation has been gradually changing, however, with several forces converging to highlight the work–family interface. These forces include: (1) the influx of women into the workforce, (2) new life styles which attempt to integrate work, family, and leisure in different ways, (3) increases in single-parent families, (4) increases in dual-career couples, and (5) a greater realization that events in one sphere are likely to influence, and be influenced by, events in another sphere, i.e. the open systems concept.

DEFINITIONS

Work is equated with paid employment in this review. While the focus here is on paid employment, it is acknowledged that there is valuable work being done which is non-remunerative in nature such as housework and volunteer work. The fact that the focus is on paid employment is not meant to detract or undervalue in any way unpaid work. Reference to unpaid work will be made only in so far as it relates to our understanding of work and family. *Family* is limited to husband, wife, and children in this chapter. This ignores family of origin (parents) and extended families. The latter will be referred to only as they relate to our understanding of work and family.

WORK AND FAMILY—MUTUAL INFLUENCES

There is an integral relationship between one's work and family such that experiences in one cannot help but influence the other domain. Problems and difficulties at one's job can also be lessened by familial support. As Gilmer (1971) has stated, employment problems are almost inevitably shared with one's family, and familial feedback affects one's job functioning. Let us consider a few studies which provide a general sense of mutual influence of work and family.

Research from a variety of diverse sources suggests that job satisfaction is often affect by familial demands and conflicts as well as the adjustment of family members, especially one's spouse. For example, a study of female and male military personnel (Nieva, 1979) reports that job satisfaction and job involvement were both negatively related to general familial demands, such as the family's need for time and energy; to work–family bidirectional conflict (pulled in opposite directions by family and job); to work–family conflict (demands of job interfere with family life) and to family–work conflict (vice versa). In a survey of 1800 male executives of a major international company, Guest and Williams (1973) concluded that the two most important influences on overall satisfaction with the overseas assignment were the job itself and, more importantly, the adjustment of the executives' wives to the foreign environment. From the company's point of view, the way in which a wife does adjust to her new environment can affect her husband's work performance.

In a study of Schneider and Dachler (1978), family satisfaction was significantly positively related to organizational and job satisfaction as well as to task, career, and life satisfaction. These investigators identified five issues concerning the relationship between work and family. These dealt with the impact of the organization on financial concerns, involvement of the employee in everyday family activities, the social life of the family with respect to activities involving others, the autonomy of the spouse, and feelings of status of the family. A factor analysis of 27 items written to tap these five dimensions yielded three factors which the labeled: 'time contraints,' 'activities level,' and 'security concerns'. A comparison of males and females showed that these family issues were equally important for both sexes.

Work, Family, and Life Satisfaction

Research findings indicate that men and women who are satisfied with their jobs tend to be more satisfied with their lives. For example, Rice, Near, and Hunt (1980) reported the results of a survey of more than 350 job satisfaction / life satisfaction relationships reported in 23 studies that varied widely in terms of the sample, instrumentation, and date of survey. For more than 90 per cent of the cases, the direction of this relationship was positive, and none of the scattered negative relationships was statistically reliable. The magnitude of the reported zero-order relationships between job satisfaction and overall life satisfaction was typically modest, with correlations mostly in the mid-30s for males and mid-20s for females.

Andrews and Withey (1976) concluded, based on three sets of evidence, that work was one of the most important domains of life experience. The first was the relatively high positive correlation between job satisfaction and a set of extrawork variables (standard of living, housing, leisure time, marriage, and family), which in turn accounted for a high proportion of the variance (54 per cent) in life satisfaction scores; the second was the low levels of life satisfaction reported by respondents in their study who were unemployed; and the third was simply the high proportion of employed respondents' lives that was devoted to the job.

Studies have also examined the effects of extrawork variables on job satisfaction (Blood and Hulin, 1967; Hulin and Blood, 1968; Turner and Lawrence, 1965; Katzell, Barrett, and Parker, 1961). Hulin (1969) found that a multiple correlation of eight job-, economic-, and community-related variables accounted for the following variances: for 30 per cent of the variance in job satisfaction and 19 per cent of the variance in life satisfaction for male workers; 45 per cent of the variance of job satisfaction and 13 per cent of the variance in life satisfaction for female workers. Unfortunately, the correlation of life and job satisfaction was not reported.

Taken together, these findings indicate that job and life satisfactions generally are positively correlated. In addition, home and family variables are consistently related to life satisfaction, often to a greater degree than to job satisfaction, particularly for women (Near, 1984). But these conclusions, based on global measures of work, family, and life satisfaction, do not provide any information on the direction of influence, the specific areas of work and family life that are being influenced, or the process through which this influence is being exerted.

Types of Relationships between Work and Family

In what ways does work affect family? And in what ways does family affect work? Several types of relationships have been proposed (Banner, 1974; Kabanoff, 1980; Kando and Summers, 1971; Near, Rice, and Hunt, 1980; Payton-Miyazaki and Brayfield, 1976; Evans and Bartolomé, 1980; Bailyn, 1970).

Payton-Miyazaki and Brayfield (1976) identified six possible relationships between work and family life. These are: *Incompatible*—they are in conflict with each other and cannot be easily reconciled: *Independent*—they exist side by side and are divorced from each other: *Compensation*—one is a way of making up for what is missing from the other: *Instrumental*—one serves as a means to get things desired from life through the other: *Reciprocal*—one affects the other and vice versa in a positive or negative way: *Integrative*—they are so closely fused that it is almost impossible to consider them separately.

Evans and Bartolomé (1984) considered five types of relationships between work and family. In *spillover*, work and family can affect each other in a positive or negative way. For example, satisfaction in work will contribute to family life while dissatisfaction in one will contribute to dissatisfaction in the other. Work and family can also be *independent* of each other such that one can be successful or satisfied in one or the other. If work and family are in *conflict*, satisfaction or success in one will entail sacrifices in the other. Work and family may have an *instrumental* relationship such that, for example, work may be a way of maintaining a satisfying family life, or vice versa. Finally, there is *compensation* when work or family makes up for what is missing in the other.

Evans and Bartolomé (1980, 1984) conducted semi-structured interviews with 44 managers and their wives. Each was asked to describe the current relationship between their work (or their husband's work) and family. Evans and Bartolomé found that each of the five relationships was reported by at least some people, and that individuals used one type of relationship to describe the relationship of work and family in the past and another to describe it in the present. Thus there was no one permanent or single way of describing the relationship between work and family (see also Rousseau, 1978; London, Crandall, and Seals, 1977). Attempts by researchers to resolve the spillover–compensation debate by finding a single model are futile (Kabanoff, 1980; Near, Rice, and Hunt, 1980). The emphasis instead should be placed on understanding the social and psychological factors (e.g. marital status, stage in both life and career cycle) associated with different relationships between work and family.

Evans and Bartolomé also found that, in this sample, work had a much stronger influence on family than vice versa. Family life affected work only in extreme instances of crisis such as divorce. Interestingly, almost all individuals who were dissatisfied with their present distribution of time and energy between work and family felt they were spending too much of themselves in work.

Although several types of relationships between work and family have been proposed and observed, we have little conceptual understanding of how work affects family, and even less of how family affects work. The work of Evans and Bartolomé does make a contribution to the former. They identified two interacting factors which explained the experiencing of different types of work–family relationships. One involved the *emotional outcomes of work*. Managers who had positive feelings about work reported work and family to be either conflicting or independent of each other. Managers reporting mixed feelings about work saw the relationship as negative spillover of work to family. Managers reporting negative feelings about work saw work as instrumental for family. The second involved the *importance of work in the life of the individual*. Managers for whom work was very important reported work–family conflict or spillover of work to family. Managers reporting their work to be moderately important saw work and family as independent. Finally, managers reporting little importance attached to work either saw work as instrumental or saw their family as compensation for disappointments at work. These concepts provide a useful start in understanding changes in the patterns of work–family relationships as individuals develop both careers and family lives. Parker (1967) addresses this area by providing a structural conceptual scheme which emphasizes occupational type and occupational characteristics of the husband and both husband's and wife's roles.

EFFECTS OF WORK ON FAMILY

Despite the belief by organizations that work and family are separate, the structure of work influences family life in several ways. Work operates as a dominant constraint on family life as well as a source of economic and personal sustenance. Kanter (1977) has identified five aspects of the structure of work life that seem most important in shaping and influencing the family. The first is the *relative absorptiveness* of an occupation—the extent to which it draws in and demands performance from the worker and other family members. Some jobs demand the maximum commitment of the worker and define the context for family life. These jobs also tie in other family members and demand formal or informal participation in the work system (e.g. executives and their wives, farm families, owners of small restaurants or retail establishments, teachers, and police in small towns). Other jobs involve little of the person and demand little of their off-the-job life. The second aspect is *time and timing* and refers to the effects of work hours and schedules (daily, monthly, and yearly cycles including the timing of major work events). This includes the amount of time demanded by occupations, which part of the day one works, whether the hours worked intrude upon the time the family can expect to claim, how the hours which workers have available for leisure and family mesh with those of other family members (e.g. shift work); and work which does not permit stable daily rhythms to develop or disrupts daily routines (work involving a great deal of travel). The third aspect is *reward and resources*—the income provided by occupations, both economic and psychological. Income helps determine life style, consumption level, and resources that one can control. Money and prestige are two 'outputs' from work that have exchange value. These variables can influence the level of tension or integration within the family and the relative power of family members. The fourth aspect is *world view*, the cultural dimension of work—the job as a socializer of values. Work can influence child-rearing standards and values, one's orientation toward self and others, tastes, and worthwhile leisure pursuits. The fifth aspect concerns *emotional climate*, the social–psychological dimension of work—the personal experiencing of the world and of self offered by the work environment as a result of one's place in an organizational system. Work can arouse a set of feelings which are brought home and affect the tone and dynamics of family life and include such things as work satisfaction and negative emotional spillover. Some studies have shown that unpleasant, dissatisfaction-producing jobs were related to family tension (Bartolomé and Evans, 1980). Wives of men in personnel whose work involved deep involvement with others reported that their husbands were often distant and insensitive at home, as if they had been 'burned out' at work (Kanter, 1977).

There are considerable research findings illustrating the effects, mostly negative, of work on family. These effects will be examined from the perspective of individual workers, their spouse, and, to a lesser extent, their children. Features of work that have received particular attention include the nature of the work experience itself, the experience of occupational stress, emotional spillover, work schedules and shift work, and the impact of paid employment on the functioning of family roles and on well-being. We will now examine these, and other effects of work on family, in some detail.

Work, Family Competencies, and Family Commitment

The experience of working has been found by some researchers to reduce both the character traits and skills required for effective functioning in the roles of partner and parent, and the value of the family itself (Bartolomé, 1972; Steiner, 1972). Maccoby (1976) examined how capacities required and developed at work influenced the broader personality of the job incumbent. He interviewed 200 successful managers from twelve successful American corporations. They were highly successful in their careers according to income, occupational prestige, power, and responsibility. Respondents indicated how important various character traits were for the effective conduct of their work and named those that were stimulated (strengthened) by their work experiences. Maccoby found that character traits which were rated very important for their work were also stimulated or developed to a higher level by the work experience itself. He categorized these character traits as 'qualities of the head' (e.g. ability to take the initiative, self-confidence, pride in performance, open-mindedness, and flexibility). Among those character traits rated not very important for work and consequently not stimulated or developed by the work were such things as idealism, generosity, compassion, friendliness, a critical attitude toward authority. Maccoby termed these 'qualities of the heart'. On the basis of the overall interview Maccoby also rated each manager on the level of his 'productiveness' in both work and love. In general, Maccoby rated the managers in the sample more productive in the work than in the personal domain. Thus, 80 per cent fell in the 'productive' half of the work scale as opposed to only 45 per cent in the 'productive' half of the love scale.

A further glimpse at ways in which the work experience relates to family activities is offered by Bray and his colleagues (1974). They report the results of a 7-year follow-up of a group of more than 200 MBA graduates that joined A/T and T in the late 1950s and early 1960s. Each of these individuals was interviewed prior to joining the organization and annually thereafter. These clinical interviews were content-analyzed in terms of nine different life themes. Raters were then asked to indicate how important each of these nine life themes appeared to be in each person's interview. The most successful individuals were then contrasted with the least successful individuals. Success was defined using criteria (salary, number of promotions, occupational level after 7 years) that had general external validity. The largest difference between successful and unsuccessful performers was found on the occupational theme. This theme increased in importance for the successful performers and modestly decreased for the unsuccessful performers. Four of the six life themes that involved non-work were rated less important for the successful performers.

According to the authors, 'these results lead to the conclusion that job success holds one to the quite job related themes whereas lack of success permits one, or motivates him, to turn away. Success also militates against outside work themes, whereas lack of success may permit involvement in them or even drive one to them for life satisfaction.' Thus, only organizational 'failures' would be interested in devoting attention on their families, parents and relatives, leisure, recreation and social activities, and spiritual and humanistic pursuits. The authors ignore the possibility that individuals might make these choices on the basis of different value systems.

Finally, individuals in professional and managerial roles are called upon to travel in the conduct of their work and to undertake geographical relocation in the development of their careers. Anecdotal material (Culbert and Renshaw, 1972; Maccoby, 1976; Renshaw, 1975; Seidenberg, 1973; Feinberg, 1980; Greiff and

Munter, 1980) provides examples of negative effects on spouses caused by frequent geographical moves in the pursuit of one's career, and travel in the course of one's corporate duties. The empirical evidence (Brett, 1980) provides only partial support for these observations, however. Thus although job transfer can be classified as a stressful event, and disruptions associated with job transfer have been documented, several myths about the negative effects of job transfer have not been supported.

Type A Behavior and the Family

This line of research has considered the attitudes, values, and behaviors of individuals which propel organizational careers and their off-the-job experiences and satisfactions. Type A behavior, or coronary-prone behavior as it has been generally termed, has already received considerable research attention in this regard. Friedman and Rosenman (1974) present anecdotal information which suggests that Type A individuals, as opposed to their Type B counterparts, invest less time and energy in their families and have less emotionally intimate relationships with their spouses and children. In addition, Type A individuals spend less time in vocational pursuits (hobbies, reading, leisure) and are less able to cultivate and enjoy friendships.

Burke and Weir (1980) investigated the relationship in men of Type A behavior to occupational and life demands, life and marital satisfaction, and social participation measures. The results were that the more Type A the job incumbents, the greater the negative impact of the job on their personal lives, the more negative their marital behaviors, and the less their marital satisfaction.

These results confirmed the expectation that Type As would be living under more stressful circumstances than Type Bs. In spite of greater occupational demands, Type As reported greater occupational self-esteem, more job involvement, and greater organizational identification, thus supporting earlier observations that the Type A identity is heavily invested in the employment role. A similar pattern was evident on the home front and in the non-work life of Type As. They reported that work encroached substantially on their leisure, their home life, and their relationships. They indicated more negative encounters with their spouses in daily living, and had less marital satisfaction. Yet, they did not report worrying more about personal or home conditions, and they reported higher life satisfaction. It appears that the life satisfaction of Type As is highly dependent on a perception of self in the work setting and less so in the non-work setting.

Burke, Weir, and Duwors (1979) investigated the relationship of Type A behavior of 85 correctional administrators to wives' marital satisfaction and well-being. Husbands completed a paper-and-pencil measure of Type A behaviors; their wives independently providing assessments of their satisfaction and well-being. Wives with Type A husbands reported less marital satisfaction, fewer positive marital behaviors, more negative marital behaviors, more negative impact from husband's job on personal, home, and family life, more negative affective states, more psychosomatic symptoms, and less social participation with friends. Thus, wives with Type A husbands experienced less satisfaction, more stress in their lives, and had fewer resources (friends, emotional and psychological support from spouse) to cope with their stresses. A similar pattern of findings was observed when spouses' perceptions of their husbands' Type A behavior were examined (Burke, Weir, and Duwors, 1980b).

In a study of 16 married couples who filled out the JAS (Jenkins Activity Survey) Becker and Byrne (1984) report that husbands' Type A behavior was negatively related to communication frequency, incidence of marital communication, and marital sex. The desire for an increase in the duration of sexual activity was also related to Type A scores. JAS scores were positively associated with amount of time spent working around the home, and with both frequency and total amount of socializing activity, and negatively with enjoyment of social activity.

Husbands' JAS scores were positively related to wives' desire to increase both communication and sexual activity, and desire to socialize more frequently and for longer periods of time. Husbands' Type A scores were negatively related to the amount of total weekly time wives spent relaxing. And, as husbands' JAS scores increased, so did wives' desire to increase both the frequency and duration of relaxation.

Wives' Type A scores were unrelated to spouses' joint reports of communication and sexual activity. Type A scores of wives were positively associated with enjoyment of marital sex, negatively correlated with frequency, duration, and enjoyment of relaxation activities, and negatively related to their enjoyment of social activity. Finally, wives' Type A scores were associated with husbands' preference for a decrease in the frequency and duration of marital communication. And as wives' JAS scores increased, husbands' reported shorter periods of relaxation. In conclusion, these data indicate that Type A characteristics showed a consistent and somewhat negative influence on the daily activities of young married couples. Type As and their spouses spend less time in interpersonal and leisure activities, and report less enjoyment in their time away from work. It also seemed that marital concerns were less important for Type As and Type Bs.

Blaney, Brown, and Blaney (1986) examined the relationship between JAS-defined Type A behavior in upper-middle-class married couples and life stress and marital adjustment. Their results indicated substantially lower adjustment in Type A husband/Type B wife pairs than in the other three combinations. They attribute the poor adjustment of this pairing to the work rather than home and marriage orientation of the Type A husband. When a Type A man, who is likely to be highly career-committed, is married to a Type B woman, who is probably less work- and more home-oriented, the resulting poor fit leads to disillusionment and less marital satisfaction. This may be due to the unwillingness and/or inability of the Type A man to fulfill the marital and parental expectations held by the wife.

Moreover, given the salience of the hostility and anger components of the Type A behavior pattern (Williams et al., 1980), the Type A man may be unable to enter into a close and trusting relationship with a woman who expects this in a marital relationship. In the pairing of the Type A husband/Type A wife, there is greater congruence of values, sharing of goals, and, as a result, better understanding of each other's motivations. Thus, the wife may not hold unrealistic expectations of her husband's behavior, particularly in the non-work area. It is also possible that, being Type A herself, the wife does not, any more than her husband, expect a close, intimate relationship. Instead of expecting intimacy, the partners in a Type A couple may expect (and get) time and support for 'doing their own thing.'

A related study highlighted the importance of considering both marital partners' Type A behaviors in the incidence of coronary heart disease of employed men. Eaker,

Haynes, and Feinleib (1983) reported that the risk of developing coronary heart disease among Type A men, compared with Type B men, was affected by the behavior and social status of their wives. Data were collected as part of the Framingham Heart Study. Between 1965 and 1967, 269 spouse pairs in which the husbands were 45-64 were administered a lengthy psychosocial questionnaire. These pairs were followed over a 10-year period for the development of heart disease. Type A husbands were 2.5 times as likely to develop CHD as Type B husbands if married to women with 13 or more years of education, and had 3.5 times the coronary risk of Type B husbands if married to women employed outside the home. When spouse Type A behavior was considered, the highest rates of coronary heart disease were among Type A men married to Type B women; this rate was over three times the rate for Type B men married to Type B women. They explain their findings in part by postulating that a wife with particular characteristics (high education, working outside the home) may represent a psychologically threatening situation to the husband or a threat to his sense of control. A second possible explanation involved behavioral differences and potential incompatibility between Type A and Type B spouses. It may be psychologically and physiologically taxing for a Type A man (hostile, time urgent, competitive) to live with a woman who is the opposite.

Taken together, these investigations show an interaction between a particular way of behaving in work settings, Type A behavior, and family functioning. Specifically, research has shown that the husband–wife relationship and spousal satisfaction are vulnerable to a spouse's Type A behavior pattern. To the extent that a spouse, male or female, is highly Type A, systematic predictions can be made about the way that person behaves in relationships (Ditto, 1982; Yarnold, Mueser, and Grimm, 1985; Van Egeren, Sniderman, and Roggelin, 1982) and the likely effects of these behaviors on their spouse. Implications of research investigations are that the Type A behavior pattern can almost certainly be identified as a factor leading to marital dissatisfaction. What remain to be determined in future research are the processes and means by which Type A behavior functions as a stressor on the marital relationship.

Occupational Stress and the Family

This line of research has considered the relationship between specific occupational stressors, single or in combination, and family experiences and satisfactions. Thus, Burke and Weir (1981) examined the effects of various occupational stressors on non-work experience and satisfaction. The occupational stressors examined were previously considered in another investigation (Caplan, Cobb, French, Harrison, and Pinneau, 1975) but primarily as they affected work experiences. The non-work areas included marital and life satisfaction, impact of job on personal, family, and home life, negative feeling states, psychosomatic symptoms, and aspects of life style and health behaviors. Data were collected from 127 senior, mainly male administrators of correctional institutions.

The general pattern of findings indicated the existence of a negative impact of occupational stressors on non-work experiences of job incumbents. The negative impact was more pronounced in some areas (marital and life satisfaction, psychosomatic symptoms, number and degree of emotional upset of both work and non-work stressful life events) and less pronounced in other areas (social participation, social support, objective assessments of psychological indicators of stress and physical health). Occupational demands of role conflict and role ambiguity had consistently negative effects.

Burke and his colleagues (1980a) then investigated the relationship of these occupational stressors experienced by administrators and the well-being of their spouses. Data were collected by means of questionnaires completed independently by the husbands and their wives. Husbands provided data on 18 occupational stressors including: role ambiguity, job complexity, underutilization of skills, role conflict, responsibility for people, and hours worked per week. Wives separately provided information on life worries, stressful life events, negative affective states, marital satisfaction, impact of husband's job on personal, home, and family life, social support, social participation, psychosomatic symptoms, and life satisfaction. The results were that, the greater the husband's occupational stressors, the greater the spouse's life concerns, the more negative her feeling states, more negative her marital behaviors, and less her marital satisfaction. Thus, there was a negative relationship between husbands' job demands and spouses' well-being. There was no evidence of the wives' well-being being enhanced as a function of the husbands' demands.

Jackson and Maslach (1982) reported a study of 142 couples illustrating the effects of job stress of family life. Police officers and their wives described family interactions. Officers who were experiencing stress, as measured by the Maslach Burnout Inventory, were more likely to display anger, spend time away from the family, be uninvolved in family matters, and be less satisfied in their marriages.

The empirical evidence clearly indicates that individuals experiencing occupational stress are more likely to report negative family experiences. This also is the case for spouses of job incumbents experiencing greater occupational stress. What have not been identified in this body of research are the processes through which this occurs. One such mechanism is emotional spillover.

Emotional Spillover

Evans and Bartolomé (1980, 1984) reported that nearly half of the male managers and a third of their wives described the effects of work on family as one of spillover. That is, the emotional feelings generated at work spilled over into family life. In almost all cases, spillover went from work to family rather than from family to work. In addition most of the emotional feelings were negative—that is, worries, tensions, and concerns—rather than positive. Evans and Bartolomé use the phrase 'negative emotional spillover' to describe these findings.

Bartolomé and Evans (1980) noted that executives at top organizational levels, whose home lives had deteriorated, were subject to emotional spillover. Work consistently produced negative feelings that overflowed into their private lives. But some executives had learned to manage their work careers so that negative spillover was minimized, and they achieved a balance between their work and home lives. Spillover, in addition, could be positive as well as negative. In their study, work was found to spill over into home life in two ways: through fatigue, and through emotional tension and worry. To have a healthy home life, one must therefore manage negative emotions that arise at work. Among the key ingredients they identified were: adapting well to changes in jobs, finding the right job, and handling career disappointments well.

Piotrkowski (1978) considered if work affected the quality of emotional life in families, and if so, how? To explore this question, she interviewed at least one member of thirteen families, for a total of 30 men, women, and children. Two of these families were also observed at home and at work. Generally, the father–husband was employed in a working-class or lower-middle-class occupation. The concept of a family's emotional life referred not only to family members' thoughts and feelings about themselves and each other, but also to their interpersonal relationships and the processes through which they achieved intimacy, meaning, and identity.

Participants rarely mentioned the extension of positive feelings from workplace to family. It was more common to report the carry over of negative feelings to the family. Even more common were mentions of personal depletion and energy drain (tired, physically and mentally beat). The crucial link was the psychological state generated by the individuals' experience and relationships to their jobs.

Piotrkowski identified three work–family interface patterns, some of which existed simultaneously. These were:

1. *Positive carry over* Job satisfaction or gratification was critical here. Individuals who were job satisfied were also emotionally available (positive energy) and interpersonally available to their family members.
2. *Negative carry over* Stressful feelings at work were carried over into the family system. Other family members extended personal resources in helping the worker manage his strain. Individuals experiencing stress at work were emotionally unavailable and, thus, interpersonally unavailable to their family members at home. Home was seen as a haven for these job incumbents, a place to rest and. recuperate.
3. *Energy deficit* This refers quite simply to not enough psychological or physical energy to engage in family activities.

These studies, and others (Hammond, 1954; Dyer, 1964; McKinley, 1964), suggest that an emotional climate existing within an occupation or an organization can influence family life.

The Power-motivated Man and his Relationship with Women

A handful of studies conducted in the 1970s examined the impact of the need for power in men on their relationships with women. This research is relevant since the need for power is typically pursued and satisfied at work while relationships with the opposite sex occur outside work. McClelland and his colleagues have been engaged for several decades in research on the 'n Power Motive' (McClelland, 1979; Winter, 1973). Men high in n Power tend more often to be officers in organizations, to participate more in contact sports, and to accumulate more prestige possessions than do men low in n Power.

Studies of men have shown that n Power is associated with distorted views of women, exploitation of women, and difficulties in sustaining intimate relationships with them. Slavin (1972) found that college men who scored high in n Power viewed women as harming men by their very contact, exploiting and rejecting men, being unfaithful to men, or triumphing over men. In a study of dating couples, Stewart and Rubin (1976) found that hope of power (the approach element of the motive) was associated with dissatisfaction and anticipation of relatively more problems in the relationship on the part of both partners. Power-oriented men scored lower on scales assessing both their love and their liking of their partners. Couples where the man scored higher on hope for power were more likely to break up, and less likely to marry during the following 2-year period.

Studies of married men have confirmed that n Power continues to affect the marriage relationship in the same sorts of ways. In a study of middle-class and working-class men, McClelland and his colleagues (1972) found that n Power was associated with divorce. In a study of married couples, McClelland and his associates (1976) found that what they termed the 'conquistador' pattern of high n Power, low n affiliation, and low activity inhibition was associated with low ratings of marital satisfaction by both partners and low pair performance on an interpersonal game. Having power over women is therefore an expression of the power-motivated male's generalized tendency to seek impact on another, even at the cost of intimate and enduring sexual relationships. Or, fearing intimacy with a woman, because of feelings of inadequacy, the man high in n Power compensates by pseudo-aggression in the form of dominance over the woman.

Winter, Stewart, and McClelland (1977) examined the relationship of n Power of 51 male college graduates (measured in 1960) and the level of their wives' careers in 1973. The hypothesis they proposed was that n Power in men should be negatively associated with their wives' career level. Power-oriented men should be less likely to tolerate the sharing of power implied in their wives having careers. They might resent the diminished availability of their wives to provide personal service and attention. They would be less flexible and understanding, and less likely to make accommodations. As predicted, husbands' n Power as measured in 1960 was significantly negatively associated with wives' career level in 1973. In addition, wives' career level was significantly negatively associated with husbands' being business executives and husbands' conservative political views. It may be that men high in power in the first place select and marry women with lower career aspirations, perceiving as threatening women with high career aspirations of their own.

Time, Timing, and Shift Work

Time and scheduling conflicts are a major source of work–family conflict. These include the amount of time required by the job, and potential work–family schedule incompatibility. Hours worked on the job cut into hours available for home. Pleck (1979) examined the area of work interference with daily family life and reported that over one third of a national sample of workers experienced at least moderate interference of work with family life. Parents, compared to non-parents, reported significantly more day-to-day interference.

Although '9 to 5' is the usual work-day for the majority of workers, many in fact work at other times of the day and night. Individuals and their families have to adjust to schedules of work that are different from the usual pattern of working during the day time (afternoon, night, rotating schedules of work) (Staines and Pleck, 1984). Shift work must (of necessity) affect the totality of a worker's life as well as that of his family. But most of society's activities are organized as if the usual work pattern was universal. Shift work is a problem because this work pattern is out of synchrony with the time pattern of other workers' activity. Moreover, shift work is atypical because it violates societal norms about time usage.

Staines and Pleck (1986) found, however, that flexibility of work schedule moderated the effects of non-standard work schedules on family life. That is, non-standard work schedules had a less negative association with the quality of family life when accompanied by a high level of schedule flexibility. The buffering effect of flexibility against the negative effects of non-standard work schedules on family life was found to be more pronounced among working women than working men.

Mott, Mann, McLaughlin, and Warwick (1965) provide an excellent review of the effects of shift work on physical health, family relations and social participation, and attitudes and feeling states. Shift work likely influences the time-oriented body functions (particularly sleep, digestion, and elimination). There is also evidence that shift work affects the worker's family relationships, his or her social participation and opportunities for leisure activities.

Mott and his colleagues (1965) examined the physical, social, and psychological consequences of working shifts. Job incumbents worked on day, afternoon, night, and rotating shifts. They found that 66 per cent of rotating shift workers wanted to change shifts, 44 per cent of night shift workers wanted to change shifts, 38 per cent of afternoon shift workers wanted to change shifts, and 6 per cent of day shift workers wanted to change shifts. They also found that men working on the afternoon shift reported the greatest difficulty in being a companion to their wives and diverting her from household duties. Companionship with one's wife and providing diversion and relaxation from her work are typically seen as early evening activities. In addition, workers on the afternoon shift had the most difficulty with the father role, followed by rotating shift and then the night shift. Men working nights had the greatest concerns about sexual activities and protection of their wives. According to Mott and his colleagues (1965), male workers on the day shift, compared with workers on the other shifts, reported the greatest marital happiness and family integration and the least friction. Rotating shift workers had least integration and most strain as well as the least happiness.

The compressed work week (e.g. 10-hour day, 4-day week) offers potentially better use of leisure time for recreation, and for family and personal needs, providing that fringe benefits are provided. Flexible working hours (flexitime) is an alternative work schedule that allows employees certain freedom in choosing their times of arrival and departure at work and is particularly useful to both sexes given the increased participation of men in family life and the goal of an increasing number of young couples to share family responsibilities. Ronen (1984) found six studies with data on the effects of the compressed work week on the home and personal life of workers. Four of these studies reported positive findings (Ronen and Primps, 1981).

Wives' Employment and Husbands' Well-being

Considerable research has documented the significant relationship between wives' employment and their mental health (Warr and Parry, 1982; Kessler and McRae, 1982). At the same time, other research suggests that the mental health of husbands of employed women may be adversely affected (Burke and Weir, 1976; Otherson and Dill, 1983; Rosenfield, 1980). We know a fair amount about why work has positive consequences for wives (Kessler and McRae, 1982); unfortunately, we know little about why having a wife that works has adverse consequences for a husband's mental health.

Two recent studies shed some light on this issue (Kessler and McRae, 1982; Staines, Pottick, and Fudge, 1986). Kessler and McRae (1982) reported findings from a large national survey conducted in the United States which showed a significant positive relationship between spouse's employment and psychological distress among married men. They then examined several possible explanations for these findings. These included taking on new role obligations (e.g. children, housekeeping responsibilities), and loss of status and power associated with the wife's bringing money into the family. None of these explanations accounted for the greater distress of men with working wives.

Staines, Pottick, and Fudge (1986) examined this question by considering specific domains of husbands' lives, in particular work life and family life. Data for their study came from a national sample of 1515 American workers. The analysis was confined to two groups of employed husbands aged under 63: those whose wives worked for pay at least 20 hours a week, and those who wives did not work for pay (housewives). The data, once again, showed that wives' employment had negative association with husband's job and life satisfaction.

They systematically considered four possible psychological costs of wives' employment for husbands. They were: husbands' daily home life was more burdensome, complicated, and interfered with work responsibilities when their wives worked for pay; husbands of working wives were less comfortable with their wives' employment status, and this discomfort got translated into lower job and life satisfaction; husbands of working wives found it difficult to relocate in order to take advantage of job opportunities; and husbands whose wives worked felt less adequate as breadwinners. Only one of these explanations was supported. Husbands of working wives felt less adequate as family breadwinners than did husbands of housewives.

In a similar view, Pleck and Staines (1982) investigated the effects of having an employed spouse on one's own work schedule, the degree of work-family conflict, and the relationship between work schedule and work-family conflict. They expected that having an employed spouse would cause a worker to seek simpler patterns of days and hours, to work fewer hours per week, and to experience more work-family conflict. Their data on the effects of spouses' employment status revealed an asymmetry along gender lines that represented an inequity. That is, within the domains of work schedules and conflict, the only demonstrated effect on working husbands of having an employed wife was the positive one of having an easier work schedule. In contrast, within the same domains, the only effect on working wives of having an employed husband was the negative one of higher levels of schedule conflict. This result is due largely to the societal expectation that is internalized by women themselves that they shoulder the primary responsibility for the home and family. As a result, employed women who are also mothers are seen as adding an additional role (worker) to the roles they have (wife, mother). Men, on the other hand, see themselves as primarily identified with the work rather than the non-work domain and, in contrast to women, are not only permitted but are also often expected to place their work roles ahead of their family ones.

Work and the Experiences of Children

In a chapter entitled 'The children of "God," ' Feinberg (1980) indicated some of the difficulties children of driven high achievers must endure. These included the experience of excessively high standards, an inability to please or be good enough, and stinging criticism. A common reaction of this kind of environment is to try to get back at the father. One tragic symptom of such 'revenge' may be reflected in the frightening growth in the number of teenage suicides. A 1979 report in the *Journal of the American Medical Association* revealed an increase in the rate of suicide among 15–24-year-olds of 124 per cent since 1961, making it the third ranking cause of death in that age group.

Sostek and Sherman (1977) recently published the results of an 8-year study of executives' children which examined their attitudes toward parents and their behavior. The reaction of most of these children to their extremely successful parents and to parental authority was bitter resentment. The self-confidence, achievement orientation, and pride in workmanship of this group was significantly lower than in control groups of children with less affluent or important parents. The biggest complaint of the children of executives was the rigid, non-negotiable demands for compliance with the point of the view of parents who at the same time showed little interest or understanding of the children's views. These children often chose failure rather than aggressive, socially acceptable goal-seeking behavior. According to Sostek and Sherman, over half of the children of upper-middle-class families choose the failure route. Thus, the factors which enable the male executive to achieve financial success at the same time contribute to the development of a non-academic, suffering child with a fear of failure and a low aspiration behavior pattern.

Another outcome may be that few of the children of executives are interested in pursuing the same career as their fathers (Brooks, 1977). In a study of children whose fathers were in top or upper-middle management in a 'Fortune' 500 US corporation, only 15 per cent planned a corporate or business career. At the same time, the children may have been rejecting a particular set of values—those typically held by executives, such as the pursuit of money, status, and power. It is conceivable that high-achieving parents may pursue other goals, including service to others and intellectual accomplishment. Given a greater congruence between the values held by parent and offspring, children should be less likely to reject parents and their values.

Other research (Burke and Weir, 1977a, 1977b) has examined the support mothers, fathers, and peers give to adolescents in dealing with their problems and anxieties. The sample consisted of 273 adolescents ranging in age from 13 to 20, and represented diverse backgrounds. Adolescents were least likely to inform their fathers (as opposed to mothers or peers) about their problems and anxieties, and were least satisfied with the help they received from their fathers. What seemed particularly noteworthy was that fathers were more frequently seen as disinterested, unresponsive, unapproachable, and likely to be embarrassed by the discussion of certain problems. In addition, the adolescents reported being more embarrassed about talking over particular problems with fathers than with mothers and peers. The helping 'style' offered by fathers was seen as one of lecturing their children; trying to influence them with facts, arguments, and logic; ordering or commanding them to do something; and criticizing or blaming them. Fathers were seen as responding in ways which diminished or 'put down' the adolescent and which acted to control or exhibit authority. The relatively poorer performance of the fathers as helpers was not affected very much by father's age, education, and income.

It is interesting that the behavior attributed to fathers in their helping relationships with their adolescents in behavior which is prevalent in most work environments. The work world tends to be characterized by impersonal relationships, and respect is granted on the basis of power, authority, logic, and facts. It is possible that fathers may be attempting to relate to their adolescents and their personal problems in the same way as they relate to coworkers and handle problems at work. The latter type of behavior in a personal life context may do little but set up barriers between fathers and their children.

In her study of work and family in which she conducted interviews and family observations, Piotrkowski (1978) reported that children connected their fathers' jobs to their fathers' bad moods. When unable to do this, children blamed themselves for difficulties with their fathers and they also got angry with them. Three other areas in which work influenced children's reactions were: they connected work (income) and family financial security, they worried about their fathers' physical safety, and father absence negatively affected the process of identification by which young boys acquired their mature masculine identity.

EFFECTS OF FAMILY ON WORK

Kanter (1977) discusses four broad ways in which family patterns may impact on work systems. First in the role of membership in ethnic groups and families which represent certain cultural traditions. In particular ethnic groups, family life may be carried out independently of workplace influences and also seriously affect members' behavior as workers. Second, a family can directly define the operations of a workplace in a family- owned or family-dominated business. Third, Kanter discusses the situation of the 'corporate wife', her impact on her husband's career opportunities, and her possible influences on relationships within the work organization (Whyte, 1963). Fourth, she points out that family situations can define work orientation, motivation, abilities, emotional energy, and the demands people bring to the workplace. Issues such as the demand for childcare can also affect career decisions and the willingness or ability of the worker to travel. Such demands frequently lead to conflict between roles of parent vs. employee. While such conflict is typically found more in female employees than in their male counterparts, men also experience conflict between familial and work roles (Greenhaus and Beutell, 1985).

While acknowledging that family experiences could affect work, Bartolomé and Evans (1980) conclude that work experiences were more likely to affect family. The only times that family life was believed to affect work life involved instances of major career and life decisions. Thus, they state that work affected family on a day-to-day basis. But the reverse was not true; family only affected work in extreme situations. They may reflect the relatively low priority given to children and family life in some industrialized countries (Bronfenbrenner and Crouter, 1982).

Spillover from Family to Work

Crouter (1984) conducted an exploratory field study of the extent to which family effects on work were part of the day-to-day conscious experience of working adults.

semi-structured interviews were conducted with 55 employees from a large manufacturing plant both on the job and at home. The sample included 38 men and 17 women who ranged in age from 21 to 40. Thirty-seven of the 55 individuals reported that their family life had some sort of impact on their work life. Those who reported no effects of family or personal life on work were typically young unmarried men and women without children.

Examples of both positive and negative spillover were provided. Positive spillover involved the supportive nature of one's family and the chance to use skills and attitudes acquired at home in one's work. Negative spillover included inhibiting influences of family on work (e.g. restrictions on travel, shift schedule, and hours that can be worked) and energy and mood (e.g. bring home worries to work, times of crisis). For negative spillover, mothers reported significantly greater difficulties than did fathers. Additional analyses indicated that women with young children at home reported the highest levels of spillover.

Crouter categorized the types of spillover from family to work into two themes: educational spillover and psychological spillover. Educational spillover occurred when the individual learned something at home that could be applied on the job. Educational spillover would be relatively long lasting. Psychological spillover involved family effects on the person's energy, moods, feelings, and concentration while at work. This type of spillover was relatively brief.

Crosby (1984) was interested in understanding what contributed to a satisfying work life. Her research indicated that the best predictor of job satisfaction was a full life outside of work. She found that single people were the least satisfied with their jobs. This pattern existed for both sexes, and for both low-prestige and high-prestige workers. Crosby proposes that multiple roles offer psychological protection to individuals—a proposition consistent with other research findings (Epstein, 1981; Verbrugge, 1982; Barnett, Baruch, and Rivers, 1982). Crosby offers several speculations on why a full home life (and especially parenthood) might make people content with their roles. These include: the happiness of a home with children can block disappointments at work, a full household can also add to positive feelings as well as dissipate negative feelings, and home problems and concerns may serve to put work concerns into perspective.

Crosby (1984) also describes an ongoing research program investigating the effects of divorce on the workplace. She is examining two basic questions. First, what specifically happens in the work life of professional and managerial workers when their home and family life is disrupted? Second, what role does work play in the adjustment of professional and managerial workers to disruptions in their home and family life?

Family Stress and Work Experiences

In the course of daily living, individuals experience a variety of events or life changes which may be potential stressors. This list includes such diverse major events as death of one's spouse, separation and divorce, serious illness of family members, and the assumption of large financial indebtedness. These events often require significant social readjustments and adaptations on the part of the individual undergoing such life experiences (Holmes and Rahe, 1967). No one is immune from these events, although some groups are more likely to report higher incidences of such events (Dohrenwend and Dohrenwend, 1974; Johnson and Sarason, 1979). Interestingly, the events that have been examined include a combination of both work-related and non-work-related events. And although some researchers have attempted to cluster these events into various groupings, few studies have attempted to investigate the differential predictability of one grouping vs. another and various indices of illness behavior.

Holmes and Rahe (1967) were the first to indicate that a cluster of events which required 'change in ongoing life adjustment was significantly associated with time of illness onset'. Others have shown there is also a strong predictive relationship between the incidence of such events and the onset of both psychological distress and physical illness (Dohrenwend and Dohrenwend, 1974). Much of this work has focused on psychiatric disorders, anxiety, and negative feeling states. Few researchers have examined the effects of this personal life stress on performance of individuals in work settings, or on family functioning.

Vicino and Bass (1978) report that life stability, as measured by low life stress scores using a shortened version of Holmes and Rahe's social readjustment scale, was significantly correlated with managerial success and the degree of task challenge reported in a sample of managers. The higher the life stability reported by these managers, the higher their scores on assessment batteries for forecasting job success. Life change scores have also been related negatively with indices of academic performance (Harris, 1972) and with measures of teaching effectiveness (Carranza, 1972).

Bhagat (1980, 1985) has systematically attempted to develop and test a model which links the effects of stressful life events to individual performance effectiveness and work adjustment processes within organizational settings. The model proposes a series of linkages between the experience of stressful life events and the development of personal life stress. Personal life stress in turn leads to three different outcomes for the person: emotional/affective outcomes, cognitive outcomes, and behavioral outcomes. These outcomes then lead to various effects on individual work role behavior (job involvement and internal work motivation, performance effectiveness, job satisfaction, attendance or withdrawal behavior). Several conditioning variables such as coping and adaptation skills, social support, type of organizational control systems, and job or organizational stresses are proposed to mediate the link between the individual outcomes and the work role outcomes.

Sarason and Johnson (1979), in research conducted in organizational settings, found that negative personal life changes were significantly related to lower levels of satisfaction with supervision, pay, and the work itself, while positive life changes were only related to satisfaction with promotional opportunities.

In a similar vein, Bhagat, McQuaid, Lindholm, and Segovis (1985) examined the effects of work, personal, and total life stress (a combination of work and personal stress) on a range of work outcomes. The latter included job satisfaction, organizational commitment, absenteeism, and turnover intentions. There was a significant relationship between negative personal life stress and the organizational outcomes. The authors concluded that individuals do not separate their personal lives from their job lives, and there was a spillover of the effects of non-work stress on organizational outcomes.

The Family as a Support System

Several writers (Kahn and Antonucci, 1980; Cobb, 1976; Payne, 1980) have proposed that individuals cope better with work and family demands if they are well supported by the people around them. Social support was conceptualized by Kahn and Antonucci (1980) as interpersonal transactions that include one or more of the following key elements: affect, affirmation, and aid. They define affect as the expression of liking, admiration, respect, or love; affirmation as an expression of agreement or acknowledgement that another person was right in what he or she said or did; and aid as the giving of assistance such as money, time, labor, and information. Caplan and his associates (1975) identified two types of social support. The first consisted of tangible help (e.g. medical or financial), and the second consisted of emotional support (e.g. love, affection, sympathy, friendship).

The most complete attempt to conceptualize the role of the family as a social support was made by Caplan (1976). He identified the following support system functions of the family: (1) the family as a collector and disseminator of information about the world, (2) the family as a feedback guidance system, (3) the family as a source of ideology, (4) the family as a guide and mediator in problem solving, (5) the family as a source of practical service and concrete aid, (6) the family as a haven for rest and recuperation, (7) the family as a reference and control group, and (8) the family as a contributor to emotional mastery.

Burke and Weir (1977c) studied the mental hygiene function of marriage, the latent contribution one spouse made to the mental health of the other. They found that the strongest effects were evidenced when spouse helping was treated as a moderating variable between measures of experienced stress and well-being. Only modest support was indicated for preventative or therapeutic effects of spouse helping. The preventive effect was problematic, possibly because many life events were not controllable. Certainly stressors originating at work were not directly preventable by the spouse of the person who was working in that environment.

The findings of this study also showed that the greater the job stress experienced by husbands, the more likely they were to disclose their problems and tensions to their wives, but the less satisfied they appeared to be with their wives' help. The greater the job stress experienced by wives, the more likely they were to describe their husbands as active helpers. However, they did not perceive themselves as very helpful to their husbands.

Burke and Weir (1975, 1977c) also suggest that wives more easily recognize than husbands the emotional state of their spouses and respond more readily as helpers to their spouses than husbands to their wives. This may be due to social norms of femininity which prescribe that women be the emotional mainstay of the family (regardless of other roles they may occupy), nurturant and helpful at the same time. Additionally, feminine, compared to masculine, socialization places greater emphasis on the development of interdependence, the ability to express interpersonal needs, particularly in emotional relationships, and to relate meaningfully to others in interpersonal relationships (Greenglass, 1982). So important are these behavioral norms to a woman's self-esteem, that women have been found to feel that they 'ought to be able to cope' with problems that arise in the family, including problems with their husband (Stewart and Salt, 1981).

But what are the effects on the woman when she and family members alike perceive her in this helping role with all its attendant expectations? Research data suggest that while men may benefit from the support provided by their wives, giving emotional support may function as a source of strain for women, particularly for those simultaneously pursuing a demanding career. For example, in a study of dual-career couples, Heckman, Bryson, and Bryson (1977) found that one source of stress for wives derived from the disproportionate amount of time and emotional effort devoted to supporting their husband's career need vs. their own. However, when emotional support for wives' career pursuits was evident, pressures from role conflict seemed to be attenuated. For example, research findings have indicated that good relations and emotional support from families were highly negatively correlated with the experience of physical, emotional, and mental exhaustion (Pines and Kafry, 1981).

As expected, employed wives, compared to housewives, are less likely to provide emotional support for their hubands. Focusing on the husband's self-report, one study found that husbands of employed wives, when compared to those married to full-time housewives, had lower marital satisfaction, greater job pressure, and poorer mental and physical health (Burke and Weir, 1976). Moreover, when a wife holds outside employment herself, she may be less responsive to her husband's needs, as suggested in a study which found that husbands whose wives were employed were less satisfied with their wives as confidantes than those whose wives were full-time housewives (Burke and Weir, 1977c). As suggested above, because of their own pressures, employed wives (particularly those involved in demanding careers) may be unable to provide the same level of emotional support for their husbands as full-time housewives. Not only is the employed wife less likely to cater for her husband's needs in this respect, but she may even turn to her husband for support and encouragement in *her* employment role.

In summary, there is some evidence (Piotrkowski, 1978; Bronfenbrenner and Crouter, 1982) that families served a social support function for individuals at work. But other studies have produced inconclusive evidence about the role of the family as a source of social support for workers. For example, House (1981) and his colleagues studied the effects of social support on work stress, health, and the relationship between the two among male hourly workers in a manufacturing plant. They found that work-related sources of support reduced work stress and indirectly improved health but non-work sources of support (wife and friends) had little or no effect on work stress and health. More research is required to determine the conditions associated with the family functioning effectively as a social support system for its members.

Work and Career Decision Making

There are many factors that influence whether or not a women decides to take a job. These include: personal characteristics, attitudinal factors, and family circumstances. In many cases, family factors (e.g. financial need) may cause a married woman with children to obtain a job. Thus, the decision of a married woman to work is often an economic decision. In the case of married women, the decision to work may also be a function of the relationship of husband and wife. That is, the husband's attitude toward his wife's working is very important (Winter, Stewart, and McClelland, 1977; Farmer and Bohn, 1970). In addition, other family factors such as the number and ages of children, the need for availability of childcare, and the mobility of the wife influence this decision. Decreasing family size has been discussed as both a cause and an effect of women's employment (Greenglass, 1982).

Women's family roles also affect their labor force attachment with many exhibiting an intermittent work pattern. This involves career interruption and combinations of work and family cycles (Waite, 1980). Age at marriage and childbearing influence women's labor force participation over time (Lopata and Norr, 1980). Early marriage and childbearing increase the likelihood of limited work experience. Decisions to take part-time work are also heavily influenced by women's family roles. Moreover, the lack of good childcare facilities generally is another obstacle to women's greater participation in the labor force (Kanter, 1977).

The recent General Mills (1981) survey of workers reported that at least two-thirds of the sample considered family factors important in making decisions about hours worked (overtime, full-time, or part-time), distance to commute, accepting promotions, on-the-job travel, relocation. More women thought these factors important than men.

Family roles have also been found to be important factors in workplace lateness and absenteeism. Steers and Rhodes (1978) conclude that women are absent more frequently than men due to women assuming the traditional family responsibilities assigned to them. The family has also been given as one of the major reasons for employees refusing job transfers (Brett, 1980). The transfer is turned down because it would interfere with the career development of one's spouse (Costello, 1974).

ROLE CONFLICT

While there is increasing recognition that one's work life cannot be understood outside the context of the family, research has tended to treat the two domains quite separately. But because, increasingly, women and men are occupying both roles simultaneously, it is important to examine its psychological implications. One of the most salient of these is role conflict. Kahn and his colleagues (1964) define role conflict as the 'simultaneous occurrence of two (or more) sets of pressures such that compliance with one would make more difficult compliance with the other' (p. 19). While role conflict may be found in either work or family domains, to date research has tended to focus mainly on work to the relative exclusion of role conflict in the family. Another kind of role conflict identified by these authors is interrole conflict, where the role pressures associated with membership of one organization are in conflict with pressures stemming from other group memberships. So, for example, pressures to spend long hours at the office may conflict with demands or expectations from family members to spend time at home. Role conflict can occur at work, within the family, and between work and family roles.

Kopelman, Greenhaus, and Connolly (1983) provide a theoretical model for describing the relationship between role conflicts at work, in the family, and between the two, as well as satisfaction at home, at work, and with life in general. They define *work conflict* as the extent to which an individual experiences incompatible role pressures within the work domain, and *family conflict* as the extent to which incompatible role pressures are experienced within the family. For both types of conflict, the model postulates that incompatibility may arise from multiple role senders, one role sender, or a lack of fit between the focal person and role requirements. The model also includes *interrole conflict*, which is described as the extent to which a person experiences pressures within one role that are incompatible with pressures from another role. In two studies which tested the theoretical model, Kopelman and his colleagues (1982, 1983) report strong links between domain conflict and domain satisfaction (e.g. work conflict and job satisfaction), and between domain satisfaction and life satisfaction. The investigators, however, failed to find a significant relationship between interrole conflict and domain satisfaction. This may be due to the operation of unmeasured, mediating variables, namely coping strategies, given that previous research has found a significant relationship between effective coping with interrole conflict, and role and life satisfaction.

Another theoretical model of role conflict (Greenhaus and Beutell, 1985) suggests that pressures from work or family can heighten conflict between work and family roles. Greenhaus and Beutell (1985) identified three ways that role pressures can be incompatible: (1) time spent in one role may leave little time to devote to other roles, (2) strain within one role domain may 'spillover' into another one, and (3) behavior appropriate to one role domain may be dysfunctional in another, i.e. shifting gears from work to family. Thus, variables that have an impact on time, strain, or behavior can heighten work–family conflict. The model proposes that any role characteristic that affects a person's time involvement, strain, or behavior within a role can produce conflict between that role and another role.

The model provides a useful integration of empirical research on work–family conflicts, their sources, and consequences. An important assumption associated with this model is that simultaneous pressures from both work and family roles are necessary to arouse conflict between work and non-work areas. While this may seem obvious, existing research has typically examined the impact of either work pressures *or* family pressures on work–family conflict. The interactive effect of work and family pressures is seen, for example, in the case of the female manager who is required to put in long hours at the office. She would not experience work–family conflict if, at the same time, she did not also perceive her children's expectations to spend time with them.

On the negative side, the model does not allow us to disentangle the sources of conflict within the employment domain. For example, time-based and strain-based conflict share several common sources within the work domain, i.e. a lot of time involvement at work can produce strain-based conflict. And secondly, if coping resources are poor, the result may be poor coping with all three types of conflict. Nevertheless, empirical studies using the model are being conducted. For example, Beutell (1986), in a sample of 115 married couples with children, reported that the best predictor of conflict involving the work role was the wife's employment status, with women highly involved in their employment experiencing more conflict with home maintenance and parental roles. These findings are consistent with the notion that time-based conflict is the most prevalent type of work–family conflict.

Sources of Role Conflict

Hall (1972) suggested that conflicts arise in married women because of multiple roles (interrole conflict) rather than within a given role (intrarole conflict). So far, research has used a global measure of work–family incompatibility or treated the family in general terms without acknowledging that the family domain consists of a number of distinct roles such as spouse, parent, and maintainer at the home. Therefore, it is surprising that so little research has studied the sources of conflict between work and specific family roles (i.e. parent vs. employee). Since each role that a person enacts differs with regard to role perceptions, role expectations, role behaviors, a conflict between the roles of employee and parent would have different antecedents from a conflict between employee and home maintenance roles. And, since role behaviors are almost inevitably affected by gender, antecedents of conflict between specific roles would vary according to the person's sex.

Holahan and Gilbert (1979), in one of the few studies of its kind, investigated sex differences in specific pairs of work and family roles and their relationship to attitudinal, self-concept, and satisfaction variables. Focusing directly on relevant life roles (Professional, Spouse, Parent, and Self as Self-actualized Person) rather than on time demands, Holahan and Gilbert constructed six scales to measure potential role conflict in those areas represented by specific pairs of those roles (e.g. Professional vs. Parent). In a study of 28 dual-career couples, Holahan and Gilbert (1979) investigated the relationship between being a parent and various role conflicts. They report that the area of Professional vs. Self was associated with the highest conflict for the non-parent and parent groups alike, with conflict in the areas of Professional vs. Parent, and Self vs. Parent, as equally conflict-related for the parent group, as was Professional vs. Self. Thus, the addition of the parent role provides additional conflict to each of the roles in the area of most conflict, namely Professional vs. Self.

Pleck, Staines, and Lang (1980), in an analysis of the 1977 Quality of Employment Survey data, report that 34 per cent of the men believed that their job and family lives interfered with each other. Greenhaus and Kopelman (1981) studied 229 male alumni of an eastern US technical college. Subjects were employed in technical, administrative, and marketing positions as well as being self-employed. Using responses to open-ended items, Greenhaus and Kopelman report that approximately one half of the sample experienced interrole conflict. They found that conflict between one's work and family was positively related to work-role salience. While the wife's employment status had no effect on conflict, men whose wives were employed in managerial/professional positions experienced significantly more intense work–family conflict than men whose wives were employed in non-managerial/non-professional positions. Further results indicated that incidence of work–family conflict was higher when all children were preschoolers rather than when children were older. As expected, men who placed a lot of importance on work and men whose children were young and living at home were the most likely to experience work–family conflict. Expectations from the man's family including his young children may be incompatible with work-role demands. The finding that men whose wives were employed in managerial/professional positions experienced more intense conflict suggests that the work involvement of women in high-level positions places demands on husbands to participate more actively in home and family roles, thereby generating more role conflict for the man.

Another factor that has been found to relate significantly to role conflict is that of career commitment. Individuals who place high priority on their careers may invest more time and energy in their work role, expect more of themselves, and undertake more challenging assignments than those who are less career-committed. Holahan and Gilbert (1979) demonstrated that career aspirations were positively correlated with role conflict for females in dual-career couples but negatively correlated with role conflict in males. A normative explanation of these findings suggests that men with high career aspirations, in placing such high priority on their career, are behaving in a way congruent with societal norms for the masculine role. Thus, career-committed men would experience little role conflict. On the other hand, women in a dual-career couple who are highly career-committed, are going against societal expectations for women by adding a non-traditional role, thus heightening their role conflict. They found that when husband's career salience was high, and there were children present in the home, working women experienced greater role conflict than when their husband's career salience was low. They also report that when the work role was of equally high importance to both husband and wife, role conflict was low relative to those couples with disparate work salience. The authors argue that highly career-committed couples may have worked out a system of mutual understanding and accommodation.

Role conflict may be exacerbated by other factors, including certain personality characteristics. For example, research has shown that role conflict correlates positively with Type A behavior (Eberhardt and Eberhardt, 1983). The explanation of these results can be found in the Type As high expectations—expectations which include greater pressures to perform on the job and greater pressures to meet the demands of spousal and parental roles. This, in turn, likely leads to greater role conflict.

Coping with Role Conflict

Not surprisingly, individuals generally try to reduce role conflict since it is a negative experience (Kahn *et al.*, 1964). Given the three levels of the role process described by Levinson (1959)—structurally imposed demands, personal role conception, and role behavior—Hall (1972) has logically derived coping mechanisms which intervene in the role process at each level. These are: structural role redefinition, personal role redefinition, and reactive role behavior. Structural role redefinition (Type I) is a strategy which involves actively attempting to alter the incoming demands by reducing, reallocating, and rescheduling. This process involves coping in the strict sense of the term as opposed to defence, which involves altering one's feelings or perception in response to a situation. An example of structural role redefinition would be a person who works out an agreement with her employer that she be allowed to stay at home on days when her children are ill. She agrees to make up her lost time by working late on certain days.

The second type of coping involves changing one's personal concept of the role demands made by others and is termed personal role redefinition (Type II). An example of this process would be to set priorities among and within roles, being certain that priority demands are met (i.e. caring for a sick child) while others have lower priority (i.e. entertaining one's husband's clients). The third type of coping (Type III) is reactive role behavior which entails improving the quality of role performance so that one can better satisfy all of the demands of one's role senders. Implicit in this strategy is the assumption that one's role demands are unchangeable and that one's task is to find ways to meet them.

Hall (1972) tested his model with a sample of 170 married women. In addition to identifying the coping strategies used by these women, Hall also examined the effectivess of the strategies by relating them to a measure of satisfaction with their roles in life. Since many people used more than one type of coping, Hall examined the relationship of a mix of coping types to satisfaction. He found the strongest relationship between coping and satisfaction for the combination of the presence of Type I and the absence of Type III coping. That is, the most effective coping pattern would appear to involve actively altering incoming demands while at the same time not actively changing one's role performance. Moreover, Hall (1972) found that women who used Type I and Type II coping strategies were more satisfied with the way they handled their life roles than women who relied on Type III coping.

In a study of female doctors, lawyers, and professors, Gray (1983) examined use of various coping strategies and how each related to personal satisfaction with life roles. In general, the results showed that professional women used Type I coping strategies more often, Type II strategies next, and Type III least often. Specifically, over 80 per cent of the people reported receiving help from role senders in order to meet role demands, eliminating certain activities within roles, and hiring outside help. They were found to use many of the Type II strategies, including reducing standards somewhat within certain roles, rotating attention among roles depending on which need was most pressing, and developing new attitudes to reduce conflicts. The women in this sample derived more satisfaction from their life roles when they utilized Type I and Type II coping strategies. In this regard, the most effective strategy was having family members share in household tasks.

In a direct test of Hall's coping model, Beutell and Greenhaus (1983) examined role conflict between home and non-home roles in 115 married female students with at least one child. They found that role conflict intensity was related to Type III coping only among women with relatively traditional attitudes—a finding consistent with that Frieze, Parsons, Johnson, Ruble, and Zellman (1978) who stated that rigid sex role attitudes may be related to the development of inflexible coping techiques. In finding that Type I and Type II coping strategies were seen as more successful than Type III strategies, the authors suggest that trying to be a 'supermother' is not likely to be effective as a coping technique.

Studies of coping with role conflict have tended to focus primarily on married women. While, in general, it is true that married women experience role conflict more than their male counterparts, there is a need for more empirical investigations of coping in men—both married men and male single parents. Also, it is worth noting that the correlational design typically employed in studies on coping does not permit intferences regarding causal relationships. Longitudinal studies are thus needed on the correlates and effectiveness of various coping strategies, and particularly how they are affected by the type of interrole conflict experienced.

Role Conflict and Multiple Roles

It should be pointed out, however, that experiencing multiple roles simultaneously does not necessarily lead to negative psychological consequences. For example, Thoits (1983) has reported that, regardless of gender, occupancy of up to seven roles was positively associated with mental health. In another study, higher levels of self-esteem were found among women who occupied the three roles of wife, mother, and employee than among women with fewer roles (Barnett and Baruch, 1985). The latter study showed that there was no increase in reported stress associated with a greater number of roles, and the more roles a woman occupied, the more sources of pleasure she reported in her life. The more roles one has, the more potential sources of self-esteem, stimulation, privileges, social status, and social identity (Thoits, 1983). However, as Baruch, Biener, and Barnett (1985) argue, it is likely that involvement in multiple roles is most beneficial to women when the role set includes that of paid worker. In fact, the presumed overemphasis on jobs as a source of stress (as concluded from research primarily on men) has obscured the benefits of employment for women, involving greater physical and mental health (Kessler and McRae, 1982).

THE DUAL-CAREER COUPLE

The two-career couple presents a particularly interesting and vivid juxtaposition of work and family. The notion of tradeoffs (Greiff and Munter, 1980) becomes particularly important when both partners are pursuing careers. The assumption is that people have a fixed amount of time and energy to allocate to their various roles. As Hall and Hall (1980) point out, the more a person invests in and identifies with his or her career role, the less time and energy there is to invest in the roles of parent, partner, or keeper of the house. Critical to the two-career couple is the fact that there is no longer a full-time parent, spouse, and homemaker.

There has been little theory and empirical work devoted to the dual-career couple (Gupta and Jenkins, 1985). Hall and Hall (1979) developed a typology of dual-career couples with specific reference to role conflict, role overload, work–family integration, and stress. Members of a dual-career couple were classified on the basis of ego involvement in work and family roles. Four dual-career types were noted. *Accommodators* had one member high on work involvement and low on family involvement while the other member was low on work involvement and high on family involvement. *Adversaries* had both members high on work involvement and low on family involvement (but with a high value for a well-ordered home). *Allies* had both individuals low on work involvement and high on family involvement or both high on work involvement and low on family involvement (like the Adversaries, but with a low alue on a well-ordered home). *Acrobats* were both highly involved with work *and* family.

Hall and Hall hypothesize that the greatest stress would be experienced by Acrobats. This is because there are several role demands placed on them as they attempt to have successful careers, be good parents, run a well-ordered home, and provide support for their spouses. Role overload would be their greatest source of stress, with little extra energy available for coping with unpredictable events. The next highest stress level would be experienced by Adversaries. This couple is competing over priorities. Both want their career to come first, and both place low priority on the home, family, and partner support roles. Despite this, it is important for them to have a well-ordered home. Role conflict would be high, and both partners experience high career demands resulting in stress. Allies, would experience the next highest level of stress. Both individuals share the same work and home orientation and would experience less role overload as a result. But Allies having high work involvement and low family involvement may experience stress due to lack of time for their relationship and may have less predictability because of career demands, work overload, and frequent work-related changes. Accommodators would experience the least stress. They have compatible complementary career and family orientations resulting in low role conflict and role overload coupled with high predictability and control.

Hall and Hall (1980) indicate that stress among dual-career couples is caused by overload, conflict, and change. Overload arises from demands and pressures as a result of the number of roles played by the couple. Conflict results from conflicting demands, such as a scheduled business trip conflicting with a spouse's birthday, or from the problems of meshing careers of two people, for instance scheduling vacations together. Another example of conflict results from unmet expectations or the feeling that one person is not living up to the standards the couple has set for itself. Change itself is a source of stress, in that the couple must constantly adapt and respond to transitions in their work, personal, and family lives.

Rapoport and Rapoport (1976) identified various problems or dilemmas for dual-career couples: overload, normative, identity, social network, and role-cycling. Overload dilemmas resulted from lack of time and energy when heavy scheduling demands prevented day-to-day domestic chores from being done. Normative dilemmas resulted from disparities between personal norms of the dual-career couple and general societal norms. Identity dilemmas resulted from 'discontinuities between internalized early experiences and current wishes' (Rapoport and Rapoport, 1976, p. 310). Social network dilemmas resulted from problems dual-career couples had in maintaining relationships outside their immediate family. They had limitations on the time available for interacting with friends because of overload dilemmas. Role-cycling dilemmas refer to attempts by the dual-career couple to integrate their different individual career cycles with the cycle of their family. Each of the above created stress for dual-career couples.

In addition, when both individuals are pursuing careers and raising children, certain inequities may arise. These inequities, in turn, may lead to stress in the woman, the man, or both. One of the most salient of these inequities involves how time for home and work activities is divided between the members of the couple.

Division of Time Among Dual-Career Couples

Research shows that employed wives and husbands do not share household activities (Berk and Berk, 1978; Pleck, 1977; Bryson and Bryson, 1978). In an intensive study of organization of the household day among a cross-section of urban families, Berk and Berk (1979) found that in two-thirds of the wife-employed families studied, husbands contributed no more to after-dinner chores than husbands of non-employed wives. Moreover, home responsibilities and family factors affect the jobs women take, the satisfactions they receive from their work, their salary, and many job-related behaviors.

Because employed women, more than their husbands, are likely to maintain primary responsibility for the home, they may be more vulnerable to 'weekend stress syndrome'. This syndrome is characterized by tension, irritability, and occasionally physical malaise (Szinovacz, 1978). It is more easily recognized by its periodicity — symptoms peak every Monday, Friday, and Saturday, diminish on Sunday, and are hardly noticeable from Tuesday through Thursday. The syndrome presumably stems from the woman's knowledge that she actually holds not one but two jobs—breadwinner and housekeeper. 'Blue Monday' comes about because of the anxious feelings most people, regardless of sex, experience when anticipating another hard week at the work place. But, whereas men cheer up as the weekend approaches, employed women become tense because they feel they have to catch up on all the childcare and housework they put off during the week. Moreover, research shows that although the number of husbands participating in housework increased between 1960 and 1980, there is little evidence that household tasks are being shared equally when the wife is employed. Husbands generally contribute almost the same amount of time to family tasks whether their wives are employed or not (Meissner, Humphreys, Meiss, and Scheu, 1975; Robinson, Juster, and Stafford, 1976).

It may be that husbands, while accepting their wives' employment grudgingly, have more trouble than their wives in enacting non-stereotypical roles (which include doing housework). There are some who argue that the increase in employment among married women has been accompanied by an increase in an egalitarian pattern in which husbands increase their participating in the home and assume some of the domestic and childcare responsibilities which customarily fall exclusively on the wife (Rapoport and Rapoport, 1969; Garland, 1972). Or, as Young and Willmott (1973) put it, the family becoming more symmetrical, i.e. evolving toward a pattern in which each marital partner has a significant role in both paid and family work. But research findings generally do not support the new egalitarian pattern, rather they support the traditional and conventional one. For example, Pleck (1978) found that family tasks were strongly segregated by sex and that husbands' time in family tasks did not vary in response to changes in wives' family work that result from wives' paid employment. Gender accounts for more of the variance in an individual's time in family work than does his or her employment status. Weingarten (1978) confirmed this in a study which found that couples negotiated a division of labor that allowed women to compensate for the time they spent away from the family and that allowed men to choose the family work that was less threatening to their masculine selves.

Yogev (1981) studied marital dynamics of 106 married faculty women at a large American university where she focused on the wives' perception of time spent on housework, childcare, and career by their spouses and themselves. Results showed that all women estimated that their husbands devoted more weekly hours to their careers than did the wives. Husbands were also reported to spend less time engaged in housework and childcare. Despite these discrepancies in time spent working in the home, only a few women felt that their husbands were not doing enough in the home. The research clearly indicates that wives did not expect an egalitarian pattern where husbands do half of the housework and childcare chores. These results are congruent with findings by Rice (1979) who notes that women in dual-career families do more housework than their husbands but at the same time they do not complain. Additional findings in this study indicated that the wives perceived their husbands in a way that assumed egalitarian relationships, i.e. they did not perceive their husbands to be 'superior' to them; rather they perceived themselves to be basically equal to their husbands. But, at the same time, these women were adhering to a traditional model in that they assumed most of the responsibilities for housework and childcare. These women were undergoing role expansion which allowed them to expand their horizons and roles while not abandoning traditional functions and obligations.

The present expansion may be only the first step in preparation for a role definition which will involve a complete egalitarian marital relationship, i.e. equality in sharing housework and childcare as well as in the perception of each other. In a study of 164 faculty women's estimation of the time spent on their professions, housework, and childcare, Yogev (1982) found that, even though they were working over 107 hours per week, these women did not feel overloaded. Professional women with children would appear to have very high standards about combining career and family. They seem to feel that they can and should be able to be successful in their career, be feminine, be good mothers, and have happy marriages, all without feeling overworked. But perceiving a problem is a necessary prerequisite for change. If people are not aware and/or do not admit they are overworked, they will not attempt to alleviate this pressure which will inevitably affect their health adversely.

The problem of role overload worsens in the relatively small contingent of families in which the woman is raising a family and simultaneously occupying a career role which demands a high level of commitment. Although she is more likely than her less affluent counterpart to be able to afford outside help with housework, nevertheless, she and her husband will likely have high achievement aspirations for both their marriage and their children's psychological development. Since normative expectations disproportionately place the responsibility for children's psychological development on the mother, these pressures will be felt more by the woman involved in a demanding career than the man (Johnson and Johnson, 1976). Moreover, previous research on dual-career families indicates that conflicts between professional and parental roles are especially stressful for the female spouse (Bryson and Bryson, 1978; Heckman et al., 1977; Holahan and Gilbert, 1979).

The problem of role overload and its physical effects on women is illustrated very well in a study, this time on clerical workers. In their analysis of the findings over a 9-year period, Haynes and Feinleib (1982) found that while employment per se, even in a clerical job, was not an additional risk factor in the development of coronary heart disease in women, certain role combinations increased the risk. For clerical workers who had three or more children or were married to blue-collar workers, there was a two- or three-fold increase in risk. For such women, the authors suggest, family roles entail especially heavy responsibilities since blue-collar husbands are assumed to be even more reluctant to share in family work. Thus, this study illustrates how work roles may interact with family roles in increasing the effects of stress in one role.

The primary conclusion drawn by Hall and Hall (1980) is that the stresses of dual-career couples can be reduced when either their relationship or their careers become more protean. They define a protean relationship as one where the couple invent their own flexible way of managing their lives together, rather than responding to societal norms about how they should live. Similarly, a protean career stresses autonomy and self-fulfillment. The individual takes charge of his/her own career and redirects it as needed rather than depending on an organization's career paths and timetables. The aim for the couple is to increase flexibility in their time so they can respond appropriately when unexpected changes occur in work or home activities.

TOWARD A NEW RESEARCH PARADIGM

Tables 9.1 and 9.2 summarize critical factors which need to be studied when examining work and family interactions (Burke, 1986). Table 9.1 identifies critical factors at work that impact on the family system. These factors have been broken into two types: objective and subjective. The objective factors are structural variables of the job which are amenable to measurement and quantification (e.g. hours of work, level of responsibility). The subjective factors are attitudes and behaviors of people and measurement generally requires an assessment of the individual's subjective perception of the factor (e.g. level of job satisfaction, climate of the job, amount of social support). The right-hand column in Table 9.1 identifies critical outcome variables in the family that need to be looked at in understanding the impact of the job on the family. These dependent variables have also to be broken into objective and subjective. Table 9.2 looks at the reverse interaction, the impact of critical factors in the family on the person in his or her occupational setting. Thus, both objective and subjective factors in the family and outcome measures at work are identified and categorized.

While calling for more research in this area based on the taxonomy of variables represented in Table 9.1 and 9.2, we need to go beyond research based on the traditional model of dependent and independent variables. While causality is important to understand, we also need to pursue notions inherent in systems approaches to work and family (Culbert and Renshaw, 1972). The first step in this direction has been taken in that research on work and family in breaking down the traditional closed system boundaries and looking at the relevant interactions. The myth of separate worlds is being destroyed and open systems thinking is replacing it (Piotrkowski, 1978).

We also need to move beyond the doctrines of reductionism and mechanism (Ackoff, 1974) in which scientific phenomena are reduced to their smallest parts and analysis is based only on the fundamental relationship of cause and effect. Renshaw (1975) has taken an important step in this direction. She has stated that pressures in the two systems, work and family, are cumulative and that stress in one system is not caused by events in the other system. Stress is rather a function of the interactive nature of the relationship. Thus, she recognizes the whole and looks at the problem from a higher level of systems analysis. Approaches such as stressful life events research by Holmes and Rahe (1967) and Dorhenwend and Dohrenwend (1974) may be a useful beginning in this direction but this research has only begun to look at the specific interaction between work and family factors (Bhagat, 1985). Another important beginning has been made by Paradine and his colleagues (1981) who have shown that job stress and off-the-job stress combine in a multiplicative fashion to produce worker strain (job dissatisfaction and depressed mood).

In addition, family processes can usefully be thought of using a cybernetic-like or systems model. Kantor and Lehr (1975, p. 10) define family as organizational complex, open, adaptive, and information processing.' Critical to this analysis is the understanding that families are open systems which manifest a great deal of two-directional interchange with the larger environment.

INNOVATIVE METHODOLOGIES IN THE STUDY OF WORK AND FAMILY

Lee (1984) has developed and applied an interesting methodology for representing overall patterns of structuring daily life. This involves the study of actual behavior

TABLE 9.1 — Work Impact on the Family

	CRITICAL FACTORS AT WORK (INDEPENDENT VARIABLES)	OUTCOME MEASURES IN THE FAMILY (DEPENDENT VARIABLES)
OBJECTIVE	Travel — length of time, frequency, distance Transfer — frequency, location Promotion, demotion Physical conditions Work hours and schedules Rewards and resources, pay Level of responsibility — number supervised Stage in career cycle	Use of psychiatrists/psychologists Use of drugs, alcohol Amount of time in joint family activities Health, psychosomatic symptoms Attendance at religious services Number of friends and social activities Amount of leisure time Success of children in school Number of arguments Number of stressful life events
SUBJECTIVE	Satisfaction with job Nature of job, e.g. routineness, isolation Amount of social support Amount of job security Relative absorptiveness, e.g. extent to which other family members are drawn in Turnover intentions Cultural dimension of the job and impact of personal values Climate of the job Amount of role ambiguity, job complexity, role conflict Degree of quality pressures	Wife and children's satisfaction with life Marital satisfaction Community satisfaction Peer relations of children Quality of family relationships Perceived spillover of negative emotions, e.g. fatigue, worry Amount of discussion of job-related issues Perceived stress

TABLE 9.2— Family Impact on Work

	CRITICAL FACTORS IN FAMILY (INDEPENDENT VARIABLES)	OUTCOME MEASURES AT WORK (DEPENDENT VARIABLES)
OBJECTIVE	Financial need Wife's career position Social background and class Number of children/dependents Recency of critical events, e.g. death in family, divorce, separation Quality of neighborhood Existence of child care facilities Ethnic background and traditions Family connection — social Type of marriage/family Stage in family life cycle	Absenteeism Number of rejections of promotion, transfer Level in hierarchy Performance and potential ratings
SUBJECTIVE	Degree of marital harmony/satisfaction Wife's career aspirations Degree of complementarity or conflict in couple's expectations, values and commitment to the job Wife's personal beliefs and attitudes regarding work Family demands for time and energy Degree of social support Amount of emotional bonding and family adaptability Family satisfaction with job Wife's adjustment to job location, transfers, promotion, etc.	Job satisfaction Job involvement Level of stress Work orientation Motivation Level of energy Performance Turnover intentions Willingness to travel, transfer Demands for/expectations of raises, promotions

patterns in terms of four elements: time use, spatial location, activity, and social interaction. The method examines and then categorizes the ways individuals structure their daily lives in terms of *life space structures*. A life space structure is a set of institutionalized arrangements that allows individuals to accomplish important tasks and fulfill salient personal needs.

The research involved both a series of interviews and the collection of diary records. The diary format required individuals to indicate where they were, what they were doing, whom they were with, and in what time frames those situations occurred for the waking hours of nine consecutive days. Data analysis involved the search for underlying structure. Dean identified thirteen dimensions to represent ways individuals moved through the life space. Q factor analyses were used both to determine the power of a set of dimensions to distinguish different types of life structures and to cluster individuals.

The thirteen dimensions she found are shown in Table 9.3. They encompass individual ways of combining the four primary elements (time, place, activity, people) in the life space. Subsequent analyses indicated the existence of a higher-order clustering; i.e. there were four broad basic types of life space structures: one having an above-average quality and quantity of time at home but not at work, one having an above average quality and quantity of time at work but not at home, a third having high quality and high quantity of time both at home and at work, and a fourth in which high quality and high quantity time together was not present in either home or work. Within these broad types, there were also subtypes, as shown in Figure 9.1

Learning more about how the life space structures work for or against people in particular situations (Lee, 1985) should point the way to helping people coordinate their work and personal lives more effectively.

Hall (1984a, 1984b) has proposed two interesting and different perspectives for viewing work and family. One of them (Hall, 1984a) develops the metaphor of weaving a complex life fabric out of many life threads, in place of the more common image of balancing personal and professional life. The threads (personal, professional, or family) may not be all of the same length, ply, color, texture, or fibre. Some of the threads may be tightly woven, others loose threads, some waiting to be reclaimed, others lost along the way.

The process of weaving involves setting a series of warp threads, which are usually stationary, then weaving over and under with woof and weft threads. Work (or family) can be either warp or weft threads in this metaphor. The warp provides the structure around which the other threads are woven. The finished product may highlight mainly weft, mainly warp, or both. And the pattern can change as one moves through life and career stages. In addition, the more threads with which one is working, the more complex the weaving. Hall proposed that although life fabrics are never really finished, individuals pass through three stages: finding the threads, learning to weave one's own fabric, and managing the threads as a creative act.

She (Hall, 1984b) provides an equally innovative way of describing *life space configurations* using analogs or models from the field of architecture. The concept of *living patterns* is highlighted as a critical ingredient of an architecture that provides for a quality of life. A living pattern is a configuration (in architecture) that resolves the conflicts that arise out of different contexts. The concept of living patterns translates to the area of work and family in the sense that individuals need to design

TABLE 9.3 – Critical Life Space Dimensions Identified by Lee (1984)

DIMENSION	INDICATOR
Home centrality	Percent total time spent at home
Home choice orientation	Relative amount of time spent in high-choice activities at home
Home pleasure index	Percent especially activities experienced at home
Work centrality	Percent total time spent at work
Work choice orientation	Relative amount of time spent in high-choice activities at work
Work pleasure index	Percent especially enjoyable activities experienced at work
Latitude	Total number of different places visited
Location modality	Number of type locations in which 10 per cent or more of total time is spent (e.g. home, work, places of business, others' homes, indoor places of recreation)
Overall choice orientation	Relative amount of time spent in high-choice activities
Overall instrumentality	Relative amount of time spent in high-instrumentality activities
Friendship breadth	Total number of friends engaged in dyadic interaction for 5 or more minutes
Relationality depth	Average closeness of dyadic relationships
Relationality complexity	Average variance in closeness of dyadic relations within locations where 10 per cent or more of total time is spent

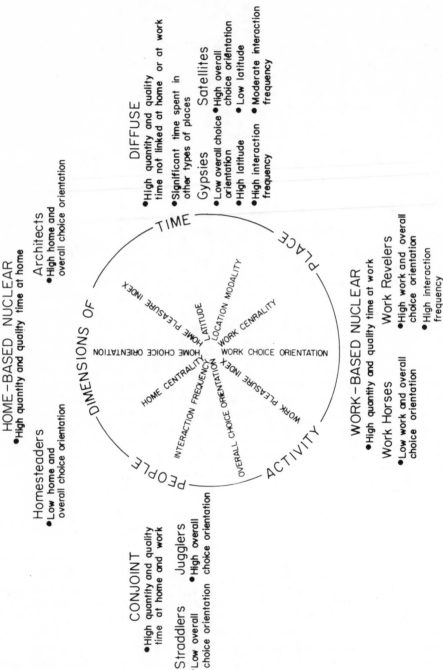

Figure 9.1 Life space structure types and subtypes identified by Lee (1984)

life space to create configurations that resolve rather than induce conflicts. These individuals can create a *personal architecture* in the way they structure living patterns in their life space.

Hall interviewed a small sample of professionals to identify the issues they experienced at the interface of their work and family lives, and the characteristics of work and family environments that contributed to the presence or absence of these issues, and to describe the life space configurations they used to resolve conflicts arising between work and family. She observed that most of the solutions people employed to manage the work–family relationship were structural in character (linked to space and boundary) rather than process oriented (interpersonal). A key distinction was whether the individual chose to integrate or differentiate work and family. Integrations were both stimulated and satisfied by the overlap of the two life domains. Differentiators needed to separate work and family and did so by creating deliberate boundaries or space.

Intervention and Policy Implications

Study of the interdependence of work and family roles is relevant for social policy and job design considerations as well as for interest in the roles of women and men (Lee and Kanungo, 1984). The reality of women's labor-force participation is that over 60 per cent of women are employed during their lifetime; women constitute nearly 50 per cent of the labor force, and at least 50 per cent are married. These percentages are likely to be increasing rather than decreasing. One of the issues that should be addressed by industry is how to alter employment demands so that they mesh more easily with family responsibilities. But, at the present time, most employers do not consider their employees' concerns as family members to be an organizational concern. Policies and practices are designed as if responsibilities outside the job were subordinate to work demands. If, rather than ignoring these, companies were to acknowledge them and assist their employees, a great deal of employment–family conflict could be alleviated (General Mills, 1981).

One area in which the company could assist is childcare. Childcare is a demand on the family that poses conflict between work and family interests, particularly in the single-parent family. Other benefits could encourage men to take a more active role in the family, i.e. the provision of paternity leave, as seen in Scandinavian countries.

A second area in which organizations could take action involves the concept of what constitutes a career. Most organizations currently define career in a narrow sense in terms of progress and upward mobility, and in so doing preclude a life style that deviates from the masculine one. For example, persons who move through the ranks efficiently and quickly are rewarded and it is almost always assumed that the highly motivated person works his or her way upwards faster than the person who is minimally motivated. As a result, the part-time worker (whether part-time for 1 year or 5) is tolerated rather than accepted and may even be referred to as a 'casual' worker. It is not recognized that individuals pursuing careers may have other commitments, i.e. family responsibilities and/or interests related to pesonal growth, that demand substantial time and energy. It is primarily during the years when women are experiencing pregnancy and childbirth and rearing young children that societal institutions should acknowledge and accommodate alternative life styles to the one currently assumed for all members of society. Lack of 24-hour childcare, inadequately paid maternity leave, and the assumption that all 'committed' employees should work an 8-hour day, constitute discrimination against women. Moreover, organizations can introduce programs which promote a climate which is responsive to the needs of women and men, particularly when they are raising a young family (Ronen, 1984). For example, flexitime can be introduced such that workers can schedule their work in different time frames, depending on their needs at particular stages in their life cycle (Best, 1978).

What is needed is greater flexibility in work schedules to allow individuals, both women and men, the freedom and opportunity to balance their work and family responsibilities in ways which are compatible with their own life style. Such changes would benefit women as well as men who may wish to take a greater role in their developing youngster's lives.

Organizations are increasingly presenting material on work and family in executive development seminars (Burke, 1980). Seminars for spouses are becoming increasingly popular. Burke describes courses on the executive family taught at the Harvard Business School and at the Faculty of Administrative Studies at York University (Canada). These courses are aimed at student couples and cover material on occupational and life stress, investments in work and family, and the inevitable tradeoffs one must make. Finally, employee assistance programs have come more and more to deal with family, and work–family interface issues.

Published reports of interventions, though rare, appear in the literature. Two such studies addressed the impact of heavy business travel on the work–family interface (Culbert and Renshaw, 1972; Renshaw, 1975). In the first example (Culbert and Renshaw, 1972) the individuals were members of a research unit whose research responsibilities required them to travel a great deal during the summer to test products under field conditions. Most of them expected heavy travel schedules when they joined the unit, but the complex problems of heavy travel surprised them all. Family problems arose from disconnected family relationships, lack of social life, shifts in responsibilities during absences, and needs for emotional support. The job incumbents also found that travel resulted in their feeling tired, lonely, and guilty to the point of depression about being away from home.

A seminar designed to address the problems of travel had three primary objectives: (1) participation in the seminar would improve problem-solving resources of the husband and wife team; (2) focusing these resources on the couple's problems with business travel would strengthen each person's capacity to cope with separation; and (3) new and strengthened resources for coping would be generalized to other organizational issues and problems. The format for the seminar consisted of a 2-day workshop in which couples engaged in activities to strengthen their analytical and problem-solving skills. Evaluation data using a control group of travellers from other units revealed that those participating in the study felt better able to cope with travel stress after participating in the seminar. In addition, the majority of the seminar participants showed a decrease in rated intensity of travel stress following the workshop.

Renshaw (1975) conducted another workshop, involving only wives, which dealt with the effects of being temporarily transferred to the United States from another country for periods of 1 to 2 years. Renshaw concluded that the key ingredient in both workshops was the amount of perceived influence individuals came to believe they had over the events in a stressful situation.

The increasingly widespread interest in the quality of working life would suggest that this area will become more and more important during the next decade. More individuals and their employing organizations will be interested in enhancing attempts to balance work and family needs (General Mills, 1981).

SUMMARY AND CONCLUSIONS

Recent years have seen increasing research conducted on the relationship between work and family (Nieva, 1984, 1985). While, in the past, each life domain was treated as a closed system, more recently there is growing evidence of the belief on the part of theoreticians and researchers alike in the interdependence of work and family. Moreover, the emphasis on the perception of interdependence of life domains coincides with the new emphasis in psychology on the total life cycle. This perception of interrelatedness also fits in with one of the basic precepts of Marxist theory, namely, the assumption of connections between occupational experiences and personal life, and the well-known propounded marxist belief that the organization of productive life relates to people's life experiences. The idea of interconnectedness is expressed by many writers in the area regardless of their academic persuasion. For example, in addition to discussing the interdependence of work and family, Kanter (1977) examines the way in which familial patterns may impact on work systems. Others argue (Evans and Bartolomé, 1986) that family life has little effect on work experiences except in extreme situations—for example, when there are instances of major career and life decisions, such as the decision to marry, divorce, or have children.

There are important sex differences in the relationship between work and family since society and individuals themselves have subscribed to double standards regarding familial responsibilities. Women employees, in contrast to their male counterparts, when they marry and have children, are seen as adding an additional role, the domestic role, to that of their employment roles. Morevoer, whatever else a woman does, her familial roles are supposed to take precedence since women are expected to take primary responsibility for the family. While women may be expected to choose between family and work roles, no such choice is expected of men. This may help to explain the findings among managers that males tend to be married with children, while among females one tends to find that less than half of such samples are married and even fewer have children (Fraker, 1984).

The approach which sees the work domain influenced by the family has another implication, this time for theoretical conceptions of sources of stress that cross domains. Thus, Kanter (1977) argues that family stressors may define the demands or pressures that people bring with them to work, thus influencing as well the degree of satisfaction they experience with their job. Data supporting this view are provided by Nieva (1979) who reports that demands made by the family, such as the family's need for time and energy, and work–family conflict were both negatively related to job satisfaction and job involvement.

Just as there is increasing recognition of the potential impact of the family on the work system, at the same time research is increasingly pointing to the negative impact the job can have on family members, familial relationships, and the family as a unit itself. Burke and Bradshaw (1981) have shown that a person's well-being can be critically affected by the occupational demands of a spouse. Thus, research in recent years supports increasing recognition of the concept of 'open systems' whereby events in one life sphere are likely to influence and be influenced by events in another one.

As has been illustrated, most of the research on work and family has approached the relationship in terms of its implications for role conflict. The trend has been to look for negative influences of family on work or of work on family rather than positive complementary influences. On the positive side, there is the family support that may be provided for workers — support which may function as a buffer against stress. There may be significant sex differences here. For example, the role of social support has been found to be important for lowering the harmful effects of stress on health, primarily in male workers, while the family and the marital relationship, in particular, can function as buffers against role conflict and its stressful effects in general. But this may be more true for men than for women. As has been suggested, because the nurturant role is prescribed and adhered to generally more by women than by men, men may benefit more psychologically from marriage than women because it provides them with an intimate relationship that they may not find elsewhere. Thus, marriage may function more as a buffer against stress in men than in women. But this too may be changing given that increasing numbers of women are seeking and obtaining employment outside the home. Given that a women is employed full-time, she may be less receptive to her husband's problems, and given the demands of her own job she may have less time and energy to act as a support to her husband than her non-employed housewife counterpart.

Our conclusions about work and family were limited by several research gaps. Most studies were restricted to white middle-class or upper-middle-class individuals in the United States, with little study of or attention to minority groups, blue- and pink-collar workers, workers from industrialized countries other than the United States, or workers from non-industrialized countries.

Another limitation of the research literature has to do with its treatment of women. In comparison to men, women tend to be undervalued and studied less. Moreover, it has only been within the last few decades that women have come to be regarded as workers in their own right, worthy of study, rather than being perceived simply in the role of wife. Implicit in the prevalent view of the family in the past was the assumption that men were married to women whose primary purpose in life was to provide a stress-free haven for their husband who did the 'real' work, i.e. was the family provider. The work that women as housewives did in the home has not been recognized as work. And while there is an abundant literature on the role of the wife as a supportive other to the husband, rarely did one find studies on the role of the husband as a support to his wife in the housewife role. This view is slowly giving way to another view, that the function of the family vis-à-vis the worker is very much affected by the worker's gender. Contrary to being a haven from stress, the home and the family, in particular, present a much greater set of demands and potential stressors to the female worker than to her male counterpart. This is due in part to the belief held by many, and even by the women herself in many instances, that the roles of wife and mother should take precedence over other roles. Given that men still do not share household and childcare responsibilities equally, women still bear the brunt of family responsibilities. The effects of having both sets of responsibilities and the role conflict this may elicit are beginning to be studied by social scientists (Holahan and Gilbert, 1979).

RESEARCH PRIORITIES

The following research directions appear to be important to our understanding of work and family in the context of the currently available literature.

1. More attention to integrating the research findings from various disciplines (psychology, sociology, economies, adult development, organization behavior) as they relate to work and family.
2. More in-depth qualitative research for generating hypotheses and theory (Piotrkowski, 1978).
3. The potential usefulness of new ways of viewing work–family relationships (Lee, 1984, 1985; Hall, 1984a, 1984b).
4. The joint (or interactive) effects of work and family on relevant outcome variables.
5. More research on the effects of family on work.
6. The potentially positive effects of work on family, and family on work.
7. Work and family in non-industrialized nations, and outside of North America.
8. Work as a creator of values and culture within families.
9. Blue-collar families (Shostak, 1980, Piotrkowski, 1978).
10. Studies involving spouses, and children.
11. How intact families manage to deal with work and family issues while remaining intact.
12. How husbands and wives can develop more satisfying marital relationships.
13. Fathers as parents.
14. Homemakers as workers.
15. Work and family in the context of feminist writing (Hewlett, 1986).
16. Evaluation research of organizational (and societal) programs—e.g. day care, flexitime.

Social scientists can make a significant contribution by conducting systematic research to disentangle factors involved in the relationship between work and family. Research in this area has additional value in its contributions to theoretical statements of work and family integration of interest to a wide variety of disciplines. In addition, systematic understanding of the ways in which individuals integrate and cope with their many roles in contemporary society will contribute to both broader knowledge and a more comprehensive view of individual functioning, a view that rests on successfully integrating research on work and family.

ACKNOWLEDGEMENTS

Preparation of this manuscript was supported in part by the Faculty of Administrative Studies and the Department of Psychology, Faculty of Arts, York University. We would like to thank our colleague Patricia Bradshaw-Camball for her helpful input to the manuscript and Betty Hagopian and Leslie Vogan for assistance in its preparation.

REFERENCES

Ackoff, R. (1974). *Redesigning the Future: A Systems Approach to Societal Problems.* New York: John Wiley.

Andrews, F. M., and Withey, S. B. (1976). *Social Indicators of Well-being: Americans' Perceptions of Life Quality.* New York: Plenum.

Bailyn, L. (1970). Career and family orientations of husbands and wives in relation to marital happiness. *Human Relations.* **23**, 97-113.

Banner, D. K. (1974). The nature of the work-leisure relationship. *Omega,* **2**, 2.

Barnett, R. C., and Baruch, G. K. (1985). Women's involvement in multiple roles and psychological distress. *Journal of Personality and Social Psychology,* **49**, 135-145.

Barnett, R. C., Baruch, G. K., and Rivers, C. (1982). *Lifeprints: New Patterns of Love and Work for Today's Women.* New York: McGraw-Hill.

Bartolomé, F. (1972). Executives as human beings. *Harvard Business Review,* **50**, 62-69.

Bartolomé, F., and Evans, P. L. (1979). Professional lives versus private lives—shifting patterns of managerial commitment. *Organization Dynamics,* **3**, 3-29.

Bartolomé, F., and Evans, P. L. (1980). Must success cost so much? *Harvard Business Review,* **58**, 137-148.

Baruch, G. K., Biener, L., and Barnett, R. C. (1985). Women and gender in research on stress. Working paper, Centre for Research on Women, Wellesley, Mass.

Becker, M. A., and Byrne, D. (1984). Type A behavior and daily activities of young married couples. *Journal of Applied Social Psychology,* **14**, 82-88.

Berk, R. A., and Berk, S. F. (1979). *Labor and Leisure at Home: Content and Organization of the Household Day.* Beverly Hills, Calif.: Sage.

Berk, R., and Berk, S. (1978). A simultaneous equation model for the division of household labor. *Social Methods and Research,* **6**, 431-467.

Best, F. (1978). Preferences on worklife scheduling and work-leisure tradeoffs. *Monthly Labor Review,* **101**, 31-37.

Beutell, N. J. (1986). Conflict between work-family and student-family roles: Some sources and consequences. Working paper, Division of Research, W. Paul Stillman School of Business, Seton Hall University.

Beutell, N. J., and Greenhaus, J. H. (1983). Integration of home and nonhome roles: Women's conflict and coping behavior. *Journal of Applied Psychology,* **68**, 43-48.

Bhagat, R. S. (1980). Effects of stressful life events upon individual performance effectiveness and work adjustment processes within organizational settings: a research model. Presented at the American Psychological Association Meeting, Montreal, August.

Bhagat, R. S. (1985). The role of stressful life events in organizational behavior and human performance. In T. A. Beehr and R. S. Bhagat (eds.), *Human Stress and Cognition in Organizations.* New York: John Wiley.

Bhagat, R. S., McQuaid, S. J., Lindholm, S., and Segovis, J. (1985). Total life stress: A multimethod validation of the construct and its effects on organizationally valued outcomes and withdrawal behaviors. *Journal of Applied Psychology,* **70**, 202-214.

Blaney, N. T., Brown, P., and Blaney, P. H. (1986). Type A marital adjustment and life stress. *Journal of Behavioral Medicine,* **9**, 201-209.

Blood, M. R., and Hulin, C. L. (1967). Alienation, environmental characteristics and worker responses. *Journal of Applied Psychology,* **51**, 284-290.

Bray, D. W., Campbell, R. J., and Grant, D. L. (1974). *Formative Years in Business: A Long Term AT and T Study of Managerial Lives.* New York: John Wiley.

Brett, J. M. (1980). The effect of job transfer on employees and their families. In C. L. Cooper and R. Payne (eds.), *Current Concerns in Occupational Stress.* New York: John Wiley.

Bronfenbrenner, U., and Crouter, A. C. (1982). Work and family through time and space. In S. Kammerman and C. Hayes (eds.), *Families that Work: Children in a Changing World.* Washington, DC: National Academy Press.

Brooks, P. (1977). Whatever happened to following in Dad's footsteps? *TWA Ambassador,* **May**.

Bryson, J. B., and Bryson, R. A. (1978). Dual career couples. *Psychology of Women Quarterly,* **3**, whole issue.

Burke, R. J. (1980). How work and the family affect each other. *Canadian Training Methods: The Human Element,* **9**, 12–14.

Burke, R. J. (1982). Impact of occupational demands on nonwork experiences of senior administrators. *Journal of Psychology,* **112**, 195–211.

Burke, R. J. (1986). Occupational and life stress and the family: Conceptual frameworks and research findings. *International Review of Applied Psychology,* **35**, 347–369.

Burke, R. J., and Bradshaw, P. (1981). Occupational and life stress and the family. *Small Group Behavior,* **12**, 329–375.

Burke, R. J., and Weir, T. (1975). Receiving and giving help with work and nonwork-related problems. *Journal of Business Administration,* **6**, 59–78.

Burke, R. J. and Weir, T. (1976). Relationships of wives employment status to husband, wife and pair satisfaction and performance. *Journal of Marriage and the Family,* **38**, 279–287.

Burke, R. J., and Weir, T. (1977a). Working men as fathers of adolescents. *School Guidance Worker,* **33**, 4–9.

Burke, R. J. and Weir, T. (1977b). Why good managers make lousy fathers. *Canadian Business,* **50**, 51–54.

Burke, R. J., and Weir, T. (1977c). Husband-wife helping-relationships: The 'mental hygiene' function in marriage. *Psychological Reports,* **40**, 911–925.

Burke, R. J., and Weir, T. (1980). The Type A experience: Occupational and life demands, satisfaction and well-being. *Journal of Human Stress,* **6**, 28–38.

Burke, R. J. and Weir, T. (1981). Impact of occupational demands on non-work experiences. *Group and Organization Studies,* **6**, 472–485.

Burke, R. J., Weir, T., and Duwors, R. E. (1979). Type A behavior of administrators and wives' reports of marital satisfaction and well-being. *Journal of Applied Psychology,* **64**, 57–65.

Burke, R. J., and Weir, T., and Duwors, R. E. (1980a). Work demands on administrators and spouse well-being. *Human Relations,* **33**, 253–278.

Burke, R. J., Weir, T., and Duwors, R. E. (1980b). Perceived Type A behavior of husbands' and wives' satisfaction and well-being. *Journal of Occupational Behavior,* **1**, 139–150.

Campbell, A., Converse, P. E., and Rodgers, W. L. (1976). *The Quality of American Life: Perceptions, Evaluations and Satisfactions.* New York: Russell Sage.

Caplan, G. (1976). The family as a support system. In G. Caplan and M. Killilia (eds.), *Support System and Mutual Help.* New York: Grune & Stratton. 1976.

Caplan, R. D., Cobb, S., French, J. R. P., Harrison, R. V., and Pinneau, S. R. (1975). *Job Demands and Worker Health.* HEW Publications (NIOSH) 75-160. Washington, DC: Government Printing Office.

Carranza, E. (1972). A study of the impact of life changes on high school teacher performance in Lansing School District as measured by the Holmes and Rahe Schedule of Recent Experiences. Unpublished Ph.D. dissertation, Michigan State University.

Cobb, S. (1976). Social support as a moderator of life stress. *Psychosomatic Medicine,* **38**, 300–314.

Costello, J. (1974). Why more managers are refusing transfers. *Nation's Business,* October, p. 4.

Crosby, F. (1984). Job satisfaction and domestic life. In M. D. Lee and R. N. Kanungo (eds.), *Management of Work and Personal Life.* New York: Praeger.

Crouter, A. C. (1984). Spillover from family to work: The neglected side of the work–family interface. *Human Relations,* **37**, 425–442.

Culbert, S. A., and Renshaw, J. R. (1972). Coping with the stresses of travel as an opportunity for improving the quality of work and family life. *Family Process*, **11**, 321-337.

Ditto, W. B. (1982). Daily activities of college students and the construct validity of the Jenkins Activity Survey. *Psychosomatic Medicine*, **44**, 537-543.

Dohrenwend, B. S., and Dohrenwend B. P. (1974). *Stressful Life Events: Their Nature and Effects*. New York: John Wiley.

Dyer, W. G. (1964). Family reactions to the father's job. In A. Shostak and W. Gomberg (eds.), *Blue-Collar World: Studies of the American Worker*. Englewood Cliffs, NJ: Prentice-Hall.

Eaker, E. D., Haynes, S. G., and Feinleib, M. (1983). Spouse behaivor and coronary heart disease in men: Prospective results from the Framingham Heart Study. II. Modification of risk in Type A husbands according to the social and psychological status of their wives. *American Journal of Epidemiology*, **118**, 23-41.

Eberhardt, B. J., and Eberhardt, M. J. (1983). The prevalence and effects of the Type A behavior pattern in men and women: A direct comparison. Paper presented at the 43rd National Meeting of the Academy of Management, Dallas, Texas.

Epstein, C. F. (1981). *Women in Law*. New York: Basic Books.

Evans, P., and Bartolomé, F. (1980). The relationship between professional and private life. In C. B. Derr (ed.), *Work, Family and Career*. New York: Praeger, pp. 281-317.

Evans, P., and Bartolomé, F. (1980). *The changing picture of the relationship between career and family. Journal of Occupational Behavior*, **5**, 9-21.

Evans, P., and Bartolomé, F. (1986). The dynamics of work-family relationships in managerial lives. *International Review of Applied Psychology*, **35**, 371-395.

Farmer, H. S., and Bohn, M. J. (1970). *Home-career conflict reduction and the level of career interest for women. Journal of Counselling Psychology*, **17**, 228-232.

Feinberg, M. R. (1980). *Corporate Bigamy*. New York: William Morrow.

Fraker, S. (1984). Why women aren't getting to the top? *Fortune*, **16 April**, 40-45.

Friedman, M., and Rosenman, R. H. (1974). *Type A Behavior and Your Heart*. New York: Alfred A. Knopf.

Frieze, I. H., Parsons, J. E., Johnson, P. B., Ruble, O. N., and Zellman, G. L. (1978). *Women and Sex Roles: A Social Psychological Perspective*. New York: W. W. Norton.

Garland, T. N. (1972). The better half? The male in the dual profession family. In C. Safilios-Rothschild (ed.), *Toward a Sociology of Women*. Lexington, MA: Yerox College, pp. 199-215.

General Mills (1981). *Families at Work: Strengths and Strains*. American Family Report conducted by Louis Harris & Associates. Minneapolis, Minn.: General Mills.

Gilmer, B. V. H. (1971). *Industrial and Organizational Psychology*. New York: McGraw-Hill.

Gray, J. D. (1983). The married professional woman: An examination of her role conflicts and coping strategies. *Psychology of Women Quarterly*, **7**, 235-243.

Greenglass, E. R. (1982). *A World of Difference: Gender Roles in Perspective*. Toronto: John Wiley.

Greenhaus, J. H., and Beutell, N. J. (1985). Sources of conflict between work and family roles. *Academy of Management Review*, **10**, 76-88.

Greenhaus, J. H., and Kopelman, R. E. (1981). Conflict between work and nonwork roles: Implications for the career planning process. *Human Resource Planning*, **4**, 1-10.

Greiff, B. S., and Munter, P. K. (1980). *Trade-offs: Executive, Family and Organizational Life*. New York: New American Library.

Guest, D., and Williams, R. (1973). How home affects work. *New Society*, **9**, 14-19.

Gupta, N., and Jenkins, G. D., Jr. (1985). Dual career couples: stress, strains and strategies. In T. A. Beehr and R. S. Bhagat (eds.), *Human Stress and Cognition in Organizations*. New York: John Wiley, pp. 141-176.

Hall, D. T. (1972). A model of coping with role conflict: The role behavior of college educated women. *Administrative Sciences Quarterly*, **4**, 471-486.

Hall, D. T., and Hall, F. S. (1979). *The Two-Career Couple*. Reading, MA: Addison-Wesley.

Hall, D. T., and Hall, F. S. (1980). Stress and the two-career couple. In C. L. Cooper and R. Payne (eds.), *Current Concerns in Occupational Stress*. New York: John Wiley.

Hall, F. S. (1984a). The interface of work and nonwork: Implications for designing life space configurations. Paper presented at the Annual Meeting of the Academy of Management, Boston. MA.

Hall, F. S. (1984b). Loose threads and life fabrics: An extended metaphor about personal, professional and organizational lives. In M. D. Lee and R. N. Kanungo (eds.), *Management of Work and Personal Life*. New York: Praeger.

Hammond, S. B. (1954). Class and family. In O. A. Deser and S. B. Hammond (eds.), *Social Structure and Personality in a City*. London: Routledge & Kegan Paul.

Harris, P. W. (1972). The relationship of life change to academic performance among selected college freshmen at varying levels of college readiness. Unpublished Ph.D. dissertation, East Texas State University.

Haynes, S. G., and Feinleib, M. (1982). Women, work, and coronary heart disease: Results from the Framingham 10-year follow-up study. In P. Berman and E. Ramsey (eds.), *Women: A Developmental Perspective*. Publication no. 82-2298, NIH Bethesda, Md.

Heckman, N. A., Bryson, R., and Bryson, J. B. (1977). Problems of professional couples: A content analysis. *Journal of Marriage and the Family*, **39**, 323-330.

Hewlett, S. A. (1986). *A Lesser Life: The Myth of Women's Liberation in America*. New York: Morrow.

Holahan, C. K., and Gilbert, L. A. (1979). Conflict between major life roles: Women and men in dual career couples. *Human Relations*, **32**, 451-467.

Holmes, T. H., and Rahe, R. H. (1967). The social readjustment rating scale. *Journal of Psychosomatic Research*, **11**, 213-218.

House, J. S. (1981). *Work Stress and Social Support*. Reading, Mass.: Addison-Wesley.

Hulin, C. L. (1969). Sources of variation in job and life satisfaction: The role of community and job-related variables. *Journal of Applied Psychology*, **53**, 279-291.

Hulin, C. L., and Blood, M. R. (1968). Job enlargement, individual differences and worker satisfaction. *Journal of Applied Psychology*, **69**, 41-55.

Jackson, S. E., and Maslach, C. (1982). After-effects of job related stress: Families as victims. *Journal of Occupational Behavior*, **3**, 63-77.

Johnson, F. A., and Johnson, C. L. (1976). Role strain in high commitment career women. *Journal of American Academy of Psychoanalysis*, **4**, 13-16.

Johnson, J. H., and Sarason, I. G. (1979). Recent developments in research on life stress. In V. Hamilton and D. M. Warburton (eds.), *Human Stress and Cognition. An Information Processing Approach*. New York: John Wiley.

Kabanoff, B. (1980). Work and non-work: A review of models, methods, and findings. *Psychological Bulletin*, **88**, 60-77.

Kahn, R. L., and Antonucci, T. (1980). Convoys over the life course: Attachment roles and social support. In P. B. Baltes and O. Brim (eds.), *Life-span Development and Behavior*, vol. 3. Boston, MA: Lexington Press.

Kahn, R. L., Wolfe, D. M., Quinn, R. P., Snoek, J. D., and Rosenthal, R. A. (1964). *Organizational Stress: Studies in Role Conflict and Ambiguity*. New York: John Wiley.

Kando, T. M., and Summers, W. C. (1971). The impact of work on leisure: Toward a paradigm and research strategy. *Pacific Sociological Review*, **14**, 310-327.

Kanter, R. M. (1977). *Work and Family in the United States: A Critical Review and Agenda for Research and Policy*. New York: Russell Sage.

Kantor, D., and Lehr, W. (1975). *Inside the Family: Toward a Theory of Family Process*. San Francisco: Jossey-Bass.

Katzell, R. A., Barrett, R. S., and Parker, T. C. (1961). Job satisfaction, job performance and characteristics. *Journal of Applied Psychology*, **45**, 65-72.

Kessler, R. C., and McRae, J. A. (1982). The effect of wives' employment on the mental health of married men and women. *American Sociological Review*, **47**, 216-227.

Kopelman, R. E., Greenhaus, J. H., and Connolly, T. F. (1983). A model of work, family, and interrole conflict: A construct validation study. *Organizational Behavior and Human Performance*, **32**, 198-215.

Kopelman, R. E., Rosenzweig, L., and Lally, L. H. (1982). Dual-career couples: The organizational response. *Personnel Administrator*, **27**, 73-78.

Lee, M. D. (1984). Life space design. In M. D. Lee and R. N. Kanungo (eds.), *Management of Work and Personal Life: Problems and Opportunities*. New York: Praeger.

Lee, M. D. (1985). Probing behavioral patterns of structuring daily life. *Human Relations*, **38**, 457-476.

Lee, M. D., and Kanungo, R. K. (1984). *Management of Work and Personal Life*. New York: Praeger.

Levinson, D. (1959). Role, personality, and social structure in the organizational setting. *Journal of Abnormal and Social Psychology*, **58**, 170-180.

London, M., Crandall, R., and Seals, G. (1977). The contribution of job and leisure satisfaction to quality of life. *Journal of Applied Psychology*, **62**, 328-334.

Lopata, H. Z., and Norr, K. F. (1980). Changing commitments of American women to work and family roles. *Social Security Bulletin*, **43**, 3-14.

McClelland, D. C. (1979). *Power: The Inner Experience*. New York: Irvington.

McClelland, D. C., Coleman, C., Finn, K., and Winter, D. G. Motivation and maturity patterns in marital success. Cambridge, Mass.: Harvard University Laboratory for Social Relations (unpublished manuscript).

McClelland, D. C., Davis, W. N., Kalin, R., and Wanner, E. (1972). *The Drinking Man*. New York: Free Press.

Maccoby, M. (1976). *The Gamesman*. New York: Simon & Schuster.

McKinley, D. C. (1964). *Social class and family life*. New York: The Free Press.

Meissner, M., Humphreys, E. W., Meiss, S. M., and Scheu, W. J. (1975). No exit for wives: Sexual division of labour and the culmination of household demands. *Canadian Review of Sociology and Anthropology*, **12**, 424-439.

Mott, P. E., Mann, F. C., McLaughlin, Q., and Warwick, D. P. (1965). *Shiftwork: The Social, Psychological and Physical Consequences*. Ann Arbor, Mich.: University of Michigan Press.

Near, J. P. (1984). Predictive and explanatory models of work and nonwork. In M. D. Lee and R. N. Kanungo (eds.), *Management of Work and Personal Life: Problems and Opportunities*. New York: Praeger.

Near, J. P., Rice, R. W., and Hunt, R. G. (1980). The job satisfaction/life satisfaction relationships: A review of empirical research. *Basic and Applied Social Psychology*, **1**, 37-64.

Nieva, V. F. (1979). The family's impact on job-related attitudes of men and women: report of work in progress. Presented at the American Psychological Association Annual Meeting, New York, August.

Nieva, V. F. (1984). Work and family roles. In M. D. Lee and R. N. Kanungo (eds.), *Management of Work and Personal Life: Problems and Opportunities*. New York: Praeger.

Nieva, V. F. (1985). Work and family linkages. In L. Larwood, A. H. Stromberg, and B. A. Gutek (eds.), *Women and Work: An Annual Review*. Beverly Hills, Calif.: Sage Publications.

Osherson, S., and Dill, D. (1983). Varying work and family choices: Their impact on men's satisfaction. *Journal of Marriage and the Family*, **45**, 339-346.

Paradine, P., Higgins, R., Beres, J., Szeglin, A., and Kravitz, R. (1981). The job stress-worker strain relationship moderated by off-the-job experience. *Psychological Reports*, **53**, 108-119.

Parker, S. R. (1967). Industry and the family. *The Sociology of Industry*. New York: Praeger.

Payne, R. (1980) Organizational stress and social support. In C. L. Cooper and R. Payne (eds.), *Current Concerns in Occupational Stress*. New York: John Wiley.

Payton-Miyazaki, M., and Brayfield, A. H. (1976). The good job and the good life: Relationship of characteristics of employment to general well-being. In A. D. Biderman and T. F. Drury (eds.), *Measuring Work Quality for Social Reporting*. New York: Sage Publications, pp. 105-150.

Pines, A., and Kafry, D. (1981). The experience of tedium in three generations of professional women. *Sex Roles*, **7**, 117-134.

Piotrkowski, C. S. (1978). *Work and the Family System*. New York: The Free Press.

Pleck, J. H. (1977). The work-family role system. *Social Problems*, **24**, 417-427.

Pleck, J. H. (1979). Men's family work: Three perspectives and some new data. *Family Coordinator*, **28**, 481-488.

Pleck, J. H., and Staines, G. L. (1982). Work schedules and work-family conflict in two-earner couples. In J. Aldous (ed.), *Two Paychecks: Life in Dual-Earner Families*. London: Sage, pp. 63-87.

Pleck, J. H., Staines, G. L., and Lang, L. (1980). Conflicts between work and family life. *Monthly Labor Review*, 29-32.

Rapoport, R., and Rapoport, R. N. (1969). The dual-career family: A variant pattern and social change. *Human Relations*, **22**, 3-30.

Rapoport, R., and Rapoport, R. N. (1976). *Dual-career Families Re-examined*. New York: Harper & Row.

Renshaw, J. R. (1974). Explorations and the boundaries of work and family life. Unpublished Ph.D. Dissertation, University of California at Los Angeles.

Renshaw, J. R. (1975). An exploration of the dynamics of the overlapping worlds of work and family. *Family Process*, **14**, 143-165.

Rice, G. D. (1979). *Dual Career: Marriage: Conflict and Treatment*. New York: The Free Press.

Rice, R. W., Near, J. P., and Hunt, R. G. (1980). The job-satisfaction life-satisfaction relationship a review of empirical research. *Basic and Applied Social Psychology*, **1**, 37-64.

Robinson, J., Juster, T., and Stafford, F. (1976). *Americans Use of Time*. Ann Arbor, Mich.: Institute for Social Research.

Ronen, S. (1984). *Alternative Work Schedules: Selecting, Implementing and Evaluating*. Homewood, IL.: Dow Jones-Irwin.

Ronen, S., and Primps, S. B. (1981). The compressed work week as organizational change: Behavioral and attitudinal outcomes. *Academy of Management Review*, **6**, 61-74.

Rosenfield, S. (1980). Sex differences in depression: Do women always have higher rates? *Journal of Health and Social Behavior*, **21**, 33-42.

Rousseau, D. (1978). The relationship of work to non-work. *Journal of Applied Psychology*, **63**, 513-517.

Sarason, I., and Johnson, J. (1979). Life stress, organizational stress and job satisfaction. *Psychological Reports*, **44**, 75-79.

Schneider, B., and Dachler, H. P. (1978). Work, family and consideration in understanding employee turnover intentions. College Park, Md.: Department of Psychology, University of Maryland.

Seidenberg, R. (1973). *Corporate Wives — Corporate Casualties?* New York: AMACOM.

Shostak, A. B. (1980). *Blue-collar stress*. Reading, Mass.: Addison-Wesley.

Slavin, W. (1972). The theme of feminine evil: the image of women in male fantasy and its effect on attitudes and behavior. Unpublished Ph.D. dissertation, Harvard University.

Sostek, A., and Sherman, S. (1977). Report on children of executives. *Behavioral Science*, 8 August.

Staines, G. L., and Pleck, J. H. (1984). Nonstandard work schedules and family life. *Journal of Applied Psychology*, **69**, 515-523.

Staines, G. L., and Pleck, J. H. (1986). Work schedule flexibility and family life. *Journal of Occupational Behavior*, 7, 147-523.

Staines, G. L., Pottick, K. J., and Fudge, D. A. (1986). Wives' employment and husbands' attitudes towards work and life. *Journal of Applied Psychology*, **71**, 118–128.

Steers, R. M., and Rhodes, S. R. (1978). Major influences on employee attendance: A process model. *Journal of Applied Psychology*, **63**, 391–407.

Steiner, J. (1972). What price success? *Harvard Business Review*, **50**, 69–74.

Stewart, A. J., and Rubin, Z. (1976). Power motivation in the dating couple. *Journal of Personality and Social Psychology*, **34**, 305–309.

Stewart, A. J., and Salt, P. (1981). Life stress, life styles, depression, and illness in adult women. *Journal of Personality and Social Psychology*, **40**, 1067–1069.

Szinovacz, M. (1978). Cited in 'Health matters'. *Family Health*, **10**, 18.

Thoits, P. (1983). Multiple identities and psychological well-being. *American Sociological Review*, **48**, 174–187.

Turner, A. W., and Lawrence, P. R. (1965). *Industrial Jobs and the Worker: An Investigation of the Response to Task Attributes*. Boston; Mass.: Harvard University Press.

Van Egeren, L. F., Sniderman, L. D., and Roggelin, M. S. (1982). Competitive two-person interactions of Type A and Type B individuals. *Journal of Behavioral Medicine*, **5**, 55–66.

Verbrugge, L. (1982). Women's social roles and health. In P. G. Bermand and E. Ramey (eds.), *Women: A Developmental Perspective*. Washington, DC: National Institute of Child Health and Human Development.

Vicino, F. L., and Bass, B. M. (1978). Life space variables and managerial success. *Journal of Applied Psychology*, **63**, 81–88.

Waite, L. J. (1980). Working wives and the family life cycle. *American Journal of Sociology*, **86**, 272–294.

Warr, P., and Parry, G. (1982). Paid employment and women's psychological well-being. *Psychological Bulletin*, **91**, 498–516.

Weingarten, K. (1978). The employment patterns of professional couples and their distribution of involvement in the family. *Psychology of Women Quarterly*, **3**, 43–52.

Whyte, W. H. (1963). The wives of management. In P. Olson (ed.), *America as a Mass Society*. Glencoe, Ill.: The Free Press, pp. 478–491.

Williams, R. B., Haney, T., Lee, K., Kong, Y., Blumenthal, J., and Whalen, R. (1980). Type A behavior, hostility and coronary heart disease. *Psychosomatic Medicine*, **42**, 539–549.

Winter, D. G. (1973). *The Power Motive*. New York: The Free Press.

Winter, D. G., Stewart, A. J., and McClelland, D. C. (1977). Husband's motives and wife's career level. *Journal of Personality and Social Psychology*, **35**, 159–166.

Yarnold, P. R., Mueser, K. T., and Grimm, L. G. (1985). Interpersonal dominance of Type As in group discussion. *Journal of Abnormal Psychology*, **94**, 233–236.

Yogev, S. (1981). Do professional women have egalitarian marital relationship? *Journal of Marriage and the Family*, **43**, 865–871.

Yogev, S. (1982). Are professional women overworked: Objective versus subjective perception of role loads. *Journal of Occupational Psychology*, **55**, 165–169.

Young, M., and Willmott, P. (1973). *The Symmetrical Family*. New York: Pantheon.

International Review of Industrial and Organizational Psychology 1987
Edited by C. L. Cooper and I. T. Robertson
© 1987 John Wiley & Sons Ltd

Chapter 10

APPLICATIONS OF META-ANALYSIS

John E. Hunter
Department of Psychology
Michigan State University
USA
and
Hannah Rothstein Hirsh
Department of Management, Baruch College
City of New York University
USA

The purpose of this chapter is to locate and review studies which have applied meta-analysis to relationships in industrial and organizational psychology. Our primary focus is on substantive findings, though we will offer methodological comments at times. The chapter will be organized by dependent variable: job performance, job tenure, job satisfaction, and disruptions. All results will be converted to correlations in order in order to maximize ease of comparison.

METHODOLOGICAL META-ANALYSES

The results of primary research studies are distorted by many artifacts (Schmidt and Hunter, 1977; Hunter, 1986). Nine of these artifacts (stated in the language of validation studies) are:

1. *Sampling error.* Study validity will vary randomly from the population value because of sampling error.
2. *Error of measurement in the dependent variable.* Study validity will be systematically lower than true validity to the extent that job performance is measured with random error.
3. *Error of measurement in the independent variable.* Study validity for a test will systematically understate the validity of the ability measured since the test is not perfectly reliable.
4. *Range variation in the independent variable.* Study validity will be systematically lower than true validity to the extent that hiring policy causes incumbents to have a lower variation in the predictor than is true of applicants.
5. *Deviation from perfect construct validity in the dependent variable.* Study validity will differ from true validity if the criterion is deficient or contaminated.
6. *Deviation from perfect construct validity in the independent variable.* Study validity will vary if the factor structure of the test differs from the usual structure of tests for the same trait.

7. *Reporting or transcriptional error.* Reported study validities differ from actual study validities due to a variety of reporting problems: inaccuracy in coding data, computational errors, errors in reading computer output, typographical errors by secretaries or by printers. Note: these errors can be very large in magnitude.
8. *Variance due to extraneous factors.* Example: study validity will be systematically lower than true validity if incumbents differ in experience at the time they are assessed for performance.
9. *Attrition artifacts.* Study validity will be systematically lower than true validity to the extent that there is systematic attrition in workers on performance; as when good workers are promoted out of the population or when poor workers are fired for poor performance.

Failure to consider these artifacts leads to error in the estimation of effect sizes and a misinterpretation of the variance of effect sizes across studies. The artifacts that can be directly corrected using the methods of Hunter, Schmidt, and Jackson (1982) are sampling error, error of measurement in the independent and the dependent variable, and range variation on the independent variable. If enough studies are available, then moderator analysis would permit control of construct invalidity of selected measures and attrition artifacts. Bad data cannot be controlled in meta-analysis, though we know they are there and the error is sometimes very large. Because some of the artifacts cannot be eliminated, Schmidt and Hunter (1977) noted that even if there is no real variation in outcome across studies, some residual variation in observed results due to uncorrected artifacts will still be there. They then recommended that if known artifacts account for 75% of the observed variance, the remaining variance is probably due to the uncorrected artifacts. The 75% rule of thumb was conceived in the context of personnel selection and may not be applicable in very different areas. For example, biodata research has a much larger average sample size and hence sampling error accounts for much less variance across studies. Also, it is important to focus on the actual estimate of residual standard deviation. Even if the residual variation is not due to artifacts, it may be too small to be of practical interest. On the other hand, even a tiny variation might be of interest to some obscure theoretical point.

To correct for an artifact, that artifact must be quanitified. For sampling error, this means that the sample size for each correlation must be known — which poses only a rare problem for meta-analysis. However, in order to correct for error of measurement, reliabilities must be known. In order to correct for range restriction on the independent variable, the incumbent to applicant standard deviation ratio must be known. In early meta-analyses in personnel selection, Schmidt and Hunter (1977) used artifact distributions estimated by expert judgement. However, since that time, meta-analyses have generated empirical values for artifact distributions. These will be reviewed here. For validation studies on cognitivie aptitudes, the expert judgement artifact distributions turned out to be fairly accurate.

The most common measure of job performance is supervisor ratings. Supervisor ratings are subject to many different kinds of error; random response error in making the rating, halo — idiosyncrasy in the overall rating of each judge, leniency variation across judges, and non-work related factors common to all judges. King, Hunter, and Schmidt (1980) did a meta-analysis of studies in the civilian sector using the judge by trait by ratee design. This permits the separate quantification of several error sources. They found that 38.4% of the variance in a single rating is due to random response error on the part of the rater. This source of error can be largely eliminated if a summated rating scale is used. However, many studies continue to use only a single rating of overall performance. When only a global rating is used, then the reliability will be 61.6% lower than if a summated rating is used. They found that 30.6% of the variance is due to halo-the systematic term for the idiosyncratic rater overall impression. They found that 8.1% of the variance is due to traits. That is, departure in the rating of a given trait from the overall average rating accounts for only 8.1% of the variance. Finally, 22.9% of the variance is due to the consensus rater overall judgement.

The reliability of a rating depends on its form. For single ratings on a particular trait, the interrater reliability would be $(22.9 + 8.1)/100 = 0.31$. If several rating scales for each trait were summated, then this reliability would rise to $(22.9 + 8.1)/(22.9 + 8.1 + 30.6) = 0.50$. For single global ratings of overall performance, the interrater reliability would be $22.9/100 = 0.29$. For overall performance ratings with a summated rating scale, the interrater reliability would be $22.9/(22.9 + 30.6) = 0.43$. If the ratings of two or more raters are averaged, then the reliability would increase from 0.43 using the Spearman–Brown reliability formula with the number of raters used in place of the length of the test. For summated ratings averaged across two raters, the reliability is 0.60. Finally, it should be noted that these figures may be different for the military. Military ratings have much lower correlations with all other variables (see Hunter and Hunter, 1984) and are suspected to suffer from ceiling effects, rater hostility, and other not yet quantified problems (Vineberg and Joyner, 1982).

In many meta-analyses, citation is made to King et al. (1980) as showing that the reliability of summated ratings by single supervisors would be at most 0.60. This stems from an arithmetic error made by Hunter some time ago. The calculations shown in the previous paragraph show that the reliability of summated ratings by a single supervisor would be 0.43 rather than 0.60. If all studies were done with single supervisors, then the overstatement of reliability would be by a factor of the square root of the ratio of 0.60 to 0.43 (i.e. 18%). Corrected effect sizes would then be understated by 18%. However, some studies are done with two or more raters. The reliability for two raters is 0.60 and the reliability for three raters is 0.69. Thus a mean of 0.60 for the general literature is not that far off.

Correlations between raters are somtimes higher than 0.43. However, these are cases where the ratings are not independent. For example, a second rater is sometimes the supervisor's supervisor. That is, the second rater is a level removed from the worker. In many cases, the supervisor's supervisor obtains most of his or her information from the immediate supervisor and thus obtains biased information. The remote supervisor's ratings would then correlate more highly with those of the immediate supervisor than would ratings by a second independent immediate supervisor.

Correction for attenuation using the interrater reliability corrects for most of the unsystematic error in supervisor ratings. However, there is the problem of non-work related factors used in judgements by all or nearly all raters; factors such as personal appearance, moral conventionality, etc. Ratings are not perfectly construct valid. Quantification of the extent of departure from construct validity can be obtained by correlating ratings with objective measures of job performance. Hunter (1983a) did a meta-analysis of correlations between ratings and content valid job sample measures of performance. For incumbents, the corrected correlation was 0.42 for civilian work and 0.27 for military work. For an applicant population (Hunter, 1984, 1985a, 1985b, in press), the corrected correlation between ratings and job sample performance is 0.52 for civilian work and 0.31 for military work. Some have argued that content valid job sample measures may not be perfectly construct valid either, though they offer no evidence to support these arguments. In any case, the corrected correlation of only 0.52 between objective and subjective measures of performance shows the construct validity of ratings to be only moderate.

There are two issues to be considered in terms of work sample measures of performance: content validity and feasibility. A work sample measure is only content valid if the tasks assessed are a representative sample of the tasks on the job. If the work sample uses a systematically deviant subset of tasks, then content validity is compromised. For example, a typing test may be a content valid measure of performance for a secretary whose only work is to type routine correspondence. But for a secretary who also does filing, scheduling, answers questions from clients, etc., the typing test is only a fragment of performance and is probably not the most important fragment.

In some court cases, lawyers have argued that since a work sample is a better performance measure than supervisor ratings, then studies using ratings should be disallowed. The problem with this recommendation is that work sample performance measures are often extremely expensive. In the case of a job such as police officer, which has as many as 160 tasks, it would be virtually impossible to do complete work samples. Thus work samples are usually infeasible. Furthermore, the fact that ratings are imperfect does not make them unusable. Much of the problem with ratings is that they cause the effect size to be underestimated. This problem is greatly reduced by correction for attenuation. Use of ratings just means that the effect size is probably underestimated. While work samples are preferable when resources permit, ratings are usually the only feasible performance measure for validation research. For validation research, performance ratings are a reasonable performance measure if validities are properly corrected for attenuation.

The extent of range restriction in incumbent populations depends on the variable in question and varies across settings depending on the selection methods and attrition rates in each setting. Hunter (1980b) did a meta-analysis of range restriction using the 515 validation studies done by the US Employment Service. The range restriction parameter used was u: the ratio of the standard deviation in the incumbent population to the standard deviation in the applicant population. Across 415 proficiency studies, Hunter found the average value of u to be 0.67 (s.d. = .083) for general cognitive ability, 0.82 (s.d. = .083) for general perceptual ability, and 0.90 (s.d. = .082) for general psychomotor ability. Across 90 training success studies, he found the average value of u to be 0.60 (s.d. = .071) for general cognitive ability, 0.76 (s.d. = .076) for general perceptual ability, and .89 (s.d. = .080) for general psychomotor ability. The empirical range restriction distribution for cognitive ability is very similar to that derived from expert judgement by Schmidt and Hunter (1977) for cognitive aptitude tests. The preceding range restriction distributions are for civilian settings; military settings often have much larger multivariate range restriction (Schmidt, Hunter, Croll, and McKenzie, 1983).

PERFORMANCE

There are three different kinds of determinants of job performance: (1) knowledge, skills, abilities, and other characteristics brought to the job, (2) knowledge, skills, abilities, and other characteristics developed on the job, and (3) conditions that affect the nature of the job. Psychological interventions can alter any of these determinants. Selection studies focus primarily on characteristics brought to the job. Studies of promotion and certification focus primarily on characteristics developed on the job. Other interventions vary. Training develops job knowledge which is a characteristic also developed on the job. Predictors can be classified as to whether they assess prejob or on-the-job determinants of performance.

Studies can also be categorized on the basis of their statistical design; i.e. correlational versus experimental. Here, correlational results will first be considered in the two main contexts: selection in an entry level context (where the person is to be trained for the job after hiring) verus certification, promotion, or lateral transfers (where the person is currently performing the same job or a job very similar to the job in question). Hunter and Hunter (1984) found that in going from one job to a very similar job, the validity of current performance as a predictor of future performance can be very high. The higher the quality of the measure of current performance, the higher the validity. After the correlational studies, the experimental studies will be reviewed.

Selection — Comprehensive Studies

The scientific study of selection can be cast in the form of prediction: how well do characteristics at the time of hiring predict later job performance? This chapter will consider only criterion related validity studies since they produce quantitative results. This section of the chapter will consider comprehensive meta-analyses and the next section will consider special studies. The section after that will review studies devoted to the issue of situation specificity and validity generalization.

There have been a number of comprehensive reviews of validation studies. Most of them were reviewed and quantified by Hunter and Hunter (1984); including Ghiselli (1963, 1963), Dunnette (1972), Reilly and Chao (1982), and Vineberg and Joyner (1982). Hunter and Hunter also added a number of new meta-analyses. There has been a subsequent comprehensive review of published research by Schmitt, Gooding, Noe, and Kirsch (1984); though they made no corrections for unreliability or restriction in range. Validity is not accurately given unless proper corrections for error of measurement and range restriction have been made. Hunter and Hunter made these corrections while Schmitt et al. did not. The proper corrections to the Schmitt et al. findings have been made here. Schmitt et al. thought that they had found inconsistencies between their results and those of Hunter and Hunter. However, the values in the following tables show that the discrepancies stem from the fact that Schmitt et al. made no corrections.

The results of validation studies differ according to the measure of performance. Most studies have used performance ratings, many studies have used training success, a few studies have used promotion or job level, and a tiny trickle of studies have used work sample measures of performance. Table 10.1 presents a summary of the findings for performance ratings for various predictors. Table 10.2 presents a summary of the findings for training success for various predictors. Table 10.3 presents a summary of the findings for promotion for various predictors. Table 10.4 presents a summary of the findings for work sample performance for various predictors. Table 10.1 presents the results from Hunter and Hunter (1984) and from Schmitt *et al.* (1984) predicting performance ratings. The average correlations for Schmitt *et al.* were corrected for error of measurement in performance ratings using a

TABLE 10.1—The average validity predicting performance ratings of various predictors as found in meta-analyses by Hunter and Hunter (1984) and by Schmitt, Gooding, Noe, and Kirsch (1984). Values for Schmitt *et al.* were corrected for attenuation due to error of measurement in performance rating using a reliability of 0.60. The value for ability was corrected for range restriction using a value of $u = 0.67$

PREDICTOR	HH VALIDITY	SGNK VALIDITY
Ability	0.53	0.41
Biodata	0.37	0.41
Personality		0.27
Reference checks	0.26	
Education	0.22	
Special aptitude		0.21
Interview	0.14	
T&E ratings[a]	0.13	
College grades	0.11	
Interest	0.10	
Age	−0.01	

[a] Training and experience ratings

TABLE 10.2—The average validity predicting training success of various predictors as found in meta-analyses by Hunter and Hunter (1984) and by Schmitt, Gooding, Noe, and Kirsch (1984). The correlations from both studies have been corrected for attenuation using a reliability of 0.81. The correlations for cognitive ability have been corrected for range restriction using $u = 0.67$

PREDICTOR	HH VALIDITY	SGNK VALIDITY
Ability	0.63	0.63
College grades	0.33	
Biodata	0.33	0.25
Special aptitude		0.31
Physical ability		0.31
Education	0.27	
Reference checks	0.26	
Interest	0.20	
Personality		0.17
Interview	0.11	
Age	0.02	

TABLE 10.3 — The average validity predicting promotion or status change of various predictors as found in meta-analyses by Hunter and Hunter (1984) and by Schmitt, Gooding, Noe, and Kirsch (1984). The correlation for mental ability was corrected for range restriction using $u = 0.67$

PREDICTOR	HH VALIDITY	SGNK VALIDITY
Physical ability		0.61
Mental ability		0.40
Biodata	0.26	0.33
Interest	0.25	
College grades	0.21	
Personality		0.13
Reference checks	0.16	
Interview	0.08	

TABLE 10.4 — The average validity predicting work sample performance of various predictors as found in meta-analyses by Hunter (in press) and by Schmitt, Gooding, Noe, and Kirsch (1984). All correlations were corrected for attenuation in the work sample measure using an average reliability of 0.81. The correlation for cognitive ability was corrected for error of measurement on ability and corrected for range restriction using $u = 0.67$

PREDICTOR	HH VALIDITY	SGNK VALIDITY
General cognitive ability	0.75	0.71
Physical ability		0.47
Special aptitude		0.31

reliability of 0.60. The correlation for general mental ability was corrected for range restriction using $u = 0.67$. The validities for education and age were updated from Hunter and Hunter by breaking down the US Employment Service data for proficiency and training success separately. The validity of ability was a bit smaller in Schmitt et al. and the validity for biodata was a bit higher. However, in the case of ability, the Schmitt et al. value was based on far fewer data. The construct nature of biodata predictions is unknown at present.

Table 10.2 presents the average validity predicting training success using various predictors from Hunter and Hunter (1984) and from Schmitt et al. (1984). The values from both studies have been corrected for attenuation in training measures using a reliability of 0.81 (Hunter and Hunter, 1984). The correlation for general mental ability in Schmitt et al. was corrected for range restriction using $u = 0.60$. There is little difference between the two meta-analyses. In particular, the validity of general cognitive ability is 0.63 in both. In a summary of over 500 military studies involving nearly half a million personnel, Hunter (in press) found an average validity of 0.62. Since the validity in Hunter and Hunter was based entirely on civilian training, this means there is almost perfect agreement between military and civilian training success validity. The validity of general cognitive ability predicting training success is far higher than the validity of any other predictor: 0.65 versus the nearest alternative, 0.33.

There are some interesting comparisons between validity predicting performance ratings versus validity predicting training success. The validity of cognitive ability goes up a bit: 0.53 to 0.63. The validity of college grades increases substantially: 0.11 to 0.33. The validity of interest increases from 0.10 to 0.20. The validity of the interview goes down from 0.14 to 0.1. The high value of 0.31 for physical ability probably reflects a very selected set of jobs.

Table 10.3 presents the validity predicting promotion or status change for various predictors in the meta-analyses by Hunter and Hunter (1984) and by Schmitt *et al.* (1984). The validity for cognitive ability in Schmitt *et al.* was corrected for range restriction using $u = 0.67$. These validities are noticeably smaller than those predicting better measures of performance. The highest validity is the correlation of 0.61 for physical ability. This high value was based on only three jobs and may represent very special jobs. Either that, or modern corporations determine promotion at the tennis court.

Table 10.4 presents the validity for the best extant measure of performance — work sample performance. The value for general cognitive ability is from Hunter (in press); i.e. the value from Hunter (1983a) corrected for restriction in range. Though the fourteen studies in Hunter (1983a) do not provide a representative sample from the whole job universe (there are no feeding or off-bearing jobs), there is a considerable spread in character: from physicians to cooks. The value for cognitive ability from Schmitt *et al.* was corrected for attenuation in work sample performance and in cognitive ability using reliability 0.81. It was corrected for range restriction using $u = 0.67$. The correlations in Table 10.4 were computed for path analysis and therefore the correlations for ability were corrected for error of measurement in the cognitive ability measure. In a practical selection application, these values must thus be corrected downward by the reliability of the test in use in the selection setting. The validity of general cognitive ability is 0.75 in Hunter (in press) and 0.71 in Schmitt *et al.* (1984). This is far higher than any known alternative predictor.

In summary: the performance measures can be rank ordered from the extremely subjective promotion to still subjective performance ratings to objective training success to work sample performance. The validity of general cognitive ability becomes higher and higher as objectivity becomes higher and higher; from 0.40 for promotion to 0.53 for ratings to 0.63 for training success to 0.75 for work sample performance. The validity of the interview is low across all objectivity levels: from 0.08 for promotion to 0.14 for ratings to 0.10 for training success. Biodata has a consistent moderate validity of 0.26 for promotion to 0.37 for ratings to 0.30 for work sample performance. In terms of characteristics that are brought to the job, general cognitive ability has far higher validity than any known alternative. Hunter and Hunter (1984) note that adding other predictors in selection will only increase validity if the less valid predictor is given a suitably smaller weight in the composite. If the less valid predictor is given too much weight, it can reduce the validity.

Selection — Special Studies

This section will review specialized meta-analyses on a number of issues including training and experience ratings, the interview, leadership and personality in management, race and financial analysts.

Training and experience ratings

McDaniel and Schmidt (1985) performed a more extensive meta-analysis of training and experience ratings than did Hunter and Hunter (1984). Hunter and Hunter distinguished sharply between two uses of training and experience ratings: (1) traditional ratings where there is a sharp difference between old jobs and the job for hire (the 'point method') and (2) Behavioral Consistency Experience Ratings (or their equivalent) where current job performance estimated from self-report data is used to predict performance at the same or a similar job. Validity predicting performance ratings for traditional T&E ratings is 0.13 while the validity for BCER ratings is 0.49. These studies form the bulk of the McDaniel and Schmidt meta-analysis, though they also analyze other less well known methods. Their results were similar to those of Hunter and Hunter.

The interview

McDaniel, Whetzel, Schmidt, Hunter, Maurer, and Russell (1986) did a much more extensive meta-analysis of the interview than Hunter and Hunter (1984); locating far more studies than were found by previous narrative reviewers. The vast bulk of the studies were very low validity studies such as have dominated reviews of the interview in the past. All of the studies reviewed by Hunter and Hunter were from this population. However, a minority of the McDaniel *et al.* studies showed higher validity. Thus their average validities are higher, but their standard deviations are also much higher. Predicting performance ratings, their average validity was $r = 0.29$ (s.d. $= 0.19$). Predicting training success, their average validity was slightly lower, $r = 0.25$ (s.d. $= 0.14$). The type of interview made little difference predicting training success, but there was some difference predicting supervisor ratings: a validity of 0.30 (s.d. $= 0.19$) for job related interviews and a validity of 0.21 (s.d. $= 0.04$) for the psychological interview. This comparison is greatly complicated by the very high standard deviation for job related interviews. While the mean validity is lower for the psychological interview, the 90% credibility level is $0.21 - 0.05 = 0.16$ while the 90% credibility value for job related interviews is $0.30 - 0.24 = 0.06$ which is one third the size. That is, there is so much variance in the validity of job related interviews, that the poorer cases are lower than those for the psychological interview which has a lower mean validity. Thus it is only some job related interviews that have higher validity.

The largest identified moderator variable was the difference between police studies and other occupations. Predicting ratings, the average validity was 0.12 (s.d. $= 0.11$) for police studies and 0.32 (s.d. $= 0.18$) for others. The correlations for all predictors are lower for police ratings (e.g. Hirsh, Northrop, and Schmidt, 1986). This suggests a problem with police ratings. Other moderator variables were much smaller. There was a very small difference between structured and unstructured job related interviews: an average of 0.32 (s.d. $= 0.21$) for structured versus 0.26 (s.d. $= 0.12$) for unstructured. Within the structured job related interviews, but nowhere else, there was a lower validity for administrative ratings than for research ratings.

An important moderator variable that did not show up was the predicted difference between jobs that require social skill and jobs that do not. The validity was not different for the two types of jobs. This tends to disconfirm the hypothesis that the interview measures social skills.

On the other hand, interview evaluations are correlated with general cognitive ability: an average correlation of 0.20. Since cognitive ability correlates 0.63 with training success (Table 10.2), path analysis would show that the interview predicts training success through its correlation with cognitive ability by $(0.63)(0.20) = 0.13$; a value which is lower than the observed correlation of 0.25. For multiple regression on ability and the interview using these average figures, the beta weight for the interview is only 0.13. That is, the average incremental validity of the interview is only 0.13.

The impact of cognitive ability on the prediction of supervisor ratings is more complicated. The correlation for the interview is not dropped too far on average: the beta is 0.19 where the correlation was 0.29. However, McDaniel et al. also found that it was those interviews that had high correlations with cognitive ability that had the higher validity predicting ratings. Thus if cognitive ability could be partialled out for the minority of high validity interview studies, the incremental validity might drop to the level of the low validity studies. That is, the value given by Hunter Hunter (1984) — i.e. $r = 0.14$ — may be accurate as the incremental validity of all interviews. It is crucial that future studies on the interview report the correlation between general cognitive ability and the interview.

Finally, there is the problem of construct validity in performance ratings. Even ideal ratings correlate only 0.52 with objectively measured performance. Thus it may be that the interview predicts the non-work related components of ratings rather than actual job performance. This fits the very low validity predicting training success and the low incremental validity predicting ratings. This hypothesis states that the incremental validity of the interview predicting performance is 0. This hypothesis would explain the fact that the interview does not predict ratings any better for jobs with a high social skill requirement than for jobs with no social skill requirement.

The question of the construct measured by the interview is clearly the key issue for the interview. This is also brought out clearly in the meta-analysis on the interview done by Wiesner and Cronshaw (1986). Without correction for restriction in range, they found a validity of 0.13 for unstructured interviews and 0.40 for structured interviews. The validity for unstructured interviews matches that found by Hunter and Hunter (1984).

There is a strong argument to be made that the structured interview does not measure the same construct as the unstructured interview. Wiesner and Cronshaw (1986) followed Pursell, Campion, and Gaylord (1980, p. 908) to define the 'structured' interview as composed of 'job related questions with predetermined answers that are consistently applied across all interviews.' In addition, they required the rating scale to be the summated rating of the ratings of the answers to each question separately. Where structured interviews are used for lateral transfer or promotion, the format is exactly that of a verbally administered job knowledge or work sample test. Where the interview is used for entry level hiring, hypothetical job questions are often used. In this case, the interview is a verbally administered intelligence test using items tailored to the job. This suggests that many structured interviews are not 'interviews' in the traditional sense, but are intelligence tests or job knowledge tests or are verbal forms of work sample tests. Evidence for this argument can be found in the standard deviation of validity for structured interviews.

Wiesner and Cronshaw (1986) found a mean validity of 0.40 but a corrected standard deviation of 0.26. The 90% range of validities thus runs from 0.07 to 0.73 which spans the range from unstructured interviews predicting ratings (mean r = 0.14) to general cognitive ability predicting training success (mean r = 0.63).

Wiesner and Cronshaw (1986) found that 10% of the studies presented restriction in range information. The studies which reported such information showed a very great deal of restriction. The median study showed hiring of the top third; a range restriction parameter of $u = 0.50$. However, this may have been a biased subset of interview studies because the range restriction corrected correlations are frequently extreme in both mean and variance. For example, in structured interviews that used formal job analysis to build the questions, the mean corrected validity was 0.87 with a corrected standard deviation of 0.30. Since correlations are bounded above by 1.00, it is hard to imagine such a distribution.

Wiesner and Cronshaw (1986) also found that an interview by a board has higher validity than an interview by a single interviewer. For unstructured interviews, the validity rises from $r = 0.13$ for single interviewers to $r = 0.24$ for a board. They interpret this increase as representing an increase in the reliability of the interview.

Assessment centers

Gaugler, Rosenthal, Thornton, and Bentson (1986) conducted a meta-analysis of assessment center validities, based on 107 correlations from 50 studies. Gaugler *et al.* (1986) yielded somewhat lower validity estimates than did Hunter and Hunter (1984)—0.63 versus 0.53 for management potential, 0.43 versus 0.36 for performance ratings—although they are in the same general range. These values are also very close to those found by Schmitt *et al.* (1984).

Lowenberg, Loschenkohl, and Faust (1985) also meta-analyzed assessment center validities. However, instead of looking at the overall assessment center evaluation, they looked at single assessment center dimensions. In view of the high degree of halo in the dimension ratings, it seems very unlikely that there would be any gain in scoring separate dimensions. Lowenberg *et al.* provide no evidence that anything was gained by their analysis.

Leadership

The assessment center validity strongly suggests that classic narrative reviews were wrong in their conclusions about leadership. For example, Stogdill (1948) and Mann (1959) wrote narrative reviews that concluded that there are no personality traits consistently linked to leadership. A meta-analysis by Lord, DeVader, and Alliger (1986) showed that the inconsistency in past results was largely due to sampling error; the residual variance is small for four of the six traits studied. The small size of observed correlations was largely due to low reliabilities. They do not say where their distributions for reliabilities and range restriction came from, but they may have used the Schmidt and Hunter (1977) expert judge estimates. While those distributions have proved to be fairly accurate for validation studies on cognitive ability, the accuracy is unknown in the leadership study context. The reliability distributions are similar to those in the field as a whole and are probably close. However, the range restriction distribution is for cognitive ability and may not apply to other personality characteristics. The correlations for traits other than intelligence may be overcorrected. They found correlations of 0.52 (s.d. = 0.03) for intelligence, 0.34 (s.d. = 0.09) for masculinity, 0.22 (s.d. = 0.00) for conservatism, 0.21 (s.d. = 0.07) for adjustment, 0.17 (s.d. = 0.19) for dominance, and 0.15 (s.d. = 0.15) for extraversion. The high correlation for intelligence is consistent with the high validity of general cognitive ability predicting managerial performance ($r = 0.53$) in the Hunter and Hunter (1984) reanalysis of Ghiselli (1973).

The two dimensions found by Lord et al. (1986) to be variable across settings are dominance and extraversion. These are precisely the dimensions that would be predicted to be situation dependent by Fiedler's (1965, 1978) contingency model of leadership. Fiedler (1965) classifies leadership situations according to three dimensions: group morale may be high or low, the task may be structured or unstructured, and leader position power may be high or low. If these dimensions are dichotomized, then there are eight combinations or 'octants'. In four of these octants, Fiedler predicts that a dominant leader will be effective: the two octants where morale is good and the task is structured, the octant where morale is good and the task is unstructured but leader position power is high, and the octant where morale is low and the task is unstructured and leader position power is weak. In the other four octants, a warm and extraverted leader should be effective; especially if morale is high and the task is unstructured and leader position power is weak.

In a narrative review, Fiedler (1978) found considerable support for his model. Strube and Garcia (1981) did a meta-analysis using Rosenthal's (1978, 1979) methods for combining p values. They claimed strong support for Fiedler's model and suggested areas for further research on co-acting and training groups. Peters, Hartke, and Pohlmann (1985) did a meta-analysis using effect sizes and controlling for sampling error. They found that in the studies used by Fiedler to derive his model, the sign of the effect size was as predicted in all eight octants and sampling error accounted for over 60% of the variance in all eight octants. When all the subsequent validation data were pooled, the sign of the effect size was in the right direction in all eight octants, but sampling error accounted for 60% of the variance in only three of the eight octants. They then broke the data down into lab and field studies. For the lab studies, the sign of the effect size was right in seven of the eight octants (all but Octant II) and sampling error accounted for over 60% of the variance in six of the eight octants. For the field studies, the sign of the effect size was right in seven of the eight octants (all but Octant VI) and sampling error accounted for over 60% of the variance in three of the eight octants. Peters et al. then criticized the Fiedler model on this basis.

While Peters et al. (1985) used the Hunter et al. (1982) procedure to estimate the variance in effect sizes, they did not consider the small total sample size for the average effect size within each octant. Consider the field validation studies. There were 54 effect sizes with a median sample size of 12, so that the average total sample size for each octant was only 81. For the problem octant, the total sample size was only 60. For a population effect size of $-.10$, the standard error of the mean effect size is 0.26 and the observed effect size could be as large as $+.21$ with probability 12%. Given eight chances to make an error with probability 12%, the total probability of an error—that is, capitalizing on chance—is 64%. Thus because of the small sample sizes, there is very high probability that one of the eight octants would come out in the wrong direction by chance. Consider the field studies. The total sample size in the problem octant is only 43 and the observed mean effect size is $-.01$ rather than positive. If the population effect size were $+.10$, the standard error for a sample size of 43 is 0.31 and the probability of a value as far off as $-.01$ or farther is 36%. With an error rate of 36%, the probability that one of the eight octants would come out in the wrong direction is 97%. Thus for the field studies there is also an extremely high probability that one octant would go in the wrong direction by chance.

Since examination of the data for lab and field studies in Peters *et al.* (1985) shows only random differences, we believe that the combined validation studies provide the best estimate of mean effect size. That analysis clearly supports the Fiedler contingency model. This also reconciles the findings of the Fiedler contingency model with the results of the meta-analysis of leadership traits done by Lord *et al.* (1986).

Hunter (1982) did a meta-analysis of nine validation studies predicting management performance in Sears. Sears had data of general cognitive ability (using the ACE), four personality batteries: the Guilford–Zimmerman, the Guilford–Martin, the Allport–Vernon, and the Kuder interest inventory. Cognitive ability had a validity of 0.44 predicting future performance ratings. Thirteen of the twenty-eight personality scales had a validity of 0.15 or more, though seven of the scales had indirect rather than direct impact. The six scales with direct effects were put together in a personality index which was uncorrelated with general cognitive ability. The index appears to measure blandness—a set of values and attitudes which do not promote argument or conflict; e.g. there is a negative weight for strong religious interests or strong political interests. The personality inventory had a validity of 0.48 and the combination of cognitive ability and personality had a validity of 0.64 predicting future performance ratings.

Race

There is a vast theoretical and empirical literature on the issue of test bias. The consensus conclusion in this literature is that cognitive aptitude tests are not biased against minority applicants (National Academy of Science, 1982). Meta-analyses have been performed on single group validity, differential validity, and predictive bias (reviewed in Hunter, Schmidt, and Rauschenberger, 1984). Consideration of bias requires the simultaneous comparison of the group difference on the predictor and the group difference on the criterion, with respect to the predictor criterion correlation and with proper consideration of predictor unreliability. Regression equations which also control for other predictors are better yet. Piecemeal consideration of these numbers is known to lead to erroneous conclusions. Yet meta-analyses of the separate numbers are being done and the predicted erroneous conclusions are being made. That is, meta-analyses on race are now repeating errors that had earlier been made in primary research.

Bernardin (1984) did a meta-analysis of race differences on work sample performance, performance ratings, job knowledge, and withdrawal measures (tenure, turnover, absenteeism, etc.). The mean for whites was higher than the mean for blacks on each measure. He reported his results as d statistics. These results will be transformed to equal frequency point biserial correlations in order to use path analysis. He found an average r of 0.26 (s.d. = 0.06) for work sample performance, 0.23 (s.d. = 0.05) for job knowledge, 0.15 (s.d. = 0.14) for performance ratings, and

0.025 (s.d. = 0.095) for withdrawal measures. The large standard deviation for withdrawal measures suggests that not all of his criterion variables were measuring the same thing. He made no comment on the high standard deviation for ratings.

According to the research showing that there is no bias in ability tests, Bernardin's (1984) results can be explained by the fact that differences in ability are causally translated into differences in job performance. To show this, we use the path analysis results of Hunter (1983a). He started with a meta-analysis of the correlations between general cognitive ability, job knowledge, work sample performance, and supervisor ratings taken from fourteen studies. He found a major path from general cognitive ability to job knowledge to work sample performance. The correlation between race and general cognitive ability is about 0.45. The correlation between ability and work sample performance for job incumbents across all studies was 0.53. Thus the correlation between race and work sample performance predicted from the path analysis is 0.45 (0.53) = 0.24 which is almost exactly equal to the value of 0.26 found by Bernardin. The correlation between ability and job knowledge was 0.61 which leads to a predicted correlation between race and job knowledge of $r = 0.27$ which is higher than the 0.23 found by Bernardin. Given correlations of 0.26 on work sample performance and 0.23 on job knowledge, the path analysis predicts a correlation of $r = 0.11$ between race and performance ratings which is lower than the value 0.15 observed by Bernardin. Half of the discrepancy between 0.11 and 0.15 stems from the discrepancy between in the observed correlation between race and job knowledge. If the predicted correlation of 0.27 is substituted for the unexpectedly low observed correlation of 0.23, then the path analysis predicts a value of 0.13 for ratings which almost exactly matches the observed value of 0.15. Thus the racial differences found by Bernardin are in accord with Hunter's path model. This in turn means that the size of each difference is the size that would be predicted by the hypothesis of no test bias. In addition, the observed differences are of exactly the size predicted by the hypothesis that there is no racial bias in supervisor ratings.

Bernardin (1984) reaches somewhat different conclusions. He interprets the withdrawal measures of tenure, turnover, and absenteeism to be 'objective' measures of performance while ignoring work sample measures as objective measures of performance. He then contrasts the small differences found on 'objective performance measures' with the large differences found on 'less direct' performance measures. Examination of Bernardin's references shows that the work samples in those studies were based on job analysis (e.g. Campbell, Crooks, Mahoney, and Rock (1973)). That is, in the studies analyzed by Bernardin, the work sample measures were content valid behavior samples based on extensive job analysis. According to the usual standards of scientific measurement (and the Principles of Division 14 of the American Psychological Association), this means that the work sample measures are construct valid measures of job performance. Bernardin presents no empirical evidence to suggest that absenteeism or tenure or turnover are construct valid measures of performance. The fact that blacks differ from whites by less on work withdrawal than on work performance is not relevant to the issue of racial bias in performance ratings.

Problems with construct validity have also plagued three recent meta-analyses by Ford, Kraiger, and Schechtman (1986; Kraiger and Ford, 1985; Ford, Schechtman, and Kraiger, 1985). Ford et al. (1986) sought to provide evidence regarding possible racial bias in ratings by comparing racial differences on objective and subjective measures. For absenteeism, they had good construct validity and found no significant difference ($r=0.11$ for objective, $r=0.15$ subjective). For 'cognitive' measures — training success and job knowledge — they had good construct validity and found differences on objective measures to be substantially larger than differences on subjective measures ($r=0.34$ for objective, $r=0.23$ for subjective). However, under the rubric 'performance', they compared apples and oranges. The subjective measure for performance is the rater's judgement of overall job performance, but the objective measures were fragmentary, low reliability partial indicators: accidents, customer complaints, shortages. The fact that the difference is quite low on each fragmentary indicator ($r=0.16$) does not mean that the difference on a proper composite might not be much higher. For example, if the correlation between these four indicators were 0, then the difference on the composite would be $r=0.32$ which is higher than the difference for ratings ($r=0.22$). Evidence that this is true can be found in the research on work sample performance which they ignored. Bernardin (1984) found a correlation of $r=0.26$ for work sample performance; an objective measure of overall performance. This correlation is larger than the correlation for the subjective measure of overall performance; i.e. the Ford *et al.* ratings correlation of 0.22 or the Bernardin correlation of $r=0.15$. Thus where objective and subjective measures both assess overall job performance, the difference on objective measures is larger than the difference on subjective measures. This is consistent with the extensive research showing that cognitive aptitude tests are not biased against blacks.

Ford *et al.* (1985) also did a meta-analysis on the correlation between objective and subjective measures for whites and blacks separately. For 'cognitive' measures, the correlations were the same ($r=0.31$ for blacks, $r=0.30$ for whites). However, their 'performance' indicators were again fragmentary partial indicators rather than construct valid work sample measures. For these fragmentary measures, the correlation was 0.23 for blacks and 0.06 for whites. Since these fragmentary measures are not known to be linearly related to performance, the difference in correlation could be an artifact of the difference in means.

Age

Hunter and Hunter (1984) did a meta-analysis of the correlations between age and performance ratings for 419 validation studies carried out by the US Employment Service. They reported an average correlation of -0.01 (s.d. $=0.12$). In data not reported, they found little variation across job complexity: $r=-0.02$ (s.d. $=0.14$), $r=0.00$ (s.d. $=0.11$), and $r=0.01$ (s.d. $=0.09$) for low, medium, and high complexity jobs respectively.

Waldman and Avolio (1986) also did a meta-analysis relating age to performance though on far fewer studies. For performance ratings, they had thirteen non-professional jobs ($r=-0.18$) and five professional jobs ($r=-0.05$). They interpreted their findings as proving a general negative correlation between age and performance ratings. Instead, the negative correlations show that they had a biased sample of studies of performance ratings. The US Employment Service correlated age with performance in every study. Since all correlations with age are reported, those analyzed by Hunter and Hunter (1984) are an unbiased sample of correlations. On the other hand, most published studies do not report correlations for age. Thus those few published studies which do report these correlations may well do so because the correlation seemed unusual; a prescription for fluke results. This may be a case where there is a 'file drawer' problem (Rosenthal, 1979).

Waldman and Avolio (1986) also found studies assessing performance using productivity and peer ratings. For productivity, the correlation between age and performance was consistency positive: both for professionals ($r=0.27$, s.d.$=0.16$) and for non-professionals ($r=0.26$, s.d.$=0.11$). For peer ratings, the correlation was positive for professionals ($r=0.30$, s.d.$=0.04$) while for non-professionals the correlation was negative ($r=0.32$, s.d.$=0.06$).

Miscellaneous

There is a job which current economic theory says cannot be done: the job of financial analyst. A typical analyst keeps track of 30 or 40 stocks. At the beginning of each quarter, the analyst predicts future return on each stock. The correlation between predicted and actual return is called an 'information coefficient'. In some trust companies, the raises for individual analysts are determined by that correlation. However, according to the 'efficient market' hypothesis, all relevant information about companies is assimilated instanteously by all investors. Thus prediction of return should be impossible. Information coefficients should all be 0 and there should be no individual differences between analysts. Coggin and Hunter (1983) used meta-analysis to test these hypotheses. In one trust company, they found a mean correlation of $r=.10$ with a standard deviation of 0.00; i.e. no individual differences between information coefficients once sampling error is removed. They then went to an independent service firm which made a national sample available. The mean correlation was 0.00 with a standard deviation of 0.00; i.e. the finding predicted by the efficient market hypothesis. Dimson and Marsh (1984) replicated the Coggin and Hunter study on a national sample of British analysts. They too found no individual differences in correlations after sampling error was removed, though they found a mean correlation of about 0.10. Thus all three data sets found no individual differences in the information coefficient, but two of the three data sets did find a mean correlation greater than the 0.00 predicted by the efficient market hypothesis.

Jackson and Schuler (1985) reported average correlations of -0.12 and -0.11 between role ambiguity and role conflict with performance ratings. They reported correlations of -0.10 and $+0.02$ with 'objective' measures, not further defined. Mabe and West (1982) did a meta-analysis of self-ratings of performance. However, they did not break their findings down by criterion measure. Brown (1981) reported that the validity of a biodata form was moderated by 'quality of management practices', but gave no definition of these practices nor any theoretical basis for such a finding. Rodgers, Helbrun, and Hunter (1986) used meta-analytic raw score regression line methods to look at the relationship between seniority and performance for workers who were or were not exonerated in grievance proceedings.

Situation Specific Validity and Validity Generalization

The first comprehensive meta-analyses of validity were done by Ghiselli (1966, 1973) who used the method later called 'meta-analysis' by Glass (1976). Like Glass, Ghiselli made no correction for sampling error, or error of measurement, or range restriction. The failure to correct his variances for sampling error was a grievous error. Ghiselli simply took sampling eror at face value and was thus faced with random variation that seemed to have no explanation. He concluded with his law of situation specific validity: that validity coefficients vary across settings for unknown reasons. As a consequence, he also believed that a local validation study should be run to see if an instrument is valid in the local setting.

Schmidt and Hunter (1977) noted that Ghiselli's 'unexplained' variation could be explained by artifacts in study results. Most of the variation is just the high degree of sampling error to be expected in small sample statistics such as the correlations in personnel selection research. They also noted that even if statistical artifacts did not explain all variation across studies, it might still be possible to generalize validity across settings if the residual variance (the variance after subtracting the effect of correctable artifacts) was small enough. They then set an agenda to use meta-analysis to study the two issues: situation specific validity and validity generalization. These issues have now been thoroughly explored for cognitive aptitude tests; the investigation is proceeding more slowly for other predictors.

Not everyone believes that sampling error exists, though there have been thousands of physical experiments showing the random variation predicted by statistical equations. There is now direct evidence of sampling error in personnel selection research. Schmidt and Hunter (1984) located an organization where a succession of validity studies had been done. They showed that (1) the amount of variation across studies was the amount predicted by the sampling error formulas of meta-analysis and (2) the amount of variation across studies within that setting was comparable to the amount of variation found across settings in other personnel selection research. Schmidt, Ocasio, Hillary, and Hunter (1985) showed the same thing using an empirical Monte Carlo method. They took very large sample data from one organization and randomly broke them up into subsets that acted like small sample 'studies'. Again the random variation was as predicted from sampling error formulas. Dunnette et al. (1982) also used the Monte Carlo technique to show that variation across settings in their data was no larger than variation across random subsets of the data formed with the same sample size.

More than 200 meta-analyses have now been done looking at the validity of specific cognitive aptitudes predicting performance in specific jobs. Correctable study artifacts account for about 80% of the variance across studies. Since there are many artifacts such as computational and transcriptional errors whose variance is not known and which is not subtracted, the 20% of the variance which is left may all be due to those uncontrolled artifacts. Schmidt and Hunter have concluded that these data show that there is no situation specificity for the validity of specific test-job combinations. However, even if all the residual variance were situational, it is small enough to leave overwhelming evidence for validity generalization. Some of the areas used in this research includes: technical occupations where apprentices are employed (Northrop, 1986); clerical occupations (Dye, 1984; Pearlman, Schmidt, and Hunter, 1980; Schmidt, Hunter, Pearlman, and Caplan, 1980); computer programmers (Schmidt, Gast-Rosenberg, and Hunter, 1980); health science and engineering aides and technicians (Lilienthal and Pearlman 1983); law enforcement personnel (Hirsh, Northrop, and Schmidt, 1986); mechanical repairers (Schmidt, Hunter, Pearlman, and Caplan, 1980); petroleum industry operations and maintenance personnel (Callender and Osburn, 1981; Schmidt, Hunter, and Caplan, 1981); power plant operators (Dunnette *et al.* 1982); semi-professional occupations (Trattner, 1985); and sales clerks (Schmidt, Hunter, and Caplan, 1981). There is also evidence of generalizability of the validity for general cognitive ability across jobs of entirely different content as shown in Tables 10.1–10.6.

There is now a professional consensus on part of the Schmidt and Hunter (1977) agenda. In response to Schmidt, Hunter, Pearlman, and Hirsh, (1985), a blue ribbon panel of experts in personnel selection research (Sackett, Schmitt, Tenopyr, Kehoe, and Zedeck, 1985) agreed that the validity of cognitive aptitude tests generalizes across settings in all cases. They agreed that if there is situation specificity, the variation is very small. There is still some question as to whether the residual variation is absolutely 0. They were not ready to draw a consensus conclusion as to the generalizability of validity of other predictors though there is now substantial evidence there too. Even Schmidt and Hunter are not yet prepared to argue that situation specificity will be totally absent for other predictors.

Concommitant Determinants of Job Performance — Job Knowledge

This section will consider the prediction of job performance from characteristics acquired on the job. For example, the most important determinant of job performance is job knowledge. These are the characteristics used for certification, lateral transfers, and promotion. These characteristics can rarely be used for entry level hiring because they usually do not exist until the person has worked at the job. However, the correlations for these characteristics are very important for building a theory of job performance. The review will begin with comprehensive meta-analyses and then continue with special cases.

Hunter and Hunter (1984) noted that if a person is already working at a job that is very similar to the job to be predicted, then current performance can be used to predict future job performance. The better the measure of current performance, the better the prediction of future performance. This hypothesis was confirmed by the validity findings for performance ratings. The results for performance ratings are shown in Table 10.5. Table 10.5 also presents the results from Schmitt *et al.* (1984) and presents the validity of general cognitive ability for comparison purposes. The results for work sample performance are shown in Table 10.6.

Table 10.5 presents the meta-analyses predicting supervisor ratings from characteristics acquired on the job. The correlations for Schmitt *et al.* (1984) were corrected for error of measurement on ratings using a reliability of 0.60. The correlation under 'peer ratings' for Schmitt *et al.* also includes supervisor ratings. The findings confirm the Hunter and Hunter hypothesis. Measures of current performance predict in order of the quality of measurement of current performance: work sample performance (0.54) higher than peer ratings (0.49) as high as behavioral consistency experience ratings higher than job tryout (0.44) assessed by supervisors. The indirect indicators of current performance have varying success. Job knowledge (0.48) predicts almost as well as current work sample performance. Assessment centers (0.43) are only slightly lower. However, experience on the job (0.20) predicts much more poorly.

TABLE 10.5—The validity predicting supervisor ratings for characteristics acquired on the job; from Hunter and Hunter (1984) and Schmitt, Gooding, Noe, and Kirsch (1984). All correlations were corrected for error of measurement in the ratings using a reliability of 0.60. The correlations for cognitive ability have been corrected for range restriction using $u = 0.67$

PREDICTOR	HH VALIDITY	SGNK VALIDITY
Work sample performance	0.54	0.41
General cognitive ability	0.53	0.41
Peer ratings	0.49	0.41
Behavioral consistency e.r.[a]	0.49	
Job knowledge test	0.48	
Job tryout	0.44	
Assessment center	0.43	0.55
Experience on job[b]	0.20	

[a] Behavioral consistency experience ratings
[b] For a representative sample of jobs studied using concurrent validity studies

TABLE 10.6—The validity predicting work sample performance for characteristics acquired on the job; from Hunter's (in press) civilian work correlations and Schmitt, Gooding, Noe, and Kirsch (1984). All correlations have been corrected for error of measurement in both predictor and criterion and all were corrected for restriction in range

PREDICTOR	HH VALIDITY	SGNK VALIDITY
General cognitive ability	0.75	0.71
Job knowledge	0.80	
Supervisor ratings		
Consensus summated ratings	0.52	
Single supervisor summated rating	0.40	
Single supervisor global rating	0.32	
Experience[a] on the job	0.56	

[a] From Schmidt, Hunter, and Outerbridge (1986); for a special sample of military personnel with a very low mean experience and a very high standard deviation

Table 10.6 presents the meta-analyses predicting work sample performance. In this table, the correlations have also been corrected for predictor unreliability. The correlations are from Hunter (in press; corrected for range restriction from Hunter, 1983a) and from Schmitt et al. (1984). The correlation for experience is from Schmidt, Hunter, and Outerbridge (1986) and represents a special military population with a very low mean and very high standard deviation on experience. Thus this value is much higher than the correlation for a representative civilian job and population (average 6 years experience rather than 2 years).

The most striking findings from Table 10.6 are the very high validities for job knowledge (0.80 and general cognitive ability (0.75). People who do not know what to do will not do it very well. The much lower correlation for even ideal supervisor ratings (0.52) shows that ratings are relatively poor measures of performance. The quality of ratings drops still further under ordinary measurement conditions: 0.40 for single supervisor summated rating scales and 0.32 for a single supervisor global rating. There is reason to believe that the correlation for operational ratings would be lower yet (Landy and Farr, 1980).

Hunter (in press, 1983a) used path analysis to show that much of the high validity for general cognitive ability is due to the fact that it predicts job knowledge. General cognitive ability predicts job knowledge with a correlation of 0.80: the classic finding that general cognitive ability measures learning ability. If cognitive ability were only relevant because it predicts job knowledge, then the correlation between ability and performance would be (0.80) (0.80)=0.64. The actual correlation is 0.75 which is higher. The beta weights for performance predicted from ability and knowledge together are 0.31 and 0.56 respectively. Thus cognitive ability predicts job performance above and beyond the extent to which it predicts the learning of job knowledge. This confirms the many construct and content validity studies showing that the major cognitive skills are used in everyday job performance.

Schmidt, Hunter, and Outerbridge (1986) extended the Hunter (in press, 1983a) work to include experience on the job. There were two important new findings. First, experience has its main impact on performance through job knowledge; though there is also a direct effect of experience on performance itself. Second, experience effects performance ratings only through job knowledge and work sample performance. This further confirms the hypothesis that performance ratings are an imperfect reflection of work performance which is measured near perfectly by work sample performance.

Further work on experience was done by McDaniel (1986). Schmidt, Hunter, and Outerbridge (1986) noted that using experience as a predictor is comparable to looking at learning curves. They therefore hypothesized that performance is a non-linear function of experience. They also hypothesized that differences between ability groups would be maintained over time. McDaniel tested these hypotheses in a series of meta-analyses done on the US Employment Service 'revalidation' data: i.e. the large database gathered to check for potential test bias against minority applicants. Both hypotheses were confirmed for the Employment Service data. The learning curves extended much farther in time than was anticipated. There was still growth — though very slow growth — at 20 years. Schmidt, Hunter, Outerbridge, and Goff (1986) are in the process of extending the analysis of learning curves to job knowledge and work sample performance using the military data gathered by Vineberg and Taylor (1972). The results are similar to those for the US Employment Service though their data are distorted by attrition artifacts past 5 years.

Similar findings are emerging from the US Army Project A data. Borman, White, Gast, and Pulakos (1985) confirmed the Hunter (in press, 1983a) path model both for supervisor ratings and for peer ratings. White, Borman, Hough, and Hoffman (1986) have extended the model to include personality variables (which they call 'temperament).

The findings for work sample performance cast a new light on the findings of Hunter and Hunter (1984) looking at performance ratings. They found that measures of current job performance predict future performance ratings. The better the measure of current performance, the better the prediction of future performance ratings. Current work sample performance was hypothesized to be the best measure of current performance and was found to be the best predictor of future performance ratings, confirming that hypothesis. However, the correlation of 0.54 for future ratings greatly understates potential validity because future performance is only imperfectly measured by ratings. If future performance were well measured, i.e. measured by work sample performance, all the validities in Table 10.5 would be much higher. The correlation between current work samples and future ratings is 0.54 which is about the same as the concurrent work sample correlation with ratings. If there is little change in rank order of actual performance in the shift between jobs, then current work sample would predict future work sample performance nearly perfectly. General cognitive ability would predict with validity near 0.75, and current job knowledge would predict with validity near 0.80.

Hunter (in press) also summarizes a series of meta-analyses of military data (Hunter, 1983b, 1983c, 1984a, 1984b, 1985a) looking at the issue of the predictive power of specific cognitive aptitudes. The findings were similar to the meta-analytic findings for the US Employment Service (Hunter, 1980a): cognitive aptitude composites tailored to the job do not predict performance any better than general cognitive ability. Specific aptitudes do not add to the prediction by general cognitive ability except in a handful of special jobs.

To summarize: the most important determinant of individual differences in job performance now known is job knowledge. The correlation between job knowledge and job performance in civilian work is 0.80 on average. The correlation between general cognitive ability and job knowledge is 0.80. This explains much of the high validity of cognitive ability predicting job performance: $r = 0.75$. The indirect causal effect of ability on performance through job knowledge is $(0.80)(0.56) = 0.45$ while the direct effect is 0.31. Since job knowledge determines job performance in all jobs, it is no surprise that general cognitive ability predicts performance on all jobs.

Organizational Interventions

There has been one comprehensive meta-analysis of organization interventions: that done by Guzzo, Jette, and Katzell (1985). Their results for performance are presented in Table 10.7. The results are given as correlations to make it easy to enter them into path models.

The highest correlation is $r = 0.73$ for financial compensation. However, this figure does not represent only individual compensation but also includes studies in which there are incentives for group or plant performance. Thus the massive effect may reflect changes in organizational or work strategy rather than an increase in effort. The next highest effect is $r = 0.39$ for training. The high payoff for training is consistent with the high correlation between job knowledge and job performance ($r = 0.75$; Hunter, in press). All of the interventions have very large effects in dollar terms (Hunter and Schmidt, 1983).

Management by objectives

The effect of management by objectives (MBO) is severely understated in Table 10.7. Rodgers and Hunter (1986) found that if the MBO program has strong support from top management, then there is a 42% (s.d. = 18%) increase in productivity, while if there is not high top management commitment, there is only a 4% (s.d. = 9%) increase which is not significantly different from control group change. Schmidt and Hunter (1983) found that the typical performance standard deviation on a ratio scale is 20% of the mean. Thus an increase of 42% in productivity corresponds to a d of 42/20 = 2.1 or a correlation of $r = 0.72$.

An earlier widely cited narrative review by Kondrasuk (1980) concluded that there was little evidence for a positive effect for MBO. Rodgers and Hunter (1986) showed that he was led to this false conclusion because he threw out all studies without control groups. The only studies with control groups were those where there was weak commitment from top management. The reason for this is that control groups for a whole organization intervention can only mean subdivisions of the main organization. But if top management is committed to MBO, then they apply it to the whole organization and not to divisions piecemeal.

Goal setting

Most studies of goal setting do not look at total job performance. Laboratory studies consider a single task. Many field studies consider one aspect of a task. Locke (1986) noted that field studies are often as artificial as lab studies. Kopelman (1986) makes this point in listing some of the work behaviors studied: smiling at customers, reducing interruptions by hotel clerks, handwashing by kitchenworkers, other safety acts. It may be better to think of goal setting research as task performance rather than job performance.

Guzzo *et al.* (1985) report a grand average correlation of $r = 0.31$ for goal setting. However, the moderator effects are so great that this average means very little. In addition to the Guzzo *et al.* global meta-analysis, there have been four meta-analyses

TABLE 10.7 — The average effect on output of various organizational interventions expressed as point biserial correlations as found in meta-analyses by Guzzo, Jette, and Katzell (1985)

INTERVENTION	CORRELATION
Financial compensation	0.73
Training	0.39
Decision making strategies	0.33
Organizational development	0.31
Goal setting	0.31
Work redesign	0.25
Supervisory methods	0.25
Management by objectives	0.22
Appraisal and feedback	0.20
Work rescheduling	0.15

devoted exclusively to goal setting. Each of the four focused on potential moderator variables (Chidester and Grigsby, 1984; Mento, Steele, and Karren, in press; Latham and Lee, 1986; and Tubbs, 1986). All four studies make the same mistake in analysis: they look at each moderator separately using all studies instead of breaking down the studies by combinations of moderators. This would work only if there were additivity of moderating effects; and that has not been true of most studies where multiple moderators have been considered in combination (e.g. see the discussion of participative decision making below). Differences on one potential moderator variable may be confounded with effects due to another moderator. This is especially true of the smaller moderators.

Some methodological moderators can be best dealt with by segregating studies. For example, Tubbs (1986) found that studies with subjectively estimated goal effects radically understated the effects of goal setting in comparison to studies with direct measurement. The average effect was $r = 0.38$ for direct measurement but only $r = 0.09$ for survey measurement. He then looked at other moderator variables only for studies with direct measurement. The other authors did not note this distinction. On the other hand, Mento et al. (in press) noted that three experimental studies instructed subjects to stop working once they reached their goal, thereby guaranteeing very large differences between easy and hard goal groups. Mento et al. dropped these studies, but Tubbs seems to have missed them.

Latham and Lee (1986) did not do a quantitative meta-analysis. They merely counted significance test results to see if lab studies ever indicated results in the opposite direction from field studies. In the goal setting area, the population correlations are all positive and hence there are no differences in direction to be found. On the other hand, counting significance test results loses too much information to detect the whopping difference in effect size between lab and field studies.

The moderator analyses for Chidester and Grigsby (1984); Mento, Steele, and Karren (1986); and Tubbs (1986) are summarized in Table 10.8. All three meta-analyses broke the data down between goal difficulty studies and goal specifity studies, though there is little difference between results; especially for field studies. Chidester and Grigsby found only 41 studies while Tubbs found 121 and Mento et al. found 129. The one consistent difference found by all investigators is the massive difference in effect size between lab and field studies. Lab studies typically have effects about 50% larger than the effects in field studies. Tubbs found a very large difference between studies that set a quantity goal and studies that set a time goal. Averaging across all studies, the quantity goal studies found an effect of $r = 0.32$ while time goal studies found an effect of $r = 0.17$; a difference of nearly 2 to 1 in magnitude. Mento et al. found that studies done on workers with high education found about 50% larger effects than studies done with less educated workers ($r = 0.27$ versus $r = 0.18$). If all three effects are independent, then a field study using a time goal for blue-collar workers should have an effect of $r = 0.13$ while a lab study on students with a quantity goal would have an effect of $r = 0.58$. That is a very large spread across effect sizes. If there is further variation within these sets of studies, then there may be field settings in which goal setting has even smaller effects.

Furthermore, goal setting has not been tried for a random selection of jobs. Rather, goal setting is tried for those jobs which appear to be promising for goal setting. Thus the effects studied may overstate the general effectiveness of goal setting in

TABLE 10.8—The average effect size for goal setting in different kinds of studies as found by Chidester and Grigsby (1984); Mento, Steel, and Karren (in press); and Tubbs (1986)

	GOAL DIFFICULTY			GOAL SPECIFICITY		
	CG	MSK	T	CG	MSK	T
Laboratory	0.25	0.31	0.41	0.25	0.27	0.28
Field	0.19	0.24	0.25	0.24	0.17	0.21
Education — High		0.29		0.24	0.24	
Education — Low		0.18		0.22	0.19	
Quantity goal			0.39			0.24
Time goal			0.21			0.12
Feedback given		0.29	0.38	0.34	0.24	0.24
not given		0.28	0.17	0.22	0.20	0.25
Incentive given		0.24	0.24		0.31	
not given		0.29	0.29		0.21	
Overall effect	0.27	0.28	0.38	0.30	0.22	0.24
Number of effects	19	70	65	22	49	48

new and less promising circumstances. While there is no doubt that goal setting has a positive effect, the size of the effect ranges down to very small effects in certain field settings ($r = 0.13$, s.d. = unknown). Given the size of the moderator variables, it is very important that future research on goal setting focus on the intervening variables that determine the bottom line effect. At present, the construct meaning of goal setting is unknown.

Objective feedback

The meta-analyses on goal setting found no moderating effect for feedback. However, Kopelman (1986) found that objective feedback increased performance even without setting goals. It may be that the goal setting tasks studied are usually such that people can tell for themselves how well they are doing. Kopelman found that objective feedback increased corresponding work behaviors by 43.4%, increased performance criteria by 46.5%, and increased output by 15.2%. Using the output standard deviation ratio of 20% found by Schmidt and Hunter (1983), a 15.2% increase in output corresponds to a d of $15.2/20 = 0.76$ or $r = 0.36$. That is, Kopelman found that objective feedback alone generated as high an increase in output as goal setting.

Participative decision making

Miller and Monge (in press) did a meta-analysis of the effect of participative decision making on performance. They found large moderator effects. First, participation in goal setting yields only a small effect (as noted in Table 10.8); $r = 0.11$. In settings where workers participate in a variety of decisions, there was a sharp difference between field and lab studies. When leadership behavior was manipulated in the lab, participative decision making led to a decrease in performance: $r = 0.33$. When task or group structure were manipulated in the lab, there was no effect; $r = 0.01$. However, in field studies, extensive participation in decision making produced a large increase in performance: $r=0.27$. Miller and Monge interpreted this increase as due to improved flow of information.

TURNOVER

When people terminate employment, the organization loses their training and experience. Replacement of these losses costs money and thus turnover has usually been viewed as a negative event. However, McEvoy and Cascio (1986) have noted that the impact of turnover may not be negative; it may be positive. There is a very important prior question which must be answered before this issue can be addressed: is it the good or the poor performers who leave? To the extent that it is poor performers who leave early, then their termination provides the opportunity to replace poor workers by good workers. The resulting increase in productivity may more than compensate for the loss in experience and training. Thus the relationship between performance and turnover will be addressed before looking at other predictors of turnover.

There is also an important methodological caveat to be placed on turnover correlations. It is important to make the technical distinction between 'turnover' and 'tenure'. Tenure is the length of time an employee stays with an organization. Tenure is a continuous variable. Administrators define 'turnover' by counting the number of people who leave the organization during a given time period. Thus they count the number of people whose tenure has run out during that period. Among other things, this converts the continuous variable of tenure into the dichotomous variable of turnover. Many psychologists have mirrored this shift by dichotomizing their tenure data. They define some threshold such as 1 year or 6 months and then label the person as stay or leave. This is statistically the same as replacing correlations computed using a continuous variable by correlations computed using a dichotomous variable. This systematically reduces the correlation as in the distinction between 'biserial' and 'point biserial' correlations. If the dichotomization were at a median split—i.e. a 50-50 split—then the correlation would be reduced to 80% of its original value and could be corrected by a corresponding 25% (i.e. $1.00/0.80 = 1.25$) increase. However, if the split is extremely deviant from the median, then there is a further reduction. For a 90-10 split, the further reduction is an additional 40%. Turnover splits are frequently very extreme and the corresponding correlations are therefore extremely low. The implications of this will be spelled out for the McEvoy and Cascio (1986) study where it was possible to pull out the data for even splits and generate a corrected value. In the other meta-analyses reported here, no such correction was made. Thus most of the correlations reported here are underestimates.

Tenure and Performance

Turnover can result from either of two decisions: (1) management may decide to fire or lay off an employee or (2) the employee may decide to quit. Low performance would be expected to influence either decision. Thus one would expect a high correlation between performance and tenure. This is exactly what was found in the meta-analysis done by McEvoy and Cascio (1986). Analyzing all data together, they found an average correlation of 0.54 (s.d. $=0.10$) between performance ratings and tenure for involuntary termination and an average correlation of 0.21 (s.d. = 0.15) between performance ratings and tenure for voluntary termination. However, these values are severely flawed by an artifact in the computation of turnover correlations: the dichotomization of tenure. Correlations based on extreme splits are necessarily much smaller than correlations based on near even splits. These 'bad data' create the appearance of a moderator variable where there is none.

McEvoy and Cascio (1986) found that nearly half the studies used very uneven splits. The correlations for uneven splits were severely depressed as predicted from the algebra of the biserial correlation as noted here. They found an average correlation of 0.40 for the studies with approximately even splits and an average correlation of only 0.21 for the studies with extreme splits. However, the effect of the extreme splits on variance is even greater. Nearly all the variance across studies other than sampling error is due to the uneven split studies. McEvoy and Cascio thought they had identified three moderator variables in analyses combining good (near even splits) and bad data (extreme splits). However, in each case, the alleged moderator variable was confounded with the evenness of split. When only the even split data are considered, there is no evidence of moderator variables.

A reanalysis of the McEvoy and Cascio (1986) data considering only even split data shows an average correlation of 0.51 (s.d. = 0.00) between performance ratings and tenure for involuntary termination and an average correlation of 0.31 (s.d. = 0.09) between performance ratings and tenure for voluntary termination. These correlations are for the dichotomous turnover variable. Had tenure been correctly left continuous, these correlations would have been about 0.64 (s.d. = 0.00) for involuntary termination and 0.39 (s.d. = 0.11) for voluntary termination. For total termination, the average correlation between performance ratings and tenure would be about 0.52 with variation depending on the relative proportion of voluntary and involuntary termination.

To summarize: properly corrected, the meta-analysis on turnover and performance done by McEvoy and Cascio (1986) shows that the correlation between tenure and performance ratings is 0.64 for involuntary termination and 0.39 for voluntary termination. Thus it is those with poor performance ratings who leave early. Unless there is an extremely expensive training program involved or unless there is extremely high administrative cost for termination (as in frequent court cases), this means that turnover is positive for the organization. Turnover provides the opportunity to replace poor performers by good performers. However, it should be noted that the turnover studies in the McEvoy and Cascio (1986) meta-analysis were not studies of companies in crisis. If high turnover were a sign of bad management or if the organization is going through extreme contraction because of economic circumstances, the correlations reported here might not apply.

Other Predictors of Turnover

There have been two comprehensive meta-analyses of predictors of tenure: Hunter and Hunter (1984) and Schmitt et al. (1984). Table 10.9 presents the average correlations from those two studies. The correlation for general cognitive ability in Schmitt et al. was corrected for restriction in range using the value $u = 0.67$. The other correlations have not been corrected in any way. In particular, Table 10.9

has no correction for the fact that the correlations are point biserial correlations including studies with extreme splits. Thus all the correlations are at least 25% too small.

The positive correlation for general cognitive ability is particularly noteworthy. Many people have speculated that there would be a negative correlation between cognitive ability and tenure because bright workers would leave early to find better jobs. The correlation is positive: an observed average of 0.21 for dichotomous scoring which represents a correlation of at least 0.26 for continuous scoring. Thus the brighter workers stay longer. This is consistent with the fact that it is the workers with poor performance ratings who leave early.

The correlation of 0.21 for biodata from Schmitt et al. (1984) is based on far more studies than the 0.26 for Hunter and Hunter (1984) and should be regarded as the more accurate figure. This correlation for tenure is as high as for general cognitive ability; which was not true of biodata predicting performance. However, biodata keys for tenure raise even uglier ethical questions than does the racial difference on cognitive ability. Inspection of the keyed items where available suggests that biodata keys would cause employers to avoid hiring young women with children, especially if they are unmarried or black. Note also that the biodata key is rejecting workers directly on demographic characteristics rather than rejecting people incidentally because they are low on a job related qualification.

Interests predict tenure with a biserial correlation of at least $1.25(0.22) = 0.28$, which is far higher than the correlation between interests and performance ratings which is 0.10. Thus people whose interests do not fit the job may register their lack of fit by leaving early rather than in reduced performance. Since interests are not highly correlated with general cognitive ability, the correlation of 0.28 may well be the incremental validity of interests in combination with ability.

The employee's decision to terminate is preceded by a conscious intention to quit. Steele and Ovalle (1985) found an average correlation of 0.50 between intentions and turnover. They also found average correlations between tenure of 0.38 with organization commitment, 0.31 with work satisfaction, and 0.26 with job satisfaction. They found that the correlation between intention and turnover decreases as the time interval between intent and turnover increases. That is, those who do not quit right away often change their minds.

Fisher and Gitelson (1983) reported average correlations of -0.13 and $+0.03$ between tenure and role ambiguity and role conflict respectively. Using more studies, Jackson and Schuler (1985) found average correlations of -0.16 and $+0.02$.

Organizational Interventions

There is one comprehensive review of the impact of interventions on tenure: the review by Guzzo, Jette, and Katzell (1985). Their results expressed as correlations are presented in Table 10.10.

The largest effect is for training, $r = 0.30$. Since training increases performance, this is consistent with the finding that poor performers leave early. Work design has an impact of $r = 0.14$. McEvoy and Cascio (1985) also did a meta-analysis of the effect of job enrichment on tenure. They found $r = 0.17$ which is very close to the Guzzo et al. value of 0.14 for work redesign.

TABLE 10.9—The average validity predicting job tenure of various predictors as found in meta-analyses by Hunter and Hunter (1984) and by Schmitt, Gooding, Noe, and Kirsch (1984)

PREDICTOR	HH VALIDITY	SGNK VALIDITY
Reference checks	0.27	
Interests	0.22	
General cognitive ability		0.21
Biodata	0.26	0.21
Physical ability		0.15
Personality		0.12
College grades	0.05	
Interview	0.03	

TABLE 10.10—The average effect on tenure of various organizational interventions expressed as point biserial correlations as found in meta-analyses by Guzzo, Jette, and Katzell (1985)

INTERVENTION	CORRELATION
Training	0.30
Financial compensation	0.17
Work redesign	0.14
Organizational development	0.09
Appraisal and feedback	0.09
Supervisory methods	0.05
Work rescheduling	0.05
Goal setting	0.05
Management by objectives	0.00
Realistic job preview	−0.01

Table 10.10 shows a correlation of only $r=0.17$ between financial compensation and tenure. Thus increasing wages does little to prolong tenure. This is consistent with the fact that most of those who leave early leave because of poor performance rather than to seek a higher paying job.

Realistic Job Preview

Premack and Wanous (1985) conducted a meta-analysis of realistic job preview (RJP) experiments which they viewed as an attempt to resolve the inconsistencies in five recent narrative reviews of the RJP. They found a correlation of $r=0.06$ with tenure. A second meta-analysis of the RJP restricted to field settings was done by McEvoy and Cascio (1985). They found an average impact of $r=0.09$; though this was moderated by job complexity as hypothesized by Reilly, Brown, Blood, and Malatesta (1981). The correlation for the higher complexity jobs was $r=0.12$ while the correlation for the lower complexity jobs was $r=0.02$.

JOB SATISFACTION

This section will review meta-analyses related to job satisfaction. The relationship between job satisfaction and job performance is put in this section rather than under performance because we believe that the causal arrow runs from performance to satisfaction. We may be wrong. We also believe the causal arrow runs from role ambiguity and role conflict to satisfaction. In the case of satisfaction and unionization, the arrow is probably from satisfaction to unionization. We also believe that the arrow runs from satisfaction to absenteeism. In the case of the Job Diagnostic Survey (JDS), there is much room for argument as to the causal relationship. The question is: does the JDS measure job complexity or does the JDS measure work satisfaction? We also review meta-analyses of the impact on satisfaction of two interventions: participative decision making and MBO.

Job Performance and Job Satisfaction

Petty, McGee, and Cavender (1984) found an average correlation between job performance ratings and overall job satisfaction of 0.31. With even more studies, Iaffaldano and Muchinsky (1985) found a correlation between performance ratings and overall satisfaction of 0.29; a virtually identical figure.

However, Iaffaldano and Muchinsky (1985) also did meta-analyses on the components of overall satisfaction: pay satisfaction, co-worker satisfaction, etc. For components, the average correlation is, of course, much lower: $r = 0.17$. This figure for components is the only figure that they cite in their abstract or discussion. Thus this was the value found by Guzzo, Jackson, and Katzell (1986). Guzzo et al. then compared the $r = 0.17$ instead of the $r = 0.29$ to the correlation of 0.31 in Petty et al. (1984). They then falsely concluded that the two meta-analyses had generated conflicting results.

Role Ambiguity and Role Conflict

Fisher and Gitelson (1983) found average correlations of -0.25 and -0.35 between role ambiguity and role conflict respectively with overall job satisfaction, where neither correlation is corrected for attenuation. Jackson and Schuler (1985) found more studies and corrected for attenuation. They found correlations of -0.46 and -0.48 for role ambiguity and role conflict respectively.

Unionization

Premack (1984) found a correlation of -0.38 between overall job satisfaction and membership in a union. Prior narrative reviews had argued that the correlation between satisfaction and unionization varied greatly from one setting to the next and there was considerable speculation as to possible moderator variables. But in fact, nearly all of the variance across studies was found to be due to sampling error.

Absenteeism

Across 31 studies, Hackett and Guion (1985) found a correlation between overa
satisfaction and absenteeism of −0.14. Terborg, Lee, Smith, Davis, and Turbi
(1982) did a meta-analysis of absenteeism for six stores in a national chain. The
looked only at facets of satisfaction and provided no value for overall satisfactio
However, their values seem to be consistent with the findings of Hackett and Guio

The JDS

Hackman and Oldham (1976) developed the Job Diagnostic Survey (JDS) in hop
of measuring properties of the job. They hoped that workers could faithfully recor
five job dimensions: task identity, task significance, skill variety, autonomy, an
feedback. They hoped that the total score across the dimensions would measur
'job complexity'. Stone (1986) adopts this same hopeful position in naming th
summated score 'job scope'. However, there is ample reason to question th
assumption. We will call the summated score 'JDS' as a neutral label.

Stone's (1986) own meta-analysis calls the label 'job scope' into question. He foun
an average correlation between JDS and work satisfaction to be $r = 0.88$. Furthermor
this value was not corrected for attenuation. Thus the corrected value is probab
1.00. That is, Stone found JDS to be identical to work satisfaction. Few would arg
that work satisfaction is identical to job complexity.

Stone (1986) also looked at the correlation between JDS and overall job satisfactio
$r = 0.63$. This is the level that would be expected from the correlation between wo
satisfaction and overall satisfaction. Stone also looked at the correlations for th
component scales of the JDS. Here the correlations were lower as would be expecte
from measurement theory: $r = 0.65$ for work satisfaction and $r = 0.53$ for overa
satisfaction.

Loher, Noe, Moeller, and Fitzgerald (1985) also did a meta-analysis betwee
JDS components and overall job satisfaction. They reported a somewhat lower valu
$r = 0.39$ instead of $r = 0.53$. They also looked at studies where the data were broke
down by growth needs strength in accordance with the Hackman and Oldham (197
hypothesis. They found an average correlation of $r = 0.38$ for those low in growt
needs and a much higher correlation of $r = 0.68$ for those high in growth needs. Th
bears out the Hackman and Oldham prediction. Note that the moderator correlatio
0.38 and 0.68 are not consistent with their overall correlation of 0.39. On the oth
hand, the average $(0.38 + 0.68)/2 = 0.53$ exactly matches the average correlatio
reported by Stone (1986). Thus their reported figure of 0. 39 was probably off becau
of an outlier or a computational error.

Participative Decision Making

Miller and Monge (in press) performed a meta-analysis on the effect of participativ
decision making on job satisfaction. They found strong moderator effects. For la
studies, they found a uniformly high relationship: $r = 0.38$. For field studies, the
was a difference between studies which assessed actual participation (fie

experiments) and those which assessed perceived participation (correlational studies). In the actual participation studies, the effect was lower: $r=0.16$. In the perceived studies, the size of the effect depended on the number of issues on which participation was measured. For specific issue studies, the correlation was $r=0.21$ while for multiple issue studies the correlation was much higher: $r=0.46$.

Management by Objectives (MBO)

Rodgers, Rogers, and Hunter (1986) did a meta-analysis of the impact of MBO on job satisfaction. They found an impact of $r=0.14$ in organizations where the MBO project had a high level of top management commitment and a correlation of $r=0.07$ where top level commitment was lacking.

DISRUPTIONS

This section uses the Guzzo, Jette, and Katzell (1985) definition of 'disruption' to include accidents, strikes, and other costly disturbances. Indeed, their set of meta-analyses are the only ones we found for disruption. Those meta-analyses are reviewed in correlational form in Table 10.11.

TABLE 10.11 — The average effect on disruptions of various organizational interventions expressed as point biserial correlations as found in meta-analyses by Guzzo, Jette, and Katzell (1985)

INTERVENTION	CORRELATION
Goal setting	0.64
Appraisal and Feedback	0.58
Training	0.27
Management by objectives	−0.15

Table 10.11 presents the meta-analyses of the effects of various organizational interventions on disruption. Disruption is reverse coded so that a positive correlation represents a decrease in disruption. Goal setting and appraisal/feedback both have very large effects: $r=0.64$ and $r=0.58$ respectively. Training also reduced disruption, though less strongly. The figure for MBO must be considered in the context of the fact that Guzzo et al. considered only studies with control groups. Rodgers and Hunter (1986) found these studies to have only weak top level management commitment and to have virtually no effect on productivity. Rodgers, Rogers, and Hunter (1986) found almost no increase ($r=0.07$) in job satisfaction in the low commitment studies. The effect on disruptions may be quite different in organizations with top management commitment where MBO was successful in increasing productivity and satisfaction.

CONCLUDING REMARKS

This chapter is the first review of meta-analytic studies in Industrial and Organizational psychology ever written. We have attempted to show the impact of meta-analytic methodology on the knowledge base of our field. Because the review covers all of Industrial/Organizational psychology, it has been necessarily superficial in some respects. The scope of our review prevented us from being as definitive as we may otherwise have been regarding the resolution of some long-standing problems addressed in the research we reviewed. We felt that it would be more instructive to showcase the many exciting new findings that were uncovered by the studies reviewed here, and thus illustrate the potential for discovery of new knowledge that is inherent in the meta-analytic method.

Although it is not true that all issues covered in this chapter have been decided, it appears that more questions are nearer to being answered than would have been apparent from a narrative review. Furthermore, interesting new questions were raised that might otherwise not have been asked. Meta-analysis has already changed the nature and level of knowledge in the field, and the rate of this change should increase in time, as more meta-analyses are conducted.

REFERENCES

Bernardin, H. J. (1984) An analysis of black–white differences in job performance. *Academy of Management Proceedings*.

Borman, W. C., White, L. A., Gast, I. F., and Pulakos, E. D. (1985) Performance ratings as criteria: What is being measured? Paper presented at the 93rd Annual Convention of the American Psychological Association, Los Angeles, CA.

Brown, S. H. (1981) Validity generalization and situational moderators in the life insurance industry. *Journal of Applied Psychology*, **66**, 664–671.

Callender, J. C., and Osburn, H. G. (1981) Testing the constancy of validity with computer-generated sampling distributions of the multiplicative model variance estimate: Results for petroleum industry validation research. *Journal of Applied Psychology*, **66**, 274–281.

Campbell, J. T., Crooks, L. A. Mahoney, M. H., and Rock, D. A. (1973) *An Investigation of Sources of Bias in the Prediction of Job Performance: A Six Year Study*. Princeton, NJ: Educational Testing Service.

Chidester, T. R., and Grigsby, W. C. (1984) A meta-analysis of the goal setting-performance literature. *Academy of Management Proceeding*.

Coggin, T. D., and Hunter, J. E. (1983) Problems in measuring the quality of investment information: The perils of the information coefficient. *Financial Analysts Journal*, **39**, 3–10.

Dimson, E., and Marsh, P. (1984) An analysis of brokers' and analysts' unpublished forecasts of U.K. stock returns. *Journal of Finance*, **39**, 1257–1292.

Dunnette, M. D. (1972) *Validity Study Results for Jobs Relevant to the Petroleum Industry*. Washington, DC: American Petroleum Institute.

Dunnette, M. D., Rosse, R., Houston, J. S., Hough, L. M., Toquam, J., Lammlein, S., King, K., Bosshardt, M. J., and Keyes, M. (1982) *Development and Validation of an Industry-wide Electric Power Plant Operator Selection System*. Minneapolis, MN: Personnel Decisions Research Institute.

Dye, D. (1982) Validity generalization analyses for data from 16 studies participating in a consortium study. Unpublished manuscript. George Washington University, Washington, DC.

Fiedler, F. E. (1965) Engineer the job to fit the manager. *Harvard Business Review*, **43**, 231–239.

Fiedler, F. E. (1978) The contingency model and the dynamics of the leadership process. In L. Berkowitz (ed.), *Advances in Experimental Social Psychology*. New York: Academic Press.

Fisher, C. D., and Gitelson, R. (1983) A meta-analysis of the correlates of role conflict and ambiguity. *Journal of Applied Psychology*, **68**, 320-333.

Ford, J. K., Kraiger, K., and Schechtman, S. L. (1986) A study of race effects in objective indices and subjective evaluations of performance: A meta-analysis of performance criteria. *Psychological Bulletin*, **99**, 330-337.

Ford, J. K., Schechtman, S. L., and Kraiger, K. (1985) The relationship among criteria as a function of subgroup membership: An integrative review. Paper presented at the 93rd Annual Convention of the American Psychological Association, Los Angeles, CA.

Gaugler, B. B., Rosenthal, D. B., Thornton, G. C., and Bentson, C. (1986) Meta-analysis of assessment center validity. Unpublished manuscript. Colorado State University.

Ghiselli, E. E. (1966) *The Validity of Occupational Aptitude Tests*. New York: Wiley.

Ghiselli, E. E. (1973) The validity of aptitude tests in personnel selection. *Personnel Psychology*, **26**, 461-477.

Glass, G. (1976) Primary, secondary, and meta-analysis of research. *Educational Researcher*, **5**, 3-8.

Glass, G. V., Smith M. L., and McGaw, B. (1981) *Meta-analysis in Social Research*. Beverly Hills, CA: Sage Publications.

Guzzo, R. A., and Bondy, J. (1983) *A Guide to Worker Productivity Experiments in the United States, 1976-81*. New York: Pergamon.

Guzzo, R. A., Jackson, S. E., and Katzell, R. A. (1986) Meta-analysis analysis. In L. L. Cummings and B. M. Staw (eds.) *Research in Organizational Behavior*, vol. 9. Greenwich, GT: JAI Press.

Guzzo, R. A., Jette, R. D.., and Katzell, R. A. (1985) The effects of psychologically based intervention programs on worker productivity: A meta-analysis. *Personnel Psychology*, **38**, 275-292.

Hackett, R. D., and Guion, R. M. (1985) A reevaluation of the absenteeism–job satisfaction relationship. *Organizational Behavior and Human Decision Processes*, **35**, 340-381.

Hackman, J. R., and Oldham, G. R. (1976) Motivation through the design of work: Test of a theory. *Organizational Behavior and Human Performance*, *16*, 250-279.

Hirsh, H. R., and McDaniel, M. A. (1986) Developing decision rules for meta-analysis. Paper presented at the first annual conference of the Society for Industrial/Organizational Psychology, Chicago, IL.

Hirsh, H. R., Northrop, L. C., and Schmidt, F. L. (1986) Validity generalization results for law enforcement occupations. *Personnel Psychology*, **39**, 399-420.

Hunter, J. E. (1980a) *The Dimensionality of the General Aptitude Test Battery (GATB) and the Dominance of General Factors of Specific Factors in the Prediction of Job Performance*. Washington, DC: US Employment Service.

Hunter, J. E. (1980b) *Test Validation for 12,000 Jobs: An Application of Synthetic Validity and Validity Generalization to the General Aptitude Test Battery (GATB)*. Washington, DC: US Employment Service.

Hunter, J. E. (1982) Personality, cognitive ability, and executive performance. Unpublished manuscript. Michigan State University.

Hunter, J. E. (1983a) A causal analysis of cognitive ability, job knowledge, job performance, and supervisor ratings. In F. Landy, S. Zedeck, and J. Cleveland, (eds.), *Performance Measurement Theory*. Hillsdale, NJ: Erlbaum, pp. 257-266.

Hunter, J. E. (1983b) *Validity Generalization of the ASVAB: Preliminary Report*. Rockville, MD: Research Applications.

Hunter, J. E. (1983c) *Validity Generalization of the ASVAB: Higher Validity for Factor Analytic Composites*. Rockville, MD: Research Applications.

Hunter, J. E. (1984a) *The Prediction of Job Performance in the Civilian Sector using the ASVAB*. Rockville, MD: Research Applications.

Hunter, J. E. (1984b) *The Validity of the Armed Services Vocational Aptitude Battery (ASVAB) High School Composites*. Rockville, MD: Research Applications.

Hunter, J. E. (1985a) *Differential Validity Across Jobs in the Military*. Rockville, MD: Research Applications.

Hunter, J. E. (1985b) Are validities generalizable? An empirical assessment. Paper presented at the American Educational Research Association, Chicago.

Hunter, J. E. (1986) A rebuttal of Dr Novick's false allegations about validity generalization and the validity of general cognitive ability predicting job performance. Paper presented at the first Annual Conference of the Society of Industrial Organizational Psychology, Chicago.

Hunter, J. E. (1987) Cognitive ability, cognitive aptitudes, job knowledge and job performance. *Journal of Vocational Behavior* (In press).

Hunter, J. E., and Hunter, R. F. (1984) Validity and utility of alternative predictors of job performance. *Psychological Bulletin*, **96**, 72-98.

Hunter, J. E. and Schmidt, F. L. (1983) Quantifying the effects of psychological interventions on employee job performance and work force productivity. *American Psychologist*, **38**, 473-478.

Hunter, J. E., Schmidt, F. L., and Jackson, G. B. (1982) *Meta-analysis: Cumulating Research Findings Across Studies*. Beverly Hills, CA: Sage Publications.

Hunter, J. E., Schmidt, F. L. and Rauschenberger, J. (1984) Methodological, statistical, and ethical issues in the study of bias in psychological tests. In C. R. Reynolds and R. T. Brown (eds.), *Perspectives on Bias in Mental Testing*. New York: Plenum Press.

Iaffaldano, M. T., and Muchinsky, P. M. (1985) Job satisfaction and job performance: A meta-analysis. *Psychological Bulletin*, **97**, 251-273.

Jackson, S. E., and Schuler, R. S. (1985) A meta-analysis and conceptual critique of research on role ambiguity and role conflict in work settings. *Organizational Behavior and Human Decision Processes*, **36**, 16-78.

Katzell, R. A., Bienstock, P., and Faerstein, P. H. (1977) *A Guide to Worker Productivity Experiments in the United States, 1971-75*. New York: New York University Press.

King, L. M., Hunter, J. E., and Schmidt, F. L. (1980) Halo in a multidimensional forced choice performance evaluation scale. *Journal of Applied Psychology*, **65**, 507-516.

Kondrasuk, J. N. (1981) Studies in MBO effectiveness. *Academy of Management Review*, **6**, 419-430.

Kopelman, R. E. (1986) Objective feedback. In E. A. Locke (ed.) *Generalizing from Laboratory to Field Settings*. Lexington, MA: Lexington Books.

Kraiger, K., and Ford, J. K. (1985) A meta-analysis of ratee race effects in performance ratings. *Journal of Applied Psychology*, **7**, 56-65.

Landy, F. L., and Farr, J. L. (1980) Performance rating. *Psychological Bulletin*, **87**, 72-107.

Latham, G. P., and Lee, T. W. (1986) Goal Setting. In E. A. Locke (ed.), *Generalizing from Laboratory to Field Settings*. Lexington, MA: D. C. Heath, pp. 101-118.

Lilienthal, R. A. and Pearlman, K. (1983) *The Validity of Federal Selection tests for Aid/technicians in the Health, Science and Engineering Fields*. Washington, DC: US Office of Personnel Management.

Locke, E. A. (1986) Generalizing from laboratory to field: Ecological validity or abstraction of elements? In E. A. Locke (ed.), *Generalizing from Laboratory to Field Settings*. Lexington, MA: Lexington Books.

Loher, B. T., Noe, R. T., Moeller, N. L., and Fitzgerald, M. P. (1985) A meta-analysis of the relation of job characteristics to job satisfaction. *Journal of Applied Psychology*, **70**, 280-289.

Lord, R. G., DeVader, C. L., and Alliger, G. M. (1986) A meta-analysis of the relation between personality traits and leadership perceptions: An application of validity generalization procedures. *Journal of Applied Psychology*, **71**, 402-410.

Lowenberg, G., Loschenkohl, G. H., and Faust, B. D. (1985) Meta-analyses demonstrating validity generalization for managerial assessment center dimensions. Paper presented at the 93rd Annual Convention of the American Psychological Association, Los Angeles, CA.

Mabe, P. A., and West, S. G. (1982) Validity of self-evaluations of ability: A review and meta-analysis. *Journal of Applied Psychology*, **6**, 280-296.

Mann, R. D. (1959) A review of the relationships between personality and performance in small groups. *Psychological Bulletin*, **56**, 241-270.

McDaniel, M. A. (1986) The evaluation of a causal model of job performance: the interrelationships of general mental ability, job experience and job performance. Unpublished doctoral dissertation. George Washington University.

McDaniel, M. A., Hirsh, H. R., Schmidt, F. L., Raju, N. S., and Hunter, J. E. (1986) Interpreting the results of meta-analytic research: A comment on Schmitt, Gooding, Noe, and Kirsch (1984). *Personnel Psychology*, **39**, 141-148.

McDaniel, M. A., and Schmidt, F. L. (1985) A meta-analysis of the validity of training and experience ratings in personnel selection. Paper presented at the 93rd Annual Convention of the American Psychological Association, Los Angeles, CA.

McDaniel, M. A., Whetzel, D. L., Schmidt, F. L., Hunter, J. E., Maurer, S., and Russell, J. (1986) The validity of employment interviews: A review and meta-analysis. Unpublished manuscript, Washington, DC: US Office of Personnel Management.

McEvoy, G. M., and Cascio, W. F. (1985) Strategies for reducing employee turnover: A meta-analysis. *Journal of Applied Psychology*, **70**, 342-353.

McEvoy, G. M., and Cascio, W. F. (1986) A meta-analysis of the relationship between employee performance and turnover. Unpublished manuscript. Utah State University, Logan, UT.

Mento, A. J., Steele, R. P., and Karren, R. J. (in press) A meta-analytic study of the effects of goal setting on task performance: 1966-1984. *Organizational Behavior and Human Decision Processes*.

Miller, K., and Monge, P. (in press) Participation, satisfaction, and productivity: a meta-analytic review. *Academy of Management Journal*.

National Academy of Sciences (1982) *Ability Testing: Uses, Consequences, and Controversies*. Washington, DC: National Academy Press.

Northrop, L. C. (1986) *Validity Generalization Results for Apprentice and Helper-trainee positions*. Washington, DC: US Office of Personnel Management.

Pearlman, K., Schmidt, F. L., and Hunter, J. E. (1980) Validity generalization results for tests used to predict job proficiency and training success in clerical occupations. *Journal of Applied Psychology*, **65**, 373-406.

Peters, L. H., Hartke, D. D., and Pohlmann, J. J. (1985) Fiedler's contingency theory of leadership: An application of the meta-analysis procedures of Schmidt and Hunter. *Psychological Bulletin*, **97**, 274-285.

Petty, M. M., McGee, G. W., and Cavender, J. W. (1984) A meta-analysis of the relationship between individual job satisfaction and individual performance. *Academy of Management Review*, **9**, 712-721.

Premack, S. L. (1984) Prediction of employee unionization from knowledge of job satisfaction. *Academy of Management Proceedings*.

Premack, S. L., and Wanous, J. L. (1985) A meta-analysis of realistic job preview experiments. *Journal of Applied Psychology*, **70**, 706-720.

Pursell, E. D., Campion, M. A., and Gaylord, S. R. (1980) Structured interviewing: Avoiding selection problems. *Personnel Journal*, **59**, 907-912.

Reilly, R. R., Brown, B., Blood, M. R., and Malatesta, C. Z. (1981) The effects of realistic job previews: A study and discussion of the literature. *Personnel Psychology*, **34**, 8-34.

Reilly, R. R., and Chao, G. T. (1982) Validity and fairness of some alternative employee selection procedures. *Personnel Psychology*, **35**, 1-62.

Rodgers, R. C., Helbrun, I. B., and Hunter, J. E. (1986) The relationship of seniority to job performance following reinstatement. *Academy of Management Journal*, **29**, 101–114.

Rodgers, R. C., and Hunter, J. E. (1986) The impact of management by objectives on organizational productivity. Unpublished manuscript. Management Department, University of Texas at Austin.

Rodgers, R. C., Rogers, D. L., and Hunter, J. E. (1986) The impact of MBO of job satisfaction. Paper presented at the Academy of Management, San Diego.

Rosenthal, R. (1978) Combining results of independent studies. *Psychological Bulletin*, **85**, 185–193.

Rosenthal, R. (1979) The 'file drawer' problem and tolerance for null results. *Psychological Bulletin*, **86**, 638–641.

Rosenthal, R. (1984) *Meta-analysis procedures for social research*. Beverly Hills, CA: Sage Publications.

Rosenthal, R., and Rubin, D. (1982) Comparing effect sizes of independent studies. *Psychological Bulletin*, **92**, 500–504.

Sackett, P. R., Schmitt, N., Tenopyr, M. L., Kehoe, J., and Zedeck, S. (1985) Comment on forty questions about validity generalization and meta-analysis. *Personnel Psychology*, **38**, 697–798.

Schmidt, F. L. Gast-Rosenberg, I., and Hunter, J. E. (1980) Validity generalization results for computer programmers. *Journal of Applied Psychology*, **65**, 643–661.

Schmidt, F. L., and Hunter, J. E. (1977) Development of a general solution to the problem of validity generalization. *Journal of Applied Psychology*, **62**, 529–540.

Schmidt, F. L., and Hunter, J. E. (1980) The future of criterion related validity. *Personnel Psychology*, **33**, 41–60.

Schmidt, F. L., and Hunter, J. E. (1983) Individual differences in productivity: An empirical test of estimates derived from studies of selection prodedure utility. *Journal of Applied Psychology*, **68**, 407–414.

Schmidt, F. L., and Hunter, J. E. (1984) A within setting test of the situational specificity hypothesis. *Personnel Psychology*, **37**, 317–326.

Schmidt, F. L., Hunter, J. E., and Caplan, J. R. (1981) Validity generalization results for two jobs in the petroleum industry. *Journal of Applied Psychology*, **66**, 261–273.

Schmidt, F. L., Hunter, J. E., Croll, P. R., and McKenzie, R. C. (1983) Estimation of employment test validities by expert judgement. *Journal of Applied Psychology*, **68**, 590–601.

Schmidt, F. L., Hunter, J. E., and Outerbridge, A. N. (1986) The impact of job experience and ability on job knowledge, work sample performance, and supervisor ratings of job performance. *Journal of Applied Psychology*, **71**, 432–439.

Schmidt, F. L., Hunter, J. E., Outerbridge, A. N., and Goff, S. (1986) The joint relation of experience and ability with job performance: A test of three theories. Unpublished manuscript, University of Iowa.

Schmidt, F. L., Hunter, J. E., Pearlman, K., and Caplan, J. R. (1980) Validity generalization results for three occupations in the Sears, Roebuck, Co. Unpublished manuscript, US Office of Personnel Management.

Schmidt, F. L., Hunter, J. E., Pearlman, K., and Hirsh, H. R. (1985) Forty questions about validity generalization and meta-analysis. *Personnel Psychology*, **38**, 697–798.

Schmidt, F. L., Hunter, J. E., and Raju, N. S. (1986) Validity generalization and situational specificity: A second look at the 75% rule and the Fisher's Z transformation. Unpublished manuscript. Department of Industrial Relations and Human Resources, University of Iowa.

Schmidt, F. L., Ocasio, B., Hillery, J., and Hunter, J. E. (1985) Further within-setting tests of the situational specificity hypothesis in personnel selection. *Personnel Psychology*, **38**, 509–524.

Schmitt, N., Gooding, R. Z., Noe, R. A., and Kirsch, M. (1984) Meta-analyses of validity studies published between 1964 and 1982 and the investigation of study characteristics. *Personnel Psychology*, **37**, 407–422.

Schuler, R. S., Aldag, R. J., and Brief, A. P. (1977) Role conflict and ambiguity: A scale analysis, *Organizational Behavior and Human Performance*, **20**, 111-128.

Steele, R. P., and Ovalle, N. K. (1984) A review and meta-analysis of research on the relationship between behavioral intentions and employee turnover. *Journal of Applied Psychology*, **69**, 673-686.

Stogdill, R. M. (1948) Personal factors associated with leadership: a survey of the literature. *Journal of Psychology*, **25**, 35-71.

Stone, E. F. (1986) Job scope — job satisfaction and job scope — job performance relationships. In E. A. Locke (ed.), *Generalizing from Laboratory to Field Settings*. Lexington, MA: Lexington Books.

Strube, M. J., and Garcia, J. E. (1981) A meta-analytic investigation of Fiedler's contingency model of leadership effectiveness. *Psychological Bulletin*, **90**, 307-321.

Terborg, J. R., Lee, T. W., Smith, F. J., Davis, G. A., and Turbin, M. S. (1982) Extension of the Schmidt and Hunter validity generalization procedure to the prediction of absenteeism from knowledge of job satisfaction and organizational commitment. *Journal of Applied Psychology*, **67**, 440-449.

Trattner, M. H. (1985) *Estimating the Validity of Aptitude and Ability Tests for Semi-professional Occupations using the Schmidt-Hunter Interactive Validity Generalization Procedure*. Washington, DC: US Office of Personnel Management.

Tubbs, M. E. (1986) Goal setting: A meta-analytic examination of the empirical evidence. *Journal of Applied Psychology*, **71**, 474-483.

US Department of Labor (1977) *Dictionary of Occupational Titles*. Washington, DC.

Vineberg, R., and Joyner, J. N. (1982) *Prediction of Job Performance: Review of Military Studies*. Alexandria, VA: Human Resources Research Organization.

Waldman, D. A., and Avolio, B. J. (1986) A meta-analysis of age differences in job performance. *Journal of Applied Psychology*, **71**, 33-38.

White, L. A., Borman, W. C., Hough, L. M., and Hoffman, R. G. (1986) A path analytic model of job performance ratings. Paper presented at the 94th Annual Convention of the American Psychological Association, Washington, DC.

Wiesner, W. H., and Cronshaw, S. F. (1986) The moderating impact of interview format and degree of structure on interview validity. Unpublished manuscript. Guelph, Canada: University of Guelph.

INDEX

Cooper & Robertson, **International Review of Industrial and Organizational Psychology 1987**
ISBN 0 471 91352 9

Erratum
p. 367, Replace the whole page with the following:

*International Review of Industrial
and Organizational Psychology*
1986

CONTENTS